Managing Investment Portfolios

A Dynamic Process

SECOND EDITION

STUDENT EDITION

Managing Investment Portfolios

A Dynamic Process

SECOND EDITION

Edited by

John L. Maginn, CFA
Donald L. Tuttle, CFA

Sponsored by

The Institute of Chartered Financial Analysts

A subsidiary of THE ASSOCIATION FOR INVESTMENT MANAGEMENT AND RESEARCH

STUDENT EDITION

 **WARREN, GORHAM & LAMONT**
BOSTON • NEW YORK

PRINTED IN THE UNITED STATES OF AMERICA

Contributors

Keith P. Ambachtsheer is president of K.P.A. Advisory Services Inc. in Toronto, publisher of *The Ambachtsheer Letter*, and publisher of the *Canadian Investment Review*. He received a B.A. in economics and finance at the Royal Military College of Canada, earned an M.A. from the University of Western Ontario, and did additional graduate work at McGill University. He was an investment analyst with Sun Life Assurance Company from 1969 to 1972 and a partner and research director of Canavest House, a brokerage firm specializing in investment technology services for institutional investors, from 1972 to 1981. From 1981 to 1984 he was a partner and senior consultant with Pension Finance Associates, a firm offering advisory and information services to pension plan sponsors. He founded his own firm in 1984. A respected author and commentator on pensions and investment topics, his articles have appeared regularly in the *Financial Analysts Journal, The Journal of Portfolio Management*, and other professional journals. He is a three-time winner of the *FAJ*'s Graham and Dodd Award, and he won the Institute for Quantitative Research in Finance's Roger Murray Award in 1983. He has written one book on pension investment management, contributed chapters to two popular investment texts, and had a number of his articles included in the *Institutional Investor* book series. Mr. Ambachtsheer is chairman of the Financial Research Foundation of Canada. He is on the advisory board of a major U.S. investment management firm and the editorial board of the *Financial Analysts Journal*. K.P.A. Advisory Services Inc. provides strategic advice on pension governance, finance, and investment matters to governments, industry associations, pension plan sponsors, and organizations providing services to pension plan sponsors. The primary outlet for this advice is *The Ambachtsheer Letter*, which in 1989 regularly reached 130 corporate and institutional clients in the United States and Canada.

Robert D. Arnott joined First Quadrant Corp. in 1988 as president and chief investment officer. The author of over three dozen research articles in various professional journals, he has twice won the *Financial Analysts Journal*'s Graham and Dodd Award for articles on strategic asset allocation and the relationship between the business cycle and security selection. He is a member of the editorial board of *The Journal of Portfolio Management*. Mr. Arnott is also the author of numerous monographs and book chapters on a wide variety of investments subjects, and he coedited the book *Asset Allocation*. Mr. Arnott joined First Quadrant from Salomon Brothers Inc., where he was vice president and strategist. He developed the Salomon Tactical Asset Allocation product and produced the "Equity Risk Premium Review" and "Passive Management Focus" publication series. While at Salomon, he also developed and published research in a variety of areas relating to pension sponsor activities, equity strategy, asset allocation strategy and investment theory. Mr. Arnott was previously president and chief investment officer of TSA Capital Management, where he designed the firm's asset allocation and equity strategies.

Kathleen A. Condon, CFA, is managing director—structured products at Bankers Trust Company. The activities of the Structured Products Division, which she manages, include index fund, option, futures, and other quantitative strategies. She joined the bank in 1970 as an equity portfolio manager and has since had experience with index fund development, performance measurement, and investment process consulting. Ms. Condon received a B.A. from Mount Holyoke College and an M.B.A. from New York University. She is a past recipient of the *Financial Analysts Journal*'s Graham and Dodd Award for an outstanding *FAJ* article. Ms. Condon serves on the Board of the Institute for Quantitative Research in Finance and is a former member of the Board of Trustees of The Institute of Chartered Financial Analysts. She is a member of the New York Society of Security Analysts.

Charles A. D'Ambrosio, CFA, earned his B.S.C. from Loyola University, Chicago, and his M.S. and Ph.D. from the University of Illinois at Urbana. He joined the University of Washington's finance faculty in 1960, where he is currently professor of finance. Professor D'Ambrosio was the 1988–89 president of the Financial Management Association and is a past president of the Western Finance Association. He is a member of the Board of Directors of the Institute for Quantitative Research in Finance, the Board of Trustees of the Research Foundation of The Institute of Chartered Financial Analysts, and the ICFA's Continuing Education and Research Committee. He has been education director, member of the Board of Directors, and treasurer of the Seattle Society of Financial Analysts. His consulting experience includes being a trustee of a $160 million pension plan, an investment manager for pension and profit-sharing plans, a consultant to numerous companies and investment firms, and an expert witness in a number of antitrust and damage suits. Professor D'Ambrosio's research and writing includes being the cofounder and managing editor of the *Journal of Financial and Quantitative Analysis* and serving on the editorial boards of the *Review of Social Economy*, *The Financial Review*, and the *Journal of Financial Education*. He is presently editor-in-chief of the *Financial Analysts Journal*, editor-in-chief of the *CFA Digest*, and the director of the ICFA's Research Foundation. His publications include six books and numerous articles on investments and business finance. He writes occasional editorials for the *Financial Analysts Journal* and is McGraw-Hill Book Company's consulting editor in finance.

Jeffrey J. Diermeier, CFA, is managing director and division head of the Domestic Equity Division of First Chicago Investment Advisors. He is responsible for the management of $3 billion of discretionary, actively managed domestic equity assets, supervising a staff of 12 investment researchers and traders. Mr. Diermeier is also a member of the senior management team that develops and coordinates the firm's overall business and investment strategy. Mr. Diermeier joined First Chicago Corporation in 1975 after receiving B.B.A. and M.B.A. degrees from the University of Wisconsin. He began in the Trust Department, principally conducting economic and investment studies. From 1981 to the end of 1986 he was chairman of the Asset Allocation Committee. In addition, he was product and investment manager of the Multi-Asset Portfolio Fund and codeveloper of the Multiple Markets Index. In 1987 he launched the EXDEX fund, a sell-oriented active alternative to stock indexing. Mr. Diermeier has made several contributions to investment journals and has lectured at universities and professional investment forums on global asset allocation, investment objective setting, and performance analysis and attribution. He is the chairman of the Economics Section of the ICFA's Candidate Curriculum Committee and is a member of the Board of Directors of the Investment Analysts Society of Chicago.

Peter O. Dietz is a consultant and retired senior vice president at Frank Russell Company, advisor for large international pools of capital. Dr. Dietz holds an A.B. from Dartmouth College, an M.B.A. from the Amos Tuck School at Dartmouth, and a Ph.D. from Columbia University. From 1960 to 1969 he taught at Northwestern University, and from 1969 to 1976 he taught at the University of Oregon, becoming department chairman in 1973. He is currently chairman of the Research Committee and a member of the Board of Directors of the Institute for Quantitative Research in Finance. Dr. Dietz has written numerous articles on the subjects of setting investment objectives and measuring investment performance, including several articles with a Japanese focus. He is a member of the Seattle Society of Financial Analysts and is an associate editor of the *Financial Analysts Journal*.

David M. Dunford, CFA, is vice president—diversified financial services and chief investment officer, Merrill Lynch & Co., Princeton, N.J. Mr. Dunford is responsible for the investment activities of the Diversified Financial Services units of Merrill Lynch Consumer Markets, which includes insurance and banking operations. He joined Merrill Lynch in 1989. Prior to his current position, Mr. Dunford was responsible for the activities of Travelers Investment Managers Company (TIMCO) at The Travelers Corporation. He joined The Travelers in 1972 as a financial analyst in the Common Stock unit of the Securities Department and five years later was named assistant investment officer. In 1979 he was promoted to vice president in Travelers Investment Management Company and portfolio director of pension asset management operations. In 1980 he was named senior vice president. He was appointed corporate vice president and head of the Public Bond and Portfolio Management Division of the Travelers Securities Department in 1984. In 1986 he was appointed president and chief investment officer of TIMCO. Mr. Dunford received an A.B. degree in economics from Princeton University in 1970 and an M.B.A. degree from New York University in 1972. He is a member of the Hartford Society of Financial Analysts and a member of the Council of Examiners of The Institute of Chartered Financial Analysts. In 1983 he was appointed to the Financial Products Advisory Committee of the Commodity Futures Trading Commission. Mr. Dunford is a frequent speaker at industry and professional forums.

H. Gifford Fong is president of Gifford Fong Associates, an investment technology consulting firm with a specialty in fixed-income portfolio analysis and asset allocation strategies. He is a graduate of the University of California, Berkeley, where he earned his B.S., M.B.A., and J.D. degrees. Mr. Fong is a member of the editorial boards of *The Journal of Portfolio Management* and the *Financial Analysts Journal*, the Board of Directors (and Program Chairman) of the Institute for Quantitative Research in Finance, and the editorial advisory board for *The Handbook of Fixed Income Securities*. He has served on the Board of Directors of the Financial Management Association and the advisory board for the Investment Technology Association. He is a contributor to a number of professional books and journals and is the co-author of a book on fixed-income portfolio management.

William S. Gray, III, CFA, is a consultant to the Trust Department of Harris Trust and Savings Bank. He joined the bank in 1950 and worked as a securities analyst there for 15 years and in various capacities after that. For 19 years prior to his retirement in 1985, he was the senior investment officer in the Trust Department and chairman of the Trust Investment Committee. His professional activities include president of the Investment Analysts Society of Chicago (1965–1966), chairman of the board of the Financial Analysts Federation (1975–1976), chairman of the Investment Committee, Trust Division, American Bankers Association (1975–1978), and president of the Financial Analysts Research Foundation (1979–1981). He is the recipient of a Graham & Dodd Scroll for an article that appeared in the *Financial Analysts Journal*. He has written numerous other articles published in leading finance journals, as well as chapters and sections in investments books and monographs. The FAF honored him with its Distinguished Service Award in 1980. Since 1985, he has been chairman of the Board of Trustees of the American Red Cross Retirement System. He received a Ph.B. degree in 1948 and an M.B.A. degree in 1950, both from the University of Chicago.

Ronald W. Kaiser is co-founder, senior vice president and director of Bailard, Biehl & Kaiser, Inc., a financial advisory and investment counseling firm that provides services in investment counsel, financial planning, and personal financial education/publishing. Mr. Kaiser received both a B.S. in Geology and an M.B.A. from Stanford University, and he did additional graduate work at Yale University. Upon graduation in 1969, he and two fellow classmates, Tom Bailard and Larry Biehl, formed Bailard, Biehl & Kaiser, Inc. In 1989, the firm managed $700 million for 250 individuals, $300 million for 25 tax-exempt accounts, and $100 million in a no-load mutual fund. BB&K also advises as a consultant in asset allocation to major U.S. corporate, state, and municipal institutions. In addition to managing portfolios for clients, Mr. Kaiser serves as a member of the Investment Research Group of BB&K and is a director of Western Real Estate Fund, a publicly registered company sponsored by the Landsing Corporation. In addition, Mr. Kaiser is co-author of a leading college textbook in personal finance. He has published several articles on individual investing, macro financial analysis, and real estate investing, and he has lectured widely on personal financial planning.

Jeannette R. Kirschman, CPA, is a senior vice president and a client executive of Frank Russell Company, asset strategy consultants. She has been in the consulting business for more than 20 years and has developed and directed Frank Russell Company's portfolio monitoring and performance analysis systems. Ms. Kirschman attended Western Washington University and the University of Washington. She is a member of the American Institute of Certified Public Accountants, the Washington Society of Certified Public Accountants, the American Women's Society of Certified Public Accountants, and the American Society of Women Accountants. She is also a member of the advisory board of the University of Washington Center for the Study of Banking and Financial Markets.

Robert M. Lovell, Jr. is chairman and chief executive officer of First Quadrant Corp., an institutional investment management subsidiary of Xerox Financial Services, Inc. He entered the investment field in 1955 as a trainee at Halsey, Stuart & Co. and subsequently served as an investment advisory associate and associate director of the Lehman Brothers Investment Advisory Service. He was an officer and shareholder of New Court Securities, and, until 1985, he was senior vice president, financial of Crum & Forster, an insurance holding company. A contributor of articles to professional journals, he is a trustee and member of the finance committee of the College Retirement Equities Fund and a director of Princeton Bank. A member of the New York Society of Security Analysts and Insurance Investment Officers, he received his B.A. degree in history from Princeton University.

John L. Maginn, CFA, is senior executive vice president, chief investment officer, and treasurer of Mutual of Omaha Insurance Company and United of Omaha Life Insurance Company. He is also the president of Mutual Asset Management Company. Mr. Maginn received a B.S.B.A. degree from Creighton University and an M.S. degree in finance from the University of Minnesota. He began his investment career as a research analyst at CNA Financial Corporation, Chicago, and subsequently joined the investment staff of Mutual of Omaha. His investment experience has included common stock and bond analysis as well as the management of insurance company, mutual fund, and endowment fund portfolios. In his current position, he is responsible for the management of the investments of Mutual and United and their affiliated insurance companies. Mr. Maginn is a past chairman of the Board of Trustees of The Institute of Chartered Financial Analysts and a past member of the Institute's Council of Examiners and Candidate Curriculum Committee. He is a former director of the Financial Analysts Federation and a past president of the Omaha-Lincoln Society of Financial Analysts. Mr. Maginn is a co-editor of two multi-author investments books and wrote the insurance company section of *The Determinants of Portfolio Policy*, published by The Institute of Chartered Financial Analysts.

William F. Sharpe is chairman of the board of Sharpe-Tint, Inc. and Timken professor emeritus of finance at Stanford University's Graduate School of Business. He joined the Stanford faculty in 1970, having previously taught at the University of Washington and the University of California at Irvine. An originator of the capital asset pricing model and its beta and alpha concepts, Dr. Sharpe developed a widely used method for the valuation of options and other contingent claims as well the computer algorithm used in many asset allocation procedures. Dr. Sharpe has published numerous articles in a number of professional journals, including *Management Science*, the *Journal of Business*, *The Journal of Finance*, the *Journal of Financial Economics*, the *Journal of Financial and Quantitative Analysis*, *The Journal of Portfolio Management*, and the *Financial Analysts Journal*. He has also written six investments books, including the landmark *Portfolio Theory and Capital Markets* in 1970 and his *Investments* textbook, in its fourth edition, in 1990. Dr. Sharpe is a past president of the American Finance Association. He has also served as consultant to a number of corporations and investment organizations.

Jack Treynor is president of Treynor Capital Management, Inc. He was previously a partner and chief investment officer of Treynor-Arbit Associates, Inc. For many years editor-in-chief of the *Financial Analysts Journal*, he has also contributed prolifically to a number of leading practitioner and academic journals and is co-author of two books. Formerly a trustee of the Financial Analysts Research Foundation and a director of the American

Finance Association, Mr. Treynor is currently a director of the Institute for Quantitative Research in Finance, a member of the Visiting Committee to the Graduate School of Business of the University of Chicago, and a member of the editorial board of the *Financial Analysts Journal*. He is a director of certain of the Vance-Sanders mutual funds and a general partner of two partnership funds. He is a member of the Indianapolis Society of Financial Analysts and has received five *Financial Analysts Journal* Graham and Dodd Awards and the Nicholas Molodovsky Award from the Financial Analysts Federation. A graduate of Haverford College and Harvard Business School, he enjoys teaching investments when the opportunity arises. Mr. Treynor's teaching affiliations have included Columbia University and the University of Southern California.

Donald L. Tuttle, CFA, is professor of finance in the Graduate School of Business at Indiana University. He received his B.S.B.A. and M.B.A. degrees from the University of Florida and his Ph.D. degree from the University of North Carolina at Chapel Hill. He has previously taught at the University of North Carolina and has been a visiting professor at the European Institute of Business Administration (INSEAD), University of Florida, Georgetown University, and University of Virginia. He has served as an investments and capital markets consultant to corporations, government agencies, and professional organizations. He is the author of 22 articles in leading finance journals and 5 books on security analysis and portfolio management. Dr. Tuttle is the former president, vice president, and executive director of the Financial Management Association, national professional society of finance teachers, researchers, and practitioners. He is also a former associate editor of *The Journal of Finance* and *Financial Management*. He is a member of the ICFA's *CFA Digest* Editorial Board and is a former member of the Institute's Board of Trustees, Candidate Curriculum Committee (chairman, 1982–1985), and Council of Examiners. He has been chairman of the ICFA's Select Committee to Evaluate the CFA Program and a member of its Admissions, Curriculum, and Examination Review Committee. He is also a member of the Board of Trustees of Bison Money Market Fund, the Board of Trustees of the Research Foundation of The Institute of Chartered Financial Analysts, and the Board of Regents of the College for Financial Planning. He is a former member of the Board of Directors of the Federal Home Loan Bank of Indianapolis. He holds membership in the Indianapolis Society of Financial Analysts.

Jay Vawter, CFA, is a senior vice president of Stein Roe & Farnham, investment counselors. He has been in the investment mangement business for over 30 years and has specialized in the management of institutional funds, particularly endowment and retirement funds. Mr. Vawter holds B.B.A. and M.B.A. degrees from the University of Michigan. From 1978 to 1982 he served as chairman of the ICFA's Council of Examiners, and from 1982 to 1988 he served as a member of the Institute's Board of Trustees (chairman, 1984–1985). He has been a trustee of a public pension plan and a large religious endowment fund and is currently a trustee of the Princeton Theological Seminary. Mr. Vawter is a frequent speaker and lecturer on the economy, financial markets, and personal and institutional investing, both in the United States and abroad. He is a member and past chairman of the ICFA's International Affairs Committee. He is also a member and past president of the Washington Society of Investment Analysts and is a past director of the Financial Analysts Federation. He was the 1989 recipient of the ICFA's C. Stewart Sheppard Award.

Wayne H. Wagner is a partner of Plexus Group, a Santa Monica–based investment advisor and provider of trading services and trading advisory services to institutional investors and pension plan sponsors. Plexus Group also provides marketing services to The Crossing Network, offered by Instinet Corporation. Mr. Wagner was a founder of Wilshire Associates and previously served as chief investment officer of Wilshire Associates' Asset Management Division, where he managed over $2.5 billion. He also created and operated the Trust Universe Comparison Service (TUCS), the Index Fund Management Service, and the Special Consulting Division at Wilshire. Before joining Wilshire Associates, Mr. Wagner designed quantitative investment systems at Wells Fargo Bank, where he participated in the design and operation of the first index funds. Mr. Wagner is editor and an author of *The Complete Guide to Securities Transactions: Improving Performance and Reducing Costs*, published in 1989. Mr. Wagner has written and spoken frequently on many trading and investment subjects. He has received two Graham and Dodd Awards for excellence in financial writing from the *Financial Analysts Journal*. Mr. Wagner has an M.S. degree in statistics from Stanford University and a B.B.A. degree from the University of Wisconsin.

Randall C. Zisler is president of Russell-Zisler, Inc., a Princeton-based real estate subsidiary of Frank Russell Company, specializing in real estate and corporate financial analysis of real estate portfolios on behalf of retirement plans, corporations, and other institutional investors. Before founding Russell-Zisler, he was vice president and director of real estate research, Goldman Sachs & Co. As a senior vice president of Landauer Associates, Inc. and, prior to that, as a partner of Jones Lang Wootton, an international real estate consulting firm, he advised some of the largest developers, syndicators, and corporations in the United States. Dr. Zisler has also been an assistant professor at Princeton University, where he taught economics and finance in the urban planning program. He received his A.B., M.A.U.P., and Ph.D. degrees from Princeton University, and he also received an M.S.E. in structural engineering from The Catholic University of America.

Foreword

THE FIRST EDITION OF THIS BOOK ON PORTFOLIO MANAGEMENT was published in 1983 under the sponsorship of The Institute of Chartered Financial Analysts. Much has happened to the techniques of portfolio management and to the Institute in the following years.

In the title of the book, *Managing Investment Portfolios: A Dynamic Process*, the word *dynamic* really has a dual definition. *Dynamic* as applied to the portfolio managment process itself means that once a portfolio is constructed to meet given objectives, constraints, and preferences, there must be ongoing monitoring and evaluation of the many variables involved, and appropriate changes must be made to assure attainment of the results being sought. Also, *dynamic* conveys the sense of continuing developments in the elements of the portfolio management process, including, among many others, refinements and new methodologies in asset allocation, risk control, and measurement procedures.

This second edition of *Managing Investment Portfolios: A Dynamic Process* addresses these dynamic characteristics in a comprehensive and logical fashion. In addition, it fully meets the basic criteria established for the first edition for its overall content and authorship; namely, it:

1. Describes and demonstrates that portfolio management is a dynamic decision-making process that is based on fundamentally sound and recognizable investment considerations and is one that lends itself to equally sound and recognizable principles of organizational behavior;
2. Demonstrates that this process is applicable to any category or combination of investment assets—stocks, bonds, real estate, mortgages, and so on;
3. Draws heavily on the collective wisdom and experience of well-recognized professionals and is written by and for practitioners; and
4. Represents a rigorous combination of theory and practice, but at the same time avoids jargon and ambiguity.

In helping to meet the foregoing criteria, the editors and contributing authors of this second edition have drawn on information contained in a number of ICFA seminar proceedings. Since 1983, the Institute has conducted more than 20 seminars, the primary purpose of which has been to add to and enhance the body of knowledge applicable to all aspects of the investment process. The seminar proceedings, which cover a diverse list of subjects, have been distributed to all CFAs, as part of the ICFA Continuing Education Program, introduced into the ICFA Candidate Program, and made available to other investment constituencies and the academic community. Also enhancing the body of knowledge are research monographs funded by the Research Foundation of The Institute of Chartered Financial Analysts. Earnings from the Foundation's endowment fund are financing projects ranging from reexamination of basic core issues to the study of theory having potential practical application in the future.

The first edition of this book was introduced into the curriculum for the 1983 CFA Study and Examination Program as a key knowledge source of the portfolio management process. At the time somewhat less than 4,000 candidates were enrolled at all 3 levels of the program. Enrollments for the 1989 program exceeded 10,000 candidates at all 3 levels, a 150 percent increase in 6 years. During this same time frame approximately 4,000 candidates successfully completed the program and were awarded the CFA charter. From the inception of the Institute in 1963 through 1989, more than 12,000 persons were awarded the CFA charter. Thus the word *dynamic* as referred to previously also can be used to measure the progress of the Institute.

Part of the rapid growth in the number of Institute candidates and members reflects fast-expanding interest in the CFA program by investment professionals outside of North America. From a relatively small handful in the early 1980s, the number of international candidates in 1989 was approximately 1,000, or 10 percent of the total. International interest in the Institute is more than just candidate participation. Under the sponsorship of Nikko Securities in Tokyo, the first edition of *Managing Investment Portfolios: A Dynamic Process* has been translated into Japanese and is being used by the Security Analysts Association of Japan and other educational training entities in Japan as a basic learning source on the subject of portfolio management. Also, the Society of Investment Analysts in the United Kingdom is using the first edition as part of the syllabus for that organization's study and examination program. Again, the word *dynamic* applies to international interest in this book.

On behalf of the Institute Board of Trustees, considerable gratitude is extended to the editors and authors of this second edition. Collectively and individually they have built on the strong foundation of the first edition and have created in this volume an even more useful and practical source of knowledge. We are convinced that all readers will applaud and benefit from their accomplishment.

Alfred C. Morley, CFA
President
The Institute of Chartered Financial Analysts

Gary P. Brinson, CFA
1989–90 Chairman of the Board of Trustees
The Institute of Chartered Financial Analysts

James R. Vertin, CFA
Chairman of the Council on Education and Research
The Institute of Chartered Financial Analysts

Preface

THE MANAGEMENT OF INVESTMENT PORTFOLIOS is a rapidly growing and increasingly sophisticated professional endeavor serving a broad array of investors—both individual and institutional—with investment portfolios ranging in asset size from thousands to billions of dollars.

Portfolio management is both an art and a science. It is much more than the application of a formula to a set of data input from security analysts. It is a dynamic decision-making process, one that is continuous and systematic but also one that requires large amounts of astute managerial judgment.

This book is neither a "cookbook" nor a "bible" of investment management. Rather, this book documents the portfolio management process, blending academic theory with the experience of noted practitioners. The language of the book is that of the investment community rather than that of the scholar. It was written by and for portfolio managers and those whom they serve.

This second edition is both an updating as well as a broadening of the scope of the material covered in the first edition, reflecting the myriad of changes in the investment markets over the past few years. New financial instruments, techniques, and strategies are being developed at an accelerating pace as investment managers adjust to the increasing volatility and globalization of the capital markets.

The pioneering efforts of the contributing authors to the first edition once again are acknowledged. In the second edition, each author was again chosen from among the leading professionals in his or her subject area. Each author's contribution was highly directed in order to blend his or her collective insights into the context of the portfolio decision-making process logic. The result is a uniquely readable book, rich in its real life perspective and in its exposition of the subject.

Such a book represents untold hours of effort by authors, editors, and reviewers who have joined together in this common cause. The editors wish to acknowledge the contribution of the authors and to thank their families and associates for allowing these busy people to share their talents. The members of the editorial review board read and reread manuscripts and contributed greatly to the refinement and polishing of each chapter. Their knowledge of the profession and the process was of great value in the preparation of this book. Special recognition is due board member James R. Vertin, CFA, Alpine Counselors, for his diligent editing and insights, which have enhanced authors' contributions throughout the book.

The editors also acknowledge the comments, criticism, and guidance provided by the following individuals: Marvin D. Andersen, CFA, Mutual of Omaha Insurance Company; Peter L. Bernstein, Peter L. Bernstein, Inc. and *The Journal of Portfolio Management*; Richard M. Bliss, Mutual of Omaha Insurance Company; Royce L. Bluhm, Mutual of Omaha Insurance Company; Philip W. Carmichael, Putnam, Hayes & Bartlett, Inc.; Charles A. D'Ambrosio, CFA, University of Washington and *Financial Analysts Journal*; William G. Droms, CFA, Georgetown University; William S. Gray, III, CFA, Harris Trust and Savings Bank; Michael L. McCowin, CFA, Harris Trust and Savings Bank; John W. Peavy, III, CFA, Southern Methodist University; Jeffry F. Sailer, CFA, Mutual of Omaha Insurance Company; Fred H. Speece, Jr., CFA, First Asset Management; Gary G. Schlarbaum, CFA, Miller Andersen & Sherrerd; Katrina F. Sherrerd, The Institute of Chartered Financial Analysts; George H. Troughton, CFA, California State University at Chico; and Richard A. Witt, CFA, Mutual of Omaha Insurance Company. Special thanks also go to students at Georgetown University and Indiana University who were exposed to earlier versions of this text for their valuable feedback.

We also want to recognize Alfred C. Morley, Jr., CFA, President of The Institute of Chartered Financial Analysts, and the Institute's officers and trustees for their strong encouragement and financial support throughout this project. We are also appreciative of the physical facilities and staff support of the Institute, especially the extensive manuscript preparation work done by Diane Hamshar. Finally, on a personal note, we want to thank our families, especially Carol and Peg, for their support throughout the many months it took to produce this book.

JOHN L. MAGINN, CFA, *Associate Editor*
DONALD L. TUTTLE, CFA, *Editor-in-Chief*

October 1989

Table of Contents

Part II   Investor Objectives and Constraints: Determination of Portfolio Policies

3   Individual Investors
Ronald W. Kaiser

Part III   Expectational Factors

Part V Managing the Investor's Portfolio

13 Monitoring and Rebalancing the Portfolio
Robert D. Arnott and Robert M. Lovell, Jr.

14 Evaluating Portfolio Performance
Peter O. Dietz and Jeannette R. Kirschman

Part I

Principles of Financial Asset Management

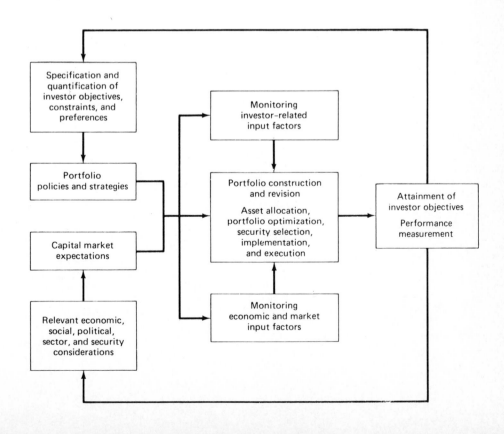

The Portfolio Management Process and Its Dynamics

John L. Maginn, CFA
Donald L. Tuttle, CFA

OVERVIEW

Investment management is an old profession, the growth of which has paralleled the accumulation of wealth and the evolution of our civilization. Investors have sought assets that would grow in value and/or provide income. Over the centuries, the investment assets selected have been encyclopedic, reflecting the culture and commerce of the times. In essence, investment management practices have evolved in a long-term trend with a more populous and more prosperous world community of investors. Today the number of investors and investment managers continues to grow rapidly on a worldwide basis. As with many things in life today, the technology of investment management is changing and developing rapidly. Advances in theory, new financial instruments, innovative global markets, and instantaneous worldwide communications are among the factors shaping the dynamics of the investment process.

Since the seminal work of Harry Markowitz in the early 1950s, the practice of investment management has undergone revolutionary change. His was a watershed contribution to investment theory, identifying the collective importance of all the investor's holdings—the portfolio of investments. The interrelationships of individual asset holdings was identified by Markowitz in the context of the classic investment trade-off between risk and return. Over the past four decades, investment management attention has been shifting from primary emphasis on asset selection to a more balanced emphasis on diversification and the interrelationship of individual asset characteristics within the portfolio. Thus, the theory of building port-folios has significantly altered the practice of investment management. In fact, portfolio theory has broadened the concept of investment management to that of portfolio management.

All these changes were taking place at a time when two other trends were unfolding within the investment community: first, the emergence of institutional investing as a new, yet large and rapidly growing business that essentially reflects the growth of pension funds in the United States; second, the professionalization of the investment management field. Forty years ago, investment analysts were considered compilers of statistics and portfolio management was the province of senior management or committees. The phenomenal growth of investment assets, coupled with pressure from reg-ulatory bodies such as the Securities and Exchange Commission, motivated the Financial Analysts Federation in the early 1960s to establish a profes-sional accreditation program and the Chartered Financial Analyst (CFA) designation under the auspices of the Institute of Chartered Financial An-alysts.

Through the Institute, a common body of knowledge has been identified and continuously updated as explained by Pete Morley in the Foreword of this book. That body of knowledge verifies the fact that the end result of the analysis of economic, accounting, and capital market information is the investment decision making that determines the portfolio of the investor. Even a decision to take no action is a decision. Thus, the cumulation of all investment analysis is portfolio management.

PORTFOLIO MANAGEMENT AS A PROCESS

Despite its growth and importance, the subject of portfolio management historically was not treated comprehensively in the literature. Much of the traditional literature was based on an "interior decorator/catalog approach" in which management was explained in terms of classes of assets matched with classes of investors on an almost ad hoc basis. Overlooked was the fact that, through the eyes of the practitioner, portfolio management is a *process*, an integrated set of activities that combine in a logical, orderly manner to produce a desired product. This concept of portfolio management as a process is so basic, so intuitively correct, so intellectually satisfying, and so pragmatically useful that it can be accepted under virtually any cir-cumstances. It is a *dynamic* and *flexible* concept, and it is an accurate de-scription for any portfolio function, regardless of the portfolio investments—bonds, stocks, real estate, gold, collectibles, or whatever; regardless of or-ganizational type—trust company, investment counsel firm, insurance com-pany, mutual fund, or whatever; regardless of customer orientation—personal, pension, endowment, foundation, insurance, bank, or whatever; and regardless of manager, location, investment philosophy, style, or approach. Portfolio management is a process that, complete with feedback loops and monitoring and adjustment, is *continuous* and *systematic*. The process can be as loose or as disciplined, as quantitative or as judgmental, and as simple or as complex as its operators wish it to be.

Whatever its construct in a particular application, the process at work is the same as in every other application: an integrated set of steps undertaken in a consistent manner to create and maintain appropriate combinations of investment assets. The process starts with the identification and specification of an investor's objectives, preferences, and constraints and the development of appropriate investment policies and strategies. The next step is the implementation of the process in the marketplace for the choice of an optimal combination of investment assets that are selected on the basis of capital market and individual asset expectations. Then, through the monitoring of market conditions, relative asset values, and the investor's own circumstances, the process comes full circle when changes in these variables result in the need to rebalance the portfolio. Then the cycle begins anew.

THE PROCESS LOGIC

Given the process idea, the necessary steps for the conduct of the portfolio management function, as well as the logical sequence of these steps, the nature of the decisions to be made, and the ordering of these decisions, are immediately apparent. Different organizations reach differing conclusions as their unique judgments are applied at various points in the process. These organizations place different emphasis on different aspects of the process because acceptance of the notion demands no uniformity in decision content. Rather, recognition of the process simply permits any manager to organize for, identify, and execute the necessary decisions in an orderly, consistent manner that ensures comprehensive attention to all of the areas relative to portfolio creation, maintenance, and adjustment.

In sum, the process logic shown in the diagram in Figure 1-1 is incorporated in the following definition, which is the cornerstone for this book. Portfolio management is an ongoing process by which:

1. An investor's objectives, preferences, and constraints are identified and specified to develop explicit investment policies;
2. Strategies are developed and implemented through the choice of optimal combinations of financial and real assets in the marketplace;
3. Market conditions, relative asset values, and the investor's circumstances are monitored; and

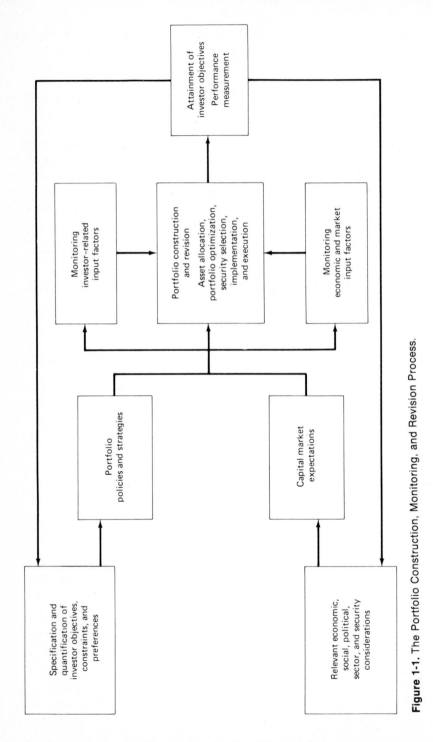

Figure 1-1. The Portfolio Construction, Monitoring, and Revision Process.

4. Portfolio adjustments are made as appropriate to reflect significant change in any or all of the relevant variables.

This book makes no judgments and voices no opinions about how the process should be organized, who should make which decisions, or any other process operating matter. Each management organization—indeed, each manager within an organization—has a preferred operating course that is uniquely its own, which is as it should be. The book clarifies the fact that *the process itself is common to all managers everywhere*. Systematic exploitation of this underlying reality is as readily accomplished at a one-manager shop in which a hand-held calculator is used as it is by an industry giant employing the latest in real-time, on-line, interactive computer systems. The *dynamic* is there, and it is useful and fundamental.

THE DYNAMICS OF THE PROCESS

One of the truly satisfying things about portfolio management as a professional activity is the existence of the underlying logic and the dynamism of the process notion. In a broad sense, the work of analysts, economists, and market strategists is all a matter of "getting ready." The work of portfolio management is where the action is: taking the inputs and moving step by step through the orderly process of converting this raw material into a portfolio that maximizes expected return relative to the investor's ability to bear risk, that meets the investor's constraints and preferences at the same time that it executes the strategy, and that integrates portfolio policies with expectational factors and market uncertainties. This is where the payoff is, because this is where it all comes together. Of course, it is the result of this process that is judged: the performance of the portfolio relative to expectations and comparison standards.

Professionalism is enhanced and practice is improved by visualizing and operating the portfolio management function as a process that:

- Consists of the steps outlined in this book
- Flows logically and systematically through an orderly sequence of decision making
- Moves from the final step of monitoring back to the first step of policy determination in an ongoing way, so that, once put into motion with respect to a given investor, the process is continuous

This view sees portfolio management not as a set of separate elements operating by fits and starts as intuition or inspiration, but as an integrated whole in which every decision moves the portfolio down the process path and in which no decision can be skipped without sacrificing functional integrity.

Principles of Asset Management

The initial building blocks of the portfolio decision-making process are the basic concepts of the trade-off between risk and return under conditions of uncertainty. In Chapter 2, Chuck D'Ambrosio provides a concise but comprehensive discussion of the basic financial concepts that are the foundation for portfolio theory. In addition, D'Ambrosio includes a discussion of international return and risk and develops return/risk considerations for real estate. This fully integrated discussion of risk and return provides a highly appropriate foundation for this second edition of *Managing Investment Portfolios*.

Determination of Portfolio Policies

With the basic financial principles and variables specified, the process begins to unfold in Chapter 3 as Ron Kaiser explains how the objectives, preferences, and constraints of individual investors are identified and specified to develop explicit personal investment policies. Kaiser makes a unique contribution in his coverage of determination of risk tolerance for individual investors. He logically sorts out individual investors by risk type and goes well beyond the traditional life cycle approach to individual investing found in most investment texts. In effect, he uses psychological factors to identify the risk tolerance level of various individual investors, regardless of age or wealth position. In this respect, Kaiser truly begins to bridge the gap between individual and institutional investors and opens up opportunities for development of explicit investment policies for individual investors.

In Chapter 4, three authors—Keith Ambachtsheer, Jay Vawter, and John Maginn—explain how the objectives, constraints, and preferences of institutional investors determine portfolio policies. Ambachtsheer provides a different perspective on pension funds. He broadens the traditional coverage of this class of institutional investors to include corporate and national socioeconomic policy considerations, which are becoming an increasingly important aspect of pension fund policy setting. Vawter discusses endowment funds and funds managed for associations, which are important classes of institutional investors that are often ignored in the traditional investment literature. He brings years of experience and unique insights to the shaping of investment policy for endowment funds. Maginn revises and updates the section on insurance companies, commercial banks, and mutual funds with considerable discussion of the asset/liability management goals of insurance companies and banks. An additional feature of Chapter 4 is the inclusion of a number of investment policy statements that can serve as guidelines and models for trustees, investment committees, investment managers, and consultants.

Expectational Factors

Investment strategies developed from these policy statements are used, together with the investment manager's expectations for the capital markets in general and for individual sectors and assets in particular, to choose a portfolio of assets in a simultaneous equation type of solution process. In Chapter 5, Jeff Diermeier develops insights into the macroexpectational factors influencing the market for bonds, stocks, and real estate on both a domestic and international basis. Diermeier develops, in a comprehensive and systematic manner, the macroeconomic processes and phenomena that affect the money and capital markets. He extends the original work done by Peter Bernstein in the first edition of this book. One of Diermeier's major contributions is the systematic associations that he makes that attempt to identify cause-and-effect relationships on a global basis. This chapter develops the foundation for the implementation aspects of portfolio management. In effect, Diermeier identifies the environmental inputs for the asset allocation model discussed in Chapter 7.

Bill Gray, in Chapter 6, calls on his years of securities research and investment management experience to develop the other half of the expectational picture: the microenvironmental inputs for building portfolios. Gray identifies the microanalytical construct and the causative variables that underlie the desired return and risk estimates. The formation of microexpectations influences the selection of each investment asset to be included by the portfolio manager in a specific portfolio.

Integrating Policies and Expectations

The most difficult and important phase of the portfolio management process is the integration of macro- and microexpectations with the investor's objectives, constraints, and preferences as defined in the policy statement. This operational process is covered in five critically important chapters dealing with the asset allocation decision; the construction of fixed-income, equity, and real estate portfolios; and the role of derivative securities. Bill Sharpe, in Chapter 7, makes a major contribution to detailing the asset allocation considerations that are applicable to any investment portfolio as well as the most recent developments in operational approaches to asset allocation. Sharpe systematically identifies and sorts out four major, distinct approaches to asset allocation: integrated, strategic, tactical, and insured. Furthermore, he develops and categorizes the techniques to implement these approaches: mathematical programming, Monte Carlo simulations, investor preferences, and quadratic programming. In sum, the chapter represents one of the most comprehensive, almost exhaustive, treatments of a subject that far outweighs all others in determining ultimate portfolio performance.

In Chapter 8, Gifford Fong updates his first edition effort and focuses on the critical issues involved in fixed-income management. Fong sorts out and categorizes active, semiactive, and combination techniques and identifies and describes the situations to which each best applies. In addition, he examines the pros and cons of these techniques, based on his years of fixed-income portfolio consulting experience.

Chapter 9, written by Kathy Condon, develops a comprehensive description of active and passive equity portfolio practices and principles. Reorienting the treatment of this subject as it appeared in the first editon, Condon develops the newer approaches being used in equity portfolio management while retaining the discussion of styles and other aspects of traditional equity management. Importantly, Condon clearly contrasts the motivations for selecting active versus passive management. She enhances the coverage of passive portfolio management processes and techniques and elaborates on the newer, quicker, and cheaper techniques that are being used in this approach. In her discussion of active management, she focuses on the factors that matter and comments on their importance. Finally, Condon broadens the content of this chapter to include global considerations and to introduce some of the newer trading techniques, such as package trading.

The first edition of this book included real estate as a portfolio asset and introduced it to the CFA study curriculum in a systematic and comprehensive manner for the first time. This innovation is further developed in Chapter 10, in which Randy Zisler makes a substantial contribution. He develops a clearly identifiable portfolio approach to real estate investing and pointedly demonstrates the benefits of diversification both by and for a real estate portfolio. Zisler provides concrete examples of the kind of diversification that tends to add value—namely, geographic diversification—and the kind that is of less significance—namely, property type. In addition, to alleviate the perennial problem of appraisal-based values in the real estate market, Zisler provides adjusted data that reflect the risk and return trade-off more realistically and more comprehensively both by geographic location and by property type. Another important contribution is his description of the importance of leasing arrangements and terms and their effect on the volatility of the cash flow stream valued by real estate investors. Zisler argues that the role of the property leasing manager is extremely critical to shaping and maintaining the continuity and stability of the cash flow stream, especially via escalator clauses to pass through inflation effects. In theory, consistency of cash flow is a key characteristic that is attributed to real estate. Zisler's work further suggests that the lack of volatility or sluggishness of real estate returns reflects achievement of lease terms and lease portfolios that produce steady and constant cash flow growth. Thus, it is possible for real estate cash flows to be more predictable, more stable, and more inflation-proof than cash flows from alternative equity investments such as dividends on common stocks.

Dave Dunford, in Chapter 11, provides a thorough yet concise exposition of the role of derivative securities in the portfolio management process. His examples outline the major derivative securities strategies in comprehensive fashion. Dunford expands the work that he and Bob Kopprasch developed for the *1985–1986 Update* to the first edition of this book. In addition to a discussion of international currency hedging, Dunford has added a section on global investing and rebalancing through currency markets that can serve as an active strategy proxy for foreign market investing, at least on a temporary basis. He also further develops the role of bond and stock synthetic securities and the technique of portfolio insurance. In his discussion of portfolio insurance, Dunford talks about its dynamic properties and its put protective characteristics and indicates that, except in periods of market disruption such as October 1987, dynamic hedging can be done effectively with futures contracts.

Execution and Trading

The implementation or execution phase of the process is one of the most critical but least understood aspects of portfolio management. This major gap in the literature has been filled by Jack Treynor and Wayne Wagner, who have teamed up in an expanded Chapter 12, which continues to be one of the best expositions of how markets work. Treynor explains the motivations of the various types of transactors, and Wagner demonstrates how those motivations are implemented in the markets. Wagner also describes the role of the trading function and provides pointers on how the trader can analyze the motivations of the transactor or manager for whom he is executing. In addition, the chapter includes a discussion of trading costs and the components thereof as an indication of the efficiency of trading.

Restructuring the Portfolio

Despite the fact that portfolio managers spend most of their time monitoring and rebalancing existing portfolios, the literature traditionally had focused almost exclusively on the creation of portfolios. In Chapter 13, Rob Arnott and Bob Lovell combine their insights and experience to explain how the elements of the portfolio management process are applied to the actual day-to-day monitoring and adjusting of portfolios. Rebalancing is the heart of the portfolio managing dynamics. Arnott and Lovell lay out a systematic process, identify the critical elements, and evaluate the cost effectiveness of rebalancing. Furthermore, Arnott and Lovell analyze market, economic, and investor utility function factors as they affect rebalancing decisions,

primarily by seeking out useful correlation and elasticity coefficient relationships. Because it has been difficult to get adequate data to measure many
of these factors, these authors' efforts reflect a pioneering exposition that
will be further enhanced as better data and more analysis provide additional
discriminatory evidence.

Performance Evaluation

Portfolio managers are not measured by how well they prepare, but rather
by how well they perform. Chapters 3 through 13 describe a logical, sys-
temic, and continuous decision-making process. In Chapter 14, Peter Dietz
and Jeannette Kirschman provide a strong blend of academic insight and
practitioner craftsmanship to examine performance measurement and its
uses and abuses. Their work on the subject continues to be the state of the
art. In Chapter 14, they refine and restate the issues, emphasizing practical
solutions to thorny problems that have developed in assessing performance
management. They segment and customize measurement approaches by
class of assets and discuss the trend of moving from "benchmark" to more
focused, "normal" portfolios. The latter more clearly reflect the mandates
given to the manager. Dietz and Kirschman also offer a good schematic
example of attribution for asset allocation.

PORTFOLIO MANAGEMENT COMES OF AGE— CHALLENGES OF THE FUTURE

Portfolio management has come of age as a profession in the past quarter
century. The evolution and advancement of the theory and practice of portfolio management during this period have been shaped by many factors,
including the following:

- Increased institutionalization of money management
- Growth in the number and size of investable pools of money,
  which in turn reflects the growth in population, wealth factors, and
  social changes, particularly retirement benefits
- Spread of communications and information dissemination
  technology, which is shrinking the world and expanding global
  investing
- Greater use of computers for processing masses of data and as a
  tool in both the management of information and performance of
  functional activities
- Increased emphasis on the use of quantitative techniques in the

decision-making process of business in general and of finance in particular
- Larger direct and indirect costs of errors or shortfalls in meeting portfolio objectives

While it is unknown whether these same factors will be the principal shapers of the future investment environment or if an entirely different set of influences will come into play, change will occur, probably with increasing frequency and severity. Given the enhanced sophistication and competitiveness of the portfolio management community, reaction to change will be increasingly swift and resolute. Only managers with a solid grounding in dynamic, systematic decision-making processes such as those described here will be able to adapt to, master, and thrive in such a volatile and competitive environment.

CHAPTER 2

Portfolio Management Basics

Charles A. D'Ambrosio, CFA

OVERVIEW

The purpose of this chapter is to introduce the reader to basic portfolio management concepts. It covers several major topics that form building blocks for further study. The chapters that follow make use of the principles and theories as well as the tools and techniques discussed in this chapter. The goal of portfolio management is client satisfaction and, more specifically, client results that are attractive and appropriate. Successful investment management rests on a theoretical and empirical foundation of knowledge about the world of investing. The focus in this chapter is more on investment diversification, pricing, and management than on which investment assets to select or when to buy or sell them. Although the chapter focuses primarily on domestic common stocks in discussing the principles of portfolio management, these principles are applicable to all classes of investments.

The chapter begins with a brief discussion of time and investment and continues with discussions of capital markets and their efficiency, calculating returns, risk analysis, modern portfolio theory, the capital asset pricing and arbitrage pricing theories, and investor risk aversion.

Portfolio techniques are another essential element of portfolio management, and passive and active strategies, as well as top-down and bottom-up approaches, are discussed briefly. Chapters 8, 9, 10, and 11 discuss portfolio management strategies in greater detail.

The final two topics of the chapter focus on real estate and international investing. These two investment areas are separated from the others because they possess characteristics that differ from those of domestic bonds and stocks. Both will be seen as desirable components of a portfolio because each tends to reduce portfolio risk without penalizing returns.

TIME AND INVESTING

Time Value of Money

There are two dimensions in which time and investing are discussed in this chapter. The first begins with savings. The simple view is that when saved money is invested, more money will be available in the future than is saved now. To obtain that greater future sum a trade-off is made: One gives up certain consumption today for the prospect of uncertain future consumption, that is, the prospect of using money today to buy goods and services vis à vis the possibility—not the certitude—of being able to buy more goods and services in the future. The process, involving multiple future time periods, of compounding and compound interest is described in any basic finance or investment text.

To illustrate present and future value, assume that $1,000 is invested today at 9 percent for 10 years. What will that $1,000 grow to by the end of that time period? The answer is $2,100. This is called the future value of the amount of money invested today. Alternatively, if an investor expects to receive $2,100 in 10 years and the required rate of return on investments of this level of risk is 9 percent, by reversing the process that future amount is worth $1,000 today. The value today of money to be received in the future is called its *present value*.

Time as a Risk Moderator

There is a second sense in which time and investing must be considered, namely the damping effect that time seems to have on the riskiness of investments. As investments are held for longer and longer periods, the old saw that "the market will come back" seems to capture this concept. If one is patient, the long-run benefits of investing will be realized. The idea of all investing is to let time work in the investor's favor. The power of compounding returns is strong enough to warrant taking the long-term view of investing. For not only are reasonable returns likely to be forthcoming, but the risk of the portfolio also is likely to be less than it would be with a strategy that focused on short-term performance.

ASSET MARKETS

Investments are made in markets. The motivation of all participants in financial markets is presumed to be the same: to earn a return at least commensurate with the level of risk assumed. It can be postulated that most major capital markets seem to be relatively efficient most of the time; that is, in most cases they have returns appropriate for the risk borne. Not too long ago a much stronger efficiency statement would have been made, but an onslaught of studies has suggested that markets are not nearly as efficient as they were once thought to be. As indicated previously, *efficient markets* are those in which the expected return from investing is commensurate with the risk assumed—no more, no less. *Abnormal* (or *excess*) *returns* are those beyond those warranted by the level of risk assumed.

Efficient Market Hypotheses

Markets have been studied under three forms of the *efficient market hypothesis* (EMH): weak, semistrong, and strong. Each differs from the other in terms of its assumptions about the amount and kind of information that comes to the marketplace *and* the rate at which it is reflected in price. The more quickly information comes to the marketplace and the more rapidly it is reflected in market prices, the more highly efficient is the market.

Weak Form EMH. The weak form of the EMH states that, using yesterday's prices only, one cannot foretell what tomorrow's prices are likely to be and thereby make unusual returns. These studies that tested the weak form EMH indicate that a simple trading rule, in a trend-extrapolating or trend-reversing sense, cannot be invoked after trading costs to garner those elusive, abnormal returns. None of the weak form EMH studies claim that no trading rule will work (one might).

Semistrong Form EMH. The semistrong form of the EMH states that no publicly available information, such as earnings and dividends, can be used consistently to earn returns in excess of those warranted by the level of risk assumed. Most recent EMH studies focus on this form, and it is the one of greatest interest to portfolio managers because portfolio managers rely so heavily on publicly available information for making decisions.

What do the studies reveal? Among the findings are the following:

- Stock prices react favorably to dividend announcements when the dividend is increased, unfavorably when the dividend is decreased, and virtually not at all when dividends are unchanged.
- Macroeconomic data announcements such as changes in the money supply, the Federal Reserve discount rate, or monetary or fiscal policy do not contain sufficient information to enable one to earn abnormal returns.
- Stock splits, in and of themselves, do not have an exploitable impact on rates of return, although stock splits that are accompanied by dividend changes may be exploitable because a

change in dividends seems to signal management's confidence in
higher future earnings.

- Stock prices seem to be slightly influenced by sales of large blocks
  of stocks; the pressure of large-block sales tends to lower share
  prices.

- Stock prices seem to be affected by quarterly earnings surprises.
  That is, if quarterly earnings changes differ from the consensus
  projection, positive or negative unusual returns seem to persist for
  several quarters thereafter.

- Small firms tend to earn returns in excess of those warranted by
  the level of risk, a phenomenon not associated with large firms.
  This effect has not disappeared, although there is some debate
  about whether this effect is an aberration, a statistical artifact, or a
  different way of pricing risk.

- There seem to be market "seasonalities," such as a weekend
  effect, with positive rates of return on Fridays and negative returns
  on Mondays being far more numerous than expected, and a turn-
  of-the-year effect, with abnormally large returns in early January
  relative to other times.

Strong Form EMH. The strong form of the EMH states that no information, regardless of whether it relates to earnings and dividends or price
and volume and regardless of whether it is public or private, may be used
consistently to earn rates of return consistently in excess of those warranted
by the level of risk assumed. The results of the studies of this phenomenon
are mixed. Overall the studies suggest in the aggregate that only those with
truly private information—insiders and specialists—may consistently exploit it to earn abnormal returns. Several basic investment texts provide a
detailed review of the numerous EMH studies that have been done.

What may be concluded about the behavior of financial asset markets?
The safe, initial assumption is that markets are mostly efficient most of the
time and that the market for assets, and therefore their prices, are "fair
game" markets. That is, one gets what one pays for, and there are no free
lunches. This is the safe *beginning* assumption. If the portfolio manager
discovers that the markets in which he is trading are not efficient, the analytical framework used to assess financial markets must be adjusted to reflect
that new insight.

CALCULATING ASSET RETURNS

Returns consist of dividend or interest income plus principal or market price.
But there are returns and there are returns. That is, there is much more to
the story.

Total Return vs. Mean Returns

Total returns consist of all price changes and income received during a specific interval. For example, $100 invested in stock *A* that increases in price to $110 in one year and pays $5 in cash dividends during the year has a total return of 15 percent.

$$\text{Total return} = (\text{Change in price} + \text{cash received})/\text{Beginning value}$$
$$= (\$110 - \$100 + \$5)/\$100$$
$$= \$15/\$100$$
$$= 15\%$$

But this one-period total return may not tell the story that is relevant here. For example, the Ibbotson Associates data in Figure 2-1 indicate that a dollar invested at year-end 1925 in common stocks grew to $406.45 by the end of 1988. A similar investment in a portfolio of small stocks grew to $1,478.14. Those are the aggregate dollar returns. The annual percentage returns are derived as follows:

$$1 + R = (406.45)^{1/63}$$
$$= 1.1001$$

and

$$R = 0.1001, \text{ or } 10.01\%$$

This is the annual *geometric mean rate of return,* or the annual *compound rate of return.* According to this measure, $1 invested at the rate of 10.01 percent, compounded annually for 63 years, will grow to $406.45. For small stocks, the equivalent calculation results in an annual compound (geometric) return of 12.28 percent.

Figure 2-2 contains geometric and arithmetic returns. *Arithmetic mean returns* are just that: the simple averaging of each period's rates of return. For example, yearly returns of 10 percent, 12 percent, − 5 percent, 2 percent, and −6 percent average to 2.6 percent per year [(10 + 12 − 5 + 2 − 6)/5]. This is the annual average return for the period. For all common stocks and small stocks, the annual average returns are 12.1 and 17.8 percent, respectively.

The compound average (geometric mean) return indicates the rate at which wealth grows; the arithmetic mean return indicates the annual average return from investing. Because investors want to know the rate at which wealth grows over time, the geometric mean return is preferred to the arithmetic mean return. This example tells the story. If a portfolio increases in value from $100 to $150 and then decreases to $100, the first change is a 50 percent increase and the second is a 33 percent decrease. The arithmetic average change is +8.5 percent. But it is obvious that there has been no

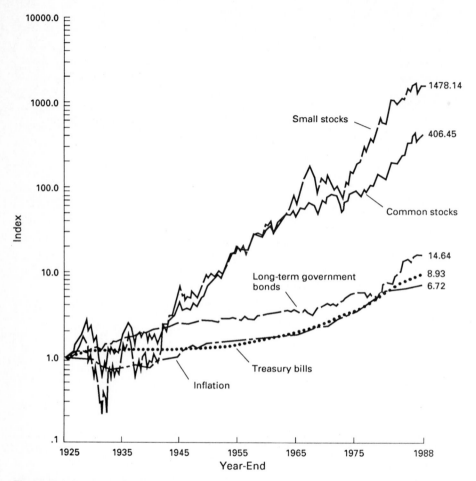

Figure 2-1. Wealth Indices of Investments in the U.S. Capital Markets, 1926–1988 (year-end 1925 = $1.00). SOURCE: Ibbotson Associates [1989].

change in the value of the portfolio, so the return must be zero. This is the value of the geometric mean, and it is therefore the best measure of wealth change.

Net Returns

Rarely is there a problem with determining total returns. It is when investors try to determine net returns that problems arise. Managerial and custodial fees, trading costs, taxes, and inflation each call for adjustments to total returns. The various ways to obtain net returns are discussed here, and the data in Table 2-1 are used to illustrate the points.

Series	Geometric Mean	Arithmetic Mean	Standard Deviation	Distribution
Common stocks	10.0%	12.1%	20.9%	
Small-company stocks	12.3	17.8	35.6	
Long-term corporate bonds	5.0	5.3	8.4	
Long-term government bonds	4.4	4.7	8.5	
Intermediate-term government bonds	4.8	4.9	5.5	
U.S. Treasury bills	3.5	3.6	3.3	
Inflation rates	3.1	3.2	4.8	

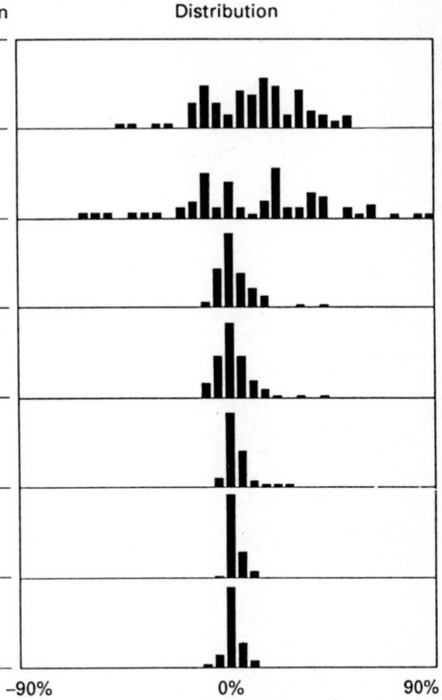

-90%   0%   90%

Figure 2-2. Basic Series: Summary Statistics of Annual Returns, 1926–1988. SOURCE: Ibbotson Associates [1989].

The total return on the portfolio is equal to the sum of (1) the difference between the ending and beginning values of the portfolio and (2) the dividend and interest income earned, all divided by the beginning value, or

$$R = [(\$1{,}053{,}250 - \$1{,}000{,}000) + (\$32{,}250 + \$64{,}500)]/\$1{,}000{,}000$$
$$= \$150{,}000/\$1{,}000{,}000$$
$$= 15\%$$

To obtain the net return after management costs, reduce total dollar income in the numerator of the preceding calculation by the amounts of custodial and management fees and trading costs. The calculations are as follows:

$$R = [\$150{,}000 - (\$5{,}375 + \$5{,}375 + \$10{,}750)]/\$1{,}000{,}000$$
$$= (\$150{,}000 - \$21{,}500)/\$1{,}000{,}000$$
$$= \$128{,}500/\$1{,}000{,}000$$
$$= 12.85\%$$

TABLE 2-1. A Typical Portfolio

Beginning market value	$1,000,000
Ending market value	1,053,250
Dividend income	$32,250
Interest income	64,500
Custodial fees	5,375
Trading costs	10,750
Management fees	31,750
Change in CPI	5.2%
Tax rate	28.0

This is the net return of a nontaxable fund, such as a pension fund that pays no income taxes. If the owner of this portfolio were taxable, however, a tax adjustment would be necessary. Assume for purposes of this example that the marginal tax rate on dividends, interest, and capital gains is 28 percent. To determine the net after-tax return, first determine how much tax must be paid. With net income and realized capital gains of $128,500 and a tax rate of 28 percent the tax due is $35,980, so the arithmetic becomes:

$$R = (\$150,000 - \$21,500 - \$35,980)/\$1,000,000$$
$$= (\$150,000 - \$57,480)/\$1,000,000$$
$$= \$92,520/\$1,000,000$$
$$= 9.25\%$$

Inflation Adjustment

Inflation requires another adjustment to returns. All of the above returns are *nominal returns* because they capture the dollar changes in the fund; they do not account for changes in the purchasing power of those dollars. Returns adjusted for inflation are called *real returns*. The adjustment is made by subtracting the inflation rate from the nominal return.

The Consumer Price Index (CPI) is usually used to adjust the calculations. In Table 2-1, the CPI changed by 5.2 percent, and all returns should be adjusted accordingly. Total return in real or constant purchasing power terms then becomes 9.8 percent (15 − 5.2); net return becomes 7.35 percent (12.85 − 5.2); and after-tax return becomes 4.35 percent (9.55 − 5.2). While these returns are illustrative of markets during the late 1980s, longer-term returns are illustrated in Tables 2-2 and 2-3.

Table 2-2 indicates the relative importance of the sources of total returns for various asset classes: income or capital appreciation. Table 2-3 shows the inflation-adjusted returns for several asset classes. The Ibbotson Associates studies present an important frame of reference for evaluating the

TABLE 2-2. Total Returns, Income, and Capital Appreciation on the Basic Asset Classes: Summary Statistics of Annual Returns, 1926–1988

Series	Geometric Mean	Arithmetic Mean	Standard Deviation
Common Stocks			
Total returns	10.0%	12.1%	20.9%
Income	4.8	4.8	1.3
Capital appreciation	5.0	7.0	20.1
Small Company Stocks			
Total returns	12.3	17.8	35.6
Long-Term Corporate Bonds			
Total returns	5.0	5.3	8.4
Long-Term Government Bonds			
Total returns	4.4	4.7	8.5
Income	4.8	4.9	2.9
Capital appreciation	−0.7	−0.4	7.3
Intermediate-Term Government Bonds			
Total returns	4.8	4.9	5.5
Income	4.5	4.5	3.3
Capital appreciation	0.1	0.2	4.1
U.S. Treasury Bills			
Total returns	3.5	3.6	3.3
Inflation rates	3.1	3.2	4.8

SOURCE: Ibbotson Associates [1989].

long-term rates of return on investment assets typically held by portfolio managers. The only important fact not presented in these tables is that reinvestment of dividend income, because of the compounding effect involved, has accounted for almost half of the long-term wealth accumulation of common stock portfolios in which dividend reinvestment has been practiced.

TABLE 2-3. Inflation-Adjusted Series: Summary Statistics of Annual Returns, 1926–1988

Series	Geometric Mean	Arithmetic Mean	Standard Deviation
Inflation-adjusted common stocks	6.7%	8.8%	21.1%
Inflation-adjusted small stocks	8.9	14.3	34.9
Inflation-adjusted long-term corporate bonds	1.9	2.4	10.0
Inflation-adjusted long-term government bonds	1.2	1.7	10.1
Inflation-adjusted intermediate-term bonds	1.7	1.9	7.0
Inflation-adjusted U.S. Treasury bills (real interest rates)	0.5	0.5	4.4

SOURCE: Ibbotson Associates [1989].

RETURN EXPECTATIONS[1]

Historical vs. Expected Returns

Still another way to assess returns is to compare *historical* and *expected returns*. Historical returns are just that: the history of the performance of an investment decision over a specified time period. Expected returns are best estimates (guesses) of what returns might be over some future time period. Historical returns are known with certainty. Expected returns are fraught with uncertainty; that is, they are probabilistic in nature. Figure 2-2 shows the variation around average historical returns as indicated in the columns labeled "Standard Deviation" and "Distribution."

Scenario Analysis

Tomorrow's returns are the meaningful ones for decisions made today. The client in possession of the preceding taxable portfolio may be curious about a portfolio manager's return expectations for the year ahead, if not for the next several years. What is the sensible way of approaching this matter? *Scenario analysis* is the one most often used. In this scheme several possible scenarios are set forth, and a probability is assigned to each scenario. The result of weighting each scenario by its probability of occurrence is the expected (most likely) scenario for the period being studied. The end result of the entire process is an expected return and distribution of returns. Chapter 5 presents an extensive scenario analysis for a representative macroeconomic/macromarkets situation.

Expected Returns and Risk Premiums

An important use of expected return is to compare values across asset classes and across time. Some asset allocation decisions are based on the risk premium differential, which is the difference between the expected return on assets such as stocks, bonds, or real estate and the expected return on a risk-free asset such as a Treasury bill. For example, in the coming holding period, the expected risk premium of stocks over Treasury bills might be estimated to be 8.1 percent. Such an estimate should be compared with the historical average. Severe deviations from historical norms raise questions that the investment policy committee must be prepared to answer. For example, Ibbotson Associates reports (in Table 2-4) a 1926 to 1988 compound annual equity premium of 6.2 percent.

---

[1] Adapted from Keith P. Ambachtsheer and James H. Ambrose, "Basic Financial Concepts: Return and Risk," in Maginn and Tuttle [1983]. See also Farrell [1983].

TABLE 2-4. Risk Premium Series: Summary Statistics of Annual Returns, 1926–1988

Series	Geometric Mean	Arithmetic Mean	Standard Deviation
Equity risk premia (stocks to Treasury bills)	6.2%	8.4%	20.9%
Small-stock premia (small stocks to stocks)	2.1	3.8	18.8
Default premia (long-term corporate bonds to long-term U.S. Government bonds)	0.6	0.7	3.0
Horizon premia (long-term U.S. Government bonds to Treasury bills)	0.8	1.1	7.9

SOURCE: Ibbotson Associates [1989].

While the premiums are important in several contexts, two stand out. First, they are used to make overall decisions to allocate money between equities and debt investments. When the equity risk premium is "low" (e.g., 4 percent) relative to returns on Treasury bills, a shift from stocks to debt may be called for. Second, premium data are used to determine the allocation within both stock and bond classes. An above-average small stock premium, for example, may indicate an opportunity to shift a portfolio into that set of securities. A low horizon (i.e., maturity risk) premium may call for shortening the maturities of debt securities.

The nominal before-tax expected return matrix produced by the manager's investment policy committee is of limited value to a client interested in real returns. The economic scenario may well bring out a particular inflation estimate. The expected inflation rate is then deducted from each of the asset class expected returns to obtain real expected returns. Taxable funds must further adjust the results for their expected tax rate so that real after-tax expected returns are used.

RISK ANALYSIS

Investment risk is categorized according to the two sources of investment return: a macro, pervasive factor such as the national economy and micro, localized factors such as the company itself. The risk associated with macro factors is called *systematic risk*; returns depend in a systematic and associative way on that factor. If the economy does well, returns on assets are likely to do well too.

The micro risks associated with factors particular to a company are called *unsystematic risks* or *unique risks*; investment returns are uniquely determined by the firm's underlying earning power, such as its turnover of assets, its operating margin, and its return on assets and equity. As discussed in the section that follows, investment managers can do little about systematic risk, although there is much they can do about unique risks, namely diversify them.

Pervasive Risks

Purchasing Power Risk. Some risks are pervasive and applicable to all investments. One risk is *purchasing power risk*. This is the chance that investment returns will be better or worse than expected because of the sole influence of price inflation (or deflation). Because the only reason to invest is to earn a positive real rate of return, purchasing power risk is a major concern for all portfolio managers and clients. This risk transcends international boundaries.

Political Risk. The chance that returns will be affected by the policies and stability of nations is termed *political risk*. The danger of debt repudiation or failure to meet debt service, expropriation of assets, differences in taxes, restrictions on repatriating funds, and the prohibition against exchanging foreign currency into domestic currency are typical political risks. Chapter 6 broadens the discussion of political risk into *country* and *sovereign risks*.

Currency (Exchange) Risk. The chance that returns will be affected by changes in rates of exchange because investments have been made in international markets whose promise to pay dividends, interest, or principal is not denominated in domestic currency is called currency risk or exchange risk. Concerns regarding currency risk have long been an impediment to global investing because fluctuations in relative foreign exchange values tend to accentuate return and risk in domestic currency terms. This problem and its disposition are dealt with in greater detail in Chapters 8, 9, and 11.

Systematic Risks

The three somewhat interrelated systematic risk factors that are common to all assets are inflation, interest rates, and movements in the markets in which a particular asset or portfolio of assets is traded.

Interest Rate Risk. The chance that returns will be better or worse than expected because of changes in the level of interest rates in called *interest rate risk*. The prices of all investment assets tend to rise as interest rates decline, and vice versa. This inverse relation pervades all investments, although not to the same degree. Pure interest moves are associated with default-free investments, such as U.S. Treasury securities. But the effect on other investments is present as well, because the discount rate—the required rate of return used to place a value on an asset—consists in part of the return available on a default-free investment. The problem with extending interest rate risk to other assets, such as equities, lies in the other component of the discount rate, namely the required risk premium over and above the default-free rate, consisting of compensation for default risk and equity market risk. If the default-free rate dominates the total discount rate, such as in the case of high-grade bonds or utility equities, interest rate risk is more influential than if the default-free rate is small in comparison to the risk premium, such as that for junk bonds or growth equities.

Market Risk. Another pervasive risk associated with the equities market is *market risk*. It is the chance that market influences will affect expected returns of all equities in ways that were not anticipated. In the equities market, the returns on individual stocks are influenced by the price movements of the marketplace in which they are traded, depending on their sensitivity to the overall movement of the market. For example, if the market were to rise by 20 percent, the chances would be great that any one stock or a portfolio of stocks would rise as well. The extent of the increase would depend on the sensitivity of an individual stock or stock portfolio to movements in the stock market. The sensitivity measure is *beta,* a concept to be developed more fully in a later section of this chapter.

Real Estate Risk. Real estate possesses five types of risk not found in most other investments:

1. Real estate is less liquid—in some instances much more illiquid—than financial instruments.
2. Because no continuous auction trading market exists, quoted prices may not represent properties' intrinsic value.
3. The difficulty of finding a buyer and seller raises the cost of transacting.
4. Real estate markets are likely to be segmented and therefore not as efficient as the markets for other assets, so the cost of acquiring information is greater.
5. Real estate values are more influenced by changes in interest rates than are other equities, because so much of their return is determined by the going rate on default-free assets.

Chapters 6 and 10 discuss systematic risk factors for real estate in greater detail.

Unsystematic Risks

An investment asset's unsystematic risks consist of two major components: credit (or company) risk and sector (or industry) risk.

Credit/Company Risk. Credit risk consists of a firm's business and financial risks. *Business risk* is the risk inherent in the nature of the business. *Financial risk* is the risk in addition to business risk that arises from using financial leverage. For example, many electric power companies, especially those not heavily dependent on nuclear energy, are considered to have low business risk because of predictable demand and profit margins. Their total unqiue risk is increased, however, because of their extensive use of debt to finance their operations. An example of high business risk is a manufacturing firm that manufactures products for which demand is highly sensitive to macroeconomic activity and has small profit margins. Its total unique risk would be increased by adding debt to an already unpredictable business.

It can be stated, then, that credit risk is associated with the ability of the firm that issues securities to meet its promise on those securities. The fundamental promise of every investment is a return commensurate with its risk. So the credit risk analyzed is the ability to deliver returns that are consistent with the risk assumed. The risk stems from the firm's basic productivity and the way in which it finances its operations.

Sector/Industry Risk. Sector risk is the risk of doing better or worse than expected as a result of investing in one sector of the economy instead of another. It is often called industry risk, although in the investment environment of the late 1980s that was a misnomer. For example, Value Line Investment Survey classifies the 1,700 companies it follows into 92 industries. For many portfolio management purposes, this may be a useful differentiation. However, many portfolio managers may find 92 classes to be too many; other classification schemes may be more suitable.

Portfolio managers who prefer far fewer classifications cluster stocks into a handful of sectors. Sector investing implicitly acknowledges that the impact of individual investment decisions is less critical, certainly to large portfolios, than investing in the proper sector at the proper time. Sector rotation, then, is a portfolio management style that shifts resources to sectors that are expected to be more promising and are overweighted in a portfolio (relative to their normal market value fractional weighting) in contrast to other sectors, which are underweighted.

There are at least three ways to view sectors. For example, Farrell [1975] found that the stocks he studied could be classified by the way in which their characteristics grouped. Four predominant groups emerged: growth stocks, stable stocks, oil stocks, and cyclical stocks.

Still another way of classifying sectors is along lines of major economic activity. Typical classifications include capital goods, consumer durables, consumer nondurables, energy, financial, transportation, utilities, and raw materials and intermediate goods.

A variation around that theme is to classify assets by some other criterion, such as small versus large capitalizations, dividend yields, price/ earnings ratios, or betas.

Real Estate Investment Risk. As in the case of systematic risk, real estate requires a separate discussion because, as Ibbotson and Brinson [1987] point out, residual risk is endemic to real estate. Real estate possesses not only macro risks not found in financial assets but also some unusual residual risks. Indeed, much of the systematic risk of real estate may be viewed as residual risk as well, such as illiquidity, lack of a continuous auction trading market, and quoted prices that may not represent intrinsic value. But there is also the large size of real estate projects, which may limit the portfolio manager's ability to diversify adequately and thereby mitigate any tendency to reduce total portfolio risk. Because real estate markets are likely to be segmented, the risk of imperfect information is present; also, of course, real estate is nonhomogeneous and not easily divisible. Investors do not care which share of IBM they hold. After all, a rose is a rose is a rose. But the nonhomogeneity and indivisibility of real estate give rise to a unique risk that may not be fully canceled through diversification.

MEASURING RISK

Systematic and unsystematic risks are measured differently. Investment returns are not known in advance and therefore are risky. Before the investment is made, one can only guess at what those risks might be. Although a guess is the best one can do, good guesses are possible. One approach is to couch the guess in statistical terms. A return that you expect to receive from investing probably will not be the return that you actually receive. It will probably be higher or lower than expected. Accordingly, variation exists around the expected return.

Standard Deviation Calculation

Expected returns are estimated by analyzing a reasonable set of possible returns, attaching probabilities to their occurrence, weighting each return by that probability, and adding them up. Variation around the expected return is measured statistically by either the variance or the standard deviation. Refer to the example in Table 2-5. The upper portion illustrates the calculation of expected returns: each of the possible returns is multiplied by its probability of occurrence, and all of the products of the possibilities multiplied by chances are added to obtain an expected return of 30 percent. The same methodology can be used to derive the expected return for any investment or portfolio of investments.

TABLE 2-5. Expected Return and Risk Calculations for a Common Stock

Possible Return	Chance of Occurrence	Possibilities × Chances
−25%	0.12	−3.0%
0	0.08	0.0
10	0.15	1.5
30	0.25	7.5
50	0.30	15.0
90	0.10	9.0
	1.00	30.0% Expected return

Possible Return	Expected Return	Deviation From Expected Return	(Deviation)^2	Chance of Occurrence	(Deviation)^2 × Chances
−25%	30%	−55%	0.3025	0.12	0.0363
0	30	−30	0.0900	0.08	0.0072
10	30	−20	0.0400	0.15	0.0060
30	30	0	0.0000	0.25	0.0000
50	30	20	0.0400	0.30	0.0120
90	30	60	0.3600	0.10	0.0360
				Variance	0.0975

The lower portion of Table 2-5 shows how to calculate the variance for the expected return. First, take the differences (column 3) between possible returns (column 1) and the expected returns (column 2). Second, square the differences (column 4). Next multiply that by the probabilities or chances of occurrence in the upper portion (column 5). Add the results (column 6), and the variance of returns is obtained. The square root of the variance is the standard deviation, and the standard deviation of the illustrated expected return is 31.22 percent (the square root of 0.0975). The standard deviation measures the total risk of an asset and a portfolio.

Two more aspects of measuring risk need to be discussed. First, the probability distribution of returns and the decomposition of risk measurements can be divided into measurements associated with the market in which the asset is traded and those associated with the asset itself. The probability distribution of *ex ante* or potential future returns is assumed to be bell-shaped (statistically "normal"). Figure 2-3 is such a bell-shaped curve. If returns are normal, about 68 percent of the time all the returns that are relevant for decision making will fall within plus or minus one standard deviation of the expected return. About 96 percent of the time all of the relevant returns will fall within plus or minus two standard deviations of the expected return. Three standard deviations on either side of expected return encompasses

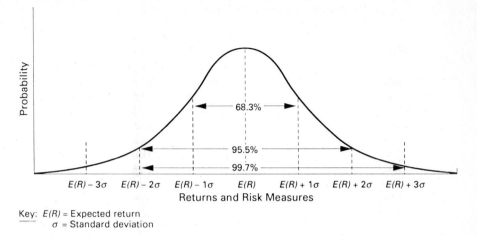

Key: *E(R)* = Expected return
     σ = Standard deviation

Figure 2-3. A Bell-Shaped (Normal) Distribution of Returns.

almost all of the relevant information.[2] Second, because the risk of single assets differs from the risk of a portfolio, different measures are needed. As illustrated in the next section, diversification may eliminate most of the unique or company-specific risk. So the total risk consists of that which is diversifiable and that which is not. The standard deviation picks up total risk.

Beta Calculation

Beta picks up the risk that cannot be diversified away. Because effective diversification eliminates almost all of an asset's unique risk, the relevant measure of a single asset's risk is not its standard deviation, but its beta (β_i). Beta indicates an asset's contribution to the total risk of a portfolio. The formula for an asset's beta is as follows:

$$\beta_i = cov\ (R_i, R_M)/\sigma^2 R_M$$

where

$$\beta_i = \text{beta of asset } i$$
$$cov\ (R_i, R_M) = \text{the covariance of the return on asset } i \text{ with the return on the market } (M)$$
$$R_i = \text{the return on asset } i$$

---

[2] If the distribution of returns is not normal, different analytical assumptions are necessary. Studies of past returns suggest that return distributions are not normal, although the normality assumption is used extensively in practice.

TABLE 2-6. Perfectly Offsetting Expected Rates of Return for Two Assets

Variation in E(R₁)	Variation in E(R₂)
+0.10	−0.10
−0.10	+0.10
+0.02	−0.02
+0.04	−0.04
+0.01	−0.01
−0.05	+0.05
+0.03	−0.03
−0.08	+0.08
−0.02	+0.02

R_M = the return on the market (M)

σ^2 = the variance (the standard deviation squared) of the market

MODERN PORTFOLIO THEORY

Modern portfolio theory (MPT) deals with the rationale for and methods of diversifying portfolios. The rationale is straightforward: to obtain the best possible expected return, given the level of risk assumed. The process of achieving this desired goal is a matter of minimizing the risk of the portfolio for each level of desired risk and return combination. The method focuses on combining assets whose expected returns are not highly correlated. The elements, then, that go into MPT are each asset's expected risk and expected return and the estimated covariances of each pair of asset returns.

Covariance measures the extent to which pairs of asset returns are likely to move together. The object always is to obtain efficient portfolios, the criterion for which is either of the following:

- For a given level of expected return, there is no portfolio with a lower risk.
- For a given level of risk, there is no portfolio with a higher expected return.

An extreme example of this is contained in Table 2-6, the data from which are plotted in Figure 2-4. Note from the table that the expected returns on the two assets are perfectly offsetting; as one increases by a given amount, the other decreases by the same amount, and vice versa. Figure 2-4 shows the same result: The expected rate of return on asset 1, $E(R_1)$, varies exactly in the opposite direction as that of asset 2, $E(R_2)$. In other words, the return on one exactly offsets that of the other. When combined in equal weights

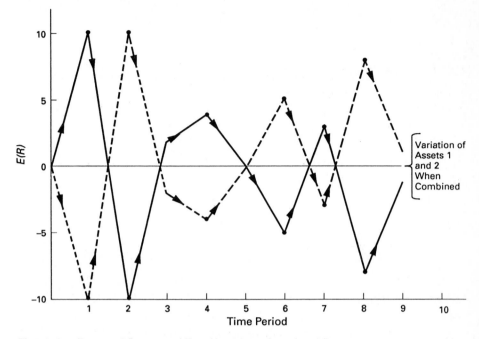

Figure 2-4. Expected Returns of Two Negatively Correlated Returns.

the total portfolio risk is zero, because the covariance of the assets is negative—their beta is -1. Naturally most real world portfolios are not likely to have such completely and perfectly offsetting effects, a topic discussed in more detail in a later section.

Portfolio Expected Return

The expected return on a portfolio of assets is the weighted average of the expected returns of the portfolio's component assets. For example, if Hot-Shot, Inc.'s expected return were 20 percent and if that of Mildly Hot, Inc. were 15 percent, an equally weighted portfolio return would be 17.5 percent. That figure is derived as follows:

$$E(R_p) = (20\% \times 50\%) + (15\% \times 50\%)$$
$$= 10\% + 7.5\%$$
$$= 17.5\%$$

where $E(R_p)$ is the expected return of the portfolio.

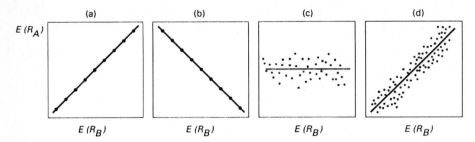

Figure 2-5. Illustrations of Expected Returns on Two Assets That Are (a) Perfectly Positively Correlated, (b) Perfectly Negatively Correlated, (c) Zero Correlated, and (d) Highly Positively Correlated.

Portfolio Risk

The risk of a single asset is measured in two ways: by its standard deviation of expected return and by its comovement with the expected return of the assets in the market in which it is traded. The standard deviation measures the total risk of an asset and covariance measures the risk of the asset's comovement with the other assets in the market.

Although the return on a portfolio is a simple weighted average of its components, the risk of a portfolio is complicated because the rates of return of the assets in the portfolio are not likely to move together perfectly. If they do not, the risk of the combined set of assets cannot be estimated by simply averaging their individual risks. Not only must the risk of the individual assets be incorporated into the analysis but the extent of the comovement of the pairs of expected returns must also be accounted for. The extent to which pairs of assets move together is measured by their covariance. Alternatively, and more intuitively, the comovement is picked up by the correlation of returns to two assets.

Correlation Effects. To understand the risk of the portfolio more clearly the essence of portfolio diversification must be reviewed. Refer to Figure 2-5. Panel (a) represents two assets, A and B, whose expected rates of return, $E(R_A)$ and $E(R_B)$, move together exactly; that is, if the rate of return on one is expected to go up, the other return is expected to go up by the same amount. When the returns of two assets are expected to move exactly alike—up or down—their returns are said to be perfectly positively correlated with each other.

The exact opposite of a perfect positive correlation is perfect negative correlation, which is depicted in panel (b). "Perfect negative correlation" means that if the return of one asset is expected to go down, the other is expected to go up.

The zero correlation case is depicted in panel (c). "Zero correlation"

TABLE 2-7. Basic Series: Cross-Correlations for Historical Yearly Returns of Security Groupings and Inflation, 1926–1988

	Common Stocks	Small Stocks	Long-Term Corporate Bonds	Long-Term Government Bonds	Intermediate-Term Government Bonds	U.S. Treasury Bills	Inflation
Common stocks	1.00						
Small stocks	0.82	1.00					
Long-term corporate bonds	0.19	0.08	1.00				
Long-term U.S. Government bonds	0.11	−0.01	0.93	1.00			
Intermediate-term U.S. Government bonds	0.03	−0.07	0.89	0.89	1.00		
U.S. Treasury bills	−0.07	−0.08	0.19	0.22	0.50	1.00	
Inflation	−0.02	0.06	−0.17	−0.17	0.01	0.41	1.00

SOURCE: Ibbotson Associates [1989].

means that no association of returns exists between the assets. If the return on one increases, it cannot be predicted what is likely to happen to the return on the other. It is just as likely to decrease as it is to increase.

As might be suspected, perfect correlation, either positive or negative, is not likely to exist in reality. Rather, most stocks move together, but not perfectly; that is, the correlation of returns between all possible pairs of assets is likely to be less than perfectly positively correlated. This phenomenon is depicted in panel (d). Moreover, rarely are negative correlations between assets found. Historical correlations of returns are measurable, and the technique may be found in Fuller and Farrell [1987] and Sharpe [1985]. Table 2-7 tabulates the correlation of past returns for various asset classes.

Figure 2-6 depicts the three correlations: perfectly positive, or +1; perfectly negative, or −1; and zero. Three important notions emerge from that picture. First, perfect positive correlation results in no risk reduction when the two assets are combined. For all practical purposes, one has bought the same asset. Indeed, one expects identically risky assets to have the same expected returns. This is represented by the straight lines (i.e., a one-for-one relation) connecting assets X and Y in Figure 2-6.

Second, perfect negative correlation has the potential for totally eliminating risk as shown in Figure 2-4. This is done by combining assets whose returns are perfectly negatively correlated and weighting them properly. With the proper combination of assets X and Y, the standard deviation can be forced to zero while the expected return remains at 15 percent.

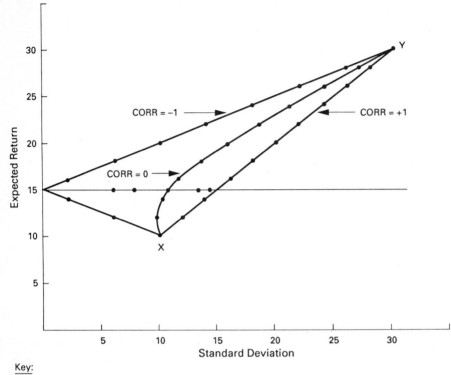

Key:

CORR = Correlation coefficient

Figure 2-6. Illustration of Risk Reduction Potential of Zero and Negatively Correlated Return Securities.

Third, the arc that connects points X and Y is the condition of less than perfect correlation (neither $+1$ nor -1). It represents zero correlation in this figure, but with a little less curvature it could represent the typical positive, but less than perfectly positive ($+1.0$), correlations for a portfolio. Indeed if one were to plot all assets, including single assets and portfolios of assets, into risk and return space as in Figure 2-7, and if one were to continue to combine all assets into portfolios, the arc AB would emerge. This arc is important to both the analytical content of MPT and the pricing of assets. It is called the *efficient frontier* of risky assets. Note that the efficiency criteria hold:

1. At a given level of expected risk there is no other combination of assets that has a higher expected return.
2. At a given level of expected return there is no other combination of assets that has a lower expected risk.

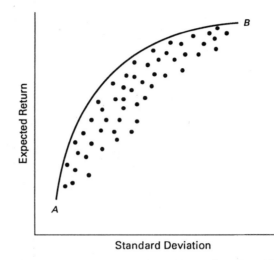

Figure 2-7. Illustration of an Efficient Frontier of Portfolios Within the Opportunity Set Available in Return/Risk Space.

Diversification Adequacy. A major insight of MPT is that a little diversification goes a long way. How little? The studies suggest that as few as 8 to 12 stocks whose returns are not highly correlated with each other would reduce the portfolio risk to approximately that of the marketplace in which they are traded. Figure 2-8 depicts the results of a typical study of this phenomenon.

Although diversification beyond 8 to 12 stocks seems superfluous, not many professional managers have so few stocks in their portfolios. There are many reasons for this, but the major one is that the studies deal with average past performance. Those who deal with real portfolios sense that, looking ahead, the relationships and therefore the results of a portfolio that consists of just 8 to 12 stocks are not nearly as predictable as those of a larger portfolio and that such a policy is not prudent. Even at that, Value Line recommends forming portfolios of about 15 stocks spread across 8 different industries. (It should be noted that this recommendation includes stock selection based on Value Line's own system of ranking stocks' expected performance.)

International Investing

One cannot conclude the diversification discussion without at least some discussion of international investing. The lure of rapidly growing international investing is the same as that of investing in purely domestic markets: to package assets that are not highly correlated so that risk reduction ensues,

Figure 2-8. Illustration of Rapidity of Unsystematic Risk Reduction as Additional Randomly Selected Stocks Are Added to an Equity Portfolio.

without limiting expected returns. International investing carries with it, however, two risks that domestic investing does not: political risk and currency risk, which were identified earlier as pervasive risks. Both historical and expected rates of return must be adjusted for exchange rate differentials. Forecasted returns especially must account for the return on both the currency and the asset to be bought. This complication of the investment process is necessary, but its costs are likely to be mitigated by the extensive risk reduction that ensues from international investing.

The rationale for international investing is not hard to discern. If one invests in domestic assets only, too much of the universe of potential assets is left out of the portfolio and more risk than necessary is assumed, perhaps with a penalty to returns as well. International investments expand the universe of assets to include in the portfolio. When the expanded set of assets has returns whose correlations are lower than those in the domestic set alone, the potential for risk reduction is great. The opportunity set of assets is expanded because the average correlation of international asset returns with those in the United States is lower (as low as 0.35) than the average for domestic assets alone (about 0.50 in the United States).

The studies that have produced these results are of historical correlations of returns between international markets with a broad-based index of global capital markets, such as the Morgan Stanley Capital International (MSCI) World Index or Morgan Stanley's EAFE Index (Europe, Asia, and

Far East Index), which is the same as MSCI World but leaves out the United States and Canada. Table 2-8 indicates some of the historical correlations that make international investing so enticing. Figure 2-9 indicates what happens to a portfolio's total risk when international stocks are added to a portfolio of U.S. stocks only. Not only is total risk reduced dramatically but the effort required to do so is not great in terms of the number of stocks one must hold.

Can the same risk-reducing results be achieved by investing in domestic companies that have extensive international operations? The studies suggest that by and large investing in such companies does not produce much risk reduction. Indeed, national risk seems to dominate so much that investing in multinational corporations provides precious little international diversification. See Solnik [1988], Senchak and Beedles [1980], and Jacquillat and Solnik [1978]. Further discussion of international diversification appears in various sections of the text, but especially in Chapters 5 through 10.

Modifying Portfolio Risk

Although modifying portfolio risk is discussed in far more detail in Chapters 6 and 11, it is important to point out here that a portfolio's risk may be modified by using either financial futures or options to hedge present positions. For example, options may be used to offset long positions in stocks. If a portfolio manager were uncertain about the direction the equity market might take, taking an option position in some broad-based index would hedge his position. Financial futures accomplish roughly the same thing, except that the obligation incurred and the settlement procedures employed with futures are different.

ASSET PRICING THEORIES

Asset prices are not determined simply by magic. To capture the logic and rationale for asset pricing, models have been developed. The models are important because they:

1. Help portfolio managers understand the nature of the investment environment.
2. Focus on the things that are worth worrying about, such as efficient diversification, and not on the things that may be relegated to a position of lesser importance, such as some, but not all, market idiosyncrasies.
3. Allow a portfolio manager to question constantly the efficacy of his firm's policies in light of both the models and their empirical content.

TABLE 2-8. Correlation Matrix of Stock Markets, 1971–1986 (monthly returns in U.S. dollars)

	West Germany	Belgium	Denmark	France	Italy	Norway	Netherlands	United Kingdom	Sweden	Switzerland
West Germany	1.00									
Belgium	0.63	1.00								
Denmark	0.42	0.47	1.00							
France	0.55	0.62	0.31	1.00						
Italy	0.33	0.41	0.29	0.43	1.00					
Norway	0.33	0.51	0.32	0.44	0.24	1.00				
Netherlands	0.66	0.65	0.48	0.57	0.35	0.48	1.00			
United Kingdom	0.41	0.51	0.36	0.52	0.35	0.34	0.61	1.00		
Sweden	0.36	0.42	0.38	0.31	0.30	0.32	0.42	0.36	1.00	
Switzerland	0.69	0.64	0.43	0.59	0.32	0.41	0.68	0.52	0.44	1.00
Spain	0.34	0.36	0.25	0.35	0.37	0.20	0.34	0.26	0.29	0.28
Australia	0.26	0.28	0.28	0.35	0.26	0.36	0.36	0.41	0.30	0.36
Japan	0.45	0.44	0.36	0.40	0.38	0.10	0.44	0.32	0.31	0.41
Hong Kong	0.18	0.23	0.31	0.21	0.18	0.20	0.34	0.29	0.17	0.26
Singapore	0.07	0.14	0.20	0.14	0.10	0.15	0.24	0.40	0.16	0.21
Canada	0.28	0.32	0.31	0.42	0.25	0.36	0.52	0.50	0.32	0.44
United States	0.32	0.36	0.31	0.40	0.23	0.37	0.55	0.47	0.35	0.44
Gold Mines	0.11	0.23	0.01	0.21	0.13	0.25	0.17	0.08	0.10	0.22
Gold	0.19	0.29	0.11	0.25	0.18	0.28	0.22	0.08	0.15	0.24
World Index	0.55	0.57	0.44	0.60	0.44	0.44	0.73	0.65	0.45	0.61
EAFE Index	0.64	0.62	0.44	0.62	0.52	0.35	0.70	0.69	0.43	0.61

	Spain	Australia	Japan	Hong Kong	Singapore	Canada	United States	Gold Mines	Gold	World Index	EAFE Index
West Germany											
Belgium											
Denmark											
France											
Italy											
Norway											
Netherlands											
United Kingdom											
Sweden											
Switzerland											
Spain	1.00										
Australia	0.22	1.00									
Japan	0.34	0.27	1.00								
Hong Kong	0.15	0.29	0.28	1.00							
Singapore	−0.02	0.29	0.21	0.41	1.00						
Canada	0.19	0.56	0.25	0.22	0.29	1.00					
United States	0.15	0.47	0.27	0.26	0.37	0.66	1.00				
Gold Mines	−0.01	0.15	0.09	−0.08	−0.04	0.23	0.10	1.00			
Gold	0.13	0.32	0.17	0.07	−0.07	0.26	0.01	0.58	1.00		
World Index	0.35	0.56	0.60	0.32	0.39	0.70	0.87	0.17	0.16	1.00	
EAFE Index	0.43	0.46	0.77	0.28	0.31	0.48	0.47	0.14	0.22	0.83	1.00

SOURCE: Solnik [1988].

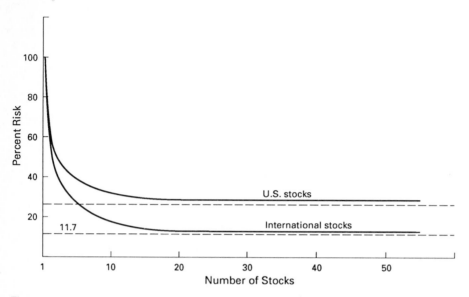

Figure 2-9. Illustration of Risk Reduction for U.S. Stocks From International Diversification. SOURCE: Solnik [1974].

4. Reinforce the work of both fundamental analysts and technicians, who continually compare their value estimates with the prices of the assets.
5. Tell portfolio managers how to estimate risk (e.g., beta) and return (estimates of a default-free rate of return and expected return on factors that influence returns).
6. Show portfolio managers how to evaluate the performance of portfolios.

The two main forms of asset pricing models are the capital asset pricing model (CAPM), the traditional version, and the arbitrage pricing theory (APT). Although conceptually asset pricing and MPT are separable, they are viewed here as being parts of a cohesive whole.

Capital Asset Pricing Model

The MPT exercise is important, for if the existence of a default-free asset, such as U.S. Treasury bills, is postulated, it can be plotted along the vertical axis in a graph such as that in Figure 2-10. Assume that it plots at point R_f. If one were to form a portfolio consisting of the default-free asset and a risky bundle of assets, which would be the best risky bundle? Without going into the mathematics, one continues to combine the risk-free asset with some

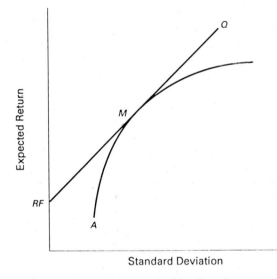

Figure 2-10. Illustration of the Risk-Free Rate, Market
Portfolio, and Capital Market Line.

risky asset on the arc *AB* until a line combining both is tangent to the efficient
frontier. Call it point *M*, for the market portfolio.

Figure 2-10 illustrates two important MPT concepts. The first is the
concept of the market portfolio itself. Point *M* indicates that a market portfolio exists, that it consists of all risky assets in proportion to their market
values, and that if one is to hold a risky portfolio of assets, given the alternative of holding a default-free asset, one will hold only the market portfolio.
The second MPT concept is illustrated by the line $R_f MQ$.

Capital Market Line. The line $R_f MQ$ represents the best combination
of risk and expected return in the capital markets. It is called the *Capital
Market Line* (CML). No other combination of the default-free asset and a
risky bundle of assets is superior to any combination along the CML. By
definition, no other risky assets exist above the arc *AB*, the efficient frontier
of only risky assets. Any point below the CML is undesirable, because it
will have either more risk at a given level of return or less return at the given
level of risk.

The important thing about the CML analysis is that it establishes the
presence of a combination of risky assets, *M*, that is preferred over all other
combinations of risky assets. It also helps when the portfolio manager wishes
to expand the analysis to include all assets, both single assets and portfolios
of assets, which are the commonplace arrangements in everyday portfolio
management.

At this point it is important to repeat that an investment's total risk is

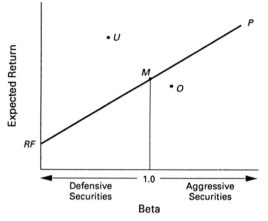

Figure 2-11. Security Market Line.

measured by its standard deviation of return. Because some of that total risk—sometimes a lot of it—may be diversified away by combining it with other assets, the standard deviation of return is not the risk measure to be applied to single assets or to portfolios that are not well diversified. Beta is the proper measure of the risk that cannot be diversified away as measured by the asset's responsiveness to market factors. Beta measures an asset's sensitivity relative to the marketplace in which it is traded. It contains only market-related risk. Therefore, diversifiable risk is not a factor in this analysis.

Security Market Line. Given this new measure of risk and the presence of a default-free asset, a new analytical picture emerges. It is depicted in Figure 2-11. The market portfolio, M, is taken from the CML and plotted. Adding the default-free rate and connecting the two points, the line that emerges is called the *security market line* (SML), or simply the *market line*.

The market line discloses several important things. First, all individual assets may be viewed as some combination of the default-free asset and the market portfolio. Second, all assets, in equilibrium, plot on the SML. Because equilibrium is a condition from which there is no tendency for change to occur, all of the assets are priced correctly. Rewards will be proportional to the risk exposure.

The SML and Asset Selection. If assets were temporarily below or above the SML, investors would identify them and correct the mispricing. For example, were an asset to plot above (or below) the SML, such as asset U (or asset O), it would be expected to earn a return in excess of (or less than) that warranted by its level of risk. It is undervalued (or overvalued), because its expected return differs from the SML prediction of return. Investors search for such phenomena and when they are discovered the assets are bought (or sold), driving up (or down) their prices. If all else stays the same, the expected return of the asset will subsequently decline (or rise), most likely until it converges vertically in an arbitrage-type process onto the SML.

This depiction is the CAPM, one of the major paradigms in financial analysis. The equation of the SML is

$$E(R_i) = R_f + [E(R_m) - R_f]\beta_i$$

The equation illustrates that an asset's expected return, $E(R_i)$, equals the risk-free return, R_f, plus an increment representing the anticipated equity market risk premium, $E(R_m) - R_f$, adjusted for the riskiness of the asset, β_i.

The SML also illustrates how to describe assets and portfolios. Inasmuch as the beta of the market is one, that serves as the *benchmark* by which to assess other assets: Those assets with a beta risk of less than one are called *defensive* and those assets with a beta risk of greater than one are termed *aggressive*.

Estimated Market Line. The CAPM has its flaws, many associated with its simplifying assumptions, but its strengths are compelling for the practice of investment management. Nevertheless, knowledge of the model's flaws is important. First, one clearly cannot borrow all that one wants at the default-free rate, although one can lend (buy bonds) at that rate. But the difference that this may make in an operational context is not material, especially for those investors who cannot by law or policy borrow. The point R_f may also be called a zero-beta asset, so that all one needs to do to develop the SML is to identify a zero-beta asset. Also, one way to develop an operational, ex ante (or projected) SML is to estimate the returns and risk for all assets in the manager's universe, statistically fit a line through the data points, and isolate all assets that plot above the estimated SML as potential candidates for inclusion in the portfolios. This approach dispenses with the need to identify whether a risk-free or zero-beta asset exists.

To illustrate this approach the data in Table 2-9 were arbitrarily assembled, and the estimated return was regressed against the estimated risk (beta). The plot of the results of the regression are depicted in Figure 2-12. Those assets that plot above the regression line would be candidates for purchase, and those plotting below the line would not be considered. (Note that the downward-sloping regression line, while theoretically unsupportable, does occur occasionally in certain market environments.)

Most of the CAPM holds up under most of the preceding criticism. Portfolio managers recognize that the trade-off between risk and expected return exists; that most of the time most assets seem to be fairly priced; that

TABLE 2-9. Hypothetical Data for Estimated Return/Risk Market Line

Stock	Estimated Return	Estimated Beta
1	12.00	1.00
2	1.00	1.25
3	2.00	1.05
4	5.00	0.55
5	−4.00	0.75
6	9.00	1.10
7	16.00	0.85
8	2.30	0.85
9	4.50	0.90
10	6.70	0.95
11	8.90	1.00
12	1.20	1.05
13	2.10	0.80
14	3.20	0.70
15	4.30	0.60
16	5.40	0.55
17	6.50	0.75
18	−7.60	1.05
19	−8.70	1.10

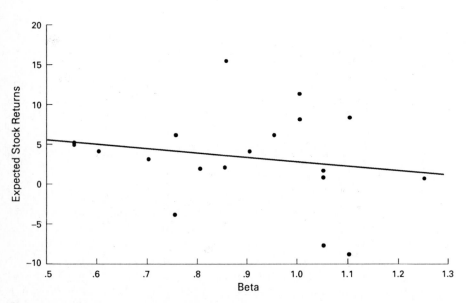

Figure 2-12. Estimated Market Line of Expected Returns and Risk.

unusual performance is difficult to attain in most markets; and that investors do not pay for something that they do not need (which is a simple way of saying that diversifiable risk is not compensated for by financial markets, or that only nondiversifiable risk counts when constructing a portfolio).

Market Model

One derivative of the CAPM is called the *market model*, which states that the rate of return on an asset depends on the rate of return on the market in which that asset is traded, plus a host of other considerations. The market model can be stated mathematically as follows:

$$E(R_i) = \alpha_i + [\beta_i \times E(R_M)] + e_i$$

Stated verbally, the market model is the expected return, $E(R_i)$, on any asset over some time period equals some constant (α_i) plus the expected return on the market, $E(R_M)$, multiplied by the sensitivity (β_i) of the asset's return with the market return, plus a host of other things as represented by an "error term" (e_i). Alpha (α_i) represents the asset's unique return or the return apart from any market return factor. Beta (β_i) measures an asset's expected return response per unit of market expected return. The error term (e_i) represents the asset's residual risk or uncertainty of return not associated with the market. It is the asset's unsystematic risk that can be reduced or eliminated by portfolio diversification.

Much has been written about the various components of the market model, especially about the estimation and stability of the systematic risk component of return, beta. The reader is referred to any of the standard investment textbooks for a more complete exposition of these investigations.

Arbitrage Pricing Model

The arbitrage pricing theory, or APT, is another asset pricing model. It differs from CAPM in that the latter relies heavily on the market portfolio, whereas APT may be totally silent on that issue. APT assumes nothing about which factors influence asset prices, except that they exist, can be found, will be priced by market participants, and, if divergences from equilibrium occur, arbitrageurs will eliminate the pricing disparities by buying and selling, thereby returning asset prices to their equilibrium value. That is, APT merely states that if such-and-such factor is causing assets to be mispriced, thus plotting them above or below some market line, arbitrageurs will enter the marketplace to eliminate such mispricing. APT does not explain which factors tend to influence the price of an asset most, although studies suggest

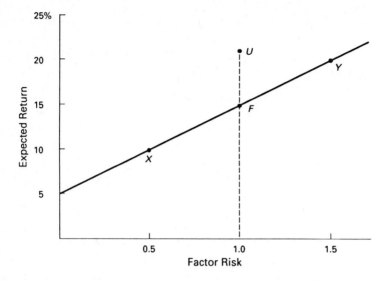

Figure 2-13. Illustration of a Mispriced Asset in a One-Factor Arbitrage Pricing Model.

that four factors tend to dominate and explain behavior. These factors are identified later in this section.

Pervasive Factors. APT is a form of multifactor asset pricing model, except that it deals with factors that are pervasive to all assets. In this context, the single-factor market model is a special form of APT. The APT model is of the following form:

$$E(R_i) = R_f + \beta_1 F_1 + \beta_2 F_2 + \ldots + \beta_m F_m$$

where

m = number of factors

$E(R_i)$ = expected return on the asset

R_f = return on the risk-free asset

β = sensitivity of the asset to its associated factor

F = factor

The single factor model's equation is

$$E(R_i) = R_f + \beta F$$

If F were the market portfolio, this would be the equation of the expected SML for the period under analysis.

The arbitrage in the APT model is similar to that of the SML analysis. For example, in Figure 2-13, the trade-off is between that of expected return

TABLE 2-10. Example of Risk-Free Arbitrage Profits Available for a Mispriced Asset in a One-Factor Arbitrage Pricing Model

	Investment	Expected Return	Factor Risk
Short sale of F	+ $100	+ 21%	− 1.0
Purchase of U	− 100	− 15	1.0
U and F net result	$ 0	6%	0.0

and some factor, with the extent of the relation being measured by the asset's sensitivity to the factor believed to determine prices and returns. Table 2-10 shows how the arbitrage could work: Sell short[3] the factor asset, F, using the proceeds to buy the mispriced asset with the same level of risk, U. The result of the process is to pocket the difference of $6, or, in other words, to earn 6 percent, which is the difference between the returns on U and F. The process continues until no more profits exist, or alternatively until all assets at the same risk level are selling at prices to produce the same expected return. In this idyllic analysis, the entire process is accomplished without assuming risk; the sensitivity of the portfolio of the long and short positions in U and F, respectively, nets to zero. Moreover, no cash is required. The point of the example is that assets with the same sensitivity to the same factors tend to sell at the same price.

Factor Identification. The most difficult aspect of APT and all multifactor models is to identify the factors that are to be priced. This is an empirical question primarily, and to date the studies suggest that the following four factors essentially determine asset prices:

1. Unanticipated changes in inflation
2. Unanticipated changes in industrial production
3. Unanticipated changes in risk premiums (the spread between yields on low- and high-grade bonds)
4. Unanticipated changes in the slope of the term structure of interest rates

Is APT better than CAPM? Investment professionals continue to debate this question. One can say that more factors are likely to be better than fewer and that settling on the set that seems to do the job is likely to make portfolio managers better at their task. In the portfolio management environment of the 1990s, a thorough understanding of both CAPM and APT is essential.

---

[3] A short sale is one in which an investor sells assets that he does not deliver to settle the trade; rather, he borrows them. The hoped-for result is a decline in the asset's price. The profit from the trade occurs when the sale price exceeds the price at which the investor buys back the asset to repay the loan of the original stock.

International Asset Pricing

Asset pricing models also exist for international assets. Many of them turn on whether international markets are segmented or integrated. The difference that this makes for decisions is great because if markets are segmented, the differentials in risk and return are not likely to be arbitraged away easily, whereas in integrated markets arbitrage tends to eliminate mispriced assets. Solnik [1988] suggests that the psychological barriers, legal constraints, transaction costs, taxation issues, political risks, and exchange risk might militate against international integration of capital markets. Wheatley [1988] found that the cost of capital for assets of similar risk was not the same in various countries, thereby indicating a lack of integration. In sum, the evidence suggests that international markets are more segmented than one would expect, but not completely so.

REAL ESTATE

Real estate investments, including mortgages, are important not only because they constitute 45 percent of investable U.S. assets (stock and bonds are about 55 percent) but also because of their important risk-reducing characteristics. About 3.5 to 4.0 percent of the total holdings of pension fund investors were in equity real estate in the late 1980s. The usual classes in which institutional investors invest are office and apartment buildings, hotels, shopping centers, industrial property, and less frequently, raw land. Institutional investors tend to favor office buildings (about 45 percent of total real estate commitments), industrial complexes (16 percent). and retail complexes (16 percent).

Measuring Returns and Risk

Real estate returns and risks are not as easily measured as those on financial assets, because, although the cash flows are identifiable, market prices are not. Discounted cash flow analyses using appraisals are commonly used to estimate market values but are flawed because they do not represent the prices at which actual transactions took place or can take place. Appraisal values are biased because the estimated values tend to be smoothed; they do not change much, or at least not unpredictably, from one appraisal to the next. Moreover, financial leverage tends to magnify return calculations. There are a number of other problems associated with real estate investing,

TABLE 2-11. Correlations of Real Estate Sectors and Composite Total Returns With Various Other Assets, 1947–1984

	Real Estate Sector			Real Estate Composite
	Business[a]	Residential	Farmland	
S&P 500 common stocks	0.14	−0.08	−0.05	−0.06
Small-company stocks	0.16	0.04	0.02	0.06
Long-term corporate bonds	0.05	0.06	−0.31	−0.08
Long-term U.S. Government bonds	0.04	0.06	−0.33	−0.09
U.S. Treasury bills	0.68	0.53	−0.10	0.38
Inflation rates	0.57	0.80	0.50	0.85

SOURCE: Ibbotson and Brinson [1987].
[a] Correlations with business real estate are for 1960–1984.

including extreme illiquidity at various times, no continuous market, large size of individual projects, nonhomogeneity of properties, large search costs for buyers or sellers, and other large transactions costs.

MPT and Real Estate Investing

With all of the negatives of real estate noted in the prior section, one wonders if a real case can be made to include it in professionally managed portfolios. Luckily, the principles of MPT apply to real estate, and they come in two steps: (1) overall diversification of a portfolio of multiple asset classes and (2) diversification of only real estate assets.

Studies show that real estate returns are not highly correlated with other assets typically found in portfolios, such as stocks, bonds and money market instruments. Tables 2-11 and 2-12 replicate the correlations that Ibbotson and Brinson [1987] and Firstenberg et al. [1988] found. Most of the Ibbotson and Brinson correlations in Table 2-11 are quite low and sometimes even negative, the stuff of which good portfolio candidates is made. The Firstenberg et al. results in Table 2-12 show low correlations among regions, even among some property types, indicating diversification of investments by region and property type within the real estate portfolio would reduce residual risk. These results tell us that real estate tends to expand the opportunity set of total investing. In effect the efficient frontier without real estate is likely to be inefficient relative to one that contains real estate. Much more will be said about real estate analysis and portfolio management in Chapters 6 and 10.

INVESTOR RISK AVERSION

Investing consists of a trade-off between risk and expected return. The feelings of investors toward risk and expected return must be integrated into

TABLE 2-12. Correlations of Real Estate Portfolio Returns for Different Geographic Regions and Property Types, 1978–1985

	Regional Correlation Matrix			
Region	East	Midwest	South	West
East	1.00			
Midwest	0.16	1.00		
South	0.25	0.04	1.00	
West	0.32	0.14	0.46	1.00

	Property Type Correlation Matrix				
Property Type	Apartments	Hotels	Industrial	Office	Retail
Apartments	1.00				
Hotels	0.56	1.00			
Industrial	0.41	0.17	1.00		
Office	0.21	0.11	0.65	1.00	
Retail	0.13	−0.01	0.59	0.21	1.00

SOURCE: Firstenberg et al. [1988].

the portfolio manager's analysis. Because one cannot expect ever higher returns without assuming ever more risk, one has to decide what combination of the two to assume. For every incremental dose of expected return, there is an incremental dose of risk. Most investors are assumed, correctly most of the time, to be risk averse. *Risk aversion* means a preference for return and a dislike for risk. Chapters 3 and 4 provide an extensive discussion of the risk/return trade-off considerations for individual and institutional investors. These considerations include asset growth, legal constraints, liquidity needs, adequate income, taxation, social investing criteria, wealth preservation, price volatility, and reinvestment rates, among others.

Only when all of these considerations and many others are melded into one final conclusion, may an investor be located on the SML. The object is to select that level of risk which makes one the most comfortable. The resulting returns are those that ensue from that risk level. Put still another way, the question is, how much more incremental risk is one willing to assume to achieve an incremental return?

Conceptually, the issues are as follows. Because most portfolios are well diversified, the non-market-related risk is eliminated. (The average R-squareds[4] of institutional portfolios are typically in the neighborhood of 0.90 to 0.94, which means that market movements are likely to explain 90 to 94

---

[4] R-squareds measure the percentage of the dependent variable that is explained by the independent variable. For example, a portfolio's R-squared of .90 means that 90 percent of the return on the portfolio was explicable by the return on the market.

percent of the changes in the value of the portfolio, with the remaining 10 to 6 percent not being explained by the market return.) So the issue of substance is whether the beta of the portfolio is less than, greater than, or equal to that of the market. As shown in Figure 2-11, portfolios with a beta of less than one are less risky than the benchmark and are considered defensive; those with betas greater than one are more risky and are considered aggressive; those that are equal to one are in a neutral territory. The decision to be made, if the portfolio is well diversified, is whether to be more or less risky than the benchmark portfolio.

An additional important issue is *whose risk aversion one assumes*. For example, the risk aversion of a pension fund sponsor may differ from that of the portfolio manager. The issue is often resolved by hiring a manager whose risk aversion matches that of the sponsor, but that approach may be flawed. A manager will tell a sponsor that he will adjust the portfolio he manages to meet the risk needs of the sponsor. Yet most managers package portfolios whose risk, and therefore expected return, are likely to be about the same. This not-unexpected result follows because the sponsor's risk aversion is not well specified and the portfolio manager's risk aversion seems to dominate; sponsors hire him based on his announced investment style, which has a built-in risk aversion. This is fine as long as the portfolio manager selection process is well executed.

To get some idea of how this matter is resolved in practice, refer to the client survey in Table 2-13 used by Batterymarch Financial Management to derive a risk profile. As can be seen, the queries evoke responses that help the manager assess the needs of the plan sponsor. This approach is a move in the right direction. The material developed in Chapters 3 and 4 on individual and institutional preference and recommended policy statements based on those preferences will further elaborate on this topic.

PORTFOLIO MANAGEMENT

Portfolio management is the art of packaging and maintaining the proper set of assets to maximize the goals and objectives of the client, given the constraints imposed. To see portfolio management in its proper perspective, it is necessary to first assume that the risk aversion of the client is specified.

Two not necessarily mutually exclusive themes exist in investment management: individual asset selection and portfolio analysis. The management of either may, in varying degree, be active or passive.

Asset Selection

Fundamental Approach. The fundamental approach to asset selection assumes that assets do not always sell at their intrinsic value, that such

TABLE 2-13. Items From Survey to Determine Institutional Investor/Pension Plan Sponsor Risk Aversion Profile

In order to help us match our communication to your individual needs, we have developed the survey that follows. Please place a check mark next to the 20 items of greatest interest to you.

1. ..... Absolute vs. relative performance
2. ..... Active management
3. ..... Avoiding typical mistakes
4. ..... Management firm's mistakes
5. ..... Management firm's organization
6. ..... Management firm's research
7. ..... Management firm's stance for the future
8. ..... Below-target returns
9. ..... Betting on unique ideas
10. ..... Biases in judgments
11. ..... Capitalizing on opportunities
12. ..... Capitalizing on undervaluations
13. ..... Career consequences of performance shortfalls
14. ..... Careful buying
15. ..... Comparisons with competitors
16. ..... Consensus portfolios
17. ..... Conservative management
18. ..... Contrary management
19. ..... Creativity in portfolio management
20. ..... Defense of management firm
21. ..... Disciplined selling
22. ..... Diversification techniques
23. ..... Fear of losses
24. ..... Fear of random events
25. ..... Finding chances worth taking
26. ..... Global strategies
27. ..... Going for the "sure thing"
28. ..... Good luck vs. good judgment
29. ..... Group decision making
30. ..... Hedging extreme thinking
31. ..... High-stake choices
32. ..... International diversification
33. ..... Investment losses
34. ..... Investor anxiety
35. ..... Investor willpower

36. ..... Justification of choice of management firm
37. ..... Likelihood of potential losses
38. ..... Limiting possible outcomes
39. ..... Long-run records
40. ..... Making too much of recent trends
41. ..... Market judgments that are wrong
42. ..... Negative surprises
43. ..... Nonconsensus portfolios
44. ..... Normal portfolios
45. ..... Not following the crowd
46. ..... Novel ideas for portfolios
47. ..... Outwitting the crowd
48. ..... Overcoming irrational fears
49. ..... Passive management
50. ..... Past vs. future performance
51. ..... Patterns that mislead
52. ..... Perceived price inconsistencies
53. ..... Personalized portfolios
54. ..... Placating the investment committee
55. ..... Portfolio characteristics
56. ..... Portfolio construction
57. ..... Positive surprises
58. ..... Prizing certainty
59. ..... Psychological phenomena behind investor behavior
60. ..... Randomness of returns
61. ..... Reliance on consultants' opinions
62. ..... Resources for the investment committee
63. ..... Rewards for patience
64. ..... Rewards for taking chances
65. ..... Short-term setbacks
66. ..... Short-term vs. long-term performance
67. ..... Skillful valuation
68. ..... Stable returns
69. ..... Target rates of return
70. ..... Use of the watch list to detect bankruptcy
71. ..... Valuation model development
72. ..... Willingness to be different

SOURCE: Farrelly and LeBaron [1989] and LeBaron, Farrelly, and Gula [1989].

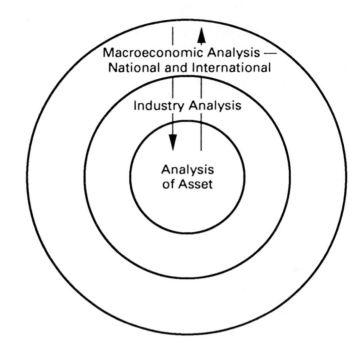

Figure 2-14. The Top-Down and Bottom-Up Approaches to Portfolio Management.

discrepancies exist and may be found, and that the search for the discrepancies is worth it. In the context of MPT and asset pricing, it indicates that unique risks are manageable and profitable. The fundamental approach may take a top-down or bottom-up orientation. Assuming that investments can be viewed in terms of three concentric circles, the inner core consists of the intrinsic value of the asset. See Figure 2-14.

Bottom-Up Fundamentals. The bottom-up approach uses a variety of fundamental economic and financial factors to determine whether a single asset is priced properly. At the extreme of this approach the manager does not care what is going on in the industry (the center circle) or in the economy (the outer circle). This approach assumes that value is value, and that eventually it will be recognized by all market participants. The portfolio is packaged so that only those assets selling below their estimated intrinsic value will be purchased. When assets exceed their intrinsic value, they are sold. Thus two of the major problems, how to select investment assets and when to buy and sell them, are solved by this approach. A third problem, how to package assets, may be solved either ad hoc or with a portfolio optimizer. Use of the ad hoc approach ensures that the portfolio contains a large but undefined number of assets and that the assets cross industry lines (in the case of stocks) or cross grades or maturities (in the case of bonds). The optimizer approach mathematically determines the best allocation of resources among the set of analyzed assets, given their expected returns, risk, and covariance with some economywide factor(s).

Top-Down Fundamentals. The top-down approach tries to achieve the same results by different means. The aggregate economy, national and international, is analyzed first, industries are identified as being prosperous relative to the overall economic cycle next, and then firms within the industries are selected based on the extent to which they are assumed to be mispriced. The portfolio is packaged in roughly the same way as in the bottom-up approach.

Technical Analysis. An altogether different approach, technical analysis, also assumes asset mispricing but it attempts to identify asset mispricing by discovering trends and turning points in asset prices. The analysis is based primarily on past prices but also on volume. The approach may be applied to the market as a whole and to single assets. Its major applications are found in stock and commodity markets. Technical methodologies abound and are used extensively. Long-term, intermediate, and short-term trends are divined from past prices and form the basis for decisions. Assets that are technically strong are bought, and those that are technically weak are sold. The construction of portfolios using technical analysis is essentially the same as that for fundamental analysis.

Portfolio Analysis

Passive Approach. Portfolio approaches also differ somewhat, depending on one's underlying assumption about the efficiency of the market in which one operates. If one assumes that the markets for assets are reasonably efficient, so that almost any search for mispriced assets is not wise, packaging a portfolio that mimics some broad-based index of the market, such as the S&P 500, makes sense. Such is the nature of index funds. The beauty of this approach is that the risk of the market is approximated and the management process is reduced to skeletal proportions, thereby reducing fees and trading costs to the minimum.

Active Approach. If the view is that mispriced assets exist and are worth seeking out, once they are found, regardless of the underlying approach, the packaging may be ad hoc, such as plenty of assets spread across a large number of industry groups, or it may be more sophisticated, concentrating or overweighting the portfolio in certain sectors, industries, or individual securities and underweighting others. If the expected return and potential risk of the assets are estimated, a *portfolio optimizer* may be used to determine the best combination of risk and expected return. Such optimizers are widely used by the professional managers. For common stocks, the inputs are the expected returns and the beta for each asset. The process of optimization is not discussed in detail here, but suffice it to say that the goal is to minimize risk for each level of return. The process requires manipulating the weights allocated to each asset being considered for inclusion until both the set of assets and the weights of each are the best possible in light of the estimated returns and risk. A picture such as that in Figure 2-7 emerges.

An alternative to using optimizers is to equally weight each asset in each asset class. This places a constraint on the percentage allocated to each asset, and it tells how many assets in each class to hold. For example, if the weights are 4 percent, 25 individual assets are to be held. Many optimizers contain a weighting constraint such as a limit of 3 percent of any one asset in the portfolio. When the constraints are exceeded, a decision to rebalance the portfolio is necessary.

Rarely are the extreme approaches used to manage portfolios. Index funds are passively managed in practice, but even then total passivity is impossible. If the weightings of the assets change, for example, portfolio rebalancing is needed.

Portfolio Performance Measurement

After having invested, it is necessary to measure the results, based on some benchmark, the analytical thrust of which is usually a variant of the proposition that returns are proportional to the risk assumed. The measures are derived from asset pricing models. Portfolio performance measurement is intended to pick up the idiosyncratic behavior of portfolio managers and exploitable market characteristics. Ability to select stocks, timing purchases and sales, and rotations among sectors are some of the things performance measures try to pick up. This topic is covered in Chapter 14 and is an extremely important although sensitive and vexing component of the portfolio management process.

SUMMARY

This chapter covered several major topics that form building blocks for further study. It began with asset markets and their efficiency. Portfolio managers have to make assumptions about the efficiency of the markets in which they are trading. The best that this chapter can do is to present the nature of the studies that have been made of market efficiency. The essential conclusion one comes away with is that most asset markets seem to be highly efficient, although not nearly as efficient as once thought.

Calculating asset returns seems a lot more simple than it is, but the important concept to carry away from this chapter is that the compound return is the proper universal return measure because it tells the rate at which wealth grows. Getting to returns that make sense requires adjustments such as those for taxes and inflation.

The discussion of return expectations touched on scenario analysis, a format in which portfolio managers are forced to assess the likely prospects of various asset classes under varying economic scenarios. Historical risk premium data were presented for the purpose of adding perspective and because those premiums are used so extensively in asset allocation models.

The discussion of risk analysis began with a delineation of risks—pervasive, systematic, and residual (although the first two are frequently combined into one for analytical purposes).

Then the knotty problem of measuring risk was discussed. It was determined that the proper measure of an asset's total risk is its standard deviation. Because of diversification, however, the risk that counts is that measured by beta: an asset's sensitivity to the returns on the market in which it is traded. This is so because reasonably complete diversification eliminates most of an asset's residual risk, so that only the contribution of an asset's market-related risk counts when constructing a portfolio.

Next modern portfolio theory was reviewed, along with its emphasis on the necessity to diversify into a set of assets whose returns are not highly correlated with each other. The same diversification principles that apply to domestic assets apply also when international portfolios are built. The likely benefit is further portfolio risk reduction, without reducing expected return.

Having reviewed MPT principles, the next step was to discuss how asset prices are determined. Portfolio managers can no longer survive without understanding the fundamentals of asset pricing. The Capital Asset Pricing Model and its associated Security Market Line concept are the major models for portfolio analysis, yet there are those that seem to think that an improvement in the original asset pricing models of CAPM is in place: Arbitrage Pricing Theory, the major appeal of which is its less-restrictive assumptions. The major shortcoming of APT to date, however, is determining the factors that truly explain asset prices. For the moment, CAPM still holds forth with considerable vigor, although the insights of APT are significant and are likely to be studied in greater depth in the future.

Real estate was next treated in a brief, separate section, not because it does not belong in other parts of the chapter but because it possesses characteristics that differ from financial assets and because it is relatively new to most portfolio managers. Basically, including real estate in a typical stocks, bonds, and bills portfolio may reduce the portfolio's risk without penalizing returns. The same was said in other parts of the chapter about the inclusion of international as well as domestic assets in investment portfolios.

In reviewing asset selection techniques, it was shown that fundamental analysis—whether top-down or bottom-up—and technical analysis are useful. The same is true of either active or passive portfolio packaging approaches.

FURTHER READING

There are a number of standard textbooks and broad-based monographs that cover general topics in investment basics. Three of the latter that are quantitatively oriented and practitioner-oriented are Brown and Kritzman [1987], Fogler and Bayston [1984], and Ibbotson and Brinson [1987].

An excellent review of historical returns and risk for domestic U.S. and international classes of assets can be found in Ibbotson Associates [1988] and Ibbotson, Siegel, and Love [1985].

Some important extensions of CAPM can be found in Breeden [1979]. A review of the various capital asset pricing theories can be found in Fuller [1981]. A straightforward development of arbitrage pricing theory is contained in Chen, Roll, and Ross [1983] and Roll and Ross [1984].

Individual risk aversion is discussed at length in Droms [1987] and as well in Farrelly and LeBaron [1989] and LeBaron, Farrelly, and Gula [1989]. Institutional portfolio management is addressed in Brinson, Diermeier, and Schlarbaum [1986], Joehnk [1987], and Vertin [1985].

Real estate as a portfolio investment is covered in Firstenberg, Ross, and Zisler [1988], Ibbotson and Siegel [1984], and Zisler and Ross [1987].

A number of pieces on international investing have appeared over the past several years and include Black [1974], Ibbotson, Carr, and Robinson [1982], Jacquillat and Solnik [1978], and Lessard [1976, 1978]. There are also two ICFA seminar proceedings in this area, one edited by McEnally [1986] and one by Vertin [1984]. The topic is likewise treated in two important books, one by Ibbotson and Brinson [1987] and one by Solnik [1988].

This chapter benefited greatly from the counterpart chapter written by Keith P. Ambachtsheer and James H. Ambrose, titled "Basic Financial Concepts: Return and Risk," in the first edition of this book, Maginn and Tuttle [1983].

BIBLIOGRAPHY

Black, F. "International Capital Market Equilibrium With Investment Barriers." *Journal of Financial Economics*, December 1974.

Black, Fischer. "Capital Market Equilibrium With Restricted Borrowing." *Journal of Business*, July 1972.

Brealey, Richard. *An Introduction to Risk and Return from Common Stocks,* 2nd ed. Cambridge, Mass.: MIT Press, 1983.

Breeden, Douglas T. "An Intertemporal Asset Pricing Model with Stochastic Consumption and Investment Opportunities." *Journal of Financial Economics,* September 1979.

Brinson, Gary P., Jeffrey J. Diermeier, and Gary G. Schlarbaum. "A Composite Portfolio Benchmark for Pension Plans." *Financial Analysts Journal,* March/April 1986.

Brown, Stephen J., and Mark P. Kritzman, eds. *Quantitative Methods in Financial Analysis.* Homewood, Ill.: Dow Jones-Irwin, 1987

Chen, Nai-Fu, Richard Roll, and Stephen A. Ross. "Economic Forces and the Stock Market: Testing the APT and Alternative Asset Pricing Theories." Working Paper No. 20-83. Graduate School of Management, UCLA, December 1983.

Cohen, K.J., and J.A. Pogue. "An Empirical Evaluation of Alternative Portfolio-Selection Models." *Journal of Business,* April 1967.

Diermeier, Jeffrey J., Roger G. Ibbotson, and Laurence B. Siegel. "The Supply of Capital Market Returns." *Financial Analysts Journal,* March/April 1984.

Droms, William G., ed. *Asset Allocation for the Individual Investor.* Seminar Proceedings, Institute of Chartered Financial Analysts. Homewood, Ill.: Dow Jones-Irwin, 1987.

Ellis, Charles D. *Investment Policy: How to Win the Loser's Game.* Homewood, Ill.: Dow Jones-Irwin, 1985.

Elton, E.J., and M.J. Gruber. *Modern Portfolio Theory and Investment Analysis,* 3d ed. New York: John Wiley & Sons, 1987.

Farrell, James L., Jr. "Homogeneous Stock Groupings—Implications for Portfolio Management." *Financial Analysts Journal,* May/June 1975.

———. *Guide to Portfolio Management.* New York: McGraw-Hill Book Company, 1983.

Farrelly, Gail, and Dean LeBaron. "Assessing Risk Tolerance Levels: A Prerequisite to Personalizing and Managing Portfolios." *Financial Analysts Journal,* January/February 1989.

Finnerty, J.E. "Insiders Activity and Inside Information: A Multivariate Analysis." *Journal of Financial and Quantitative Analysis,* June 1976.

Firstenberg, Paul M., Stephen A. Ross, and Randall C. Zisler. "Real Estate: The Whole Story." *The Journal of Portfolio Management.* Spring 1988.

Fogler, H. Russell, and Darwin M. Bayston, eds. *Improving the Investment Decision Process: Quantitative Assistance for the Practitioner—And for the Firm.* Seminar Proceedings, Institute of Chartered Financial Analysts. Homewood, Ill.: Dow Jones-Irwin, 1984.

Fuller, R.J. *Capital Asset Pricing Theories—Evolution and New Frontiers.* Charlottesville, Va.: The Financial Analysts Research Foundation, 1981.

Fuller, Russel J., and James L. Farrell, Jr. *Modern Investments and Security Analysis.* New York: McGraw-Hill Book Company, 1987.

Ibbotson Associates. *Stocks, Bonds, Bills, and Inflation: 1989 Yearbook: Market Results for 1926–1988.* Chicago: Ibbotson Associates, 1989.

Ibbotson, Roger G., and Gary P. Brinson. *Investment Markets.* New York: McGraw-Hill Book Company, 1987.

Ibbotson, Roger G., Richard C. Carr, and Anthony W. Robinson. "International Equity and Bond Returns." *Financial Analysts Journal,* July/August 1982.

Ibbotson, Roger G., Jeffrey J. Diermeier, and Laurence B. Siegel. "The Demand for Capital Market Returns: A New Equilibrium Theory." *Financial Analysts Journal,* January/February 1984.

Ibbotson, Roger G., and Laurence B. Siegel. "Real Estate Returns: A Comparison With Other Investments." *AREUEA Journal,* Fall 1984.

Ibbotson, Roger G., Laurence B. Siegel, and Kathryn S. Love. "World Wealth: Market Values and Returns." *The Journal of Portfolio Management,* Fall 1985.

Jacobs, Bruce I., and Kenneth N. Levy. "Disentangling Equity Return Regularities: New Insights and Investment Opportunities." *Financial Analysts Journal,* May/June 1988, pp. 18–43.

Jacquillat, B., and B. Solnik. "Multinationals Are Poor Tools for International Diversification." *The Journal of Portfolio Management,* Winter 1978.

Jensen, M.C. "Risk, the Pricing of Capital Assets, and the Evaluation of Investment Portfolios." *Journal of Business,* April 1969.

———. "Capital Markets: Theory and Evidence." *Bell Journal of Economics and Management Science,* Autumn 1972.

Joehnk, Michael D., ed. *Asset Allocation for Institutional Portfolios.* Seminar Proceedings, Institute of Chartered Financial Analysts. Homewood, Ill.: Dow Jones-Irwin, 1987.

LeBaron, Dean, Gail Farrelly, and Susan Gula. "Facilitating a Dialogue on Risk: A Questionnaire Approach." *Financial Analysts Journal,* May/June 1989.

Lessard, Donald F. "World, Country, and Industry Relationships in Equity Returns: Implications for Risk Reduction Through International Diversification." *Financial Analysts Journal,* January/February 1976.

———."Why Not Diversify Internationally Rather Than Domestically?" *Financial Analysts Journal,* July/August 1978.

Lorie, J.H., and V. Niederhoffer. "Predictive and Statistical Properties of Insider Trading." *Journal of Law and Economics,* April 1968.

Lorie, James H., Peter Dodd, and Mary Hamilton Kimpton. *The Stock Market: Theories and Evidence,* 2d ed. Homewood, Ill.: Dow Jones-Irwin, 1985.

Maginn, John L., and Donald L. Tuttle, eds. *Managing Investment Portfolios,* 1st ed. Boston: Warren, Gorham & Lamont, Inc., 1983.

McEnally, Richard W., ed. *International Bonds and Currencies.* Seminar Proceedings, Institute of Chartered Financial Analysts. Homewood, Ill.: Dow Jones-Irwin, 1986.

Modigliani, F., and G.A. Pogue. "An Introduction to Risk and Return," Parts 1 and 2. *Financial Analysts Journal,* March/April 1974 and May/June 1974.

Reilly, F.K., and E.F. Drzycimski. "Exchange Specialists and World Events." *Financial Analysts Journal,* July/August 1975.

Report of the Special Study of the Security Markets. Washington, D.C.: Securities and Exchange Commission.

Roll, Richard, and Stephen A. Ross. "The Arbitrage Pricing Theory Approach to Strategic Portfolio Planning." *Financial Analysts Journal,* May/June 1984.

Rosenberg, B., and J. Guy. "Beta and Investment Fundamentals," Parts 1 and 2. *Financial Analysts Journal,* May/June 1976 and July/August 1976.

Rosenberg, B., and V. Marathe. "The Prediction of Investment Risk: Systematic and Residual Risk." *Proceedings of the Seminar on the Analysis of Security Prices,* Graduate School of Business, University of Chicago, November 1975.

————."Common Factors in Security Returns: Microeconomic Determinants and Macroeconomic Correlates." *Proceedings of the Seminar on the Analysis of Security Prices,* Graduate School of Business, University of Chicago, May 1976.

Ross, Stephen A. "The Arbitrage Theory of Capital Asset Pricing." *Journal of Economic Theory,* December 1976.

————. "Return, Risk and Arbitrage," in I. Friend and J. Bicklser, eds. *Risk and Return in Finance.* Cambridge, Mass.: Ballinger, 1976.

Senchak, A., and W. Beedles. "Is International Diversification Desirable?" *The Journal of Portfolio Management,* Winter 1980.

Sharpe, William F., "Capital Asset Prices: A Theory of Market Equilibrium Under Conditions of Risk." *The Journal of Finance,* September 1964.

————."Mutual Fund Performance." *Journal of Business,* Jan. 1966.

————."Factor Models, CAPM, and the APT." *The Journal of Portfolio Management,* Fall 1984.

————. *Investments,* 3d ed. Englewood Cliffs, N.J.: Prentice-Hall, 1985.

Solnik, Bruno. *International Investments.* Reading, Mass.: Addison-Wesley Publishing Co., 1988.

Spicer & Oppenheim International. *The Spicer & Oppenheim Guide to Securities Markets Around the World.* New York: John Wiley & Sons, 1988.

Thaler, Richard, and Hersh Shefrin. "An Economic Theory of Self-Control." *Journal of Political Economy*, April 1981.

Treynor, Jack, and Fischer Black. "How to Use Security Analysis to Improve Portfolio Selection." *Journal of Business,* January 1973.

Vertin, James R., ed. *International Equity Investing.* Homewood, Ill.: Dow Jones-Irwin, 1984 (sponsored by the Institute of Chartered Financial Analysts).

————, ed. *Improving the Investment Decision Process: Applying Economic Analysis to Portfolio Management.* Seminar Proceedings, Institute of Chartered Financial Analysts. Homewood, Ill.: Dow Jones-Irwin, 1985.

Wheatley, Simon. "Some Tests of International Equity Integration." *Journal of Financial Economics,* September 1988.

Zisler, Randall C., and Stephen A. Ross. "Stock and Bond Market Volatility and Real Estate's Allocation." *Real Estate Research,* Goldman Sachs & Co., November 16, 1987.

Part II

Investor Objectives and Constraints

Determination of Portfolio Policies

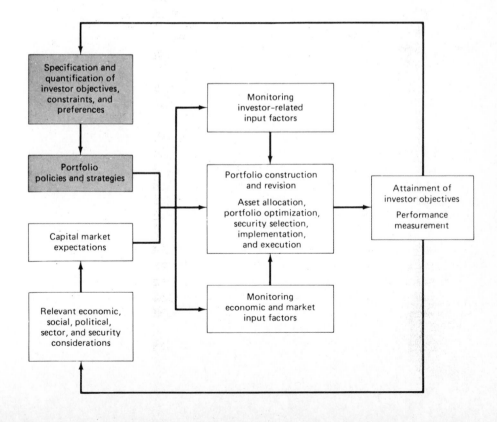

CHAPTER **3**

Individual Investors

Ronald W. Kaiser

OVERVIEW

Before an appropriate investment program can be established for an individual investor, careful consideration must be given to the investor's specific objectives and constraints. Investment program objectives are goals that are generally defined in terms of return requirements and risk tolerance. Constraints are limitations, such as liquidity, time horizon, taxes, and legal or regulatory matters, imposed on the portfolio management process within which the investor or his advisor must operate to achieve the program's objectives. Preferences are constraints that are self-imposed and may be unique to the investor.

The combining of objectives and constraints leads to the development of a set of investment policies for each investor—an operational statement or set of guidelines that specify the actions to be taken to achieve the investment objectives within the constraints imposed.

In other words, behind all investment portfolios lie flesh-and-blood investors, each of whom is unique. Many portfolio investment considerations are qualitative, but all lead to a quantification of risk and return and ultimately to the development of an efficient portfolio geared to the specific needs and objectives of the investor.

This chapter focuses on the individual investor, including personal trust. By contrast, Chapter 4 deals with objectives, constraints, and policies of institutional investors, with particular attention being given to pension funds, endowment funds, insurance companies, banks, and investment companies.

INTRODUCING THE INDIVIDUAL INVESTOR

Imagine the range of human beings you have ever met, read about, or seen on the screen—all their styles of personalities: confidence or fear; aggressiveness or conservatism; their introversion or extroversion; plodding compulsiveness or quick impetuousness; optimism or pessimism. The ap-

3-1

proaches to portfolio management for individual investors are just as varied and just as rich.

Individuals Contrasted With Institutions

Before dismissing the idea of professional portfolio management for individuals as being hopelessly bogged down in the complicated psychology of people and relationships and too enmeshed in an "eager to please" service attitude, bear in mind that there are some systematic themes and methods that can be applied across a wide range of individual situations:

- Individuals define risk as "losing money" or "doing something that feels uncomfortable," while institutions define it as "standard deviation of return."
- Individuals can be categorized by their "psychographics"—that is, their personalities—while institutions can be categorized by the investment characteristics of those who have a beneficial interest in the portfolios of pension funds, endowment funds, banks, insurance companies, and mutual funds.
- Individuals can be defined financially by their assets and goals (particularly as related to their stage in their life cycle), while institutions are a generally more precise package of assets and liabilities (or endowment funding requirements).
- Individuals are free to act as they see fit (either singly or as couples or families), while institutions are managed by committee and regulated by the Employee Retirement Income Security Act of 1974 (ERISA) or other legislation. Of course, personal trusts may be subject to legal constraints and trust department committees as well.
- Individuals have the added complexity of being subject to income taxes and estate taxes, while some institutions are free from such issues as long as they comply with certain regulations.

This chapter, then, explores some of these common elements of individual investors—their risk definitions, psychographics, demographics, goals, as well as legal and tax issues—in order to provide a framework for policy definition and portfolio management for the investment professional.

What Is Risk?

Although most individual investors do not think in terms of volatility of return, it is useful for the professional to try to relate to what the client says and feels in response to these concepts because the response provides a common reference point for discussion. For example, the portfolio manager might describe two portfolios as follows: "This multi-asset portfolio, because of its diversification, will generally go up or down only about half as much as the stock market does," or "This high-tech stock portfolio is likely to go up or down a bit more than the overall stock market." Increasingly, individuals of wealth and sophistication can converse in such concepts; some even understand "standard deviation of return."

However, the vast majority of individual investors, particularly those who engage a professional money manager, are too busy or too uninterested in investing to be so sophisticated. For them, the following are some *commonly held definitions of risk*.

Losing Money. "Losing money" is the most commonly expressed definition of "risk" among individual investors. It is most acutely felt *after* the loss has occurred. Usually, the investor is aware of such losses only when they have a monthly or quarterly report to review or only because they have realized losses to report on their tax return. Some individuals fret over money lost in any one security (and as a result are always giving their portfolio manager a lot of grief), while others more reasonably look at the bottom-line value of the portfolio.

Some measure losses only against original cost ("As soon as that stock gets back up to break-even, let's sell it."), but most are more reasonable in comparing current value to the prior value (or perhaps to a prior report or to the year-end balance sheet). Even then absolute amounts are often more meaningful than are percentages. The author recalls a client who suffered only a 7 percent decline in the crash of the fourth quarter of 1987 because he held a broadly diversified multi-asset portfolio; yet because of the great size of the account, he angrily exploded, "Don't you ever lose a million dollars for me again!"

Still others feel they have lost money only when they sell the security. It may be hopelessly underwater, but for them it is only a paper loss until it is realized. Such investors are content to clip coupons, even though their bond portfolio is declining in value as interest rates rise. After all, they would just as soon hold those bonds until they mature—where is the loss then? It is difficult for the portfolio manager to explain to such an investor why he is taking the loss in a bond (or stock) even if later the same security or a similar one can be bought back at a lower price. This usually involves a laborious exercise of calculating the extra cash left over as well as the difference in income received in the interim.

Unfamiliar Instruments. Most individuals have a fear of the unknown. For investors, this translates into a fear of, or at least a hesitancy to, invest in anything new or unfamiliar. This is particularly true if the investor has heard something somewhere about the risks in a certain kind of investment. As a result, while the portfolio manager might like to actually *reduce* risk through various futures hedging techniques or covered option writing, the investor only hears "futures" and "options" and remembers vaguely that these are complicated and risky techniques suitable only for aggressive professional traders. In such instances, it is only an open-minded client, combined with a patient, educational approach by the investment professional, whose perceptions of risk can be altered.

Previous Losses in Familiar Instruments. It is difficult even for the investment professional to overcome the psychological impediments to investing again in something that previously lost money. For unsophisticated individuals, this can translate into an unreasonable fear. Again, other than the passage of time, such perceived risks can be reduced only by education. An even better alternative is somehow to differentiate between the investments that lost money and the proposed new investments. For example, if the investor previously was burned by a portfolio of high-tech stocks, change the focus to the entire diversified portfolio in which high-tech stocks are only a small portion of the total and in which some of the initial holdings are blue chip stocks such as IBM and Hewlett Packard. Alternatively, if the investor was warned by his dad "never to throw money down real estate partnership ratholes" like he did, explain to the investor that the low-leverage, income-oriented partnership being recommended to him has a much lower level of risk than the aggressively leveraged tax-shelter deals that his dad lost money in. Finally, some investors can be persuaded to invest again when they are shown historical results over a long period of time and if it is explained to them that their experience was simply a case of bad breaks in investing in one of the negative periods for that kind of investment.

Contrary Investing. Some confident, sophisticated investors perceive much lower risk in contrarian investment strategies. But for many others, the idea of investing in an area that has been losing money for investors for some time is an exercise in high risk foolishness. This is particularly true for individuals who like the feeling of belonging in the "crowd." Such investors perceive little risk when they are buying into popular, high priced investments, and they believe that they are also reducing risk when they sell investments that everyone else is equally discouraged about.

For the professional manager trying to pursue somewhat contrarian, value-oriented strategies, there are two potentially useful antidotes to such client risk perceptions. One is to resort to value discussions. Point out that there is less risk when the market is at a price/earnings ratio of 10 than a P/E of 20, because 90 percent of the time the historical range has been between 8 and 23. The other strategy is for the portfolio manager to give in to the investor's risk perceptions without seriously altering the strategy that the portfolio manager wishes to pursue. Hold a few token positions in popular drug stocks, for example, and use those as talking points in meetings with the client while quietly accumulating more substantial positions in out-of-favor capital goods manufacturers.

Sometimes the investment professional is faced with exactly the opposite problem: how to convince a conservative, contrarian client to stay with an increasingly popular trend a bit longer. Since the portfolio manager knows that his client will engage in Monday morning quarterbacking if the portfolio manager overstays his position, it is probably wise for him to engage in at least token selling to keep the client's emotional reactions in check.

Risk: Potential vs. Actual. The fact that stocks have a historic standard deviation of return of 18 percent does not mean that the client will actually experience volatility in the coming year. In addition, the fact that in 1989 the national level of nonfinancial debt was at record levels as a percentage of the gross national product does not mean that there will be an economic depression and a wave of defaults in the early 1990s. While a portfolio manager may believe that it is prudent to hedge against such risks for a given client, there is a chance that the client will, with the benefit of hindsight, say, "What risk? I never saw it." Again, this boils down to an issue of educating the client, of helping the client to see the issues that the professional portfolio manager is concerned about.

In short, dealing with an individual investor's risk perceptions is a task that requires good counseling skills. First, the professional must listen to the client and ask questions to understand fully what the client fears and why. Then it is a matter of combining an educational approach (as much as possible) to try to modify the client's perceptions, with perhaps a modification of strategy (as little as is required) in order to show that the client's needs are being addressed.

THE PSYCHOGRAPHICS OF THE INDIVIDUAL INVESTOR

Psychographics describe psychological characteristics of people. This is not the same as demographics, which involves the fairly straightforward classification of people based on facts and circumstances such as age, wealth, income, family situation, and occupation. Psychographics involves the somewhat fuzzier process of classifying people based on their personalities and the needs that derive from them.

While much market research is done via demographic approaches (investment counselors will find a higher proportion of qualified clients in midtown Manhattan than in Brooklyn), it is also known that any two individual investors can have very different needs in the way that their money is invested and in how their money manager communicates with them. This chapter focuses on two useful psychographic classification schemes (there are certainly others) that are being used by investment firms to help them better understand and serve their clients.

Barnewall Two-Way Model

Marilyn MacGruder Barnewall of the MacGruder Agency, Inc. has put 13 years of research into studying various occupational groups and developing a superficially simple, yet surprisingly useful model of passive and active individual investors. The following are Barnewall's [1987] definitions of passive and active investors.

Passive Investors. "Passive investors" are defined as those investors who have become wealthy passively—for example, by inheritance or by risking the capital of others rather than risking their own capital. Passive investors have a greater need for security than they have tolerance for risk. Occupational groups that tend to be passive investors include corporate executives, lawyers with large regional firms, certified public accountants with large CPA firms, medical and dental nonsurgeons, individuals with inherited wealth, small business owners who inherited the business, politicians, bankers, and journalists. The smaller the economic resources an investor has, the more likely the person is to be a passive investor. The lack of resources gives individuals a higher security need and a lower tolerance for risk. Thus, a large percentage of the middle and lower socioeconomic classes are passive investors as well.

Active Investors. "Active investors" are defined as those individuals who have earned their own wealth in their lifetimes. They have been actively involved in wealth creation, and they have risked their own capital in achieving their wealth objectives. Active investors have a higher tolerance for risk than they have a need for security. Related to their high risk tolerance is the fact that active investors prefer to maintain control of their own investments. If they become involved in an aggressive investment of which they are not in control, their risk tolerance drops quickly. Their tolerance for risk is high because they believe in themselves. They get very involved in their own investments to the point that they gather tremendous amounts of information about the investments and tend to drive their investment managers crazy. By their involvement and control, they feel that they reduce the risk to an acceptable level.

Occupational groups that tend to be active investors include small business owners who start rather than inherit their businesses, medical and dental surgeons, independent CPAs, independent lawyers, entrepreneurs, self-employed consultants and advisors, and non–college graduates. Non–college graduates represent 75 percent of the new self-made millionaires each year.

Using the Active/Passive Classifications. From the investment counselor's perspective, there are some strong implications for policy formulation and account handling for active and passive investors.

Passive investors make the best clients in that they tend to delegate; they trust their advisor to do a good job. Because they are risk averse, they much prefer a broadly diversified, quality-oriented investment portfolio. Because they tend not to have much personal experience in investing, they often perceive risks as being greater than they are and they need additional education and counseling in unfamiliar investment areas. Finally, passive investors also tend to be group oriented and seek approval by others. This characteristic makes them more comfortable with trend following, or "staying with the herd," than with being courageously contrarian.

Active investors represent a more challenging type of client because they like to get personally involved in their financial affairs and often think they know more than their advisors do. In fact, in areas in which they feel they have personal expertise, they are unlikely to delegate those investments to professional management. The advisor of such a client constantly negotiates for his share of the investment portfolio to manage and must constantly display his expertise and defend his performance. As these clients get older, their energy level may wane a bit, and they will be more likely to turn over portions of their net worth to professional management. But because of this type of client's natural instinct to be personally involved, the wise professional seeks the client's input in policy formulation and major strategy changes. Finally, as a result of the active investor's willingness to take greater risks, he is more likely to prefer a focused investment strategy, rather than diluting any potential results by being too diversified.

The Bailard, Biehl & Kaiser Five-Way Model

Bailard, Biehl & Kaiser (BB&K) classifies investor personalities by focusing on two aspects of personality: the level of confidence and the method of action. BB&K's style of being broadly diversified among five or more asset classes and being somewhat contrarian has attracted mainly careful, risk averse investors. The five-way model refines some of the reasons why some clients are more difficult for the firm to satisfy than are others, although in many ways BB&K's work reflects some of the same thinking as found in Barnewall's work.

The BB&K personality classification focuses on two elements of an investor personality as shown in Figure 3-1. The first deals with how confidently the investor approaches life, regardless of whether it is his approach to his career, his health, or his money. These are important emotional choices, and they are dictated by how confident the investor is about some things or how much he tends to worry about them. The second element deals

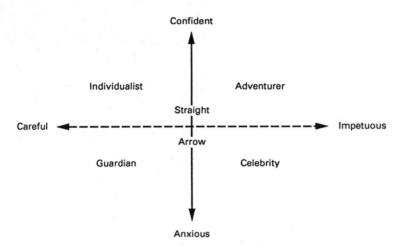

Figure 3-1. Investor Personality Characteristics.
SOURCE: Bailard, Biehl & Kaiser [1986].

with whether the investor is methodical, careful, and analytical in his approach to life or whether he is emotional, intuitive, and impetuous. These two elements can be thought of as two "axes" of individual psychology; one axis is called the "confident–anxious" axis, and the other is called the "careful–impetuous" axis (or the compulsive–impulsive axis).

Simply because an investor would be plotted in one location on the axes for one kind of choice—for example, a career choice or a marriage partner choice—does not mean that he would be in the same position when it came to managing money.

The Five Personalities

The upper-right-hand corner of Figure 3-1 represents the *adventurer*—people who are willing to put it all in one major bet and "go for it" because they have confidence. As far as they are concerned, it is a carefully considered decision. They are confident as well as intuitive or impetuous. In that quadrant, one typically will find entrepreneurial people, people who are willing to stick their necks out in their careers or in their money management strategies. These are much like Barnewall's active investors.

The lower-right-hand quadrant of Figure 3-1 is the *celebrity*. These people like to be where the action is. They are afraid of being left out. These are often people such as doctors and dentists, as well as typical celebrities such as sport or entertainment figures. These clients will keep bringing up the latest hot topic, asking, "Should I be in this, or should I be in that?"

The *individualist* is in the upper-left-hand quadrant. These people tend to go their own way and are typified by the small business person or an independent professional such as a lawyer, CPA, or engineer. These are people who are out trying to make their own decisions in life, carefully going about things, having a certain degree of confidence about them, but also being careful, methodical, and analytical.

The lower-left quadrant represents the *guardian* personality. Typically as people get older and begin considering retirement they approach this personality profile. They are careful and a little bit worried about their money. They recognize that they face a limited earning time span and have to preserve their assets.

Finally, there are always people who are so well balanced that they cannot be placed in any specific quadrant, so they fall near the center; this investor is called a *straight-arrow* client.

It is also worth noting that each investor at times exhibits some characteristics of personalities other than his normal one. This can be particularly influenced by his most recent investment experience. A guardian can become more aggressive for a time, like an adventurer, if he is on a winning streak. Conversely, most investors become more guardianlike just after an event like the October 1987 stock market crash.

Using the Five-Way Classification Model

Experience has shown that each of the five types of investors requires a different approach in portfolio management and communications.

Adventurers. Those with the adventurer personality are typically entrepreneurial and strong-willed. They are difficult to advise, because they have their own ideas about investing. They are willing to take risks, and they are volatile clients from an investment counsel point of view. They prefer concentrating their bets. A well-diversified, multi-asset approach often can be boring for the adventurer. An adventurer is often somebody who says, "Right now I think that the next big move is going to come in small cap stocks, and I want to find myself a small cap specialist." He typically stays with that specialist for two or three years, until he decides that the next big move is in real estate, at which point he will hire a real estate specialist.

One approach is to have the client acknowledge that a "financial independence" portfolio is too important to risk with adventurer-style management. Instead this core portfolio should be professionally handled by a balanced money manager. Even then the portfolio manager might have to run a less completely diversified portfolio than he might for a guardian personality, for example.

Celebrities. Celebrities are fashion followers who are worried about being left out. They really do not have their own ideas about investments. They may have their own ideas about other things in life, but not investing. As a result, they are the best prey for maximum turnover brokers. They are the most difficult clients to please for the contrarian portfolio manager, because he is the one who must say, "Now is the time to invest in international securities because the dollar is so strong that it must go the other way at some point." The celebrity then responds, "Hey, that's been losing money for the last three years. I don't want to be in that. You're crazy." Those clients can be difficult to deal with. An approach that can work with celebrities is to convince them that they need to be saved from themselves and that they should have their core financial independence portfolio handled in a more balanced, professional way.

Individualists. Individualists are also strong-willed and confident, but not rash. These are the ideal clients whom everybody is looking for—rational investors with whom the portfolio manager can talk sense. Individualists like to do their own research, are thoughtful people by nature, and tend to avoid extreme volatility. They are often contrarian investors because they do sit back and think about where they want to go and which investments make good value sense (individualists are typically value investors), but they are only good investment counsel clients if they are too busy to do it themselves. Fortunately, the world of investments is becoming so fast-paced, so complicated, and so dynamic, and most of these people are so busily engaged in their own careers, that they can make very good clients. Often when these clients retire counselors lose part or all of the account, because individualists get interested in doing it themselves.

Guardians. Guardians are people who are cautiously trying to preserve their wealth. They are definitely not interested in volatility or excitement. Guardians lack confidence in their ability to forecast the future or to understand where to put money, so they look for guidance. They tend to be very careful about selecting their investment advisor, but once they have chosen you, as long as you don't ever surpprise them with something too dramatic or disappointing, they could be loyal to you for the rest of their lives. Interestingly enough, this seems to be where most people fall when it comes to styles of money management. In 401(k) or profit-sharing plans in which individuals have a choice of how to allocate their money, they sometimes will allocate a little more of their portfolio to whatever is currently hot. But mostly they will have a fairly high proportion of their money allocated to money market funds, guaranteed investment contracts, bond portfolios, or balanced funds. They tend to take a fairly conservative posture. They tend to be highly loss averse.

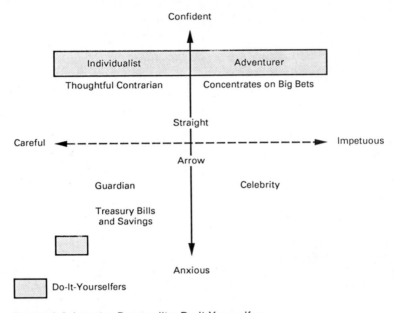

Figure 3-2. Investor Personality: Do-It-Yourselfers.
SOURCE: Bailard, Biehl & Kaiser [1986].

Straight Arrows. Straight-arrow clients do not fall into any of the personality extremes of the individualist, adventurer, celebrity, or guardian. On average, this group of clients is the average investor, a relatively balanced composite of each of the other four investor types, and by implication a group willing to be exposed to medium amounts of risk.

Who Are the Potential Clients?

Given the various individual investor types discussed, how are they likely to carry out their investment programs? Who do they typically seek out for advice and counsel in devising and executing their investment strategies?

The investor types represented by the shaded area in Figure 3-2 are "do-it-yourselfers." The individualists are the thoughtful contrarians. The adventurers concentrate on big bets. The really careful, worried guardians (the ones represented in the small box in the lower-left quadrant) also are do-it-yourselfers because they invest all of their money in certificates of deposit, Treasury bills, and money market funds, and never talk to investment counselors, unless their trust agreement requires them to.

The celebrities, represented by the shaded area of Figure 3-3, particularly the ones way out on the impetuous axis who are also anxious, are willing to listen to the current hot stories of the financial markets. They want

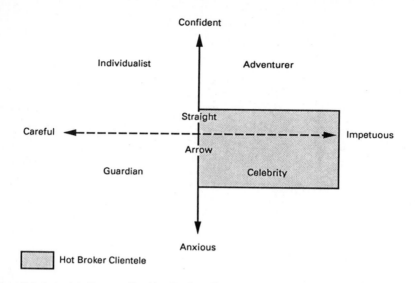

Figure 3-3. Investor Personality: Hot Broker Clientele. SOURCE: Bailard, Biehl & Kaiser [1986].

somebody else to relieve them of the burden of making investment decisions. They want to be sold. They want somebody to say, "This is where it's at. This is what everybody else is doing. It's a great bet." So the celebrities buy even if they are about to follow the herd over the next cliff. Counselors do not see many of these clients, because they do not accumulate a lot of wealth.

Finally, the largest portion of investment counsel clientele is shown in the shaded area in Figure 3-4. These investors tend to be heavily oriented toward the typical guardian personality. They often are people who have made a lot of money and want to take good care of it. This category of clientele also may extend significantly into the individualist area, particularly if they are too busy to do it themselves.

Scoring Systems

A straightforward approach to the evaluation of return/risk trade-offs for individual investors is a scoring system that relies on the responses from investors to several key questions about their return desires and risk aversions.

Such a system has been developed by William Droms of Georgetown University for several bank trust departments and insurance companies to use in advising their clients. Called the Portfolio Allocation Scoring System (PASS), this approach attempts to capture in a simple and straightford manner two important lessons of modern portfolio theory:

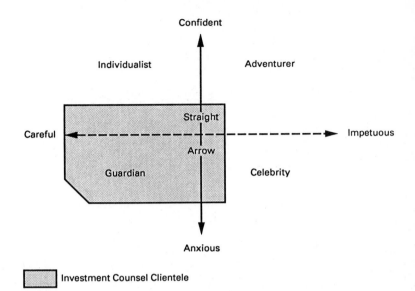

Figure 3-4. Investor Personality: Investment Counsel Clientele. SOURCE: Bailard, Biehl & Kaiser [1986].

1. Risk/return trade-offs do in fact exist.
2. Investors should diversify to reduce investment risk.

The planning constraints built into PASS look like most lists of typical individual investor planning constraints and include the investor's return objectives, risk tolerance, time horizon, income needs, and tax status.

As shown in Table 3-1, PASS is essentially a kind of "aggressiveness index" in that the more aggressive the investor's return objectives and risk tolerance are, the more points will be scored on PASS and the more the portfolio will be oriented toward aggressive investments and away from conservative ones.

The first three items on PASS deal with return objectives. If an investor ranks high long-term total return, large long-term capital gains or interest deferral, and low current (interest or dividend) income as most important, each of these objectives would receive five points toward the PASS score. Item 4 attempts to assess the length of the investor's time horizon, with a long-term horizon receiving maximum points.

Items 5 and 6 on PASS measure risk tolerance. Investors who can tolerate substantial return volatility and are willing to trade short-term losses for higher long-run returns will again be awarded a large number of PASS

TABLE 3-1. Return/Risk Assessments for the Portfolio Allocation Scoring System

Investment Objective	[Circle one.]				
	Strongly agree	Agree	Neutral	Disagree	Strongly disagree
1. Earning a high long-term total return that will allow my capital to grow faster than the inflation rate is one of my most important investment objectives.	5	4	3	2	1
2. I would like an investment that provides me with an opportunity to defer taxation of capital gains and/or interest to future years.	5	4	3	2	1
3. I do not require a high level of current income from my investments	5	4	3	2	1
4. My major investment goals are relatively long term.	5	4	3	2	1
5. I am willing to tolerate sharp up and down swings in the return on my investment in order to seek a potentially higher return than would normally be expected from more stable investments.	5	4	3	2	1
6. I am willing to risk a short-term loss in return for a potentially higher long-run rate of return.	5	4	3	2	1
7. I am financially able to accept a low level of liquidity in my investment portfolio.	5	4	3	2	1

SOURCE: William G. Droms, Copyright © 1988.

points. Finally, item 7 measures liquidity needs, with low desired liquidity receiving maximum points.

Once the investor has responded to each of the seven key questions, points are totaled to determine his relative investment aggressiveness. Investors with point totals over 30 are considered highly aggressive and could orient their portfolios heavily toward aggressive (generally equity-type) instruments, perhaps 70 to 80 percent, and can include more aggressive assets such as small cap stocks or zero-coupon bonds or illiquid investments such as venture capital or real estate. Investors with point totals under 15 are at the other end of the return/risk spectrum and should probably have only 20 to 30 percent of their portfolios in aggressive investments. Those that fall in between should vary their portfolio aggressiveness, depending on whether their point totals are closer to the lower or higher end of the 15-to-30-point range. Actual asset allocations prescribed by the PASS system are more precise, although they should be adjusted and refined based on assessment of individual circumstances by qualified counseling professionals.

Special Concerns of Inherited Wealth

In addition to considering the personality characteristics of an individual, it is important to evaluate the influence of inherited wealth. Excessive guilt, low self-esteem, indecisiveness, or suspicion should be recognized as possibly being born out of the inheritance and must be dealt with by the money manager as part of fostering a positive client relationship.

Society has always had ambivalent feelings concerning inherited wealth. This ambivalence is often felt by inheritors. Wealth is at times accompanied by *guilt*, with the inheritor feeling that this good fortune is unmerited. *Low self-esteem* is sometimes exhibited, as the inheritor may feel overshadowed by a very successful ancestor. Ironically, even personal success may be tainted by the fear that it can be attributed to the inherited wealth. This low self-esteem can also exhibit itself in a *fear of failure* and *lack of motivation*. Fear of failure can cause the inheritor to be indecisive, feeling that no decision or action is better than making a mistake. Finally, being wealthy often involves relationships built around the factor of wealth. This can lead to the inheritor becoming *suspicious of the motives of others*, sensing that they may be either envious or attempting to take advantage of him or her.

This is not meant to imply that everyone who inherits wealth necessarily exhibits any or all of these characteristics. However, inherited wealth does highlight an issue that counselors should keep in mind: Wealth may have either positive or negative effects upon the client. Wealth can be perceived as a burdensome responsibility, or it can be integrated into a client's values. Hence, charitable gifting or creative spending or investing (such as venture capital) may be ways that money can serve to make the inheritor feel positive about wealth as well as being beneficial to others. In dealing with inheritors, it is wise to set achievable goals that involve the active participation of the inheritor, such as working together on a program of charitable gifting.

Inheritors can be very risk averse because, not having earned the wealth themselves, they may be very fearful about what they would do without it. The professional would do well to listen to these fears and make an extra effort to educate the client. Establish contact with the inheritor's other professionals. In taking the initiative without being domineering, the counselor can establish a relationship built upon mutual trust and accomplishment without fostering dependence. Finally, the counselor must be patient because it can take a long time for client attitudes to evolve.

THE DEMOGRAPHICS OF THE INDIVIDUAL INVESTOR

The Wealth of American Citizens

On the surface, it seems that the universe of potential investment management clients is large enough for all investment firms to have plenty of busi-

TABLE 3-2. Percentage Asset Class Breakdown of Top Wealthholders With Gross Assets Over $1 Million, 1976 and 1982

Asset Class	1976	1982
Cash	5.7%	6.0%
Corporate stock	42.0	31.2
Bonds	12.3	7.8
Life insurance (cash value)	0.5	0.6
Notes and mortgages	3.1	4.5
Real estate	14.7	23.6
Noncorporate business assets	3.8	9.9
Other assets	17.9	16.4
	100.0%	100.0%

SOURCE: Estimates of Personal Wealth, 1982 [1985].

ness. The New York Stock Exchange reported that there were over 47 million individual shareholders in the United States in 1985, up from 30 million in 1980. Excluding children, this works out to one in four adults directly owning some common stock.

In looking behind the broad numbers, however, a different picture emerges. The average new shareholder in the 1980s had an account valued at an average of $2,200—approximately the balance needed to open an individual retirement account (IRA). In fact, of all adult shareowners, only 8 million had portfolios of stock worth more than $25,000.

Extrapolating from estate tax return data, the Internal Revenue Service periodically estimates the wealth of that portion of the U.S. population wealthy enough to provide detailed return data. In the report for 1982, the IRS estimated that there were 4.4 million people with gross assets (not net worth) of $300,000 or more. These top wealthholders represented only 2.8 percent of the adult population. Their net worth aggregated $2.4 trillion, or 28 percent of the personal wealth in the United States.

Of these top wealthholders (410,000 people), 10 percent had a net worth of over $1 million. Given the higher levels of financial and real estate markets since 1982, the number of millionaires is doubtlessly larger.

The typical millionaire, however, had only $450,000 in liquid assets (cash, stocks, and bonds), with the rest in real estate, personal business assets, and other assets. Table 3-2 details the breakdown of assets in two studies.

Another perspective on the concentration and distribution of personal wealth comes from trust department reports to the Federal Reserve Board. In combining the reports by commercial banks, savings banks, and other qualified trust institutions in a publication by the Federal Financial Institutions Examination Council [1986], the following picture emerges for personal trust accounts. Spread among 23,459 reporting trust institutions in

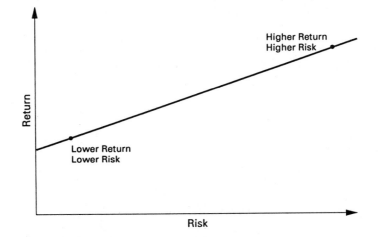

Figure 3-5. Risk/Return Trade-Offs for Investors.

1986, there were 862,891 accounts totaling $367 million under management. The average size of these accounts was $425,400. Of course, these accounts were concentrated in the largest institutions. The three largest personal trust institutions—Wells Fargo Bank, Morgan Guaranty Trust, and Citibank— each managed over $7 billion in personal trusts. The 500th-largest managed well under $100 million. The policies, strategies, and legal issues of personal trusts and trust departments are discussed later in this chapter.

Life Cycle View

In addition to the demographics of wealth, there are the demographics of age, or, more appropriately, of various stages in the life cycle. These stages are important to understand because of the impact they can have on an individual's risk and return preferences. Absent a life cycle view, we can think of the range of risk/return opportunities for individuals as being de- scribed by the line in Figure 3-5.

Each investor has feelings about where he might be along that line, especially when the points are described in terms of expected returns and volatility for specific kinds of investments. However, a broad generalization can be made that younger individuals who are just beginning to earn money and accumulate assets tend to find their preferences farther to the right on the line, while older individuals move increasingly to the lower left on the line. Older individuals not only have assets to lose but also have experienced some investment losses during their life, which adds to their risk averseness. It is useful to break up this continuous line into four different phases in

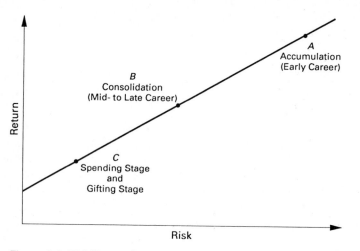

Figure 3-6. Risk/Return Position at Various Life Cycle Stages.

which individuals exhibit one dominant motif for how they view their wealth: the accumulation, consolidation, spending, and gifting phases.

Accumulation Phase. In the accumulation or early career situation, net worth is typically small relative to liabilities, especially when the latter include a large house mortgage and other debts from credit purchases. Assets are typically either nondiversified, with home equity the largest asset, or illiquid to the point of inaccessibility in the form of employee retirement programs. Priorities include savings for liquidity, children's educations, a larger home, life and disability insurance for loss-of-income protection, and, if possible, investments for future financial independence. But because the individual has a very long time horizon and a potentially growing stream of discretionary income, he can undertake more high-return, high-risk capital gain-oriented investments. Point *A* of Figure 3-6 describes this accumulation-stage person.

Consolidation Phase. The consolidation or mid-to-late-career stage of the typical life cycle is characterized by the period when income exceeds expenses, either because income has grown to outstrip expenses or because expenses have declined, typically after children have left home or after the need for larger homes and more things to fill them has finally become sated. As a result, this stage is characterized by the accumulation of an investment portfolio. Home equity and retirement program benefits are becoming substantial as well. At the same time, while the time horizon to retirement (and loss of earned income) is still relatively long (10 or 20 years), it is not so long that some risk control or capital preservation is unimportant. High capital gain investments are balanced with some lower-risk assets to achieve a portfolio close to point *B* in Figure 3-6.

Spending Phase. The "spending phase" is defined here as the period when one is financially independent; that is, living expenses are covered not from earned income but from accumulated assets such as investments and retirement programs. Because of the heavy reliance on personal investments in this phase (and the unlikelihood of going back to work), the focus is definitely on assets with relatively secure values, with more emphasis on dividend, interest, and rental income. Of course, the individual's time horizon may still be well over 10 or 20 years (even an 80-year-old has a life expectancy of 9.5 more years), so some investments in the portfolio should continue to have growth and inflation-hedge potential. Overall, the risk/return preference for such individuals falls near point *C*.

Gifting Phase. The final life cycle stage of gifting occurs when the individual comes to realize that he has more assets than he will ever need for personal spending and personal security. In such cases, while the risk/return preference may not be different from the previous stage, the attitudes about the *purpose* of investments does change. Investments are seen at that stage as having the potential to influence the change for the individual, whether to provide a home or business capital for an heir, to support a charitable cause, or to foster the growth of high-risk new businesses that the investor believes in.

Of course, it is important to remember that any person can be a composite of several life cycle stages at one time, although one will likely dominate the others. Further, the boundaries between the stages are fuzzy zones of transition that take years to complete. Finally, the basic personality that each investor brings to his stage in the life cycle greatly influences where he falls on the risk/return continuum.

GOAL ACHIEVEMENT: THE RATIONAL PORTFOLIO APPROACH

Rationally explained, all personal investing is designed to achieve a goal, whether it is a tangible goal such as a new home or a college education for a child, or an intangible goal such as security or status, which may be difficult to quantify in a meaningful way. In the following sections, the topic of how individuals might rationally approach various types of goals is briefly explored.

Types of Goals

Near-Term High Priority Goals. These are goals such as a new home or educational expenses, which have a high emotional priority and which the investor wishes to achieve within just a few years at most. As a result, investment vehicles for these goals tend to be either cash equivalents or fixed-income instruments with maturity dates that match the goal date. For people of limited to modest means, the cost of not achieving those goals is just too great to take a risk with more-volatile approaches once the goal is in sight.

Long-Term High Priority Goals. For most people this goal is typically some definition of financial independence (e.g., a level of independence measured in dollars per year, at a point a number of years in the future). Because of personal preferences, or perhaps because the discounted present value is so large relative to their resources, the time of realization for such goals is set at around age 60 for people of modest means. This gives enough time to accumulate the money and to be able to supplement the ability to meet one's needs with social security and corporate retirement benefits. Other important long-term goals might be a college education fund for a three-year-old, or the establishment of a charitable foundation during one's retirement years.

Because of the long-term nature of such goals, more-aggressive investment approaches are usually taken (except for, perhaps, the last 5 to 10 wage-earning years). Even then a diversified approach utilizing several different classes of assets is usually preferred.

Lower Priority Goals. For people of moderate to substantial wealth, there are often lower priority goals that are not particularly painful if they are not achieved. These could range from a luxury cruise to bragging rights about success in backing local business ventures to having extra funds to leave to charity. As a result, the sums for these goals are often invested in speculative kinds of investments, often more for the fun of the process than for the achievement of the goals. In fact, it is not at all unusual for professional money managers to have clients who reserve some funds that they can afford to lose just for the fun of trying their hand at some aspect of the investment process.

Entrepreneurial or Money Making Goals. To this point goals appropriate only to money management have been discussed. What about those hard-charging individuals who aspire to substantial wealth and who cannot be satisfied by conventional save-and-invest approaches? These are typical entrepreneurs, and for them a concentrated game of putting all (or nearly all) the eggs in one basket and then watching them intensely is the only possible avenue of satisfaction. These people usually start (or work for) a small company and put nearly everything they have into that firm's stock, leaving it there (no matter how undiversified and risky that approach may seem to someone else) until it reaches some level at which the individual either believes it to be enough or becomes afraid of losing what has been built up. Even then the process of diversification into a conventional portfolio is usually a lengthy one involving a series of opportunistic sales spread over many years.

INVESTMENT CONSTRAINTS

Liquidity: Real Needs and Perceived Needs

"Liquidity" is usually defined as an asset's ability to be sold and converted to cash approximately at current market prices. It can range from one day for quality cash equivalents to a week for listed stocks, to a few weeks for large blocks of slowly traded stocks and bonds, to a few months or a year for real property, to nonexistent for most partnership investments. In fact, buyers often do exist for interests in large, well-known partnerships, but only if the seller is willing to accept a 30 to 50 percent discount from underlying asset value. The leveraged buyout and merger game demonstrates that a 30 percent premium for control of an entire asset, when compared to the trading value of a minority interest, is not an unreasonable differential. At these discounted values, then, the liquidity of some partnership interests can be measured in terms of a few weeks or a few months.

The real needs for liquidity fall into five categories:

1. *Emergency Cash.* The emergency cash reserve is usually measured at two to three months' spending, but it could be more if the individual's source of income is at risk or volatile. This sum is usually set aside in money market funds and is not considered part of the investment portfolio.
2. *Goal Spending.* These needs vary with the individual, but for known goals due within five years, at least the amount needed to achieve these goals should be in assets with relatively good liquidity.
3. *Income Taxes.* Known lump-sum tax payments are usually set aside in cash equivalents maturing no later than the tax due date.
4. *Estate Transfer Taxes.* For individuals wealthy enough not to need life insurance for loss-of-income protection, the money for estate taxes must come out of the estate's assets. Aside from some long-term tax payment plans for estates involving family farms and businesses, this argues for sufficient funds to pay whatever estate taxes will be due nine months after the date of death.

5. *Investment Flexibility*. The ability to take advantage of market opportunities as asset classes become overvalued and undervalued would argue for the greatest degree of liquidity. Perhaps two-thirds of a portfolio should be able to be liquidated within a matter of weeks for optimum liquidity. This would still allow for some substantial commitment to illiquid opportunities such as real estate and venture capital.

Personal Trust Considerations

A personal trust is simply an amount of money set up by a grantor as a separately managed entity. It is often managed by a third-party fiduciary (trustee), usually an individual or a bank trust department, with whatever constraints the grantor can write into the trust document. It is managed for the financial benefit of beneficiaries (usually individuals or charities) during its existence, with the remaining principal going to remaindermen (individuals or charities) at the termination of the trust.

The various legal forms and details of trust provisions in the United States have evolved over time as laws have changed and lawyer and grantor creativity has expanded.

Revocable vs. Irrevocable Trusts. These trusts are the key distinctions to bear in mind. Revocable trusts usually remain under the control of the grantor during his or her lifetime, and their assets are often indistinguishable, in the investment manager's view, from the individual's own assets. Irrevocable trust management is subject to the trustee's interpretation of the trust document, prevailing law, the skill of the manager, and the pressures brought to bear on the trustee by the beneficiaries and remaindermen.

The Evolving Prudent Man Rule. Legal considerations play a large role in the personal trust area, in contrast to the situation with individual investors. Unlike the legal environment of pension trusts, state law rather than federal law governs personal trusts in the United States. State law is often common law, with the law being made and modified in the courts, based on results of decisions in cases typically brought by remaindermen plaintiffs against trust department defendants. Some states have codified the law into *prudent man statutes* outlining the role and duties of personal trustees.

In some states, there have been law changes affecting trustees. In California, the prudent man standard of judgment and care has been modeled upon the prudence rule of the Employee Retirement Income Security Act of 1974. This changing standard has altered the definition of "skill" for the trustee as well as the "standard of care" that must be used in making investment decisions.

Traditionally, the standard of skill required by the trustee was that of a prudent man handling his own affairs. Currently, the law is shifting to a dual standard differentiating between "professional trustees" and "ordinary trustees." If the professional trustee is an investment advisor, he will be judged by the higher level of professional skill attained by an investment advisor. It is important to remember that this "expert" standard seems to imply that the trustee must guarantee not superior results, only prudent management. To make matters more complex, it could be argued that a professional who specializes in a specific area, such as fixed-income portfolio management, would be held to an expert standard only in that area; he would be held only to "ordinary" standards in all other areas.

In addition, the standard of care that the trustee must use in making investment decisions has evolved. The present standard allows the trustee to consider each investment in a portfolio in light of an overall investment strategy. Previously, each investment was considered separately for its probable safety of capital as well as for its income.[1] A trustee can now acquire virtually any kind of investment, even if considered speculative, providing the overall mix of the portfolio is prudent. Finally, there is also an emphasis on *process*: Was the investment decision soundly conceived?

However, most states have not yet developed a new code to govern trustees of personal trusts. Further, there is such a paucity of case law that rejects or redefines obsolete interpretations of prudence that most fiduciaries continue to play it safe by investing trust assets *only* in conservative securities such as blue chip stocks, government bonds, and the like.

Income Beneficiaries vs. Remaindermen. Another area in which legal considerations play a major role is situations involving both life (or other limited period) income beneficiaries and remaindermen beneficiaries (who receive the residual estate when the life income beneficiaries die). This is so because trust law perpetuates the dichotomization of total return into dividend or interest income and capital gain (net of loss) income. The former goes to the income beneficiary, whereas the latter accumulates to the benefit of the remainderman as do unrealized gains net of losses.

This situation presents the trustee with an inherent conflict between the interests of the two sets of beneficiaries. Often the conflict is resolved almost totally in favor of the income beneficiary, with portfolio investments favoring income, especially tax-sheltered income from assets such as municipal bonds, to the almost complete exclusion of consideration of the remainderman. This lack of impartiality between income beneficiaries and remaindermen has been the source, if not the basis, for numerous lawsuits brought by remaindermen.

Hence, only if the income beneficiary has a limited need for income is

---

[1] *Estate of Talbot*, 141 Cal. App. 2d 309 (1956).

the trust focused on long-term growth. For the typical case in which the life beneficiary has substantial needs for income, there is pressure on the trustee to invest heavily in fixed-income securities or high dividend yielding, low or no growth preferred or common stocks, such as stocks of public utilities. In times of prolonged inflation, this may result in a reduction of the real value of the trust. A better approach is to invest in a portfolio of securities that provides the largest after-tax expected total return at the level of risk desired and to take advantage of the limited ability to pay out trust principal to life beneficiaries, a provision that is included in most current agreements.

Income Tax Considerations

The last few years have seen great changes in both federal and state tax laws in the United States. Yet even with all of the changes in the law, there are still some elementary principles that the counselor should keep in mind. No matter how complex tax issues become, they have their roots in three general sets of solutions: deferring taxes, avoiding them, or having a taxable item treated at a favorable rate (deduction at highest rate, income at lowest rate).

For example, the Tax Reform Act of 1986 (TRA 86) reduced the maximum ordinary income tax rate from 50 percent in 1986 to 38.5 percent in 1987 and to 28 percent in 1988. Looking forward from 1986 the tax-planning professional would have preferred to take deductions in the higher-tax years, 1986 and 1987, and defer income to the lower-tax years, 1987 and 1988. Conversely, the capital gains rate was increased from 20 percent in 1986 to 28 percent in 1987 and after. If an investor was indifferent to the timing of the sale of the capital asset, it may have been appropriate to have the capital gain taxed in the lower tax year, 1986.

The integration of investment advice and tax counseling is one of the most challenging problems for the advisor. Even with the changes in tax law, there is still friction between investments and taxes. The bias is sometimes in favor of tax counsel, because it is simpler and more certain to quantify the tax ramifications in a sale vs. no sale decision than it is to delineate the future uncertain investment risk/reward trade-off. Complicating matters is the fact that taxes are an emotional issue for many clients. It is important for the advisor to realize that this is a counseling issue that has many intuitive, nonquantifiable aspects. The counselor must not only integrate the appropriate tax considerations into a client situation, but do so in such a way that the client will be comfortable with the outcome.

Role of Tax Counsel. Depending on the complexity of an individual's situation, a tax advisor such as a CPA, financial planner, or attorney may be retained. Tax counseling can help the individual to decipher complicated tax laws and protect himself from inadvertent illegality. Well-trained, experienced financial planners are useful in tax planning because they have the benefit of being able to view the situation from a broader, long-term perspective. The planner can also recommend a specialist to further research initial findings. Perhaps as important as who constitutes the investment counsel "team" is how they work together. A free flow of information between professionals is vital. Depending on the situation, it may be the accountant, attorney, or investment advisor who leads in formulating and implementing a tax strategy, but regardless of who takes the lead, the coordination of professionals is most important.

Capital Gains: Tax Timing vs. Investment Timing. This is a U.S. tax that was altered greatly by tax law changes in the mid-1980s. Capital gains, both short and long term, are no longer treated differently from ordinary income. Even though rates are in general the same, there still may be advantages to capital gains when compared to ordinary income. The most important advantage is that the timing of when to realize capital gains is much more in the control of the investor than it is for ordinary income. The investor has the option of withholding a sale until it will be taxed at a more favorable rate. This can occur because of law changes, alteration in the client's situation, or alternative minimum tax (AMT) liability.

The decision to sell a stock with a low cost basis that would trigger a large capital gain is another aspect of the tax timing versus investment timing analysis. At first glance it may appear appropriate to defer the taxable event indefinitely. However, often the risk of loss from holding a large concentrated stock position outweighs the tax timing decision. In this situation, it is prudent to diversify the concentrated assets by selling portions of the low-basis stock over a period of time. This strategy reduces the investment risk inherent in concentrated positions. Again, this analysis is predicated on melding tax and investment planning strategies.

Tax-Free vs. Taxable Interest: Trade-Offs of Yield, Liquidity, and Quality. The choice between taxable and tax-free investments is based on the interaction of three factors: after-tax yield, differing investment characteristics, and investor emotion.

Under current U.S. tax rates, most investors are subject to a combined state and federal rate ranging from 30 to 40 percent. In AMT situations or in states with no tax, this rate could be less. There is also great diversity in how states treat municipal bonds. Using the investor's tax rate, a comparison can be made between taxable and tax-free yields. For example, in California in 1988 the maximum combined federal and state rate was 35 percent (28 percent federal tax rate plus 9.3 percent California tax rate, less the deduction for state tax, 28 percent of 9.3 percent). Therefore, the analysis of taxable and tax-free yields is as follows:

	After-Tax Yield
Corporate bond yielding 10%	6.50%
California municipal bond yielding 7%	7.00
Difference	0.50%

It should be noted that most states tax the interest income received by residents on holdings of out-of-state municipal bonds.

Municipal bond yields tend to outpace Treasury bond and corporate bond yields on an after-tax basis. However, they are less liquid (larger bid-ask spread) and offer less quality control than do Treasuries; hence, the higher after-tax yield. They also tend to have different investment characteristics than Treasuries do (such as call provisions, which can limit upside potential in bond bull markets), so the analysis is not limited to after-tax yield; the investor must weigh all the investment and tax considerations. Finally, paying taxes is sometimes an emotional issue, and aversion to taxes is not always quantifiable. To many investors tax-exempt funds simply "feel" better, regardless of the after-tax yield.

Year-End Tax Planning. Traditionally year-end has been the time for investors to put their tax planning into effect. Late November has always been a good time to meet with counsel to discuss tax savings ideas. However, given the increasing complexity of both an investor's personal tax situation and the political environment causing tax law to be in seemingly constant flux, it is advisable that tax planning be a *continuous* process. Planning in many cases must stretch over a series of years, such as in the case of limited partnerships. As mentioned previously it is especially important that all professionals involved in an investor's finances take coordinated action concerning taxes. By taking an overall view of an investor's tax situation, no individual professional will be in a knowledge vacuum, thereby acting in good faith but causing damage to an investor's overall financial well-being.

Consideration must be given to changes in tax rates on both an individual and statutory level. If Congress is expected to pass a bill lowering the capital gains rate, there will be greater savings for the investor in postponing the sale of an asset. For example, the federal capital gains rate is currently 28 percent. If Congress were contemplating reducing the rate to 20 percent, there would be the possibility of an 8 percent savings, or $4,000 of tax savings on a $50,000 capital gain. Conversely, an individual with unrealized losses may want to take them in the current year. As always, considerations of investment risk must be weighed against the dictates of tax planning.

In addition to planning for capital gains and losses, there are issues such as deferral of income, exercise of stock options, and prepayment of state taxes (state taxes should be paid in the year in which the greatest federal deduction can be realized). Retirement and estate planning opportunities should also be considered at this time. Although April 15 of the next year is the due date for making deductible IRA contributions, all 401(k) contributions must be made by year-end. The amount of pretax retirement contributions made for the tax year's filing purposes is important to determine because it will affect the taxpayer's adjusted gross income. To qualify for the $10,000 annual gift exclusion, the gift must be made by year-end; otherwise, it will count under the next year's annual gift exclusion.

IRAs and 401(k) Plans. Ironically, the very system in the United States that seeks to encourage individuals to be financially responsible for their own future well-being has greatly constrained these limited retirement savings plans. For most taxpayers, this means maximum annual pretax IRA contributions of $2,000 and 401(k) employee contributions of $7,300 (as indexed into the future for inflation). At higher levels of taxable income, IRA contributions are nondeductible. For comparison, under 1986 rules, the benefits of contributing to an IRA were very obvious. The individual was contributing to his future savings while receiving a tax deduction. However, now under 1988 rules, the limitations on contributions for most individuals with moderate to high incomes disallow the tax deduction. In addition, it may be better to take ordinary income in a low tax year like 1988 than risk the vagaries of future tax changes which may increase the ordinary income rates on future IRA withdrawals. Why did Congress limit contributions? It is the consensus that those who can afford to save more have less need for the additional deduction. Whether the contributions are made from pretax income or from post-tax income, the accumulated return on this initial outlay will remain untaxed until withdrawal.

Withdrawals from qualified plans (i.e., from an IRA or 401(k)) carry penalty taxes in addition to income tax if complex rules are not followed. For example, there is a 10 percent early withdrawal tax, which is based on the gross amount of the withdrawal, if a withdrawal occurs prior to the individual reaching age 59½. There are additional penalties if withdrawals do not meet the minimum or maximum guidelines or if withdrawals occur too late. The complexity of these rules dictates that a tax specialist be consulted when substantial retirement plans exist for the client.

Passive Loss Rules. Tax reform has completely altered the environment for tax shelters in the United States. Typical tax shelter products previously worked in the following manner: An investor invested an amount up front, and in turn the shelter would yield *passive losses* for years. These passive losses offset active, or earned, income that would otherwise be taxable at rates as high as 70 percent. Many oil drilling and leveraged real estate limited partnerships generated tax savings well in excess of the amount originally invested. The tax losses did lower the tax basis on the investor's interest, creating a potential capital gain liability. It would be the partnership's intention to continue functioning, at least on paper, into the foreseeable future in order not to trigger a capital gain tax event for the investors.

Tax reform cracked down on this strategy in two ways. For partnerships entered into before October 23, 1986, passive loss deductibility is subject to a five-year phase-in. After passive losses have been netted with all the passive income then remaining, they have partial and declining deductibility: 65 percent in 1987, 40 percent in 1988, 20 percent in 1989, 10 percent in 1990, and 0 percent in 1991. Nondeductible passive losses remain "suspended." In future years in which there is passive income that cannot be offset with current passive losses,the suspended losses can be used. Upon the sale or dissolution of a limited partnership, any capital gain from the transaction can be offset with remaining suspended losses. For partnerships entered into after October 22, 1986, current passive losses will be netted with the net passive income; all remaining passive losses will then become suspended until they can either be used to offset passive income in future years and/or until the capital gains sale of these interests.

Rental real estate property (e.g., rented condominiums) by nature are classified as "passive activities." Special allowances are made for directly held rental property such that passive losses (in excess of passive income) are deductible for a maximum of $25,000, given that the taxpayer's total earned and unearned income is less than $100,000. For income levels of $100,000 to $150,000, all passive losses from the rental real estate are suspended, once again, until passive income is generated or the property is sold.

Passive income generators (PIGs), new investment vehicles that began to appear on the market in 1988, generate passive income that can be used to offset passive losses that would otherwise remain suspended. PIGs should be evaluated not only upon their apparent tax advantages but also upon their underlying economic merit. Tax and investment counsel should be consulted before such investments are made.

Splitting Money Into Different Pots vs. Economy of One Pot. In past years, it was often beneficial from a tax viewpoint for an individual to place investments into multiple trusts in order to realize income in lower marginal brackets. For example, in 1986 trust tax rates ranged from 11 to 50 percent, with 14 different tax brackets. In 1988, tax rates ranged from 15 to 28 percent, with two tax brackets. Not only have the trust marginal brackets compressed but the IRS has now taken the position that all trusts are counted as one in terms of calculating federal income tax, so it is no longer possible to spread income into several low-bracket trusts. This does not include permanent gifts made by the use of trusts or other irrevocable transfers in which the grantor does not retain any beneficial interest or strings of ownership. Shifting income to minors also is severely restricted; for minors under age 14, all income earned on such transferred assets is taxed at the parent's marginal tax bracket.

These tax law changes attempt to take the tax decision out of the investment vehicle or gift. Congress lowered brackets and melded earned income and capital gain income. Gifts to children should increasingly be made based on the grantor's personal wishes or desires, not merely as a way to reduce an income tax burden.

Alternative Minimum Tax. Particularly with the reduction of the regular tax brackets, the phase-in of the passive loss deduction (a percentage of passive loss is deductible for regular tax calculation and completely nondeductible for alternative minimum tax) and the inclusion of incentive stock options (ISOs) at the time of exercise in alternative minimum tax calculations (the difference between the market value and the cost of the exercise is now treated as an additional preference item), a greater percentage of U.S. taxpayers have potential exposure to the AMT than ever before. While AMT calculates tax based on the lower tax rate of 21 percent, once taxable income exceeds $310,000 (married, filing jointly), the effective rate becomes 26.25 percent. Because state taxes are not deductible in the AMT calculation, the AMT can be more expensive than the regular tax. However, some relief from the AMT may be available via the AMT credit equal to the regular AMT minus the AMT calculated by excluding "timing" preference items.

Planning for AMT is especially important because there are a large number of sensitivity analyses that tax counsel can prepare to answer important questions. Realizing income, prepaying state tax, exercising ISOs, and donating appreciated property are all decisions that can either avoid or cause AMT exposure, and it is only through early, thorough planning that the taxpayer can strategically position himself by year-end.

Estate Taxes

The IRS imposes a transfer tax on the gift of property to others. If the transfer is made during one's lifetime, the transfer tax is a gift tax; with a transfer made at death, the tax is an estate tax.

The *gross estate* is the estate of the decedent before reduction for the deductions allowed in arriving at the *taxable estate*. The value at which property is included in a decedent's gross estate is its fair market value.

The estate tax is computed by applying the unified rate schedule to the aggregate of cumulative lifetime transfers made after December 31, 1976. Each recipient can be given up to $10,000 per year free of tax, and that transfer does not have to be included in the cumulative lifetime transfer calculation. Once the tax on the taxable estate is determined, it is reduced by the credits available, the unified credit, state death tax credit, gift tax credit on pre-1976 gifts, credit for foreign death taxes, and previously taxed property credit.

The maximum unified credit for 1987 and after is $192,800. This is equivalent to a tax-free estate of $600,000.

The marital deduction is one of the most important estate tax savings concepts available to married couples. Any property passing to a surviving spouse is a deduction for the gross estate of the decedent. If the entire estate is passed to the spouse, the result is zero estate tax.

Considerable death tax savings can result from the use of a trust that bypasses a taxpayer. A *bypass trust* typically holds the property that is not part of the marital deduction transfer. The amount of property in the bypass trust will usually be enough to absorb the exemption equivalent credit of the unified credit. Under a typical bypass trust arrangement, the surviving spouse receives a lifetime income interest in the trust and is known as the income beneficiary. At the surviving spouse's death, the principal is distributed to the remaindermen without being taxed on the second death.

The *generation-skipping transfer tax*, which was revised in the 1986 tax act, imposes a tax on transfers that attempts to avoid estate and gift tax in a generation below the transferor. A generation-skipping tax is applied whenever a taxable distribution, taxable termination, or a direct skip occurs. Each transferor is entitled to a $1 million exemption against generation-skipping transfers. In addition, if one makes a direct skip to one's grandchild before 1990, up to $2 million per grandchild is untaxable.

Gift and Estate Planning—Overview

When a client is considering gifting to an individual or charity, the interplay of at least four basic areas should be addressed before the gift is made.

Method of Transfer. How does the client want the individual or the charity to receive the gift? Is he willing to hand over complete control of the assets gifted? Will the individual or charity be able to responsibly manage and utilize the gifted funds? Has the individual looked at the potential for appreciation in the gifted assets and the effect that asset appreciation would have on the recipient?

Transfer Tax. The maximum federal gift and estate tax rate is currently 55 percent. One tax reduction strategy involves maximizing the gift exclusion by transferring assets out of the estate early to avoid a future estate tax. The strategies for implementation are complex, so estate and/or tax counsel should be consulted when substantial gifts are being considered.

Remaining Wealth. Has the client assured himself that he can attain his personal goals (e.g., financial independence or company control) as well as fund a gifting program to the individual or charity? With the future unknown, can the client maintain the resources and flexibility necessary to support his lifestyle?

Income Tax Effect. With the Tax Reform Act of 1986, bracket compression has diminished the motivation to gift assets to other family members for income tax purposes. The client, however, can minimize his income tax with charitable contributions. Likewise, the strategy of gifting appreciated assets out of his estate can minimize the potential for capital gains taxes. The client should consult with his tax counsel when substantial gifts are being made to individuals or charities.

Asset Selection for Gifts to Children. One strategy has been to gift a low-basis stock to a child or grandchild, with the subsequent sale of the gifted asset occurring in a lower tax bracket. However, bracket compression has occurred since the implementation of tax reform, and the client cannot assume that a child or grandchild is in a dramatically lower tax bracket.

If a client were to gift a low-basis stock to a child or grandchild and have him turn around and sell the asset, thereby incurring a tax liability, the client has minimized the allowable $10,000 annual exclusion. The client and advisor should focus on transferring the maximum amount of wealth from one generation to the next. For example, if a client transfers stock worth $10,000 with a cost basis of $0, and the child, who is in the maximum bracket, 28 percent, turns around and sells the asset, he will pay $2,800 in tax. In other words, the $10,000 gift has been reduced to $7,200.

An alternative asset selection strategy is to gift assets that could appreciate at a higher rate than other assets the client owns. By gifting these assets, the client has moved any future appreciation out of his portfolio and therefore out of his estate and into the child's portfolio. This strategy applies only when the child is planning on holding the asset for a length of time. One caveat to this strategy is that if an asset is gifted in trust to a child who will receive these funds at a given age and the asset appreciates at a substantial rate, the child will be receiving substantial wealth at an early age. The client should make sure that this result is consistent with his initial purpose.

Each individual has a $10,000 annual gifting exclusion per person per year. Any annual gift over this amount will incur a gift tax. However, each individual has a unified credit of $600,000, which can be used during his lifetime for gift tax or used at death as an estate planning tool. If a gifting program is being considered for a child, the client should consult with an estate planning attorney to design the appropriate vehicle and trust document.

The money manager/financial planner can assist the client by pulling together the players (CPA and estate planning attorney), reviewing the estate plans for investment management considerations, and handling the transfer of gifted assets.

Asset Selection for Gifts to Charitable Organizations. When gifting assets to charity from an investment portfolio, the issue of asset selection is very important. The conventional temptation is to gift a low-basis asset and then have the donee turn around and sell the asset. When the gift is made to a tax-exempt charity there will be no capital gain tax. However, the Tax Reform Act of 1986 changed this simple assumption. Under the alternative minimum tax calculation, the difference between the cost basis and the market value of an asset gifted to a charity is a preference item, which increases the possibility that the AMT will apply for the client.

When a gift is made to a charity there are limits to the amount allowed for a charitable deduction based on the donor's adjusted gross income (AGI) and the type of charitable organization. Contributions to charitable organizations such as churches, educational institutions, and hospitals are deductible up to 50 percent of a taxpayer's AGI. Contributions to nonoperating foundations such as war veterans' and fraternal organizations are deductible up to a maximum of 30 percent of the taxpayer's AGI. However, any unused charitable contribution can be carried forward to future tax years.

In considering the timing of gifts, the donor, money manager and tax counsel need to find a balance between tax certainty and implementation. As the tax year progresses, there is greater certainty to the client's tax situation and strategy. However, the process of gifting and transferring assets may take longer than expected. Therefore, it is preferable to establish the tax and gifting strategy several weeks before the end of the year so that implementation of the gifting strategy can occur.

The investment sale judgment on the securities gifted can determine the timing of the gift as well. When gifting to a charity it is important to gift at a "high-water mark" or the highest expected value or price during the year to increase the amount of the gift to the charity as well as the amount of the charitable deduction for the donor. However, when gifting to an individual who is planning to hold the asset it is preferable to transfer the asset at a "low-water mark" or at a low value or price to maximize the $10,000 exclusion effect.

Tax Basis of Property Transferred at Death. To compute the capital gains tax on the sale of property acquired from or passing from a decedent, the property's cost basis (or tax basis) is its fair market value at the date of death or the alternative valuation date (six months after the date of death). Any appreciation in value prior to this date is not subject to income or capital gains tax. The new tax basis of property acquired from a decedent is often referred to as the *stepped-up basis*. To determine the property that is given a stepped-up basis, the test is generally whether the property is included in the gross estate of the decedent for federal estate tax purposes. A special rule that applies only to community property gives a stepped-up basis in property to both halves (spouses) of the community, even though only the decedent's half was included in the decedent's estate for estate tax purposes.

Predeath Estate Tax Planning. If your client is older and/or is in questionable health, it may be appropriate to hold low-cost-basis assets until death so that the assets receive a *step-up in basis* before they are transferred to others. It would be unwise to reduce the value of an estate by an unnecessary capital gains tax payment. An analysis of the trade-off between gifting/selling the asset immediately or waiting until death should be reviewed with counsel before any major decisions are made.

Flower bonds or specially designated low-coupon Treasury bonds may be purchased in advance of death to fund the estate tax. Although they sell at a discount to par, they can be used to pay estate taxes at their full par value (thus saving money that could be used to pay for flowers at the funeral of the deceased). However, this practice has diminished as a planning tool because of the shrinking supply of these specially designated bonds.

Postdeath Estate Taxes. At death the assets that pass through probate will get a step-up in tax basis. The money manager will want to stay in touch with the estate planning attorney during the interim between the death of the client and the transfer of assets. Portfolio changes should not be made until a study of asset valuation, funding of trusts, and payment of taxes has been completed. It is important to know which tax valuation date will be used: the date of death or the alternative valuation date. Expected movements in prices of the assets as well as the use of trusts in the estate plans can determine which valuation date is preferable. A money manager should also be aware that estate taxes must be paid nine months after death. Usually the funds come from the portfolio, so the money manager should establish liquidity within the portfolio for this payment.

After death the assets may be transferred in many directions, such as bypass trusts and marital trusts. One strategy calls for placing higher-growth assets in the bypass trust so that subsequent appreciation bypasses the estate tax at the second (spouse's) death. Additional issues that need to be discussed with the estate planning attorney and beneficiaries include tax implications of the subsequent death of an heir and beneficiary versus remainderman investment strategies.

Personal Trust Tax

For the investment advisor who manages money contained in a trust, it is important to understand the characteristics of the trust, thereby melding investment and tax imperatives with the wishes and needs of grantors and beneficiaries.

As noted earlier, there are two general types of trusts that need to be considered: revocable and irrevocable trusts. The revocable is the most simple because all income and tax ramifications flow to the grantor. In other words, such a trust is normally indistinguishable from the rest of the client/ grantor's finances. An irrevocable trust is more complex because the advisor is dealing to some degree with at least two people: the grantor and the beneficiary. Furthermore, it is important to understand whether all income, or a portion, flows to the beneficiary. At what point the income is taxed depends on what the documents say and where the flows actually go.

Regardless of the type of trust, it is important to understand how it operates. There are both tax considerations and the needs of grantors/beneficiaries to consider. With the melding of personal and trust tax rates, as well as bracket compression, tax ramifications are not as large as they once were.

Tax Risk: Another Uncertainty for Investors

Adding a dimension to investment risk and the vagaries of an individual investor's tax situation has been the specter of tax laws in almost constant change. U.S. tax law changes in 1981 and 1986 have created an entirely new environment for many investments. In addition, there has been significant lag time in interpretation by the IRS and tax courts. In practice this has meant that looking into and preparing for the future is extremely difficult. Year-to-year forecasts of capital gain and income tax rates have become very problematic. If an investor arbitrarily defers taking a capital gain, he may later take this gain at higher rates. Increasingly tax planning has been in error. There is no easy remedy for this situation. Competent tax counsel is vital, with open communication between an investor's professionals being of the utmost importance. Finally, if the tax issues are not compelling, given the uncertainty of future tax law, the optimal investment judgment should clearly dominate the decision.

Integration With Outside Assets

To completely fulfill the charge to investment counselors, all of the client's resources and needs should be considered. This is in contrast to the more narrowly based investment advisory role relating to a specific set of securities or policies. In the counseling role, one of the thorniest issues is how to deal with substantial assets on the investor's balance sheet that are outside the professional's control. Examples of such assets are an inherited family farm that the family says will never be sold, illiquid partnership investments, and stock and options in the individual's company.

A normal first reaction to such large holdings is to underweight comparable holdings in the managed portfolio. For example, if a client's stock and options in his employer company amount to 50 percent of his net worth, and if the normal target for the client is to hold 50 percent of his portfolio in domestic stocks, it could be argued that the managed portfolio should hold no stocks until some of the employer company stock can be sold.

The problem with this approach is that such nonmanaged assets are typically nondiversified. In the case of employer stock, particularly in a smaller company, overall market conditions may have only a modest and random impact on changes in the market value of that security. Rather than capturing a stock market effect, the correlation of the stock's returns with those of the market in general may be so weak that only a more narrowly based industry or management effect is captured.

The solution usually lies in some compromise and depends heavily on the objectives of the individual. For example, a very wealthy person may wish to view the managed portfolio as a "stand-alone" financial independence portfolio, in which the nonmanaged assets are viewed merely as potential surplus funds, but are not relied on for core goal satisfaction. In such cases, the manager's job is easy: Ignore the outside asset effect. In other cases, such as where all assets are necessary for goal achievement, but for tax or personal or business reasons the outside assets cannot be sold and diversified, the manager's job is more complicated. If, for example, the investor holds a farm or other real estate, perhaps the managed portfolio should hold somewhat less than a normal weighting in real estate assets, but not zero. The managed portion should be well diversified (different in return patterns from the nonmanaged assets) in order to increase the assurance that the investors' overall balance sheet will actually experience some of the desired effect of holding nonstock equities such as real estate.

Income vs. Principal: The Traditional View and Its Limitations

It is a long-held view that if one spends only investment income and never dips into principal, then one's wealth will not be dissipated. In *nominal* terms, this is true and is the reason why so many trusts are set up to provide income only to the current beneficiaries, with the principal to be passed on to future generations.

In *real* terms, however, this traditional view has limitations. It is possible to invest the principal all in fixed-income interests to maximize spendable income, but the principal will decline in purchasing power—that is, in *real* value—during extended periods of inflation.

Instead, it is useful (though not always possible) to counsel clients to think in terms of a prudent annual rate of withdrawals, perhaps 3 to 5 percent per year, regardless of the actual portfolio income. There will be times when the portfolio may yield more and times when it will yield less because of the investments that are appropriate for a given environment and a given total return objective. It is not unreasonable to plan for long-term rates of return of 7 to 12 percent, depending on the assets chosen. Thus, whatever rate of spendable income is required serves to reduce the amount that can be reinvested to preserve the purchasing power of the principal.

Tying All This Together

A long list of possible constraints, including liquidity needs, tax issues, and goals integration, have been discussed. As noted, there rarely are hard-and-fast rules to follow. Individuals and their needs are a complex and continually evolving mélange of issues that require good judgment, which can be delivered only by an experienced, intelligent human being. Further, many of the issues covered in this section were discussed not because they are necessarily inherently important in the portfolio management process, but because the individual may *perceive* them to be so. They may be important and emotional issues for the investor, and therefore the management of counseling on and integration of these issues into the portfolio may be the most important part of the relationship between the money manager and the client.

DETERMINATION OF PORTFOLIO POLICIES

How are all of the constraints, interests, and needs of individual investors put together into a coherent portfolio policy? Three avenues of thought are possible:

1. Selecting "good investments" without any overall plan
2. Following the traditional approaches of focusing on characteristics such as income, growth, and the like
3. Pursuing a modern multi-asset, total return policy that is commensurate with the individual's risk tolerance

Absence of Policy: Issue-by-Issue Selection

Although difficult to comprehend from the professional's point of view, probably the most common form of policy statement among individuals is, "I just want to make good investments." As a result, the investor picks and chooses among the opportunities that present themselves and, over time, a portfolio is collected. Typically, such portfolios are oriented toward what the investor knows about or feels most comfortable with, and they might be almost entirely in stocks, or bonds, or real estate. Deeper scrutiny of the collected assets might indicate the presence of a subconscious portfolio policy: perhaps an aggressive or conservative bias, long- or short-term maturity, income or capital gain potential, and so forth. At other times there is no apparent policy other than what has been imposed on the investor by a collection of salesmen, brokers, and investment advertising.

Traditional Policy Approaches

Traditionally, policy has been classified under these headings: income, income and growth (or conservative growth), growth, and aggressive growth.

Income. Income portfolio policies arise from the traditional notion that only income can be spent and capital gains must be reinvested. Often this is a legal requirement of a trust, as discussed earlier. The portfolio resulting from this notion can range from safe, high yields in bonds and money market instruments (though with some inflation risk) to a portfolio having some high-yielding stocks (such as utilities) and real estate (such as mortgage real estate investment trusts), in which the potential risk (dividend or other payment cuts) and reward (growth in income) can be greater.

Income and Growth. Income and growth portfolio policies generally refer to both fixed-income and equity portions of the portfolios. However, because of the "income" component, the stock and/or real estate portions of the portfolio tend to have a conservative income bias. The thinking behind this policy is that investors who want to spend only income but who have a long time horizon can have a blend of spendable income and still have the potential for modest growth in income or assets (as opposed to a portfolio with a more fixed-income orientation that seeks only to maximize current yield).

Growth. Growth oriented policies tend to show fixed income as a relatively small factor in the portfolio, and focus instead on equity plays in stocks, including foreign stocks, and real estate. These are typically favored by younger or wealthier investors who do not need income, and therefore have a longer-term horizon and are able to weather the setbacks of bear markets. Historically, most studies suggest that such equity oriented policies offer the highest return in the long run, but also involve greater risk, or standard deviation of return.

Aggressive Growth. Aggressive growth policies are simply a higher risk, potentially higher return variant of a growth policy. They are appropriate for those investors most emotionally able to endure risk and volatility of return. Such portfolios are built on some combination of small capitalization equities, high beta stocks, aggressive foreign stocks, venture capital, or highly leveraged real estate.

It should be noted that all forms of traditional policy approaches envision diversification within the chosen asset class in order to reduce the potential for specific or unsystematic risk.

The limitation of the traditional approaches lies in their relatively narrow definition of "appropriate assets." There may be times when the best returns, even for a growth oriented investor, are to be found in bonds. These traditional approaches often tend to ignore newer areas of opportunity, such as venture capital or real estate partnerships. As a result, they are less able to take advantage of the changing environment than is a more flexible, multi-asset policy.

The appeal of traditional policies is that they are easy to understand and conceptualize, and they represent the conventional wisdom, having been handed down from generation to generation. They continue to be confirmed by the mutual fund industry's classification schemes and brokerage house publications.

A Multi-Asset, Total Return Policy

A multi-asset policy offers the most flexibility in reacting to the environment, has the possibility of offering enhanced returns if sound tactics are chosen, and yet has the highest potential for satisfying the risk averseness inherent in most individual investors. Such a policy is broadly written to include as many asset classes as can be handled by the investor or the professional manager, including cash equivalents, domestic and foreign bonds, domestic and foreign stocks, venture capital, precious metals, real estate, oil drilling, and farming. Such approaches have become available in a few total return mutual funds as well.

Such a multi-asset policy can offer the flexibility to take advantage of different environments. For example, during the inflationary 1970s, such a portfolio could have emphasized real estate and precious metals. In the disinflationary early 1980s, the focus could have been on long bonds and cash equivalents. Later in the 1980s, a growing low inflation economy offered opportunities in stocks, and a declining dollar offered rewards in foreign stocks and bonds.

Obviously, with such a policy the income generated by the portfolio can vary greatly. Thus, investors needing to support their lifestyle out of their investment portfolio have to be counseled on taking a fixed percentage monthly or yearly withdrawal from the portfolio without regard to whether such sums came from income or principal. As long as the total withdrawal (including income taxes) is less than the total long-term return (i.e., less than 8 to 12 percent, depending on the objectives of the portfolio), there will be something left over for portfolio growth.

The policy decisions that need to be carefully delineated in a multi-asset, total return approach, therefore, are the following:

- Which asset classes are to be included? Assume that there should be some inclusion of both debt and equity instruments.
- How much flexibility should there be in varying the asset mix?
- Which kinds of securities are to be considered (from conservative to aggressive) in each asset class?
- What trade-off of withdrawals versus reinvestment is appropriate?

The answers to these issues lie in properly addressing the individual's psychographics, peculiar risk preferences, and goals and are further dictated by the capabilities of the manager of the investments. The investor can implement the policy either by managing everything himself, by managing the asset mix policy himself but delegating the investment management to specialist managers of mutual funds, or by delegating the entire task to a multi-asset management firm.

Risk Control Issues. As shown in Table 3-3, a multi-asset portfolio can actually have lower risk (as measured by standard deviation of return) for any required level of return than that achievable by most traditional approaches focusing on only one asset class. This exhibit shows the 1966-to-1987 return and risk levels for five common asset classes (cash, bonds, domestic stocks, foreign stocks, and real estate), as well as for various combinations of these classes. The power of the combination in achieving superior return/risk trade-offs lies in two fundamental investment principles. First, asset class returns are not perfectly correlated with each other: multi-asset class diversification has less volatility than most single asset class approaches do. Second, these combinations all presume a fixed mix with periodic rebalancing as markets move the portfolio away from the policy mix. In this case, portfolios are presumed to be rebalanced each January 1, thereby enforcing the discipline of buying more of those asset classes that underperformed in that year (i.e., buying low) and selling off some of those asset classes that outperformed the portfolio (i.e., selling high), a discipline that most professional money managers wish that they could regularly achieve. The overall risk/return trade-offs of multi-asset and single asset class approaches are charted in Figure 3-7.

The *investor psychographics* are quite likely to be adequately addressed by a multi-asset portfolio. Since most private clients are generally risk averse (falling mostly in the guardian or passive investor classifications) a multi-

DETERMINATION OF PORTFOLIO POLICIES

TABLE 3-3. Annual Risk/Return Data[a] on Single Asset and Multi-Asset Portfolios, January 1, 1966 to June 30, 1989

	Single Asset Portfolios					Multi-Asset Portfolios		
Year	S&P 500[f]	EAFE[h]	Treasury Bill[i]	Real Estate[j]	Shearson Lehman Hutton Bond[g]	BB&K 20/20 Index[b]	Conservative Portfolio[c]	Aggressive Portfolio[d]
1966	-10.1%	-4.0%	4.9%	7.1%	3.7%	0.3%	1.2%	-2.3%
1967	23.9	15.7	4.3	7.3	-9.2	8.4	4.9	14.0
1968	11.1	31.7	5.3	8.1	-0.3	11.2	6.2	13.2
1969	-8.5	6.8	6.5	9.7	-5.1	1.9	0.2	0.4
1970	4.0	-10.1	6.6	10.8	12.1	4.7	7.1	4.0
1971	14.3	30.1	4.4	9.2	10.6	13.7	9.8	15.6
1972	18.9	37.1	4.1	7.5	8.1	15.1	10.1	18.1
1973	-14.8	-12.8	6.9	7.5	2.3	-2.2	0.2	-6.0
1974	-26.5	-21.6	7.9	7.2	0.2	-6.6	-2.8	-12.7
1975	37.3	37.0	5.8	5.7	12.3	19.6	15.6	25.2
1976	23.6	3.8	5.1	9.3	15.6	11.5	12.1	14.6
1977	-7.4	19.4	5.2	10.5	3.0	6.1	3.0	4.4
1978	6.5	34.3	7.1	15.9	1.2	13.0	7.0	14.4
1979	18.5	6.2	10.0	20.6	2.3	11.5	9.7	15.0
1980	32.5	24.4	11.4	17.9	3.1	17.9	14.1	23.5
1981	-5.0	-1.1	14.2	16.6	7.2	6.4	7.6	3.5
1982	21.6	-0.8	10.9	9.3	31.1	14.4	18.4	14.4

1983	22.5	24.6	8.9	13.3	8.0	15.4	12.3	18.7
1984	6.2	7.9	9.9	12.9	15.0	10.4	10.7	9.4
1985	31.7	56.7	7.4	9.8	21.3	25.4	19.0	29.1
1986	18.7	70.0	6.2	6.3	15.6	23.3	14.7	24.9
1987	5.3	24.6	5.9	5.0	2.3	8.6	5.6	8.8
1988	16.5	27.7	6.8	7.1	7.6	13.1	10.0	15.0
1989 [e]	16.4	-6.5	4.2	3.7	9.2	5.4	7.6	7.3
Annualized return	9.7%	15.0%	7.2%	10.1%	7.2%	10.3%	8.6%	11.1%
Standard deviation	16.5%	22.2%	2.6%	4.2%	8.8%	7.7%	5.8%	10.4%

SOURCE: Bailard, Biehl and Kaiser.

[a] Quarterly return deviations, annualized.

[b] BB&K Index consists of 20% in each of these five asset classes.

[c] Conservative portfolio: cash, 40%; bonds, 30%; S&P, 20%; EAFE, 5%; real estate, 5%.

[d] Aggressive portfolio: cash, 0%; bonds, 10%; S&P, 40%; EAFE, 20%; real estate, 30%.

[e] Through June 30, 1989, annualized.

[f] Standard & Poor's 500 Composite Stock Price Index.

[g] Shearson Lehman Hutton Government/Corporate Bond Index.

[h] Europe, Australia, Far East Stock Market Index (EAFE International Index).

[i] One-month Treasury bill offering.

[j] Ibbotson and Fall [1979], 1966–1970; JMB Institutional Realty Corp. [1986], 1971–1977; Frank Russell Company Property Index, 1978–1989.

Note: The real estate portfolio and the multi-asset portfolios containing real estate likely have a downward-biased standard deviation because of the smoothing effect of *appraisal-based* return calculations (as opposed to *transaction-based* return calculations).

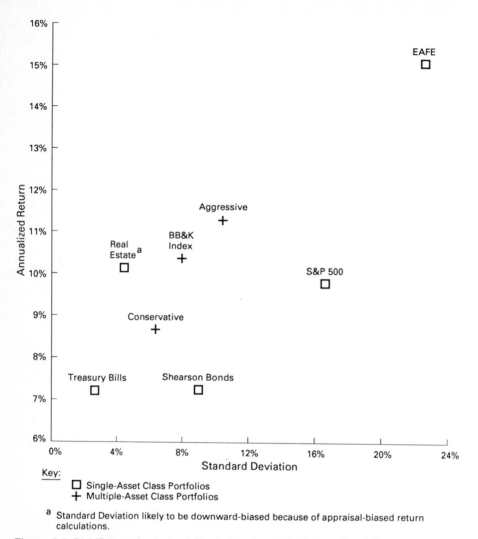

Figure 3-7. Risk/Return Analysis of Single Asset and Multi-Asset Portfolios, January 1, 1966 to June 30, 1989. SOURCE: Bailard, Biehl & Kaiser.

asset approach appears to be fundamentally sound, although it may take considerable counseling to get the investor to comprehend how a *mixture* of individual risky asset classes can actually pose less bottom line risk than a traditional "low risk" approach involving only bonds or only blue chip stocks (i.e., those included in the S&P 500).

The degree of risk desired can be adjusted by varying three elements of the portfolio:

1. The choice and basic mix of asset classes

2. The flexibility allowed to the investment manager
3. The risk level of individual issue selection

For the most conservative investors, the mix of asset classes is usually weighted most heavily toward cash and bonds, with some representation in domestic stocks and perhaps small amounts in real estate (via partnerships or real estate investment trusts), foreign stocks, and precious metals (either bullion or gold-mining company common stocks). Investors who want more moderate risk increase the relative amounts invested in equities of all kinds and reduce the amounts committed to debt instruments. The most adventuresome investors add assets such as investments in venture capital, oil drilling, or foreign stocks and bonds if they feel the timing is right (i.e., if there is a large expected return for the risk borne during the coming holding period(s)).

Another way to vary the risk level of an individual's portfolio is in the latitude that is allowed for asset shifts within the portfolio. The most conservative investors will not allow market judgment risk to enter into their portfolio decision making and will opt for a fixed mix of assets, with quarterly rebalancing. Less conservative investors might allow a range of 15 to 30 percent of their portfolio for domestic stocks, for example, and 5 to 10 percent for foreign stocks, while more adventuresome investors might allow a range of 5 to 50 percent for each, depending on the outlook for a given asset class. The potential rewards are greater for getting it right, as are the risks of getting it wrong.

Finally, the risk/return level of the portfolio can be altered by the choice of securities allowed by the investor. The following table illustrates two possible sets of choices, one for lower-risk-oriented and one for higher-risk-oriented investors.

Asset Class	Lower Risk	Higher Risk
Cash equivalents	Treasuries only	Commercial paper allowed
Bonds	Short-term Treasuries	Long-term, Baa-quality bonds allowed
U.S. stocks	Large capitalization issues	Small capitalization issues allowed
Foreign stocks	Diversified mutual fund securities	Individual stocks, some small
Real estate	Unleveraged investments only	Leveraged partnerships

Goal Integration. At times an investor's portfolio strategy must be altered somewhat, depending on the needs for some of the money. For example, taxes due the following April should normally be set aside in quality, liquid cash equivalents. For individuals of lesser means, some important goals can loom relatively large in the portfolio. For example, if an investor has several children who will be entering college over the next few years, he might invest in a portfolio of bonds with amounts and maturities matching the amounts and years of need in order to remove the uncertainty of having the funds available at the right time.

The largest goal for most people is financial independence at retirement age, or perhaps earlier for persons of substantial wealth. In cases in which the investor's investment portfolio is already comfortably larger than the discounted present value of his needs, he is free to choose the investment approach that suits his psychological profile (provided it is reasonably diversified and judged reasonably likely to succeed over time). For persons of more modest means, those for whom the investment return must equal or exceed the discount rate used in calculating the needs, the selection of an appropriate investment strategy is important. If this calls for a more aggressive asset mix than the investor is comfortable with, the professional must offer counsel regarding two possible trade-offs: (1) Learn to live with a somewhat more aggressive approach, entrusting investment decisions to professional management, or (2) either settle for a more modest level of financial independence in the future or spend less and save more for those future needs.

In short, a portfolio policy that meets the needs of a given individual must address these issues:

- Asset class selection
- Normal asset mix target
- Range of mixes allowed about the target
- Risk level of individual securities selected for the portfolio

Counseling the risk averse investor should involve attempts to add more classes of assets in order to reduce overall risk through diversification, rather than taking more narrowly based traditional approaches in which perceived risk may be low but actual portfolio volatility is higher.

SUMMARY

Individuals are freer to act out their own impulses or beliefs regarding the management of their money than are pension or endowment funds, which have fiduciary rules, specific objectives, and committee oversight. Yet individuals do have a rationale for their financial goals. The successful integration of the personality differences, goals, and various constraints (e.g., income taxes) is an exciting challenge facing the portfolio manager. Because of these various needs and the basic risk averseness of individuals, the portfolio manager is most likely to succeed by broadening the selection of asset classes in the portfolios, rather than by confining them to the conventional stock and bond approach of years past.

FURTHER READING

Much of the literature has historically been dominated by traditional trust department thinking involving conservative stock and bond approaches for widows and orphans. However, some of the newest materials are worth reading. Tuttle [1982] remains the best concise summary to that date. The Institute of Chartered Financial Analysts seminar proceedings, edited by Droms [1987] and Bayston [1988], are worth reviewing in their entirety, even though only a few topics are directly referenced in this chapter. For those interested in reviewing the financial planning issues surrounding individual investment management (i.e., insurance, budgeting, debt management, taxes, goal planning, estate transfer, and so forth), the Bailard, Biehl and Kaiser [1986] text provides comprehensive, modern coverage. Finally, the often-confusing prudent man rule issues are more completely reviewed by Longstreth [1986].

BIBLIOGRAPHY

Bailard, Thomas E., David L. Biehl, and Ronald W. Kaiser. *Personal Money Management*, 5th ed. Chicago: Science Research Associates, Inc., 1986.

Barnewall, Marilyn MacGruder. "Psychological Characteristics of the Individual Investor," in W. Droms, ed. *Asset Allocation for the Individual Investor*. Charlottesville, Va.: The Institute of Chartered Financial Analysts, 1987.

Bayston, Darwin M., ed. *Serving the Individual Investor*. Charlottesville, Va.: The Institute of Chartered Financial Analysts, 1988.

Droms, William G., ed. *Asset Allocation for the Individual Investor*. Charlottesville, Va.: The Institute of Chartered Financial Analysts, 1987.

Droms, William G. "Investment Risk and the Individual Investor," in W. Droms, ed. *Asset Allocation for the Individual Investor*. Charlottesville, Va.: The Institute of Chartered Financial Analysts, 1987.

"Estimates of Personal Wealth, 1982." *Statistics of Income Bulletin, Winter 1984– 85*. IRS Publication No. 1136. Washington, D.C.: Internal Revenue Service, 1985.

Ibbotson, Roger G., and Carol L. Fall. "The United States Market Wealth Portfolio." *The Journal of Portfolio Management*, Fall 1979.

Kaiser, Ronald W. "The Dynamics of the Investment Decision Making Process for the Individual Investor," in W. Droms, ed. *Asset Allocation for the Individual Investor*. Charlottesville, Va.: The Institute of Chartered Financial Analysts, 1987.

Longstreth, Bevis. *Modern Investment Management and the Prudent Man Rule*. New York: Oxford University Press, 1986.

New York Stock Exchange Fact Book 1988. New York: New York Stock Exchange, 1988.

Trust Assets of Financial Institutions—1986. Washington, D.C.: Federal Financial Institutions Examination Council, 1987.

Tuttle, Donald L. "Individual and Personal Trusts," in *Determinants of Investment Portfolio Policy*. Charlottesville, Va.: The Institute of Chartered Financial Analysts, 1982.

CHAPTER 4

Determination of Portfolio Policies: Institutional Investors

Keith P. Ambachtsheer
John L. Maginn, CFA
Jay Vawter, CFA

OVERVIEW

Management of institutional portfolios has become increasingly complex and challenging. Portfolio theory, performance pressures, and an increasing array of new instruments surround the portfolio manager and both test and enhance his investment management skills.

This chapter focuses on the institutional investor from five perspectives: those of pension funds, endowment funds, insurance companies, commercial banks, and mutual funds. The factors that determine the investment policy objectives and constraints of each of these classes of institutional investors are reviewed by experienced investment professionals.[1]

These five classes of institutional investors cover a wide spectrum of investment policy considerations and illustrate the challenges and complexity of the institutional portfolio manager's task. It should be obvious but bears repeating that behind all investment portfolios lie flesh and blood investors who benefit directly or indirectly as beneficiaries, policyholders, stockholders, or members of an institution.

---

[1] Keith Ambachtsheer provides an in-depth and thought-provoking perspective on the role of pension funds and their sponsors, and translates those factors into investment policy considerations. Jay Vawter explains the unique investment policy considerations that characterize endowment funds and professional and trade associations. John Maginn traces the evolution of asset/liability management for insurance companies and the impact it has had on the investment policies of life and nonlife companies. The discussion of commercial bank and mutual fund portfolio policies, originally written by Jay Vawter in the first edition of *Managing Investment Portfolios*, has been updated in this edition by John Maginn.

EMPLOYEE BENEFIT FUNDS

Pension funds have existed since the late 1800s, but it is their two-times-GNP growth during the past 25 years that has catapulted these assets to "star" status on the world investments stage. Figure 4-1 shows that just the four economies with the largest pension asset pools—the United States, Japan, the United Kingdom, and Canada—had about $3.25 trillion in segregated, employment-based pension assets by the end of 1988.

Well over 90 percent of the pension assets in Japan, the United Kingdom, and Canada are related to mid-size and large private and public sector employee pension plans where the benefits are defined (i.e., "defined benefit

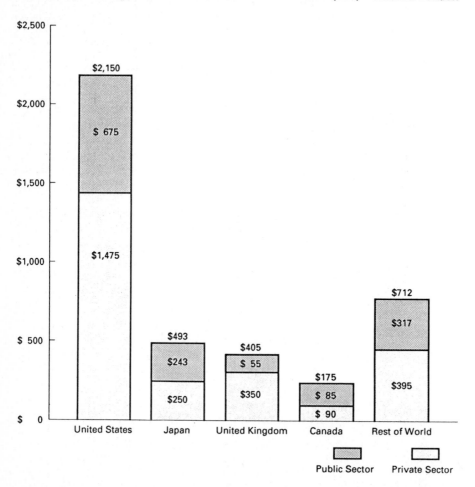

Figure 4-1. Estimated Pension Assets at the End of 1988[a] (in billions of U.S. dollars).
[a]Does not include insured plan assets. SOURCE: InterSec Research Corp.

TABLE 4-1. A Breakdown of U.S. Pension Assets at the End of 1988 (in billions of dollars)

Defined Benefit Plans	
State and local governments	$ 609
Private insured	460[a]
Private trusteed—Multi-employer	131
Private trusteed—Single employer	707
	$1,907
Defined Contribution Plans	
Large plans	$ 211
Small plans	224
	$ 435

SOURCE: Employee Benefit Research Institute, Washington, D.C.
[a] End of 1987.

plans''), usually in relation to individuals' earnings and length of service. That percentage is lower in the United States, closer to 80 percent.

Table 4-1 shows that in the United States, assets related to pension plans where only the contribution rate into the plan is defined (i.e., ''defined contribution plans'') amounted to $435 billion at the end of 1988.

Asset mixes for pension funds vary both by country and by type of plan. While precise, comparable data are not yet available, the following broad comments may be made:

- United Kingdom pension funds have the highest equity exposure, with 65 percent in stocks and 10 percent in real estate typical.
- Japanese pension funds have the lowest equity exposure, with 25 percent in stocks and 3 percent in real estate typical.
- North American asset mixes tend to be in between these extremes, with public sector funds generally having lower equity weightings (30–40 percent) than private sector funds (50–60 percent) for defined benefit plans.
- Where individuals are given the choice in defined contribution plans, they tend to opt for asset mixes with a high proportion of guaranteed investment contracts (GICs) issued by life insurance companies (60–70 percent).

Pension Assets Attract Increasing Attention

The enormous accumulations of pension assets are attracting increasing attention. Over most of the past 25 years, that attention came mainly from interested *agents*: private and public sector executives, actuaries, consultants, investment managers, accountants, and investment dealers, as well as regulators and legislators. Their roles in the governance and management of pension assets are described later in this chapter.

More recently, the *principals* themselves have become increasingly interested in the investment governance and management of employment-based pension assets. Who are these principals and what exactly is their interest in pension assets? This question is addressed first.

Pension Asset Principals

The "know your client" rule is fundamental in the investment business. Without knowing his clients, the investment manager cannot properly manage their assets. To understand how the know your client rule applies to pension assets, one must first understand the nature of pension "contracts" between employers and employees.

As noted previously, there are two basic types of pension arrangements: (1) *defined benefit* and (2) *defined contribution*. Practically, there are additional types; but on careful examination, these additional types turn out to be variations on one of the two basic themes, or combinations of them. The nature of the pension contract defines who the pension asset principals are.

Defined Benefit Pension Plans

Most pension plan participants are covered by defined benefit plans, even in the United States. A key characteristic here is that pension benefits are defined independent of the value of plan assets. Benefits are based on formulas, usually related to employee earnings and length of service or some combination of the two. First, benefits may be a flat percentage of earnings, such as "50 percent of the average salary for the last five years of service." Second, benefits may be defined as a specified dollar amount per year of service, such as "$15 per month times the number of months of service." Third, benefits may be stated as a percentage of employment earnings times the number of years of service. For example, a typical formula is an annual pension credit of 1.5 percent of final earnings times the number of years of service. Thus, an employee with 30 years of uninterrupted service would retire with an employment-related pension equal to 45 percent of final earnings under this plan. Other retirement income sources, such as social security and private savings, could raise this employee's overall income replacement ratio to 70 to 80 percent of preretirement employment income.

From a financial perspective, employers are effectively issuing pension debt to their employees in defined benefit plans. This pension debt can be serviced (1) on a *pay-as-you-go* basis or (2) on a *funded* basis. In the latter case, sufficient monies are set aside in a pension fund each year to match the estimated present value of the debt accrued that year. Calculations of the needed amounts must be made by qualified actuaries. Included in their calculations are such factors as mortality, employee turnover, salary escalation, and the likely return on a pool of assets mirroring the financial characteristics of the pension obligations.

Government regulations and tax legislation have strongly pushed private sector employers in North America, in the United Kingdom, and, to a lesser degree, in Japan, toward this "funded basis" option. More recently, public sector employers and employees have also put considerable emphasis on funding pension entitlements for benefit security and fiscal responsibility reasons. These private and public sector developments were major factors in the massive pension asset buildup during the past 25 years.

Ownership of Defined Benefit Plan Assets

There is no clear legal answer to the question "who owns the assets?" in many defined benefit pension plans. The reasons for this are twofold. First, plan documentation is often ambiguous on the asset ownership question. Second, the laws governing pension plans have ambiguities of their own. For example, in the United States, the Employee Retirement Income Security Act of 1974 (ERISA) requires pension funds to be managed "solely in the interest of plan participants." Yet ERISA permits plan sponsors to benefit from good investment performance by taking contribution holidays (i.e., forgo making regular pension contributions for some period of time) and claiming surplus asset reversions on plan termination. The "solely in the interest of plan participants" language comes from trust law tradition. The plan sponsor's rights under ERISA come from bankruptcy law tradition. Trust law and bankruptcy law make odd bedfellows.

Fortunately, economic analysis is more helpful than legal analysis in understanding how investment risk and reward are typically allocated in defined benefit pension plans. In the pure defined benefit model, the plan sponsor (and ultimately shareholders or taxpayers) bears all investment-related risks and hence should garner all investment-related rewards. Plan participants are simply owed a defined amount of pension debt by the plan sponsor.

The fact that this debt is being serviced through a separate legal entity called a pension plan would be of little economic significance *except* for the funding factor that leads to the existence of a pension fund. The fund is the plan participants' first line of defense against plan sponsor insolvency. So the economics of the pure defined benefit model suggest an interesting dichotomy. In a going-concern mode, the plan sponsor legitimately lays claim to pension fund investment return to help service pension debt as it falls due. But, in a termination mode, the shoe is on the other foot. Plan participants have first claim on pension assets. Only if there are assets in excess of the amount needed to settle all outstanding pension debt does the plan sponsor have any claim on pension assets.

Defined Benefit Plan Controversies

Excise Tax on Surplus Assets. The lack of alignment between the economic and legal models of defined benefit plans is causing considerable discord in the pensions field. There regularly are cases before the courts where the ownership of surplus pension assets is in dispute. The U.S. Congress placed a 10 percent excise tax on surplus pension asset withdrawals in 1986. Draft legislation has been introduced in the U.S. Congress that would effectively lock surpluses into both ongoing and terminating plans, thus making them no longer available to the sponsor for other corporate purposes.

Funding Regulations and Benefit Insurance. Other areas of controversy in the United States include pension funding regulations and pension benefit insurance. The Omnibus Budget Reconciliation Act of 1987 addressed both of these issues. The Act provides for normal funding by corporate plan sponsors within a relatively narrow channel. For example, if a pension plan has assets in excess of 150 percent of the accumulated benefit obligations, the sponsor is effectively barred from making any further funding payments. During periods of high inflation, this ceiling will result in serious underfunding of corporate pension plans. Conversely, if the pension plan has assets below 100 percent of the accumulated benefit obligation, very rapid funding is required to bring assets above the 100 percent mark. Meanwhile, the government-sponsored pension benefit guaranty scheme run by the Pension Benefit Guaranty Corporation (PBGC) also continues to be controversial. Despite some adjustment in premiums to reduce its deficit, the PBGC's critics contend that it is still simply a mechanism that transfers financial resources from financially strong plan sponsors to weak ones.

Inflation Protection. The number one pension issue in Canada in 1989 was mandated inflation protection in employment-based pension arrangements. Draft legislation was introduced in early 1989 that would require registered pension plans to provide a minimum level of inflation protection to retirees. The proposed formula of 75 percent of the Consumer Price Index (CPI) increase minus one percentage point would apply only to the first $16,620 of pension payments at the start. The ceiling would increase with inflation over time. The maximum CPI increase to which the formula would apply in any one year is 8 percent, but there would be a carryforward provision for the excess over 8 percent. Equivalent alternate formulas were to be permitted. Given that this requirement mirrors what many Canadian plan sponsors were already doing on an ad hoc basis, private sector resistance to the proposal was likely to be minimal.

Defined Contribution Plans

The fundamental difference between defined benefit and defined contribution plans is that with the latter, the employer has no financial obligation beyond making regular contributions on behalf of qualifying employees into a pension plan. These contributions are usually calculated as a percentage of current pay or as a percentage of profits. The defined contribution pension plan does not promise benefits in relation to final earnings, or against any other yardstick for that matter. Each plan participant's pension depends on the size of the annuity that that person's accumulated pension assets can buy at retirement. The investment risk in a defined contribution arrangement is borne entirely by the individual participants.

The statistics indicate that defined contribution plans are still largely a U.S. phenomenon. They come in a bewildering number of legal forms. The plain *money purchase pension plan* has been joined by the *401(k) plan*, the *employee stock ownership plan* (ESOP), and other forms of savings and thrift plans. Although they are still considerably smaller, pension assets under these various defined contribution schemes have been growing much faster than those of defined benefit plans in recent years.

In the United States, private sector defined benefit plan membership remained constant at 24 million during the 5 years from 1982 to 1987, but membership where the primary plan is a defined contribution plan doubled from 6 million to 12 million over the same period. Knowledgeable observers expect this trend to continue into the 1990s. They point to two reasons that explain the phenomenon and its expected continuance.

First, employers feel increasingly burdened by legislation and regulation that make the sponsorship of defined benefit plans both costlier and riskier as time passes. In fact, a significant number of U.S. employers have terminated their defined benefit plans, in most cases by purchasing annuities for covered employees, and have replaced these plans with defined contribution plans.

Second, younger employees have become increasingly disenchanted with the fact that they get little economic benefit from defined benefit plans until they reach the status of long-service employees—which many of them, correctly, never expect to become. Defined contribution plans, by contrast, regularly deposit contributions into the employee's account, and the contributions remain the employee's assets even if he or she moves on to another employer, usually after a short vesting period.

The Defined Contribution Plan Model

There is no collective pension plan balance sheet to manage when the pension plan has a defined contribution focus. Plan participants are the only principals. The employer is an *agent*, along with the investment manager, the asset custodian-recordkeeper, and other plan agents.

While the employer plays the important role of setting up the plan and ensuring the availability of an adequate range of investment vehicles for participant use, participants should make their own investment policy decisions. That is, they should allocate their pension assets according to a carefully thought out financial plan.

In fact, while participants usually direct their own contributions into the provided investment vehicles (typically GICs, and pooled stock, bond, and balanced funds), employers still direct employer contributions into these vehicles as much as 50 percent of the time. This continued employer involvement reflects the fact that the challenge of effectively delivering financial planning and investment counseling to thousands of plan participants at an acceptable cost has yet to be met. Doing so is one of the great challenges facing employers and investment professionals today. Chapter 3 has much to say to these employers and investment professionals on the topic of individual investor investment policy objectives and constraints.

Other Types of Pension Plans

There are hundreds of pension plan designs in actual use. Virtually all can be categorized as basically defined benefit, basically defined contribution, or some hybrid of the two. The simplest and most popular variation on the two basic themes is for an employer to offer a basic defined benefit plan supplemented with some form of defined contribution plan into which the employee can also contribute.

Multi-employer or *union* plans often encompass a combination of defined benefit and defined contribution features within a single plan. A union might negotiate for an employer or group of employers to contribute defined amounts into the pension plan. Instead of allocating these contributions to individual plan participant accounts, however, plan participants receive a defined benefit on retirement based both on the value of plan assets and on an appropriate balance between the financial interests of current retirees and future retirees, as determined by the plan trustees through the payout decision. The more that is paid out today, the less there is for tomorrow.

Floor plans are defined contribution plans with a guaranteed minimum defined benefit. *Cash balance plans* are essentially defined contribution plans, but with the employer crediting plan member cash balances with a predetermined interest rate. The employer also has the option to increase plan member cash balances over and above the increases due to regular contributions and the interest thereon. With both floor and cash balance plans, the plan sponsor maintains control of the pension fund's investment policy.

Another variation on the defined benefit/defined contribution theme is sometimes seen in public sector plans. These plans tend to be *contributory plans*, with the employer and the employees often contributing equal percentages of current pay. Some plans recognize that where this "equal sharing" philosophy exists, it should be carried through to risk sharing as well. Suppose, for example, that good investment results produce a plan surplus. Then the contribution rate should be reduced equally for the employer and for employees. Of course the reverse also holds: A plan deficit should lead to an increase in the contribution rate for both parties. Where both investment risks and rewards are shared, pension fund governance should also be shared by the plan sponsor and plan members.

Health Care Benefits

In the absence of a universal national health care plan, U.S. employers have been providing health care coverage to employees—and to retirees. As with pensions, the provision of these benefits started off informally as employer "gratuities." However, just as pensions have evolved over time to become legally enforceable employee entitlements, health care benefits are in the process of doing so. Estimates suggest retiree health care liabilities were in the $200 billion range for U.S. corporations at the end of 1987. Unlike pension liabilities, there are no corresponding retiree health care assets of any consequence. Thus, these liabilities represent a direct charge against corporate equity.

The retiree health care situation facing U.S. corporations has at least two material implications for investment professionals. First, they must ask themselves to what degree reported corporate earnings should be adjusted to reflect the cost of health care entitlements that accrued during the year. The Financial Accounting Standards Board's (FASB's) new accounting standards for health benefit liabilities should help clarify this question.

Second, there is a possibility that the U.S. Congress will come to the view that if funding pension entitlements is in the public interest, so is funding health care entitlements. Such a development would give a significant boost to the growth rate of contributions into employee benefit funds in the United States at a time when that growth rate is starting to flatten. However, a number of observers argue that such tax assistance would have to wait for (1) a significant reduction in the U.S. government's budget deficit and (2) some form of health care coverage for the 37 million Americans currently without any form of medical coverage.

TABLE 4-2. The Pension Debt-Servicing Financial Institution Balance Sheet

Assets	Liabilities
• What is the immunizing or guaranteed return asset mix policy?	• What is the pension "contract"?
• Should the actual asset mix policy attempt to earn a "spread" over the return on the immunizing asset mix policy?	• How much pension debt is currently outstanding against that pension "contract"?
• How should the actual asset mix policy be implemented?	*Surplus* • By how much *do* assets exceed pension debt outstanding? • By how much *should* assets exceed pension debt outstanding?

RETURN OBJECTIVES OF EMPLOYEE BENEFIT FUNDS

The Defined Benefit Plan Model

Broad adoption of what has been called the *economic model of a defined benefit pension plan* would go a long way toward solving many of the current controversies just touched on. That economic model is useful in understanding how questions regarding investment of pension assets ought to be addressed. If defined benefit plans are in fact pension debt-servicing financial institutions, pension assets should be managed in the context of the pension plan balance sheet. It follows that the riskiness of a pension fund should not be assessed in absolute terms or in relation to other pension funds. Instead, that assessment should be made in the context of the nature of plan liabilities, and in the context of the cash flow and balance sheet characteristics of the employer issuing the pension claims.

Thus, pension fund investment policy for defined benefit plans should reflect the economic interests of both sets of plan principals: the plan participants and the employer. Ultimately, "the employer" is not its senior executives, but the shareholders (for private plans) or taxpayers (for government-sponsored plans) on whose behalf those executives are making decisions. The defined benefit pension plan economic model and the issues it raises are illustrated in Table 4-2.

RISK TOLERANCE OF EMPLOYEE BENEFIT FUNDS

Defined Benefit vs. Defined Contribution Risk

The undeniable *trend toward defined contribution* at the expense of defined benefit pension arrangements in the United States raises an important question: Are defined contribution schemes the better way to go from everyone's viewpoint? It would be a mistake to assume this is necessarily so. Defined *contribution* arrangements *have some serious shortcomings* as pension delivery vehicles. First, the long-term rate of return a given savings flow will generate can be a big question mark. If the savings flow is invested largely in GICs, the return is fixed and predictable. If it is invested largely in stocks, the risk-return trade-off is uncertain. If it is invested largely in the employer's stock in an ESOP, lack of diversification (undue concentration) is a serious issue. Clearly, a wide range of investment outcomes is possible, depending on which one or what combination of these three policies is chosen.

A second potential problem is that large percentages of the assets are withdrawn from defined contribution plans in lump sum form prior to retirement, typically on termination of employment. The proportion of these withdrawals that ultimately end up being converted to periodic pension payments is an open question, but probably is quite small.

By contrast, defined benefit arrangements require the former employer to continue to manage the vested benefits of terminated employees, assuming that annuities have not been purchased for this employee group. Thus, there are no annuity pricing risks for the participants. Also, there are no rate of return risks on the investment side of the equation. The plan sponsor continues to bear those risks. But the sponsor can win too. The ongoing, long-term nature of defined benefit plans permits the adoption of a high return investment policy with the plan assets. If the policy is successful, the sponsor's contribution rate for the plan could be quite modest.

Thus, the current trouble with defined benefit arrangements in the United States and Canada is not that these arrangements do not make economic sense. They do. The trouble is that plan sponsors, plan members, politicians, and the courts are too often at odds about what the formal arrangement, the "pension contract," actually is for defined benefit plans. Only a consensus on what constitutes a legitimate defined benefit pension arrangement can arrest the previously noted steady decline in the popularity of this type of plan.

ROLE OF CAPITAL MARKET EXPECTATIONS IN PENSION INVESTMENT POLICY

In addition to return objectives and risk tolerance for various pension plan types, capital market expectations must be considered—and integrated—in determining appropriate pension investment policy. For example, a view on the long-term prospects for returns on the major asset classes is important—but only in the context of consistent long-term wage and price inflation prospects. Another important forward-looking dimension is potential economic experience and uncertainty around the long-term expectations. Then, too, there is the question of the shorter-term capital value volatility of these asset classes. Not only is the impact of this volatility on total return volatility important, but so is the question of how those return outcomes might be correlated.

Another key dimension is the differential return between the asset that most closely mirrors pension liabilities and other investment classes. For example, the asset that most closely mirrors economic, going-concern pension liabilities and is also default-free is probably (in the absence of long-term, inflation-indexed debt) a short-term government bond. How much more can be earned by taking on maturity risk? Or default risk? What about the likely equity risk premium? What can be said about prospective equity risk premium differentials between, for example, large capitalization common stocks, small capitalization common stocks, and equity real estate?

Where do these views on economic and capital market prospects come from? In a general sense, they always come from some blend of our understanding of historical experience, current capital market prices, and our best judgment on how the future might be different from the past. More specifically, forecasters can bring a battery of techniques into play to help construct a set of sensible, operational economic and capital market expectations. Chapter 5 is devoted to this topic.

PENSION PLAN INVESTMENT POLICY

The pension plan investment problem usually takes on one of two basic forms. The first is the "individual investor" form, where the plan sponsor provides the appropriate array of investment vehicles and where either individual plan participants fashion their own investment policy or employers do it for them. The second is the "institutional investor" form, where pension plan assets are not individualized, but instead collectively support the payment of pension obligations incurred by a corporation, a public sector entity, or by some other legal entity, possibly created specifically for the purpose. The individual investor form of the investment policy problem is examined in Chapter 3; the problem in its institutional investor form is discussed in the following sections.

As with any investment problem, solving the pension investment problem is a two-step process: first decide on investment policy, and then implement it. Pension fund investment policy and its implementation are examined in turn. In doing so, this chapter anticipates the more detailed treatment of many aspects of establishing and implementing investment policy in subsequent chapters.

Pension Fund Investment Policy in the Institutional Investor Context

Pension fund investment policy for defined benefit plans should be addressed in a balance sheet context, as shown in Table 4-2. Given that the plan's *raison d'etre* is to pay benefits, it follows that the plan's asset policy should be set in the context of the plan's liability (i.e., benefits) policy—and not vice versa. In short, informed asset policy decisions require a sound knowledge of plan benefits policy, or what is called "the pension contract" in Table 4-2.

A further important contextual consideration for framing investment policy arises out of the reality that a pension plan does not necessarily live forever. Plan sponsor insolvency is not the only reason a pension plan might at some point cease to exist. In many plans, the employer has the option to terminate even if not forced to by insolvency. Just as pension liability characteristics that fall out of the pension contract (i.e., the benefit promise) impact on asset policy, so does the *going-concern* versus *termination* question. In the going-concern case, there is no finite investment horizon; in the termination case, there is.

Beyond the going-concern versus termination discontinuity question lies the broader question of plan liquidity needs. Generally, young, growing work forces imply many years of net positive contributions flowing into the pension plan. Conversely, older, declining work forces imply material year-to-year liquidity needs because benefit payments exceed new contributions. Thus, informed asset policy decisions require a prior decision as to whether they are being made in a going-concern or termination context. A further assessment of plan liquidity needs in the going-concern mode must also be made.

From the three contextual considerations (i.e., type of liability, type of planning horizon, and type of liquidity needs), three further important asset policy considerations flow: (1) the importance of plan asset and liability value fluctuations, (2) the degree of main business and pension plan integration, and (3) views on capital market expectations.

Importance of Plan Asset and Liability Value Fluctuations

How much the values of plan assets, plan liabilities, and the difference between them (i.e., plan surplus) fluctuate in any given time period may be more or less important in any given pension plan context. The degree of importance attached to controlling the balance sheet volatility (usually at the expense of reducing long-term asset return prospects) depends on the following factors:

- The nature of the pension contract. Generally, if plan participants are directly affected in some financial way by balance sheet volatility, it is likely to be more tightly controlled.
- The financial strength of the plan sponsor. Generally, financially strong plan sponsors worry less about controlling pension plan balance sheet volatility than financially weak plan sponsors.
- The tolerance of plan sponsor management for pension plan-generated volatility in the sponsor's own financial statements.
- The tolerance of plan sponsor management for volatility in the sponsor's required contribution rate into the plan.

Having the plan sponsor's senior management "know thyself" with respect to these factors is one of the great challenges facing pension fund executives, their consultants, and their investment managers.

Pension Industry Balance Sheet Volatility Debate. A "perception versus reality" debate has emerged in the pension investment industry about this pension asset and liability volatility question. A positive aspect of this debate is the general recognition that pension fund asset value volatility by itself is not the central issue. Rather, the issue is the potential contribution of this asset value volatility to benefit security, to contribution rate volatility, and to financial statement volatility. The first two impacts have direct economic consequences for plan members and the plan sponsor. If asset value volatility is such that it endangers the benefit security of plan members, then plan fiduciaries in the United States are arguably in contravention of ERISA. If pension fund asset value volatility is such that it creates massive swings in contribution rates into the plan, then fund fiduciaries may not be properly reflecting the needs of the plan sponsor.

New Accounting Rules. Interestingly, the asset or balance sheet volatility debate was not sparked by these two potential direct economic impacts. Rather, it was sparked by the introduction of a new set of pension accounting rules (Financial Accounting Standard No. 87 (FAS 87) in the United States and Canadian Institute of Chartered Accountants (CICA) 3460 in Canada). Much of the debate has focused on the merit of structuring the pension fund asset mix to minimize financial statement volatility (e.g., the impact of pension plan asset and liability variations on reported plan sponsor profits and the plan's own balance sheet), or alternatively, structuring pension fund asset mix primarily in relation to the economics of the plan and the plan sponsor.

Leibowitz initiated the debate with a series of articles in the *Financial Analysts Journal*, showing that a long bond portfolio best matches the pension liability if that liability is taken to be what FAS 87 called the *accrued benefit obligation* or ABO. This ABO is the value at which plan sponsors have historically been able to discharge their pension obligations when terminating a defined benefit pension plan. Others pointed out that this apparent match disappears if the pension liability is taken to be an ongoing payment stream, the value of which depends on wage inflation prior to retirement and on price inflation after retirement. In the latter case, long bonds are no longer the "risk-free asset." Indeed, because of their fixed return and inflation exposure, they become the opposite: a quite risky asset.

Readers wanting a closer look at this debate should read the articles by Ambachtsheer [1987], Arnott and Bernstein [1988], Bookstaber and Gold [1988], Ippolito [1986], Leibowitz [1987a, 1987b], Malley and Jayson [1986], Sharpe [1987], and Wagner [1988] referenced in the bibliography at the end of this chapter. In early 1989, the impact of FAS 87 and CICA 3460 was still being debated.

The Degree of Main Business and Pension Plan Integration

From a financial planning perspective, should the pension plan be viewed as an independent, stand-alone financial institution? Or, at the other extreme, as a wholly owned subsidiary of the plan sponsor? For most plan sponsors, whether they have formally confronted this issue or not, the answer lies somewhere in between these two extremes.

On the one hand, special laws and regulations prevent plan sponsors from treating the pension plan as just another wholly owned subsidiary. On the other, plan sponsors would be foolhardy not to recognize the financial interdependence of their financial affairs and those of the pension plan. If plan asset growth exceeds liability growth, the sponsor's required contributions into the plan eventually are reduced as balance sheet surplus builds. The accounting rules ensure that this happy development is eventually reflected in corporate earnings. Conversely, if liabilities grow faster than assets, the eventual result is a balance sheet deficiency, a rising contribution rate, and a negative impact on reported earnings. In either case, the financial dynamics of the pension plan are clearly impacting plan sponsor finances.

As an example, consider the impact of a sudden surge of inflation in the economy. Taking the experience of the 1970s as a guide, pension liabilities can be expected to rise more rapidly than assets for most plans in this kind of environment because of inflation's positive effect on wage rates and negative effect on many asset values and returns. As a result, the required contribution rate rises. The main business/pension plan integration question is this: How does this sudden surge of inflation affect the main business?

If main business revenues are closely tied to inflation (e.g., for oil companies or governments), the rising required pension contribution rate might not be a major concern. On the other hand, if main business costs are more likely to be impacted than revenues with an inflation surge (e.g., for airlines or automobiles), a requirement to put more money into the pension plan in such an environment could further aggravate an already serious cash flow squeeze. What is the pension investment implication of all this? The answer is that some plan sponsors should put greater emphasis on acquiring inflation-hedged pension assets than others.

Thus, one type of main business/pension plan interdependency is the impact of *unanticipated inflation*. For another example, the reader may wish to trace through the interdependency logic for categories of plan sponsors where the surprise event is *recession* rather than inflation. Again, insights into a logical basis for pension investment policy differences between plan sponsors will likely be uncovered.

The Tax Arbitrage Argument. Corporate finance theorists have pointed out that taxable corporations can save taxes by arranging their corporate and pension balance sheets in a particular fashion. Generally, assets with income subject to a high tax rate should be placed in a tax-sheltered environment, while zero or low tax rate assets can be placed in a taxable environment at no or little tax penalty. At the same time, as much external financing as possible should be done with debt rather than equity.

Specifically, under U.S. tax regulations, pension funds should have only fixed-income assets, while any equity-oriented investments should be on the asset side of the main corporate balance sheet, and of course fixed-income on the liability side. For more on what its authors call "an irresistible plan to increase the corporation's value without increasing its risk," the reader is referred to the Black and Dewhurst article [1981].

In practice, there are very few all-debt corporate pension funds. This suggests chief financial officers have yet to be persuaded that they can push the integration of main business and pension plan to the extreme suggested by the tax arbitrage argument. If many did, their actions would be certain to draw the attention of the taxation and regulatory authorities, who would likely not be sympathetic to such practices being carried out on a large scale.

The Asset Mix Policy Decision

The discussion thus far shows that a number of factors come into play in making pension fund asset mix policy decisions. These factors have been categorized into five areas:

1. The plan sponsor's pension benefits policy;
2. Capital market expectations;
3. The plan sponsor's decision whether to invest pension assets on a

TABLE 4-3. Portfolio Composition of U.S. Pension Plans, December 31, 1988

	Private			State and Local Government
	Defined Benefit		Defined Contribution	
Asset	Single Employer	Multiemployer		
Cash items	5%	11%	18%	4%
Government and corporate bonds	16	39	7	57
Corporate equity	35	26	39	36
Other assets[a]	44	24	36	3
Total	100%	100%	100%	100%

SOURCE: Employee Benefit Research Institute [1988].
[a] Includes bank pooled funds and unallocated insurance accounts.

going-concern basis or on a termination basis (and the associated liquidity implications);

4. The sensitivity of the plan sponsor (and, possibly, of plan members as well) to plan asset and liability value fluctuations; and

5. The nature and appropriate degree of integration between sponsor main business and pension plan.

Obviously, plan sponsor pension committees need help if they are to responsibly bring all the information relevant to the pension fund asset mix policy decision together and process it in such a way that the analysis results in insights rather than information overload. This recognition is one of the reasons for the birth of a new profession. Many large plan sponsors now have *pension fund executives* who advise the pension committee on asset mix policy. More and more, these professionals are the ones who bring together all relevant information and judgments, process them, and recommend an appropriate asset mix policy for the plan sponsor to pursue. Chapter 7 expands on many of the issues and techniques that constitute pension fund asset allocation. For perspective, Table 4-3 reflects the asset mix of U.S. pension funds as of the end of 1988. In this table, the Private Defined Benefit columns have sizable "Other Assets" components, largely reflecting pooled funds and insurance accounts that are themselves invested in major asset classes in undefined allocations. GICs are the principal "other asset" in defined contribution plans.

Implementing Asset Mix Policy

As recently as a decade ago, even many large plan sponsors simultaneously dealt with both asset mix policy and its implementation by hiring one or more balanced managers and allowing these managers to invest pension assets within a broad stock-bond weighting range. Usually, the pension committee would both do the hiring and set the asset mix guidelines.

The rapid growth of pension assets during the 1980s and the heightened awareness that these assets should be managed with the same intensity and professionalism as other plan sponsor assets has changed this traditional setup. The pension fund executives who advise pension committees on pension fund asset mix policy are also being given the authority to implement the policy. This organizational development has already had a major impact in shaping pension fund investing in recent years, and it will continue to do so into the 1990s.

Pension Fund Organizational Issues

The responsibility for pension fund investing is increasingly being assigned to people with titles such as *Director–Pension Investments* or *Vice President–Pension Asset Management*. One consequence of this development is a serious review of the plan sponsor's information needs in the pension finance and investments area. There has long been a focus problem here. Often, the traditional services being offered by actuarial firms on the liability side and by performance measurement firms on the asset side are being found wanting. The result is that information needs are being redefined—as are the sources of the information and where and how it is processed.

One positive aspect of the new pension accounting rules is that they have brought the importance of managing the plan balance sheet to the fore. The implication is that the information focus should be there as well. Liability and asset related changes over time can be analyzed in the same balance sheet context. The changes can be decomposed into components that reflect organizational responsibilities. For example, it is important to distinguish between the impact of asset mix policy itself and the implementation of that policy when analyzing total fund asset value changes. Policy is set by one group of individuals; it is implemented by another. Without the critical decomposition of total fund return reflecting that reality, performance data would have no information content. Any decisions based on such data would have no factual foundation. Chapter 14 discusses measuring and interpreting investment results.

Cost Control in Pension Fund Management. Another consequence of the professionalization of the pension investment function inside plan sponsor organizations is a movement of some of the actual pension investment functions traditionally carried on outside the organization to the inside. Thus, it is becoming more commonplace among large plan sponsors to have some or all of the pension fund's stock money or bond money managed by internal portfolio managers working for the pension fund executive. This movement is part of a larger phenomenon that focuses on improving the bottom line through cutting the costs of pension fund management.

Significant economies of scale can be realized in managing pension plans. On a per dollar basis, small plans may be very expensive to operate. Most of the needed outside experts use fee schedules that have a minimum base and become cheaper at the margin only for larger numbers of dollars and/or plan participants. This is so for actuaries, accountants, consultants, master trustee/custodians, investment managers, and stockbrokers. The combined charges of all this outside talent can easily exceed 2 percent of assets per annum for small pension plans. At the other extreme, a multibillion dollar self-managed pension plan can get its total operating costs below 25 basis points per annum. This question of operating costs is high on the agenda of many pension fund executives, and the concern it implies will undoubtedly impact the evolution of the pension investment industry over the coming decade.

Changes in Asset Allocation. Pension fund executives are implementing change both at the asset class level and within asset classes. The old asset mix policy based principally on domestic stocks and bonds is rapidly giving way to a much broader-based policy. Nondomestic stocks and bonds are making their way into pension portfolios. Pension funds are also investing in real estate equity and in venture capital, and money for such investments is now flowing over domestic borders into other countries. The liquidity of the U.S. derivative securities (i.e., futures and options) markets has permitted the pursuit of specific policies for each of the basic stock-bond-cash asset classes and shifts in the pension fund exposure to these asset classes simultaneously.

This heightened interest by pension fund executives in asset mix shifts away from a static policy asset mix deserves further comment. There has always been an interest in making such shifts opportunistically in anticipation of significant price movements in the stock and bond markets. But, when this activity is approached in a casual, nonrigorous way, evidence that it loses rather than adds value has become impossible to ignore. At the same time, new, disciplined quantitative approaches to *tactical asset allocation* designed to optimally time asset class shifts that are implemented in the futures markets have been meeting with a measure of success in the United States. However, part of that success may lay in the fact that less than one percent of U.S. pension assets were estimated to be subject to this discipline as 1989 began.

The mid-1980s also saw the introduction of asset mix shifting based on a different kind of discipline. The rationale underlying *dynamic asset allocation* or *portfolio insurance* strategies is that it is important to maintain some minimum level of return, or asset value, or pension plan surplus. In each case, a risk-free asset is identified. The strategies move the pension fund asset mix either away from or toward the risk-free asset, depending on whether the prespecified minimum return, asset value, or surplus requirement is secure with a margin of safety or is close to being violated.

Thus, dynamic asset allocation strategies are the reverse of tactical asset allocation strategies. Generally, the former are geared to buy risky assets in rising markets and sell them in falling markets; the latter tend to sell in rising markets and buy in falling markets. The value of dynamic asset allocation strategies in the management of pension funds is still being debated. Ultimately, it is a question of the appropriate length of the planning horizon and what constitutes risk over that horizon. See Chapters 7 and 13 for further discussion of this issue.

Changes in Within Asset Class Management. The changes occurring in within asset class management are no less dramatic. *Passive management* is no longer a dirty phrase. Its combination of predictable performance and low cost is proving an irresistible combination to an increasing number of pension fund executives. Passive management now offers almost as many choices as active management. Selection universes go beyond domestic large capitalization stocks into orientations that include small capitalization, growth, yield, and specific industry group, in any geographic coloring one wishes. Nor has the fixed-income field been immune from this passive investment products explosion. Products exist to replicate most of the major bond indexes, and the spectrum extends to passive bond funds with specific durations and/or a focus on specific types of issuers. Increasingly, "passive" components are being combined with "active" components to produce hybrid, highly structured vehicles seeking to add value in their operation.

Active managers are under increasing pressure to define themselves in terms of their "value added." Just as the tactical asset allocators are a clearly defined species of active manager, so are domestic and global stock, real estate, venture capital, and fixed-income specialists required to explain more carefully what they are trying to do and how they do it. Specialization by research and portfolio management methodology and by new definitions of investment universes is becoming more prevalent. In addition, fee arrangements based on performance in relation to carefully defined investment universes are being used more often. Chapters 8, 9, and 10 elaborate on portfolio management within asset classes.

PENSION PLAN CHARTER

Defined benefit pension plans are complex organisms. Ultimately, they exist to pay retirement benefits to plan members. But the exact nature of the pension promise is often ambiguous, and this contributes to the difficulty of precisely defining the nature of the pension fund investment problem. Legally and organizationally, the pension fund is not quite like other plan sponsor businesses—although in many ways it can be managed as though it is one. These factors combine to create a need for a document that puts all the facets of managing defined benefit pension plans together: a *pension plan charter*. Table 4-4 provides a sample of such a charter. One benefit of this kind of pension plan charter is that it gives a very clear context for writing a pension fund's statement of investment policies and goals.

Statement of Investment Policies and Goals

A statement of investment policies and goals translates the charter's provisions regarding the pension contract, plan governance, investment policy, and information generation and its disclosure into a more detailed, investment-specific context. Table 4-5 is a sample of such a statement.

Investment Management Mandates

The pension plan charter defines the linkages between plan members, the plan sponsor, the committee charged with deciding and monitoring the financial policies of the plan, and the executive responsible for implementing those policies. The statement of investment policies and goals defines the linkages between the charter, pension fund investment policies, and the implementation of those policies. Effective policy implementation requires further clear understandings between the chief implementor and the team of investment managers charged with actually managing the plan's assets on a day-to-day basis. These understandings should be set out in a set of guidelines called *investment management mandates*.

While the specifics vary depending on the asset class and the type of investment manager, all *investment management mandates* should deal with certain essentials, including:

- The connection between a specific mandate and the overall pension fund policies and goals;
- The characteristics of the relevant selection universe and how one or more passively implemented portfolios might be constructed to act as fair performance benchmarks;
- Any constraints the portfolio manager must observe in managing the actual portfolio;
- A reasonable (given the constraints), time-bounded performance target in relation to the performance benchmark(s);

TABLE 4-4. XYZ Corporation Pension Plan Charter

SECTION I: THE PENSION CONTRACT

- The intent is to provide plan participants with a post-retirement income defined in relation to (a) a stated percentage of wages per year of service with the Corporation, and (b) the actual number of years of service.
- There is a further intent to update pension payments periodically for actual inflation experience; however, the Corporation cannot guarantee the *degree* to which it will be able to maintain pension purchasing power.
- The Corporation's funding policy is to have plan assets exceed the best estimate of accrued going-concern plan liabilities by a modest margin.
- While the intent is to run both the Corporation and the pension plan as going concerns, there is always a possibility of a plan termination; if termination occurs, the Corporation will endeavor to pay plan participants the best estimate of the accrued value of going-concern plan liabilities, with any excess plan assets reverting to the Corporation.

SECTION II: PLAN GOVERNANCE

- The Corporation will appoint a *Pension Plan Governance Committee* empowered to ensure that the Plan's financial practices and its financial relationship with the Corporation are consistent with this Charter. This committee will effectively act as the plan's board of directors and will be bound by all laws governing the behavior of fiduciaries.
- The Plan's financial operation will be directed by a senior corporate officer with the title *Vice President–Employee Benefits Investments*, appointed by the Pension Plan Governance Committee.
- The Committee will ensure the existence of a Plan *conflict of interest policy* that will cover Committee members, Plan operations personnel, and third party fiduciaries such as external investment managers.
- The voting of shares held by the Plan must be done in the best economic interest of the Plan by those fiduciaries best able to make such judgments; normally, this would be the portfolio manager who bought the stock for the Fund.

SECTION III: INVESTMENT POLICY

- The Plan, and therefore Plan assets, will be managed on a going-concern basis; this implies that, subject to meeting periodic Plan solvency tests, the *goal* of Plan assets is to earn the highest possible long-term rate of return.
- The primary mechanism through which the appropriate balance between the Plan solvency and asset growth goals is struck is the Fund *asset mix policy*; this policy will be decided by, and regularly reviewed by, the Pension Plan Governance Committee.
- The Vice President–Employee Benefits Investments (a) will advise the Committee on asset mix policy and (b) will be responsible for effectively implementing the Committee's decision.

SECTION IV: FINANCIAL INFORMATION AND ITS DISCLOSURE

- The Plan will be subjected to periodic independent audits.
- The Corporation will disclose the Plan balance sheet annually to Plan participants.
- The Corporation will account separately for (a) the cost of the issuance of pension entitlements under the Plan using a risk-free discount rate and (b) any profits or losses arising from the earned spread between pension investments and that risk-free rate.
- The earned spread between Fund total return and the discount rate used to cost the issuance of pension entitlements will be regularly decomposed into components due to (a) the Committee's decision on asset mix policy and (b) the implementation of that policy decision through investment operations.

TABLE 4-5. XYZ Corporation Statement of Pension Fund Investment Policies and Goals

---

SECTION I: PENSION FUND GOALS

- The pension plan, and therefore the Fund, will be managed on a going-concern basis.
- The primary goal of the Fund is to ensure the solvency of the pension plan over time and to meet pension obligations as required.
- The secondary goal of the Fund is to earn the highest (net of all costs) rate of return possible, without taking excess risk and thereby jeopardizing its primary goal and/or subjecting the Corporation to an undue amount of contribution rate volatility.
- Fund returns will be used to help finance pension obligations, thus reducing the level of contributions into the plan XYZ Corporation must make.

SECTION II: GOAL ACHIEVEMENT—ASSET MIX POLICY

- XYZ Corporation recognizes that the Fund's long-term investment results will in large measure be determined by the Fund's long-term asset mix policy; given its decision to manage the pension plan and the Fund as going concerns, and given its decision to maintain the plan well-funded, the long-term investment bias in the Fund will be toward equity investments, subject only to the needs to avoid plan insolvency and to control extreme contribution rate volatility.
- The Vice President–Employee Benefits Investments will advise the Pension Plan Governance Committee on the asset mix policy weightings most consistent with the pension plan's and the Fund's goals. As part of this advice, he or she shall present long-term economic and capital markets projections, and the most likely financial impact on the plan and on XYZ Corporation of the recommended asset mix policy, as well as a reasonable range of possible outcomes around the expected outcome.
- The asset mix policies will be expressed in terms of these asset classes:

Equity Oriented	*Debt Oriented*
—Large capitalization domestic stocks	—Corporate bonds
—Small capitalization domestic stocks	—Long-term government bonds
—Foreign stocks	—Foreign bonds
—Real estate	—Mortgages
—Venture capital	—Treasury bills

- There will at all times be a Fund asset mix policy expressed in terms of policy weights; these policy weights will be reviewed at least once per year. The rate of return on the passively implemented policy asset mix will be estimated by calculating the rate of return on an appropriately weighted blend (with quarterly rebalancing) representing these 10 asset classes:

Equity Oriented	*Debt Oriented*
—S&P 500 Stock Index	—Shearson-Lehman-Hutton Corporate Bond Index
—Russell 2000 Small Stock Index	
—Financial Times Actuaries Euro-Pacific Index	—Shearson-Lehman-Hutton Long-term Government Bond Index
—Equitable Real Estate Group's Prime Property Fund	—Salomon Brothers Non-U.S. Government Bond Index
—First Chicago Investment Advisors' Institutional Venture Capital Fund	—Shearson-Lehman-Hutton Mortgage-backed Securities Index
	—Salomon Brothers 90-day Treasury Bill Index

(continued)

TABLE 4-5. (*continued*)

- The return on the passively implemented policy asset mix will be used as a benchmark for evaluating the effectiveness with which the Vice President–Employee Benefits Investments actually implements the Fund's asset mix policy.

SECTION III: GOAL ACHIEVEMENT: ASSET MIX POLICY IMPLEMENTATION

- The Vice President–Employee Benefits Investments shall have the responsibility and the authority to implement the decided asset mix policy.
- In implementing the Fund asset mix policy, the Vice President–Employee Benefits Investments is empowered to employ prudently the following techniques and outside services:
  —Subject up to 10 percent of the Fund to active tactical asset allocation techniques either through the cash or derivatives markets.
  —Subject up to 10 percent of the fund to foreign currency exposure.
  —Engage asset class investment specialists either internally or externally to manage specific Fund components. Each such component will have its own investment management mandate describing its purpose, goals, and constraints. A component may relate to just one of the 10 asset classes defined above, or some combination of them.
  —Engage one or more master trustee/custodian(s) capable of meeting the Fund's custodial and information needs in an accurate and timely fashion. This custodian may be given authority to engage in security lending activities on behalf of the Fund to generate incremental revenues.
  —Engage such other information and/or consulting services as are deemed needed to effectively manage the Fund.

SECTION IV: GOAL ACHIEVEMENT: MEASUREMENT AND COMPENSATION

- Total Fund return will be measured regularly and broken down into three basic components: (1) the risk-free rate of return, (2) the asset mix policy return impact, and (3) the asset mix policy implementation return impact. Component 1 will be the one-year Treasury bond rate, component 2 will be the difference between the rate of return on the passively implemented policy asset mix (defined above) and the risk-free rate of return, and component 3 will be the difference between the actual Fund return and the return on the passively implemented policy asset mix.
- Fund results will be evaluated with a multi-year perspective. Generally, component 1 (i.e., the risk-free return) indicates how much return the capital markets are providing for the investment policy that most closely matches going-concern pension liabilities; component 2 (i.e., the asset mix policy-related return increment or decrement) indicates how much of a premium the capital markets are providing for adopting the chosen asset mix policy; and component 3 (i.e., the implementation return increment or decrement) indicates how effectively the chosen policy is being implemented.
- The Pension Plan Governance Committee and the Vice President–Employee Benefits Investments will agree on a realistic target for the return component 3. Compensation for the employee benefits investments team will be based in part on the actual performance of component 3 in relation to target performance.
- The Vice President–Employee Benefits Investments has the discretion to negotiate performance-based fee arrangements with outside investment managers if such arrangements are deemed to be in the best interest of the Fund.

- Time-bounded tolerance for underperformance, given the nature of the mandate;
- The nature and frequency of sponsor-manager information flow;
- Share proxy voting responsibilities in the case of stock portfolio managers; and
- Fees and soft dollar arrangements where security transactions generate commissions.

Mandates that cover these bases ensure a clear understanding between the plan sponsor and the investment manager as to their respective expectations and responsibilities in relation to the pension fund's overall goals and policies.

Making Private and Public Interests Converge

The focus of this section now shifts from the microeconomics of employment-based retirement systems to a consideration of some macroeconomic implications of funding pension entitlements on a large scale. Specifically, three implications merit attention: (1) the potential impact of funding pension entitlements on national savings and capital formation, (2) the impact of funding on the security of future pension claims, and (3) the direct impact of pension funding on the economics of the financial services industry.

An ongoing debate concerns whether funding pension entitlements enhances the national savings rate and the capital formation process. Some economists believe it does. Others argue it merely replaces other forms of saving that would take place in the absence of pension funding. Perhaps the issue is less one of quantity than of quality. Pension funds have the ability to be truly long-term investors. Thus, they can provide a measure of patient risk capital to an economy that neither individual investors nor other financial institutions could contemplate. To the degree that this type of investment leads to more wealth to distribute down the road, there might well be a direct link between the productivity of pension fund investing and the productivity of the economy.

Pension entitlements today become someone's current income tomorrow, and that current income becomes a claim on actual goods and services tomorrow. Generally, funding pension entitlements makes them more secure and therefore more likely to be convertible into a cashable claim on goods and services down the road. Thus, funding represents a form of securitization of claims on future national income. To the degree funded claims replace unfunded claims, that funding is helping to ensure that tomorrow's pensioners will get the deferred income they bargained for during their working years.

Finally, servicing employment-based retirement systems has become a big business in its own right. Adding together the resources allocated directly by plan sponsors and those they buy from the financial services industry for actuarial, accounting, custodial, consulting, investment management, and transactional services, an average cost estimate of one percent of assets per annum is not unreasonable. Taking the global estimate of $3.9 *trillion* in assets from Figure 4-1, that one percent translates into an annual cost of global pension-related services of $39 billion. Pensions *have* become a big business in their own right!

ENDOWMENT FUNDS

As endowment funds have moved out of treasurers' back offices—where in many cases they were ignored, ill-treated, and poorly managed and generally failed to accomplish their intended purposes—they have increasingly been recognized by the investment community as a vast and fertile area for professional investment management. Much of the credit for this recognition can be given to the Ford Foundation [1972] study conducted in the late 1960s. Although some of the philosophies and approaches espoused by that study have been challenged by endowment experts and found wanting by actual experience, many of the principles have proved to be valid. Of particular note is the strong admonition that such funds utilize professional management, in recognition of the fact that the funds' basic structures and various finance and investment committees have not always successfully managed their assets.

The Ford Foundation's emphasis on utilizing a total rate of return concept for endowment funds proved to be highly controversial, not so much because the concept itself was unsound, but rather because the report, by happenstance, was published virtually at the peak of the late-1960s bull market. The report emphasized investing in rapidly growing companies where dividends were reasonably low but where capital appreciation and strong growth of dividends were anticipated. The low dividend payouts were to be supplemented by cashing in part of the growth and using it for spending purposes. However, as the stock market declined by some 50 percent through 1974, funds that adopted this approach found they were selling equities at distressed prices to supplement income and meet spending requirements. With the subsequent significant recovery of stock prices, the total return concept again gained adherents. However, a number of methods have been developed to smooth out the use of capital and mitigate distress selling. Some of these techniques are discussed later in this chapter.

SCOPE OF ENDOWMENT FUNDS

Endowment funds, which held more than $133 billion in assets in 1988, encompass a broad range of institutions. (See Table 4-6.) Among these are

TABLE 4-6. Total Assets and Number of Endowment Funds (as of 1988)

	Number of Institutions	Total Assets

Endowment funds
  College, private school,
  museum, and hospital
  endowments over $1 million
	520	$ 66 billion

Foundation funds
  Charitable organizations with
  over $1 million
	608	67 billion

Total	1,128	$133 billion

SOURCE: *The Money Market Directory of Pension Funds and Their Investment Managers*, Charlottesville, Va. [1989].

religious organizations, educational institutions, cultural entities such as museums and symphony orchestras, private social agencies, hospitals, and corporate and private foundations. Another rapidly growing area of endowment investing is nonprofit organizations, such as trade and professional associations, that often have significant endowment or reserve assets.

Although often compared in terms of investment objectives and constraints, endowment funds and retirement funds in fact have only two major similarities. Both are usually long-term in nature and—with few exceptions—are not taxable. But their differences are far more important than their similarities. The range of objectives of endowment funds is extremely broad and the objectives themselves are often highly qualitative in nature. In this sense, endowment funds resemble individual investors. The determination of investment policy for an endowment fund can be viewed as the resolution of a *creative tension* existing between the highly demanding need for immediate income and the pervasive and enduring pressures for a growing stream of future income to meet future needs. Many of the institutions sponsoring these funds, particularly those in the fields of education, health care, and the performing arts, have suffered even greater distress at the hands of inflation than other investors, even during the slow inflation period of the 1980s. Religious organizations, too, face demands to provide increasing funds for their various purposes. Thus, perhaps the most important factor in determining endowment investment policies is resolving the tension between short-term needs and long-term requirements.

Return Requirements

Frequently, the determination of an endowment fund return requirement is a tenuous compromise between the sponsoring institution's unrealistic demands for current income and the more realistic probabilities of achieving reasonable returns on invested capital over time consistent with risk-taking ability. This determination is further complicated by the fact that, unlike retirement plans, there may be no cash inflow and, because income is usually spent, the fund does not enjoy the benefits of reinvestment and compounding returns.

The development of an endowment fund return requirement may involve determining specific dollar outlays, with a predetermined progression of income growth, from which the asset mix may fall out naturally depending on the yields available in various types of acceptable investment instruments. For example, a $1 million educational endowment may be required to generate a $60,000 annual income and may be expected to increase that income by 5 percent annually. If interest rates are in a range of 9 percent and the portfolio manager's typical stock portfolio for such a fund yields 3 percent, the maximum equity position can easily be determined by applying these rates to alternative mixes of stocks and bonds to achieve the desired amount.

In this example, if approximately $500,000 is invested in stocks yielding 3 percent to produce $15,000 of annual income, and the remaining $500,000 is invested in bonds yielding 9 percent to produce $45,000 of annual income, the annual income objective of $60,000 is met with this 50/50 asset mix. Additionally, to meet the desired 5 percent annual growth rate in income, stocks with a strong emphasis on expected dividend growth should be selected, recognizing that the fixed-income portion will show no increase in income.

Total Return Approach. Many endowments have adopted a total return approach to their spending policies, using the basic concept suggested by the Ford Foundation. The total return of a portfolio is the combination of interest, dividends, and other current earnings, plus capital appreciation (or less capital depreciation) for the period. Thus, a fund utilizing the total return concept may spend not only current investment income but may over time also use a portion of capital appreciation as a part of its spending rate. In the above example, a 70/30 stock/bond asset mix provides only $48,000 of annual income; this amount is supplemented each year with $12,000 of long-term capital appreciation to meet the $60,000 budget requirement. This approach allows the fund to have a greater amount in common stocks, historically the higher return asset over time.

Relationship to Spending Rate. A variety of formulas have been developed by different endowments to establish their total return objective, generally inclusive of the rate of inflation and a compatible maximum spending rate. Such formulas indicate how much of the total return may be used for the endowment's current needs as opposed to being reinvested. The spending rate can be thought of as a specific portion of the total return—for example, 5 percentage points—applied to a moving average of asset values over any period desired, such as the past three years, five years, or other period. The desired rate of return and spending rate require careful consideration and thought, although many endowments tend to pick these rates somewhat arbitrarily and to set them at levels too high to be justified by historical experience. Over long periods of time, spending rates much over 5 percent ultimately result in erosion of the purchasing power of the principal, as the spending rate plus inflation begin to exceed actual rates of return. Endowments with higher proportions invested in common stock and real estate have less risk in this regard because equities provide higher returns than fixed-income securities over longer periods of time.

However, one should not be misled by the unusually high equity and bond returns of the 1980s, returns that clearly exceeded historical norms. To do so could well lead to establishing spending rates significantly above the 5 percent range, quickly leading to erosion of capital as actual rates of return fall back to or below historical average levels.

Return Objective

Some endowment funds take the approach of establishing their total return objective by summing the maximum spending rate—the percentage amount actually taken out of the fund and spent by the endowed institution each year—and the expected inflation rate. This approach assures maintenance of the real value of the endowment if this total return objective is actually achieved.

In their attempt to reach total return objectives, endowment funds have taken some creative approaches in determining overall asset mix. Many endowments today are including investment vehicles that would once have been off limits, including venture capital, various options contracts and other derivative securities, real estate, securities lending, and financial futures hedging. An example of how this total return-spending rate concept can be used is illustrated in Table 4-7.

It is important to understand that the return objectives derived from this method are just that—objectives. They may or may not actually be realized in practice, but at least they provide the endowed institution and the investment manager with a known target.

Risk Tolerance

The creative tension concept discussed earlier is helpful in analyzing and understanding risk tolerance for endowments. As shown in Figure 4-2, endowment fund return objectives encompass a broad spectrum, ranging from maximum income at one end to maximum growth at the other. In fact, this spectrum's breadth rivals that for the most risk-heterogeneous of all investors, the individual. Thus, the portfolio manager must be concerned about

TABLE 4-7. XYZ University Endowment Fund Investment Objectives

I. Achievement of a total annual return, measured on a five-year moving average basis, equal to the spending rate (as determined from time to time by official university action) plus the inflation rate (calculated on a consistent basis by national government sources).

II. Within the total return objective, stability and maximization of current income, consistent with the need and opportunity for long-term capital appreciation, is desired. Current income in each year shall constitute no less than 75 percent of the annual spending rate, the balance coming from capital appreciation.

Definitions:

a. *Total annual return* equals the sum of dividends, interest, and other current income, plus the net impact of price change, time-adjusted for capital additions and withdrawals, all after transaction costs and management fees, for a given fiscal year.

b. *Spending rate*, which is equivalent to the sum distributed annually to endowment fund participants, is calculated as a percentage of the average market value as of the preceding five fiscal year-ends, adjusted for capital additions and withdrawals during the period. The spending rate for 1989 has been set at 5.5 percent by the Investment Committee.

c. *Inflation rate* is the Consumer Price Index as calculated and reported by the U.S. Department of Commerce.

Average for Five-Year Period to Indicated Date

Date	Spending Rate	Inflation Rate	Total Annual Return Objectives
12/31/85	5.00%	3.40%	8.40%
12/31/86	5.10	3.28	8.38
12/31/87	5.20	4.38	9.58
12/31/88	5.50	3.60	9.10

the *type* of risk assumed as well as the *amount* of risk. For example, where maximum income is the objective, and thus long-term fixed-income securities with holding periods to maturity tend to predominate, purchasing power risk generally must be accepted because little or no opportunity for growth in principal is provided. Where maximum growth is the objective, and thus equity-type investments such as common stocks and real estate

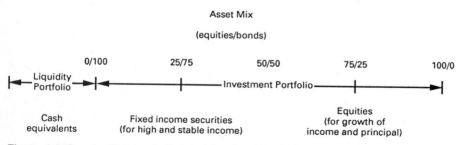

Figure 4-2. Creative Tension in Determining Portfolio Policy.

tend to predominate, market risk generally must be accepted. For a fund with a short time horizon because of a near-term capital outlay or other immediate purpose, preservation of capital is primary and thus principal risk cannot be accepted. In this case, funds would be invested in high quality money market instruments with no chance of default and with little prospect for market value loss, even if interest rates rise. At the other end of the spectrum, where growth is paramount and little income is needed for current purposes, the primary risk is purchasing power risk. Such funds are concerned more with a moderate, but growing, stream of income to meet future needs, and they are fully able to accept high volatility of returns in the short run to maximize capital appreciation and income growth over the long run.

Most funds fall somewhere between these extremes. Assessing the type and amount of risk a fund can tolerate is really a balancing act in which a variety of risks are considered and investment policies are established to deal with them.

The risk tolerance of endowments is often quite different from that for defined benefit retirement funds and more similar to that for individual investors or defined contribution retirement plans. Nevertheless, endowments, particularly those at the growth end of the creative tension spectrum, generally use the same financial instruments as retirement funds. Even venture capital has been added as an appropriate vehicle for some endowments where long-term growth is an important objective and risk tolerance is high. The difference between endowments and pension funds is in the lower percentage of assets endowments allocate to equity type investments, because most endowment funds need high levels of investment income.

Relationship to Overall Budget

An important factor in weighing risk tolerance of endowments is the relative importance of the endowment fund in the sponsoring institution's overall revenue picture. Where the endowment's distributions, whether from interest, dividends, or capital appreciation, play a relatively minor role in the institution's overall operating budget, risk tolerance may be relatively high, suggesting more aggressive policies in an effort to promote the internal growth of the fund to absorb possible future demands greater than those of the present. Contrarily, where the institution is heavily dependent on the return from its endowment (such as one Midwest university that derives about one half of its operating revenues from its endowment), there is a major constraint on investment policy, not only in terms of the stability of returns but also their minimum magnitude. While it might be said that all endowment funds seek a stable, growing stream of income, the achievement of this goal over time, and with little straying from the intended trend line, becomes increasingly important where the institution is heavily dependent on the return from its endowment. In such cases, the institution may have to settle for a lower level of total return (because of lower risk tolerance) to obtain the necessary certainty of that return.

Liquidity Requirements

Because most endowed institutions have long-term charters, despite their sometimes short-term thinking, their objectives tend to be very long-term in nature. As a result, little liquidity is needed except, perhaps, to meet emergency needs and to fund the periodic distributions prescribed by the spending rate. Contributions are made by donors in the form of property or securities, with a strong obligation to keep these donations intact on a more or less permanent basis. Other donors may restrict their contributions, allowing the distribution of income only and prohibiting the "invasion" of the principal of the donated funds.

There are important exceptions, however, such as capital contributions made for specific projects where it is known in advance that the funds will be expended (for instance, to build a new hospital, add a new educational wing to a church, and so on). Liquidity is a critical element for such special projects, and investment policies must be established to provide it. Income production, while not to be ignored, takes a back seat during the period in which the funds are expended.

Tax Considerations

The endowment income of all but private, nonoperating foundations is tax exempt. Thus, investments such as tax-exempt bonds and preferred stocks (convertibles excepted) usually are not appropriate investment vehicles for endowments. Private foundations are required by law to pay out investment income equal to 5 percent of their assets annually or face penalty taxes on the undistributed portion; to the extent that income is insufficient, the difference must be paid out of principal. Assets used in the normal course of operations—office, furniture, and the like—are excluded from the asset base for purposes of making this 5 percent calculation. In addition, 1.5 percent of assets may be excluded as a cash balance for normal operating purposes. Investment income of private foundations is taxed currently at a rate of 1 percent, provided certain distribution requirements are met (otherwise 2 percent). In determining investment income for tax purposes, long-term capital gains are excluded but short-term capital gains are taxable. Capital gains can be offset by capital losses. Investment management and custodial expenses are deductible from investment income before taxes, as are other reasonable costs. On balance, tax considerations are not a major constraint for the manager.

Regulatory and Legal Considerations

Other than the regulations discussed above concerning taxation of charitable foundations, endowment funds are subject to little in the way of federal regulation. However, many states have very specific rules and regulations concerning the management and administration of such funds. Cemetery maintenance funds that provide for perpetual care, for example, generally are scrutinized very closely by state regulatory bodies due to the public interest aspects of such funds. The portfolio manager responsible for any endowment fund should be aware of state or local regulations and carefully review them with the endowed institution to determine their impact on the investment program. Many states that formerly had very rigid rules and regulations concerning the types of investments that could be used by endowments, along with very specific requirements as to dividend history, consecutive years of positive earnings, rating by outside investment advisory services, and so on, have modified these rules largely to include the standard prudent man rule.

As noted earlier, restrictions imposed by the donor may pose a legal constraint on the management of, and distributions from, some portion of the endowment fund. Typically, restricted and unrestricted funds are managed with these constraints in mind.

Unique Needs, Circumstances, and Preferences

Because endowment funds are generally controlled by a broad array of trustees and investment committees, each with different levels of investment skill and understanding, they have a very wide range of unique needs, circumstances, and preferences. This unevenness of approach to endowment administration has a major impact on investment policies as well as on results. Personal prejudices, fears, and anxieties concerning difficult market climates, and other emotional elements frequently overwhelm a reasonable, logical approach to the investment management of endowment funds. Some committees may force liquidation of equities as the market collapses and then jump on the bandwagon once stocks have risen for extended periods.

This is not to say that all emotional elements have no validity. A number of endowments today, particularly in the religious and educational spheres, reflect thoughtful, deep-seated concerns about a variety of social issues in their investment programs. These range from the obvious concerns of a religious organization regarding ownership of tobacco or liquor stocks to the more subtle nuances of such concerns as defense policies and racial policies, which are often difficult to monitor on a company-by-company basis. In recent years, many funds have precluded the use of the securities of companies doing business in South Africa. Some funds choose to voice their objections by excluding certain investments from their portfolios; others prefer to use their investments in such companies to give them a voice for change. Some professional managers do not accept responsibility for determining which companies may fail to meet the institution's requirements, leaving that to the institutions themselves.

All of this points up very clearly the need of such funds to have highly qualified and skilled professional managers and to assure that such managers are not overly constrained by emotional issues. It is likewise important to develop a clearly defined plan of investment and to stay with it despite other variable factors, so long as the fundamental assumptions on which it is based can be shown to have continuing validity.

Movement Toward Total Return Approach. Today many endowment committees use imaginative and creative approaches to setting investment policies, establishing a meaningful spending rate, and using a variety of formulas to incorporate these factors into a total rate of return approach. Nevertheless, there is still strong reticence on the part of many committees to move away from traditional methods; this itself becomes a major constraint on the investment policy of such institutions. But funds using the newer techniques have benefited from the achievement of consistently above-average returns over time. In terms of the real (inflation-adjusted) objectives of these funds, risk has not been significantly increased, but rather has been modified. With the erosion of inflation-adjusted capital values effectively stemmed in the 1980s, the risk of greatest concern has been significantly reduced. The damage done to the total return approach by the stock market in the mid-1970s may have slowed the process, but in many instances enlightened management has prevailed, with attendant excellent long-term investment results.

Effect of Inflation. Whether managements' other concerns are short-term or long-term oriented, one problem that must be faced by all is the requirement that, whatever the level of stable income desired, it must grow to compensate for inflation.

Perhaps the most obvious difference between endowment investing and pension fund investing shows up in this area. Whereas a pension fund generally does not depend on current income, nor do changes in level from year to year significantly affect its overall, long-term objectives, endowment funds are very dependent on their returns on an ongoing, continuous basis. Consider the fixed-income portion of the fund, for example. While a retirement fund can easily change both bond maturity structure and coupon/price relationships—actions that often result in large changes in current income—an endowment fund has far less ability to effect such changes. Fluctuation in principal can be tolerated, but fluctuation of income generally cannot. The cash flow volatility of short-maturity instruments caused by fluctuations in interest rates is usually too high a price to pay for the potential of increased total returns. Thus, an endowment fund may have to emphasize longer-term bonds on a more or less permanent basis to maintain the necessary level and predictability of interest income. This policy is strengthened when the fund has a fairly high cash flow from donations and can average out changes in interest rates through continuous new investment in bonds. If adequate call protection is provided, emphasizing long-term bonds when interest rates are high reduces the risk of significantly lower yield and lower cash flow on maturity rollovers in a subsequent and perhaps prolonged period of declining interest rates.

The disadvantage of an emphasis on longer-term bonds is the opportunity cost of income during a period of rising interest rates, such as the 1965–1981 period, because such a trend is usually the result of rising inflation that adversely affects the operating costs of the endowed institution. An interesting variation of fixed-income policy designed to deal with this and maintain the traditional "real" income on bonds—that is, the difference between yield and the inflation rate—is to use a laddered or spaced maturity schedule ranging perhaps from 2 to 10 years. During periods of rising interest rates, rollover of maturities provides funds to take advantage of higher yields and the short average maturity (duration) limits price decline. Although this policy works in reverse during periods of falling interest rates, with rollover occurring at lower and lower yields, inflation rates are presumably declining as well, so the institution's costs would also be expected to grow less rapidly, enabling the institution to maintain the spread between inflation and return.

Desire for Income Stability. The desire for income stability may suggest a policy of purchasing discount bonds and holding them to maturity; the interest-on-interest element is of little consequence because all coupon income will be spent and it is desirable to assure returns on a continuing basis. The endowed institution must understand, however, that use of discount bonds may reduce both current yield and yield to maturity somewhat, and that the deeper the discount the greater the potential loss of income. However, a carefully structured fixed-income portfolio with spaced maturities and moderate discounts for call protection can provide a very high and stable level of income to the endowed institution, and that consideration may be decisive.

The desire for income stability also suggests that even with a total return concept there should be a solid anchor of current income to avoid the wide fluctuations of spendable returns that could result, given the high volatility of common stock prices, from a great dependence on capital appreciation over time. The farther the total return moves from this income anchor, the greater is its potential volatility and the greater the risk of not meeting the required return. Thus, if a spending rate is established at 5 percent, with an asset mix of 25 percent in bonds yielding 9 percent and 75 percent in stocks yielding 3 percent, providing a portfolio yield of 4.5 percent, almost all of the current income needs are obtained from dividends and interest, leaving most of the growth in principal from equities to accumulate and generate a higher level of income in the future. If, however, the spending rate is established at 8 percent with the same mix and yield, nearly half the required total return has to come from capital appreciation from the equity portion, increasing the potential volatility of the income stream or forcing liquidation of stocks at distressed prices on occasion. To some extent, this negative prospect can be mitigated by a formula designed to smooth the use of appreciation over a market cycle.

Inherent in this discussion is the implication that the types of securities employed, as well as the asset mix, are influenced by the basic policies of the fund with regard to spending rates, total return, and so forth. Thus, a fund with a longer time horizon, emphasizing reasonable current income production (but not at the expense of long-term growth of principal and income), may hold more volatile, aggressive securities than a fund in which the time horizon is short.

A sample statement of investment policy developed from these considerations is shown in Table 4-8.

PROFESSIONAL AND TRADE ASSOCIATIONS

A related, but somewhat different form of "endowment" investing is that of professional and trade association reserve funds. Although these funds do not strictly meet the usual definition of endowments—funds with capital that has been donated, often with restrictions as to the use of principal—they are managed in much the same way as the typical college or hospital endowment fund. Usually these funds are not donated, but are accumulated through an excess of revenues over expenditures by the organization. Like endowments, their investment objectives may cover a broad range, from high income for current needs through capital appreciation for future needs, but essentially their purpose is to provide for continuity of operations should there ever be an extended operating revenue shortfall.

One of the major determinants of risk tolerance for such funds is the source and stability of revenue flows (dues, seminars, trade shows, and the like). As a rule of thumb, such organizations aim to have their reserves equal to 6 to 12 months of budgeted revenues. Those associations targeting in the lower end of this range represent industries or professions that are highly stable and usually growing. For example, associations representing the medical profession or the pharmaceutical industry may well afford to have somewhat smaller reserves against impairment of future revenue streams than an association representing the steel industry or the construction machinery industry.

TABLE 4-8. XYZ University Endowment Fund Investment Policies

I. A portfolio balance, to be averaged over time, of a maximum position of 70 percent in equity-type investments and a minimum position of 30 percent in fixed-income investments.
II. Qualified equity and fixed-income investments to consist of the following:

Equity Related	Fixed-Income Related
Common stocks and warrants	Government and federal agency
Convertible securities	bonds
Option writing	Corporate bonds
Venture capital	Real estate mortages
Real estate	Private placement bonds
Securities lending	Securities lending

III. In the case of convertible securities and corporate obligations carrying a credit rating, qualified for purchase are such securities rated no less than BBB ("regarded as having an adequate capacity to pay interest/dividends and repay principal") as defined by Standard & Poor's or its equivalent as defined by other recognized rating agencies.
IV. No more than 10 percent of the average maximum equity position (7 percent of total marketable endowment funds) to be invested in venture capital and real estate equity participations, combined. No more than 20 percent of the maximum fixed-income position (6 percent of total marketable endowment funds) to be invested in real estate mortgages and private placements combined.
V. The Office of the Treasurer to have direct responsibility for no more than 50 percent of total marketable endowment funds. Remaining funds to be the responsibility of outside managers as selected from time to time. All managers to have full investment discretion within defined statements of objectives and policies.

A second element in determining risk tolerance is whether or not the association actually uses all or most of its income. Many of these associations, particularly those with more stable and growing revenue flows, tend to generate excess operating revenues that are used to build up their capital and thus they are able to reinvest 100 percent of income. Obviously, this scenario is extremely rare in the typical endowment situation. Other associations, particularly those that might be characterized as quasi-public, almost charitable in nature, may have great demands for current income and thus require more conservative investment policies or, like many endowments, may use a total return approach.

DETERMINATION OF PORTFOLIO POLICIES FOR ENDOWMENTS AND PROFESSIONAL/ TRADE ASSOCIATIONS

The portfolio policies established by endowments and association reserve funds depend on how the creative tension anomaly is resolved. Such policies may range from a 100 percent position in fixed-income securities—to maximize current income for present needs—all the way to a 100 percent position in common stocks—with growth as a primary objective and a total concern for future needs. Most endowments fall somewhere in between, trading off present and future needs in some balance specifically designed to meet their own objectives. The greater the focus on immediate demands for current income, the higher the fixed-income portion of the asset mix; contrarily, the greater the emphasis on long-term growth of principal and income, the greater the emphasis on common stocks.

As discussed earlier, frequently these decisions are arbitrary and based primarily on the emotions and prejudices of the investment committee. Endowment investing for many years focused almost entirely on risk aversion in nominal terms; this focus resulted in not only unproductive but counterproductive investment policies. In the 1970s, emphasis on fixed-income securities in the overall asset mix and on high yield stocks in the equity portion resulted in extremely low overall returns in an environment of high inflation and rising interest rates. In many instances this not only was tantamount to not preserving capital in nominal terms, but actually contributed toward consuming it. Many of the stocks paying high dividends were, in fact, companies that borrowed heavily in the fixed-income market—essentially to maintain those high dividends—and this activity gradually eroded the capital base of the underlying investor. Increasingly, it became apparent that the major risk not being dealt with was the loss of purchasing power of endowment capital and income.

Endowment Management Observations

To summarize, endowment funds have become an increasingly important area for the professional investment manager as these funds have found that using outside management is desirable in achieving goals. Investment policies determined by these funds depend on a variety of factors, including the temperament and emotional involvement of the trustees or investment committees, the trade-off between short-term demands for income and long-term needs for a growing stream of income and enhancement of capital in real terms, and an awareness of the social issues that may or may not be part of the organization's philosophy.

INSURANCE COMPANIES AND BANKS

Thus far, this chapter has considered what might be characterized as the two major private, nonprofit institutional investors—retirement plans and endowment funds. Now attention is directed to the two major financial institutions that operate for profit and, thus, must reflect in their investment policies the elements of competition and tax considerations—insurance companies and banks. While some interesting innovations in both the endowment and pension fields have been noted, none of these can be considered nearly as revolutionary or far-reaching as the trends in banking and insurance over the past decade or so. The inflation, higher interest rates, and general turbulence of the economy during the decades of the 1970s and 1980s, along with regulatory and tax law revisions, caused major changes in the investment policies and strategies of these major financial institutions. Sophisticated asset/liability management policies and procedures have been developed to control interest rate risk, as credit risk is no longer the only concern of bank and insurance company portfolio managers.

In a sense, all investing can be thought of as a matching of assets with liabilities. In the case of individual investors, endowments, defined contribution retirement plans, and investment companies (mutual funds), this process may involve a number of highly qualitative judgments because the liabilities are not obvious or clearly definable for these classes of investors. Contrarily, as has been noted, most defined benefit retirement plans have more clearly determinable liability structures, which in turn lead to more clearly definable investment policies and allocation of invested assets. Perhaps this matching of assets and liabilities is nowhere clearer or more quantifiable than in banks and insurance (especially life insurance) companies. Of particular interest with regard to these two major institutions has been the dynamic change in the patterns and durations of their respective liability structures, which in turn have caused dramatic responses in terms of asset deployment and investment policy. Asset/liability management has become the dominant theme guiding the investment policies and procedures within the insurance and banking industries, as they have struggled to deal with interest rate risk.

SIZE AND SCOPE OF THE INSURANCE INDUSTRY

Insurance companies are a major source of investment funds for the world capital markets. On a worldwide basis, the year-end 1988 invested assets of insurance companies were estimated to be approximately $2 trillion, with U.S. and Canadian companies accounting for approximately half of the total. Insurance companies in four other industrial countries—Japan, West Germany, the United Kingdom, and France—represent the next largest segment of the industry, accounting for about one third of the world total. Although insurance enjoys a world market, only a very small number of the approximately 10,000 insurance companies conduct business on a worldwide basis. However, current globalization trends in the financial markets may promote international competition in the commercial and, eventually, individual insurance markets.

The economic significance of the insurance industry is its unique role as an absorber of personal and business risks. By providing financial protection, the industry plays a key role in the growth and development of a country's economy. Because of the risk aspects of the business and the contractual obligations to policyholders, the traditional investment practices of the insurance industry have been characterized as conservative.

The insurance industry is complex but can be divided into three broad product categories: life insurance, health insurance, and property and liability insurance. For purposes of considering investment policy, it is sufficient to narrow the categories to life and nonlife (casualty) insurance companies. This division of the insurance business is consistent with the major classifications established by the insurance regulatory bodies and some, if not most, taxing authorities in the industrialized countries of the world.

Insurance companies, whether life or casualty, are incorporated either as stock companies or as mutuals (i.e., companies that have no stock and are owned by their policyholders). Mutuals have a long tradition and play a major role in certain segments of the insurance industry, but stockholder-owned companies have become the primary form of entry into the industry. While there is little difference in the investment operations between mutual and stock companies, the differences between life and nonlife insurers are substantial, as is illustrated in the following sections.

LIFE INSURANCE COMPANIES

The high and volatile interest rates that have characterized the past decade sensitized financial institutions and their clients to interest rate risk. For example, life insurance companies experienced unprecedented disintermediation in the early 1980s. As interest rates reached record high levels, policyholders took advantage of the option to borrow some or all of the accumulated cash value in their policies at the below-market policy loan rates (generally 5 to 9 percent) that are contractually defined in their whole life policies. The policy loan feature has long been considered an important life insurance policy provision. The true cost of this option became clear to the industry, as cash available for investment at the then prevailing double-digit interest rates was siphoned off in part to fund policy loans. In 1981 policy loans peaked at a post–World War II high of 9.3 percent of total industry assets, and by the end of 1988 they had declined to 4.6 percent, the lowest level in almost two decades.

An even more damaging interest rate risk exposure for life insurance companies is the surrender of policies in return for their accumulated cash values. Events of the past decade have broadened the array of financial alternatives and heightened the insurance buyer's financial awareness and sophistication level. Traditional cash value accumulation rates or policy credited rates (i.e., rates of interest credited to a policyholder's reserve account) of 4 to 5 percent that characterized the pre-1980s are no longer competitive. Voluntary termination rates (i.e., the ratio of the number of policies lapsed or surrendered to the number of policies in force) almost doubled from 6.6 percent in 1978 to a peak of 12.3 percent in 1985. This surrender experience transcends mere interest rate cycles and more accurately reflects what some have defined as a product revolution for the life insurance industry.

Universal life, variable life, and variable universal life represent the industry's response to the long-standing competitive appeal of "buying term insurance and investing the difference." These new products provide the life insurance buyer with a convenient and competitive means of purchasing varying amounts of protection along with an opportunity to save/invest at rates that vary with capital market and competitive conditions.

Asset/Liability Management

These developments have reshaped the liability structure of the life insurance industry. In portfolio management terms, the duration of the liabilities of the industry have been shortened because policyholders are now more prone to exercise their option to surrender in an effort to seek the most competitive credited rates and/or policy benefits. Surrender rates triggered by interest rate changes are more difficult to predict than mortality rates, and thus have become the more critical variable for many interest-sensitive life insurance products. The shortening of liability durations has necessitated the shortening of the duration of life insurance company portfolios, or at least those segments that are designed to fund these interest-sensitive product liabilities.

Matching or managing asset and liability durations has long been an implicit, but not necessarily explicit, aspect of insurance company portfolio management. Today asset/liability management is extremely important because of the increased volatility of both asset and liability durations caused by turbulence in the economy and reflected in the capital markets. Accumulation rates or policy credited rates are competitive among life insurance companies, but of equal importance, they are competitive with other financial alternatives. This new competitiveness is influencing the return objectives and risk tolerance of the industry, and especially the major companies. These large and medium-size companies are in the forefront of this product and portfolio management revolution. Many smaller companies are unwilling or unable to change; they continue to emphasize traditional non-interest-sensitive products and have not felt the need for modern approaches to asset/liability management. However, even if these companies are able to maintain a special niche (e.g., with traditional whole life products), they can achieve added protection for their operation via modern asset/liability management.

This new competitiveness has changed investment policies and challenged investment managers of major life insurance company portfolios. In essence, return requirements and risk tolerance specifications have changed dramatically and are continuing to change.

Return Requirements

Historically, return requirements for a life insurance company have been specified primarily by the rates used by actuaries to determine policyholder reserves or accumulation rates for the funds being held by the company for future disbursement. In effect, a rate continues as specified for the life of the contract or may change to reflect the actual investment experience of the company. Interest is then credited to the reserve account at the specified rate; this rate can thus be defined as the minimum return requirement. Failure to earn the minimum return results in an increase in liabilities by accrual of interest that is greater than the increase in assets. The shortfall is reflected in a decrease in surplus or surplus reserves, assuming the simplest case. Needless to say, the adequacy of reserve funding is monitored carefully by management, regulatory commissions, and insurance rating agencies such as *Best's Insurance Report*, and through the claims paying rating services that have been initiated by Moody's, Standard & Poor's, and Duff & Phelps.

With traditional whole life insurance policies, the minimum statutory accumulation rates for most life insurance contracts range between 3 and 5.5 percent. Thus, in the higher interest rate environment of the past two decades, the spread between life insurance companies' return on new investments and even the return on their entire portfolio exceeded the minimum returns by a widening margin. However, as growing sophistication and competition in insurance markets has led to higher credited rates, the net interest spread (the difference between interest earned and interest credited to policyholders) has narrowed quickly and dramatically.

Spread Management

Historically, the return objectives of life insurance companies have not been well defined. Today, many companies are pricing policies assuming continuation of current and competitive interest rates. Consistently above-average investment returns should and do provide a company with some competitive advantage in setting premiums. The total portfolio returns for most life portfolios are more similar than different as shown for three major U.S. life companies in Table 4-9. To a large extent, this reflects the role regulation plays in constraining the asset mix and quality characteristics of every life

TABLE 4-9. Portfolio Yields of U.S. Life Insurance Companies, Selected Years, 1970–1988[a]

Year	Industry Rate	Major Life Companies		
		Prudential	Lincoln National	Equitable-NY
1970	5.34%	5.56%	5.47%	5.32%
1975	6.44	6.47	6.98	6.22
1980	8.06	7.85	8.09	8.18
1983	9.06	8.22	8.10	9.07
1984	9.65	8.82	8.41	8.90
1985	9.87	9.07	8.49	8.72
1986	9.64	8.87	8.27	8.32
1987	9.39	8.66	8.36	8.09
1988	9.37	8.81	10.12	9.13

SOURCE: *Life Insurance Fact Book* [1989]; *Best's Insurance Management Reports* [1989].
[a] Ratio of net investment income (after expenses but before income taxes) to mean cash and invested assets.

insurance company portfolio and the historical evolution of portfolio asset allocation in that regulatory environment. Heretofore the fact that benefits were payable in fixed dollar amounts had limited the motivation to assume additional risk in an effort to achieve portfolio returns in excess of current inflation or average industry experience. By contrast, a comparison of new money rates (i.e., the yields on new investments acquired during a specified period) for all or some portion of the major life companies' portfolios would reflect striking differences in investment returns. Competition has modified the traditional conservatism of life insurance company portfolios and motivated companies to accept and manage varying degrees of risk in pursuit of more competitive investment returns.

The new interest-sensitive policies being offered by the life insurance industry require a more aggressive approach to investment risk in an effort to achieve above-average returns. To the extent that above-average returns can be earned, they can be translated into wider margins and/or higher crediting rates for a particular company's policies, providing a pricing advantage to such companies. To reflect the trend of interest spreads for the insurance industry, Figure 4-3 shows a comparison of crediting rates on certain policies relative to selected U.S. Treasury and corporate bond yield levels. This figure was prepared by a consulting actuarial firm, Tillinghast & Co., as part of its monthly survey of crediting rates for universal life policies.

More Competitive Returns

For companies selling annuity and guaranteed investment contracts, competitive investment returns have also become a necessity and narrow spread

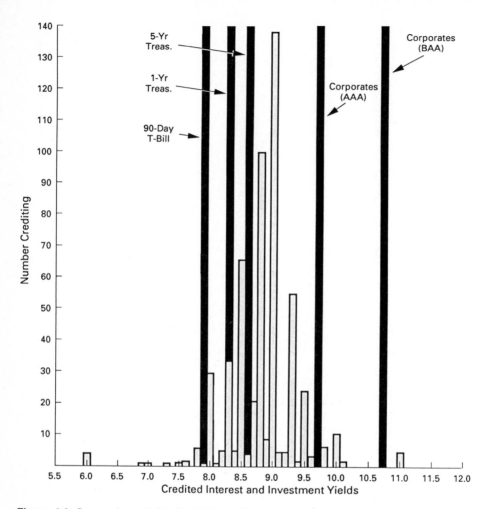

Figure 4-3. Comparison of Credited Interest Rate Distribution on Life Insurance Products With Selected Fixed-Income Yields, December 1, 1988. SOURCE: Tillinghast Universal Life Analytic Service.

margins a reality. As an indication of its importance, this major segment of the life insurance business accounts for 65 percent of total industry reserves (see Table 4-10).

For these lines of business, competition comes from outside as well as from within the industry. These competitive pressures create a dilemma for insurance companies. From a risk control perspective, they require insurance companies to match more closely or align the timing of asset and liability cash flows through asset/liability management techniques to enhance risk adjusted returns. From a competitive return perspective, however, many

**TABLE 4-10. Reserves for Annuities and
Guaranteed Investment Contracts for the U.S.
Life Insurance Industry, Selected Years,
1970–1988**

Year	Percentage of Total Reserves
1970	26.6%
1980	45.4
1982	51.8
1984	57.8
1985	61.0
1986	63.4
1987	64.4
1988	65.3

SOURCE: *Life Insurance Fact Book* [1989].

companies feel compelled to mismatch asset/liability durations or downgrade the credit quality of their investments in an attempt to achieve higher absolute returns.

Many companies have *segmented* their portfolios to assure maintenance of a competitive return under volatile market conditions. For example, insurance companies issuing GICs must invest cash flow in a portfolio of securities to assure the maintenance of guaranteed rates during the life of the contract, which is generally from 2 to 10 years. Such bond portfolio techniques as immunization, discussed in Chapter 8, have been used widely in this regard. In addition, futures and option strategies, discussed in Chapter 11, have also been used by some companies. Segmentation is discussed in more detail later in this section.

New Policy Forms

New life insurance forms, such as universal life and variable life, have been created to enable the industry to compete for the consumers' protection and savings/investment dollars (see Table 4-11). The most recent and revolutionary forms are the so-called universal life policies that provide the policyholder with a flexible, investment-oriented package. The policyholder pays a specified amount for the insurance protection desired. For a separate fee, he or she can deposit funds in a savings-type fund that provides the benefit of a competitive interest rate, the income from which is tax deferred under current tax law in the United States.

In essence, a trend toward unbundling insurance risk management and investment management is developing. Each of these new policy forms requires competitive rates of return. Thus, the major life insurance companies

TABLE 4-11. Analysis of Ordinary Life Insurance Purchases in the United States, 1978 vs. 1988

Type of Policy	Percentage of Dollar Amount of Life Insurance Purchases	
	1978	1988
Term life	38%	34%
Straight life	27	21
Universal life	—	20
Variable life	—	9
Combination policies	12	7
Limited payment life	6	2
Endowment and retirement income	3	1
Other	14	6
Total	100%	100%

SOURCE: *Life Insurance Fact Book* [1989].

find themselves specifying return requirements by major line of business, the result being that multiple return objectives may be incorporated into a single company's investment policy. Furthermore, many companies have established separate investment policies, as well as strategies, for each segment of their portfolios.

Growth of Surplus

Another important function of the investment operation is to provide growth of surplus to support the expansion in insurance volume; common stocks, equity investments in real estate, and venture capital have been the investment alternatives most widely used to achieve surplus growth. Surplus adequacy is a growing concern for the life insurance industry. Companies are looking at more aggressive capital appreciation-oriented strategies as well as financial leverage to supplement the narrowing contributions to surplus from the newer product lines.

Risk Tolerance

The investment portfolio of an insurance company (life or nonlife) is looked upon from a public policy viewpoint as a *quasi-trust fund*. Accordingly, conservative fiduciary principles limit the risk tolerance of an insurance portfolio. Confidence in the ability of an insurance company to pay benefits as they come due is a crucial element in the financial foundation of the economy. Thus, insurance companies are sensitive to the risk of any significant chance of principal loss or any significant interruption of investment income.

To absorb some modest loss of principal, life insurance companies are required to maintain a mandatory securities valuation reserve (MSVR), a reserve established by the National Association of Insurance Commissioners (NAIC). Annual contributions to and maximum amounts of the reserve are determined by specific "quality tests" delineated by the NAIC for bonds, preferred stocks, and common stocks. Net realized capital gains are also credited to the reserve as long as the reserve is below the maximum. All realized capital losses are charged to the reserve, as are all unrealized capital losses on common stock holdings—the principal class of assets carried at market value by life insurance companies. The maximum amount of the reserve varies by the class and/or quality of the invested assets: bonds of investment grade—2 percent of their total cost; bonds of lower grade—10 to 20 percent; preferred stocks in good standing—10 percent; and common stocks—33⅓ percent. These maximum rates suggest a substantial margin for absorbing losses. However, with a growing portfolio and relatively small annual contribution rates to the reserve, varying from 0.1 percent (bonds) up to 1 percent (common stocks), the security valuation reserves of most life companies are well below the maximum. Thus, surplus is vulnerable to write-down if significant losses occur.

Valuation Concerns. Surplus write-downs did occur at the end of 1974, when the cumulative effect of two years of sharply declining common stock prices resulted in a capital adequacy problem for the insurance industry. Unrealized capital losses on stocks exceeded the amount of the MSVR for many companies, with the excess being a direct reduction of surplus. As a result of that experience many insurance companies, willingly or at the urging of the NAIC, reduced the percentage of assets invested in common stocks. Today most life companies have established investment policies that limit holdings of common stock (at market value) as a percentage of surplus rather than as a percentage of assets as specified in the statutes.

In the early 1980s, the statutory surplus of life insurance companies in general was overstated, because bonds, mortgages, and preferred stocks were not (and still are not) valued at market for statement purposes. For example, at the 1980 and 1981 interest rate peaks, the consequent decline in market value of bonds would have wiped out the surplus of the life insurance industry if these fixed-income securities had been valued at market value rather than at amortized cost.

However, the liabilities of insurance companies also have not been marked to market. To add further perspective to the interest rate peaks of the early 1980s, the reduction in the market value of liabilities would have offset to a large extent, if not completely, the reduction in the market value of assets. In effect, the companies were earning interest on new investments during that period far in excess of the rates of return factored into the insurance reserve calculations. Thus, the market value of the liabilities of the companies would have been substantially reduced based on these higher market level accumulation rates.

While actuarial valuation methods have been focusing on the market value aspects of both sides of the balance sheet, no accepted or approved procedure for marking life insurance company liabilities to market has been developed. In fact, techniques for measuring the duration of life insurance company liabilities were still new in early 1989 and in need of further refinement. If and when reliable valuation methods are perfected for both assets and liabilities, life insurance companies will be able to measure and monitor the market value of surplus on a multi-interest rate scenario simulation to determine interest rate risk exposure.

Finally, the market value of a life insurance company's bond portfolio is significant from an asset/liability management perspective. Generally, limited liquidity reserves are maintained, and most companies depend on their maturity schedule or their ability to control interest rate risk and thus the market value of the bond portfolio to assure that surrenders and/or policy loans can be funded with little or no loss of principal or income.

Cash Flow Volatility. Loss of income or delays in collecting and reinvesting cash flow from investments is another key aspect of risk for which life insurance companies have low tolerance. Compounding (interest-on-interest) is an integral part of the reserve funding formula and a source of surplus growth. The actuaries assume that investment income will be available for reinvestment at a rate at least equal to the assumed (minimum return) rate. Traditionally, most companies seek investments offering a minimum risk of volatility (disruption) of both income and principal. In the case of those companies that are assuming additional credit risk to support competitive returns or widen spread margins, the much higher yields provided by investments in "junk bonds," for example, are expected to compensate for the increased risk of loss or disruption of income or principal.

Reinvestment Risk. For many life insurance companies, especially those competing for annuity and GIC business, yet another risk factor can be significant—reinvestment risk. Reinvestment risk is defined as the risk of reinvesting coupon income or principal at a rate less than the original coupon or purchase rate. For GIC or annuity contracts on which no interest is paid until maturity (terminal date) of the contract, the guaranteed rate typically includes the insurance company's best estimate of the rate(s) at which interest payments will be reinvested. Thus, an unexpected decline in interest rates can jeopardize the profitability of these contracts. However, many GIC contracts provide for annual disbursement of interest; this, of course, reduces or eliminates reinvestment risk. As discussed earlier, competitive conditions dictate maintenance of the guaranteed rate for GICs and the flexibility to adjust the rates paid on annuities and universal life policies. The quest for competitive returns, especially for unbundled policies, requires an increased risk tolerance on the part of insurance companies and some broadening of asset mix to the extent permitted by regulation.

Credit Risk. Insurance companies have been traditional buyers of investment grade bonds (Baa or higher), with emphasis on Baa and A quality bonds. Many companies have also been occasional purchasers of bonds of Ba/BB quality. Because of the importance of private placement bonds in life insurance company portfolios, credit analysis has long been considered one of the industry's strengths. In recent years, many insurance companies have been avid buyers and advocates of the so-called high yield or junk bonds. As of year end 1988, U.S. insurance companies held one third of the total high yield or junk bonds outstanding.

Arguably, major life insurance companies have the asset size to diversify a portfolio of junk bonds and the analytical staff to pick and choose among this type of security. Further, historical default rates support an expectation for the realization of a significant net yield advantage over U.S. Treasuries over the holding period. This projected advantage, of anywhere from 300 to 600 basis points (net), is well in excess of the spreads over Treasuries available from Baa securities and even mortgage loans. However, recent changes in New York regulations limit junk bonds to 20 percent of assets for those insurance companies doing business in that state. Also, recent research studies report junk bond experience that has modified upward the default risk expectations for these bonds.

Liquidity Requirements

Traditionally, life insurance companies have been characterized as needing minimal liquidity. Except during the depression of the 1930s and the disintermediation of the early 1980s, annual cash inflow has far exceeded cash outflow. Thus, the need to liquidate assets has been negligible, reflecting the growing volume of business, the longer term nature of liabilities, and the rollover in portfolio assets from maturing securities and other forms of principal payments. For many years, investment focus was concentrated on seeking the highest yield for the longest period of time.

Disintermediation. Times have changed. On four different occasions in the past 25 years (1966, 1970, 1974, and 1979–1981), inflation and high interest rates have forced life insurance companies to take measures to accommodate extraordinary net cash outflows. Initially, policy loan drains in conjunction with heavy forward commitment positions forced some remedial but temporary changes in investment strategies. Likewise, the trend of surrenders has caused (1) actuaries to reevaluate and reduce their estimates of the duration of liabilities and (2) portfolio managers to reduce the average duration of the portfolio and in some cases provide for additional liquidity reserves. Multi-scenario forecasting, similar to that developed in Chapter 5, is becoming an accepted technique used by life insurance companies to measure interest rate risk exposure and liquidity needs. In a recent survey, 58 percent of the companies responding indicated that they are using multi-scenario models.

The most recent cash flow gap (in 1979–1981) was further complicated by (1) a disruption in the flow of pension monies into GICs or separate accounts and (2) an increase in surrenders of life insurance and annuity policies. The cumulative effect of these disruptions in policy loan outflows was a scramble for liquidity. Some companies delayed the takedown of previously committed investments, many ceased making new investments for a period of months, and some sold portfolio assets to raise cash. A few major life insurance companies were even forced to borrow from banks or issue commercial paper at the prevailing high rates of 15 to 20 percent to meet record cash outflows.

Importance of Maturity Schedules and/or Marketability. These volatile economic and capital market conditions, along with increased competition, have heightened liquidity requirements and thus further constrained insurance companies' ability to use higher yielding long-term bond and mortgage loan investments. Whereas the new fixed-income investments of life companies were at one time concentrated in 20- to 30-year maturities, now they are concentrated in a 3- to 10-year maturity range. In addition, marketability of investments is receiving increased attention in an effort to insure ample liquidity. Also, forward commitment activity has been slowed by liquidity considerations. Such commitments represent agreements by life insurance companies to purchase private placement bonds or mortgages, with part or all of the settlement typically delayed from 6 to 18 months. The traditional stability and growth of cash flow fostered this practice in the 1960s and 1970s, but disintermediation has undermined the predictability of life companies' cash flow. Thus, forward committing has waned in importance.

To deal with the change in liquidity requirements, life insurance companies are paying more attention to maturity and duration characteristics. As discussed earlier, asset/liability management strategies and changing investment policies are being adopted to match or manage more closely the maturity or duration of assets with liability reserves.

Time Horizon

Life insurance companies have long been considered the classic long-term investor. Traditionally portfolio return objectives have been evaluated within the context of holding periods as long as from 20 to 40 years. Furthermore, with annual cash available for investment ranging from hundreds of millions of dollars to several billions of dollars for each of the top 50 life companies (which account for over half of industry assets), the need to put that money to work created an internal pressure to seek an adequate number of investment outlets. Thus, most life insurance companies traditionally sought long-term maturities for bond and mortgage investments. Equity investments (real estate, common stocks, convertible securities, and venture capital), with long-term capital appreciation and inflation (purchasing power) risk protection characteristics, have also been attractive to life insurance companies. Such investments are receiving increased attention as the need for growth of surplus increases in importance.

One reason that life insurance companies have segmented their portfolios is the recognition that particular product lines or lines of business have unique time horizons and return objectives. For example, GICs are generally written with maturities of 2 to 10 years. Thus, many, if not most, of the assets funding those products have comparable maturities or, more accurately, durations.

Asset/liability management practices have tended to shorten the overall time horizon of the typical life insurance company. Today portfolio segments have differing time horizons, which are reflected in the investment policies for each segment.

Tax Considerations

For approximately 25 years, from 1958 to 1982, the U.S. life insurance industry experienced a period of relative tax tranquility. Although the tax code during that period was generally described as very complex, in retrospect the laws were relatively favorable for the life insurance industry, providing opportunities and incentives for taking full advantage of the capital gains and corporate dividend exclusions provisions of the code. Investment policy during that period reflected both tax complexities and opportunities. In fact, it was not uncommon during that period for there to be swaps of securities between insurance companies with differing tax positions.

During the decade of the 1980s, three major changes were made in the U.S. tax laws as they apply to the life insurance industry. The net result of these changes has been an increase in the amount of tax paid by the industry, largely as a result of the following: (1) new code standards for establishing policyholder reserves, (2) standardization of the tax rate for life insurance companies (currently at the full corporate tax rate of 34 percent), (3) taxation of capital gains at the corporate income tax rate, (4) reduction of the corporate dividend exclusion from 85 percent to 70 percent, and (5) application of the alternative minimum tax. Space does not permit an exhaustive treatment of insurance industry taxes; suffice it to say that taxes are a key consideration for investment policy, even though the opportunity to reduce income tax through such policies has been constrained by the U.S. Tax Reform Act of 1986.

In a very simplified context, investment income of life insurance companies is divided into two parts for tax purposes: (1) the policyholders' share—that portion relating to the actuarially assumed rate necessary to fund reserves—and (2) the balance that is transferred to surplus. Under present law, only the latter portion is taxed.

One very important tax consideration that is being watched carefully by the U.S. life insurance industry relates to the tax treatment of the so-called *inside buildup* of cash values under a life insurance policy or annuity. The tax deferral as it applies to the accumulation of cash values within a life insurance contract has been a long-standing characteristic of such products. However, in 1989 Congress was reassessing the tax deferral of such inside buildup for certain single premium life products that became popular in recent years. Changes in the tax law that would reduce or eliminate the tax deferral granted to the inside buildup would create significant competitive problems for the insurance industry.

Regulatory and Legal Considerations

Insurance is a heavily regulated industry. In the United States, state rather than federal regulation prevails, and this regulation pervades all aspects of an insurance company's operations—permitted lines of business, product and policy forms, authorized investments, and the like. The NAIC, whose membership includes all 50 states, promulgates accounting rules and financial statement forms. In Canada, regulation is federal, except for those companies doing business only within a specific province. At either level—federal or provincial—Canadian regulation is as pervasive as U.S. regulation. In Japan, the Ministry of Finance regulates insurance companies, while in the United Kingdom, the Department of Trade is the responsible governmental authority.

Audit procedures of the insurance department ensure compliance with the regulations of the state or country in which the company is domiciled. In most cases, these regulations are the primary constraint affecting investment policy.

Eligible Investments. Insurance laws determine the classes of assets eligible for investment and may specify the quality standards of each asset class. For example, in the United States many states require that for a bond issue to be eligible for investment, the *interest coverage ratio* (earnings plus interest divided by interest) must meet minimum standards over a specified time period (e.g., 1.5 times coverage over each of the past five years), and that common stocks must have had a minimum amount of net earnings available for the payment of dividends over each of the past five years. Generally, regulations specify the percentage of an insurance company's assets that may be invested in a specific class of eligible assets. For example, in the United States, most states limit the value (at cost) of common stock holdings of life insurance companies to no more than 10 percent of total admitted assets. Foreign investments are also limited in most states to no more than 5 percent of admitted assets.

Prudent Man Rule. While the scope of regulation is extensive, it is important to note that the *prudent man* concept has been adopted in several key states, most notably in New York. This trend to replace traditional "laundry lists" of approved investments with prudent man logic simplifies the regulatory process and allows life insurance companies much needed flexibility to keep up with the ever changing array of investment alternatives. New York's leadership in this area is important because, traditionally, regulations of this state have been the model for insurance regulation in the United States.

Valuation Methods. In the United States, uniform valuation methods are established and administered by the NAIC. In fact, the NAIC's *Security Valuation Book*, published at the end of each year, is a compilation of the values or valuation bases to be used by insurance companies for portfolio securities. This book is the source of the valuation data listed in Schedule D of the annual statement filed by each company with the insurance departments of the states in which it operates. Schedule D is an inventory of all bond and stock holdings at year-end and a recap of all transactions during the year. Because the primary emphasis of insurance regulation is protection of the interests of policyholders, it limits investment alternatives in terms of classes of assets, quality factors, and concentration of holdings available to insurance companies. Regulation, then, has a profound effect on both the risk and return aspects of a life insurance company portfolio, primarily because it constrains the most critical aspects of portfolio management—the asset mix and asset allocation.

Unique Needs, Circumstances, and Preferences

Each insurance company, whether it be life or nonlife, may have unique preferences or needs attributable to factors over and above the insurance products the company provides. These idiosyncrasies may further modify portfolio policies. The size of the company and the sufficiency of its surplus position are among the considerations influencing portfolio policy.

By law, a committee of the board of directors, usually called the investment or finance committee, is required to establish investment policy and oversee its implementation by approving all transactions. This committee's preferences and its perception of the company's needs is influenced by the operating goals of the senior management and the size and qualifications of the investment staff.

Determination of Portfolio Policies

Life insurance companies' limited but growing tolerance for risk is the dominant factor shaping investment policy. Because of their contractual liabilities, it is prudent that interest rate risk be minimized or managed through the use of asset/liability management techniques and that credit risk be controlled through diversification via limits on individual holdings. Despite the emphasis on safety, the persistence of interest rate volatility and competition has altered traditional risk/reward relationships. The result is that life insurance companies have experienced far greater value volatility in their fixed-income portfolios than regulators or managements had ever envisioned. Under these conditions, the traditional definition of a fixed-income security, even including a U.S. Treasury bond, as a "safe" asset is less than viable. Conversely, the traditional characterizations of life insurance companies as conservative investors is no longer an appropriate definition. However, it is not likely that they will soon, if ever, be characterized as aggressive investors.

Asset/liability management within the insurance industry is evolving from a single dimensional approach that focused on yield to multi-factor approaches that include yield, duration, and, more recently, convexity (discussed in detail in Chapter 6). A recent survey of randomly selected insurance companies indicates that over 40 percent have used interest rate swaps as an asset/liability management technique and about 35 percent have used interest rate futures.

Other dimensions of asset/liability management are credit risk, liquidity risk, and even equity market risk. The latter is an opportunity risk applicable to long duration liabilities for which common stocks, with their long-term expected return superiority, are both attractive and appropriate as an alternative to fixed-income instruments.

Effect of Industry Product Trends. Of perhaps greater and more fundamental importance to the long-term investment policy of life insurance companies is the accelerating move away from whole life policies toward

TABLE 4-12. Asset Mix Changes of Life Insurance Companies

Traditional	Contemporary

Bonds—Domestic (Aaa–Baa)	Bonds
	  Domestic
	    Aaa–Ba Quality
	    Junk bonds
	  Foreign
	    Hedged
	    Unhedged

Mortgage loans—Residential	Mortgage loans—Commercial and residential
Stocks—Common and preferred	Common stocks—Domestic and foreign
Equity real estate	Equity real estate

Other—Venture capital	Venture capital
	Derivative instruments
	  Futures
	  Options
	  Interest rate swaps

SOURCE: Mutual of Omaha Companies.

term and other intermediate types of policies, specifically universal life and variable life policies. The latter products reflect an effort on the part of the industry to recapture savings/investable dollars that have been lost to other savings and investment outlets, such as certificates of deposit (CDs), Treasury obligations, and mutual funds.

Consolidation of Financial Services. These product trends might also be considered to be part of the broad consolidation of financial services that is sweeping through the industrialized countries. The acquisition of brokerage companies by insurance companies and other significant mergers, combinations, and acquisitions within the financial field are indicative of this trend. Today life insurance policies are routinely sold by investment brokerage firms in several countries. On the other hand, since the 1960s, a number of U.S. insurance companies have offered mutual funds to investors through their vast distribution networks. It appears that this trend toward a broader array of financial services will accelerate dramatically over the remainder of the century and will have a significant impact on both the life insurance industry and the capital market systems of the world.

Changing Product/Asset Mix. One major result of these industry trends is a dramatically changing asset mix for most life insurance companies. Table 4-12 illustrates the change now taking place. These product and asset mix trends can be expected to continue and perhaps accelerate over the remainder of the century.

Universal life, with its important function as a savings instrument, requires insurance companies to invest significant funds in intermediate-term debt markets. To the extent that policyholders elect an equity alternative for variable universal policies, opportunities will open up for life companies to invest more funds in the equity market.

This changing mix of insurance products will have its greatest impact on investment policies through the increased risk that insurance companies assume to provide competitively attractive returns.

Portfolio Segmentation. The net result of these developments is a continued emphasis on portfolio segmentation, or the creation of subportfolios within the general account portfolio, according to the product mix for each individual company.

Portfolio segmentation has been adopted by a significant number of life insurance companies. In a recent survey of 250 randomly selected companies, 75.9 percent of the respondents indicated that they had segmented all or part of their portfolios and another 5 percent indicated that they were considering segmentation.

Prior to segmentation, the return on invested assets in the general account was allocated proportionately to various lines of insurance business (whole life, annuities, group, and so on) on the basis of the *investment year* method or based on the ratio of each line's reserves to total reserves. Allocation of investment income by the investment year method means that the cash available for investment from a particular line of business is credited with the new money rate (average yield for new investments in that year). Thus, statutory reports have not permitted insurance companies to match assets and their returns with the product line. However, the shift of the product mix to annuity and guaranteed investment contracts created a need to identify subportfolios designed to support these product lines.

Segmented portfolios provide the investment manager with a clear focus for meeting return objectives over the time horizons specified for the subportfolios. Regulators and senior management are finding that segmentation provides far more accurate measurement of both profitability by major line of business and the suitability of the investment policy defined for these subportfolios. A number of life insurance companies have received regulatory approval to segment their portfolios for statutory reporting purposes. Many others have segmented "notationally" and are reporting on a segmented basis for internal purposes only. Statutorily, all general account assets of a life insurance company back all liabilities; for reporting purposes only, insurance companies have been permitted to divide their general account portfolios into segments by line of business.

The objective of segmentation is to assure that appropriate amounts and types of assets are supporting or funding the reserves attributable to a particular product line of business. The appropriateness of the type of asset is measured on at least three bases: investment return, interest rate risk (duration), and credit risk characteristics. Each of these are evaluated relative to the competitive, actuarial, and statutory characteristics of the product line(s) being funded. From a portfolio management perspective, segmentation is a very effective tool for particularizing investments to (1) seek to construct a set of optimized portfolios, (2) measure and monitor risk adjusted returns, and (3) allocate investment income by line of business.

Life companies that have chosen to segment by line of business generally maintain four to eight major portfolio segments and possibly a few subsegments. Each segment has its own return objective, risk parameters, and liquidity characteristics. A few companies have segmented by product line and in some cases have established as many as 40 different segments. Span of control and overall suboptimization considerations increase with the number of segments.

Policy Coordination. In the final analysis, investment policy must complement the operating policy of any insurance company. Thus, investment portfolio policy seeks to achieve the most appropriate mix of investment alternatives (1) to counterbalance the risks inherent in the mix of insurance products involved and (2) to achieve the stated return objectives. Numerous factors must be considered in arriving at the appropriate mix, the most important of which are regulatory influences, time horizons, and tax considerations. Finally, competition—both within and outside the insurance industry—is expected to require yet more flexible and responsive management of insurance company portfolios.

Investment Policy Statement. The format and content of investment policy statements are unique to each insurance company. However, Table 4-13 is an example of a representative statement for a stock life insurance company.

NONLIFE INSURANCE COMPANIES

The second broad insurance industry category is the nonlife sector, which includes but is not limited to health, property, liability, marine, surety, and worker compensation insurance. For purposes of considering investment policy, these nonlife (casualty) companies are really quite similar even though the products they sell are rather diverse. However, the investment policies of a casualty company are significantly different from those of a life insurance company because the liabilities, risk factors, and tax considerations for nonlife companies are distinctly different from life companies. For example, nonlife liability durations tend to be shorter, claim processing and payment periods are longer, and some, but not all, casualty liabilities are exposed to inflation risk but are not directly exposed to interest rate risk.

TABLE 4-13. Statement of Investment Policy for ABC Life Insurance Company

ABC Life Insurance Company's investment policy may be stated in terms of the *investment objectives and constraints* under which the portfolio is managed to fund liability reserves for the policyholders and to contribute to the growth of surplus for benefit of both the policyholders and stockholders. In effect, there are five investment portfolios: short-term money market securities, bonds, mortgage loans, common stocks, and equity real estate assets.

ABC Life's INVESTMENT OBJECTIVES may be defined in terms of return requirements and risk tolerance as specified for each of the portfolio segments. The statement below reflects a common set of objectives that applies in whole or in part to each of the respective portfolio segments. More detailed policy statements exist for each segment. Capital market and insurance market conditions shape the achievement of these policy objectives.

RETURN REQUIREMENTS

Short-term portfolio. Earn a reasonable return on all funds not immediately needed to fund cash disbursements.

Bond portfolio. Earn a favorable return so as to fund interest sensitive insurance products on a competitive basis, allowing for an adequate margin.

Mortgage loan portfolio. Earn a return that on average is at least 25 basis points above that provided by A/Baa-rated private placement bonds so as to enhance the competitive returns or margins for interest sensitive insurance products.

Common stock portfolio. Meet or exceed the return of the stock market averages in up markets and maintain a positive return in down markets so as to contribute to the growth of corporate surplus.

Real estate portfolio. Earn a total return that on average is at least 250 basis points over the total return objectives of the common stock portfolio.

RISK TOLERANCE

Short-term portfolio. All commercial paper must be rated A-1/P-1 and all other short-term investments must be of comparable quality.

Bond portfolio. The emphasis is on public bonds rated Baa/BBB or higher or private placement bonds that would qualify for such ratings, with selected purchases of foreign bonds and bonds of Ba quality after obtaining Investment Committee approval.

Mortgage loan portfolio. The emphasis is on well-located, high-quality commercial properties with a strong tenant base and good long-term cash flow trends.

Common stock portfolio. The emphasis is on a diversified portfolio of established companies with annual sales of $250 million or net income of $25 million and ranked B+ or better by Standard and Poor's Dividend and Earnings Ranking service.

Real estate portfolio. The emphasis is on commercial properties that are diversified by type of property and location with a strong tenant base and underlying economic trends.

ABC Life's INVESTMENT CONSTRAINTS can be defined in terms of the following factors, as specified for each of the portfolio segments. The policy specifications below reflect the investment constraints across all product segments.

LIQUIDITY

Short-term portfolio. Liquidity and safety are the primary objectives with maturities concentrated within 30 days; the size of the portfolio reflects corporate and portfolio segment considerations.

Bond portfolio. A laddered maturity schedule is maintained with an average maturity target of approximately 7 years, which is a composite of the targets for all segments.

Mortgage loan portfolio. A laddered maturity schedule is maintained with an average maturity target of 7 years, which is a composite of the targets for all segments.

Common stock portfolio. Larger capitalization companies are emphasized to provide liquidity.

Real estate portfolio. Liquidity is not a consideration, given the long-term nature of market characteristics for real estate investments.

TAX

Income tax considerations determine the mix of investments that provides the most favorable after-tax returns.

REGULATORY

All investments must qualify under the insurance code of the state in which ABC is domiciled and the foreign insurance companies regulations in the countries in which ABC Life operates.

UNIQUE PREFERENCES

Private placement bonds and commercial mortgage loans offer returns that are important within the asset/liability management parameters and competitive objectives of the Company.

General market common stock holdings (at market value) may not exceed 35 percent of surplus to minimize the market value risk (over and above the MSVR).

Real estate holdings may not exceed 10 percent of total assets.

This policy statement will be reviewed at least annually by the Investment Committee and is subject to modification based on significant changes in insurance or tax regulations as well as significant changes in capital or insurance market conditions.

As explained in this section, the investment policies and practices of the nonlife insurance companies in the United States are evolving. These changes are brought on by both operating considerations and new tax laws. In fact, tax planning has dominated the investment policy of nonlife companies for many years, reflecting the cyclical characteristics of this segment of the insurance industry. For reasons described in the following pages, asset/liability management is receiving increased attention.

Asset/Liability Management

A unique aspect of the casualty insurance industry is what is often described as the "long tail" that characterizes the claims reporting, processing, and

payment structure of the industry. Whereas life insurance is heavily oriented
to products sold to or for individuals, commercial customers account for a
very large portion of the total casualty insurance market. The "long tail"
nature of many types of liability (both individual and commercial) and casualty insurance claims arises from the fact that months and years may pass
between the date of the occurrence and reporting of the claim and the actual
payment of a settlement to a policyholder. Many casualty industry claims
are the subject of lawsuits to determine actual or appropriate settlement
amounts. Furthermore, some of these claims require expert evaluation to
determine the extent of the damages—for example, a fire in a major manufacturing plant or damage to an oceangoing vessel. Thus, the liability structure of a casualty insurance company is very much a function of the products
that it sells and the claims reporting and settlement process for those types
of products.

From an asset/liability management perspective, most casualty insurance companies traditionally have been classified as having relatively short-
term liabilities, even though the spectrum of casualty and health insurance
policies covers a wide range of liability durations, from very short—one
year or less—to very long. One of the primary factors that limits the duration
of a nonlife company's assets is the so-called *underwriting* (or *profitability*)
cycle, generally averaging three to five years. These cycles are often coin-
cident with general business cycles and frequently require companies to
liquidate investments to supplement cash flow shortfalls resulting from the
significant underwriting losses that may occur in the low part of the underwriting cycle.

It is possible, but not easy, for actuaries to estimate the duration of a
casualty insurance company's liabilities. Using multi-scenario and multifactor models, they attempt to capture: (1) the underwriting cycle, (2) the
liability durations by product line, and (3) any unique cash outflow characteristics. Using information derived from these models, casualty insurance
companies can adapt certain of the asset/liability management policies and
practices described previously for the life insurance industry. For nonlife
companies, business cycles and not interest rate cycles, per se, determine
the need for liquidity through appropriate durations and maturities of assets.

Return Requirements

Historically, most casualty insurance companies had not implicitly taken
investment earnings into account in the calculation of premiums. This policy
was in striking contrast to the accumulation rates long factored into life
insurance premiums. For this reason, casualty insurance companies were
once thought to be operating as if they were two separate organizations—

an insurance company and an investment company operating a balanced fund.

Competitive Policy Pricing. In the late 1970s and early 1980s, many casualty insurance companies, especially the larger ones, took advantage of the high interest rates being earned on new investments, in some cases, to lower insurance premiums and, in other cases, to delay the normal pass-through of cost increases to their customers. As a result of this strategy, casualty insurance premiums lagged the otherwise high rate of inflation that characterized the early 1980s. Once interest rates started to fall, projections of high investment returns became suspect and the decline in operating margins of many casualty insurance companies collapsed. The substantial losses experienced by casualty insurance companies in the mid-1980s resulted, in part, from the mispricing of their product because of expected returns that did not materialize. An escalation of the dollar amount of court-awarded settlements added to the adversity of the period.

Today most casualty insurance companies are trying to follow a more enlightened approach to setting insurance policy premium rates. However, competitive pressures continue to be intense, and the longevity of these enlightened pricing policies is problematic.

Profitability. Investment income and the investment portfolio return are primary determinants of the continuity of profitability for the typical casualty company and, indeed, the industry. The underwriting cycle (the profit cycle of the business) influences the volatility of company and industry earnings. Return requirements for casualty companies are not framed in reference to a crediting rate for their policies. Rather, casualty insurance portfolios are managed to maximize return on capital and surplus to the extent that prudent asset/liability management, surplus adequacy considerations, and management preferences will allow.

Given the underwriting uncertainties inherent in the casualty insurance business, it is obvious that investment income provides financial stability for the insurance reserves. In fact, periodic underwriting losses (claims and expenses in excess of premium income) from the insurance side of the company are expected to be offset by investment earnings. Most products of the casualty insurance business are priced competitively and thus premium rates are not sufficiently ample or flexible to eliminate the loss aspects of the underwriting cycle.

Growth of Surplus. An important function of the investment operation is to provide growth of surplus, which, in turn, provides the opportunity to expand insurance volume. The risk-taking capacity of the casualty insurance company is measured to a large extent in terms of the ratio of premiums to capital and surplus. Generally, this ratio is maintained between two-to-one and three-to-one. Thus, each dollar of surplus generated by investment income or capital appreciation has the potential to support $2 to $3 of additional annual premiums. Common stocks, convertible securities, and venture capital have been the investment alternatives most widely used to achieve surplus growth. Their return and marketability characteristics fit well within the underwriting cycles of the industry. By contrast, real estate does not provide sufficient marketability and thus is not a favored investment alternative for U.S. nonlife insurance companies.

Traditional Asset Mix. Casualty insurance companies maintain a bond portfolio to offset insurance reserves, with capital and surplus funds invested largely in common stocks. Some portion of the maturity schedule of the bond portfolio is typically structured in line with the estimated liability cash outflows, at least over the short and intermediate term. In this manner, there is an attempt to match, either on a cash basis or a duration basis (similar to dedication or immunization discussed in Chapter 8), the assets and liabilities. If matching is not the objective, then certainly management of the mismatch is a primary function of casualty company portfolio management.

After-Tax Returns. Over the years, nonlife insurance companies have been very sensitive to the after-tax return from the bond portfolio and to the tax benefits, where they exist, of certain kinds of investment returns. In the United States, these returns have included dividend income (through the exclusion of a portion of the dividends received by one corporation on stock issued by another corporation), realized long-term capital gains, and tax-exempt bonds. The latter have been favored historically by U.S. casualty insurance companies, especially when underwriting is profitable, to achieve the highest after-tax return. Flexibility to shift between taxable and tax-exempt bonds has long been an important consideration for many casualty companies, as a key element of managing and optimizing after-tax income through the operating loss carryback and carryforward provisions of the U.S. tax code. Most companies have maintained some balance of taxable and tax-exempt bonds in their portfolios, shifting that mix as tax considerations warranted. Recent changes in the tax laws, discussed later, have diminished all of the tax benefits available to casualty insurance companies.

Total Return. Active bond portfolio management strategies designed to achieve total return, rather than yield or investment income goals only, have gained popularity among casualty insurance companies, especially the larger ones. Generally accepted accounting principles (GAAP) and statutory reporting require that realized capital gains and losses flow through the income statement. The decline in interest rates and increase in bond prices

TABLE 4-14. Pretax Portfolio Yields of U.S. Property/Casualty Companies, Selected Years, 1975–1988 [a]

	Average of Top 100 Companies	State Farm	Allstate	CNA Financial	Travelers Indemnity	St. Paul Fire and Marine	Continental Insurance
1975	5.7%	5.5%	5.1%	5.3%	7.3%	6.1%	5.5%
1980	6.9	5.9	6.3	7.3	8.0	6.1	7.2
1983	8.0	7.9	7.4	10.0	7.9	7.3	6.9
1984	8.4	8.0	7.3	11.0	8.1	8.3	8.8
1985	8.4	8.2	6.8	9.7	7.2	8.7	9.0
1986	7.8	8.0	7.2	9.4	7.3	8.6	9.4
1987	7.2	7.9	6.8	8.4	7.5	8.5	6.5
1988	7.4	7.9	6.8	8.4	7.7	8.4	7.0

SOURCE: *Best's Trend Report Property-Casualty Companies* [1989].
[a] Ratio of net investment income (after expenses but before income taxes) to mean cash and invested assets.

since 1982 have encouraged casualty insurance portfolio managers to trade actively at least some portion of their bond portfolios.

One of the most interesting characteristics of casualty insurance companies is that their investment returns vary significantly from company to company. This variation reflects (1) the latitude permitted by insurance regulations; (2) differences in product mix and, thus, in the duration of liabilities; (3) the individual tax cycle or tax status of a particular company; and (4) the emphasis placed on capital appreciation versus the income component of investment return. This contrast is illustrated in Table 4-14.

Risk Tolerance

Casualty insurance companies, like life insurance companies, have a quasi-fiduciary role; thus, safety is a dominant consideration influencing investment policy. However, the risks insured by casualty companies are less predictable. In fact, for companies exposed to catastrophic events—such as hurricanes, tornados, and explosions—the potential for loss may be significantly greater. Furthermore, casualty policies frequently provide replacement cost or current cost coverage; thus, inflation adds to the degree of risk.

Cash Flow Characteristics. Not surprisingly, then, the cash flows from casualty insurance operations can be quite erratic. Unlike life insurance companies, which historically have been able to project cash flows and make forward commitments, casualty companies must be prepared to meet operating cash gaps with investment income or maturing securities. Thus, for the portion of the investment portfolio relating to policyholder reserves, the tolerance for loss of principal or diminishing investment income is low. Predictability of investment maturities and investment income is necessary and operates as a direct offset to the unpredictability of operating trends.

Interestingly, casualty insurance companies are not required to maintain a securities valuation reserve. Evidently, the regulators feel that the surplus requirements, mentioned earlier, are sufficient. Casualty insurers' need for liquidity and a shorter time horizon (as compared to a life company) may be considered by the regulators to be an additional favorable modifier of market valuation risk.

Common Stock to Surplus Ratio. Inflation in the United States and worldwide has further reduced the tolerance for investment risk among many casualty insurers. In fact, the volatile stock market conditions in the 1970s, and in particular 1973–1974, persuaded many casualty companies to reduce the percentage of surplus invested in common stock. Up to then, it was not uncommon for a casualty insurance company to have common stock investments that were equal to or greater than its total surplus. Several major companies were forced to liquidate large portions of their common stock holdings near the end of the 1974 bear market because of a significant erosion of surplus. This impaired their ability to increase volume and, in some cases, to provide sufficient financial stability for existing volume.

Essentially, the regulators gave such companies the option of reducing common stock holdings or of temporarily ceasing or curtailing the issuance of new policies. Needless to say, this experience reduced casualty companies' risk tolerance for the portion of the investment portfolio related to surplus. By 1989, although there was no absolute rule, many casualty insurance companies had adopted self-imposed limitations restricting common stocks at market value to some significant but limited portion (frequently one half to three quarters) of total surplus.

The surplus of casualty insurance companies, like that of life companies, is often overstated because bonds are not carried at market value for statement purposes. If bonds had been valued at market rather than amortized cost, the 1980–1981 increase in interest rates and the consequent decline in bond prices would have reduced the aggregate surplus of the industry by approximately 50 percent.

Liquidity Requirements

Given the uncertainty of the cash flow from casualty insurance operations, liquidity has always been a paramount consideration. This is in sharp contrast with the relative certainty—excluding policy loans and surrenders—of life company cash flows.

In addition to meeting cash flow needs, liquidity has also been a necessary adjunct of the variable tax status of the casualty company. Historically, casualty companies have found it necessary to liquidate portions of their bond portfolios to shift between tax-exempt and taxable classes of bonds as underwriting cycles swung between profits and losses. Liquidity continues to be a necessity for casualty insurance companies, to provide portfolio flexibility under changing tax, underwriting, and interest rate conditions.

Marketability and Maturity Considerations. To meet its liquidity needs, the typical casualty company does several things. Quite often it maintains a portfolio of short-term securities, such as commercial paper or U.S. Treasury bills, as an immediate liquidity reserve. In addition, it may also hold a portfolio of readily marketable U.S. Government bonds of various maturities (as much as 20 percent or more, versus less than 5 percent for life companies); maintain a balanced or laddered maturity schedule to insure a sufficient rollover of assets; match some assets against seasonal cash flow needs; and, finally, concentrate some portion of the bond portfolio in higher quality bonds that are generally more marketable.

Needless to say, such attention to maturity and marketability complements the limited risk tolerance and further modifies the return objectives of casualty insurers.

Time Horizon

As the discussions of liquidity and asset/liability management suggest, the time horizon of a casualty insurance company is typically shorter than that of a life company because the durations of casualty liabilities are typically shorter than the duration of life insurance liabilities, and because underwriting cycles affect the mix of taxable to tax-exempt bonds. Ironically, the bond portfolios of some typical casualty companies have average maturities of 9 to 18 years as compared with approximately 7 to 9 years for the typical life company (see Table 4-15).

Differences in average maturity are a reflection of the emphasis by casualty companies on longer-term (10- to 30-year) tax-exempt bonds to maximize after-tax income. They also reflect the companies' willingness to accept interest rate risk via asset/liability duration mismatches and trade at least some portion of their portfolios through a market or underwriting cycle. As noted in the following section, tax law changes in the United States are reducing the after-tax benefits of municipal bonds for casualty insurance companies. To the extent that taxable bonds predominate in the portfolios of casualty insurance companies, the average maturities of those portfolios are likely to fall to a range of from 6 to 10 years.

In terms of common stock investments, casualty companies historically have been long-term investors, with growth of surplus the primary return

TABLE 4-15. Comparison of the Average Maturity of Bond Portfolios of Selected Nonlife and Life Insurance Companies, Year-End 1987

Companies	Average Maturity of Bond Portfolio, Year-End 1987
Nonlife	
SAFECO Corporation	18 years
Home Group, Inc.	17
Continental Corporation	9
USF&G Corporation	11
Life	
Lincoln National Life Insurance Co.	9 years
Prudential Insurance Co. of America	9
Equitable Life Assurance Co. of New York	7
John Hancock Mutual Life Insurance Co.	7

SOURCE: *Best's Insurance Reports* [1988].

objective of the stock portion of the portfolio. As noted earlier, realized gains and losses flow through the income statement. In recent years, especially during the bull market in common stocks dating from 1982, casualty insurance companies have used realized capital gains as part of a strategy to manage overall earnings. Thus, the long-term equity investor status of the industry has been modified by objectives related to current reported earnings that has in turn led to some additional turnover in the common stock portfolio and more active management of that portion of the total portfolio.

Tax Considerations

Tax considerations have long been an important factor in determining investment policy for the nonlife segment of the insurance industry. Prior to changes in the U.S. laws in 1986, nonlife companies operated under a relatively simple and straightforward set of tax provisions. Under those laws, investment policy was directed to achieving the appropriate balance between taxable and tax-exempt income on one hand, and taking advantage of the lower capital gains tax rate and corporate dividend exclusion, where possible, on the other.

As a result of the 1986 changes, tax-exempt bond income is subject to tax for nonlife insurance companies; it will become increasingly so under tax law changes that become effective in 1990. Application of current tax provisions requires a series of calculations to determine the net tax being levied on tax-exempt bond income. Because both the operating profit or loss characteristics of the nonlife insurance company and alternative minimum tax provisions of the Code are factored into the equations, a computer model is needed to determine the appropriate asset allocation, if any, between tax-exempt and taxable securities both for new purchases and for existing holdings. With the further changes effective in 1990, the tax on tax-exempt bond income will negate much of the tax planning attraction of these securities. However, the complexities and implications of the taxation of tax-exempt bond income for nonlife companies is beyond the scope of this chapter.

The reduction in the corporate dividend exclusion under current tax laws in the United States, and the application of ordinary income tax rates to capital gains, has further reduced the importance of tax considerations in establishing investment policy for nonlife insurance companies. Like the life insurance industry, the nonlife insurance industry is likely to be subjected to further modification of the tax code, leaving the investment manager with greater uncertainty as to the tax consequences of certain portfolio activities or alternatives when measured over a longer time horizon.

In other countries, tax considerations can and do shape the investment policy of nonlife insurance companies. Portfolio managers typically work closely with the companies' tax advisors to measure and monitor the tax implications of various portfolio strategies.

Regulatory and Legal Considerations

While the insurance industry in general is heavily regulated, regulation of casualty company investments is relatively permissive. On the one hand, classes of eligible assets and quality standards for each class are specified just as they are for life companies. Also, the New York law, which is considered the most restrictive, requires that assets equal to 50 percent of unearned premium and loss reserves combined be maintained in "eligible bonds and mortgages." However, beyond these general restrictions, casualty insurance companies are permitted to invest the remainder of their assets in a relatively broad array of bonds, mortgages, stocks, and real estate, without restriction as to the amount invested in any particular class of assets (except that certain states impose limitations on real estate holdings).

A casualty company is not required to maintain a valuation reserve but is required to value both preferred and common stocks at market value. (Life companies, by contrast, are required only to value common stocks and non-sinking fund preferred stocks at market value.) In essence, then, the full impact of increases and decreases in the market value of stocks is reflected in the surplus of the casualty company.

Determination of Portfolio Policies

As in the case of life insurance companies, a limited tolerance for risk is the dominant factor determining investment policy for casualty companies. Because of contractual liabilities and difficulty in forecasting the cash flow from insurance operations, casualty companies seek some degree of safety from the assets offsetting insurance reserves. Indeed, the willingness to assume risk with the assets offsetting surplus has been moderated, or is at least subject to more careful management, as a result of the market volatility of recent years.

Over and above liquidity needs, which are clearly important, casualty insurance companies develop a significant portfolio of stocks and bonds and generate a high level of income to supplement or offset insurance underwriting gains and losses. Capital appreciation builds the surplus base and supports additional investment in the business. The structure of the bond portfolio between taxable and tax-exempt securities depends on the results of underwriting experience and tax regulation. In the past, when the insurance operation was profitable (and taxable), tax-exempts were sought; when the insurance operation was unprofitable (and taxes were minimized), taxable bonds were the choice. Under current (1989) tax regulations, casualty insurance companies derive far less of a tax advantage from tax-exempt securities at a time when underwriting results are favorable and the company overall is taxable.

To the extent that insurance operations were profitable and tax rates were relatively high, common stock policy in the past tended to emphasize yield to take advantage of the corporate dividend exclusion provisions of the U.S. tax code. Under recently changed U.S. laws, the tax benefits of dividend income and tax breaks for capital gains are limited. Common stocks do play a key role in the longer-term growth objectives of the casualty insurance industry as a source of both capital appreciation and expansion of the surplus base to support higher aggregate premium income levels. Also, as noted, the management of earnings as a result of flowing through realized gains and losses increases the importance of the managed common stock portfolio and creates the opportunity for using a total return or active management approach for some portion of the bond portfolio.

COMMERCIAL BANKS

Bank investment management is truly unique among the various institutions considered in this chapter. Unlike pension funds, endowment funds, and nonlife insurance companies, banks do not deal with essentially cost-free funds that are invested at a rate of return adequate to meet a specific purpose. Rather, generally they must purchase funds, often at considerable cost, with the expectation of reinvesting those funds at a rate higher than the borrowing cost. This spread, or margin, becomes the gross return to the bank.

Prior to the rapid inflation of the 1970s and early 1980s, investment portfolio management for banks around the world was largely a passive exercise. Liabilities, consisting of deposits and savings, were mostly uncontrollable, so asset management involved providing for primary and secondary reserves to meet legal requirements and providing liquidity for deposit withdrawals; the balance was then either lent in the form of commercial loans or consumer loans, or invested in fixed-income securities. However, the rapidly increasing rate of inflation, starting in the mid-1960s in the United States, created immense loan demands that could be met only by purchasing liabilities and managing both assets and liabilities to minimize interest rate risk and maximize the spread between interest rates. In fact, banks were the early pioneers of asset/liability management. Today investment management of banks has been further complicated by changing regulations and increasing competition, both within the banking industry and from insurance companies, brokerage houses, and other financial institutions.

Risk-Return Trade-Off

For practical purposes, money is a commodity and, thus, to a large extent, an undifferentiated product. This means that it is highly price sensitive—and price is the interest rate. In a perfect world, if interest rates were known to be rising, a lending institution would borrow long and lend short, thus freezing the cost of borrowed funds while the price of the product being sold—money—would rise, increasing the spread between the borrowing cost and the interest rate realized on assets. Contrarily, if interest rates were known to be falling, the bank would borrow short and lend long, freezing the return received while the cost of funds fell, again widening the spread between the two. However, the world is neither perfect nor predictable, as the wild fluctuation of interest rates in recent years has demonstrated.

In an effort to maximize profits in terms of the interest spread between borrowed liabilities and investable assets, banks around the world have undertaken to manage carefully both their assets and liabilities. This has led to the development of an interest *sensitivity ratio*, which is the ratio of interest sensitive assets to interest sensitive liabilities. The definition of this ratio is somewhat arbitrary. Whatever the definition, the lending institution makes its projections for interest rates and establishes this sensitivity ratio accordingly. For example, if interest rates are expected to rise, the ratio should be raised above parity or neutrality (1.0), to a point where interest sensitive assets moderately exceeded interest sensitive liabilities. This action would freeze the cost of liabilities (by borrowing more longer-term funds) while allowing the interest rate on earnings assets to rise on the faster rollover, with the result that the spread between the two would widen. Contrarily, if interest rates are expected to fall, the proportion of interest rate sensitive assets should be below parity, thus locking in high returns on the asset side (by lending long) while allowing the cost of liabilities to fall more rapidly (by borrowing and reborrowing short).

The risks inherent in these strategies are obvious. If the interest rate forecast is incorrect, the opposite result of what is intended occurs. During periods of unstable or uncertain interest rates, lending institutions generally try to equalize interest rate sensitive assets and liabilities to maintain the spreads at a constant level and reduce the risk of error. Doing so is not as simple as it seems because interest rates on assets tend to be more sensitive to change than are rates on liabilities. For example, many loans are tied to the prime rate; as the prime rate fluctuates so does the return on assets. Contrarily, interest rates on CDs are fixed for the entire maturity of the CD, and the lending institution must wait until maturity before that rate can be adjusted. Many banks have developed deposit instruments with variable rates to deal with this problem, but customer resistance has limited their acceptance. Customers prefer fixed-rate obligations and/or investment.

As the sensitivity ratio concept has evolved, banks have made a greater effort to manage spreads across specific maturity categories, not just in those that are purely interest rate sensitive, by changing the terms of the asset mix to conform more closely to those of the liability mix.

Liquidity Requirements

Banks maintain liquidity primarily to meet withdrawals of funds by depositors or provide loans to customers. In the latter case, the amounts may be controllable by the bank (e.g., in the case of making a new loan) or uncontrollable (e.g., in terms of customers drawing down lines of credit). There are two forms of liquidity for banks—internal and external. Internal liquidity refers to highly liquid assets that can be converted to cash quickly and made available to meet liquidity demands. Banks are generally in the fortunate position of having access to considerable external liquidity, either by borrowing under standby loan agreements with other institutions or by issuing securities such as CDs.

Banks must be careful not to overuse these various external sources, or they may impair their overall capital position to the detriment of the shareholders and perhaps even depositors. Impairment can result either from an excessive increase in debt relative to equity, placing the bank in a higher risk position, or from borrowing at high rates of interest relative to lending rates, which results in net losses, or from both. Thus, the manner in which liquidity is managed has an important role in the bank's overall profitability and stature with regulatory agencies, shareholders, and depositors.

In the final analysis, while it is important for a bank to have adequate liquidity, it is also important to diversify sources of liquidity to avoid undue leveraging of the bank's capital position.

Time Horizon

The time horizon for banks is obviously short term. Although some loans, particularly mortgages, are made over longer terms, the high volatility of interest rates over the past several years has changed the pattern of even this type of lending. Variable rate mortgages, short-term renewable mortgages with long-term amortization schedules, floating rate notes, and other creative types of instruments have helped to match the maturities or durations of assets and liabilities to reduce the interest rate risk. In the late 1980s, the typical U.S. bank was reluctant to issue CDs with a term beyond five years.

Regulatory and Legal Considerations

As U.S. banks made the transition from passive management of assets to far more sophisticated matching of assets and liabilities, one regulatory aspect created considerable difficulty. This was Regulation Q, which fixed the interest rates banks could pay on many of their liabilities. As interest rates rose rapidly in the 1970s and early 1980s and savings depositors became more aware of alternative, higher yielding investment opportunities, the whole complexion of liability management changed drastically. By the same token, usury laws in many states restricted the level of interest rates banks could charge on assets and also impacted on lending policies. Regulation eventually did provide for certificates of deposit tied to Treasury bill rates with maturities of six months to two-and-one-half years. To some extent, this enabled banks to compete for deposits that were being lured away from low-rate passbook savings accounts. The advent of money market funds provided further competition. Smaller low-rate passbook savings accounts were reduced or closed, to be replaced by large denomination, high-yielding CDs issued by the banks and bought by the money market funds. (In part, this was a recycling of funds, because many former passbook holders became money market fund holders.)

Regulation Q has been phased out and investment policies have been modified accordingly. Banks offer competitive interest-bearing deposit accounts to their customers and some banks are allowing proprietary money market funds (for which they are an investment advisor or subadvisor) to solicit certain of their customers.

In the late 1980s international regulatory requirements regarding capital adequacy (ratio of capital to assets) were increased and began to be phased in. These requirements are yet another constraint under which banks operate worldwide.

Unique Needs, Circumstances, and Preferences

Differences in unique needs, circumstances, and preferences revolve primarily around the size of banks, their localities, the mix of their uncontrollable liabilities (core deposits), and their individual skills in matching assets and liabilities in the most productive way. Small community banks, for example, may well have significant core deposits of relatively unsophisticated individual depositors that will stay with them. By the same token, they will likely be denied opportunities to purchase liabilities available to large money center banks.

Determination of Portfolio Policies

The success of a bank in increasing or maintaining profitability depends on its ability to manage its assets and liabilities in an environment of widely fluctuating interest rates. Portfolio policies reflect directly this central fact. Scenario forecasting has become an important decision tool, with bank economists developing several different interest rate scenarios based on forecasts of the economy and other factors bearing on interest rates and then assigning varying probabilities to these different scenarios. These scenarios then bear directly upon the investment policies established in terms of sensitivity ratios and the gaps between assets and liabilities at different maturity levels. It is desirable, where possible, to fix the spread between the cost of funds borrowed and the return on loans, thereby increasing the stability or predictability of bank earnings.

INVESTMENT COMPANIES

Investment companies, most of which are open-end or mutual funds (as contrasted with closed-end funds), are important institutional investors. However, because they are regarded more as conduits for investment funds—and thus more like actual investment vehicles—rather than as institutional investment entities, they are discussed only briefly here.

There are more than 2,000 mutual funds in the United States. Each has its own statement of objectives and policies. These may range from short-term liquidity, as in the case of money market funds, to more specialized objectives in such funds as aggressive growth, leveraged, option-using, specialized industry, single-asset category, or country focused funds. The latter are a relatively new but increasingly popular form of specialty fund. The objective of the country fund is to manage a portfolio of stocks or bonds originating in a particular country. These country funds provide investors with an avenue for global investing. Investors, whether individuals or institutions, may use mutual funds in various combinations to implement investment programs designed specifically to meet their own particular investment goals and objectives. By doing so, they are able to obtain diversification and professional management at a reasonable cost. Whether the investor's objectives require the use of cash equivalents, equities, real estate, fixed-income securities, foreign stocks, or foreign bonds, appropriate mutual fund vehicles are available.

The development of the money market fund will certainly be recorded as one of the great investment innovations of the 1970s, and perhaps even of the twentieth century. By Fall 1989, these funds exceeded $350 billion in total assets and were sponsored by a wide variety of investment management organizations, banks, and brokerage firms. They allow investors to pool their resources and, at modest cost, participate in (often) high-yielding, short-term investment instruments that previously would have been available only to large individual or institutional portfolios. Country funds may well emerge as yet another significant development in the annals of investment innovations.

The variety of mutual funds is impressive, indeed. Mutual funds, like portfolios of individual securities, may be used by individual and institutional investors to accommodate risk-return trade-offs as well as differential time horizons, liquidity needs, diversification, and tax requirements.

SUMMARY

Understanding the investment objectives, constraints, and policies of institutional investors is essential to understanding the portfolio management process.

Using the traditional building block analogy, the evaluation of investment objectives, constraints, and policies may be characterized as the foundation building stage of the portfolio management process. Construction begins with the establishment of objectives (the risk/return trade-off), followed by consideration of various investment constraints—including liquidity requirements, time horizon, taxes, regulatory and legal considerations, and the unique needs, circumstances, and preferences of each investor—and how these constraints affect or modify the risk/return relationship. This foundation is completed with the establishment of investment policies designed to meet each investor's objectives as modified by the constraints.

In discussing the broad variety of institutional investors, distinctions are drawn between those where the asset/liability relationships are rather clear and quantifiable, such as defined benefit pension plans, insurance companies, and banks, and those where these distinctions are far less clear and

less indentifiable, such as defined contribution retirement plans, endowments, and investment companies. All, however, can be accommodated
within the basic objectives and constraints framework.

FURTHER READING

When the Institute of Chartered Financial Analysts' Portfolio Management Review
Subcommittee reviewed the then-existing resources for the Chartered Financial Analyst (CFA) examination program, the whole area of investor objectives, constraints,
and policies—the subject of Chapters 3 and 4 of this revised edition—evidenced a
serious dearth of good material. While there were many good examples dealing with
specific, narrow subjects, the committee found no single source material that
"brought it all together." This chapter and the previous one represent a comprehensive effort to fill this gap and update the discussion of this subject as well as
capture the evolution of investment policies and procedures.

An enduring textbook on the subject of portfolio management, with particularly
good material on investor objectives, constraints, and policies, is Sauvain [1973].
Another important text, which has served as a major study resource for the CFA
program, is Cohen, Zinbarg, and Zeikel [1987].

Material about retirement funds generally tends to focus on a single subject such
as ERISA regulation, actuarial funding methods, and the like. One area that has been
almost totally lacking in coverage is profit-sharing (defined contribution) plans. Particularly useful in the preparation of this chapter were Ambachtsheer [1986] and Ezra
[1979]. Other background material on pension fund portfolio management can be
found in Vawter [1983]. The Employee Benefit Research Institute, Washington,
D.C., regularly produces a number of relevant employee benefits investments publications, including the *EBRI Quarterly Pension Investment Report* and the monthly
Issue Brief.

The rapid evolution in the management of endowment funds seems to have left
the written material behind, although there are occasional articles and chapters from
texts available. For good background material, Ford Foundation [1972], Kittell
[1987], and Williamson and Sanger [1980] are recommended.

If there has been a rapid evolution in the management of endowment funds,
then the changes in the management of insurance company assets can only be characterized as a revolution. Again, the written materials have not kept up with these
changes. Primary source materials are in the form of journal or newspaper articles.
Particularly useful in describing new techniques is Platt [1986]. Also useful are research papers produced by Atwood and Ohman [1983], Norris [1985], Tilley [1988],
and Weinberger and Kaminski [1989], as well as the ICFA seminar proceedings on
asset/liability management edited by Troughton [1986]. For background material on
insurance companies, see Maginn [1981].

Banks are also in a rapidly developing stage of asset/liability management and
Platt [1986] covers the current technology. Again, periodicals are a useful source.
See especially Binder [1980] and Miller [1980].

BIBLIOGRAPHY

Ambachtsheer, Keith P. "Pension Funds: Rich or Poor?," *Financial Analysts Journal*, March/April 1985.

———. *Pension Funds and the Bottom Line*. Homewood, Ill.: Dow Jones-Irwin, 1986.

———. "Pension Fund Asset Allocation: In Defense of a 60/40 Equity/Debt Asset Mix." *Financial Analysts Journal*, September/October 1987.

Andrews, Emily S. *The Changing Profile of Pensions in America*. Washington, D.C.: Employee Benefit Research Institute, 1985.

Arnott, Robert D., and Peter L. Bernstein. "The Right Way to Manage Your Pension Fund." *Harvard Business Review*, January/February 1988.

Arnott, Robert D., and Frank J. Fabozzi. *Asset Allocation*. Chicago: Probus, 1988.

Atwood, James A., and Carl R. Ohman. "Segmentation of Insurance Company General Accounts," in *Transactions of the Society of Actuaries*. Vol. 35, 1983.

Best's Insurance Management Reports. Oldwick, N.J.: A.M. Best Co., August 1989.

Binder, Barret F. "Asset/Liability Management." *The Magazine of Bank Administration*, November 1980.

Black, Fisher, and Moray Dewhurst. "A New Investment Strategy for Pension Funds." *The Journal of Portfolio Management*, Summer 1981.

Bodie, Zvi, and John B. Shoven. *Financial Aspects of the U.S. Pension System*. Chicago: The University of Chicago Press, 1983.

Bookstaber, Richard, and Jeremy Gold. "In Search of the Liability Asset." *Financial Analysts Journal*, January/February 1988.

Brenner, Lynn. "Can the Life Insurance Industry Survive?," *Institutional Investor*, September 1981.

Cohen, Jerome B., Edward D. Zinbarg, and Arthur Zeikel. *Investment Analysis and Portfolio Management*, 5th ed. Homewood, Ill.: Dow Jones-Irwin, 1987.

Doran, Phyllis A., Kenneth D. MacBain, and William A. Reimert. *Measuring and Funding Corporate Liabilities for Retiree Health Benefits*, an EBRI-ERF Study. Washington, D.C.: Employee Benefit Research Institute, 1987.

Drucker, Peter F. *The Unseen Revolution: How Pension Fund Socialism Came to America*. New York: Harper & Row, 1976.

Employee Benefit Research Institute. *EBRI Quarterly Pension Investment Report*. Washington, D.C., Fourth Quarter 1988.

Ezra, Don D. *Understanding Pension Fund Finance and Investment*. Toronto: The Pagurian Corp. Ltd., 1979.

———. "Economic Values: A Pension Pentateuch." *Financial Analysts Journal*, March/April 1988.

Ford Foundation Advisory Committee on Endowment Management. *Managing Education Endowments*, 2d ed., 1972.

Friedland, Martin. *Report of the Task Force on Inflation Protection for Employment Pension Plans*. Toronto: Queen's Printer for Ontario, 1988.

Frinquelli, A. Michael, and Margaret M. Alexander. "Investment Portfolios and Yields of Leading Publicly Held Property/Casualty Insurers: 1983–87." New York: Salomon Brothers, Inc., August 1988.

Gray, William S. III. "Pension Funds," in *Determinants of Investment Portfolio Policy*. Charlottesville, Va.: The Institute of Chartered Financial Analysts, 1981.

Harbrecht, Paul P. *Pension Funds and Economic Power*. New York: The Twentieth Century Fund, 1959.

Hendriksson, Roy D. "Portfolio Optimization Within a Surplus Framework," *Financial Analysts Journal*, March/April 1988.

Investment Bulletin. Washington, D.C.: American Council of Life Insurance, December 1988.

Ippolito, Richard A. *Pension, Economics, and Public Policy*. Homewood, Ill.: Dow Jones-Irwin, 1986.

———. "The Real Economic Burden of Corporate Pension Liabilities." *Financial Analysts Journal*, January/February 1986.

Joehnk, Michael D., ed. *Asset Allocation for Institutional Portfolios*. Seminar Proceedings. Charlottesville, Va.: The Institute of Chartered Financial Analysts, 1987.

Kittell, Cathryn E., ed. *The Challenges of Investing for Endowment Funds*. Seminar Proceedings. Charlottesville, Va.: The Institute of Chartered Financial Analysts, 1987.

Leibowitz, Martin L. "Total Portfolio Duration: A New Perspective on Pension Fund Asset Allocation." *Financial Analysts Journal*, September/October 1986.

———. "Pension Fund Asset Allocation Through Surplus Management." *Financial Analysts Journal*, March/April 1987a.

———. "Liability Returns: A New Look at Asset Allocation." *The Journal of Portfolio Management*, Winter 1987b.

———. *A New Perspective on Asset Allocation*. Charlottesville, Va.: The Institute of Chartered Financial Analysts, 1987c.

Life Insurance Fact Book. Washington, D.C.: American Council of Life Insurance, 1989.

Mall, Robert T. "A Plan Sponsor's View of Asset/Liability Integration." *The Investment Management Review*, November/December 1987.

Malley, Susan L., and Susan Jayson. "Why Do Financial Executives Manage Pension Funds the Way They Do?" *Financial Analysts Journal*, November/December 1986.

Maginn, John L. "Insurance Companies," in *Determinants of Investment Portfolio Policy*. Charlottesville, Va.: The Institute of Chartered Financial Analysts, 1981.

Miller, Donald C. "New Opportunities in Liquidity Management." Paper presented at a symposium on future sources of lendable funds for agricultural banks, Kansas City, Mo., December 9, 1980.

Mitchell, Karlyn. "Interest Rate Risk Management at Tenth District Banks." *Economic Review*, The Federal Reserve Bank of Kansas City, May 1985.

Noris, Peter D. "Asset/Liability Strategies for Property and Casualty Companies." New York: Morgan Stanley & Co., May 1985.

Platt, Robert B. *Controlling Interest Rate Risk*. New York: John Wiley & Sons, 1986.

Rowan, Malcolm. *In Whose Interest?: A Report on Public Sector Pension Fund Investing*. Toronto: Queen's Printer for Ontario, 1987.

Sauvain, Harry C. *Investment Management*, 4th ed. Englewood Cliffs, N.J.: Prentice-Hall, 1973.

Segerstrom, John R. "Use Net Interest Margin to Manage Interest Rate Risk." *ABA Journal*, July 1984.

Sharpe, William F. "Integrated Asset Allocation." *Financial Analysts Journal*, October/November 1987.

Shultz, Robert E. "The National Investment Sponsor Federation Comes of Age." *The Investment Management Review*, March/April 1988.

Tilley, James A. "The Application of Modern Techniques to the Investment of Insurance and Pension Funds." New York: Morgan Stanley & Co., November 1988.

Treynor, Jack L., Patrick J. Regan, and William W. Priest. *The Financial Reality of Pension Funding Under ERISA*. Homewood, Ill.: Dow Jones-Irwin, 1976.

Troughton, George H., ed. *Asset/Liability Management*. Seminar Proceedings. Charlottesville, Va.: The Institute of Chartered Financial Analysts, 1986.

Vawter, Jay. "Endowment Funds," in *Determinants of Investment Portfolio Policy*. Charlottesville, Va.: The Institute of Chartered Financial Analysts, 1981.

Wagner, Wayne H. "The Many Dimensions of Risk." *The Journal of Portfolio Management,* Winter 1988.

Weinberger, Alfred, and Vincent Kaminski. "Investment Strategy for Property/Casualty Insurance Companies: The Fixed-Income Portfolio After Tax Reform." New York: Salomon Brothers, Inc., March 1989.

Williamson, J. Peter, and Hazel A.D. Sanger. "Educational Endowment Funds," in Summer N. Levine, ed. *The Investment Manager's Handbook*. Homewood, Ill.: Dow Jones-Irwin, 1980.

Part III
Expectational Factors

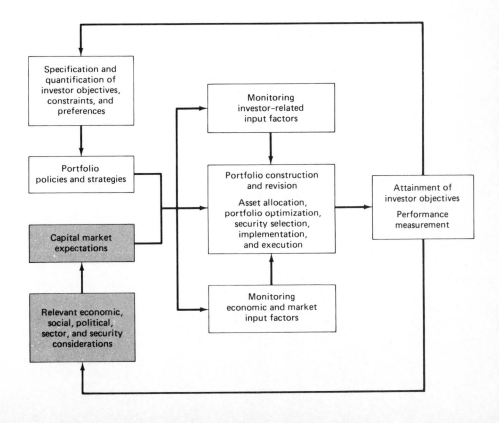

CHAPTER 5

Capital Market Expectations: The Macro Factors

Jeffrey J. Diermeier, CFA

OVERVIEW

Having explored the preferences of individual and institutional investors, it is time to turn to the other major set of inputs to the portfolio decision-making process: expectations of returns and risk available in the marketplace. The process of forming expectations is a two-step process. The first step, forming macro or capital market expectations, is covered in this chapter and is heavily used in the asset allocation process discussed in Chapter 7. The second step, forming micro or individual asset expectations, is covered in the next chapter and is critical to the bond, stock, and real estate portfolio decisions discussed in Chapters 8, 9, and 10.

In the first section of this chapter the expectational needs of the analyst and portfolio manager are spelled out. The second section frames the forecasting of asset class returns by creating a mechanism to generate aggregate capital market expectations and then dividing returns among the asset classes. Global output limits the "returns" available to all of the components in the production process. Once the aggregate return is defined, what remains is a competition within and across national boundaries for share among equity shareholders, debt holders, landowners, laborers, and the tax authorities—the factors of production.

The third section addresses long- and short-term expectations regarding the macroeconomic variables that feed into the framework. The fourth section delves into a particularly powerful macrovariable, inflation, and its impact on the capital markets. Finally, the fifth section describes the use of scenario forecasting of macro variables as a convenient way to organize the input of economic expectations into the investment process.

THE EXPECTATIONS-FORMING PROCESS

Investing requires forming expectations about the risks and rewards associated with the outlay of capital. In fact, the decision of whether or not to invest requires weighing the expected benefits of investing against the pleasures of consuming. Two key aspects of economic expectations involve the importance of consensus expectations and the macro variables that produce those expectations.

The Consensus Process

The aggregate consensus sets the market prices for all securities in capitalistic systems. This is done under the relatively democratic approach of one dollar, one vote. The consensus judges the positives and negatives of each security and sets prices accordingly. If the consensus opinion proves to be correct, returns are as anticipated. If consensus expectations are not met, the consensus outlook is revised and security prices change as a new consensus expectation emerges. It is through changes in consensus expectations that windfall profits or losses are made. These windfall profits are the stuff of successful professional active management.

A relatively small set of key macro variables will drive the performance of broadly diversified portfolios. This assertion is supported by a substantial body of research describing period to period changes in security returns. (See Sharpe [1964], Lintner [1965], Mossin [1966], King [1966], Black, Jensen, and Scholes [1972], and Farrell [1975].) As a result, the investor can focus his attention on a relatively small list of macro variables and their associated expectations for maximum efficiency.

How expectations are formed is a subject of much study in the field of cognitive psychology. Unfortunately, the study of macroeconomic expectations is seriously hampered by a lack of good quality expectational data bases. Empirical testing of economic theory relies heavily on actual data with only proxies for what expectations might have been. Only when macroeconomic expectational data bases have been more fully developed will there be a much better understanding and verification of the linkage of economic expectations and capital market returns.

FORECASTING THE CAPITAL MARKET ENVIRONMENT

There are two distinct and different needs for expectations in the investing process. The first involves the needs of the security analyst, whose job it is to correctly evaluate the return and risk potential of the individual security. The second involves the needs of the portfolio manager, whose job it is to organize client objectives and security return/risk input into the building and maintaining of portfolios. Both have specific but overlapping macro expectational needs.

Forecasting Inputs for the Analyst

The primary macro-expectational needs of the security analyst can be determined by reviewing a standard valuation model used to make security valuations. A general model that covers all securities must include the forecasting of cash flows generated by the security and a discount mechanism to bring those future cash flows back to a present value. The requirements hold for bond, real estate, and other analysis as well as equities, as discussed in Chapter 6.

   The Standard Valuation Model. Table 5-1 displays a generalized valuation model that should be viewed as an elaboration on J.B. Williams's [1938] net present value model. Williams's model is a perpetual or infinite-life model where every cash flow to the investor is discounted back to the present. Table 5-1 simplifies Williams's model by providing for specific point forecasts of cash flows in the first N years and then adopts the conventional perpetual model simplification at the end of year N to generate a discounted present value for all cash flows beyond year N.

   This two-stage model is used by practitioners as a way to take current cash flows and grow them at some abnormal rate to a period in which normal growth would occur. The focus of the model is on the expected cash flow to the investor. There are terms to convert each cash flow to the investor's desired currency. Cash flows here are defined as the income that can be expected to be returned to the investor after all appropriate senior payments have been satisfied and an allowance for capital replacement and growth is made.

   The analyst is charged with generating the inputs to this model. What macro variables will be of interest to him? Clearly, macro variables impacting cash flows, foreign exchange rates, and discount rates are important.

   Cash Flow Forecasting. The forecasting of cash flows requires the analyst to determine the revenue stream to be generated by the underlying company and to simultaneously and iteratively apportion the company's revenue across competing inputs of labor, raw materials, rents, interest, taxes, and profits. Because these inputs are often dictated in good measure by the macro environment, a hierarchy of expectations is needed. A forecast of the national income accounts sets the economy-wide environment for the basic demand for the company's products as well as supply/demand interaction of labor income, rents, interest, taxes, and profit. Table 5-2 displays

TABLE 5-1. Standardized Valuation Model

V_E	$=$	V_{S1}	$+$	V_{S2}

or in words,

estimated value of asset	$=$	discounted value in growth to normal stage	$+$	discounted value of normal stage

where,

$$V_{S1} \quad = \quad \sum_{T=1}^{N} \frac{CF_T(\$/FX)_T}{(1+k)^T}$$

discounted value of growth to normal stage	$=$	each period's cash flow in local currency adjusted to the currency of investor's choice (e.g., dollars), as shown below, discounted to the present at an appropriate discount rate for the investor

where,

$$(\$/FX)_T \quad = \quad \left(\prod_{T=1}^{N} (1 + (I_{US})) \right) \Big/ \left(\prod_{T=1}^{N} (1 + I_{FOR}) \right)$$

currency adjusted in time T	$=$	cumulative growth of U.S. inflation from time 0 to time T divided by the cumulative growth of local currency inflation over the same period

and where,

$$V_{S2} \quad = \quad \frac{(CF_{N+1}(\$/FX)_{N+1})/(k_L - (G + ((\$/FX) - 1))}{(1 + k)^N}$$

discounted value of normal stage	$=$	cash flow in the first period of the normal stage, adjusted to the currency of choice for inflation up to that point, divided by the difference between the appropriate long-term discount rate and the normal growth rate of the asset plus an adjustment for long-term relative currency movement; this quantity discounted back from period N to the present at an appropriate discount rate.

recent proportions and historical growth of the major segments of the U.S. national income accounts, deflated by subtracting the Consumer Price Index (CPI) across the board. It illustrates the dominance of labor income relative to income paid out in the form of net interest, corporate profits, rent, or proprietor's income, as well as growth since 1929, the earliest date for the data.

Underlying the forecast of the national income accounts must be a forecast of growth typified by a forecast of the Gross National Product (GNP).

TABLE 5-2. 1988 National Income Accounts and Their 1929–1988 Growth

	1988 Level (Billions)	1988 Percentage of Total	Inflation Adjusted Annual Growth[a]			
			1929–1988	1929–1945	1945–1970	1970–1988
National Income	$3,968.2	100.0%	3.4%	4.5%	3.1%	2.7%
Compensation of employees	2,904.7	73.2	3.8	5.3	3.5	2.6
Wages and salaries	2,436.9	61.4	3.5	5.0	3.2	2.2
Supplements including employer contribution to Social Security	467.8	11.8	12.8	13.7	7.1	5.0
Proprietor's income	324.5	8.2	2.1	4.6	0.6	1.7
Farm	36.3	0.9	-0.2	4.1	-2.5	-1.2
Nonfarm	288.2	7.3	2.9	4.9	1.8	2.2
Rental income	19.3	0.5	-0.9	-0.3	2.1	-6.1
Net interest	391.5	9.9	4.5	-5.0	9.2	6.9
Corporate profits	328.1	8.3	2.9	4.2	2.3	2.2
Profits tax liability	142.6	3.6	4.9	13.1	1.6	1.8
Profits after tax	163.8	4.1	1.8	0.0	3.1	1.5
Dividends	104.5	2.6	1.7	-1.8	3.4	2.5
Undistributed profits	59.2	1.5	2.0	2.6	2.8	0.1
Inventory valuation adjustment	-23.8	-0.6	b	b	b	b
Capital consumption adjustment	45.6	1.1	b	b	b	b
Consumer Price Index	b	b	3.3	0.4	3.2	6.4

SOURCE: Bureau of Economic Analysis, U.S. Department of Commerce [1986 and 1989], Economic Report of the President [1989], and First Chicago Investment Advisors.
a Deflated by subtracting CPI.
b Entry not meaningful.

TABLE 5-3. 1988 Gross National Product and Its Components and Their 1929–1988 Growth

	1988 Level (Billions)	1988 Percentage of Total	Inflation Adjusted Annual Growth[a]			
			1929–1988	1929–1945	1945–1970	1970–1988
Gross National Product	$4,864.3	100.0%	3.0%	4.1%	2.3%	2.8%
Personal consumption	3,227.5	66.4	2.9	1.4	3.8	3.1
Durable goods	451.1	9.3	4.0	-2.1	7.2	5.3
Nondurable goods	1,046.9	21.5	2.5	2.7	2.7	2.0
Services	1,729.6	35.6	3.0	0.6	4.3	3.4
Gross private domestic investment	766.5	15.8	2.8	-3.7	6.6	3.6
Nonresidential	488.4	10.0	2.8	-1.4	5.2	3.5
Structures	142.8	2.9	1.4	-4.3	5.8	0.7
Equipment	345.6	7.1	3.9	1.3	4.8	4.9
Residential	229.7	4.7	2.9	-7.2	9.7	3.2
Change in business inventories	48.4	1.0	b	b	b	b
Net exports of goods and services	-94.6	-1.9	b	b	b	b
Exports	519.7	10.7	4.3	-1.1	6.7	6.0
Imports	614.4	12.6	4.8	2.3	5.5	6.1
Government purchases	964.9	19.8	3.7	13.4	-0.8	1.7
Federal	381.0	7.8	5.0	24.8	-3.4	1.1
National defense	298.4	6.1	NA	NA	NA	NA
Nondefense	82.6	1.7	NA	NA	NA	NA
State and local	583.9	12.0	3.1	-0.5	6.0	2.2

SOURCE: Bureau of Economic Analysis, U.S. Department of Commerce [1986 and 1989] and First Chicago Investment Advisors.
a Deflated using GNP Deflators.
b Entry not meaningful.

See Table 5-3. This forecast of the total growth of the economy, when put into some detail, also provides forecasts for various sectors of the economy. For example, the typical economic forecast will provide detail at several levels of personal consumption and capital expenditures. This requires an understanding of the linkages between aggregate growth in output and the growth of sectors. Sectoral growth can be further disaggregated to obtain industry growth. The analyst then forecasts specific company revenues and resulting cash flows on a micro basis.

The domestic sector/industry analyst can, after making adjustments for accounting and reporting convention purposes, directly translate aggregate economic activity and national income forecast into forecasts of cash flows appropriate to a sector or industry.

The global analyst must go a step further and translate foreign cash flows into the currency of choice. This is purely a macro variable phenomenon based on forecasts of foreign exchange rates. Foreign exchange rates are written as a function of differential inflation rates in the standardized valuation model.

Comparability of Cash Flows. The global analyst must deal with an additional level of complexity when forecasting cash flows: comparability. First, the analyst must be able to convert forecasted cash flows into the specified currency of interest if cross-market comparisons are desired. It is crucial that the inputs to valuation be constructed so that meaningful comparisons can be derived. Second, reported cash flows across countries are not comparable because of different international accounting conventions, and therefore adjustments need to be made. The following list shows a number of accounting items where differences frequently arise. Many of these differences arise because U.S. firms have two sets of books, one for tax purposes and one for reporting. In most other countries, only one set of books is maintained.

- Consolidation
- Goodwill
- Depreciation
- Foreign currency
- Deferred taxes
- Reserves
- Inventory
- Asset revaluation
- Extraordinary items
- Earnings per share

For example, major differences in U.S. versus Japanese accounting relate to depreciation method, deferred income tax, foreign exchange gain or loss recognition and, until recently, methods of consolidating statements. The lack of comparability is illustrated in Table 5-4, which indicates the proportion of U.S. and Japanese firms using accelerated and straight line depreciation for reporting purposes. In Japan, reported earnings are based on accelerated depreciation, whereas U.S. firms use straight-line depreciation

TABLE 5-4. Comparison of Japanese and U.S. Depreciation Techniques in the Mid-1980s

Japan Method	1983		United States Method	1986	
	No.	Percentage		No.	Percentage
Declining balance	209	69.7%	Declining balance	49	6.4%
Straight line	19	6.3	Straight line	561	73.7
Combination					
Declining balance					
and straight line	53	17.7	Sum of the year's digits	14	1.8
Other	19	6.3	Accelerated method	77	10.1
			Unit of production and other	48	6.3
			Other	12	1.6
Total companies	300	100.0%	Total companies	761	100.0%

SOURCE: Nikko International [1989] and *Accounting Trends & Techniques, 1987* [1988].

for reporting purposes. In 1987, Nikko Securities estimated that earnings in the Nikkei 225 would have been 78 percent higher had depreciation techniques been comparable to those used in the United States.

The major accounting differences between the United Kingdom and the United States are U.K. purchase accounting, deferred taxes, and foreign exchange gain/loss recognition. For example, as in Japan, U.K. companies recognize foreign exchange (forex) gains and losses only at the resolution of a multiperiod contract rather than at the end of each reporting period, the method used in the United States. In West Germany, depreciation is highly accelerated relative to the United States. Other West German differences arise in treatment of investment in subsidiaries and reserving for contingency losses not allowed in the United States. For example, when showing consolidated statements only, domestic German subsidiaries must be consolidated under current accounting rules (scheduled to change in 1990). However, worldwide consolidation is required in the United States. Furthermore, until 1990, investment in subsidiaries is accounted for at book value with no "goodwill" technique to expense outlays greater than book value. As to reserving for contingency losses, German companies can provide reserves that reduce income and raise liabilities when a loss or future expense appears possible. In the United States, contingency reserves are prohibited, but reserves can be made when a loss is probable and estimable.

Overall, earnings tend to be overstated in the United Kingdom relative to the United States and understated in Japan and West Germany.

The Discount Mechanism. The analyst must also determine the rate at which to discount future cash flows. As originally suggested by Fisher [1930], the convention is to break down the discount rate into three key components.

Discount Rate (DR) = Real Risk-Free Interest Rate (RRFR)

+ Inflation Premium (IP) + Risk Premium (RP)

The real risk-free rate of interest and inflation premium forecasts combine to provide the analyst with the nominal risk-free rate. All that is needed is a forecast of an appropriate risk premium for the security or asset class. This requires a forecast of risk and a theory for describing what types of risk are likely to be compensated for in the marketplace. All methods of risk assessment make the assumption that risk results from changes in the consensus opinion of the variables that impact the standardized valuation model. For example, future cash flows, inflation rates and even the perceived real risk-free rate of interest are not known with certainty and may therefore shift in an unexpected manner. Shifts in the consensus can result in losses to the investor. The prospect of loss is what risk is all about.

Total risk can be separated into subcomponents that relate to the types of risk involved.[1]

Total Risk (TR) = Inflation Risk (IR) + Currency Risk (CR)

+ Cash Flow Risk (CFR)

Cash flow risk can, in turn, be broken down into two more subcomponents.

Cash Flow Risk (CFR) = Sovereign Risk (SR)

+ Private Cash Flow (Default) Risk (PCFR)

Because of the need to develop estimates of appropriate risk premiums, it is not enough for the analyst to have only point forecasts of key macro variables. He also needs to know a probabilistic range of outcomes for the critical variables in his analysis because this will impact his analysis of risk and risk premiums.

The investor should also know the covariance or correlation matrix of the underlying macro variables. For example, if high inflation is almost always related to a slowdown in cash flows available to investors, the risk to investors of an unexpected surge in inflation is transmitted through both the numerator and denominator of the standardized valuation model. To date, such matrices do not generally exist. The investor should also know about other variables related to the risk premium such as liquidity premiums, tax premiums, and the like, which are beyond the scope of this section. (See Ibbotson, Diermeier, and Siegel [1984].)

Bond and Real Estate Analysts

The same general expectations must be set for the analyst of bonds and real estate as well, although focus points may vary. The valuation formula in Table 5-1 is just as appropriate.

Bond Analysis. The cash flows of fixed-income securities are generally relatively easy to identify, with the last cash flow, the repayment of principal, typically being large relative to the regular coupon payments. The discount rate is composed of a real risk-free interest rate, an inflation premium, and a risk premium.

The risk premium is potentially a function of the four components of risk listed earlier. Bonds can be categorized by the risk matrix in Figure 5-1.

---

[1] Note that because the real risk-free interest rate varies over time it can be argued that it is a source of uncertainty and, hence, a source of risk premium. It is not included here for the purpose of simplicity.

	Government	Nongovernment
Domestic	Inflation Risk	Inflation Risk Private Cash Flow Risk
Foreign	Inflation Risk Currency Risk Sovereign Risk	Inflation Risk Currency Risk Sovereign Risk Private Cash Flow Risk

Figure 5-1. Bond Risk Matrix.

Included in this matrix are the types of risks that feed into the estimates of risk premiums for bonds of various types.

Private cash flow risk (PCFR) in bonds is typically called default risk. Because the number of company defaults is highly correlated with the condition of the economy, this variable is highly influenced by forecasted economic conditions. The distribution of potential value from default does not follow a normal bell-shaped distribution, but instead is more amenable to option pricing theory. This is because, in essence, shareholders own a put contract with which, at a certain value of the firm, they can put the firm to the bondholder and violate their principal obligation. In a portfolio context, however, according to the Central Limit Theorem, the portfolio's default risk may more closely resemble a normal distribution.

Real Estate Analysis. The real estate analyst also uses a valuation model similar to that in Table 5-1. In practice, it is not unusual for the first stage of the valuation model to be 10 years in length. Often the second stage in the equation reduces to capitalizing the expected net operating income from a real estate project by a "cap" rate. As discussed in Chapter 10, the cash flow section of real estate analysis is more subject to regional conditions than national or global conditions because of the lack of mobility and substitutability of the basic product. This means that macroeconomic forecasts must be translated into regional consequences using regional economic data for proper analysis.

To sum up, the analyst needs to have at his disposal a set of macroeconomic expectations that establish:

1. The future amount of income an economy can generate, allocated across the factors of production and different productive sectors;
2. The prospects for growth of the economy;
3. The potential for shifts in the share of income within the economy;

4. A way to translate future cash flows into the currency of choice; and

5. Assumptions for future rates of interest and inflation.

In addition, he needs to know the risk associated with these expectations, because those fundamental risks will translate into the risk premium of the individual security.

Forecasting Inputs for the Portfolio Manager

The macro needs of the portfolio manager come from his duty to match the goals of the investor with the appropriate set of available investment vehicles. Under ideal conditions, this involves working with the client to determine the proper amount to be invested, how assets are to be allocated across class lines, and whether to use active versus passive management. It may also involve how assets are to be invested across economic factor lines. For example, some investors, such as life insurance companies, want to control their exposure to changes in interest rates for asset/liability management purposes.

Client Preferences. A portfolio manager works with the client to make the difficult decision of how much to consume today versus investing for consumption later. The portfolio manager needs to provide a set of expectations and associated probabilities for the relevant set of investment vehicles, at least at the asset class level. Through one or more optimization techniques, the manager can show the client, for an array of different risk levels, potential returns in exchange for current consumption. It is imperative that the data are inflation-adjusted so that the client can see the trade-off between present and future consumption of real goods and services.

A specific time horizon constraint is sometimes imposed when the client needs to have money withdrawn at set dates. This requires the portfolio manager's set of macro expectations to be very time specific. The development of a solid set of macro expectations is extremely important in deciding whether the investment portfolio should be handled under a "going concern" or "liability matching" philosophy as discussed in Chapter 4. For example, the decision to buy a five-year bond with a known nominal payoff to meet estimated pension payments in year five should be weighed against the probability of generating a better nominal return with a more risky portfolio for the same time horizon. Capital market expectations for the more risky portfolio are crucial.

Furthermore, at the institutional level, many of today's investment portfolios are pension funds created under legal requirements to meet the needs of present and future retirees. In the development of projections of future benefit payments, macro forecasts of inflation and wage/salary growth are crucial assumptions.

Requirements for Asset Allocation. The portfolio manager is faced with four key questions.

1. What asset classes should be included or excluded from investment consideration?
2. How should the selected asset classes be weighted?
3. How should the sectors or groupings of securities within the asset classes be weighted?
4. What specific securities should be held and in what amounts?

The first two are asset allocation questions. *Asset class* refers to investments that are of a common financial form such as common stocks, bonds, and real estate. Substantial empirical evidence has demonstrated that investments of a common financial form perform in a significantly similar fashion. The first question involves determining what asset classes are worthy of potential investment. A satisfactory answer requires being able to put together an adequate set of capital market expectations for each asset class.

The second question involves asset class weightings and can be broken down into two components. The first has to do with setting long-range investment policy. Take, for example, a pension situation where there is a corporate pension committee and one or more investment managers investing the pension's assets. For purposes of planning and control, the committee representatives establish policies so that the managers will know what the strategic, long-run, or normal policy asset allocation is to be.

The second component involves establishing policies that define the degree to which asset allocation weights can deviate from normal to reflect interim investment strategy. This deviation from the normal or strategic is termed active or tactical asset allocation. See Chapter 7 for a complete discussion of these issues.

One of the approaches typically used to determine policy weights is mean-variance optimization as developed by Markowitz [1959]. This requires relatively long-term estimates of return, standard deviations, and cross-correlations for each asset class. Long-term estimates are used because the policy setting process by nature requires some continuity over time.

Active asset allocation is undertaken when asset class weights are shifted away from the normal policy allocation to take advantage of shorter-term opportunities. Referring back to Table 5-1, the basic model provides a framework for strategic asset allocation based on intrinsic values.

Factor Forecasts. The third question faced by the portfolio manager is how to invest in sectors or groupings of securities within or across asset

TABLE 5-5. Regression Coefficients for Selected Independent Economic Variables and the Associated Return Performance of 20 Equally Weighted Portfolios Based on 1958–1984 Monthly Data

Independent Variable	Coefficient (t Statistic)
Month-to-month growth in industrial production	13.589
	(3.561)
Change in expected inflation	−0.125
	(−1.640)
Unanticipated inflation	−0.629
	(−1.979)
Unanticipated change in spread in return between low- and high-grade bonds	7.205
	(2.590)
Unanticipated changes in the spread in return of the long government bond and Treasury bill	−5.211
	(−1.690)
Constant	4.124
	(1.361)

SOURCE: Chen, Roll, and Ross [1983].

classes. Researchers have long noted that securities having common characteristics perform similarly. King [1966] found this for the common characteristic now known as the industry factor. Farrell [1975] showed strong commonality of performance across securities falling into cyclical, growth, defensive, and energy sectors. Rosenberg [1974], Sharpe [1982], and others found other common characteristics to be useful in explaining security performance.

Arbitrage Pricing Theory (APT) as developed by Ross [1976] suggests that there are a limited number of nondiversifiable factors that drive security prices. Exposure to them means exposure to a potentially adverse shift (i.e., to risk). Nondiversifiable or systematic risk is part of the justification for the risk premium. The initial work of Ross [1976] and Roll and Ross [1980] established the theory and presence of factors but did not relate specific economic variables to the factors themselves. Later work has attempted to do so.

Most attempts at relating macro variables to the capital markets in the APT sense have involved tests of the U.S. stock market. Chen, Roll, and Ross [1983], in a key piece, built upon the basic structure of APT to relate relatively independent macro variables that could be expected to have broad influence over many companies' cash flows and discount rates. The macro variables found to be useful in describing stock market portfolio returns are shown in Table 5-5.

Their work suggests that unexpected changes in economic activity, inflation expectations, quality spreads, and the term structure of interest rates will directly affect stock portfolio performance. The table indicates that portfolios that were estimated to have a concurrent positive beta on unanticipated changes in industrial production have, over time, been compensated for the exposure to that economic factor. This suggests an awareness by the aggregate market of credit or default risks or, in our terms, cash flow risk. Similarly, securities whose returns respond in the same direction as the spread in return on low-grade versus high-grade bonds have been compensated in a statistically significant fashion.

Stocks, which historically have done well when inflation jumps in an unanticipated manner, underperformed. This suggests that companies that are in fact viewed as relative inflation hedges are desirable. By contrast, stocks that are perceived to not be inflation hedges are undesirable and therefore systematically compensated for that risk. The change in the expected inflation variable provides a similar interpretation. The interpretation of the term structure variable is less clear, given the interaction with the other independent variables in the regression analysis.

Kim and Wu [1987], using a different approach, concluded that there are classes of macro variables influencing systematic stock returns. These classes include a general economy-wide group, an interest rate/money supply group and a labor group. Cho, Eun, and Senbet [1986] attempted to estimate common factors applied to international stock markets. Their work suggests that there may be three or four worldwide common factors and, furthermore, that the degree to which two countries may have factors in common may depend on the degree of economic integration between the two countries.

Finally, most of the APT tests use concurrent data to uncover the relationship of economic macro variables and security pricing. There is, however, some suggestion that these same variables, possibly due to auto-correlative structures of economic and market variation, may have predictive power over market returns. Harvey [1988], using lagged variables, found significant relationships between stock portfolio returns and a version of Chen, Roll, and Ross' term premium and default premium. These results imply that when bond quality spreads are unusually wide, the likelihood of positive subsequent stock market performance is higher than when spreads are low. This suggests a business cycle influence on the market. See Chapter 13 for some additional statistical evidence of the relationship of changes in macro variables and changes in capital market return/risk expectations.

In summary, the portfolio manager needs economic input to: (1) address the four key questions inherent in portfolio management and (2) provide assistance in the ultimate determination of the client's willingness to trade off current for future consumption. Macroeconomic variable expectations are crucial in establishing long-term asset class returns and risk expectations for policy asset allocation purposes as well as for active or tactical asset allocation. Macroeconomic expectations may lead directly to portfolio decisions concerning investment factors or groupings of securities that are sensitive to changes in the economic landscape. Finally, through the efforts

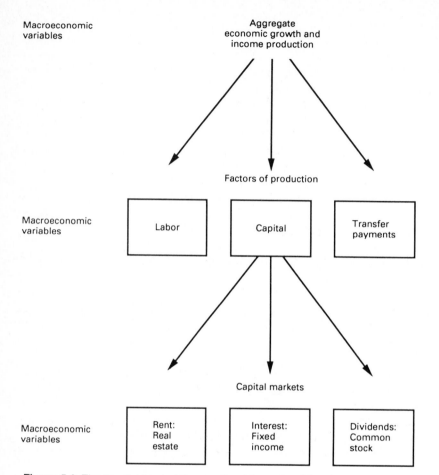

Figure 5-2. The Capital Market Forecasting Hierarchy. SOURCE: First Chicago Investment Advisors.

of the analyst and his use of macroeconomic information, the portfolio manager makes investment-specific decisions.

FRAMING THE FORECAST BY ASSET CLASS

Having identified the macro forecasting needs of the analyst and the portfolio manager, a structure is needed to organize macroeconomic input into the capital market return forecasting process. Figure 5-2 breaks the capital market forecasting process into three levels: (1) aggregate output and income production; (2) allocations to key factors of production; and (3) income distribution to the broad categories of the capital market. In the next section

of this chapter, the forecasting of macroeconomic variables as they relate
to the three levels of the hierarchy will be addressed.

In Figure 5-2, *the hierarchy begins with the fact that total output defines
and constrains the income and hence the return available to all economic
participants.* All subsequent analysis is, in essence, a form of competitive
analysis, to determine who gets what share of the aggregate pie. At the first
level down, the competition is at the factor of production level. At the lowest
level in the figure, the returns to the capital market are subdivided by asset
class primarily as a function of the demand for the characteristics of the
asset classes.

This framework is useful in understanding how forecasts of long-term
returns can be put together on a conceptual level. At the end of this section,
the empirical investment characteristics (i.e., risk, return, cross-correlation,
and autocorrelation) of the major asset classes will be expanded.

The Long-Term Setting

The secular setting in which investment expectations are set will follow the
three-pronged approach of determining aggregate economic output, shares
to the factors of production, and allocation by asset class.

Aggregate Economic Output. Williams' [1938] Law of the Conservation of Value, like the Law of the Conservation of Matter, states that real
wealth can only be derived from the production of goods and services. The
packaging of wealth, or the form it is in, does not affect its total real value.
For example, debasing the currency or inflating prices does not create or
destroy value in the first order. To understand and forecast growth in wealth,
the investor must be able to forecast aggregate output. In equilibrium, the
return potential from the aggregate capital market will be governed by the
ability of the economy to produce output, as empirically documented by
Ibbotson, Diermeier, and Siegel [1984].

Real Interest and Growth Rates. It is no accident that Irving Fisher
suggested 3 percent as the real risk-free rate of interest. Fisher was con-
ditioned by the ability of the broad economy to generate a real return on
capital. Three percent was chosen as it roughly corresponded to the historic
real growth of aggregate economic output.

A supply side view is taken in forecasting long-term output growth. That
is, the focus is on the ability of the factors of production to generate goods
and services, hence income and wealth. The supply of total income and
therefore returns available to investors is related to the productivity of all
labor and capital. Putting this idea in notational form will be helpful when
comparing aggregate economic returns to the more limited case of capital

market returns. Equation 5-1 below states that the return in the aggregate economy is a function of society's current consumption and the growth in wealth.

$$R = (C + \Delta W) / W$$

| R Society's return | C Society's current consumption | ΔW Change in the volume of society's wealth | W Society's wealth | (5-1) |

Economic Wealth. Wealth is defined as including all human capital, as well as conventional notions of wealth. Society's dividend (or current income not reinvested) is properly labeled "consumption," because it is the true net income yield that is taken out of the system and used up. It includes measures of personal consumption, depreciation, and government consumption.

By making simplifying assumptions of constant growth and discount rates, as in the Gordon-Shapiro dividend discount model, society's wealth from period to period will grow with the expected consumptive power of the economy, which should grow in line with the overall economy. Constant growth and discount rate assumptions are not unreasonable when working with long-term forecasts. Therefore:

$$G = \Delta W/W$$

| G Growth in GNP | $\Delta W/W$ Growth in society's wealth | (5-2) |

Country Specific vs. Global. Ideally, forecasts of aggregate growth would be done at the global level. Growth and income could then be subdivided into country components much like the income of the United States can be divided into components by state. Unfortunately, most aggregate forecasting is done at the country (national) level, with the foreign component treated as an exogenous factor of production and source of demand. This analysis will follow the national convention, but will consider global ramifications.

One of the difficulties arising from starting the process at the national level involves binding local country returns too tightly to local growth. For example, a 6 percent growth economy would then generate aggregate returns to its society of roughly 6 percent per annum. A one percent growth economy would generate a return of one percent. Clearly, if capital and product mobility existed between two such countries, capital and goods would flow so as to even out the returns of the two countries. The issue is the degree of integration of the global economy. Without integration, unbalanced return opportunities could exist for lack of means of arbitrage.

Shares to Factors of Production

The factors of production, which share in the income produced by the aggregate economy, are capital, (broadly defined) labor, and nonlabor. Capital income is defined as the flow of all rents, interest, and dividends accruing to the providers of investment capital. Labor can be broken down into two categories: wage and proprietor's income. The sum of these two components describes the amount of national income that is paid for the expenditure of local human effort. The present value of human capital in the free world was estimated to be over $100 trillion by Ibbotson and Siegel [1983]. It has long been presumed that human capital overshadows investment capital because of the preponderance of income flowing to labor over time, as documented by Kuznets [1966].

Nonlabor income is that income that the government redistributes to parts of the populace on the basis of hardship or need rather than on the basis of productivity. In the United States, the category is primarily composed of transfer payments and is one of the fastest growing and most successful competitors for share in the economic derby. Figure 5-3, using national income account data for the United States, shows the various factor income shares since 1929. The major secular shift over time involves the growth of nonlabor income and a decline of proprietors' income. The point of primary interest is that despite its ups and downs, the share of income flows to the investor in the form of rents, interest payments, and cash dividends has stayed relatively constant at about 20 percent.

If the income flow to capital assets maintains a constant share, its growth rate will be the same as the growth in society's overall wealth. Therefore:

$$g = G$$

Growth in $\qquad$ Growth in GNP
aggregate capital market wealth $\qquad\qquad\qquad\qquad\qquad\qquad$ (5-3)

This equation is supported by historic data since 1926, which reveals that growth of capital market values in the United States has been quite similar to growth in aggregate GNP. As shown in Table 5-6, this relationship holds up reasonably well in shorter time spans as well.

Capital Market Returns. With the relationships established thus far, a forecast for the aggregate capital market can be framed. All that is needed is a formula for aggregate capital market return.

$$r = (d + a) / w$$

Capital	Capital	Capital	Capital market
market	market	market	aggregate
return	income	appreciation	value

$\qquad\qquad\qquad\qquad\qquad\qquad\qquad\qquad\qquad\qquad\qquad\qquad$ (5-4)

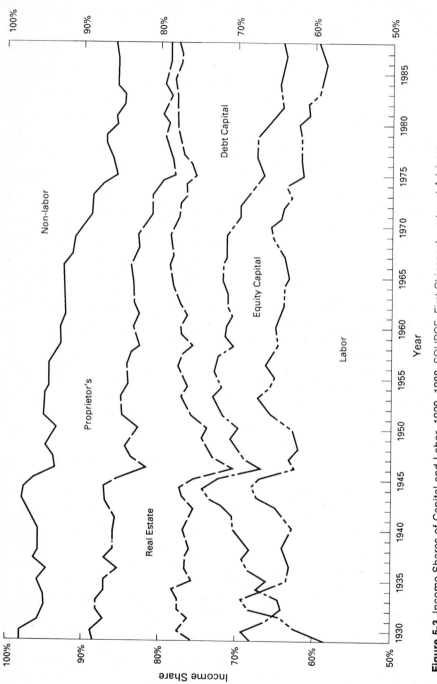

Figure 5-3. Income Shares of Capital and Labor, 1929–1988. SOURCE: First Chicago Investment Advisors.

TABLE 5-6. Real Compound Growth Rates of the U.S. Economy as Measured by Growth of GNP and the Capital Markets for Selected Periods, 1926–1988

	Compound Annual Rates of Growth in Real (Inflation-Adjusted) Terms[a]			
	1926–1988	1947–1988	1959–1988	1970–1988
U.S. capital market				
Aggregate value growth (*g*)				
Stocks	3.1%	5.0%	2.7%	2.1%
Bonds and cash equivalents	4.4	3.0	4.7	5.0
Real estate	2.9	3.3	3.4	3.6
Market value weighted total	3.5	3.5	3.8	3.7
U.S. Gross National Product (*G*)	3.6[b]	3.3	3.1	2.6

SOURCE: First Chicago Investment Advisors.
[a] (1 + Nominal Growth)/(1 + CPI Percent Change).
[b] 1929–1988.

Investment or capital market returns usually are not stated on a gross basis but on a *per share basis* that takes into account new contributions or withdrawals of capital. Part of the growth of the aggregate value of the capital market results from economy-wide new contributions, which usually come in the form of net new issues introduced into the capital markets, *n*. The net new issues are appropriately viewed as decrements to aggregate capital market income because they represent withdrawals from the income stream. As a result, Equation 5-4 can be rewritten as:

$$
\begin{aligned}
r &= d/w &+ a/w \\
&= (d - n)/w &+ (a + n)/w \\
&= (d - n)/w &+ g
\end{aligned}
$$

(5-5)

where *n* represents net new issues of stock, debt, and real estate. Together, capital market appreciation and net new capital market issues equal the growth in aggregate capital market wealth, *g*. Substituting *G* for *g* as per equation 5-3 produces a simple yet important starting point for further analysis:

$$
\underset{\substack{\text{Capital} \\ \text{market return}}}{r} = \underset{\substack{\text{Net capital} \\ \text{market income} \\ \text{yield}}}{(d - n)/w} + \underset{\text{Growth in GNP}}{G}
$$

(5-6)

As a result, a forecast of return for the U.S. capital market could proceed as shown in Table 5-7. Net capital market income yield is made up of an estimate of the weighted current gross yield less an estimate of net new

TABLE 5-7. Forecast of Equilibrium Real Pretax U.S. Capital Market Returns

Net Capital Market Income:

Gross Income Yield: *Asset Class*	*12/31/88* *Asset Class* *Weight*	*Forecast* *Long-Term* *Income Yield*	*Weighted Forecast* *Income Yield or* *Contribution*
Equity	29.0%	4.5%	1.3%
Fixed income	42.6	8.1	3.5
Real estate	15.3	6.0	0.9
Cash equivalents	13.1	6.4	0.8
	100.0%		6.5%
Less: Net new issues			5.0
Equals: Net capital market income			1.5%
Real market value growth:			
Real GNP growth		3.0%	
Less: Factor share adjustment		0.0	
Equals: Real market value growth			3.0%
Sum equals: Real pretax capital market return			4.5%

issues of stock, debt, and real estate. The latter is estimated at 5 percent for the period covered, reflecting the relative volume of new financing and rising trend of interest rates. The next step is to add a forecast of real GNP growth to get an estimate of real pretax capital market return. No adjustment to real GNP was made under the assumption that the long-term division of income between investable and human factors of production would be reasonably constant. Note that the numbers in the table are not necessarily absolutely correct, but rather they give the investor a framework by which to derive a supply of capital market returns.

Ideally, the table requires two adjustments. The first would reconcile pretax and post-tax returns to the capital market. Such adjustments have been complicated in the United States by the numerous changes in the tax laws and rates that characterized the decade of the 1980s.

The second adjustment requires applying this U.S. analysis on a global scale. One approach would be to assume that the United States, after considering the degree of integration in the global economy, is a fair sample of the world at large and therefore no adjustment may be necessary. A second approach would consider the potential lack of integration on a global scale and significant differential growth rates of differing economies. A third approach would consider the perception of relative riskiness of U.S. versus other country investments. If the United States were perceived to be a safe haven, its capital assets may offer a smaller return as investors heavily invest in U.S. securities and bid up their prices. In general, practitioners fall into two camps on this issue: those that believe that U.S. and non-U.S. returns are similar and those that believe that U.S. assets earn a smaller return because of the maturity of its markets and a lack of sovereign risk.

Allocating Returns Across Asset Classes

Once an aggregate long-term capital market return forecast is established, expectations of returns to common stocks, fixed-income securities, and real estate can be derived. Whereas the aggregate figure was more of a supply driven estimate, the allocation of return across the asset classes is more of a demand driven process. This does not suggest that pricing is not a function of the interaction of the supply and demand for capital market securities, rather it is the demand window that is used to frame the generation of market expectations.

The Capital Asset Pricing Model (CAPM) as per Sharpe [1964], Lintner [1965], and Mossin [1966], Arbitrage Pricing Theory (APT) as per Ross [1976], and New Equilibrium Theory (NET) as per Ibbotson, Diermeier, and Siegel [1984] all view the equilibrium returns that a security or asset class has to offer as a function of demand characteristics. If investors dislike the bundle of characteristics that a security offers, then it will be priced at a relatively low price to clear the market, resulting in a higher subsequent return. The CAPM and APT allocate equilibrium returns in accordance with the systematic risk of the security. Riskier assets, however defined, offer greater equilibrium returns than less risky assets. NET broadens the list of characteristics beyond systematic risk to include pricing of nonsystematic risk, taxability, marketability, and miscellaneous factors. All the theories distribute relative returns from the vantage point of the demander of returns according to the degree of his distaste for a security or asset class.

Demanders of return expect to receive from each investment an appropriate real risk-free rate, an inflation premium, and a risk (or distaste) premium. The real risk-free rate should be common to all investments and reflects a pure time premium payment. Similarly, all investors in the United States (and around the world if purchasing power parity holds) will suffer consumption erosion from the ravages of inflation and therefore require compensation for the expected loss of purchasing power. Therefore, the first two components, the real risk-free rate and the inflation premium, are embedded in the pricing of all assets.

The third component of the equilibrium return is the risk premium. In a world of risk-averse investors, risk premiums should be positively related to risk. As defined earlier, this premium is composed of four different components. The first is common to all investments: inflation risk. The next two are common to investments of a given country: currency risk and sovereign risk. The last is unique to the individual investment: private cash flow risk.

**TABLE 5-8. Segmented and Integrated Risk Premiums for the Investable Capital
Market**

	Segmented Risk		Integrated Risk	
Asset Class	Standard Deviation	Risk Premium = Std. Dev. × .4	Beta	Risk Premium = Beta × 3.6
Domestic stocks	17.5%	7.0%	1.5	5.3%
Non-U.S. stocks	13.5[a]	5.4	1.2[a]	4.5
Venture capital	40.0	16.0	1.2	4.3
Real estate	12.0	4.8	0.6	2.3
Dollar bonds	7.5	3.0	0.5	1.6
Nondollar bonds	4.7[a]	1.9	0.4[a]	1.3
30-day Treasury bills	1.5	0.6	0.0	0.0
Investable capital market	9.0[b]	3.6[c]	1.0	3.6

SOURCE: First Chicago Investment Advisors.
[a] Weighted average of local currency standard deviations and betas.
[b] Standard deviation to the U.S. investor; includes use of correlation matrix to reflect diversification effects.
[c] Includes the diversification effects of correlation/covariance estimates.

All risks and risk premiums exist because of the uncertainty that a given forecast will materialize as expected.

Segmented vs. Integrated Approaches to Risk

Two methods are typically used to generate expectations of long-term risk premiums. Both involve generating estimates of risk, but they view risk from two different but related philosophical standpoints. Using a convention employed by Lessard [1980] and Brinson, Diermeier, and Schlarbaum [1986], risk is approached from a *segmented* and an *integrated* viewpoint.

Under the segmented approach, the focus is on the risk of the security or the asset class viewed in isolation. This assumes that investors in risky assets limit their focus to one asset class. This is as if the segmented investor was not aware of opportunities for diversification. In this case, the standard deviation of return for the asset class is an appropriate risk measure. A linear relationship between standard deviation and risk premium is assumed as shown in Table 5-8. The pricing factors of .4 for segmented risk and 3.60 for integrated risk will be explained shortly.

Under the integrated approach, capital markets are assumed to be perfectly integrated. Investors view risk from the context of the portfolio, taking into account the lack of perfect correlation between markets. This approach requires a forecast of the correlation between each asset class and the market so as to be able to compute the beta of the asset class with the aggregate capital market as follows:

$$\beta_{im} = \frac{\rho_{im}\sigma_i}{\sigma_m} \qquad\qquad (5\text{-}7)$$

β_{im} = Beta of asset class i with the market
ρ_{im} = Correlation of asset class i with the market
σ_i = Standard deviation of asset class i
σ_m = Standard deviation of the market

Once again, a linear relationship is assumed to exist between the beta of the asset class and the risk premium. The two approaches, segmented and integrated, provide a demand driven way of allocating the return expected from the aggregate capital market. The forecaster can then select values from within the integrated and segmented boundaries, add a real risk-free rate assumption, and reconcile the resulting weighted aggregate with the capital market real return forecast from Table 5-7.

In Table 5-8, the price of segmented risk of 40 basis points and the price of integrated risk of 360 basis points for a 1.0 beta portfolio were chosen so that the resulting aggregate capital market risk premium would be consistent with Table 5-7. Given those operational assumptions, a long-term risk premium is selected for each asset class that lies between the segmented and integrated figures. Each individual selection is made to the degree the asset class is believed to be segmented as an asset class or fully integrated as an asset class. The result, when added to a *real* risk-free rate assumption of 140 basis points, is a weighted total that matches the real pretax return estimate found in Table 5-7 of 450 basis points.

Risk, Return, Correlation, and Autocorrelation

Typically, *risk of loss* is provided for by using volatility or standard deviation in the segmented case and by a broad market beta in the domestic CAPM or international CAPM structures. Factor betas are used in APT structures. All structures require a reliance on standard deviation of returns as a key measure of risk. Assuming that return distributions are normally distributed (or normally distributed in logarithms of returns), the standard deviation statistic gives a good summary description of the risk of loss. The beta calculation requires, as in equation 5-7, an estimate of covariances across asset classes.

There are three general methods by which standard deviations and covariances can be estimated. The first involves a historical empirical estimate and the assumption that history repeats. The second is a partitioned view of history where the forecaster analyzes history and discards periods believed to be irrelevant to the future and focuses on periods of future relevance. The third uses the technology of econometrics whereby an attempt is made to understand underlying causal factors, so as to build a predictive model.

The state of the art of forecasting volatility and (particularly) correlations is not very well developed. A key problem arises because of a relative paucity of data and because of autocorrelation of returns. Autocorrelation measures the correlation of a time series with a lag unto itself.

Because the raw data unit typically used for empirical analysis is monthly, any forecast of a longer horizon requires the expansion of the short interval data to a longer interval. Because of autocorrelations within the series itself, the expansion procedure is difficult at best. It becomes even more difficult as further evidence is gathered because for some asset classes, such as common stocks, there are tendencies for short-term positive autocorrelations and long-term negative autocorrelations. Put another way, historically stock returns may have shown a tendency for trends in the short run but for reversals over longer intervals. As a result, standard deviations and correlations calculated from monthly data may be materially different from standard deviations and correlations calculated over, say, five-year observations of data.

This problem is further compounded because short interval data estimation puts enormous stress on data gathering methods. U.S. stock investors are blessed with the best economic and capital market data in the world. Even this data, because of problems of nonsynchronous trading, transaction costs, and the like, have trouble standing up to statistical analysis on a daily, weekly, or to a lesser degree, monthly interval. Data on other asset classes, such as real estate, suffer by comparison and therefore do not stand up as well to intensive statistical scrutiny.

Fundamentally, the forecaster should generate a risk forecast on the basis of economic variables impacting the standardized valuation model. The variability in cash flow expectations for each asset class, discount rate expectations for each asset class, and the correlation of the volatility of cash flow expectations with the volatility of the discount rate expectations can drive a fundamental risk forecast. It is incumbent upon the knowledgeable forecaster to understand and translate macroeconomic uncertainty into forecasts of cash flow and discount rate risk.

Investable Capital Market. The investable capital market should have a return commensurate with the supply of returns as offered to a pretax investor. Figure 5-4 shows the estimated composition by market value of that portfolio as of the end of 1988. The pie is made up largely of fixed-income instruments with the combination of U.S. cash equivalents, domestic bonds, and nondollar bonds accounting for 50.5 percent of the total global

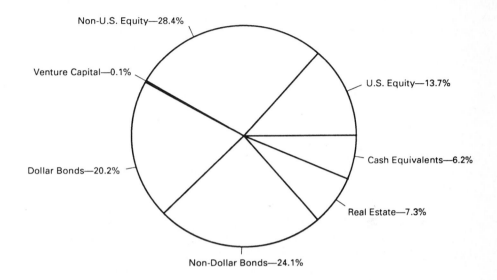

Non-U.S. Equity—28.4%

Venture Capital—0.1%

U.S. Equity—13.7%

Cash Equivalents—6.2%

Dollar Bonds—20.2%

Real Estate—7.3%

Non-Dollar Bonds—24.1%

$22.2 Trillion

Figure 5-4. Percentage Breakdown of Value of Total Investable Capital Market, December 31, 1988. SOURCE: First Chicago Investment Advisors.

portfolio. The common stock proportion amounts to approximately 42 percent of the total, with the remainder in U.S. equity real estate and U.S. venture capital (non-U.S. real estate and non-U.S. venture capital are excluded because of a lack of data). Note that the real estate segment contains only investable real estate owned by noncorporations. The venture capital market value estimate is biased downward because it represents only those venture investments that are under the care of professional venture capitalists. More proprietor assets would be included if good data were available.

This portfolio, whose weights shift over time, has provided a geometric real return of 4.7 percent per annum over the period 1970 through 1988. It has done so with a standard deviation of 9 percent. This volatility figure is an understatement because of data limitations on the real estate component as explained in Chapter 10. Adjusted for that limitation, the risk experience was probably closer to 10 percent, suggesting that a real return of 4.7 percent could have been obtained at a volatility of 10 percent or a payoff in addition to the inflation rate of 47 basis points for each unit of standard deviation.

Note that Ibbotson, Siegel, and Love [1985], using less satisfactory annual data available starting in 1960, made an estimate of what they called the world market wealth portfolio that includes precious metals. This estimate of real return over the 1960 through 1984 period was 3.1 percent when the personal consumption deflator is used to adjust for inflation. A standard deviation in the aggregate portfolio of 5.8 percent was found, which reflects the relative calm of the 1960s market environment versus that of the 1970s and 1980s. This 5.8 percent is a downward biased estimate because of data limitations, primarily in the real estate segment.

Asset Class Statistics. Table 5-9 provides a summary of the return, risk (standard deviation and beta), and correlation characteristics of various asset classes for the period 1970 to 1988. In Chapters 8, 9, and 10, the authors comment further on the risk/return profile of bonds, stocks, and real estate. Also, the several Ibbotson (with various coauthors) studies of risk and return by asset class provide a wealth of information to assist in the formation of macro-expectational inputs for portfolio managers.

The following points should be made regarding the data in Table 5-9:

1. The period (1970–1988) covered by the data was an extremely volatile and inflation-sensitive period of capital market experience.
2. Although the standard deviation for 90-day U.S. Treasury bills was 1.3 percent for this period, Treasury bills still serve as a usable proxy for the risk-free asset. Note that the real return to Treasury bills of 1.4 percent per annum is well above the near-zero return cited in early Ibbotson-Sinquefield studies. The 1970 through 1988 period is probably more representative.
3. The domestic bond market has been and continues to be highly sensitive to inflation. For example, using data on long-term bonds provided by Shearson Lehman Hutton, the standard deviation of quarterly returns ranged from about 2 to 6 percent over the decades of the 1930s through the 1960s, but increased to about 6 to 19 percent during the inflationary 1970s and 1980s.
4. Nondollar bonds differ from domestic (U.S. dollar) bonds based on government economic policies and currency movements. The standard deviations and correlations for nondollar bonds are shown in both U.S. dollar and local currency terms in Table 5-9. On a five-year moving average basis, the standard deviation of quarterly nondollar bond returns, converted to U.S. dollars, ranged from about 8 to 15 percent over the 1975 through 1988 period.
5. Domestic common stock risk and return evolve fundamentally from expectations of changes in real output of the economy (real cash flows) and changes in the rate of inflation (as reflected in fluctuations in the expected discount rate). Generally, small-capitalization stocks are more volatile than large-capitalization stocks because the returns on these stocks tend to have a larger response to changes in economic output and inflation. It should be noted that crude data for common stocks going back to 1970

TABLE 5-9. Annualized Quarterly Returns, Standard Deviations, Correlations, and Betas for Various Asset Classes, December 31, 1969 to December 31, 1988

	Investable Capital Market	Cash Equivalents[d]	U.S. Bonds[b]	Nondollar Bonds U.S. $	Nondollar Bonds Local Currency[c]	U.S. Common Stocks	Non-U.S. Common Stocks U.S. $	Non-U.S. Common Stocks Local Currency[c]	Real Estate	Venture Capital
Mean annual returns										
Geometric—Nominal	11.0%	7.5%	9.4%	12.1%	10.8%	10.6%	15.5%	19.1%	10.5%	12.1%
—Real[a]	4.7	1.4	3.2	5.8	4.5	4.3	9.0	12.4	4.2	5.8
Arithmetic—Nominal	11.5	7.6	9.7	13.0	11.0	12.6	17.6	20.3	10.5	19.2
—Real[a]	5.2	1.5	3.5	6.6	4.7	6.2	10.9	13.5	4.2	12.5
Standard deviation	9.0%	1.3%	8.0%	12.3%	5.8%	19.5%	19.3%	14.6%	2.4%	35.1%
Correlations with:										
Investable capital market	1.00	-0.20	0.64	0.69	0.69	0.81	0.87	0.63	-0.01	0.59
Cash equivalents[d]	-0.20	1.00	-0.03	-0.30	-0.15	-0.11	-0.27	-0.12	-0.58	-0.07
Domestic bonds	0.64	-0.03	1.00	0.50	0.72	0.41	0.33	0.23	-0.11	0.12
Nondollar bonds	0.70	-0.30	0.50	1.00	1.00	0.22	0.62	0.14	-0.12	0.24
Domestic equity	0.81	-0.11	0.41	0.22	0.28	1.00	0.68	0.75	0.06	0.66
International equity	0.87	-0.27	0.33	0.62	0.43	0.68	1.00	1.00	-0.07	0.52
Real estate	-0.01	0.58	-0.11	-0.12	-0.22	0.06	-0.07	-0.13	1.00	0.16
Venture capital	0.59	-0.07	0.12	0.24	0.22	0.66	0.52	0.41	0.16	1.00
Beta coefficient with investable capital market	1.00	-0.03	0.57	0.95	0.49[e]	1.75	1.85	1.12[e]	0.00	2.28

SOURCE: First Chicago Investment Advisors.
[a] Adjusted by the personal consumption deflator.
[b] Shearson Lehman Hutton/Salomon Broad Investment Grade (BIG) linked index.
[c] Data is for 1974–1988 based on market weighted average of the individual countries.
[d] 30-day U.S. Treasury bills.
[e] First Chicago Investment Advisors estimate with own capital market.

suggest real returns of near 7 percent and standard deviations of 20 percent are typical of the domestic market.

6. Nondomestic common stocks, like nondollar bonds, reflect the differences in socio/political/economic climate as well as currency variations. Japan represents the largest segment of the nondollar stock market, comprising over 60 percent of that market with the United Kingdom and West Germany trailing well behind at 13.5 and 8.5 percent, respectively. The effects of currency variations are reflected in the difference between the standard deviation of returns measured on a dollar basis (19.3 percent) and a local currency basis (14.6 percent), as shown in Table 5-9.

7. Venture capital data are not robust because of the industry's youth and its private nature. The volatility of venture capital returns is reflected in the standard deviation statistic: 35.1 percent.

8. Although real estate is a worldwide investment alternative, because of data limitations, the data in Table 5-9 are for noncorporate, nonfarm U.S. real estate. Appraisal techniques tend to significantly smooth the reported returns data. Thus, the usefulness of the real estate standard deviation, correlations, and beta in Table 5-9 is limited. Much more will be said on this topic in Chapter 10.

9. The historic correlations of the asset classes are highly impacted by the economic environment. For example, in the 1960s, when inflation expectations were stable, domestic stock and bond markets showed low correlations. In the 1970s, when inflation expectations were unstable, the correlation between these markets was much higher.

10. The highest correlations across the asset classes were found in the U.S./non-U.S. common stock and U.S. nondollar bond pairs, suggesting some degree of global integration. The lowest correlations are often found where the data are poor and do not stand up well to statistical analysis.

With this brief summary of asset class risk and return characteristics, the broader macroeconomic variables and relationships that shape expectations can be explored.

MACROECONOMIC VARIABLES

This chapter's focus is on the creation of a framework that analysts and portfolio managers can use to set capital market expectations. Macroeconomic variables enter the process at two different levels. The first level deals with how economic expectations impact expectations of longer-term capital markets. The second level deals with short-term macroeconomic expectations. In the real world, an extraordinary—if not excessive—amount of effort goes into making short-term economic forecasts.

The Long-Term Setting

As indicated earlier in Figure 5-2, the capital market return hierarchy is composed of three different tiers. The highest involves the supply of aggregate returns. The middle involves the dividing up of aggregate income (returns) across the factors of production. The lowest breaks up the return to the capital factor of production across investment classes on the perception of risk or distaste. The focus here will be on long-term expectations of real growth, income share ownership, and longer-term stability.

Real Economic Growth. Real output is the key variable determining the amount of real returns available to all economic participants. The formulation of longer-term real economic growth expectations tends to be fairly uniform across economic forecasters. The constraints on growth in the long run are perceived to be those of supply. As a result, the forecasts are supply oriented. Supply is characterized by the factors of production available for work and the environment for work. The major determinants of long-term growth are listed in Table 5-10. This is an expansion of the simplified version that suggests growth is a function of labor productivity and the number of hours worked.

Denison [1985] attempted to break down the component contributions to real economic growth from 1929 to 1982. His results are shown in Table 5-11. Real potential national income growth over that period was 3.2 percent for the economy as a whole. Denison contends that the largest contributor to growth was increased labor input. Ranking in order thereafter are advances in knowledge, the provision of capital, and training/education.

The huge econometric models at places such as Data Resources (DRI), Wharton, Interactive Data, and UCLA regularly crunch out detailed long-term forecasts premised on the basic supply expectations of demographics and capital. DRI, for example, has been making long-term projections (25-year outlooks) since 1978. It is interesting to note the changes in their forecast between 1978 and 1988 as shown in Table 5-12. For example, expectations of annual real GNP growth declined from 2.7 to 2.3 percent with the decline due to lower productivity (output per worker) expectations of 1.4 percent versus 2.0 percent. Some of the decline in productivity expectations is a result of the growth of the service sector. As the United States becomes the banker and entertainer of the world, productivity has tended to suffer. Optimists will point out that important measurement problems arise in service economy productivity estimation, with the result that confidence in the estimates of productivity has declined.

TABLE 5-10. Sources of Long-Term Economic Growth Expectations

Labor effort:
  Population
  Labor participation rate
    Labor force
    Percentage employed
      Work force
      Hours worked per employee
        Total hours worked
        Business training
        Education
Capital effort:
  Capital stock (net)
    Capital employed
    Technology/R&D
    Capacity utilization
Contributing factors:
  Economic mix (manufacturing vs. service)
  Peace expectations
  Energy availability
  Economic stability
  Foreign competition
  Incentives
    Regulation
    Tax mix
    Government share of output

SOURCE: First Chicago Investment Advisors.

An important variable in estimating productivity growth is the willingness to expand plant and capacity and to put them at the disposal of labor. Table 5-13 from Barro [1984] shows the global relationship of real output to the ratio of investment to output. A strong positive relationship is found in the data.

Part of the U.S. productivity slowdown is attributed to the capital investment slowdown of the 1970s following the expansion of the 1960s. Concern for future productivity exists because capital expenditures spurred by tax cuts in the early 1980s were of a short-term nature, such as for microcomputers and trucks, and were not likely to add materially to productivity.

Key among the forces influencing future economic growth rates are government policies. Of the 17 primary variables listed in Table 5-10, six are heavily influenced by government policy. These direct variables include education, peace, economic stability, regulation, tax mix, and government share of output.

Long-term real growth expectations are also influenced by inflation. In particular, Fama [1981] demonstrated a seemingly persistent negative re-

TABLE 5-11. Contributions of Various Factors to Potential and Actual National Income Growth Rates, 1929–1982

Contributions to 1929–1982 Growth Rates

	Potential National Income				Actual National Income			
	Total		Per Person Employed		Total		Per Person Employed	
	Whole Economy	Nonresidential Business	Whole Economy	Nonresidential Business	Whole Economy	Nonresidential Business	Whole Economy	Nonresidential Business
Growth rate	3.2%	3.1%	1.6%	1.7%	2.9%	2.8%	1.5%	1.6%
Percentage of growth rate								
All sources	100	100	100	100	100	100	100	100
Labor input except education	34	25	-13	-23	32	20	-12	-25
Education per worker	13	16	26	30	14	19	27	34
Capital	17	12	15	10	19	14	20	13
Advances in knowledge	26	34	54	64	28	39	55	68
Improved resource allocation	8	11	16	19	8	11	16	18
Economies of scale	8	11	17	20	9	12	18	22
Changes in legal and human environment	-1	-2	-3	-4	-1	-2	-3	-4
Land	0	0	-3	-4	0	0	-3	-3
Irregular factors	0	0	0	0	-3	-5	-7	-8
Other determinants	-5	-7	-10	-13	-5	-8	-10	-13

SOURCE: Denison [1985].

TABLE 5-12. Comparison of Data Resources Long-Term U.S. Economic Forecasts at December 1978 and July 1988

	December 1978 Outlook	July 1988 Outlook
Average Annual Percentage Increases, 1987–2003		
Real GNP	2.7%	2.3%
Industrial production	3.6	2.8
Manufacturing employment	0.4	0.2
Inflation	5.4	5.0
Real oil price	3.1	4.0
Output per hour	2.0	1.4
Potential GNP	2.6	2.3
Average Percentage Level, 1988–2003		
Federal deficit (as % of GNP)	0.0%	1.5%
Merchandise deficit (as % of GNP)	0.6	1.4
Oil imports (as % of GNP)	3.1	1.5
Federal expenditures (as % of GNP)	20.3	22.9
Unemployment rate	4.9	5.7

SOURCE: Data Resources [1988].

TABLE 5-13. Aggregate and Per Capita Real Gross Domestic Product (GDP) Growth and Net Fixed Investment Relative to GDP for Nine Countries, 1950–1979

	Real GDP Growth	Per Capita Real GDP Growth	Net Fixed Investment/GDP (Period Average)
United States	3.4%	2.0%	0.07
Austria	4.4	4.1	0.13
Denmark	3.5	2.9	0.15
France	4.6	3.7	0.11
West Germany	5.0	4.3	0.14
Italy	4.6	3.9	0.12
Japan	7.8	6.7	0.19
Spain	5.3	4.3	0.11
United Kingdom	2.6	2.2	0.08

Note: GDP is the value of output produced domestically. Investment includes purchases of capital goods by governments, except defense goods. Public investment is about 10 to 20 percent of total investment with no major differences across countries.
SOURCE: Barro [1984].

lationship between the level of inflation and real output growth. Difficulties in nominal contracting, uncertainty of real payments, effort expended to anticipate and respond to inflation, and dislocations caused by the inability to index whole economies are strong reasons to expect weaker overall performance in a period of high and/or volatile inflation.

Factor Income Share. The key competitors for income are labor, transfer payment recipients, capital, and, in a narrowly viewed local economy, foreign participants. As displayed earlier, the capital market claimants in the United States have managed to hold onto their relative share since 1929. The investor implicitly must make a forecast of factor incomes and could, of course, extrapolate the past record.

A key element in that forecast would be real wages. Thus far the U.S. economy has operated, during its measured history, with a balance of labor and capital. In fact, it is difficult to see how labor's share could gain materially without substantial disruption to the economy. A substantially higher share suggests that investors would be willing to accept systematically lower returns on investment while continuing to provide capital. Conversely, a substantially lower labor share might invoke the return of unionism. A key risk in the future, however, lies with a large potential buildup of corporate liabilities to workers in the form of health and retirement benefits. Some current guesses as to the ultimate liability suggest a growing, but currently hidden, share gain by labor at the expense of investors.

Nonlabor or transfer payments in the United States continue to grow as greater income share is allocated to the disadvantaged and nonworking. This is a trend that should continue, given three crucial factors: (1) longer lifespans, (2) greater health rights and demands, and (3) the institutionalization of retirement needs. With people living longer, a sticky retirement age of 65 in the United States, systems in place to provide extraordinary health care on the basis of need (not means), and many citizens expecting government support in retirement years, this trend is very likely to continue. The government operationalizes this trend through its taxing and redistribution power. Key to investors is how the incidence of taxation falls upon individuals, corporations, and investors. If the incidence falls only on wages, investors would be unaffected. If the incidence falls primarily on cash flows available for investors, the present value of future cash flows would drop.

The offset to nonlabor income has been a shrinking of the proprietary share of total labor income. This shrinkage reflects the reduction in small, private businesses such as the small farmer, retailer, grocer, brewer, publisher, and the like. This trend is likely to continue as the United States prepares for more diverse global competition.

Capital Income Shares. Within the capital market sphere, income is divided into rents, interest, and profits. Figure 5-3 displayed how these components have changed through time. Rent share has declined through time. This is likely due to the fact that in an advancing, sophisticated economy raw human needs, such as the need for physical space, decline relative to total output.

Conversely, interest payments have grown as a percentage of capital income, primarily because of an increased leveraging of our corporate structure and a large accumulated government deficit compounded by high current interest rates. Knowledgeable observers believe that this expansion of debt accumulation is not sustainable and at some point it must stop, if not reverse.

Overall, the equity capital share of income, as measured by dividends and retained earnings, has been reasonably steady over the long history of the measured data. Based on the evidence, it is reasonable to assume that the corporate profits share will be maintained.

Stability of Long-Term Expectations. Critical to the risk forecasts used by investors is the perception of economic stability. Risk averse investors would demand an extra return premium from common stocks if fundamental economic risk were expected to be high. If economic risk were high, consumers would consume more today and save less for the future.

In the 1960s, inflation was low and stable. This led some economists and businessmen to believe that through demand management of the economy the business cycle could be repealed. Tobin's "q" ratio, which measures the market value of debt and equity in the economy and divides it by the replacement cost of capital in the economy, was estimated by Malkiel [1979] to be at historically high levels in the 1960s. This occurred, according to Malkiel, because of a belief in general stability, so that risk premiums and hence required rates of return declined, causing an upward revaluation of the existing stocks and bonds.

Overall, with the exception of the Great Depression, a decade-by-decade review of U.S. real GNP growth reveals relative long-term stability. Of the 10 decades of recorded U.S. experience, fully 7 of the 10 decades had growth that lay within one percentage point of the 3.3 percent trend over the entire history. (See Table 5-14.)

Sources of Instability. The three primary sources of economic instability are: (1) natural disasters, (2) business forecasting errors, and (3) government policy errors. Natural disasters involve either the destruction of capital or the overabundance or scarcity of some key good by way of an event in nature. Some of this is to be expected. Preparation for disaster is a matter for business and government strategy and policy.

Business forecasting errors most conventionally take the form of overestimating expected sales, which leads, in aggregate, to an economy that overinvests in inventory, whether consumer or capital goods. It is difficult

TABLE 5-14. Compound Annual Rates of Change in U.S. Real Gross National Product, by Decades, 1890–1988

Decade	Rate of Change
1890–1899	4.3%
1900–1909	4.6
1910–1919	2.3
1920–1929	3.4
1930–1939	0.3
1940–1949	4.5
1950–1959	3.9
1960–1969	4.3
1970–1979	3.1
1980–1988	2.9

SOURCE: First Chicago Investment Advisors.

to say if the U.S. economy, as a whole, is better today at managing inventory risk. A look back over a long history by Schwert [1988] suggests that economic volatility, as measured by an estimate of volatility of monthly industrial production in Figure 5-5, has been reduced since the Great Depression. One must be careful not to overinterpret the data, however, because old,

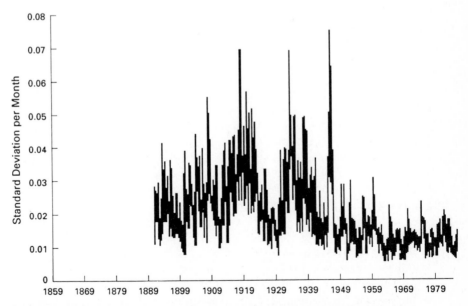

Figure 5-5. Historic Volatility of U.S. Economic Output Growth as Measured by an Estimate of the Standard Deviation of Monthly Industrial Production, 1890–1986. SOURCE: Schwert [1988].

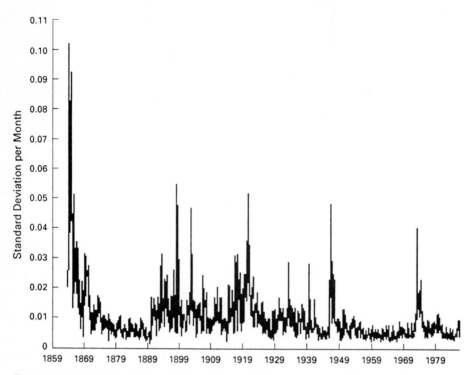

Figure 5-6. Historic Volatility of U.S. Inflation as Measured by an Estimate of the Standard Deviation of the Monthly Producer Price Index, 1864–1986. SOURCE: Schwert [1988].

poorly constructed data tend to be noisy by nature. Schwert's estimation of the volatility of inflation rates, as indicated in Figure 5-6, shows some smoothing in the past several decades but still contains the occasional spikes that have dominated the long-term past.

The third source of economic volatility lies with government policy errors. Much of the focus of government policy is geared towards stability. Stability of the economy is desired so that the citizenry can plan for the future. The issue is whether or not the following policies will stabilize, continue at the current level of uncertainty, or become explosively volatile.

- Policies on national defense and encouraging/discouraging war
- Policies designed to free the economy from regulation
- Policies on demand management of the economy and the prevention of boom and bust cycles
- Policies on maintaining the price level
- Policies on stabilizing the currency
- Tax policies that alter incentives in the system

As government officials vacillate on their views of such policies and with a constant shuffling of government personnel, a certain amount of policy volatility is to be expected (and probably desirable). On the other hand, tax policy experience in the first eight years of the 1980s was not encouraging given the four major tax bills that were passed, three of which contained significant reversals of prior legislation.

The importance of policy volatility is particularly important in the realm of national security. History is replete with politically motivated closings of capital markets for extended periods. War is the most common culprit. Clearly, the ultimate risk for the capital investor is not a depression, which leaves the system intact, but a threat to the system itself.

Short-Term Expectations

Most of the practicing economics profession is absorbed in making short-term forecasts of the economy. Most professional investors either make these forecasts or pay to obtain them. Considerable intellectual effort is geared to gaining short-term incremental advantage. But gaining a short-term advantage is difficult because so many intelligent, well-trained professionals are in the pursuit of the same advantage.

In this section, four aspects of the setting of short-term expectations are dealt with: (1) the techniques of short-term forecasting, (2) the private sector, (3) the public sector, and (4) the international sector.

Short-term forecasting is much different from long-term forecasting. Whereas long-term expectations are set primarily on the basis of supply considerations, *short-term expectations are demand driven*. The focus is on the path of aggregate demand as related to overall supply capacity. Forecasts of the private sector are geared towards shocks that might cause a divergence from trend. The focus in the public sector is policy management of demand. The international sector greatly complicates the analysis by introducing, in the limited view, exogenous supply and demand variables and the difficulties of multiple currencies.

Forecasting Techniques. There are several techniques used to make short-term forecasts of the economy. For the sake of convenience, these will be defined as leading indicators, flow of funds, econometric, and time series techniques.

Leading Indicators Approach. The National Bureau of Economic Research (NBER) designates the beginning and end of recessions and depressions (i.e., business cycle turning dates). Since 1790, there have been an estimated 45 recessions in the United States. These recessions have involved, on average, a decline in industrial production of 17 percent with an

TABLE 5-15. Leading Indicators of Economic Activity

- Average weekly hours of production of nonsupervisory workers, manufacturing
- Average weekly initial claims for unemployment insurance, state programs
- Manufacturers' new orders, in 1972 dollars, consumer goods, and materials industries
- Vendor performance, percentage of companies receiving slower deliveries
- Contracts and orders for plant and equipment in 1972 dollars
- New building permits, private housing units
- Change in sensitive materials prices
- Stock prices, 500 common stocks
- Money supply, M-2, adjusted for inflation
- Index of consumer expectations from the University of Michigan[a]
- Factory orders for durable goods[a]

SOURCE: National Bureau of Economic Research.
[a] Added in January 1989 to replace change in business and consumer credit outstanding and change in manufacturing and trade inventories on hand and on order in 1972 dollars.

average length of 19 months. The NBER has selected 11 economic indicators that, taken together, come the closest to providing a reliable and leading relationship to the general movement of the economy. These are listed in Table 5-15.

The leading indicator series is shown in Figure 5-7. The index of leading indicators has, on average since 1950, signaled the onset of recessions 9.6 months in advance and the coming of recovery 3.1 months beforehand. Practically speaking, however, there is little advance notice coming out of recessions, given that the data are a month old before they are compiled and released as a composite.

Liquidity/Flow of Funds Approach. The second short-term forecasting technique uses a liquidity or flow of funds approach to anticipate fluctuations in general economic conditions. The rationale is that when money (i.e., liquidity) is flooded into the system via the Federal Reserve, it will first act to raise the value of financial assets and then stimulate real business activity. One of the most articulate spokesmen for this approach has been Beryl Sprinkel (See Sprinkel and Genetski [1977]). A number of others including Fama [1981] and Geske and Roll [1983] have argued that the appearance of liquidity cannot be separated from ongoing economic activity. Fama argues that lower real economic activity decreases the need for money balances and thus creates the appearance of liquidity. In this framework, inflation and not real growth will flow. Geske and Roll argue that slower output reduces government revenues and therefore boosts the budget deficit, government borrowings and pressure to relax monetary conditions. In the liquidity/flow of funds approach, it is crucial that a good understanding of

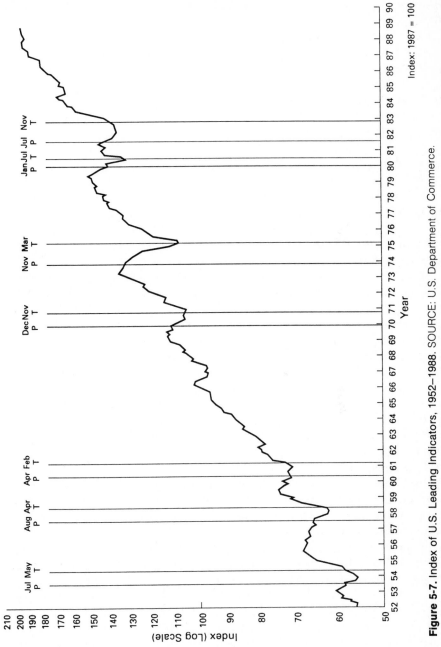

Figure 5-7. Index of U.S. Leading Indicators, 1952–1988. SOURCE: U.S. Department of Commerce.

the driving variables be assessed because of the potentially circular logic of the relationships.

Econometric and Time Series Approaches. The most formal short-term forecasting approaches involve econometric models and time series models. Econometric models attempt to describe the economy as it exists today as a function of a limited set of policies and exogenous variables and a host of economic relationships tied to these variables. Policy variables would include money supply, government spending, and tax policies. Other exogenous variables would include weather conditions, oil politics, consumer utility, and the like. Once the current economy has been reduced to its lowest and simplest mathematical form, the model is solved. The relationships embodied therein, allowing for judgmental factors, are then extrapolated forward after inputting the anticipated policy and exogenous environment. By and large, large scale econometric forecasting has lost some credibility with practitioners because of an inferior forecasting track record relative to other approaches.

The final forecasting technique involves the use of time series analysis. This approach presumes that there are important patterns in past data that repeat in some predictable fashion in the future, even if that fashion requires fairly wholesale transformation. McNees [1988] provides evidence suggesting that time series models have proven to be inferior to other forecasting techniques. This approach currently receives limited use in the investment community.

The Private Sector. The two major elements of private sector demand involve consumer and corporate activity. Consumer demand shows up in consumption of durables, especially housing, nondurables, and services. Corporate demand is reflected in plant and equipment expenditures and inventory spending.

Consumer demand is a function of two key elements, the desire for consumption and the capability to consume. Most economic forecasters focus on the second element—capability. The desire for spending as reflected in the marginal propensity to consume is governed by demographics, the attractiveness of new products (in the 1980s, health care products were a good example), the need for immediate versus future gratification, and short-term inflation expectations.

Capability is simply a function of two components, real income and borrowing capacity. Milton Friedman's permanent income hypothesis suggests that consumers view their real income in a longer-term context and will determine their consumption capability as a function of longer-range expected income. As a result, the outlook regarding future income prospects is considered vital as most consumers try to even out their consumption patterns over time. This helps establish an appropriate sense of lifestyle and belongingness. Borrowing is a form of spreading out a lifestyle, although in recent years, the new availability of credit and the presumption of future credit availability may have caused an upward shift in the propensity to spend.

Temporary disequilibrium can result from a mismatch of income and credit expectations and reality. For example, the 1980 recession is largely attributed to President Carter's restrictions placed on credit, which immediately caused a reduction in new purchases financed by borrowing. Economists spend considerable effort monitoring consumer borrowings compared to the more stable component of real income, looking for signs that an imbalance has occurred. Correction of an imbalance may cause consumers to go on a buying strike resulting in an economic contraction. Because most econometric work suggests that income is the key driver of consumer spending and attitudes, most forecasters focus the largest portion of their efforts on income growth and its components: people employed, hours worked, and earnings per hour.

Investment demand is a function of current plant and equipment utilization, the rate of technological and physical obsolescence, the level of competition (domestic or foreign), the availability of cheap labor (a substitute), and the availability of funds. Capital goods investment is seen as being part of a very long cycle, in part because of the large and long-lived nature of the expenditure. Long wave or Kondratieff cycle theory, covering time horizons of 50 years and more, sees the shifting from capital expansion to capital excess (and therefore diminished capital spending) as part of a recurring cycle. The cycle exists because capital goods are an infrastructure component with long lead times to put in place. As a result, a spurt in end product demand or a shortage in the labor pool can, using an accelerator principle, cause rapid growth in the production of capital goods. Some of the capital goods will initially be diverted into the production of other capital goods (to produce more consumer goods). This in turn creates the appearance of a shortage of production capacity and rising capital goods backlogs, a precondition to overshooting. Once consumer demand is met, it is likely that excess capacity will have been created and the whole process then works in reverse.

A short-term version of this, that primarily takes place in consumer goods production, is called the business cycle. Although many seasoned researchers doubt that anything as systematic as a cycle exists, there have been numerous occasions in history where, because of an over-optimistic set of expectations, businesses find themselves with an oversupply of consumer goods. Subsequent layoffs, intended to reduce output and inventory, result in lower demand through the lowered incomes of those laid off or those fearing for their jobs. Thus, the process feeds on itself and generates the characteristics of a cycle. This is what preoccupies most practicing economists, although because of the adaptive nature of business and consumer day-to-day decisions, economists have an undistinguished track record in anticipating business cycles.

The Public Sector. The public sector in most countries has two objectives. One is to provide certain monopolistic services such as utilities, defense, and education, where it is believed a competitive environment would be damaging to the national interest. The second is to manage the economy to ensure its survival and optimize the living standard of its populace. This is almost always interpreted to mean the promotion of stable growth.

Policymakers have two primary tools to manage the economy in the short run. Both are considered to be means of demand management, but as demonstrated by the 1981 tax act, supply side management tools are also available. The tools of demand management are those of fiscal policy and monetary policy. Both are treated by most economists as relatively exogenous or external to their forecast mechanisms. That is, their size and effect are independently determined by a government body.

Fiscal policy uses government spending, the ultimate direct demand vehicle, along with taxing and financing to affect economic activity. The United States, influenced by Keynesian theory, has tried for many decades to minimize the occurrence and amplitude of business cycles by forcing spending and borrowing, a form of dissaving. Forced dissaving, unless offset, acts to transfer consumption to the present that otherwise would have been deferred to the future as a function of the marginal efficiency of investment. The direct impact of government dissaving is to require an increase in private savings (or foreign capital flows) to finance the needed borrowing. Government borrowing is considered to be relatively insensitive to the rate of interest involved in financing. As a result, interest rates will rise, presuming no expansion of monetary policy, to induce an offsetting increase in private savings. Beyond the increase in real output caused by the increase in government spending, the rise in interest rates will work to retard real output. Real output will further suffer assuming that the government is less able than the free market to allocate its funds efficiently. In addition, to the degree that the government is too generous with its entrusted funds, it can generate a sense of permanent income and minimally satisfactory lifestyle among the nonworking and permanently impair the economy's long-term performance.

The history of monetary policy since the early 1950s and the Federal Reserve–Treasury accord has been that of targeting interest rates at a level deemed appropriate to promote or accommodate reasonably stable economic activity. Unfortunately, because of the "short-term gain, long-term pain" quality of excessive monetary stimulation, there has been a tendency to err on the side of too much ease in monetary policy. As a result, the low inflation of the late 1950s and early 1960s gave way to double digit inflation rates in the late 1970s.

Some would lay this problem at the door of our tax structure, which allows nominal interest to be deducted from income for tax purposes. As a result, and particularly with the presence of a healthy inflation to exacerbate matters, U.S. economic participants were given strong incentives to borrow. With a monetary policy driven by interest rate targeting at what was considered to be reasonable real interest rates, and with a tax structure that encouraged borrowing, the result was upward pressure on rates while simultaneously causing the Federal Reserve to supply excessive monetary reserves. This laid the groundwork for the great inflation.

In October 1979, the Federal Reserve Board, under the direction of its chairman, Paul Volcker, switched from a policy of interest rate targeting to one of money supply targeting. This new policy allowed interest rates to clear at a more natural level. Over the ensuing two years, interest rates soared and the prime rate rose above 20 percent. But, with a reasonable lag, rates on the short end fell by two-thirds and long rates fell by almost half their prior highs, reflecting much lower inflation expectations. Following Volker's resignation, the policy mode of the Federal Reserve has again changed. By 1989, technological invention in the banking industry and newly resurrected classical economic thought had the Greenspan-led board somewhere in the midst of a four-factor policy model of targeting interest rates, targeting monetary reserves, targeting commodity prices, and targeting the value of the U.S. dollar.

The International Sector. Most foreign countries have had to take seriously the nondomestic influences on their economy for a long time. The United States has remained relatively isolationist in its economic views. Nevertheless, the foreign sector is important for three reasons: (1) as a source of exogenous supply and demand, (2) as a source and use of capital, and (3) because of the difficulties and risks associated with currencies.

The presence of external markets and productive capacity, with strengths and weaknesses different from those of the United States, provides an opportunity for global integration. The law of comparative advantage suggests that, as long as goods and services are freely exchanged, the collective income, wealth, and standard of living will benefit through increased trade. This is surely one of the key sources of historical growth built into the growth records of all nations.

To the investor and the economist, international trade and exchange requires a unit of monetary account at which goods and services can be passed that somehow reconciles two quasi-independent monetary systems. That system is the system of foreign currency exchange (forex). The forex market is every bit as real as the underlying security market of the investment to investors owning foreign securities.

Forecasting Exchange Rates. Two basic approaches are used to forecast currency exchange rates: (1) the balance of payments (BOP) approach

and (2) the asset market approach. The BOP approach focuses on the relationship between balance-of-payments flows and exchange rates. BOP
tracks all financial flows crossing the borders of a country, including capital
flows that offset goods and services purchases. At any point in time, this
approach presumes that the relative values of currencies are set primarily
so that the goods and capital markets will clear by finding the point where
a country's BOP must be equilibrated to maintain the continuity of exchange
and avoid the probability of default.

Under the asset market approach, the view that flow or spot supply and
demand markets determine currency levels is rejected. Exchange rates are
viewed as relative asset prices traded in a financial market. The exchange
rate is governed by expectations about the future values of currencies and
therefore is a function of future capital and trade flows. In its broad form,
this approach sees the collective setting of the exchange rate as the present
value of the collective net assets of one country versus the collective net
assets of the other, scaled by the amount of currency in circulation.

In the narrower sense, the asset market approach can take on the form
of purchasing power parity (PPP) or interest rate parity. PPP states that spot
exchange rates adjust perfectly to inflation differentials. The purchasing
power parity relationship, in its simplest form, is written:

$$\frac{S_1}{S_0} = (1 + I_F)/(1 + I_D) \qquad (5-8)$$

or, in words, disregarding the addition of unity to the numerator and denominator of the right side,

$$\text{the change in foreign currency relative to the domestic currency} = \frac{\text{foreign inflation}}{\text{domestic inflation}}$$

A broader view of PPP adds in the differences in domestic productivity
and compares inflation only at the tradable goods level. An even broader
view sees PPP as a measure of future expected relative inflation. In this
framework, currencies are always aligning themselves in the present so that
forward purchase of goods and services across boundaries are properly
aligned. Overall, the track record of PPP suggests that it is a poor predictor
of short-term currency movements. Nonetheless, many believe it does hold
over the long run (see Solnik [1988]).

A related asset theory is that of interest rate parity. This relationship
states that for free market interest rates, the interest rate differential between
two countries must equal the percentage difference between the forward
exchange rate and the spot rate, under simplifying assumptions of relative

equality in tax and risk perceptions across the two countries. This is as much a technical arbitrage condition as it is a theory. The underlying theory is the law of one price, which suggests that a freely traded good or assets will sell effectively at one price. Failing to do so would induce buying and selling resulting in excess economic profits from low or no cost effort.

The relation is written as:

$$\frac{F}{S} = \frac{1 + r_F}{1 + r_D}$$

or, in words,

forward over one plus the foreign interest rate
spot rate = divided by one plus the domestic
interest rate

where the spot rate equals the amount of foreign currency one unit of domestic currency will buy.

If this relationship did not hold, an investor could earn an easy arbitrage profit. For example, if U.K. interest rates were 10 percent and U.S. rates were 5 percent, and the forward/spot ratio was out of line at 1.00, the U.S. investor could purchase spot pounds, simultaneously sell forward pounds at no give up, and invest the pounds at 10 percent. The result is an excess profit of 5 percent over the U.S. interest rate of 5 percent. Such a situation would cause a massive shift into spot pounds and U.K. investments and out of forward pounds until the situation was righted.

As a result, when free market interest rates change, presumably reflecting expectations of future inflation and the real interest rate, spot currency rates must also change to reflect the new information and reestablish the proper spot/forward rate spreads.

The international Fisher relation describes the theoretical difference in nominal interest rates across national boundaries. The difference is linked to expectations of relative real interest rates and inflation. This relationship has found substantial support in empirical research.

$$\frac{1 + r_F}{1 + r_D} = \frac{1 + E(i_F)}{1 + E(i_D)} \times \frac{1 + E(I_F)}{1 + E(I_D)} \tag{5-9}$$

or, in words,

foreign nominal   foreign expected   foreign expected
interest rate   real interest   inflation rate
relative to   =   rate relative to ×   relative to
domestic   domestic   domestic

Thus far, this chapter has attempted to provide a structure for analysts and portfolio managers to address capital market expectations from the vantage point of macroeconomic input. Macroeconomic variables have been postulated to enter the process at two levels. The first deals with long-term expectations of macrovariables, primarily the growth of aggregate income, its stability, and its allocation across the factors of production and investment vehicles. The second deals with short-term macroeconomic expectations, the focal point of most conventional analysis. Besides discussing the techniques used for short-term forecasting, specific attention has been paid to the private, public, and international sectors of the economy.

INFLATION AND DEFLATION: SYMPTOMS OF DISEQUILIBRIUM AND THEIR EFFECTS

This section describes the nature of the inflation/deflation problem from the standpoint of the investor and then looks at how inflation/deflation impacts the holders of equity, debt, real estate, and international securities.

Nature of the Problem

To understand the nature of the problem from the investor's viewpoint, several terms must be understood. These terms are very much in keeping with the tone of this chapter in that it is expectations that set prices in the marketplace and changes in expectations that cause prices to change. Other than expectations of real output, there is probably no more important macrovariable to investors than inflation.

Inflation, from the investor's standpoint, must be carefully delineated as to (1) expected inflation and (2) changes in expected inflation (which includes unexpected inflation). Many an error has been made by investors and researchers because of a failure to make this distinction. As a result, some studies of the levels of inflation and the relationship to security performance have uncovered results that appear at odds with experience and have caused confusion among the students of markets and inflation.

Two clearly diverging relationships should be understood between security markets and expected inflation on the one hand, and changes to expected inflation on the other. Aggregate returns are linked with aggregate output in the framework presented in this chapter. To the degree that output is framed in nominal terms, nominal output is higher with higher inflation than with lower inflation. If a higher level of inflation is expected and those expectations are relatively stable, there will be higher aggregate nominal security returns, a positive relationship. This is because, as discussed earlier, all investors in future claims demand compensation for purchasing power erosion.

However, in a period of *rising inflation expectations,* it is expected that security returns will fall, a negative relationship. As a result, the interpretation of studies on the relationship of inflation and security market returns must carefully ascertain the nature of the inflation expectation at work as to whether the level of expected inflation or changes in inflation expectations are being observed.

From this point forward, the focus will be on changes in inflation expectations. The immediate focus will be on inflation as a wealth transfer agent, on the volatility of inflation expectations, and on how inflation expectations are formed.

Debasement of Financial Claims: A Wealth Transfer. Work by Fama [1981] and Geske and Roll [1983] indicate that inflation and the real economy do interact. Fama and others have provided ample empirical support for a theory that inflation (both expected and unexpected) and real output are negatively related. Fama suggests that lower economic activity decreases the demand to hold money, and therefore, with a fixed supply of money, additional inflation will result to clear the potential demand/supply imbalance. Geske and Roll view the potential causality as starting from exogenous shocks which cause a reduction in economic activity. This in turn lowers tax revenue, increases the budget deficit, increases government borrowing and ultimately forces the Federal Reserve to supply money to the economy. This is consistent with the notion of a political process where a given level of economic growth is expected and deemed acceptable. Evidence of a potential failure to meet the real output targets puts in action machinery to attempt to boost output, creating an inflationary potential.

Beyond the real output effect, which reduces the aggregate pool of returns, changes in inflation expectations have a *wealth transfer* character. All investments convey some obligation of potential future payment in money. Increases in inflation expectations directly reduce the value of future obligations that are quoted in monetary terms. This is exactly the same phenomena that occurs when one currency declines relative to another. A rise in inflation debases money relative to real goods and services and therefore debases all future monetary obligations with respect to future opportunities to buy goods and services.

What type of wealth transfers are occasioned by increasing inflation expectations? Clearly, a bond—a fixed promise to receive a nominal dollar amount in the future—will be directly and fully debased by a rise in inflation expectations. A real estate security that involves an assortment of promises to receive future payments and to pay future expenses could be affected entirely differently. For example, if the related expenses lag the revenue stream in the passing through of inflation, the real estate owner may actually benefit from rising inflation. A human laborer who regularly renegotiates his employment contract can be impacted positively, neutrally, or negatively depending on a host of factors. Note that after allowance for the real output effect, *all wealth transfers are a zero sum game*. Were it not for the real output effect, changes in inflation and inflation expectations would only act to move wealth around among the existing economic participants: labor, government, foreign interests, and capital market investors. If one group were hurt by inflation, another would gain.

Volatility in Inflation Expectations. Changes in inflation expectations also affect expectations of future price change volatility. This may very well be the transmission mechanism for the real output effect. High levels of inflation are believed to be inherently unstable. Increased expectations of inflation volatility make it difficult for rational risk averse economic agents to make long-term capital decisions, which provide the basis for growth in productivity. At the limit, great uncertainty over future changes in prices greatly encourages current consumption at the expense of capital expenditure.

Inflation was low and believed to be predictably so in the United States in the 1960s. Capital expenditures were large, and numerous long-term contracts of 30 or more years duration were made. Today, in certain overseas markets where volatile inflation is the rule, it is difficult to float a bond with much more than a 10-year maturity.

Forming Inflation Expectations

Formal tests of inflation forecasting devices have focused on three forecasting approaches. One approach assumes that the *term structure of interest rates* contains the best forecasts of inflation. Fama [1975] uses this approach assuming the real interest rate component of Treasury bills is constant. In a variation of this approach, Fama and Gibbons [1984] allowed the real rate to follow a random walk. A problem with this approach is its circuitous nature. That is, interest rates are used to forecast inflation in order to forecast interest rates. Nevertheless, the evidence suggests that of the three approaches, this one is the most successful for short-term forecasts.

The second approach uses a *time series model* approach. Nelson and Schwert [1977] used a univariate time series model and found results that approached the results contained in the term structure of the interest rates.

A third approach uses the *consensus of inflation forecasters*. This approach can be reviewed over the longest period by using the Livingston surveys. In recent years, surveys by Robert Eggert and Richard Hoey provide a more regular and disciplined calibration of short- and long-term expectations from economists and investors, respectively. The University of Michigan surveys consumer inflation attitudes.

For the investor who does not want to use the bond market or technical models to set inflation expectations, or does not want to systematically go with consensus opinion, two individual approaches are typical. The first blends three key expectational elements. The second is in the classic National Bureau of Economic Research mode of leading indicator analysis.

Combination Expectations Approach. Resler [1980] tried to understand what caused Livingston survey inflation expectations to move around over time. He pointed out that, given the state of the economics profession, three key pieces of information affect forecasters.

1. Inflation is first, last, and always a *monetary phenomenon* and therefore inflation forecasts are anchored to a longer-term relationship of monetary growth to inflation.
2. There is great *serial correlation* in inflation so that changes in actual past inflation help determine the expectations of future changes.
3. There are *shocks*, such as the energy crises of the 1970s, that occasionally occur that cause forecasters to have *serial errors* in forecasting. Therefore, there is a tendency for expectations to be impacted by past errors.

This type of approach combined with a deeper analysis of ongoing temporary shocks provides the basis of most multiquarter inflation forecasts. This contrasts with shorter-term monthly estimates that are largely "bottom up" estimates or a summation of component-by-component estimates.

Inflation Index Approach. A discussion of forming inflation expectations is not complete without mentioning the work on leading inflation indicators by Geoffrey Moore [1983]. Using the same methodologies used to develop the composite index of leading economic indicators, Moore has in recent years put together a leading index of inflation. (See Figure 5-8). The components of this index include the following:

- Percentage of population employed
- Growth in business and consumer debt
- Growth in federal debt
- Rate of change in industrial material prices
- Rate of change in import prices excluding fuels
- Dun and Bradstreet's survey of anticipated selling prices of businessmen

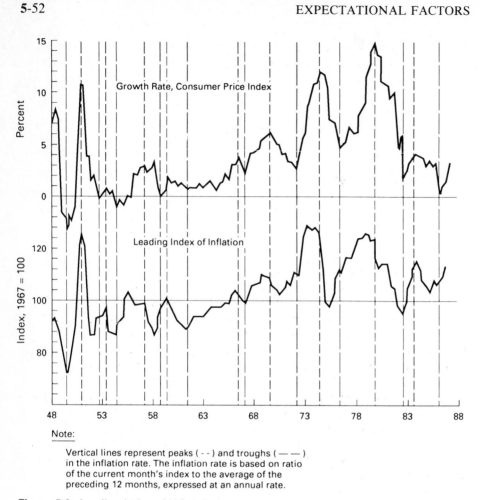

Note:

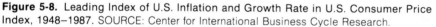

Vertical lines represent peaks (- -) and troughs (— —)
in the inflation rate. The inflation rate is based on ratio
of the current month's index to the average of the
preceding 12 months, expressed at an annual rate.

Figure 5-8. Leading Index of U.S. Inflation and Growth Rate in U.S. Consumer Price
Index, 1948–1987. SOURCE: Center for International Business Cycle Research.

The importance of fluctuations in currency values in setting inflation
expectations has only recently been realized in the United States. As with
trade, there is a direct impact from the fact that a devaluation in one country's
currency makes certain global commodity-based items immediately more
expensive. Other goods' prices will increase as a result of foreign company
pricing strategies. Survey work by Hooper and Lowrey [1979] suggests that
for each one percent decline in the U.S. dollar against a basket of foreign
currencies, U.S. inflation will ultimately rise 0.8 to 4.0 percent.

Effect on Stock Valuation

Conventional wisdom through the 1960s was that common stocks were an
inflation hedge. This was not meant to imply that stocks were an actual

hedge that excelled absolutely during periods of inflation, but that they were not adversely affected by inflation and therefore performed relatively well. To get this point across, it is useful to review the Gordon-Shapiro perpetual dividend discount model.

$$V_O = \frac{D_O}{k - g_D} \tag{5-10}$$

V_O = value at time zero

D_O = dividends received during time period zero

k = constant discount rate

g_D = constant growth rate of dividends

The inflation hedge school believes that V_O would be unaffected by unexpected inflation because the discount rate k would rise with a change in inflation expectations but by no more or less than the dividend growth rate g_D. As a result, V_O would be unaffected. For this to happen, companies must be fully capable of passing increases in costs of operations, borrowings, and taxes through to increases in selling prices. The argument that stocks show real gains in periods of unexpected inflation is one where companies could raise prices faster than costs because labor and some other costs would lag. The empirical evidence suggests, however, that stocks have not proven to be a good defense against unexpected inflation. Note that this conclusion is based on pretax returns. The results are even more striking for after-tax returns.

Why have stocks not been a good defense against inflation? Beginning with the aggregate framework, real output growth is not impervious to the ravages of inflation. As a result, in aggregate, all capital assets suffer. Common stocks suffer disproportionately because their income stream is the economy's residual income stream.

Inflation and Costs. Do other claimants hold their ground? Labor, the biggest component, actually lags in most inflationary periods because lengthy labor contracts, particularly union contracts, tend to delay adjustment of its price. Furthermore, employee benefits, which make up an increasing proportion of labor income, tend only to be reset periodically. This is a net benefit on average to corporations in terms of short-term cost pressures. Rents (as discussed later in this chapter) may, if anything, rise faster than inflation in the short term. Interest costs rise more or less instantaneously.

As for taxes, the rules in most countries require corporations to pay taxes based on original cost, not on replacement cost. As a result in a period of rising inflation, such as in the 1970s in the United States, corporations ended up paying taxes on phantom profits. Inventory profits at the national account level are measured by the inventory valuation adjustment (with a negative sign indicating phantom profit). This adjustment attempts to put all inventory on a last-in-first-out (LIFO) basis which minimizes the effect of inventory profits. In 1974, inventory profits accounted for 40 percent of U.S. book pretax corporate profit.

Capital consumption profits are measured by the capital consumption adjustment (CCA), which attempts to put all corporations on a straight-line depreciation basis at replacement cost. In the early 1980s, this item misleadingly added 8 percent to pretax profit. As a result, inflation can cause taxes to be materially higher than appropriate. However, over several years in the 1980s when inflation was declining, overdepreciation occurred, providing a tax shield and causing less than normal taxes to be paid. Book pretax profits are adjusted for inventory valuation, capital consumption, and taxes in Figure 5-9, to arrive at a net adjusted profit series over the 59-year period from 1929 to 1988.

Inflation and Management Decisions. Does the onset of unexpected inflation and deflation make for better management decisions? Assuredly not. Unexpected variation in the prices at which goods and services are transacted can impose a heavy cost on a company. First, there is a direct effect, clearly visible in Latin America, where time, resources, and effort are expended simply to keep track of and make decisions regarding steep and often accelerating price level increases. As compared to a noninflationary environment, this is unproductive. Second, there are indirect effects from making, on average, worse decisions. Companies may acquire or manufacture extra inventory, as was true in the 1970s, in the hopes of earning a windfall profit on inventory holdings. Again, as compared to a noninflationary environment, this is unproductive. Furthermore, there has been a tendency in periods of high or volatile inflation for companies to make their priorities more short-term oriented and avoid the risk-taking inherent in big project long-term decisions. These management problems are exacerbated by historical cost-based accounting, which fails to provide management with an accurate picture of how their operations are truly performing.

Historical Inflation and Stock Value Experience. The empirical evidence is quite damaging to the notion of stocks as an inflation hedge. Table 5-16 from Ibbotson and Brinson [1987] provides such evidence. The table is built in two sections. The first takes inflationary readings by year and places them in one of six categories ranging from extraordinary deflation (−4 percent and below) to extraordinary inflation (8 percent and above). The concurrent year's stock market return is placed in the cell, and the members of the cell are averaged.

Shown are results both for the long term (1790–1985) and the post World War II (1946–1985) experience. As Table 5-16 shows, very high rates of

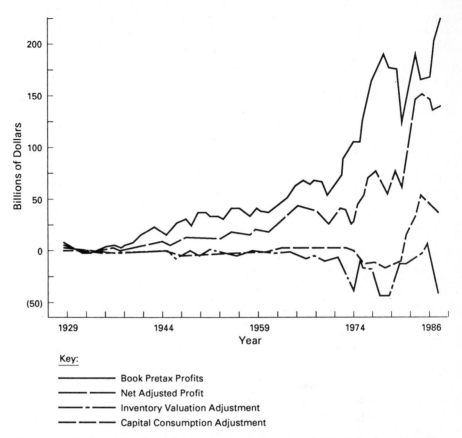

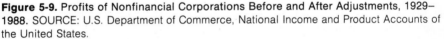

Figure 5-9. Profits of Nonfinancial Corporations Before and After Adjustments, 1929–1988. SOURCE: U.S. Department of Commerce, National Income and Product Accounts of the United States.

inflation are not healthy for stocks. Note, however, that periods of price stability to moderate deflation are associated with equity returns that nominally are a bit higher than in extraordinary deflationary periods and are fairly close to each other in real terms.

The second part of Table 5-16 shows the relationship of stock returns to periods of accelerating and decelerating inflation. Even in nominal terms, the results are striking. In 31 years of rapidly accelerating inflation (up 5 percent or more), nominal stock returns of less than 3 percent were achieved, whereas in 34 periods of rapid deceleration (down 5 percent or more) gains of over 11 percent are achieved.

The relationship of inflation and stock price changes was the topic for a number of academic studies, spurred by the development of the Center for Research on Security Prices (CRSP) data files in the 1960s and the great

TABLE 5-16. Inflation, Inflation Rate Changes, and Real Total Returns on U.S. Common Stocks Over the Long Term (1790–1985) and the Post-WWII Period (1946–1985)

	The Long Term 1790–1985		Post-WWII Period 1946–1985	
	Number of Years	Average Real Total Stock Market Return[a]	Number of Years	Average Real Total Stock Market Return[a]
Inflation Range				
Extraordinary deflation −4.00 percent and below	32	11.27%	0	N/A
Moderate deflation −3.99 to −0.99 percent	24	12.90	1	22.01%
Price stability −0.99 to 0.99 percent	35	12.53	5	23.02
Moderate inflation 1.00 to 3.99 percent	55	10.23	18	10.32
High inflation 4.00 to 7.99 percent	26	3.65	8	8.47
Extraordinary inflation 8.00 percent and above	24	−5.65	8	−7.82
Inflation Rate Changes From Previous Year				
Rapid deceleration Down 5.00 percent or more	34	11.74%	4	10.37%
Low deceleration Down 0.01 to 4.99 percent	63	10.76	17	16.91
Low acceleration Up 0.00 to 4.99 percent	68	6.87	16	0.39
Rapid acceleration Up 5.00 percent or more	31	2.69	3	−8.61
All Years	196		40	
Arithmetic mean		8.31%		7.74%
Geometric mean (compound average return)		6.28		6.02

SOURCE: Ibbotson and Brinson [1987].
[a] Arithmetic mean, except where noted.

inflation of the 1970s. Several hypotheses were generated that purport to interpret the relationship. They involved *Investor Rationality*, *Real Output Effects*, and *Nominal Contracting*.

The investor rationality, or better yet, irrationality argument, was put forth by Modigliani and Cohn [1979]. Modigliani and Cohn (MC) posited that investors make a mistake in periods of high inflation because of their tendency to compare the nominal interest rate with the earnings yield for the stock market. For example, assume that an investor arrives at the conclusion that the secular rate of inflation has moved from 5 percent to 6 percent. What should happen to stock prices as a result? MC believe that investors would appropriately increase the inflation premium in the discount rate of the bond market and of the stock market, which does two things. First, it reduces the present value in the standard valuation model for both stocks and bonds. Second, the implied lower present value will cause both the bond yield and the earnings yield of the stock market to rise, which in isolation will maintain the spread between the bond yield and earnings yield.

MC's irrationality argument is that the analysis should not stop there. Whereas a fixed coupon bond may require a full one percent increase in yield to compensate for a one percent rise in the inflation premium, the stock market may not. In fact, if the increased inflation is fully passed through in the form of product and service price increases, the cash flows to the investor in the standard valuation model should increase sufficiently to totally offset the rise in the inflation premium. The appropriate result could be no change in present value and no change in the current earnings yield.

MC surveyed memoranda from large brokerage firms that indicated that investors were using the spread between the current earnings yield of the stock market and the nominal bond yield to help determine the fair value of the stock market. If corporations can pass through inflation to some degree, or unless the brokerage firms made some adjustment to the earnings level used in the earnings yield calculation to adjust for future inflation, this kind of spread comparison would lead to a relative valuation error. If corporations can fully pass through inflation, it would be more appropriate to work with the spread between the earnings yield and the real bond rate (i.e., the bond yield with no inflation premium). This argument is heavily dependent on practitioners relying on an earnings yield type of concept and then inappropriately applying it. This is a straw man argument that has little validity.

MC go on to argue that investors fail to reduce the value of corporate nominal liabilities during periods of high inflation. They say that if investors were engaged in valuing stocks on an asset value or balance sheet basis, this argument would lead to valuation errors. Asset value analysis typically involves estimating the value of the assets of the firm and the firm's liabilities, with the equity value being calculated as the residual. There is nothing inconsistent, when properly applied, about using asset valuation in contrast to using the standard valuation model. They are two ways of viewing the equity value of the same corporation.

When using the asset value approach, however, it is important to value the assets under the same inflation assumptions as the corporation's indebtedness is valued. Failing to reduce the value of fixed coupon liabilities under assumptions of higher inflation is clearly erroneous. The decline in market value that the corporate bondholder suffers when inflation rises reflects the ability of bond issuers to pay off fixed-rate bonds in inflation-cheapened dollars.

The MC argument can be avoided, however, by using the standard valuation model as opposed to asset valuation. Under an assumption of higher secular inflation, the analyst using the standard valuation model must carefully assess: (1) the ability of the firm to increase prices; (2) the likelihood and degree of cost increases; (3) the increase in the nominal, but tax deductible, costs of future borrowings; and (4) the tax impacts created by the differences in economic versus historical cost, including bond tax accounting, profits. Proper analysis implicitly reduces the present value of the liability and avoids the MC concerns.

Summers [1981] attempted to directly test the power of MC's argument and found that, in the 1970s, a large part of the decline in the stock market was related to overpayment of taxes as a result of inflation. This overpayment apparently overwhelmed the tax savings due to inflated tax deductible interest payments.

The real output effects hypothesis was discussed earlier in terms of inflation's effect on aggregate capital market returns. The second part of this hypothesis, as it relates to common stocks, is that because the stock market is forward looking, expectations of lower future real output will be particularly injurious to stocks, the residual profit beneficiary in the economy. Gultekin [1983] extended the standard analysis to use unexpected inflation as a predictor of stock returns using the difference between realized inflation and expected inflation from the Livingston consensus data as a measure of unexpected inflation. His results show that expected inflation had an insignificant impact on the return of the Standard & Poor's 500 Composite Stock Price Index (S&P 500) over the 1952 through 1979 period. Unexpected inflation, however, had a large and statistically significant negative impact on stock returns where a one percent unexpected inflation surprise was, on average, related to a 4 percent decline in the S&P 500.

A number of the hypotheses concerning inflation and stock prices have been put under the umbrella label of nominal contracting. Because firms do most of their contracting in nominal terms and pay taxes based on nominal profits, it is expected that some contracts should prove beneficial (or harmful) to the firm's profits in periods of unexpected inflation. Contracts considered in research studies include depreciation tax shields, first-in-first-out (FIFO) inventory, and indebtedness. Extensive research has not as yet been conducted on nominal contracts involving labor and materials. Empirical studies, such as French, Ruback, and Schwert [1981], found little support for the nominal contracting hypothesis. However, more recent work by Pearce and Roley [1988], in which surveys of expected monthly CPI inflation were used instead of proxy measures of expectations to determine unexpected inflation, provides some encouragement to the nominal contracting hypothesis. Pearce and Roley's empirical results suggest that a company's

CAPITAL MARKET EXPECTATIONS

debt-to-equity ratio and level of depreciation is important in determining the company's response to inflation surprises.

Inflation in International Markets. Given the preceding, it would be surprising if international stock markets exhibited a different relationship to home country unexpected inflation. Gultekin [1983] regressed the return of 14 local stock markets against expected and unexpected inflation as provided by a time series model. The results of his research showed that in 7 of the 13 countries, excluding the United States, the sign of the relationship between stock returns and unexpected inflation was negative. In addition to the United States, only three countries' negative signs approached statistical significance: Canada, Italy, and Switzerland. However, each showed only one-half the power of the United States' negative relationship. In the United Kingdom, the relationship is actually significantly positive, possibly the result of a positive effect from oil inflation for the U.K.'s North Sea petroleum discoveries and the strong influence of import prices on its inflation rate. Higher import inflation strongly suggests an improvement in domestic export competitiveness.

Overall, these international results are much more ambiguous than the results for the United States. This may be because of the different relationships that corporations have with labor and the differences in tax codes and the fact that in most foreign countries only one set of books is kept for reporting and tax purposes. For example, Miller [1988] states that the United States has the world's only completely unintegrated tax system, whereby income made by corporations is taxed twice, once at the corporate level and again at the personal level as dividends are received. Taxing inflated dollars twice may result in the U.S. stock market being more sensitive to inflation than are overseas stock markets.

To make the picture a bit more confusing, however, there is some evidence to the contrary. Solnik [1988] argues that prior to free-floating exchange rates, there were not autonomous monetary policies and diverse independent inflation rates across countries. By focusing on the post-Bretton Woods period and using interest rates as an inflation proxy, Solnik shows, in Table 5-17, a strong negative relationship between changes in interest rates and real stock returns for all eight countries examined, holding constant the level of interest rates. Clearly, if interest rates and inflation expectations overseas are tightly linked, this provides good evidence of a U.S.-style relationship between *changes* in inflation expectations and stock market returns.

Effect on Bond Valuation

Because bond prices are linked to interest rates, the linkage between changes in inflation expectations and changes in interest rates is important. In the

TABLE 5-17. Regression Relationships Between Monthly Real Stock Returns, Interest Rates, and Changes in Interest Rates, 1971–1982

Country	Interest Rate Coefficient[a]	Change in Interest Rate Coefficient[a]	R^2
Belgium	−2.2 (1.2)	−12.7 (4.1)	8%
Canada	−2.1 (1.4)	−30.4 (6.2)	15
France	−1.1 (1.3)	−7.0 (2.8)	4
West Germany	−0.5 (1.2)	−16.1 (3.8)	11
Japan	−4.2 (1.8)	−19.3 (9.5)	6
Netherlands	−2.3 (1.5)	−8.7 (4.0)	4
Switzerland	−3.7 (1.4)	−20.2 (4.2)	16
United Kingdom	−2.0 (1.9)	−26.3 (4.8)	18
United States	−2.1 (1.1)	−15.1 (3.4)	13

SOURCE: Solnik [1988].
[a] All monthly rates of return have been annualized to be consistent with annualized interest rate quotations. Standard deviations of coefficient estimates appear in parentheses.

standardized valuation model, the discount rate for a bond is made up of a real risk-free rate, an inflation premium, and a risk premium in the Fisherian framework. For simplicity's sake, this discussion will focus on government bonds. Corporate bonds take on equity-like characteristics at lower levels of credit quality and very low quality corporate bonds will respond to changes in inflation expectations as a cross between a government bond and a common stock.

There is no disagreement that interest rates in the United States are directly linked to changes in inflation expectations. The only controversy arises out of whether all or almost all of the variation in rates on government bonds is due to changes in inflation expectations or to changes in real interest rates.

A powerful source of evidence confirming the relationship of interest rates to inflation expectations goes back to the discussion of how inflation expectations are formed. Inflation expectations derived from the term structure of interest rates, using a constant for the real rate of interest, have so far proven superior in forecasting inflation to either time series models or a consensus of forecasters. This is strong evidence that the relationship of inflation to interest rates is so strong that forecasters have a difficult time

TABLE 5-18. Average Annual Exchange Rate Movements, Inflation Rate Differentials, and Interest Rate Differentials for Six Paired Country Comparisons, 1973–1985

Countries	Average Annual Exchange Rate Movement	Average Annual Inflation Rate Differential	Average Annual Interest Rate Differential
U.S./Japan	3.6%	0.4%	2.8%
U.S./West Germany	2.4	3.1	3.8
U.S./U.K.	−2.2	−4.8	−2.2
U.S./Switzerland	5.2	3.3	5.6
U.S./France	−2.7	−2.7	−2.4
West Germany/U.K.	−4.9	−7.6	−6.0

SOURCE: Solnik [1988].

finding worthwhile information that is being missed by the bond market pertaining to inflation prediction.

International Interest Rates and Inflation Rates. Another source of support for an interest rate-inflation expectations relationship can be taken from the international Fisherian relationship. This version states that the interest rate differential between two countries is a function of differences in real interest rates and expected inflation. If real interest rates are equal in two countries, differences in nominal rates are caused by different inflationary expectations. This relationship has received much support when applied to the major currencies. Table 5-18 from Solnik [1988] illustrates how U.S./foreign inflation rate differentials tracked interest rate differentials from 1973 to 1985. The similarity of the two sets of differentials is remarkable.

Effect on Real Estate Valuation

Most investors believe that, because real estate is a tangible asset, real estate returns are positively correlated with inflation because inflation is a debasement of paper assets. This is not necessarily so, because a debasement of the currency by inflation devalues all assets stated in terms of that currency. What is really at issue is whether or not real estate as an asset class performs relatively well in inflationary periods versus other goods and services.

The standardized valuation model applied to real estate provides a framework for analysis. Without question, a permanent increase in inflation expectations reduces the value of real estate by increasing the discount rate applied to all future cash flows to the investor. If there were no offsets in the numerator of the equation, Diermeier, Freundlich, and Schlarbaum [1986] estimate that, in the mid-1980s, the impact of a one percent rise in permanent inflation expectations would be an approximate 9 to 11 percent decline in value for a typical tax-exempt real estate investment.

Real Estate Cash Flows and Inflation. However, it appears that, for real estate as an asset class, this is more than compensated for by growth in the cash flow component, the numerator. This occurs because market rents, outside of rent-controlled areas, tend to be fairly responsive to cost increases and regional inflation. Many real estate lease contracts of size are directly responsive because they have an explicit cost of living adjustment built into them. Furthermore, many contracts have clauses that pass increased costs directly to the tenant. Some key costs not directly passed through, such as maintenance, labor, property taxes, and insurance in general, tend to lag general price level changes. The end result for many real estate properties is for real cash flows to the investor to increase in periods of rising inflation because nominal cash flow growth more than offsets the increase in the discount rate.

Real Estate Leverage and Inflation. Many holders of real estate leverage their ownership by borrowing money to attain an equity interest in the property. It is not unusual for commercial real estate deals to start off with 100 percent debt financing. The form of financing does not impact the underlying asset's relationship with inflation, yet the fact that fixed-rate creditors are losers with respect to unanticipated inflation suggests that the residual real estate equity holder would be the beneficiary of a wealth transfer from the debt holder to the equity owner. Because leverage is relatively heavily used in the real estate field (although not in tax-exempt institutional investing), part of the belief in real estate as an inflation hedge arises from the use of leverage financing.

Furthermore, the structure of the U.S. real estate industry is such that real estate developers tend to cut back activity as interest rates rise. Carrying costs, with no concurrent revenue offset, rise and sources of short-term construction and bridge loans have traditionally dried up during periods of rising rates. As a result, unexpected inflation tends to encourage a cutback in expectations of new supply of developed property, which improves the utilization and rent outlook for existing properties. Conversely, lower inflation expectations and rates have been associated with flooding the market with new space and have caused serious problems with occupancy and rents, as occurred in the mid-1980s in many U.S. urban locations.

As a result, real estate as an asset class, even if it is not positively impacted by unanticipated inflation in an absolute sense, is relatively advantaged compared to other investment vehicles. The conventional wisdom, then, is for investors to flock to real estate as a safe haven when inflationary winds blow.

Effect on Exchange Rates

As previously discussed in this chapter, one of the most important determinants of changes in relative exchange rates is relative inflation. Foreign exchange rates are necessary, where political boundaries exist, to price the goods and services of one country with respect to another. Presuming a free and open market, it should be expected that an inflationary economy's currency will over time depreciate against the currency of a stable inflation country by an amount nearly equal to the difference in inflation rates.

The theory of purchasing power parity states that spot exchange rates adjust perfectly to inflation differentials. The theory relies on perfect trade and money markets. The empirical evidence finds purchasing power parity to be a poor explanation for short-term exchange rate movements. For example, Adler and Dumas [1983] found that concurrent inflation differentials explained less than 5 percent of monthly exchange rate movements in the 1970s.

Just because short-term movements in exchange rates have not been found to be closely associated with relative inflation shifts has not prevented most researchers and investors from believing that this relationship holds over the longer term. As much as anything else, the lack of a close short-term relationship may have to do with: (1) the difficulty of measuring inflation and (2) the relatively slow speed of adjustment in the goods market. Using actual inflation may be inappropriate to a degree. It is likely that the foreign exchange market, instead of balancing solely on concurrent inflation, reflects expectations of future relative inflation rates as well. In that case, current exchange rate movements are affected by future expected, rather than past, inflation rates.

SCENARIO FORECASTING AND ITS CONSEQUENCES

The set of potential economic outcomes and their implied capital market returns over any time horizon is infinite in size. In addition, it is vital that the investor recognize his forecasting limitations and those of his economic forecasters. Given this, it is naive to proceed with just one set of economic assumptions in mind when addressing the capital markets. Unfortunately, the development of expectations for every contingency can quickly become unwieldy and unbearable. Some method of managing the range of potential outcomes is necessary to prevent becoming paralyzed by having too many avenues of pursuit.

There are two methods by which the range of outcomes can be managed. The approach most widely used by practitioners involves the development of *specific economic scenarios*. A second approach is to assume that the economic variables being forecast are part of a *stochastic process* whereby statistical procedures can be used to indicate the range of outcomes.

Scenario Forecasting Techniques

Scenario forecasting fully recognizes that the future returns to be generated by the capital markets are contingent upon the state of the world. This *state contingency* can be formalized and developed into a useful set of expectations by developing alternative scenarios around the primary, or most likely, expectation scenario.

There are typically two approaches to scenario forecasting. Both require the identification of a limited set of key or driving variables. Usually these will include assumptions regarding the conduct of monetary and fiscal policy, propensity to consume and save, and the investment in capital goods. Occasionally, shock factors such as war, energy, food, wealth, or other disequilibria are introduced. The purpose is to define under different exogenous assumptions which economic environments could result.

The first approach simply identifies past economic periods with an appropriate mix of exogenous variables. For example, depression scenarios are usually patterned on the experience of the Great Depression of the 1930s. Similarly, the 1960s are used as a model for periods of declining tax rates and restrained monetary policy. The second approach is based on econometric modeling. Here economic relationships are believed to be understood. Given some key exogenous model assumptions, the model is allowed to forecast the economy.

The advantages of multiple scenario forecasting are that it:

- Allows recognition of the likelihood of error in the most likely forecast
- Affords convenience in reducing a difficult multipronged task to a manageable level
- Forces the decision maker to focus on the key variables affecting the forecast
- Provides an excellent mechanism to convey information across an investment organization and provide staff with the proper focus
- Affords particular benefits if the distribution of potential outcomes has a distinct skew to it (a single scenario approach cannot convey the skewed likelihood)
- Forces the forecaster to consider the exercise from many different angles and frames of reference

Scenarios are most useful where the economic relationships that are believed to exist are strong and relatively uncomplicated, and when the exogenous variables are highly correlated with respect to their impact on key variables. If the ''error'' terms in the assumed relationships are large, then the structure of scenario building loses much of its theoretical elegance. This is because most scenario building is based on using several different exogenous assumptions and then presuming that all other economic relationships will hold as postulated. If, in fact, the linkage of the exogenous variable is itself highly variable, or if subsequent economic relationships are also highly variable, the value of the identified scenarios is highly diluted.

Even if economic relationships are not stable, however, scenario forecasting can provide valuable self knowledge. The discipline of building scenarios of perceived low probability events can be very instructive. By going through the process of constructing extreme high and low scenarios, the forecaster is usually forced to clarify strongly held, longer-lasting beliefs, to identify and abandon more ephemeral and temporary information, and to strip away ambiguous relationships. Such an exercise may help the forecaster avoid the natural biases and erroneous tendencies that human beings, even experts, often fall prey to.

Reconciling Scenario and Stochastic Forecasting

The use of scenarios should involve, at the least, reconciling the set of scenarios with a *naive forecast distribution* because, as Tversky and Kahneman [1974] have indicated, a *bias of imaginability* can exist in which probabilities are often assigned to different scenarios not on the basis of their true likelihood but by the ease with which the scenarios can be constructed. Because the ease of constructing scenarios does not necessarily reflect actual likelihood, the scenario mode of analysis is particularly prone to bias. The use of naive forecast distributions, which statistically generate a multitude of nonspecified scenarios in the shape of a distribution, helps the investor identify any biases he may have.

One of the simplest forms of such a forecast distribution is to assume a naive model where the future will look like the past. For example, the histogram in Figure 5-10 plots the errors of a model that says this year's forecast change in inflation will equal last year's change in inflation.

Reconciliation of specific economic scenarios with a naive forecast distribution, such as the one shown, at times will show a potential characteristic of scenario-based decision making: The end decisions are often driven as much by omitted scenarios as by the scenarios present and identified. By reconciling the specific scenarios with stochastic modeling, the forecaster gets a better handle on what is driving his decision making. Scenario based decision making is fraught with potential pitfalls without this reconciliation.

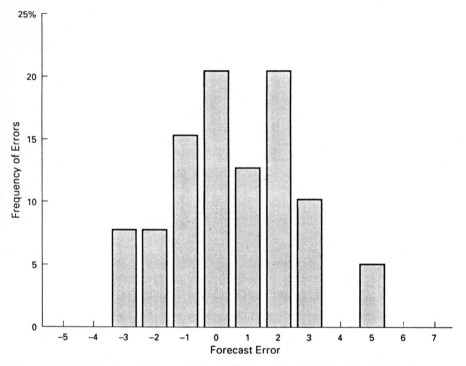

Figure 5-10. Distribution of Forecast Errors Using a Naive Inflation Model (Inflation$_t$ = Inflation$_{t-1}$ + Error). SOURCE: First Chicago Investment Advisors.

Examples of Specific Scenarios

Table 5-19 shows three economic scenarios revolving around the important macroeconomic factor, changes in the general price level, called *disinflation*, "*muddle along*," and *reinflation*. They correspond to expectations of 3 percent, 5 percent, and 7 percent inflation. For each scenario, two forward periods are defined to match the two-stage valuation model framework used throughout this chapter. The first stage covers the economic expectation for the next five years, at which time some level of normalcy is assumed to occur, setting the stage for a steady state second stage. This explains why in the second stage so many of the cells in the table show the same growth rate.

The first issue addressed in the forecast is the amount of aggregate real output to be generated under each (inflation) scenario. Following Fama [1975], the rate of growth in the real economy over longer periods is shown to vary inversely with the rate of inflation. The key determinant of that differential real growth is found in the line marked "Productivity." Higher inflation is assumed to harm the rate of output per hour worked because of

TABLE 5-19. Economic Forecasts for the U.S. Domestic Economy Under Three Inflation Scenarios and Two Periods: 1988–1993 and 1993–Forward

Economic Variable	Scenarios					
	Disinflation		Muddle Along		Reinflation	
Average Rate or Average Growth Rate per Year	1988–1993	1993–Forward	1988–1993	1993–Forward	1988–1993	1993–Forward
Inflation	3.0%	3.0%	5.0%	5.0%	7.0%	7.0%
Real GNP	3.0	3.0	2.5	2.5	2.1	2.1
Labor force	1.3	1.3	1.3	1.3	1.4	1.4
Hours worked	−0.3	−0.3	−0.3	−0.3	−0.3	−0.3
Productivity	2.0	2.0	1.5	1.5	1.0	1.0
Real national income	2.9	3.0	2.5	2.5	2.1	2.1
Compensation of employees	3.4	3.0	2.9	2.5	2.1	2.1
Proprietors' income	1.9	3.0	−1.0	2.5	2.8	2.1
Rental income	1.0	3.0	−1.0	2.5	3.7	2.1
Net interest	−0.5	3.0	4.7	2.5	6.5	2.1
Corporate profit (with inventory valuation adjustment and capital consumption allowance)	3.9	3.0	−1.2	2.5	−5.9	2.1
Tax liability	3.3	3.0	2.7	2.5	0.9	2.1
Profits after tax[a]	3.3	3.0	2.7	2.5	2.9	2.1
Dividends[a]	4.9	3.0	4.7	2.5	2.7	2.1
Undistributed profits	0.0	3.0	−1.9	2.5	−3.3	2.1
Interest rates (average):						
30-day Treasury bills (annual yield)	4.4	4.4	6.4	6.4	8.4	8.4
30-year government bond (annual yield)	6.6	6.6	8.8	8.8	11.0	11.0
Memo (real growth):						
S&P 500 earnings per share[a]	2.4	2.4	1.5	2.0	−0.7	1.4
S&P 500 dividends per share[a]	7.6	2.4	4.7	2.0	2.1	1.4

SOURCE: First Chicago Investment Advisors.
[a] Reflects accounting differences and annual dilution from new shares issued.

problems discussed earlier, such as the nonproductive effort expended just to keep track of price level changes and the errors business managers may make in mistaking inflated demand for real demand.

Once aggregate output is determined, it is necessary to allocate the income derived from that output across the claimants or the factors of production. In Table 5-19, the national income account convention is used, allocating the income generated by the domestic economy to labor, propri-

TABLE 5-20. Economic Projections for Four Countries for Two Periods: 1988–1993 and 1993–Forward

	Inflation	Real GNP[a]	Dividends[a]	Short-Term Interest Rates[b]	Long-Term Interest Rates[b]
Stage 1: 1988–1993					
Japan	2.0%	4.5%	12.0%	3.4%	5.0%
United Kingdom	6.0	3.0	6.5	7.4	10.5
West Germany	2.0	3.0	4.0	3.4	5.9
Canada	5.5	3.3	9.0	6.9	10.0
Stage 2: 1993–Forward					
Japan	3.0	3.5	8.5	4.4	5.8
United Kingdom	6.5	2.4	8.8	7.9	10.3
West Germany	2.5	2.9	4.9	9.9	5.4
Canada	5.5	3.4	9.9	6.9	9.3

SOURCE: First Chicago Investment Advisors.
[a] Annual percentage change.
[b] Average for period.

etors, real estate, and capital, whether debt or equity capital. From these forecasts, forward-looking cash flow estimates for each of the domestic U.S. asset classes can be derived, essentially addressing the numerator of the domestic version of the standard valuation model.

The forecast table goes further to include expectations of short- and long-term interest rates. It should be noted that under the higher inflation scenario, the long Treasury bond risk premium is higher than in the low inflation scenario. This reflects an underlying assumption that higher rates of inflation are inherently less stable. Much of the denominator for the long-term discount rate in the standard valuation model is provided by these interest rate expectations.

Table 5-20 provides an abbreviated version of the prior table for four of the largest non-U.S. economies: Japan, United Kingdom, Germany, and Canada. Here only the ''Muddle Along'' scenario is presented. Once again, the two-stage or two-period convention is followed to provide a feel for the valuation process.

Table 5-21 takes input directly from Table 5-19 to generate a forecast of expected return for the 1988 through 1993 time frame under the ''Muddle Along'' scenario. For example, with an early 1989 S&P 500 Index level of 287, a dividend growth of 9.7 percent to 1994 and 7 percent thereafter, and a long-term discount rate of 11.5 percent, an expected five-year annual return of 9.9 percent can be calculated. Similarly, expected rates of return of 14.9, 9.5, 8.0, and 6.4 percent are calculated for venture capital, the 30-year U.S. government bond, equity real estate, and the 30-day U.S. Treasury bill (assumed rolled every 30 days).

To illustrate the handling of the currency adjustment in the standardized

TABLE 5-21. Calculation of Domestic "Muddle Along" Expected Return (Solving for k, the Internal Rate of Return, for the Period 1988–1993)

	$\dfrac{\text{Current}}{\text{Price}}$ =	Value of Stage 1	+	Value of Stage 2
		Stage 1		Stage 2
Asset Class	Current Price	Cash Flows From 1988 to 1993 Divided by $(1+k)^T$		Cash Flow in 1994 Divided by Long-Term Discount Rate[a] Minus Long-Term Growth Rate; All Divided by $(1+k)^5$
Common stocks (S&P 500 Index)	287	1989: $10.70/(1+k)^T$ 1990: $11.76/(1+k)^2$ 1991: $12.93/(1+k)^3$ 1992: $14.21/(1+k)^4$ 1993: $15.62/(1+k)^5$ $k = 9.9\%$		$[17.18/(0.115 - 0.07)]/(1+k)^5$ = $381.69/(1+k)^5$
Venture capital	100	1989: $2.65/(1+k)^1$ 1990: $3.04/(1+k)^2$ 1991: $3.50/(1+k)^3$ 1992: $4.02/(1+k)^4$ 1993: $4.63/(1+k)^5$ $k = 14.9\%$		$[5.32/(0.185 - 0.15)]/(1+k)^5$ = $177.33/(1+k)^5$
30-year U.S. Treasury bond[b]	100	1989: $9.07/(1+k)^1$ 1990: $9.07/(1+k)^2$ 1991: $9.07/(1+k)^3$ 1992: $9.07/(1+k)^4$ 1993: $9.07/(1+k)^5$ $k = 9.5\%$		$[9.07/(0.088 - 0.000)]/(1+k)^5$ = $102.86/(1+k)^5$
U.S. equity real estate	100	1989: $5.15/(1+k)^1$ 1990: $5.30/(1+k)^2$ 1991: $5.46/(1+k)^3$ 1992: $5.63/(1+k)^4$ 1993: $5.80/(1+k)^5$ $k = 8.0\%$		$[5.97/(0.102 - 0.05)]/(1+k)^5$ = $114.81/(1+k)^5$
30-day U.S. Treasury bill	100	1989: $6.40/(1+k)^1$ 1990: $6.40/(1+k)^2$ 1991: $6.40/(1+k)^3$ 1992: $6.40/(1+k)^4$ 1993: $6.40/(1+k)^5$ $k = 6.4\%$		$[6.40/(0.064 - 0.000)]/(1+k)^5$ = $100/(1+k)^5$

SOURCE: First Chicago Investment Advisors.
[a] Long-term discount rate from Table 5-23.
[b] Bond calculation of present value for a 25-year bond with an annual coupon yield of 9.07 percent and an 8.80 percent annual yield to maturity at the end of the fifth year.

TABLE 5-22. Calculation of Expected U.K. Stock Returns in Dollars (Solving for *k*, the Internal Rate of Return for the Period 1988–1993)

Current Price	=	Value of Stage 1	+	Value of Stage 2
		Stage 1[a]		Stage 2[a]
U.K. Stocks Current Price		Cash Flows Converted to Dollars From 1988 to 1993 Divided by $(1 + k)^T$		Cash Flow in 1994 Converted to Dollars Divided by the Long-Term Discount Rate Minus Long-Term Growth Rate Plus Long-Term Inflation Differential All Divided by $(1 + k)^5$
566.50		1989: $(29.13 \times 0.9906)/(1 + k)^T$ 1990: $(31.08 \times 0.9812)/(1 + k)^2$ 1991: $(33.16 \times 0.9720)/(1 + k)^3$ 1992: $(35.37 \times 0.9628)/(1 + k)^4$ 1993: $(37.73 \times 0.9537)/(1 + k)^5$		$$\frac{[(40.25 \times 0.9403)/(0.126 - (0.0875 - 0.0141))]}{(1 + k)^5}$$ $$= $$ $$719.53/(1 + k)^5$$
			$k = 10.07\%$	

SOURCE: First Chicago Investment Advisors.

[a] Formula from Table 5-1 using assumptions of 5 percent annual U.S. inflation and 6 percent annual U.K. inflation from 1988 to 1993 and 5 percent U.S. and 6.5 percent U.K. inflation thereafter. Note: Sign on 0.0141 is minus instead of plus because the U.K. inflation rate is assumed to be larger than the U.S. inflation rate.

valuation model, Table 5-22 shows calculations of expected U.K. stock returns based on the forecasts in Table 5-20. In this case, with the Morgan Stanley U.K. Stock Index at 566.50, an expected return of 10.07 percent is derived. It is assumed that in stage one, dividends in sterling will grow by 6.50 percent per annum. Because of a forecast 6 percent U.K. inflation rate versus a 5 percent U.S. inflation rate, and assuming purchasing power parity determines relative currency movement, dividends converted to dollars grow by 5.50 percent per annum. In stage two, local currency dividend growth of 8.75 percent is converted to 7.22 percent in U.S. dollars reflecting the differential between the long-term inflation forecasts of 6.5 percent in the U.K. and 5.0 percent in the United States.

The long-term discount rate assumptions used in all the Stage 2 calculations are found in Table 5-23.[2] For all of the asset classes under consideration, the investor, who is presumed to be interested in U.S. dollar denominated returns, requires compensation for the expected U.S. level of inflation and the real risk-free rate of return. A risk premium for each asset class is selected from the integrated/segmented work provided earlier in this chapter. These payment requirements are summed to provide the long-term

---

[2] Note that some users of the model may prefer to solve for *k*, the discount rate, from 1988 to infinity, as opposed to assuming that markets will be priced at some long-term discount rate five years hence.

TABLE 5-23. Long-Term Discount Rate Assumptions

	Discount Rate	= Real Risk-Free Interest Rate +	Inflation Premium +	Risk Premium
Domestic Equities:				
S&P 500 Index	11.5%	1.4%	5.0%	5.1%
Total market	12.0	1.4	5.0	5.6
Non-U.S. equities:				
Japan	11.9	1.4	5.0	5.5
United Kingdom	12.6	1.4	5.0	6.2
Germany	11.4	1.4	5.0	5.0
Canada	12.7	1.4	5.0	6.3
Total Market	11.8	1.4	5.0	5.4
Venture capital	18.5	1.4	5.0	12.1
Dollar bonds:				
30-year U.S. Treasury bond	8.8	1.4	5.0	2.4
Total market	8.1	1.4	5.0	1.7
Nondollar bonds:				
Japan	7.8	1.4	5.0	1.4
United Kingdom	8.8	1.4	5.0	2.4
Germany	7.9	1.4	5.0	1.5
Canada	8.8	1.4	5.0	2.4
Total market	8.2	1.4	5.0	1.8
U.S. equity real estate	10.2	1.4	5.0	3.8
30-day Treasury bill	6.4	1.4	5.0	0.0

SOURCE: First Chicago Investment Advisors.

discount rate. (Note that a multiplicative and not additive combination of the components is more correct. An additive combination is used for purposes of simplicity.)

The results of carrying out the previous calculations over all asset classes and under each of the three scenarios are shown in Table 5-24. The returns for each of the scenarios have been multiplied by their respective probabilities and summed to produce the Expected Return column of numbers. The final column lists the long-term standard deviation forecasts shown earlier in the chapter. Note also the total investable capital market return row near the bottom of the table. This row results from a market capitalization weighted average of the primary asset classes, using the weights found in Figure 5-4.

From this point, most serious investors would take the expected return calculations and standard deviation assumption and combine them with a forecast correlation matrix to generate an optimal asset mix. By using a Markowitz/Sharpe style quadratic optimization routine to define a frontier of highest expected return per unit of standard deviation portfolios, a collection of relatively attractive asset class portfolios can be generated. Some investors might weight more heavily the most negative scenarios to minimize

TABLE 5-24. Projected Annual Returns and Probabilities by Global Asset Class Based on Three Scenarios for the Period 1988–1993

Asset Class	Scenarios			Expected Return	Estimated Standard Deviation
	Disinflation	Muddle Along	Reinflation		
Probability of occurrence	.33	.33	.33		
Domestic equities:					
S&P 500 Index	14.6%	9.9%	4.0%	9.5%	16.5%
Total market	15.7	10.5	3.9	10.0	17.5
Non-U.S. equities:					
Japan	−2.3	−5.1	−8.6	−5.3	19.7
United Kingdom	11.0	10.1	8.9	10.0	19.5
Germany	11.0	9.2	6.8	9.0	16.0
Canada	18.6	13.9	8.0	13.5	18.0
Total market	3.5	1.0	−2.1	0.8	19.5
Venture capital	13.9	14.9	15.9	14.9	45.0
Dollar bonds:					
30-year U.S. Treasury bond	13.7	9.5	6.2	9.8	11.0
Total market	13.0	10.5	8.4	10.6	7.5
Nondollar bonds:					
Japan	6.3	3.8	1.8	4.0	8.6
United Kingdom	10.0	6.6	4.0	6.9	9.2
Germany	13.6	11.1	8.1	11.3	5.0
Canada	13.8	9.6	6.3	9.9	9.0
Total nondollar	8.8	6.4	4.5	6.6	9.0
U.S. equity real estate	5.0	8.0	11.0	8.0	14.0
30-day Treasury bills	4.4	6.4	8.4	6.4	1.5
Total investable capital market (market capitalization weighted)	8.7	6.6	4.3	6.6	8.7

SOURCE: First Chicago Investment Advisors.

the prospect of an unpleasant return. Others might compare the five-year expected return and subtract from it the long-term discount rate or equilibrium return and calculate a *market alpha*. Markets with a negative alpha are potentially prone to a negative market correction. Markets with positive alphas have the potential for positive correction. This will be more fully demonstrated in Chapter 6.

The point of this exercise is not to suggest that the macroeconomic framework can only be used to derive asset class returns. On the contrary, the asset class framework was used only for simplicity. By taking the economic forecast to greater detail, key assumptions can be established down to the industry level and the individual security level. Industry and company revenues then can be contrasted with the general forecast of the key factor costs of labor, rents, and interest to derive forecasts of profits.

SUMMARY

This chapter focuses on two key aspects that investors need to be highly aware of as they organize their analysis of the security markets. First, there are key macroeconomic variables that drive the pricing of securities. Second, it is expectations about key macroeconomic variables that are the largest determinants of subsequent security returns. To understand this point, the investor needs to set up a macro valuation model. The essence of the model, regardless of asset class, involves a forecast of cash flows available to the investor and a mechanism to discount the value of those cash flows to the present.

The single most important determinant of all security cash flow potential relates to the economy's ability to generate goods and services and the income associated with that production. Crucial to asset class and individual security cash flow forecasts are the ability to compete for a share of total income against other factors of production, including labor and nonlabor components, as well as against other asset classes and sectors within the asset classes.

The three most crucial elements of the discounting process also involve macroeconomic expectations. These include the return called the real risk-free rate of interest, compensation for inflation expectations, and compensation for risk. The compensation for risk, or the risk premium, is primarily thought of as a function of the degree to which a security incurs systematic risk, which is risk inherent in the macroeconomy that cannot be diversified away. As a result, expectations concerning volatility in the macroeconomy and its components, such as volatility in inflation expectations, will be crucial in the market's assessment of systematic risk as it goes about setting risk premiums.

FURTHER READING

Source Material

The best sources for security returns and inflation data include Ibbotson and Brinson [1987], Ibbotson, Siegel, and Love [1985], Wilson and Jones [1987], Ibbotson and Siegel [1983], and Ibbotson and Sinquefield [1989]. U.S. economic data can be obtained from a variety of sources including the annual *Economic Report of the President* and the monthly U.S. Department of Commerce publication, *Survey of Current Business*. Internationally, the annual *World Economic Outlook* published by the International Monetary Fund is a valuable source.

Inflation Expectations

Quite literally there is no end to the work that has been done on forecasting inflation. It is hoped that the content of the chapter has pulled the reader away from the typical short-term preoccupation of near-term inflation forecasting and toward a better understanding of how inflation expectations are formed. Particularly relevant are Fama [1975], Nelson and Schwert [1977], Resler [1980], Moore [1983], and Fama and Gibbons [1984]. McNees [1988] writes regularly for the *New England Economic Review* on the forecasting success of economists, as does Zarnowitz.

Economic Factors and Security Returns

Over the past several years, the literature has begun to grow regarding the existence of nonmarket factors that drive security price and risk. Quite often these factors are found to have statistical linkages with economic variables. A good survey is found in Harrington [1987]. A fuller understanding requires reading of Rosenberg [1974], Ross [1976], Sharpe [1982], Roll and Ross [1980], and Chen, Roll, and Ross [1983].

Inflation and Security Returns

A classic article on inflation and security returns is Fama [1981], and strongly recommended readings include Sprinkel and Genetski [1977], Geske and Roll [1983], Modigliani and Cohn [1979], Summers [1981], and Gultekin [1983].

International Economics and Security Returns

The recent book by Solnik [1988] is highly recommended for understanding a number of key international investing issues. The early chapters are particularly valuable. The readings chapter by Lessard [1980] is also of substantial interest as is the article by Gultekin [1983].

BIBLIOGRAPHY

Accounting Trends and Techniques, 1987, 51st ed. New York: American Institute of Certified Public Accounts, Inc., 1988.

Adler, Michael, and Bernard Dumas. "International Portfolio Choice and Corporation Finance: A Synthesis." *The Journal of Finance*, June 1983.

Barro, Robert J. *Macroeconomics*. New York: John Wiley & Sons, 1984.

Black, Fisher, Michael C. Jensen, and Myron S. Scholes. "The Capital Asset Pricing Model: Some Empirical Tests," in Michael C. Jensen, ed. *Studies in the Theory of Capital Markets*. New York: Praeger Publishers, 1972.

Brinson, Gary P., Jeffrey J. Diermeier, and Gary G. Schlarbaum. "A Composite Portfolio Benchmark for Pension Plan Sponsors." *Financial Analysts Journal*, March/April 1986.

Campbell, John Y., and R.J. Shiller. "Stock Prices, Earnings and Expected Dividends." *The Journal of Finance*, July 1988.

Chen, Nai-Fu, Richard Roll, and Stephen A. Ross. "Economic Forces and the Stock Market." Working Paper Series B-73, University of California at Los Angeles, December 1983.

———. "Economic Forces and the Stock Market." *Journal of Business*, July 1986.

Cho, D. Chinhyung, Chaol S. Eun, and Lemma W. Senbet. "International Arbitrage Pricing Theory: An Empirical Investigation." *The Journal of Finance*, June 1986.

Data Resources (DRI). *U.S. Long Term Review*. Summer 1988.

Denison, Edward F. *Trends in American Economic Growth, 1929–1982*. Washington, D.C.: Brookings Institution, 1985.

Diermeier, Jeffrey J. "Economic Inputs and Their Effect on Asset Allocation Decisions," in James R. Vertin, ed. *Applying Economic Analysis to Portfolio Management: Improving the Investment Decision Process*. Seminar Proceedings, The Institute of Chartered Financial Analysts. Homewood, Ill.: Dow Jones-Irwin, 1985.

Diermeier, Jeffrey J., J.K. Freundlich, and Gary G. Schlarbaum. "Appendix: The Role of Real Estate in a Multi-Asset Portfolio," in Tom S. Sale, ed. *Real Estate Investing*. Seminar Proceedings, The Institute of Chartered Financial Analysts. Homewood, Ill.: Dow Jones-Irwin, 1986.

Diermeier, Jeffrey J., Roger G. Ibbotson, and L.B. Siegel. "The Supply of Capital Market Returns." *Financial Analysts Journal*, March/April 1984.

Economic Report of the President. Washington, D.C., January 1989.

Fama, Eugene F. "Short-term Interest Rates as Predictors of Inflation." *American Economic Review*, June 1975.

———. "Stock Returns, Real Activity, Inflation and Money." *American Economic Review*, September 1981.

Fama, Eugene F., and Michael R. Gibbons. "A Comparison of Inflation Forecasts." *Journal of Monetary Economics*, May 1984.

Farrell, James. "Homogenous Stock Groupings." *Financial Analysts Journal*, May/June 1975.

Fisher, Irving. *The Theory of Interest*. New York: Macmillan, 1930.

French, Kenneth R., Richard S. Ruback, and G. William Schwert. "Effects of Nominal Contracting on Stock Returns." *Journal of Political Economy*, February 1981.

Geske, Robert, and Richard Roll. "The Fiscal and Monetary Linkage Between Stock Returns and Inflation." *The Journal of Finance*, March 1983.

Gultekin, N. Bulent. "Stock Market Returns and Inflation: Evidence From Other Countries." *The Journal of Finance*, March 1983.

———. "Stock Market Returns and Inflation Forecasts." *The Journal of Finance*, June 1983.

Harrington, Diana R. *Modern Portfolio Theory, the Capital Asset Pricing Model & Arbitrage Pricing Theory: A User's Guide*, 2d ed. Englewood Cliffs, N.J.: Prentice-Hall, Inc., 1987.

Harvey, Campbell R. "Time-Varying Conditional Covariances in Tests of Asset Pricing Models." Working Paper, Fuqua School of Business, Duke University, 1988.

———. "Time-Varying Conditional Covariances in Tests of Asset Pricing Models." Working Paper Series 88-1905, Fuqua School of Business, Duke University, 1988.

Hooper, Peter, and B. Lowrey. "Impact of the Dollar Depreciation on the United States Price Level: An Analytical Survey of Empirical Estimates." International Finance Discussion Papers No. 128. Washington, D.C.: Board of Governors of the Federal Reserve System, January 1979.

Ibbotson, Roger G., and Gary P. Brinson. *Investment Markets: Gaining the Performance Advantage.* New York: McGraw-Hill, 1987.

Ibbotson, Roger G., Jeffrey J. Diermeier, and L.B. Siegel. "The Demand for Capital Market Returns: A New Equilibrium Theory." *Financial Analysts Journal*, January/Febuary 1984.

Ibbotson, Roger G., and L.B. Siegel. "The World Market Wealth Portfolio." *The Journal of Portfolio Management*, Winter 1983.

Ibbotson, Roger G., L.B. Siegel, and K.S. Love. "World Wealth: Market Values and Returns." *The Journal of Portfolio Management*, Fall 1985.

Ibbotson, Roger G., and Rex A. Sinquefield. *Stocks, Bonds, Bills, and Inflation: Historical Returns (1926–1987).* Charlottesville, Va.: Research Foundation of the Institute of Chartered Financial Analysts, 1989.

"Is the Japanese Market Overvalued?" Tokyo: Nikko International, January 1989.

Kim, Moon. K., and Chunchi Wu. "Macro-Economic Factors and Stock Returns." *The Journal of Financial Research*, Summer 1987.

King, Benjamin F. "Market and Industry Factors in Stock Price Behavior." *Journal of Business*, Jan. 1966.

Kuznets, Simon. *Modern Economic Growth.* New Haven, Conn.: Yale University Press, 1966.

Lessard, Donald R. "International Diversification," in S.N. Levine, ed. *Investment Manager's Handbook.* Homewood, Ill.: Dow Jones-Irwin, 1980.

Lintner, John. "Security Prices, Risk and Maximal Gains From Diversification." *The Journal of Finance*, December 1965.

Litzenberger, Robert H., and Krishna Ramaswamy. "The Effects of Dividends on Common Stock Prices Tax Effects or Information Effects." *The Journal of Finance*, May 1982.

Malkiel, Burton G. "The Capital Formation Problem in the United States." *The Journal of Finance*, May 1979.

Markowitz, Harry M. *Portfolio Selection: Efficient Diversification of Investments.* New Haven, Conn.: Yale University Press, 1959.

McNees, Stephen K. "How Accurate Are Macroeconomic Forecasts?" *New England Economic Review*. Federal Reserve Bank of Boston, July/August 1988.

Miller, Merton H. "The Modigliani-Miller Propositions After Thirty Years." *Journal of Economic Perspectives*, Fall 1988.

Modigliani, Franco, and Richard A. Cohn. "Inflation Rational Valuation and the Market." *Financial Analysts Journal*, March/April 1979.

Moore, Geoffrey H. "A New Inflation Barometer." *The Morgan Guaranty Survey*, July 1983.

Mossin, Jan. "Equilibrium in Capital Asset Market." *Econometrics*, October 1966.

The National Income and Product Accounts of the United States, 1929–1982. Washington, D.C.: Bureau of Economic Analysis, U.S. Department of Commerce, September 1986.

Nelson, Charles R., and G. William Schwert. "Short-Term Interest Rates as Predictors of Inflation: On Testing the Hypotheses That the Real Rate of Interest Is Constant." *American Economic Review*, June 1977.

Pearce, Douglas K., and V. Vance Roley. "Firm Characteristics, Unanticipated Inflation and Stock Returns." *The Journal of Finance*, September 1988.

Resler, David H. "The Formation of Inflation Expectations." *Review*. Federal Reserve Bank of St. Louis, April 1980.

Roll, Richard, and Stephen A. Ross. "An Empirical Investigation of the Arbitrage Pricing Theory." *The Journal of Finance*, December 1980.

Rosenberg, Barr. "Extra-Market Components of Covariance in Security Markets." *Journal of Finance and Quantitative Analysis*, March 1974.

Ross, Stephen A. "The Arbitrage Pricing Theory of Capital Asset Pricing." *Journal of Economic Theory*, December 1976.

Schwert, G. William. "Why Does Stock Market Volatility Change Over Time?" Working Paper No. GPB87-11, University of Rochester, 1988.

Sharpe, William F. "Capital Asset Prices: A Theory of Market Equilibriums Under Conditions of Risk." *The Journal of Finance*, September 1964.

———. "Factors in NYSE Security Returns, 1931–1975." *The Journal of Portfolio Management*, Summer 1982.

Shiller, Robert J. "Do Stock Prices Move Too Much to Be Justified by Subsequent Changes in Dividends?" *American Economic Review*, June 1981.

Solnik, Bruno. *International Investments*. Reading, Mass.: Addison-Wesley, 1988.

Sprinkel, Beryl W., and R.J. Genetski. *Winning with Money: A Guide for Your Future*. Homewood, Ill.: Dow Jones-Irwin, 1977.

Summers, Lawrence H. "Inflation and the Valuation of Corporate Equities." Working Paper No. 824, National Bureau of Economic Research, December 1981.

Survey of Current Business. Washington, D.C.: Bureau of Economic Analysis, U.S. Department of Commerce, March 1989.

Tversky, Amos, and Daniel Kahneman. "Judgment Under Uncertainty: Heuristics and Biases." *Science*, September 1974.

Williams, John B. *The Theory of Investment Value*. Cambridge, Mass.: Harvard University Press, 1938.

Wilson, Jack W., and Charles P. Jones. "A Comparison of Annual Common Stock Returns: 1871–1925 With 1926–1985." *Journal of Business*, April 1987.

CHAPTER 6

Individual Asset Expectations

_____ **William S. Gray III, CFA**

OVERVIEW

In Chapter 5, Jeff Diermeier provides a clear perspective on the relationship between the output of an economy, the distribution of that output to the factors of production (mainly labor and capital), and the implications for portfolio allocations to assets such as stocks, bonds, and real estate. He discusses the interplay of forces that determine the pricing of investable assets and, as a result, their respective expected returns and varying degrees of risk. Consensus expectations regarding both risks and rewards are generally perceived to play a dominant role in the pricing process. Changes in such expectations are, of course, the major source of price volatility.

Special attention is given to the impact of inflation as a key factor in the standard valuation model, which is adaptable to the payment characteristics of any asset class. Its disruptive effect on the real value of payments to capital and on changing expectations was painfully clear in the 1970s and 1980s.

These capital market factors are pervasive and, therefore, represent the environment within which all individual assets—specific stocks, bonds, and real estate—exist and behave. Because each individual asset has features that are somewhat similar to other assets but also has some uncommon elements, it is important to understand as much as possible about the determination of prices (and expected returns) under such circumstances. This is most readily accomplished by focusing on the risk characteristics of each asset and recognizing the significance of the asset's _systematic_ and _unsystematic_ components.

This chapter provides a summary discussion of the manner in which expectational factors affect the pricing of individual assets in each of the major investable portfolio investment classes. Its focus, then, is the generation of inputs by the analyst for the portfolio manager.

FIXED-INCOME EXPECTATIONAL INPUTS

The risk/return characteristics of fixed-income obligations have undergone dramatic change since the late 1960s. Until that time, yields to maturity on such obligations were only modestly greater (1 to 2 percent) than the expected rate of inflation during much of the current century. Presumably, this reflected a widely held perception of relatively low risk. Hence, such assets were being priced to provide only a small risk premium. During the 1980s, yields to maturity on similar obligations moved to levels that were considerably greater (by 4 to 5 percent) than the real risk free rate plus the expected rate of inflation. That situation still exists as of this writing in early 1989.

There are at least two possible explanations for this change. It may reflect an unusually tenacious anchoring or "rear view mirror" phenomenon in the bond market. Just as the bond market was very slow to adjust to the rising inflation of the 1970s, it may simply be very slow in responding to the subsiding inflation that took place in the 1980s. A more plausible explanation appears to be that the riskiness of bonds has increased quite a bit. This is the additional toll on bonds resulting from the risk of an uncertain inflation environment.

Figure 6-1 shows what has happened to the volatility of long-term, high grade corporate bond returns as measured by the Salomon Brothers Index. Figure 6-2 shows the frequency of their *real* return losses. Both compare the experience during the period 1926 through 1967 with that of 1968 through 1988. These figures reflect not only the absolute changes for bonds themselves but how such experiences have changed relative to those of common stocks. Both are consistent with the substantially increased risk perception of fixed-income obligations.

Intuitively, it seems wise to assume that the risk of real loss in the future will continue as long as it is clear there is an uncertain inflation environment.

It should be noted that the expected returns for bonds, especially those with medium to long maturities, would become extraordinary if there were an expected or actual reversion to a very stable (preferably low) inflation environment. A reduction in the risk premium from the current 4 to 5 percent to the former 1 to 2 percent would most likely generate a bountiful harvest in the form of capital gains and total returns for bondholders.

Interest Rate or Systematic Risk

While the total riskiness of bonds is greater (i.e., their risk premia are much larger and their returns are more volatile), the systematic risk characteristics of bonds continue much as they always have. In general, bond prices (and rates of return) are sensitive to changes in the level of interest rates. The degree of sensitivity corresponds fairly closely with the period to maturity

Volatility of Stocks and Bonds, 1926-1967 and 1968-1988

Standard Deviation of Returns

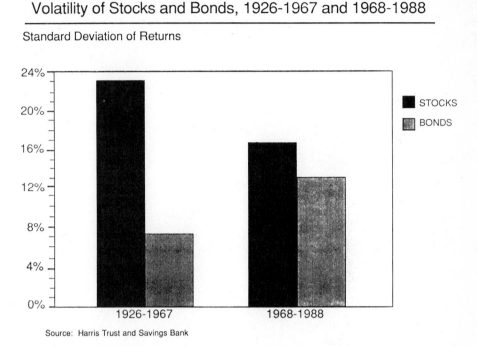

Source: Harris Trust and Savings Bank

Figure 6-1. Volatility of Stocks and Bonds, 1926–1967 and 1968–1988. SOURCE: Harris Trust and Savings Bank.

of any particular fixed-income issue. Short-term issues are relatively insensitive (low beta), while long-term issues tend to be quite sensitive (high beta). These tendencies may be magnified or diminished if a change in the general level of interest rates is accompanied by a shift in the term structure of interest rates (i.e., the shape of the yield curve changes).

Duration. Because there are factors other than maturity that affect the sensitivity of fixed-income obligations, it is best to use a measure that is most ideally suited for that purpose. The best measure is that of the *duration* of bonds. Duration is a measure that allows coupon *and* maturity to be considered simultaneously in one measure. It is defined as the weighted average time to full recovery of principal and interest payments on a fixed-income security. A simplified formula for Macauley's duration, where annual compounding is assumed, is:

$$D = \frac{\displaystyle\sum_{t=1}^{n} \frac{C_t(t)}{(1+i)^t}}{\displaystyle\sum_{t=1}^{n} \frac{C_t}{(1+i)^t}}$$

Risk of Loss on Stocks and Bonds, 1926-1967 and 1968-1988

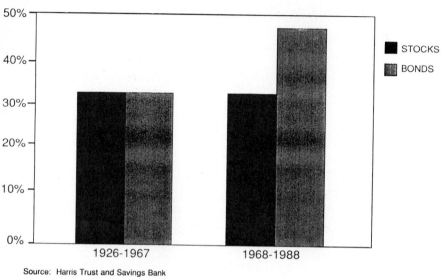

Frequency of Real Losses

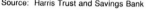

Source: Harris Trust and Savings Bank

Figure 6-2. Risk of Loss on Stocks and Bonds, 1926–1967 and 1968–1988. SOURCE: Harris Trust and Savings Bank.

where t is the time period in which coupon or principal repayment occurs, C_t is the interest or principal payment in period t, and i is the market yield to maturity for this type of bond. In other words, the formulation becomes:

$$\text{Duration} = \frac{\text{Present value of cash flows weighted to length of time to receipt}}{\text{Present value of the unweighted cash flows}}$$

where the denominator is, in effect, the current market price of the bond.

Here is an alternative way of looking at duration calculation. Assume as givens (1) the scheduled dates and amounts of each coupon payment and final redemption value (plus dates and amounts of sinking fund payments, if any) and (2) the current price of the bond. Then calculate the proportion of the current price of the bond that is contributed by each future payment equal to the present value of each payment divided by the bond's current price. That is, for a 10-year maturity bond,

P_1 = Present value contribution of first annual coupon payment as a percentage of bond price

P_2 = Present value contribution of second annual coupon payment as a percentage of bond price

$\vdots$

P_{10} = Present value contribution of tenth annual coupon payment and principal repayment as a percentage of bond price

———

100% = Sum of above

Then assign numbers to the time intervals:

T_1 = Time period 1

T_2 = Time period 2

$\vdots$

T_{10} = Time period 10

Then duration will equal the sum of the individual time-weighted present value (percentage) contributions divided by 100.

$$\text{Duration} = \frac{\sum_{i=1}^{10} P_i T_i}{100}$$

Table 6-1 illustrates the calculation of duration for two 10-year maturity bonds with different annual coupons in an 8 percent yield environment. As this table illustrates, the two bonds with different coupons have significantly different durations. In general, there are five factors that affect duration.

1. Coupon. When a bond has a coupon, duration is less than the term to maturity because duration gives weight to these interim payments. A bond with a larger coupon has a shorter duration because more of the total cash flows come earlier, in the form of interest payments. Thus, there is a negative relationship between coupon and duration. A bond with no coupons (e.g., zero-coupon bonds) has a duration exactly equal to the term to maturity because the only payment or cash flow is at maturity.

2. Maturity. There is a positive relationship, generally, between term to maturity and duration. A bond with a longer term to maturity almost always has a longer duration. The elasticity of duration with respect to maturity term varies, however. For bonds with less than 5 years to maturity, duration expands rapidly as maturity increases. From 5 to 15 years, duration expands with maturity, but at a slower rate. Above 15 years, duration increases little for normal coupon bonds, regardless of maturity. Most of these

TABLE 6-1. Calculation of Duration for Two Bonds With Different Coupons in an 8 Percent Yield Environment

	Bond A	Bond B
Face value	$1,000	$1,000
Maturity	10 years	10 years
Coupon	4%	8%

Bond A

(1) Year	(2) Cash Flow	(3) Present Value at 8%	(4) Present Value of Flow	(5) Present Value as Percentage of Price	(6) (1) × (5)
1	$ 40.00	0.9259	$ 37.04	0.0506	0.0506
2	40.00	0.8573	34.29	0.0469	0.0938
3	40.00	0.7938	31.75	0.0434	0.1302
4	40.00	0.7350	29.40	0.0402	0.1608
5	40.00	0.6806	27.22	0.0372	0.1860
6	40.00	0.6302	25.21	0.0345	0.2070
7	40.00	0.5835	23.34	0.0319	0.2233
8	40.00	0.5403	21.61	0.0295	0.2360
9	40.00	0.5002	20.01	0.0274	0.2466
10	1,040.00	0.4632	481.73	0.6585	6.5850
Sum			$ 731.58	1.0000	8.1193[a]

Bond B

(1) Year	(2) Cash Flow	(3) Present Value at 8%	(4) Present Value of Flow	(5) Present Value as Percentage of Price	(6) (1) × (5)
1	$ 80.00	0.9259	$ 74.07	0.0741	0.0741
2	80.00	0.8573	68.59	0.0686	0.1372
3	80.00	0.7938	63.50	0.0635	0.1906
4	80.00	0.7350	58.80	0.0588	0.2352
5	80.00	0.6806	54.44	0.0544	0.2720
6	80.00	0.6302	50.42	0.0504	0.3024
7	80.00	0.5835	46.68	0.0467	0.3269
8	80.00	0.5403	43.22	0.0432	0.3456
9	80.00	0.5002	40.02	0.0400	0.3600
10	1,080.00	0.4632	500.26	0.5003	5.0030
Sum			$1,000.00	1.0000	7.2470[b]

[a] Duration = 8.12 years
[b] Duration = 7.25 years

TABLE 6-2. Duration of Bonds With Various Characteristics

Maturity (Years)	No Sinking Fund, Purchased at Par, With Coupon of:				8% Coupon, No Sinking Fund, Purchased at Yield of:		8% Coupon Purchased at Par With Sinking Fund That Retires 75% of Issue From Year 5 to Maturity
	6%	8%	10%	12%	10%	12%	
1	0.96	0.94	0.93	0.92	0.93	0.92	
3	2.71	2.62	2.54	2.46	2.59	2.56	
5	4.27	4.06	3.86	3.68	3.98	3.91	
10	7.44	6.80	6.23	5.73	6.51	6.23	5.34
15	9.80	8.65	7.69	6.88	8.05	7.46	7.25
20	11.56	9.90	8.58	7.52	8.94	8.05	8.30
30	13.84	11.31	9.46	8.08	9.72	8.38	9.68
40	15.10	11.96	9.80	8.25	9.94	8.39	10.49

bonds have durations of less than 10 years, even though they may be 30-year-maturity instruments.

3. Yield to Maturity. Bonds with a higher yield to maturity have a shorter duration. Thus, the relationship is negative. For example, if yield to maturity increased from 8 to 12 percent for the bonds in Table 6-1, Bond A's duration would drop from 8.12 to 7.75, and Bond B's duration would drop from 7.25 to 6.80. Why? Because the present value of the distant cash flow payments (the ones with the heaviest weights) becomes less important relative to the present value of the nearer payments (the ones with the lightest weights).

4. Sinking Fund. A bond with a sinking fund has a shorter duration because the cash flows in the earlier years are greater than those of a non–sinking fund bond. Thus the relationship between the sinking fund feature and duration is negative. The effect of adding a sinking fund, along with maturity, coupon, and yield effects, is shown in Table 6-2.

5. Call Feature. Similar to the sinking fund feature, a bond with a call provision has a shorter duration, and thus there is a negative relationship between call and duration. The reason is straightforward: The potential maturity date for the bond has been shortened, and the principal repayment associated with it has been accelerated.

Duration is important in fixed-income analysis and portfolio management for two very different reasons. First, because duration encompasses both coupon (negative relationship) and maturity (positive relationship), it is a measure of bond price volatility. Specifically,

Change in bond price = Change in yield to maturity × Modified duration,

where

$$\text{Modified duration} = \frac{\text{Macauley's duration}}{1 + \dfrac{\text{Yield to maturity}}{\text{Number of coupon payments per year}}}$$

For example, a bond with a duration of 10 years, a yield of 9 percent, and semi-annual coupon payments would have a modified duration of 10/(1 + .09/2) = 9.57 years.

Thus, as a measure of bond price volatility, modified duration is also a measure of a bond's beta or its return elasticity to changes in interest rates, and it is thus a measure of bond systematic risk.

Second, as discussed in Chapter 8, duration is extremely useful in asset/liability matching and immunization techniques in bond portfolio management. By matching durations of asset and liability portfolios, managers are able to avoid interest rate risk.

Convexity. In addition to duration effects on systematic risk, the effects of bond pricing convexity often need to be considered.

Convexity is mathematically defined as the rate of change of duration or the second derivative of bond price with respect to yield. But for the purposes of this chapter, convexity is defined as the price change that occurs for a bond that is not accounted for or predicted by (modified) duration.

In estimating the price change of a bond for relatively small changes in yield (less than 50 basis points), duration is a fairly satisfactory estimating tool. However, for many long-maturity bonds, discrepancies begin to appear between the modified-duration-predicted price change and the actual price change for yield changes of 100 basis points or more. This is illustrated in Table 6-3. The differentials grow—the term used frequently is *accelerate*—with bigger changes in rates. The differences are 4.6 percentage points when a 300 basis point increase in yield occurs and 6.7 percentage points when a 300 basis point decrease in yield occurs for a 12 percent 30-year maturity bond. Note the lack of symmetry.

Graphically, convexity is illustrated in Figure 6-3 for a long-maturity bond. The differential between actual bond price and modified-duration-predicted price is indicated by the vertical distance between the solid and dashed lines at various yield levels away from the 12 percent starting point.

The convexity effects of various maturity bonds are shown in Figure 6-4. Short-maturity instruments such as the one-year and five-year notes exhibit small convexity effects. Duration is a useful but not perfect predictor for most yield changes for these securities. However, the figure shows that for longer-maturity securities with large yield changes, convexity effects are

TABLE 6-3. Differences in Actual Price Change and Price Change Estimated by Modified Duration of a 12 Percent 30-Year Bond for Various Instantaneous Changes in Yield From 12 Percent Base

Change in Rates (Basis Points)	Price: Initial Case of 12% Yield	Percentage Change in Value of 30-Year Bond	Percentage Change Estimated by Using Modified Duration of 8.1	Difference Between Actual and Estimated Change
+300	$ 80.261	−19.7%	−24.3%	4.6%
+250	83.017	−17.0	−20.2	2.3
+200	85.961	−14.0	−16.2	2.2
+150	89.110	−10.9	−12.1	1.2
+100	92.484	−7.5	−8.1	0.6
+50	96.105	−3.9	−4.0	0.1
No change	100.000	No change	No change	0.0
−50	104.200	+4.2	+4.0	0.2
−100	108.725	+8.7	+8.1	0.6
−150	113.623	+13.6	+12.1	1.5
−200	118.929	+18.9	+16.2	2.7
−250	124.690	+24.7	+20.2	4.5
−300	130.957	+31.0	+24.3	6.7

SOURCE: Sullivan and Kiggins [1988].

quite large, making duration *by itself* a poor predictor of bond price response to yield change. In these situations, systematic risk can be accurately assessed only by taking both duration and convexity into account. Convexity and duration relationships are also affected by call features and other factors, sometimes producing negative convexity when price increases are less or price decreases are more than those predicted by modified duration. These issues are explored in Sullivan and Kiggins [1988].

Covariance. The historical covariance of bonds (1969–1988) relative to other asset classes is shown in Chapter 5. During that period they had modest negative correlations with cash equivalents (−0.03) and real estate (−0.11). They had a positive correlation with domestic equity (0.41). For current asset mix considerations, the important question is what these relationships will be in the future. This remains a very difficult judgment. It is usually assumed that they will continue as in the past, unless specific reasons for a difference can be identified.

Determinants of Interest Rates and Their Term Structure

Chapter 5 recognizes interest payments as one of the allocations to capital from the output of the economy. The discussion of discount rate estimation focuses on two main components: the inflation premium and the risk pre-

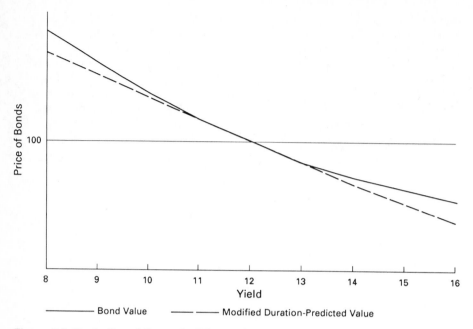

Figure 6-3. Illustration of Convexity Effect on Pricing of a Long-Maturity Bond.
SOURCE: Sullivan and Kiggins [1988].

mium. The much enlarged risk premium reflected in bond yields to maturity
is noted and discussed. Each of these perspectives helps to provide a foundation for the following discussion.

General Level of Interest Rates. U.S. Treasury bonds are often used
as a benchmark for the general level of interest rates. The going rate of
interest or current yield to maturity on such bonds may be viewed mostly
in terms of a real risk-free rate of interest, an inflation premium, and a
premium for a risk that must largely reflect risks other than cash flow risk.
In early 1989, when the going rate was about 9.0 percent, the real risk-free
rate was 3 percent, and the expected inflation rate was near 4.5 percent, the
risk premium was about 1.5 percent.

As noted earlier, the risk that probably accounts for most of the risk
premium must be the uncertain inflation environment and the concern that
it generates about the possibility of receiving future payments that have lost
more purchasing power than reflected in the inflation premium in early 1989.

Looking to the future, significant changes in the yields to maturity on
U.S. Treasury bonds are most likely to result from either a change in inflation
expectations or in the degree of uncertainty about the inflation environment.
Both fiscal and monetary policies have a crucial impact on such matters.

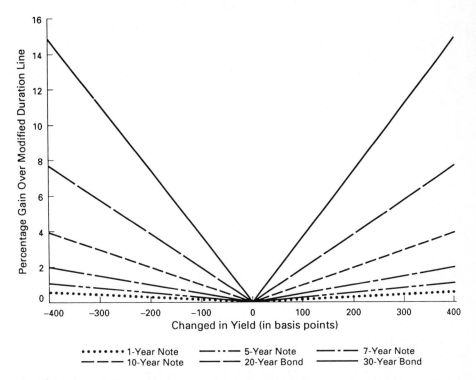

Figure 6-4. Convexity Effects in Price Changes of Selected Maturity Bonds for Various Changes in Yield to Maturity. SOURCE: Sullivan and Kiggins [1988].

For example, significant progress on reducing the federal deficit would probably reduce U.S. interest rates at least somewhat.

Changes in monetary policy—that is, the rate of growth in the money supply or changes in the level of the Federal Reserve discount rate—have become more difficult to interpret. The implications of such changes have become heavily dependent on the circumstances at the time they occur. There are times when their liquidity implications are weighted most heavily, other times when the inflationary implications dominate investor reaction, and even times when such implications essentially neutralize each other.

Other factors that now receive significant attention as barometers for the future rate of inflation are the experience of the U.S. dollar in the foreign exchange markets, the price of gold, certain indexes of the more sensitive commodity prices, and the continuity and sustainability of the current government or governmental system.

Term Structure. The term structure of U.S. interest rates indicates the pattern of such rates across the entire spectrum of maturities represented in the bond market. It is usually portrayed in the form of a *yield curve*, and almost always it is based on the interest rates on various U.S. Treasury obligations outstanding at the time.

By restricting the relevant population to U.S. Treasury issues, the problem of dealing with differences in credit risk considerations or the risk of a call for redemption is moderated or eliminated. It does not, however, avoid the problem of two or more Treasury issues with the same maturity, but with interest coupon differences (which could impact the amount of tax exposure) or special provisions (such as one that permits redemption at par if the proceeds are used to pay federal estate taxes).

There are models available to fit a yield curve to the yield to maturity data on the various individual bond issues. All use a least squares regression to fit the curve to the data. The Bradley-Crane and Elliot-Echols models are available for this purpose. See McEnally [1987].

Any U.S. Treasury yield curve provides a relatively homogeneous benchmark to which the yield to maturity on any other type of bond issue can be related. It is widely used by investors. Many Wall Street sources and institutional investment managers produce such yield curves, which are updated frequently (at least each week, and daily for some).

Slope of Yield Curve. As noted in an earlier section on the systematic risk of bonds, the shape of the yield curve is constantly changing, sometimes substantially over longer time periods. Nevertheless, the normal or upward sloping yield curve is one that reflects an ascending pattern of yield to maturity figures, starting with the shortest maturities. However, to be "normal" it need not be a straight line, not even approximately.

When the normal condition does not exist, the curve may be "flat" (which should require no further explanation) or "inverted." The latter applies when there is a generally descending pattern of yield to maturity figures starting with the shortest maturities.

There are three reasons that interest rates differ across maturity among bond issues that are similar in other respects. They may differ because of systematic risk, market segmentation, or future expectations.

The most stable reason is based on differences in *systematic risk*, or sensitivity to changes in the general level of interest rates. Everything else being equal, longer maturity/duration means greater risk and therefore greater expected return as reward for bearing that risk. If this were the only factor that influenced the shape of the curve, a rather straightforward "normal" curve would prevail. The fact that the yield curve is more or less normal most of the time suggests that the other factors do not provide significant contrary impacts most of the time.

The second reason is based on the notion that there is *market segmentation* among investors, based on differences in their investment objectives. Certain investors, such as commercial banks, wish or need to avoid exposure to longer maturities. Other investors, such as pension funds, have only a limited need to maintain significant short-term maturity positions. If there is a shift in the pattern of funds flowing to these different investors, it could reflect itself in a relative demand shift for short-, medium-, and long-term maturities, which would in turn affect the shape of the curve.

The third reason, *future expectations*, is probably the most interesting one to ponder. The expectations that seem most important are those that pertain to inflation and/or the business cycle. History strongly confirms the tendency toward recurring business cycles. Depending on where the economy is in terms of the business cycle, interest rates may be influenced up or down by relevant supply and demand factors. For example, the Federal Reserve may tighten the money supply during the late stages of the up phase of the business cycle to prevent "overheating" (excess inflationary pressure). This is likely to raise interest rates, especially short-term rates. In a similar manner, the demand for funds by consumers and business tends to weaken during a recession, and that works in the direction of lower interest rates.

Because of the ebb-and-flow pattern of interest rates, which are influenced somewhat heavily by the business cycle, there is an opportunity to improve portfolio returns by shifting maturity exposures. These opportunities have been especially significant since the late 1960s. As shown in Table 6-4, the magnitude of changes in interest rates (peak-to-trough) was greater in the late 1980s than earlier.

This has been a major factor in the development and popularity of *active fixed-income management*. Of course, the fact that an opportunity exists does not assure its successful exploitation. Judging whether or when interest rates will peak or trough remains a very challenging task.

Since the late 1960s, there have been several periods in which the yield curve was inverted; that is, short-term interest rates were higher than longer-term interest rates. Presumably, the extra yield on short-term instruments reflected investor concern about inflation intensifying during the following one to two years, but not necessarily beyond that time frame. This concern was usually related to anticipated business cycle peaks. Because such peaks are followed by recessions and some easing of inflation pressures, the lower long-term rates may have reflected some hope that longer maturity obligations would benefit ultimately from some price appreciation.

On each of these occasions, the power of such expectations was great enough to overcome the systematic risk considerations that are believed to be responsible for the normal yield curve. Table 6-5 provides a summary of when these periods reached a climax, as well as the returns during the ensuing holding periods for both 1-year and 30-year obligations.

From these past experiences, it appears that the hope of any significant appreciation from long-term obligations is not likely to be fulfilled, except in the aftermath of severe recessions such as those in 1973–1974 and 1981–1982, in which inflation pressures eased quite a bit. The reinforcement of

TABLE 6-4. High-Grade Corporate Bond Yields and Post–World War II Business Cycles

Recession	(1) Trough	(2) Succeeding Peak	(3) Basis Points Rise	(4) Basis Points Decline	(5) (4)/(3)
1953–1954	2.74 (1954:3)	4.81 (1957:6)	207	120	58.0%
1957–1958	3.61 (1958:6)	5.37 (1959:10)	176	100	57.0
1960–1961	4.37 (1961:3)	6.14 (1966:9)	177	79	45.0
1966–1967	5.35 (1962:2)	9.70 (1970:6)	435	216	50.0
1970–1971	7.54[a] (1971:2)	10.44 (1974:9)	290	254	88.0
1974–1975	7.90 (1976:12)	14.08 (1980:3)	618	296	48.0
1980–1981	11.12 (1980:6)	16.97 (1981:9)	585	568	97.0
7-cycle average					63.0%

Note: Dates in parentheses are dates of cyclical peaks and troughs in monthly interest rates.

SOURCE: *Business Conditions Digest*, U.S. Department of Commerce.
[a] Trough in 1972 was disregarded because of price controls.

subsequent secular disinflation, such as that which occurred after 1982, increases the likelihood of such an outcome. Otherwise, the premium short-term rates that occur under such circumstances are a good investment opportunity.

Forecasts of Interest Rates

At any given time there are many views on the outlook for interest rates. In some cases, these views simply represent a "feeling" that is probably based on a variety of casual observations on things that have been going on in the economic-political-sociological arena. However, other views are based on a systematic analytical process that reflects some understanding of the factors that determine interest rates. In this latter category, there are many forecasts that are available through investment banker/broker, institutional investor, and economic consultant sources.

    There is a range of opinions on this subject. Some of these differences merely reflect a lack of uniformity in the length (time period) of such forecasts. But even when the time horizons are similar there is normally a di-

TABLE 6-5. Total Returns for Various Holding Periods Following the Peak of Yield Curve Inversions

	Total Return								
	Next 6 Months		Next 12 Months		Next 18 Months	
Date of Inversion Peaks	1-Year Notes	30-Year Bonds	1-Year Notes	30-Year Bonds	1-Year Notes	30-Year Bonds
Sept. 1969	4.41%	(0.40)%	8.18%	(2.75)%	13.89%	9.47%
Sept. 1973	5.11	1.54	6.74	(8.37)	14.41	5.21
Sept. 1974	7.67	13.59	9.33	10.82	13.99	19.47
Nov. 1979	8.09	(1.78)	10.89	(8.18)	16.40	(13.52)
Dec. 1980	7.59	(0.63)	17.34	6.04	23.41	10.05
Apr. 1982	10.03	20.89	15.42	33.55	19.81	33.43

Note: Each of the time periods starts at the beginning of the month in which the ratio of 30-year to 1-year yields is at a minimum. Figures in parentheses represent negative returns.

SOURCE: Harris Trust and Savings Bank.

vergence of opinions. This reflects the degree of uncertainty about what may happen to interest rates in the future. This uncertainty is consistent with the fact that even the most respected authorities have issued interest rate forecasts that misjudged both the direction and the amount of interest rate changes.

Interest Rates as the Price of Money. The inherent difficulty of divining the future of interest rates may be diminished a bit by recognizing that it is the price of money that is being contemplated. As with anything in a free market environment, an understanding of relevant supply and demand factors is required. Of course, in trying to gauge where interest rates will be next month, next quarter, or next year, it is necessary to analyze just how the supply and demand factors will be interacting and what prices will be needed to clear the market at such points in time. In doing so, it seems very important to keep the determinants of interest rates very much in mind.

As discussed earlier, U.S. Treasury interest rates are determined mostly by views about a suitable inflation premium and an additional premium that largely reflects the degree of uncertainty about the inflation environment. In the case of corporate obligations, there is an additional element, the premium needed to recognize *credit risk* (which applies to municipal debt as well). With foreign obligations there is a fourth element, a premium for *currency risk*. While they are by no means unimportant, the premia for credit risk (except for non–investment grade bonds) and currency risk were small relative to the premia related to inflation uncertainty during the 1980s.

The Consensus Outlook. The preceding discussion of the factors that affect the outlook for interest rates is very limited. There are many other factors that are included in the more elaborate efforts to forecast interest rates. Well-directed studies of possibly relevant variables should be encouraged. They may contribute to a better understanding of how the system works. However, they may have very little to do with the ultimate accuracy of a given forecast. That is why many investors accept the *consensus outlook* or the current level of interest rates as the best view of the future and essentially avoid any great use of interest rate forecasts.

International Fixed Income Risk Factors

Although the U.S. bond market accounts for roughly one-half of the entire world bond market, foreign bonds (in the aggregate) account for well over $2 trillion when converted into U.S. dollars. The quantity of various foreign bonds is related to the size of the economies of the various countries of issue and is influenced by the relative strength and stability of their respective currencies. Japan is the largest source of foreign bonds, followed by Germany, the United Kingdom, and Italy. Other sources include France, Canada, Belgium, and Switzerland. See Chapter 10 of Ibbotson and Brinson [1987].

From a U.S. investor's point of view, foreign bonds have the same kinds of interest rate risk and credit risk that are so important in determining the yields to maturity on domestic bond issues. In addition, foreign bonds entail two other forms of risk: *sovereign risk* and *currency risk*. Sovereign risk may be viewed as a unique dimension of credit risk in cases where countries or states with sovereign powers are involved. As such, it will be discussed later as part of the sections on financial or unsystematic risk and return.

Currency Risk. Currency risk is quite another matter. Not only is it a systematic risk factor for each foreign country, but it is generally regarded as the single most important risk aspect related to foreign bond ownership.

Except in those instances in which foreign obligations are denominated in U.S. dollars, the interest and principal payments are paid in the local currency of the particular country involved or occasionally some other nondomestic currency. From a U.S. investor's point of view, any changes in the rate of exchange between the U.S. dollar and the relevant foreign currency will impact the investment experience during the period from the dates of purchase of a foreign bond and payments later received as a bondholder.

This impact can be very significant. For example, since the mid-1970s, the U.S. dollar has gone through three distinct phases relative to a "market basket" of leading foreign currencies. This is shown in part in Figure 6-5. The U.S. dollar was weakening prior to 1980 (although it was close to a low in late 1978), was strengthening from 1980 to March 1985, and was weakening thereafter through 1988. Whether from peak-to-trough or from trough-to-peak, these relative changes ranged from roughly 30 to 45 percent in magnitude. Of course, because the market basket is a weighted average of foreign currencies, the U.S. dollar's movement relative to specific foreign currencies may have been greater than or less than 30 to 45 percent.

These rather dramatic changes in exchange rate relationships create an enormous opportunity to enhance investment returns—at least from a theoretical standpoint. Unfortunately, in the real world, it is not easy to realize a return from this opportunity. First, there is a tendency for expected changes in exchange rates between two countries to be reflected in differences in interest rate levels between those two countries. If interest rates are higher in a particular foreign country than they are in the United States, it often indicates that its currency is likely to decline relative to the U.S. dollar. If that happens, the apparent rate of return advantage is diminished or offset completely. Second, trying to anticipate changes in exchange rates that the market consensus does not yet expect is very difficult.

Because U.S. investors are relatively new in the international invest-

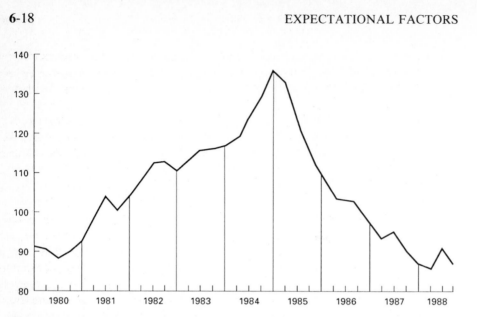

Figure 6-5. The U.S. Dollar: J.P. Morgan Index vs. 15 Currencies, 1980–1988 (Quarterly Averages, 1980–1982 = 100).

ment arena, a gigantic learning process has been under way. For example, it has become more clearly recognized that exchange rates reflect not only the relative price of internationally traded goods and services but the relative price of internationally traded financial assets as well.

A better understanding of the complex factors that determine exchange rates may or may not lead to better forecasts of unexpected rate changes in the future. Even though knowledge of various approaches to currency forecasting may not lead to better forecasts, it should be useful to comment briefly on three approaches discussed in Morrison [1986], each of which is believed to have some following:

- *Traditional*. This approach is concerned primarily with the analysis of relative inflation differentials or relative current account trade balances.
- *Monetarist*. This approach uses relative money supplies or relative interest rate differentials to predict foreign exchange movements.
- *Asset Market*. This approach requires some assessment of relative risks and returns and how these are expected to change. The most important influence is the mix of a country's fiscal and monetary policies because that mix is likely to determine the mix of real interest rates and economic performance.

The latter seems most promising. It does not require that purchasing power parity be dominant in the determination of equilibrium exchange rates. Rather, they must satisfy the interaction of all goods and financial assets affecting the balance of payments. The mix of a country's fiscal and monetary policies is probably the most important indicator of exchange rates because it is likely to determine the real and nominal economic performance, including interest rates.

Because of the magnitude of currency risk involved in foreign investing, there are compelling reasons for investors to address the problem when making portfolio investments abroad. Some U.S. investors are doing this by hedging the currency risk of foreign investment positions. However, it appears that the problem can be kept within tolerable limits through carefully structured diversification between U.S. positions and a variety of foreign investment exposures.

Financial or Unsystematic Risk

Unsystematic risk covers all of the sources of uncertainty except those factors that affect the general level of interest rates. It is composed of those more unique uncertainties that affect particular sectors of the economy, a certain industry, or, in some instances, a single company. Changes in the competitive environment for the participants in a given industry, technological breakthroughs that obsolete a product with a similar purpose, or the loss of a key person in a particular company are sources of unsystematic risk. More generally, unsystematic risk for a company is associated with a significant change in its profitability or financial stability.

Credit Risk. While it is a matter of perspective to some extent, unsystematic risk is reflected in and accounts for an important part of what is labeled credit risk. It can and does affect the ability (and willingness) of a company to make interest payments and repay the principal under the terms of a particular debt instrument. Historically, the assessment of credit risk has been based largely on past operating results and financial characteristics. This no longer applies to the analysis of most bonds, especially non–investment grade debt obligations, and particularly high-yield bonds or junk bonds.

The amount of credit risk is reflected in the yield to maturity of an issue. The larger the perceived risk, the larger the increment of yield over a no-credit-risk instrument. U.S. Treasury obligations have virtually no credit risk, while U.S. Government agency obligations have a small amount of risk. Both corporate and municipal obligations are rather diverse in credit risk, ranging from relatively small amounts to very large amounts. Foreign obligations (issued by governments or corporations) present a similar diversity in the magnitude of credit risk exposure.

Credit Ratings. There are a number of organizations that evaluate the credit risk of many of the issuing entities and publish a quality rating of the

TABLE 6-6. Yields by Quality Grade of Major Categories of New 25-to-30-Year-Maturity Corporate Bond Issues, March 31, 1989

New Issue Long-Term Corporate Bonds	Quality Grade			
	AAA	AA	A	BBB
Industrials	10.05%	10.40%	10.65%	11.15%
Utilities	10.00	10.20	10.35	10.75
Finance companies	10.15	10.40	10.65	—

SOURCE: Salomon Brothers, Inc.

debt obligations of those entities. Moody's, Standard & Poor's, Duff & Phelps, and Fitch's are well-known publishers of such ratings. Most of the ratings take the form of letter grades such as A, B, C, or D, with some further discrimination within each of those grade categories. Each of these publishers has its own method of reflecting the finer rating distinctions. For example, Moody's ratings start with Aaa (the best) and move on down through Aa, A, Baa, and so on, and the comparable ratings for Standard & Poor's an AAA, AA, A, BBB, and so on.

There are some differences among the rating agencies in how they rate any particular issue. Also, bond analysts often disagree with the ratings published by these agencies. While the assessment of credit risk tends to be a somewhat structured process, it is not a precise science and there are legitimate differences of opinion.

Yield Spreads

In spite of the differences of opinion on credit risk, the similarities far outweigh the differences much of the time. Therefore, corporate and municipal debt obligations tend to be grouped by their credit ratings. Some of the rating agencies regularly publish a matrix of current interest rate figures. These provide an approximate indication of the going market rate for each of the rating categories. Table 6-6 provides an example of how bond issues are classified by rating and what the going interest rate was for each category in early 1989.

With this kind of classified information on bond yields, it has been customary to refer to the differences as a *yield spread*. The yields from any two categories may be compared in this way. A few of the more popular combinations are U.S. Treasuries vs. Aaa Corporates, Aa Industrials vs. Aa Utilities, and Aaa Industrials vs. Baa Industrials. Even though the degree of credit risk difference between the various categories is believed to remain somewhat constant, the yield spreads do change with the passage of time. Some of these changes in yield spread may be due to market segmentation factors. However, most of them are believed to be related to changes in investor risk tolerance (aversion).

To the extent that investors are able to anticipate potential problems they try to avoid them or at least to minimize their exposure to them. The prospect of a business recession is an excellent example of such a problem. On balance, investors lighten their exposure to those companies or municipalities that are most sensitive to the business cycle when a recession appears to be forthcoming. This tends to affect adversely the price of the bonds of such entities, thereby increasing their yields at least relative to the yields of bonds with less business cycle sensitivity. Figure 6-6 provides a good example of the normal tendencies of yield spreads and, especially, how they change over the course of a business cycle.

To the extent that yield spreads tend to widen when the consensus perceives the increased likelihood of recession (usually around business cycle peaks) and the general level of interest rates is elevated, the purchase of higher-risk obligations can be especially rewarding. Because the general level of interest rates is very likely to go down, especially during the later stages of a recession, and since there may be some narrowing of yield spreads by the early stages of the ensuing business recovery, the expected return for the coming holding period may be much larger than the yield at the moment of such a timely purchase.

The investment performance of a given bond issue (or a bond portfolio) may be compared with an index of bond market returns. Perhaps the most popular index at present is the Shearson Lehman Hutton Government/Corporate Index. It represents a comprehensive picture of the entire bond market. If one accepts such an index as a suitable proxy of the bond market, one may construct a bond portfolio that is above, below, or about the same in its degree of credit risk as the bond market as a whole. History suggests that a portfolio of above average credit risk will be rewarded; that is, it will earn some incremental return most of the time.

High Yield Bonds. Typically, bonds rated below Ba are considered to be high yield bonds, although some analysts consider any bonds rated below investment grade (Aaa to Baa) to be high yield bonds.

The historical verification of an incremental return for taking credit risk in bonds, as reported in Altman and Nammacher [1985], was one of the reasons for the 1980s popularity and acceptance of high yield bonds, commonly referred to as junk bonds. However, it must be noted that as of late 1989, such high-risk bonds had *not* gone through a severe recession since they became popular. Therefore, the relatively low incidence of bankruptcies recorded in the late 1980s among junk bond issuers may not stand up when the next meaningful recession occurs. Also, more recent studies by Altman [1989], Asquith, Mullins, and Wolf [1989], and Moody's Investor Service [1989] have shed new light on the default rates of junk bond issues over

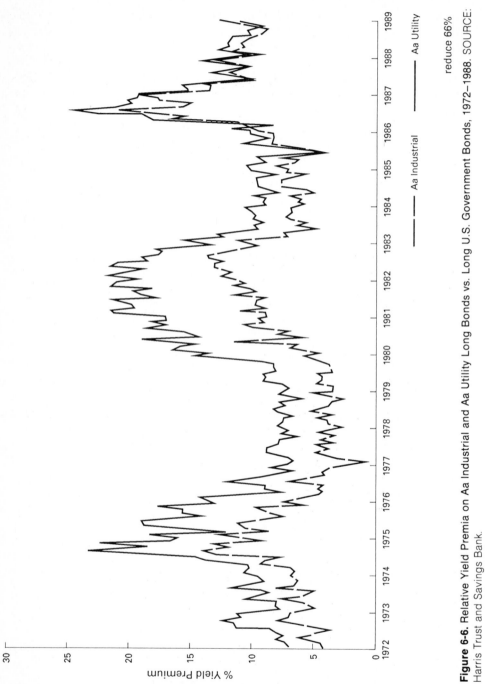

Figure 6-6. Relative Yield Premia on Aa Industrial and Aa Utility Long Bonds vs. Long U.S. Government Bonds, 1972–1988. SOURCE: Harris Trust and Savings Bank.

various holding periods. As a result of the higher default rates reported in these studies, further questions are being raised about the appropriate role for high yield bonds.

The mere prospect of additional return for taking credit risk in the bond market does not necessarily make it appropriate to do so. Such risks should be taken only if they are clearly compatible with the investment objectives and circumstances of the client.

Credit Analysis and Ratings for Domestic Corporate Securities

Credit analysis is the process by which credit risk is normally determined. It is the amount of such risk that determines the quality ratings that are assigned to many corporate and municipal debt obligations. This process has several aspects. They may be classified as follows: measurement of the ability to meet debt service requirements, evaluation of financial statements, economic characteristics of the company and the industries in which it is represented, and review of the indenture provisions pertaining to the particular fixed-income obligation.

The first aspect may be viewed as the primary focus, but the other three are essential for any meaningful credit analysis. Each requires a comparative analytical framework in which the subject issuer and its debt obligations are viewed in a perspective of alternative debtors.

Debt Service Coverage. The ability to pay interest when it is due and to make principal payments consistent with the terms of the indenture are determined by the quantity of funds available for those purposes. Measurement of that ability is often made by calculating two ratios:

1. *Interest coverage* that is equal to interest expense, inclusive of capitalized interest and some lease rental expense divided into earnings before the deduction of this interest expense and taxes; and
2. *Debt service coverage* that is equal to the sum of all fixed charges, tax-adjusted preferred dividends, and principal payments due divided into earnings available for these payments.

For details, see Chapter 7B of Maginn and Tuttle [1985] or any standard investment textbook.

The traditional (and still conservative) approach to such measurement involves a comparison of current or pro forma (when additional debt is imminent) debt service requirements with income/cash flow quantities actually available for coverage during the past 5 or 10 years. These figures are then compared with similar coverage data pertaining to other debt obligations, initially focusing on those of other issuers in the same business or industry, but quite likely extending to other situations when that is felt to be useful. As in the use of financial statement information for any other purpose, careful attention must be directed to any unusual accounting treatments and significant nonrecurring factors. The variation in interest and debt service coverage over an economic or competitive cycle are also important.

Financial Statement Analysis. A good sense of the overall health and well-being of a company may be obtained from a careful review of its financial statements. Many of the important signs are most clearly recognized in the form of ratios or percentage breakdowns. Some of the important ones for industrial companies are as follows:

- Long-term indebtedness as a percentage of total capitalization
- Ratio of total indebtedness to net worth
- Ratio of working capital to long-term indebtedness
- Ratio of cash and receivables to current liabilities
- Ratio of net income to net worth (return on equity)

Because the stock market provides a consensus view of the well-being of companies, it is useful to consider the market value of the net worth as well as the figure at which it is carried in the financial statements. Also, because of the impact of inflation on the real value of company assets, it is well to consider the replacement value of company assets, especially when the particular company has used an historical cost basis in determining its depreciation charges and the amount at which it carries its inventories. Such replacement values should be reflected in an adjustment to the net worth as well.

Probably the most important common denominator of the success of an enterprise is found in its return on equity. This return can be misleading in any given period, but its average size and trend over several years reflect the effectiveness of the use of its invested capital. Return on equity should be viewed in terms of both book value and equity and replacement value of equity. A closely related measure is the market-value-to-book-value of equity ratio or, alternatively, the "Q" ratio (market-value-to-replacement-book-value ratio), each of which provides an excellent reading of the stock market's view of the value of common equity.

Company Characteristics. As noted in the earlier section on unsystematic risk, there are many things that affect the riskiness of a particular issuer and its debt obligations. A few examples are listed there. Following is a much more complete list of the characteristics of a company (and the industries in which it participates) that may have an important bearing on creditworthiness, especially in the case of non–investment grade issuers:

- Sensitivity to ups and downs in the economy
- Competitive environment (see, for elaboration, Porter [1980])
  —Ease of entry (capital and know-how requirements)
  —Degree of concentration among leading industry participants
  —Amount of cost advantage in large scale production
  —Percentage utilization of industry capacity that is viable
  —Concentration or fragmentation of major suppliers
  —Sophistication or economic leverage of customers
  —Market share as compared with that of other participants
  —Control of raw material requirements
- Breakdown between fixed and variable operating expenses
- Amount and organization of labor supply (union versus nonunion)
- Degree, form, or uniformity of regulation
- Product liability or hazardous waste disposal liability exposures
- Research and development expenses and success record

These and any other company characteristics that may be important in a given situation should be examined from the standpoint of how they are changing. All have the potential of affecting the level of profitability (i.e., return on equity) or the extent to which profits may vary from period to period beyond changes related to the business cycle.

Indenture Provisions. The indenture provisions pertaining to a particular debt instrument cover many aspects. Some of them have little to do with the financial analysis of the company. An important example is the *redemption provision* that is found in most corporate indentures. Indenture provisions relate to the unsystematic risk of a bond issue and the investor's ability to maintain the bond's duration, credit quality, and potential for repayment.

While there are some unique standard indenture provisions for different sectors within the corporate bond market, there are important provision similarities that may be found across the entire bond market. Some common provisions are restrictions on:

- The issuance of additional debt (using a debt test or an earnings test)
- Use of assets to secure debt instruments (tangible or intangible property)
- Negative pledge clauses that limit the creation of liens on property in the future without providing the same security to bondholders
- Sale and leaseback of property
- Other property sales
- Mergers or changes in ownership

- Sinking fund requirements
- Payment of dividends under certain circumstances

Credit Analysis and Ratings for Domestic Municipal Securities

The credit analysis process has the same purpose when applied to municipal debt obligations as it does when applied to corporate obligations, that is, to determine credit risk. It is the amount of such risk that determines the quality ratings (for those issues that are rated) and the pricing (in terms of yield to maturity) of these obligations. Because there are two broad categories of municipal obligations (each having some important distinctive features), discussion of the credit analysis process is tailored accordingly.

General Obligation Bonds. Bonds, notes, and paper issued by state, county, city, and other governmental entities and backed by the full faith and credit of the issuer are called general obligation (GO) issues. In each case, the issuing entity pledges to use its taxing powers to produce the funds to pay interest and principal when due.

First, it is important to have reasonable knowledge of the characteristics of the area from which the issuing entity collects its tax revenues. Population trends (both absolute changes and changes relative to other areas), personal income and wealth accumulation trends, major employment sources and trends, and the degree of political harmony and cooperation are among the important matters in this category.

Second, it is important to have a good understanding of the municipality's financial condition and trends in that condition. The amount of debt outstanding (both direct and "overlapping"), how it has been changing over the past 5 or 10 years, the market value of real property in the tax base, and the budgetary process administered by the responsible government authorities should receive careful attention.

Revenue Bonds. Obligations issued in the United States by non–federal government entities and dependent on revenues generated by the activities being financed are called *revenue bonds*. Some of the more important activities financed in this manner are electric power, water and sewage treatment, public housing, hospitals, airports, highways (toll roads), and industrial facilities.

The economics of the activity (or project) to which the revenue bonds are related are very important. If it is a new project, a professional feasibility study is mandatory. It should include an analysis of the demand for the use of the project (or service) and a financial analysis to project revenues and costs of operation. An assessment of current or prospective competition is equally important. The creditworthiness of major lessees (as in the case of airports) or guarantors (as in the case of housing projects) may be crucial in judging the project's long-term feasibility.

Credit and Other Unsystematic International Risk Factors

In addition to the many countries participating in the international bond market, there are a variety of bond issuers that may be classified in the following categories (for elaboration, see Emmer [1986]):

- Supranational entities such as the World Bank, the Asian Development Bank, and the European Economic Community.
- Sovereign borrowers such as the Kingdom of Sweden, the Kingdom of Denmark, and companies guaranteed by sovereign borrowers.
- Political subdivisions such as the Canadian provinces, the City of Toronto, and the City of Stockholm.
- International banks such as Citibank, Barclays, Long Term Credit Bank of Japan, and National Bank of Hungary.
- Private multinational companies such as Siemens, Phillips N.V., ICL, Dow Chemical, and Moet Hennessey.

Sovereign Risk. Perhaps the most unique element is the matter of *sovereign risk*, which is an important factor in most non-U.S. bonds. Sovereign status implies freedom from external control. For example, the government of a foreign country may limit the availability of its foreign exchange reserves to make external payments on its own debt obligations or especially for those of its instrumentalities. Alternatively, it may renounce any such obligations in their entirety. Of course, such drastic measures are likely to have serious and long-lasting repercussions.

In the late 1980s, a number of less developed countries with large external debts negotiated the extension of principal maturities and the reduction of the interest rate payable. As noted in an earlier section on international risk factors of a systematic nature, sovereign risks may be viewed as a unique dimension of the credit risk of foreign bonds.

Disclosure and Comparability of Information. The risk assessment of these entities runs somewhat parallel with that of strictly domestic bonds, but with some different elements or differences in the weight given to certain aspects. Differences in the amount of emphasis given to information related to *credit risk* is largely a function of the more limited sources that are available and some very important differences in accounting treatments, which are reflected in financial statements. The latter is related to philosophy of disclosure.

In the United States, the Securities and Exchange Commission mandates extensive disclosure requirements so that participants in the financial markets can make informed price decisions in purchasing stocks or bonds. In many foreign countries, it appears that disclosure is more at the discretion of the issuer and therefore may be used to avoid political reaction (by setting up reserves in periods when profits are very good) or to allay concerns about possible financial problems (by drawing on reserves when profits are poor or nonexistent).

Credit Risk. With the variety of foreign bond issuers noted earlier, the information needed to assess credit risk is by no means the same in all cases. In view of this, it may be useful to review a list of factors that Standard & Poor's uses for assessing non-U.S. borrowers:

- Country risk or sociopolitical economic climate plus sovereignty matters
- Importance of issuer to its country of domicile
- Industry risk (both domestically and internationally)
- Issuer's industry/market position (both domestically and internationally)
- Issuer's relative operating efficiency
- Management evaluation and prerogatives
- Accounting quality
- Earnings protection
- Financial leverage and asset protection
- Cash flow adequacy
- Financial flexibility

Beyond the country risk factors, several of the above items present somewhat different perspectives than investment professionals are accustomed to in the assessment of U.S. bonds. For example, many countries provide significant support to ailing companies to avoid serious disruptions in employment, economic activity, or particular geographic regions. As a partial corollary, non–U.S. company managements may not have as much latitude to make significant adjustments in the work force or to undertake other types of major corporate restructurings.

Perhaps the most frustrating difference is to be found in the area of accounting treatments. Most foreign companies do not present their financial statements in accordance with generally accepted accounting principles accepted as norms in the United States. Therefore, treatments, such as principles of financial statement consolidation, inventory valuation, depreciation write-offs, and the reflection of pension liabilities, tend to vary widely.

While credit ratings are generally available on U.S. bond issues, the same is not true on many of the other national markets (the United Kingdom, Canada, and Japan are notable exceptions). However, Standard & Poor's and Moody's do provide such ratings on many international bonds (such as Eurobonds). For more on credit ratings of international bond issues, see Chapter 7 of Solnik [1988].

Indenture Provisions. Non-U.S. bonds (in almost any currency) tend to have unusual indenture clauses and options. New instruments appear frequently. For example, there are many *index-linked bonds* and *bonds with options*.

The most common form of index-linked bonds is *floating rate notes* (FRN). The coupon paid on these issues is tied into some variable interest rate. There has been a sizable market for such obligations in Eurosterling and Swiss francs. Generally, Eurobond FRN's are indexed to the London Interbank Offered Rate (LIBOR).

The call option is the most common clause in bonds with options. Other options found in the international bond market include bonds convertible into the common stock of the issuer, bonds exchangeable for a longer maturity, and floating rate obligations that can be exchanged for fixed interest rate bonds. In addition, there are currency option bonds that give the holder a choice of receiving payments in either of two currencies. Such variety illustrates the additional complexities of non–U.S. bond valuation.

EQUITY EXPECTATIONAL INPUTS

As discussed in Chapter 5, the value of an investable asset is largely determined by its future stream of payments and a discount rate that is appropriate for the amount of risk involved. The expectational inputs that are most germane are those that are likely to affect such future payments or the rate at which they should be discounted.

In thinking about such inputs, it is helpful to divide them by types of risk factors—systematic and unsystematic. Both kinds influence the characteristics of the payments stream, but the capital asset pricing model (CAPM) posits that only systematic factors should affect the discount rate.

The importance of systematic and unsystematic factors varies a great deal from company to company with respect to the *stream of payments* available to the common equity holder. However, the systematic factors tend to be most important in large companies, and the unsystematic factors tend to dominate in small companies. For example, changes in nominal gross national product, personal consumer expenditures, and business capital expenditures have a significant impact on most large company sales and earnings. On the other hand, the newness of a particular product and the unsaturated market for such an item are more likely to have a significant impact on the sales and earnings of a small company.

With regard to the *discount rate*, there is one systematic factor that is reflected in the pricing of the common stocks of all companies, the expected rate of inflation (4 to 5 percent in the United States in early 1989). Otherwise, the relative importance of other systematic factors differs a great deal among companies. So-called interest-rate-sensitive companies such as banks, finance companies, and home construction companies are significantly affected by changes in interest rate expectations. Oil companies, electric utilities, and airlines, by contrast, are affected by changes in the price of oil.

The CAPM does not deny impact from unsystematic factors in cases in which a stock is not held (to any great extent) in diversified portfolios. In such cases, unsystematic risk is relevant because it is not diversified away. Presumably some additional increment of required return is reflected in the discount rate in those instances.

It is believed that participants in the equity market are constantly assessing the various systematic and unsystematic factors to judge the likely impact on particular companies and their common stock shares. Presumably decisions (explicit or implicit) are made on whether total risk or systematic risk is relevant, as well as on the relative sensitivity of any given equity issue. Through this process the prices of equity issues are largely determined.

Systematic Risk and Return

There have been changes in the risk/return characteristics of equity securities, but they have been much less significant and much less dramatic than in the case of fixed-income securities between 1968 and 1988 (see Figure 6-1). In very general terms, the volatility of stock market returns was relatively high from 1926 to 1946 (a time period that included the market peak in 1929, the ensuing crash, the Great Depression of the 1930s, and World War II), relatively less from 1946 to 1966 (the reestablishment of a peacetime economy and virtually no inflation after the late 1940s), and somewhat greater from 1966 to 1988 (inflation followed by disinflation). Even though volatility was less during the period from 1946 to 1966, it was still quite substantial. For elaboration, see Fisher and Lorie [1970].

Although the *real* returns (after inflation adjustment) from diversified common stock ownership have varied a great deal over many of the short and intermediate periods of stock market history, they averaged between 6 and 7 percent from 1926 to 1988. Interestingly, they averaged just about the same between 1871 and 1925, according to Wilson and Jones [1987]. This historical experience is not different from the consensus view on common stock expected return in early 1989, which was between 10.5 and 12 percent.

After adjusting for expected inflation of about 4.5 percent, this represented a real expected return of 6.5 to 7 percent.

Even though the real returns have been rewarding over longer periods of time, it is largely due to occasional relatively short periods in which common stock returns have been extraordinary. A dramatic indication of this is the fact that the total return wealth index of the S&P 500 was 406.45 at the end of 1988 (year-end 1925 = 1.00), a return of 10.0 percent per annum, a result that could have been achieved by having a position in the market during the best 51 months of that 63-year period and keeping cash in a mattress the rest of the time as determined from data published by Ibbotson Associates [1988]. It is much the same way with many individual common stocks.

Systematic Risk. This broadly pervasive form of risk, made up of economywide factors such as changes in real growth and inflation, is generally perceived as the cause of stock market volatility. The standard deviation of annual returns in the stock market (S&P 500) is about 20 percent. This represents a rough average—but only that—of the systematic risk of the individual stock issues that make up the market. It captures but conceals the variety of systematic risk characteristics of the many individual issues. This variety comes about as a result of the differing sensitivities of each stock issue to unexpected changes in the economywide factors. There has long been an understanding of these sensitivity differences; however, modern-day statistics have documented this aspect in much more concrete form.

Historical Betas. As explained in Chapter 2, the beta of a given common stock issue represents the average sensitivity of that issue relative to the general stock market (often represented by the S&P 500) during some past period. A stock that has a sensitivity equal to the stock market has a beta of 1.00. If it is more sensitive than the stock market, the beta will be above 1.00. If it is less sensitive, the beta will be less than 1.00. Most of the individual issues that make up the stock market are distributed between betas of 0.75 and 1.33. However, there are a few betas below 0.50 and a few that are more than 2.00.

Because these historical betas are sometimes used to suggest what the future excess return experience of a particular stock issue will be (relative to the market excess return), it is important to understand their limitations. Some of the limitations are common to any statistical analysis. For example, the summary finding usually varies somewhat, depending on the particular time intervals represented in the calculation. In addition, beta calculations differ as a result of particular excess return figures chosen to represent the stock market as a whole. S&P 500 excess return figures are often used, but there are some compelling arguments in favor of broader market indexes such as the Wilshire 5000 Stock Index.

Other limitations are of a more subtle nature. As noted earlier, the beta represents an average for the period covered. This average might be quite misleading if the systematic riskiness of a given issue or the sector in which it is located were changing during the measurement period. Presumably, either of these kinds of changes would have an impact on the holding period returns of individual issues. In turn, such impacts would be likely to affect the measured relationship between the individual issue and stock market returns and, as a result, the measured beta coefficient.

With these limitations, it is not at all surprising that the actual behavior of common stock issues is often inconsistent with their historical betas. Nevertheless, there is a substantial body of empirical data that confirms the existence of a wide range of sensitivities (among individual issues) to general stock market price level changes and confirms that historical betas are often a useful guide to future behavior.

It is well established that the degree of usefulness of betas, usually based on stability, is especially good when the measurement is applied to diverse groupings of stocks. Thus, historical betas on portfolios of stocks tend to be a better guide to future market sensitivity than are betas on individual issues.

Fundamental Betas. The limitations of historical betas have not been alone in generating a quest for alternatives. In a world of curious minds, there is a constant search to understand how phenomena are related to one another, with the hope of establishing cause-and-effect relationships. Accordingly, there have been many efforts to identify what it is about individual companies and their common stock issues that determine systematic riskiness. More specifically, what measures of company operating characteristics, financial condition, and stock valuation are most closely related to stock market sensitivity? This sensitivity is called the security's *fundamental beta*.

Some of the most extensive work on fundamental betas has been done by BARRA, a firm that was founded by Barr Rosenberg, an early leader in beta technology. Some of the systematic risk factors that have emerged from the firm's work are earnings variation, financial leverage, success (as measured by return on equity and a few other variables), size, labor intensity, foreign income, growth, trading, earnings/price ratio, and price/book ratio. In general, each of these risk factors has several component measures. They have been very helpful in forecasting future market sensitivity.

While fundamental betas have many of the same limitations as do the historical betas, they have achieved acceptance among some of the institutions that attempt to structure and manage equity portfolios with the help of modern tools (i.e., at institutions in which the expected returns and systematic riskiness of individual issues are dealt with in an explicit way). They should not be ignored, because they represent an important ingredient of expectational input.

Arbitrage Pricing Theory. As Chapter 2 indicates, whereas the capital asset pricing model focuses on a single factor—a stock market index—arbitrage pricing theory (APT) asserts that an asset's riskiness is related to its sensitivities to unanticipated changes in several economic variables. Usually the number of such variables is limited to four or five. Stephen Ross [1976], who is credited with the creation of APT, suggests four economic variables or factors: unanticipated changes in inflation, industrial production, risk premiums, and the slope of the yield curve.

Empirical studies have established, not surprisingly, that particular common stock issues normally have different sensitivities to such broad economic variables. They may be quite sensitive to certain variables and not very sensitive at all to others. Although this suggests an interesting potential for a more discriminating approach to systematic risk, the added complexity of including the possible existence of other significant factors has proved to be an obstacle to effective application and wide usage among practitioners.

Return for Risk Bearing. Capital asset pricing theory holds that systematic risk is the only kind of risk for which some incremental reward is justified. Unsystematic risk, because it can be diversified away, does not receive any additional reward. Presumably diversified holders of common stocks pay up to the point at which the expected return is enough to reward systematic risk taking, with nothing left for unsystematic risk, because unsystematic risk is irrelevant to them. If diversified holders are the dominant owners of a given stock, presumably their view of relevant risk will prevail in the interplay of forces that determine price.

The history of the stock market provides strong evidence that systematic risk is rewarded. As indicated earlier, the market as a whole has experienced real returns of 6 to 7 percent per annum over the long run. This is as much as, and usually much more than, the real returns from other major classes of investable assets. Furthermore, there is a tendency for those individual issues with high sensitivity to systematic risk to have above average returns over time. Stock market price levels have an upward bias over most intermediate time periods and virtually all longer time periods. Thus, overperformance during periods of rising stock prices overwhelms the underperformance during periods of declining stock prices.

Covariance. The historical covariance of stocks (e.g., 1969 to 1988) relative to other asset classes is shown in Chapter 5. During the period from 1969 to 1988 stocks had modest negative correlations with cash equivalents (-0.11), a modest positive correlation with real estate (0.06), and a more significant positive correlation with domestic bonds (0.41). As noted in a similar earlier comment on the covariance of bonds, the important question is what these relationships will be in the future. However, knowledge of past relationships and an understanding of the likely underlying causes are essential if informed judgments are to be made.

Determinants of Stock Market Value and Volatility

The value of equity securities is determined by the expected stream of dividends (or earnings) and a discount rate that provides an expected return that is appropriate for the relevant risk involved. Value variability is a reflection of the riskiness of equities, which is magnified at times by an intense need or desire to invest (or to liquidate), during periods when market psychology has taken over.

Value. One of the embellished forms of the Gordon-Shapiro equity valuation model is useful for integrating the broad economy (including the interaction of competitive factors within it), the increments to capital that are required to sustain growth and profitability, and the value of an equity exposure to the increments of output that flow from the process (see Gordon [1962]). It is expressed as follows:

$$\text{Value} = \frac{B \times \text{ROE} \left[1 - (1 - D/E)\right]}{i - g}$$

where B represents book value, ROE is return on book equity, and $(1 - D/E)$ is the earnings retention rate. As written, the numerator is equivalent to D, the current dividend. E is earnings; i is the capitalization or discount rate for equities; and g is growth rate of dividends.

The elements of the numerator reflect the fact that dividends are paid out of earnings, earnings are a form of return on the company's investment and book value of equity is a historical cost accounting version of that investment. It is important to recognize these elements in an explicit manner because the dividend growth rate, the return on equity, and the earnings retention rate are somewhat interrelated. For example, if the competitive environment permitted an increase in ROE against the backdrop of a stable dividend growth rate, it would make easier a more than normal increase in dividends, an improvement in financial position, and increments to enlarge market share in the future. Of course, the latter may have an impact on the competitive environment.

Viewed in this manner, the value of the stock market has five determinants. The normal tendencies of each of them are discussed briefly in the list that follows.

1. Book value. Book value of equity tends to move upward in a manner that somewhat parallels corporate sales and gross national product. A notable exception to this pattern occurred between 1981 and 1986, when corporate restructuring was accompanied by write-offs that virtually offset the increments to book value that normally come from retained earnings.

2. Return on equity. For the S&P 400 Industrial Stock Index, there appears to have been an ROE equilibrium tendency of about 10 percent plus the rate of inflation (or a large fraction thereof) over a multiyear period. Actual experience varies, depending on the relative vigor (or slippage) in the economy, and it has lagged a bit in response to changes in the rate of inflation.

3. Earnings retention rate. This rate appears to have an equilibrium that corresponds with nominal growth (real growth plus inflation). This may be affected by changes in capitalization leverage over short to intermediate time periods when a disproportionate share of the funds needed for expansion come through borrowing. Ultimately, the equity must grow if the business is to remain on a reasonably sound financial basis.

4. Growth rate. The dividend growth rate closely corresponds with nominal GNP growth, what it has been doing and is expected to do over the next few years. Again, there was an important exception between 1981 and 1986, when corporate manufacturing sales lagged badly relative to nominal GNP, apparently related to corporate restructuring.

5. Discount rate. In addition to being reflective of the real risk-free rate, the discount rate is influenced by an inflation premium and a risk premium that is appropriate for the amount of risk involved. For the stock market as a whole, the relevant risk is the systematic risk as it reflects itself through the multitude of companies that make up the publicly owned economy.

While this particular expression of value provides important cross-checking features (to help assure internal consistency), many practitioners continue to assess value by noting the current level of earnings (normalized if there are nonrecurring factors at work) and applying a price/earnings (P/E) ratio that is deemed appropriate. This seems a bit treacherous unless all of the factors (and their interrelationships) that are condensed into the single P/E number have been taken into account. That is, the equivalent P/E ratio model is:

$$P/E = \frac{B \times \text{ROE}\,[1 - (1 - D/E)]/E}{i - g},$$

indicating the numerous variables and how they are related to one another, which are assumed in the single P/E variable. To deal with the P/E's determining factors explicitly seems to be the preferable approach.

Volatility. Variations in value are caused by any changes in the determining factors. However, changes in the factors represented in the numerator tend to have a small impact as compared with changes in the factors
in the denominator. For example, a year-to-year change of 7 percent in the
book value (a numerator factor) would have a similar percentage impact on
value or P/E if everything else were to remain constant. By contrast, an
increase in the discount rate (represented by i in the denominator) from 11
to 11.5 percent would drop value or the P/E by more than 14 percent, assuming a growth rate of 8 percent and everything else remaining constant.

Volatility of fundamental value (as opposed to price) tends to be somewhat moderate, but it does occur. The most significant variability results
from nonparallel changes in the two factors represented in the denominator,
the discount rate and the growth rate. The difference between these two
factors should be understood in terms of its real and inflation components
as follows:

i = inflation premium + risk premium + real risk-free rate

g = inflation premium + real growth

Because unexpected change in the rate of inflation is one of the most
disruptive factors in the financial markets, it is important to recognize that
when it happens, it may not have a parallel impact on both i and g. For
example, when such unexpected changes took the form of inflation increases
in the late 1960s, they were rather quickly reflected in higher discount rates,
but with little (if any) impact on growth rate expectations. (*Inflation flow-
through* to earnings and dividends did not begin to occur until the early
1970s.) Thus, discount rate/growth rate differential increased from about 3
to 3.75 percent, with a fairly negative impact on stock values.

Although it may be a contentious view, stock prices and returns vary
more than stock values do. This creates occasional periods of exceptional
opportunity or vulnerability. Early 1972 and mid-1987 are examples of the
latter conditions. As has been noted in the financial literature many times,
if one identifies a significant flaw in the current market consensus (and it is
later proved to be valid), the rewards are likely to be extraordinary.

Forecasts of Stock Market Value

Although there are major uncertainties related to any forecast of stock market value, there are certain things about the historical behavior of the stock
market that suggest that longer range forecasts are somewhat less uncertain
than are relatively short forecasts. Most important is the fact that the greed
and fear that magnify volatility over shorter intervals tend to cancel out over
longer periods of time. The distribution of annual returns (nominal or real)

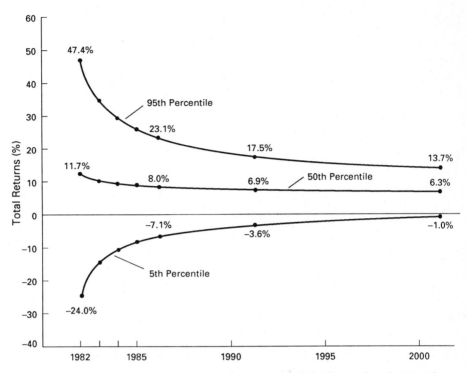

Figure 6-7. Common Stocks Inflation-Adjusted Forecast Total Return Distributions for the Period 1982–2001 Using Geometric Mean Annual Rates. SOURCE: Ibbotson and Sinquefield [1982].

tends to narrow a great deal as holding periods lengthen, as shown in Figure 6-7.

A *longer range forecast* should take into consideration the most likely development of real growth and inflation during the forecast horizon. By noting where the current ROE is relative to its equilibrium level and by projecting what it should be at the terminal date, projections of earnings and dividends can be made. The level of dividends in the terminal year may be incorporated in the Gordon-Shapiro dividend discount model to derive reasonable value at that time. A detailed discussion of the methodology is available in Gray [1979].

A *shorter range forecast* may use the same basic framework to develop a sense of possible outcomes over the next year or so. However, whether such notions of likely outcomes should be used in making strategic investment decisions depends on some additional considerations. For example, if the time interval is such that a peaking of the business cycle and an ensuing recession is likely to be involved, the typical behavior of the stock market during such periods should be taken into account. As shown in Table 6-7,

TABLE 6-7. Business Recession and Stock Market Declines

Business Cycle			Stock Market (S&P 400)					Number of Months Market Trough to Business Trough
Peaks	Troughs	Number Months	Peaks[b]	(Date)	Troughs[b]	(Date)	Decline	
Oct. 1926	Nov. 1927	13	11.01	(12/26)[a]	10.56	(1/27)	−4.1%	9
Aug. 1929	Mar. 1933	43	25.38	(9/29)[a]	3.52	(6/32)	−86.1	9
May 1937	June 1938	13	18.10	(3/37)	8.39	(3/38)	−53.6	3
Feb. 1945	Oct. 1945	8	17.06	(12/45)[a]	13.64	(11/46)	−20.0	(13)
Nov. 1948	Oct. 1949	11	16.93	(6/48)	13.23	(6/49)	−21.8	4
July 1953	May 1954	10	26.99	(1/53)	22.70	(9/53)	−15.9	8
Aug. 1957	Apr. 1958	8	53.25	(7/57)	41.98	(10/57)	−21.2	6
Apr. 1960	Feb. 1961	10	65.02	(1/60)	55.34	(10/60)	−14.9	4
Dec. 1969	Nov. 1970	11	118.03	(11/68)	75.58	(5/70)	−35.0	6
Nov. 1973	Mar. 1975	16	134.54	(1/73)	69.53	(10/74)	−48.3	5
Jan. 1980	July 1980	6	124.49	(10/79)	111.09	(3/80)	−10.8	4
July 1981	Nov. 1982	16	160.96	(11/80)	114.08	(8/82)	−29.1	3
Averages		14					−30.1%	4

SOURCE: Harris Trust and Savings Bank.
[a] Stock market peak occurred after business cycle peak.
[b] Daily closing prices.

there is a well-established pattern that stock prices decline 10 to 25 percent (and even more on occasion), usually starting sometime before the peak in the business cycle and ending sometime before the end of the recession. These tendencies result in price levels that are often well below reasonable value during the early to middle stages of a recession.

In summary, reasonable notions of the stock market outlook can be very useful in trying to gauge what a realistic expected return might be over the course of the forecast horizon. If they translate into an annualized real return that is well above (or below) the historical average of 6 to 7 percent, it represents a clear signal to move toward above (or below) normal common equity positions in investment portfolios.

It was estimated by Ibbotson, Siegel, and Love [1985] that at the end of 1984, total world wealth was about $27.7 trillion, of which 6.7 percent represented U.S. equities and 4.9 percent represented foreign equities. Thus, it appeared that U.S. stocks accounted for about 58 percent of worldwide equities at that time. During the next three years (through the end of 1987), dramatic changes occurred. While U.S. stock market indexes moved up by about 50 percent, even taking into account the October 1987 debacle, the major foreign stock markets moved up as well. Furthermore, the U.S. dollar declined significantly in the foreign exchange markets. Therefore, U.S. stocks (in U.S. dollar terms) accounted for quite a bit less than 50 percent of the worldwide total as of this more recent date.

Among the foreign stock markets, Japan is the largest by a wide margin. It probably accounts for around one-half of the foreign total. Other foreign stock markets (in approximately order of size) are the United Kingdom, Germany, Canada, Switzerland, and France. As a further indicator of relative size, on a combined basis, Australia, Italy, the Netherlands, Hong Kong, Sweden, Belgium, Singapore, Spain, Denmark, Norway, and Austria are roughly equal to the United Kingdom.

Systematic Risk. From a purely global perspective, the systematic risk factors include only those influences that are reflected in a worldwide stock market index. Morgan Stanley Capital International's EAFE (Europe, Australia, and Far East) Index is a widely used index of that sort. From that point of view, the factors that account for differences between individual foreign country stock price indexes and the worldwide index are viewed as unsystematic.

If the present movement toward international portfolio diversification continues, which seems likely, such a view of the distinction between systematic and unsystematic risks could evolve. However, the discussion here retains the traditional focus, in which the factors having a broad influence within any given country's stock market are considered systematic in nature.

The factors that are common to and broadly influence the stock market within any given country may be classified in the following manner:

| | *Systematic Risks* | |
	Internal	*External*
Economic	X	X
Political	X	X
Sociological	X	X

In viewing the systematic risk factors in the U.S. equity market, it has been customary to avoid explicit reference to those that are external. For many years after the end of World War II, the external factors seemed to be not very important most of the time. In more recent years, this has changed.

External factors tend to be much more important in foreign countries, often more nearly on a par with the internal factors. There are at least three reasons why this may occur:

1. The economies and the political power of many foreign countries (with stock markets) are relatively small.
2. Export activities tend to represent a larger portion of the total output of many foreign countries.
3. A larger portion of the large capitalization common stock issues in many foreign countries represent companies with a heavy multinational flavor.

Of course, the balance between internal and external factors within any given market may change with the passage of time. Furthermore, at any given time the particular balance within one country is very likely to differ from what it is in another country. This constitutes an extra layer of complexity for those investors who move beyond the confines of their own domestic market. While U.K. and Swiss investors, for example, have acquired much experience with such matters, U.S. investors for the most part are at an earlier stage of the learning curve.

The stock market decline of October 1987 is a dramatic example of the impact the U.S. stock market can have upon foreign stock markets. While the causes of the precipitous decline in U.S. stock prices are still in dispute, the rapid ripple effect on foreign equity markets is clear. Not all foreign markets followed or declined as much but, with about a one-day lag, the markets in Australia, New Zealand, Singapore, and Canada experienced roughly comparable declines. In addition, the markets in the United Kingdom, the Netherlands, Norway, and Malaysia were down sharply, but not by as much. The German, French, and Swiss markets did not suffer as badly, but they clearly moved in the same direction as the U.S. market. For a more detailed discussion of this topic, see Roll [1988]. Of course, there were reverse effects, with some observers claiming foreign markets led rather than followed some U.S. market declines.

Valuation. While generally less rigorous disclosure standards and less concern about trading on insider information have probably affected the trading and pricing of many foreign stocks, it appears that U.S. valuation methods are being applied. Systematic risk factors are being viewed in terms of their impact on earnings and P/E ratios, but increasingly through the projection of dividend flows and an appropriate discount rate. In the latter cases, the relative attraction of individual common stocks is being viewed within a mean-variance framework, where the level of expected return is examined in relation to relevant, mostly systematic risk.

In spite of the influence of external factors (some of which may be common in kind, though not necessarily in degree) upon most foreign economies, it appears that the internal (or domestic) factors have dominated stock price behavior in particular non-U.S. markets. This is clearly reflected in the rather divergent returns from various foreign equity markets between 1960 and 1985 as shown in Table 6-8.

It may be noted that the best returns were from Austria and Spain (1960–1964), Japan and Spain (1965–1969), Austria and Norway (1970–1974), Hong Kong and the United Kingdom (1975–1979), and Germany and Japan (1980–1985). Such changes in the "best place to be" and the inevitable difficulty in trying to anticipate these changes both lend support to a diversification approach in building international portfolios.

Unsystematic Risk and Return

If the degree of riskiness and the volatility of returns are one and the same, or if they are merely closely correlated, the risk of holding individual issues is greater than that of holding a market portfolio such as an index fund, at least in most instances. Furthermore, there is little or no opportunity for excess returns if virtually all individual issues are held in amounts representing their market capitalization weights. Therefore, to create the potential for some excess return it is necessary to maintain nondiversified portfolios.

While the quantity of funds represented in index funds has grown enormously (estimated by Salomon Brothers, Inc. at about $184 billion in mid-1987), a large portion of the market value of equity issues is held in portfolios that are less than fully diversified or as isolated holdings. Of course, most institutional investors maintain portfolios that are diversified within specified risk parameters, but usually with enough residual risk exposure to permit the realization of excess returns.

The legitimacy of such active management endeavors hinges to an important degree on the attainment of excess returns (after all transaction costs and *net* active management fees) with some consistency over reasonable time periods—usually three to five years.

TABLE 6-8. Foreign Equities: U.S. Dollar Adjusted Annual Returns for Five-Year Periods, 1960–1985 [a]

Period	Europe									Other	
	Austria	Belgium	Denmark	France	Germany	Italy	Netherlands	Norway	Spain	Australia	Canada
1960–1964	13.3%	7.2%	8.9%	2.6%	6.5%	-0.7%	7.2%	4.4%	14.7%	8.8%	12.7%
1965–1969	0.9	2.5	4.9	3.8	9.6	10.7	7.1	7.3	18.1	15.4	5.9
1970–1974	19.5	13.7	15.5	-0.6	4.8	-9.4	-0.2	19.0	14.5	-10.7	4.6
1975–1979	8.3	18.9	7.7	22.2	16.3	-1.4	23.9	17.6	-10.2	21.5	18.0
1980–1985	8.6	15.8	17.0	10.7	18.0	22.3	18.3	7.4	8.4	5.4	7.7

Period	Europe			Asia		
	Sweden	Switzerland	United Kingdom	Hong Kong	Japan	Singapore
1960–1964	11.8%	10.1%	6.6%		8.8%	
1965–1969	6.1	9.9	11.2		16.4	
1970–1974	8.2	3.7	-11.2	4.1%	15.9	11.2%
1975–1979	5.1	21.7	32.8	40.1	18.8	29.5
1980–1985	24.7	11.0	16.4	8.7	20.7	2.2

SOURCE: Ibbotson and Brinson [1988].

[a] Sample includes one six-year period, 1980–1985. Returns are compound annual (geometric mean) returns over the period indicated.

Reward for Unsystematic Risk. Prior to the advent of index funds around 1975, unsystematic risk exposure was inherent in virtually all investment portfolios. Yet the developing portfolio performance data did not indicate that unsystematic risk exposure was being rewarded with any excess return. For the most part, median portfolio returns fell below S&P 500 returns, usually by at least one percent per annum. Of course, each year there were portfolios with returns better than S&P 500 returns. However, such results appeared to be heavily influenced by temporary good luck. At least the more inquisitive studies of performance found a strong tendency for the high-ranking portfolios in one period to be distributed across the spectrum of performance in the following period.

There probably are some managers who have *consistently* achieved excess returns because of their skill in the selection of particular unsystematic risk exposures. However, they are difficult to identify prior to their achievement. Even with the benefit of hindsight, the positive identification of such skill has been questionable. During the past decade, the relationship between investment style and performance has come to be well recognized. Managers of growth stocks, blue chips, and small capitalization issues were often mistakenly thought to have skill at selecting issues, because their particular style remained in vogue for quite a number of successive years.

In light of this experience (and these problems), it is not surprising that some clients opted for the elimination of unsystematic risk exposures through the use of index funds. Ironically, after the index fund movement had gotten under way there was a period, roughly from the mid-1970s through 1982, when the median portfolio returns were often above the S&P 500 returns. Many observers construed this as a long overdue exoneration of active management.

Unfortunately, this probably represented an impetuous use of investment performance data that, during that particular period, were being affected by a historically unprecedented explosion in the performance of small-capitalization issues. Not only were many of the small-capitalization issues not represented in the S&P 500, so that beating "the market" was achieved only with a lot of help from non–S&P 500 issues, but the proportionately greater impact of small capitalization issues on smaller portfolios probably had some effect on the location of the return of the median account, raising it from below the S&P 500 to above it. Because the small capitalization issues have mostly underperformed the S&P 500 since mid-1983, it is not surprising that the median account returns have once again tended to be below the S&P 500 returns.

The historical experience of returns on less than fully diversified portfolios indicate that rewards may result from unsystematic risk exposures. However, on average, the rewards are more than offset by the penalties; that is, returns after costs have been below those of the S&P 500. Furthermore, luck or happenstance has a great deal to do with the particular outcome (reward or penalty) in any given time period. Even though the equity market is not perfectly efficient, it seems to have been sufficiently so to confound the vast majority of active management practitioners.

The growing body of literature on market anomalies, mostly published during the 1980s, does seem to offer possible solutions to the challenge of achieving rewards for unsystematic risk taking. Time alone will tell whether these anomalies will persist as more investors attempt to exploit them.

Sector/Industry Analysis for Domestic Stocks

There are many ways to classify the thousands of common stock issues that comprise the domestic equity market. Classification is usually done to simplify the study of companies that have common characteristics and price/return experiences among their common stock issues. The past price/return experience as it relates to the economic experience of such companies may be helpful in the development of expectations about the future. Some of the more widely used classification methods are:

- Economic/industry sectors
- Company size (market value of capitalization)
- Homogeneous rates of return
- Ranking by valuation yardsticks
- Relative momentum (price or earnings)

Interestingly, several of the specific classification methods are closely related to market anomalies that were identified and for the first time taken seriously during the 1980s. Each of these methods is discussed in the subsections that follow, and, where applicable, closely related market anomalies are identified.

Economic/Industry Sectors. Classification by economic sector or industry group has been used for a long time. There are important factors that affect the future course of the companies placed within such sectors/groups. Many of these factors are embodied in U.S. government economic and financial data or in the published information that comes out of industry trade associations and the like. Some of them may reflect changing competitive circumstances, relative growth, or stability within these segments. Unexpected changes in these factors represent risk, and in some degree they may contribute to the sensitivity of a particular group's stock price behavior to changes in the stock market price level.

Like most attempts to simplify, these kinds of segmentation do pose some problems. The most obvious problem is that many companies (especially larger ones) do business in more than one sector or industry. If such diversity is small in relation to a dominant product line, it is not serious. However, if a company is broadly diversified (regardless of whether it is referred to as a conglomerate), its segment classification may be largely arbitrary. Another problem is that the completely unique factors in a particular company may substantially overwhelm the common segment factors, thereby causing seemingly aberrant behavior. Many times the price/return behavior of the stocks within particular sectors or groups has been highly divergent.

There is a great deal of intuitive appeal to the use of sectors and groups as an integral part of a *top-down analysis* of future prospects. Furthermore, there is some justification for some of the widely held notions about the manner in which certain groups behave, depending on the stage of the business cycle or other longer range patterns in our economy. Nevertheless, it has not proved to be the "road to riches" for many who have used it. In some cases, the lack of success may be related to the absence of a valid value discipline in the process.

Company Size. Companies have long been ranked by size to permit the easy identification of stocks with substantial market value capitalization. This has been especially helpful to institutional investment managers handling large amounts of assets. However, during the 1980s these rankings were expanded to include virtually all publicly traded stocks. By examining these expanded rankings, it was possible to group companies by the market value of their common shares. Such groupings have enabled researchers to test for the so-called *small firm effect*. This has been one of the most extensively described anomalies.

Many articles written on the small firm effect from the late 1970s until the mid-1980s were based on studies that included small company stock market performance during much of the 1974–1983 period. That particular nine-year period witnessed extraordinary returns from small company stocks. Not surprisingly, these studies seemed to support the existence of a small firm effect and indicated this sector of the market offered extraordinary opportunity, especially in relation to the S&P 500 stocks. Many investors were lured into this sector, some of them fairly close to the time that small capitalization stocks began to have a dismal experience, from mid-1983 until the end of 1987.

A more thorough review of the history of small company stock behavior indicates a sporadic pattern of rewarding performance that was better than the S&P 500 as shown in Table 6-9. It appears that small capitalization stocks move through their own cycles of being undervalued and overvalued. In retrospect, they were unusually cheap in 1974 and extremely overpriced in 1983. It seems reasonable to assume that the Employee Retirement Income Security Act of 1974 (ERISA) contributed significantly to the extraordinary returns of that period. ERISA made it much more comfortable for trustees

TABLE 6-9. Performance of Small U.S. Company Stocks vs. S&P 500 Stocks

| Time Periods | | | Compound Annual Returns | | |
Calendar Years	Total Years	Predominant Best Performance	Small Stocks	S&P 500 Stocks	Difference
1926–1931	6	S&P 500	(20.2)%	(2.5)%	(17.7)%
1932–1945	14	Small companies	25.2	11.5	13.7
1946–1953	8	S&P 500	5.3	11.2	(5.9)
1954–1962	9	Fairly even	15.7	15.2	0.5
1963–1968	6	Small companies	30.9	12.2	18.7
1969–1973	5	S&P 500	(12.3)	2.0	(14.3)
1974–1983	10	Small companies	28.4	10.6	17.8
1984–1987	4	S&P 500	3.0	15.0	(12.0)
Summary					
1926–1973	48	Fairly even	9.8	9.3	0.5
1974–1983	10	Small companies	28.4	10.6	17.8
1984–1987	4	S&P 500	3.0	15.0	(12.0)
1926–1987	62	Small companies	12.1	9.9	2.2

SOURCE: Rate of return data is from Ibbotson Associates, Inc. [1988].

to hold small company stocks in diversified portfolios. Many portfolios that had never invested in small company stocks became new customers for such stocks. It seemed to work, so they bought more. Market momentum began to build, enticing others to join the fray. It provides a classic example of how "the herd" forms and ultimately stampedes rationality in the market.

This perspective on what happened between 1974 and 1983 does not destroy the notion of a small firm effect. There probably is an anomaly of this type, but it is sporadic and it seems to occur mostly during the month of January. Until there is better data on small company earnings growth, volatility, profitability (ROE), and related financial information, a certain uneasiness about this anomaly seems to be justified.

Homogeneous Return Patterns. Common stock issues have been put into groups on the basis of similarities in their residual return patterns. Such residual return data are determined by removing the impact of the market (S&P 500) from their respective periodic total return figures. In at least two studies in which this was done, it led to the identification of four relatively homogeneous groups: energy and three others with total return characteristics labeled growth, stable, and cyclical. For elaboration on this topic, see Farrell [1975]. With the passage of time, there has been some movement of individual issues from one group to another. This has been required to maintain the homogeneous behavior integrity of each group.

SEI Corporation has created and managed homogeneous groups of this type. For the 14-year period from 1973 through 1986, the four groups had annual compound returns as follows: energy, 13.0 percent; stable, 12.6 percent; cyclical, 10.2 percent; and growth, 6.6 percent. For elaboration, see Cottle, Murray, and Block [1988]. These differences have no particular significance in terms of future returns for each grouping. They are the product of the time period covered. However, such groupings lend themselves to the development of strategies based on the pattern of residuals.

Valuation Yardsticks. Stock issues are being grouped into quintiles or deciles according to some of the most widely used valuation yardsticks: price/earnings ratios, market-value-to-book-value ratios, Tobin's "Q" ratio (market-value-to-replacement book value), expected rates of return from multistage dividend discount models, and dividend yields. The assignment of a stock to any particular group is based on the periodic ranking of all issues according to the specific yardstick figures. All of them seem to be significant in providing an important piece in the never-ending relative value puzzle. Two of them, low price/earnings ratios and low price/book ratios, have been the focus of much attention in the anomaly literature.

Interestingly, the financial literature on low price/earnings ratios goes back at least 30 years. Among the anomalies that have been identified and tested, it has one of the most consistent and best track records in producing above-average performance. Because of all the attention it has received, one might expect it to self-destruct. But it has been difficult for professional investors to use and acknowledge publicly the use of such a simplistic technique. Because the amount of the reward for using low P/E ratio stocks is closely related to the dispersion of such ratios (which changes from time to time), the widespread adoption of this approach could diminish its value.

Momentum. Another type of classification that has proved to be quite useful is based on relative momentum. While there may be any number of things that could be examined on this basis, two that have been widely used are stock price momentum and earnings momentum. One that is somewhat related to earnings momentum is *earnings surprise*, or unexpected changes in the consensus forecast quarterly earnings level or growth rate expectations. All of these have been the subject of some attention in the anomaly literature.

The strictly momentum criteria have been useful because of the tendency for price or earnings movements to persist for some period of time. Of course, the length of any such movement can be a few weeks, a few months, or a few years. They do vary; unfortunately, they do not vary in a very predictable manner. They have no value when one is trying to determine the peak or trough in the relative performance of an issue or sector, but they can offer some assurance that performance is likely to be good or poor for awhile, once the favorable or unfavorable pattern is under way.

Company Analysis for Domestic Stocks

An individual company is analyzed for the primary purpose of determining the flow of future earnings and dividends and their present value. At this level in the development of expectational inputs, the focus is primarily on those things that are somewhat or entirely unique. Given the dynamic character of any business entity, the key issue is how any of the important unique aspects is changing. Beyond the systematic and sectoral influences to which the company is subject, how are the unique aspects likely to impact the future stream of earnings and dividends in terms of their growth and variability, and the rate at which they should be discounted? Thus, the expected future performance of the company is related to how its stock should be priced at present.

At the risk of oversimplifying, think of the company analysis in terms of three aspects: what happened, how it compared with other concurrent happenings, and why it happened. Each aspect poses some challenging information gathering and analytical problems. However, the one that is usually most difficult to solve is the third one: why it happened. The solutions to this problem require more than ordinary interpretation skills. Success in this particular aspect may be crucial to the development of credible expectations.

Financial Statement Analysis. Finding out what happened is best accomplished through a review of the corporate disclosure documents. In the United States, these include annual and quarterly shareholder reports, Form 10-K statements, prospectuses, and registration statements. The text of these reports, financial statements, and the footnotes to financial statements are all important. Whenever possible, a 5-to-10-year review of such information is desirable. Sometimes an even longer review can be useful.

With regard to the financial statements, a good understanding of accounting principles, knowledge of alternative methods of reflecting inventory, plant, and equipment costs through the income statement, and other technical accounting treatments are quite important. What has happened in terms of relationships between operating results (income statement), cash flow (flow of funds statement), and financial position (balance sheet) must be examined. Special attention should be given to the impact of extraordinary and nonrecurring events. For an extensive treatment of this subject, see Part 2 of Cottle, Murray, and Block [1988].

A fairly comprehensive "spreadsheet" of financial information is helpful in viewing the progression of sales, earnings, equity capital, and the like over a period of several years. By using this format, the pattern of profit margins, capital turnover, return on assets, leverage, and return on equity is easily derived. These company happenings should then be viewed in concert with the financial markets' assessment of what has been going on (e.g., the price history of its common stock as well as the history of total rate of return, inclusive of both dividends and price change, experienced).

Comparative Observations. Historical happenings should be compared with macroeconomic developments. The latter should include the general progression and the volatility of GNP, with some attention paid to real output and its principle sources: total hours worked and productivity. It should also include the experience of the general price level via either the Consumer Price Index or the GNP deflator, as well as interest rates. In examining such matters, an effort should be made to identify unusual circumstances at the beginning or the end of the period under review.

Next it is important to know what was happening in those industries in which a particular company is represented, what has been the unit growth and volatility of relevant products or services, and what has been the financial experience of competitors. A study of the financial experience of a company's competitors is likely to benefit from some review of the corporate disclosure documents of the significant competitors. In addition, such things as labor costs and labor unrest, cost and availability of raw materials, and government actions such as spending programs or tax rule changes may be important, depending on the particular company.

Another dimension that must not be ignored is the financial market perspective. What has happened to the stock market in terms of price level and total return? What part of the changes reflects earnings improvement, and what part reflects changes in P/E ratios? Similarly, what happened to the stock price total return of each of those companies that is most nearly comparable? Changes in bond ratings and yield spreads should be noted as well.

Answering the Question: Why? With a good picture of what happened and how it compared with concurrent events, a meaningful search for major causes may proceed. Changes in the competitive environment are often high on the list. These may take the form of supply/demand relationships (such as capacity utilization), new entrants into the field, concentration among suppliers and customers, differential product development and enhancement, and differential changes in manufacturing and delivery cost efficiency.

Changes in government regulations, environmental quality requirements, and product liability concerns may be especially important in particular cases. Differences in the level of management skills as evidenced by the use of resources for research, new product development, employee motivation, and the like should be looked for. If an accurate assessment of major causes is achieved, it should be very helpful in the formation of future expectations.

The analysis of companies (and their common stocks) does not assure that related investment decisions will produce above-average market returns. Indeed there is a great deal of academic literature and practitioner experience that suggests that it may not be worth the effort in many instances. There are several possible explanations. First, there is so much of this analytical activity going on that the pricing of many issues is quite efficient. Second, much of this activity is performed at a skill level that is not sufficient to produce good results. Third, good analytical conclusions are frequently neutralized when processed into investment accounts by the portfolio manager. Fourth, the enthusiasm that often accompanies the determination of promising future expectations overwhelms realism in judging the price that may be justified; that is, the consideration of price lacks a disciplined valuation framework.

Whatever the cause(s) may be, the experience has been sufficiently disappointing that, during the 1980s, much effort was expended in the investigation of alternative approaches. These alternatives have not necessarily excluded company analysis, but at a minimum they have supplemented such analysis with *valuation screens*, such as low P/E ratios, high dividend discount model expected returns, and the like. A comprehensive study by Reinganum [1988] singled out stocks with exceptionally high returns (1970–1983) to see whether these firms shared any common attributes. The selection strategy that emerged from this study involved the application of nine investment screens as follows:

1. The price/book ratio is less than 1.0.
2. The five-year growth rate (based on quarterly earnings) is positive.
3. Quarterly earnings are accelerating.
4. Pretax profit margins are positive.
5. Fewer than 20 million common shares are outstanding.
6. Relative price strength is at least at the seventieth percentile.
7. Relative strength in the current quarter is greater than in the previous quarter.
8. The O'Neil Datagraph (a proprietary formula) ranking is 70 or above.
9. The stock is selling at a price that is within 15 percent of its maximum price during the preceding two years.

Interestingly, several of these screens are the same as, or are closely related to, some of the efficient market anomalies previously discussed. For example, the low price/book ratio standard is similar to the low P/E ratio anomaly. In the case of the 20 million shares limit, it should be noted that the firms selected by this strategy were not necessarily small. The median stock market capitalization of the selected firms was $102.3 million, a figure close to the median capitalization of the author's seventh decile portfolio of $119 million, which was in the upper half of the capitalization ranking that included all New York Stock Exchange and American Stock Exchange companies. Nevertheless, because there were a sizable number of small companies included in the group of selected firms, it is reasonable to assume that the exceptionally high returns observed were influenced in part by the extraordinary experience of small companies between 1974 and 1983.

Sector/Industry, Company, and Other Unsystematic International Factors

By adopting the view that systematic risk is to be dealt with on a country-by-country basis (even though a worldwide view is possible and may be developing), the unsystematic risk aspects are much the same as they are for U.S. common stocks. There are sector and industry factors that influence particular groups of stocks, and the strictly company factors are somewhat unique to each individual stock.

Industry Factors. The sector/industry factors may start with the nature of the product (raw material or finished good, durable or nondurable, and consumer or industrial) because of implications for both demand and product price volatility. Related to the nature of the product is where the product is in its life cycle. This has important implications for real growth rates and whether they are likely to be accelerating, stabilized, or decelerating. Of course, to the extent that a particular product is an important source of badly needed foreign exchange in a particular country, it may carry implications with respect to the likelihood and magnitude of governmental support.

The industry's competitive environment is very important because of its impact on relative profitability. The determinants are similar to those that were discussed for U.S. companies. However, it appears that the domestic competitive environments are somewhat more controlled through various business and government arrangements in some foreign countries, most notably Japan. This may reduce somewhat the significance of competitive developments. However, because of a typically greater dependency on export markets, the worldwide competitive factors may be relatively more severe in their impact on particular foreign countries.

Because a number of major industries, such as automobiles, tires, petroleum, chemicals, steel, and consumer electronics, do have a strong international character, it is possible to approach international diversification by industry rather than by country. Because worldwide competitive factors and trade barriers normally apply somewhat uniformly to these industries, a cross-sectional view of this kind has a great deal of merit. However, it would be detrimental to ignore individual country stock market factors that could overwhelm the development of worldwide industry trends and circumstances.

Company Factors. The analysis of the unique factors in a foreign company is in many ways similar to that in a U.S. company. How are the unique aspects likely to impact the future stream of earnings and dividends, the rate at which they should be discounted, and in some cases the makeup of the company assets?

In the process of determining what happened in the analysis of a given company, the investor cannot lean as heavily on corporate disclosure documents in most foreign countries. With the notable exception of the United Kingdom and, to an increasing extent, of Japan as well, they simply do not exist in the quantity or quality that they do in the United States. As noted earlier, there are tendencies toward much more conservative reporting of earnings and a greater use of "smoothing" techniques to reduce earnings volatility in many of the important foreign countries.

In the process of determining "why it happened," the assessment of management is probably just as important, but may be more difficult, in foreign companies. Geographical, cultural, and language differences make this inevitable to some extent. In addition, many managers of foreign companies have a long-range view and are simply not as accommodating to information seekers.

REAL ESTATE EXPECTATIONAL INPUTS[1]

The purpose of real estate investment analysis is to evaluate real estate from the perspective of a particular individual or institution. It involves consideration of factors such as risk and the after-tax rate of return from the investment and how well the investment fits into an existing portfolio. The analysis is typically made relative to a presumed purchase price or estimated project construction cost. One of the primary considerations in investment analysis is whether the expected rate of return from an investment is sufficient to warrant the purchase by a particular investor or institution. Alternatively, one could determine the price necessary to provide an appropriate rate of return to justify the investment. This would indicate the value to that investor. This type of value is typically referred to as *investment value* and may be quite different from the *market value* (i.e., the most probable current selling price) of the property. Investment value is affected by factors such as the investor's objectives and constraints as discussed in Chapters 3 and 4. Sometimes an investor is willing to accept a lower return, if necessary, from one property than it could attain from another because

---

[1] This section relies heavily on analytical materials provided by Randall Zisler of Russell-Zisler, Inc. and the chapter on real estate investing by Jeffrey Fisher in Maginn and Tuttle [1983].

it has other valuable characteristics (e.g., the asset might provide more diversification, liquidity, or tax benefits).

Real estate valuation is similar to investment or security analysis, but the term "valuation" usually implies *estimating* a market value, or most probable selling price, for the property because there is no national or regional exchange for determining the market value of real estate. According to the American Institute of Real Estate Appraisers [1973], *market value* is defined as "the highest price estimated in terms of money which a property will bring if exposed for sale in the open market, allowing a reasonable time to find a purchaser who buys with knowledge of all the uses to which it has been or could be adapted and for which it is capable of being used." This estimate can be thought of as *the* relevant value for a "typical" investor in the type of property being evaluated.

Macroeconomic Factors Affecting Real Estate

Real estate prices and returns and risk for real estate investments are affected by a myriad of factors that determine the supply of and demand for different types of property (see Figure 6-8).

First, values tend to be affected by the general level of business activity, and particularly by interest rate trends. However, the housing market and the market for commercial real estate differ in the timing of their respective responses to changes in the overall economy. Historically, the housing market has tended to lead the rest of the economy into and out of a recession. The commercial real estate market, on the other hand, tends to follow rather than lead the overall economy. The difference in the reactions of these two segments of the market to conditions in the overall economy is due in large part to the fact that the housing market is very sensitive to interest rates, which tend to peak near the crest of the business cycle and bottom out near its trough. By contrast, the commercial real estate market is more responsive to the level of business activity.

Second, real estate is perhaps particularly affected by the *expected* level of inflation or deflation. In an inflationary economy, such as that during most of the 1970s and early 1980s, real estate performed relatively well. In a deflationary or, more realistically, disinflationary economy, real estate might be expected to perform less satisfactorily and might have lower returns than bond and stock investments. Chapter 10 discusses the relative rates of return from real estate in more detail.

Another category of macro factors affecting the demand for real estate is population demographics. Demand for housing, for example, is affected by factors such as the birth rate, the average number of persons living in a household, the attitudes, tastes, and preferences about consumption of housing versus other goods and services, and the average income per household.

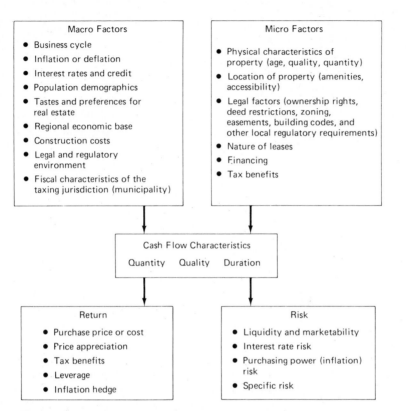

Figure 6-8. Real Estate Valuation Considerations.

Changes in lifestyle, coupled with higher energy costs, could mean that more households than in the past prefer to be close to both work and shopping. This also has implications for the location of industrial and commercial space relative to residential property.

The economic base of the geographic region in which a property is located is still another factor affecting real estate values at a macro level. Some regional and local economies are stronger than and grow faster than others. The health of a regional economy depends in part on the growth potential, stability, and diversity of its *base* employment—that is, employment in firms that export goods and services outside of the region. Examples are manufacturers who sell goods outside of the region, tourist-related businesses, large retailers or service industries that sell outside of the region, and even universities that attract students and research funding from a wide geographic area.

A region's regulatory environment is another category of macro factors affecting real estate activity. Many cities had no-growth strategies during the 1970s and 1980s that made it difficult to develop new real estate. Land use restrictions, limited access to city utilities, and the imposition of numerous development fees are some of the ways cities limited new development activities. Also, rent control regulations tended to retard the construction of new apartment properties. It is also important to note that some cities provide incentives for inner-city redevelopment.

The fiscal characteristics of a municipality, such as its property tax base and rates relative to municipal services such as fire and police, are also important. An increase in tax rates without a commensurate increase in services tends to lower property values.

Microeconomic Factors Affecting Real Estate

In addition to the macroeconomic factors discussed in the preceding section, many microeconomic factors specific to a particular property or investor also affect the value of a property. The importance of location as a distinguishing characteristic of real estate was stressed above. Real estate values are maximized when a site is used in a manner referred to as "the highest and best use." This is a use that maximizes the potential returns to the owner, subject to the constraint that such use is legally permitted, physically feasible, and economically viable. The highest and best use of a site is determined by its location relative to other parcels of real estate and economic activities, uses permitted by zoning, the accessibility of the site, amenities on or near the site, availability of utilities, and the size, shape, and topography of the site. The value of an improvement placed on a site depends on such factors as the size and design of the structure, its age and ability to function well for its intended use, and its general physical condition.

The value of a property to an investor who has leased the property to another user (a *leased fee*) is also dependent on the nature of the lease. A lease that involves a below-market rent results in some of the value of the property accruing to the lessee. The value of this *leasehold estate* is the present value of the difference between the market rent and the contract rent. Leases vary in the way that they deal with such considerations as who pays for future increases in operating expenses for the property (e.g., property taxes, insurance, and maintenance), when the lease will be renewed, and how the rate will be adjusted. Many leases also provide for lessors of retail property to receive a *percentage rent* that includes a percentage of the tenant's income over some base amount. All of these characteristics of a lease, in addition to the financial strength of the lessee, affect the value of a leased fee property as well as the extent to which it will be an inflation hedge.

If an investor has a below-market-rate mortgage on a property (perhaps because interest rates have risen), this can result in a higher selling price for the property if the loan can be assumed. That is, the favorable financing is "sold" along with the property. This assumes the absence of a *due on sale clause* in the mortgage, which prohibits sale of the financing to the new owner. The enforceability of such clauses was reaffirmed by the U.S. Supreme Court in 1982.

An important economic motivation for many taxable real estate investors, such as developers and owner-users, is the tax benefits received by investors in real properties relative to most other assets. The primary source of these benefits is the depreciation deductions that are permitted on the entire cost basis of property improvements—deductions that typically greatly exceed any economic depreciation of the value of the income property. This leads to deferral of income taxes until the property is sold.

Overview of Real Estate Investment Analysis

When inflation was low and relatively predictable, such as during the 1950s and early 1960s, typical financing included fixed-rate mortgages, tax sheltering was not considered a primary investment motive, and the valuation of income property was relatively easy. Property value in this environment could often be estimated fairly well by using simple capitalization techniques, and simple ratios could be used for measures of investment potential.

As uncertain inflation became more of a factor in the market, financing became more complex and higher taxation via "bracket creep" increasingly affected investment behavior. In this changed environment, simple traditional models for income property valuation became inadequate. Most analysts now feel that it is necessary to explicitly project the cash flows expected from a real estate investment over the anticipated holding period. Discounted cash flow analysis is then used to evaluate the cash flows, including the financing and tax benefits. Figure 6-9 shows a general model of income property evaluation.

Cost or Value Estimate. The starting point of a real estate investment analysis is normally either an estimate of the cost of developing the project or the price at which an existing property might be acquired. The purpose of the analysis is, of course, to test the feasibility of this cost or price. If financing is being explicitly considered in the analysis, the focus will be on the return on equity invested in the project (equal to the cost or price, less any debt financing).

Income/Expense Projection. The next step after making the cost or value estimate is to project operating income. This involves projecting potential gross income, vacancy and collection loss, and operating expenses (property taxes, insurance, maintenance, and so on) over a projected holding period.

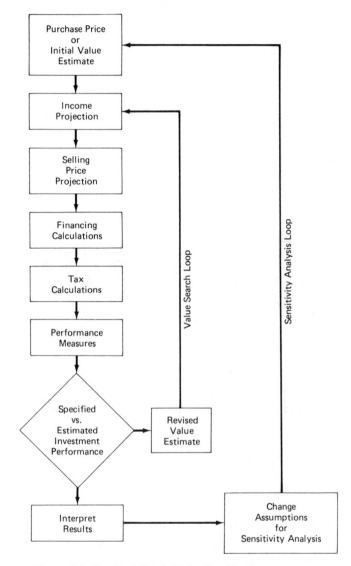

Figure 6-9. The Real Estate Valuation Process.

Projecting income requires consideration of the pattern of the expected income over time. This depends on the nature of the leases, the type of expenses, the expected increase in these expenses, and how they are related to lease income. Here analysts often make assumptions that essentially involve smoothing the income pattern.

Selling Price Projection. If the period of analysis (the holding period) is shorter than the economic life of the property, the property will have a value at the end of this holding period. This value depends, of course, on expected income that a potential buyer might receive beyond the holding period. Such income might exceed the value to the seller if the seller were to keep the property. One reason that this could occur is that the buyer would be taxed differently from the seller because a new basis for depreciation would be established. In any case, the initial or current value of the property frequently depends substantially on the anticipated value (i.e., selling price) at the end of the holding period.

For the sake of simplicity, the selling price expected at the end of the holding period is often expressed in terms of a percentage increase or decrease from the initial value. Alternatively, to estimate the selling price, a *capitalization rate* could be applied to the future stream of income expected at the end of the holding period. Capitalization rates are discussed further in a later section.

Financing Projection. The next major step in the valuation process after projecting the selling price typically involves financing projections. This includes projection of mortgage payments and the loan balance at the end of the holding period. Other financing considerations could include loan points, refinancing costs, prepayment penalties, loan participations, and possibly a sale-leaseback of the land. An investment analysis could include many combinations of loans and participations. The analyst's job here is to search for the best available financing alternative.

An important factor in choosing the best financial alternative is determining whether favorable financial leverage exists. In order for leverage to be considered favorable, the rate of return before any financing (the unleveraged or all equity return) must exceed the cost of the financing. For a taxable investor, this must be evaluated on an after tax basis.

A sale-leaseback of the land, in which the seller retains ownership of the building, can also be viewed as a way of increasing tax benefits. Because land cannot be depreciated but the entire building can be, such a sale-leaseback increases the proportion of the investment that generates a depreciation tax shelter. The lease payments on the land are tax deductible to the lessee and are taxable income to the lessor. As in the case of debt financing, it may be advantageous from a tax perspective for a lower tax bracket investor to purchase the land and lease it to a higher tax bracket investor. Some investors, such as real estate investment trusts (REITs) and pension funds, do not explicitly consider financing in the analysis. They may prefer to value a project on an unleveraged (all equity) basis.

Tax Calculations. The next step in the valuation process after the financing projection is completed involves tax calculations. This can range from making no tax assumption (i.e., doing a before tax analysis) to doing

TABLE 6-10. Projected Internal Rates of Return After Taxes for a Hypothetical U.S. Real Estate Investment Before and After the Tax Reform Act of 1986

Real Estate Investor	After Tax IRR	Leverage	Tax Rate
Taxable investor—Old law	19.8%	71.0%	40.0%
Taxable investor—1986 Tax Reform Act	11.9	71.0	28.0[a]
Tax-exempt investor—Leveraged	17.0	71.0	0
Tax-exempt investor—Unleveraged	13.6	0	0

SOURCE: Lillard [1989].
[a] Assumes investor has no passive income to shelter.

a comprehensive after tax analysis by explicitly considering the interaction of the real estate investment with the investor's or institution's other taxable income, recognizing such factors as ordinary income taxes, capital gains taxes, the alternative minimum tax on tax preferences, income averaging, and so on. An intermediate position often taken is to use a *marginal* tax rate that assumes that all taxes and tax benefits can be captured by a single tax rate. This may or may not be accurate, depending on the nature of the investment and the investor's tax status.

If taxes are not explicitly considered (i.e., if a before tax analysis is used), one must know how the tax benefits of the property are reflected in before tax yields for similar properties. For example, yields tend to be lower for tax-exempt municipal bonds than for otherwise equivalent taxable bonds, because the price of each reflects its tax status. The differential yield is in effect the price paid for the tax benefits received and reflects the marginal tax rate for the marginal taxable investor. The investor must evaluate whether he or she is in a position to receive enough tax benefits from the investment to offset the lower before tax yield. So, too, many real estate investments are more attractive to higher tax bracket investors than to lower tax bracket investors.

In 1986, Congress passed the Tax Reform Act, which eliminated many deductions and lowered tax rates. This reform had, and will continue to have, a significant impact on real estate. Until 1987, the highest tax bracket over the preceding 50 years had always been 50 percent or higher in the United States. The lower top tax rates of the 1986 law reduced the relative attractiveness of real estate to taxable investors.

Table 6-10 shows internal rate of return estimates for four investor profiles on a specific investment proposal developed by John Lillard [1989] of JMB Institutional Realty Corporation. A taxable investor under the old law in a 40 percent tax bracket—not the top bracket of 50 percent—could earn a 19.8 percent after tax internal rate of return, using a 71 percent amount of leverage. Under the 1986 law, the same investor would show an 11.9 percent return. A tax-exempt investor, using the same amount of leverage, would earn a 17 percent internal rate of return on that same property under either tax scenario and 13.6 percent on an unleveraged basis. In short, the tax-exempt investor went from being at a disadvantage under the old U.S. tax law to having a significant advantage over the taxpayer under the new law. Economic value, rather than tax benefits, have become much more important for taxable real estate investors.

In addition, many other changes made by the 1986 Act directly affect real estate return calculations. These changes are the higher capital gains tax rate, lower ordinary tax rates, longer depreciation periods, changes in the at-risk provision, and changes in the way losses can be written off against other income. They are significant and remove what has been in the past a tax subsidy for commercial property.

Valuation Measures. After the projections described in the preceding subsections are made, the analyst calculates various measures of expected investment performance. These range from simple ratios, such as the cash flow-to-equity ratio and debt service coverage ratio, to measures such as the internal rate of return (the rate that equates future cash inflows with current outflows) and net present value. Valuation measures based on estimated cash flows are then contrasted with specified investment criteria (e.g., a required rate of return) to evaluate the investment. For example, the after tax internal rate of return is compared with other investments of comparable risk. If a certain valuation measure (e.g., internal rate of return) is not equal to that required by the investor to justify the investment, a revised price estimate can be made and the process can be repeated, starting with income projections.

The valuation process suggested here is analogous to the dividend discount model and security market line (SML) approach. Using this approach, a security's internal rate of return and systematic risk are estimated and, via the SML, compared to other common stocks in the sample to determine whether, at that stock's systematic or beta risk level, it is undervalued or overvalued.

Interpretation of Results and Sensitivity Analysis. After evaluating performance measures, the analyst must interpret the results in view of overall investment criteria and risk considerations. At this point it is often desirable to evaluate the sensitivity of the results to alternative assumptions that could be made in any of the major valuation steps discussed in the preceding section. This includes alternative financing, tax assumptions, and income projections. *Sensitivity analysis* is performed for two reasons: to help determine an optimal financing or depreciation plan and to help identify the riskiness of the investment. Risk is discussed further in a later section.

Holding Period Considerations. Real estate income property is typically sold after a holding period of 7 to 10 years. One of the reasons for this is that the tax benefits of the property usually decrease over time. This occurs because, with accelerated depreciation, the depreciation deduction decreases over time, and, as the mortgage is repaid, the interest portion of the loan payment decreases and the total payment (principal and interest) usually remains constant. Because only the interest is tax deductible, tax benefits tend to decrease each year. Furthermore, as the mortgage is repaid, the investor's equity investment in the property increases and the leverage benefit decreases. After a period of time more funds may be tied up in the property than the investor prefers to have in a single project. Thus, the investor may either refinance or sell the property to receive this equity buildup.

The Appraisal Process

When securities are listed on an exchange and traded fairly often in standard units, it is relatively easy to determine what the market believes to be the value of the investment. In the case of real property, no such national exchange exists. Each parcel of real estate is unique and is not sold frequently. This creates the need for a means by which to estimate the market value of the property. For this purpose, the analyst must use a procedure known as the *appraisal process* to estimate the market value.

The appraisal process involves gathering information both about the property being valued (referred to as the *subject property*) and for other similar or comparable properties (referred to as *comps*) in the same market area. Three approaches are then typically taken to estimate the market value of the subject property. These approaches are discussed in the subsections that follow.

Cost Approach. The *cost approach* starts by estimating the cost of replacing or reproducing the improvements as if they were new. A deduction is then made for factors such as physical deterioration in the structure, obsolescence in functional design, and loss of value due to economic factors external to the property that reduce its utility for its intended use. Finally, the value of the land site is added to arrive at an estimate of the total market value. The value of the site would have to be estimated by one of the approaches discussed in the following two subsections.

Income Approach. The *income approach* starts by estimating the income from the property. The income is then converted into a present value estimate. This process is referred to as *capitalization*. There are many capitalization techniques used by appraisers. One approach is to discount the future income to arrive at a present value estimate. This is conceptually the same as discounting future dividends or earnings to arrive at an estimate of the value of a stock. The appropriate discount rate reflects the riskiness of the real estate. It represents the rate of return that can be earned on properties with comparable risk and tax characteristics.

When estimating market value, federal income taxes usually are not explicitly considered in the analysis; that is, the before tax cash flows are discounted to arrive at the value estimate. In this case, the discount rate (internal rate of return for comparable properties) must also be on a before tax basis. One must be careful that such a rate is derived from properties of comparable tax treatment, because differences in taxation might be expected to result in much different before tax rates of return for properties, even though after tax rates of return are comparable.

Income property appraisal techniques differ in whether the income stream is valued before or after deducting financing costs. If financing costs (e.g., the mortgage payments) are not deducted, the rate of return is a return on the total property. This is analogous to the return on assets. When financing is deducted, the rate of return used in the analysis is a return on equity and reflects any financial leverage that results from the financing. This will be higher (lower) than the unleveraged return on the entire property if the leverage is favorable (unfavorable). Thus, as was the case with taxes, the choice of a proper discount rate depends on the assumption made regarding the income stream.

A similar approach involves the use of the pretax ratio of net operating income to selling price for comparable properties to estimate the value of the subject property. This ratio is referred to as the capitalization rate, or *cap rate*, for the property. When adequate actual or expected income and operating expense data are available, this rate can be observed directly from the market and can be used with an estimate of operating income to estimate the value of a specific property. Cap rates can also be derived algebraically, based on assumptions about growth of future income and the required return for the holding period. This approach is analogous to using discounted cash flow analysis and is another method used as part of the income approach.

It is important to recognize that the cap rate is a *ratio* of the current operating income (before depreciation, taxes, and financing) to the value of the property. It is *not* a rate of return. Properties with the same expected after tax rate of return over a holding period may have different cap rates due to differences in the expected future income growth of the properties. A property that has a below market interest rate loan that can be assumed may also justify a lower cap rate than a property that does not have such financing. This is because the financing can be sold along with the property.

Market Data Approach. The third approach to appraisal is referred to as the *market data approach*. While all three approaches to appraisal rely on market data, this approach differs from the other two in that the data used are those directly observable in the market. There are two primary ways of applying this approach.

The first, the *direct market method*, takes sales prices from comparable properties in the area that recently have been sold and adjusts these prices for differences due to factors such as age, location, size of the site, improvements, market conditions at the time of sale, and so on.

The second, the *gross income multiplier method*, involves calculating the ratio of the observed selling price to potential gross income for the coming period from comparable properties and using this ratio to estimate the value of the property being appraised. The critical assumption is that the properties used to develop the gross income multiplier ratio are truly comparable to the subject property in terms of risk, expense ratio, taxation, financing, and so on. If enough data on these key variables can be found that are truly comparable, this approach has potential merit. It is analogous to using a price/earnings ratio of a stock listed on an exchange to establish the value of other stocks of similar risk and growth prospects that, because they have comparable key variable characteristics, should have similar price/earnings ratios.

To arrive at a final value estimate for a property, an appraiser usually uses evidence obtained by using all three major approaches (cost, income, and market data). If properly applied with sufficient and compatible data, each method should produce a value estimate that is comparable with any other. However, for income-producing properties being bought and sold as investments, most analysts believe that the income and market data approaches usually produce a more reliable and useful value estimate than the cost approach, because the former approaches more fully reflect what investors are seeking in future benefits from the property.

Real Estate Risk and Return Modifiers

Important characteristics of real estate equity investments such as diversification benefits, tax shelter benefits, and their potential as an inflation hedge are elaborated on further in Chapter 10. These characteristics all impact the risk and return of real estate equity investments relative to mortgage investments and non–real estate investments. Several additional characteristics of real estate must be discussed to evaluate fully different types of real estate investments relative to each other and relative to other assets. These are leverage potential, liquidity and marketability, the relative efficiency of real estate markets, and unsystematic risk implications.

Leverage Potential. Real estate has typically been financed with a combination of equity and debt. Leverage provides a risk/return extender.

It also increases the relative amount of tax shelter from a direct real estate equity investment because the interest is tax deductible.

Liquidity and Marketability. Earlier it was noted that real estate is not traded on a national exchange (except indirectly via real estate investment trusts or REITs), which limits its liquidity. Real estate properties cannot be moved from areas of excess supply to areas of excess demand. Moreover, at any given point in time there may be a limited number of investors in the market for a particular type of property in a particular price range and in a particular location. Thus, real estate tends to be less marketable than other investment assets. It may take several weeks or months to find a buyer for a property at a price close to what is estimated as its market value. In fact, the American Institute of Real Estate Appraisers' definition of market value, cited earlier, includes a reasonable time on the market.

The marketability of real estate depends on the restructuring of the terms of sale and the financing available. Because real estate typically cannot be sold for cash in a short period of time without (or even with) a large price concession, it is much less liquid than either equities or fixed-income securities. This adds to the risk of direct real estate investments and of course dictates a higher rate of return than for otherwise comparable but more liquid assets.

Efficiency of Real Estate Markets. The real estate market is often viewed as being less efficient than many other markets. Several reasons for this have already been discussed, including:

- Uniqueness of each parcel
- Lack of a national exchange
- Difficulty of obtaining relevant information about prices and values
- Large size of typical direct real estate equity investments
- Importance of financing for many purchasers
- Necessity for professional management
- Difficulty of applying standard valuation tools to real estate
- Potential legal complications

Thus, the real estate market appears to violate many of the conditions normally considered prerequisite to an efficient market. At the same time it is unlikely that an investor can earn a higher than normal return simply by using information about past prices and without seeing the property or knowing anything about the local market—especially when the relatively high round-trip transaction costs of a typical real estate investment are considered. Such costs include brokerage commissions, legal fees associated with verification and transfer of title, costs of obtaining financing, and taxes associated with the sale. Thus, the real estate market is likely to be weak form efficient in the sense discussed in Chapter 2.

However, an investor who has advance information about plans for future highway routings, new plant locations, and the like may be able to make a higher-than-normal return by buying land before the information is publicly available and fully reflected in land values. The use of such inside information is *not* illegal in real estate transactions as it is for trading corporate securities by those in possession of material inside information. Of course, excess returns earned by using such information may represent, in part, a return on time spent cultivating political and social relationships with the appropriate people and learning about the local market. There are also risks that time spent pursuing a strategy of trying to be at the right place at the right time will not pay off. Thus, it is still not clear that the market for information is not relatively efficient for real estate markets. What is clear is that if one decides to follow a strategy of trying to pick properties that have the potential for windfall gains, then one should be compensated for the higher risk and costs associated with following such a strategy.

Unsystematic Risk. Because of the local orientation of the real estate market, the uniqueness of each parcel, and the way that socioeconomic factors affect different types of real estate, different parcels of real estate may react differently to changing economic conditions. Properties in one area of the country may be rising in value while others are falling or stable. Similarly, office buildings may be an attractive investment at times when apartment buildings are not. At the same time, real estate in general may behave differently than stocks and fixed-income securities in response to changing economic conditions. This makes it possible to reduce total portfolio risk (variance of returns) at a given level of return for a well-diversified portfolio of real estate, stocks, and fixed-income securities. But it also leads to the potential for special sources of unsystematic risk for a portfolio that is not well diversified, both geographically and by property type.

As discussed in Chapter 10, there is some evidence of just how important it is to diversify across geographic locations and property types to minimize unsystematic risk. Intuitively, it seems that such diversification is highly desirable. If so, an investor or portfolio manager who purposely attempts to concentrate investment in geographic areas or property types that he or she thinks will outperform the market may incur additional unsystematic risk. This is analogous to choosing particular industries and companies in which to concentrate common stock investment. To compensate for the higher exposure to unsystematic risk, a commensurately higher return must be expected to justify such a strategy. As with equity securities, knowledge about the future performance of different types of property or geographic locations may already be reflected in the current price of the property.

TABLE 6-11. Matrix of Real Estate Investment Categories

Debt vs. Equity Spectrum	Directness of Investment Spectrum	
	Direct	Indirect
Debt	Mortgage loans	Mortgage-backed securities Mortgage REITs
	Mortgages with participations Convertible mortgages	Hybrid debt-equity REITs
	Joint ventures	CREFs
Equity	Limited partnership Sole ownership	Equit;· REITs

Risk and Return Trade-Offs for Alternative Vehicles

There is a myriad of real estate investment alternatives. The investor can purchase either a debt, equity, or hybrid debt-equity real estate position. Also, investment can be made directly in a property or indirectly through a number of intermediaries and security-like instruments. The major alternatives are shown in Table 6-11.

The risk and return characteristics of a particular investment vehicle depend on whether the vehicle is more in the nature of debt or equity and whether it is a direct or indirect investment vehicle. A summary of the various investment vehicles and their relative differences in potential risk and return benefits follows.

Equity Real Estate. The additional diversification benefits of real estate and its potential as an inflation hedge accrue to equity investment because the rate of return on equity depends directly on the residual performance—after leverage effects—of the property, just as it does for common stocks. Direct real estate equity investments, such as proprietorships, joint ventures, and limited partnerships, and direct investment by institutions also provide the greatest potential tax benefits to the investor.

The disadvantages of direct investments include the need for professional management, the need for a significantly large investment fund to diversify across geographic locations and property types, and the relative lack of liquidity.

Indirect investments such as equity REITs (EREITs) and commingled real estate funds (CREFs) should provide the investor with more liquidity and professional management, with open-end CREFs providing more liquidity than closed-end funds do. Furthermore, the EREIT or CREF frequently invests in a wide variety of property types and geographic locations and therefore provides diversification services. However, because of their risk-reducing properties, these more efficient vehicles are likely to be more efficiently priced (for the risk level assumed) than are direct investments, with commensurately smaller expected returns. Additionally, the investor may not be able to receive the same tax shelter benefits through an indirect real estate investment.

Real Estate Debt Investments. A pure debt investment in real estate has few, if any, of the benefits of equity real estate investments, such as tax-sheltered income, diversification potential, or as a hedge against inflation. Of course, the real property is still the underlying collateral and thus has some impact on the underlying value of the debt instruments. Still, a mortgage investment is much like any fixed-income investment, with much the same risk and return characteristics (except that it is less liquid). A standard fixed-rate mortgage is analogous to a bond that has a constantly amortizing principal value and results in a zero face value at the end of the loan term. However, the borrower can usually call the loan (like a corporation calling a callable bond) by selling the property or by prepaying the loan (although there may be a penalty for early repayment).

Because mortgage payments include both interest and principal, the *duration* of a mortgage is less than that of a bond with the same term to maturity and coupon. As discussed earlier, commercial mortgage loans in the 1980s typically had a shorter final term (3 to 10 years), with principal payments amortized over a longer period (20 to 25 years). Because of the large principal (balloon) payment at the end of the short term, such loans are even more analogous to bonds, with the bond face value being equal to the balance of the mortgage.

The use of a variable-rate mortgage is a way of transferring some of the interest rate risk to the borrower. This is one way of adjusting the degree of risk exposure of the lender. A variable-rate mortgage might therefore be expected to have a lower initial rate than a fixed-rate mortgage, unless there is a declining term structure of interest rates, because the ability to adjust the interest rate periodically produces an investment with lower risk. Although variable- or adjustable-rate mortgages have gained acceptance in the residential real estate market, they have not gained acceptance in the commercial properties market.

A major disadvantage of direct mortgage loans is the lack of liquidity, although advances in the secondary market for residential loans had helped to alleviate this disadvantage by the 1980s. Indirect mortgage investments, such as mortgage REITs or mortgage-backed securities, provide some liquidity and geographic diversification to the mortgage portfolio.

Hybrid Debt-Equity Investments. There exist several vehicles that allow for an investment that has the characteristics of both debt and equity. For example, direct real estate mortgage loans can be combined with *par-*

ticipations in either the income or price appreciation of the property in return for a lower basic mortgage interest rate. Thus, the lender exchanges some of the return in the form of fixed interest payments for a return that depends on the performance of the property. This provides the lender with a potential inflation hedge and a return with a systematic risk component much like that of an equity investor. In addition, there are direct investment vehicles, such as hybrid mortgage-equity REITs, that invest in both debt and equity, providing diversification both within and between asset categories.

Another alternative is the *convertible mortgage*. These loans typically give the lender the option of converting the debt to an equity ownership in the property after a period of time, typically about five years. The price of the option is a lower interest rate on the loan. The loan is also typically interest-only as long as it is in debt form; that is, participation is possible only via conversion from debt to equity. An interesting aspect of this arrangement is that the developer receives the tax benefits during the early years of the property (which may be more valuable to the developer than to the lender), and the lender receives an option that, like any option, is a risk/return extender but has the characteristics of a real estate equity investment.

MODIFYING EXPECTATIONS WITH FUTURES AND OPTIONS[2]

Futures and option contracts have been used for a long time, but they were not significant as compared with fixed-income or equity securities until the mid-1970s. In the United States, organized exchanges began trading options on individual stocks in 1973, and fixed-income futures contracts began trading in 1975. Debt options and equity-related futures became available in 1982. Other option instruments have been developed as well (e.g., options and futures on stock market indexes such as the S&P 500 and Value Line, and options on market subgroups).

The possible advantageous use of these relatively new derivative instruments should be viewed within the context of the basic elements of portfolio management, especially the establishment of individual asset positions with various investment characteristics, controlling risk through the management of weightings between and within major asset classes, and facilitating strategic shifts for the purpose of achieving excess return. The costs of managing these elements with derivative instruments must be compared

---

[2] This section relies heavily on material supplied by David Dunford and Robert Kopprasch, much of which appeared in greater detail in Chapters 16, 17, and 18 of Maginn and Tuttle [1985].

with the costs of dealing with them in the traditional manner through the purchase or sale of the underlying assets themselves.

The risk characteristics of stocks and bonds have had much to do with the chronology in creating and expanding the use of options and futures. Much of the total risk of individual stocks is unsystematic. Options on individual stocks (and on market subgroups of stocks) permit some modification of such unsystematic risk exposure. Most of the total risk of investment-grade bonds is systematic, as is the total risk of market indexes. Futures contracts permit a symmetrical modification of systematic risk, while options on market indexes and market index futures make possible a nonsymmetrical modification of systematic risk. All of this is discussed in considerable detail in Chapter 11.

Determining the most efficient means of dealing with these basic elements of portfolio management requires a constantly updated knowledge of the derivative instruments that are available, the volume in which they are trading (as an indication of liquidity), the manner in which their prices move in relation to the respective underlying assets, any idiosyncratic aspects that should impact the mechanics of their use, and the costs of their use, which include the costs of staffing expertise, outside services, valuation models, and so forth.

A somewhat limited discussion of the valuation of these derivative instruments follows. A much more detailed and comprehensive discussion is contained in Chapter 11.

Valuation of Futures Contracts

The purchase or sale of a futures contract represents an obligation to accept or deliver, at a price determined when the contract originates, the underlying asset or a cash settlement equivalent in certain cases on the expiration date (or during the delivery month). Assets for which there are related futures contracts include Treasury bills, Treasury notes, Treasury bonds, GNMA mortgage-backed bonds, Eurodollar deposits, the S&P 500 Index, the Value Line Index, the New York Stock Exchange Composite Index, and the Major Market Index. Contract expirations may be as much as two or more years in the future, but most of them expire within a year. Frequently, the expiration dates for the contracts related to any given asset or index are separated by two- or three-month intervals.

Rather than being based on expectations about future price levels, the pricing of futures contracts is closely related to the methodology used in the valuation of forward commitments or to the use of futures contracts in creating synthetic money market instruments. The latter is done through the simultaneous purchase of a "deliverable" Treasury bond having a maturity of 15 years or more and the sale of an appropriate number of Treasury bond futures contracts. The relevant pricing concepts are briefly discussed for Treasury bills, Treasury bonds, and the S&P 500 Index.

Treasury Bill Futures. A Treasury bill futures contract price involves one of the most direct applications of the methodology for the valuation of forward commitments, often referred to as the *arbitrage model*. It hinges on the *cost of carry* of the underlying asset, which is equal to the financing cost less the yield on the asset during the term (period to expiration) of the futures contract. Thus,

$$F = S + r^S - y^S$$

where F is the current forward price, S is the current spot or cash price, r^S is the cost of financing the underlying asset equal to the current spot price multiplied by the financing rate, and y^S is the income from the underlying asset equal to the yield multiplied by the current spot price. When the financing rate is greater than the yield, the forward price should be above the spot price, or it should *trade at a premium to cash*. When the financing rate is less than the yield, the forward price should be below the spot price, or it should *trade at a discount to cash*.

Because this particular contract calls for delivery of a 6-month U.S. Treasury bill, the spot price is the current price of a Treasury bill of that maturity (e.g., 95), the cost of the financing would probably be the repurchase agreement (repo) rate for the term of the contract (say 2.50 percent for 90 days), and the yield would be zero percent because T-bills make no income payment. The resulting forward price would be $95 + (0.025 \times 95) - 0 = 97.375$. If the contract were trading at this forward price, it would be quoted as 89.50 because a forward price of 97.375 corresponds to a quoted discount rate of 10.5 percent on the bill.

Treasury Bond Futures. A Treasury bond futures contract price is largely derived from the use of such contracts in the creation of synthetic money market instruments. It hinges on the rates available from alternative short-term instruments of like maturity. Because Treasury bonds pay interest income every six months, such payments and the accruals between payment dates do enter into the price determination process. In addition, a conversion factor must be applied if the *most deliverable bond* has a coupon other than 8 percent (the benchmark coupon adopted for the Treasury bond contract). Thus,

$$(F \times CF) + A_1 = S + A_2 + r(S + A_2) - C$$

where F is the price of the Treasury bond futures contract, CF is the conversion factor, if applicable, A_1 is the accrued interest on the most deliverable bond at the expiration of the contract, S is the current price of that bond, A_2 is the accrued interest as of the current date, r reflects the rates available from alternative short-term instruments, and C represents interest coupons received, if any.

There are three critical considerations in valuing a Treasury bond futures contract. First, if any interest coupons are received during the life of the contract, a reinvestment rate on the coupon proceeds must be assumed in considering a suitable r, the variable representing rates available. Second, the most deliverable bond is the one that produces the greatest dollar profit or the smallest loss for the holder of the short position that must deliver at the expiration of the contract. Third, the conversion factor (CF) is simply used to adjust the price of the actual coupon bond delivered to the 8 percent coupon benchmark bond adopted for this contract. The CF is above 1.0 for coupons above 8 percent and less than 1.0 for coupons less than 8 percent.

The investor who desires to achieve the going money market rate (or a bit better) through the creation of a synthetic money market instrument normally purchases the most deliverable bond at the inception of the process. If that particular bond is still the most deliverable issue at the expiration date, the futures contract CF delivery price should have converged to the price of the bond held, and the original expected return is thereby achieved.

If another bond is more deliverable at the expiration date, the investor can still achieve the original expected return by turning in the bond that was most deliverable at inception. However, the investor might do better by selling that issue and buying and delivering what has become the most deliverable issue.

There are other matters that should be taken into account in the real world use of the Treasury bond contract. These include cost/benefit aspects of the margin outflows and inflows and the ambiguity of the precise delivery date because it is ultimately determined by the holder of the short position. The specifics covered in this discussion, though incomplete, should provide a general understanding of the pricing process.

Because F does not stand alone on the left side of the equation, the A_1 must be subtracted from both sides, and then both sides must be divided by CF.[3] Treasury bond futures prices are based on the 8 percent benchmark coupon and, like the spot market, reflect changes in increments of 1/32nd of a point.

S&P 500 Stock Index Futures. A S&P 500 stock index futures contract price may be understood as another derivative of the arbitrage model. As in the case of Treasury bills, it hinges on the cost of carry for the underlying asset(s) during the term of the futures contract. Thus,

---

[3] For a more complete discussion, see Chapter 17 of Maginn and Tuttle [1985].

$$F = S + r^S - d^S$$

where F is the current futures price, S is the current spot price of the S&P 500 Index, r^S is the cost of financing the underlying asset(s), and d^S is the dollar dividend on the underlying asset(s) during the holding period.

Most of the unique problems of pricing this contract are related to the determination of the dollar dividend *and* the manner of settling the contract at the final closing date. With regard to the latter, the holder of a stock index futures contract is due an amount of cash equal to the difference between the initial futures price and the S&P 500 Index value at the expiration of the contract, multiplied by $500. This is because each of these contracts is equivalent in value to $500 multiplied by the quoted futures price.

The dollar dividend problem stems from the fact that dividend payments come from most of the 500 issues that make up the S&P 500 Index, and they are spread out unevenly over the life of a contract. During some quarters a disproportionately large dividend is received during part of the quarter because of irregular dividend payments, resulting in an unusually large effective annual dividend on the Index for that holding period. To the extent that dividends come in throughout the quarter, reinvestment income (from dividend receipt to settlement date) must be factored into the calculation. One result of the nonlinearity of the dividend flows is that this futures contract can sell at a price below that of the S&P 500 Index if the dollar dividend until settlement exceeds the cost of financing until settlement.

As in the case of Treasury bond futures, there are some additional matters that need to be considered, especially the cost/benefit aspects of the margin outflows and inflows, in the pricing of the S&P 500 futures contract. Because this contract has several features that make the underlying arbitrage difficult, actual futures prices tend to vary somewhat around the "fair" value. Thus, there are times when such contracts are quite a bargain and other times when they are quite expensive. Unfortunately, it is not possible to determine such instances from the simple relationship between the futures price and the S&P 500 Index price. The quoted prices on these contracts are expressed in the very same way as the value of the S&P 500 Index itself.

Valuation of Option Contracts

From the purchaser's point of view, an option contract represents a right to receive (a *call* option) or deliver (a *put* option) the underlying asset for a specified *exercise price* or *strike price* anytime prior to the expiration date of the option. Assets for which there are related option contracts include many individual stock issues, U.S. Treasury bonds and notes, various stock market indexes (such as oil, technology, and transportation), various U.S.

Treasury and Eurodollar obligations, and certain stock index futures contracts.

Each option contract on individual stock issues, stock market indexes, stock index futures, and Treasury bond or note futures has a specific expiration date. However, for any given underlying security or index, there is usually a choice between two or more expiration dates that normally fall at monthly or bimonthly intervals for up to 9 months. For each specific contract expiration date, there is a choice of strike prices. Individual common stocks usually have contracts covering any 1 of 2 to 5 strike prices, while stock indexes often have contracts offering any 1 of 15 or more strike prices.

Because option contracts existed and were traded over the counter long before the establishment of the Chicago Board of Options Exchange in 1973, there have been option pricing models that date back as far as 1900. However, with the creation of the Black-Scholes model in 1973, it was possible to replicate the payoff of an option by using a trading strategy in the underlying stock and an essentially risk-free asset. For details, see Berry and Sherrerd [1988]. This model has tended to eliminate excess profits in the pricing of options. Therefore, the option price, called a *premium*, should approximate the lowest cost of replicating its pattern of return.

Intrinsic Value and Time Value. It is helpful to view the value of an option contract in terms of two component parts. The *intrinsic value* component represents what the option would be worth if it were exercised today. It is determined by the difference between the current price of the underlying security and the strike price of the particular option contract. There is such value in a call option if the current price of the underlying asset is above the strike price, or, in a put option, if the underlying asset price is below the strike price. The *time value* component represents any value inherent to the continued holding of the option. Such incremental value is primarily related to the fact that the option may become more valuable in the future.

Intrinsic value is most easily visualized when it is portrayed in graphic form. Figures 6-10 and 6-11 show the relationship between intrinsic value and the price of the underlying asset for call options and put options, respectively. They also indicate terminology that is used in referring to the relationship between the price of the underlying asset and the strike price specified in the option contract, such as *in the money, at the money*, and *out of the money*.

Time value is not so easily visualized and does not lend itself to graphic representation. It is simply the difference between the total value of an option and its intrinsic value. It is largely determined by three factors:

1. The volatility of the returns of the underlying asset
2. The remaining time to expiration date
3. The risk-free level of interest rates

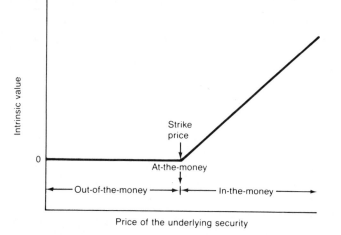

Figure 6-10. Intrinsic Value of a Call Option Contract.

Table 6-12 provides a convenient summary of the manner in which the various factors affect the value of an option contract.

As with most efforts to simplify, this one needs to be qualified. Such is the case regarding the indicated impact of the current price of the underlying asset. As long as it is not too far from the strike price, an increase or decrease in its price will increase or decrease the value of a call option

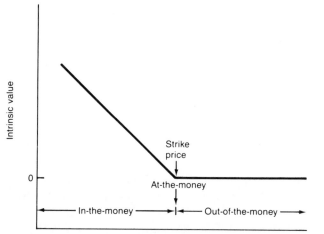

Figure 6-11. Intrinsic Value of a Put Option Contract.

TABLE 6-12. Impact of Option Valuation Factors

Valuation Factors	Characteristics That Add Value to Options	
	Calls	Puts
Intrinsic Value		
Current price of underlying asset	High	Low
Strike price	Low	High
Time Value		
Volatility of underlying asset	High	High
Time to expiration date	Long	Long
Risk-free rate of interest	High	High

and decrease or increase the value of a put option. Also, there is the indicated impact of the underlying asset volatility. Volatility may have been high, but it is trending lower. This takes away from the option premium value that is based solely on past volatility.

Because of the significant impact of the intrinsic value factors in the pricing of option contracts, such contracts are said to have a nonsymmetrical price relationship with that of the underlying asset. They tend to have a high correlation with the price of the underlying asset when they are in the money, but relatively little correlation with the price of the underlying asset when they are out of the money.

Black-Scholes Model. The Black-Scholes model can be used by inputting the facts or assumptions called for by the specified variables. The model may be expressed as follows:

Call value $= S \times N(d_1) - Ee^{-rt} \times N(d_2)$

where S = stock price

E = strike price

$N(\ )$ = the value of the cumulative normal distribution at the point ( )

$d_1 = \dfrac{\ln(S/E) + (r + .5\sigma^2)t}{\sigma \sqrt{t}}$

$d_2 = d_1 - \sigma\sqrt{t}$

ln = natural logarithm

r = short-term riskless rate (continuously compounded)

t = time to expiration (in years)

e = base of natural logarithms

σ = annual standard deviation of return (referred to as volatility)

This model suggests that the option is fairly priced if, when used in combination with the underlying asset in a riskless hedge, it earns the risk-free rate of interest. The model suggests a call price that is related to the price of the underlying asset, but it says nothing about whether the asset itself is reasonably priced.

Given the value of a call option, the value of a put option may be derived. This is based on the notion of put-call parity that posits the existence of a specific price relationship between puts and calls with the same underlying asset and the same terms.

If an asset with a current price of 40 is augmented by selling a call and buying a put on that asset (both with strike prices of 40 and the same expiration date), the combination must be worth 40 when the options expire. That being the case, the present value of that combination (discounted at the risk-free rate) would be a bit less, perhaps 39. With this present value of the "package," the value of the put option may be determined once the value of the call option has been calculated (using the Black-Scholes model). For example, if the call option has a calculated value of $2.50, then the value of the put option must be $1.50 ($39.00 + $2.50 − $1.50 = $40.00).

Problems With the Black-Scholes Model. Like most other models that attempt to explain economic behavior, the Black-Scholes model is based on several assumptions that are not entirely consistent with the real world. For example, it assumes continuous trading in the underlying asset, that there are no significant gaps in the price pattern of the underlying asset, that the asset returns will have an essentially normal distribution, and that the assets pay no dividends (or other cash income). In addition, the Black-Scholes model assumes that the options themselves involve no transaction costs and are not subject to any form of taxation. Finally, it assumes that the applicable risk-free interest rate is known and remains stable until the expiration date and that the option can be exercised only on the expiration date—a so-called *European option*, in contrast to an *American option*, which can be exercised at any time prior to the expiration date.

While these assumptions represent significant departures from reality, the Black-Scholes model has served quite well. Nevertheless, during its existence, a number of researchers have suggested modifications or particular methodologies to minimize the harm of unreal assumptions. See Merton [1988], Roll [1988a], and Whaley [1988].

In cases in which there are income payments during the life of the option contract, a reasonable modification is to subtract the present value of that payment from the price of the underlying asset. With respect to stock price dynamics, which do include occasional large changes in a short period of time, sophisticated methods have been devised to adapt the Black-Scholes model to such situations.

The fact that American options can be exercised anytime up to and including the expiration date presents only an occasional problem. The value of an option is almost always greater than it would be if it were exercised immediately. Therefore, a rational investor does not exercise an option as long as that is the case.

Apart from the assumptions underlying the Black-Scholes model, there is a problem in that one of the most important variables in the model is not really known: the volatility of the underlying asset. This is no different than the problem of determining the expected return of an individual common stock issue with the use of the capital asset pricing model. In both cases, the historical volatility is often used in the calculation process. However, it must be understood that such volatility is subject to change. The experience during the life of an option can differ from what it was during some past period.

ASSEMBLING AND INTEGRATING ASSETS INTO A PORTFOLIO

Whether managing portfolios of U.S. assets or those of global dimensions, the process involves a careful integration of the best possible expectational inputs on a broad range of assets (classes and individual) with the basic objectives and circumstances of the particular client or portfolio. The process seeks the optimal combination of the expected behavioral characteristics of the assets that make up the total opportunity set and the various needs of the client. In the most simplistic terms, this means the highest portfolio expected return for the level of risk that is appropriate. However, in many actual situations it is more complex. It may involve striving for the best balance between desired liquidity, current income, total after tax return, expected income growth, and volatility of return for any given portfolio.

Integration Across Asset Classes

As indicated in Chapter 7, integration of asset classes is accomplished through the identification of the most advantageous weightings or percentages of the total portfolio for each class. Given the expected return, expected riskiness, and expected covariance of each asset class, the chosen weights establish the best combination of expected return and riskiness of the total portfolio. Assuming that the expectational inputs prove to be fairly reasonable, the integration of assets at the class level is likely to have the major determining impact on the level and volatility of portfolio returns thereafter. Of course, any later changes in the asset mix will affect such experience.

Integration Within Asset Classes

Integration within asset classes is usually done with an initial focus on reasonable diversification and to establish a comfortable likelihood that the particular assets chosen provide a representative sample for that asset class. However, in most situations, there is another focus, which may be either secondary or coequal, that attempts to recognize strategic opportunity. This may involve the setting or adjustment of the level of systematic risk exposure within the class. Also, it may involve the establishment of the amount of residual risk to be represented within the class. The latter is particularly important within common equity and perhaps real estate equity, because it is the form of risk that can be avoided and probably will not be rewarded unless the investor knows something that is not already reflected in the market consensus. Ideally, the amount of residual risk assumed is related directly to the level of skill, not just hope, to identify undervalued situations.

SUMMARY

Each individual asset exists within a setting in which there are many factors that influence its economic experience. Historical study is helpful in providing an understanding of the impact of these factors and should contribute to the development of realistic expectations about the future. Nevertheless, expectations are inherently uncertain under the best of circumstances. Therefore, *risk*—in both amount and kind—is at center stage in contemplating the future economic performance of any investable asset and the price at which it will or may change hands.

While each asset has some uncommon features, there are many similarities between individual assets as well. Clear testimony of the latter is reflected in the long-established practice of classifying assets into a few major categories. In this chapter, each of the three major asset classes— stocks, bonds, and real estate—is discussed in terms of the important expectational factors that are believed to pertain. Because of the uncertain nature of these expectations, they are treated within a conceptual framework that recognizes the distinction between those having pervasive influence and those with only limited impact.

In the pricing of any of these assets, both the pervasive factors, designated *systematic risk*, and the more limited factors, labeled *unsystematic risk*, are examined in some detail. The kinds of information that should be considered, how the information may be best viewed and understood, and some of the more important caveats are included. Ultimately, the degree of uncertainty related to expectations and the extent to which certain risks may be diversified away are reflected in asset prices and expected returns.

The modification of expectations through the use of options and futures is of growing interest to investors. The valuation of these derivative securities is related to factors such as the current and expected values of the underlying assets. The portfolio manager uses these derivatives in combination with the underlying (and other) assets to modify the return/risk profile of a portfolio to optimally fulfill client objectives.

FURTHER READING

While much has been written on subjects that are related to the factors that affect individual asset expectations, most such literature is not intended to provide a "stand-on-its-own" comprehensive treatment. An exception is Cornish [1983], who is more traditional in his approach, with predominant emphasis on P/E ratios and dividend yields as yardsticks of value. He includes a very interesting historical perspective on the post–World War II phases of common stocks and devotes considerable discussion to the "top-down" approach to security analysis.

Fixed-Income Expectational Inputs

For some further discussion of duration and a number of charts on various combinations of maturity, yield, duration, and price relationships, Kopprasch [1987] may be helpful. Dunetz and Mahoney [1988] provide some guidance in the use of duration and convexity in the analysis of callable bonds.

Leibowitz [1987] discusses changing shapes of the yield curve, the continuous impact of the rolling yield, and how changes affect the spectrum of horizon returns. A basic treatment of interest rate forecasting by using either fundamental or technical approaches, as well as methodology for producing a forecast, is available from Woolford [1987]. Melton [1987] describes Fedwatching, covering the kinds of economic factors that the U.S. Federal Reserve watches closely, the interpretation of bank reserves, and the Fed's open market operations and the resulting projection of interest rates. Because of the volatility of interest rates, there have emerged so-called floating rate and adjustable rate debt securities, which have been discussed by Wilson [1987].

Related to the possible use of international bonds are the classical risk/return considerations and the unique dimension of currency risks. Both Carr [1986] and Treneer [1986] provide some review of the risk/return experience and how it has compared with that of U.S. bonds. Dornbusch [1987] suggests that further weakening of the U.S. dollar is needed to bring about a substantial elimination of the balance of trade deficit.

For additional perspective on the credit analysis of corporate bonds, including some of the particulars related to utility and finance issues, see Howe [1987]. The existence of a high-yield bond market in the 1920s and the high incidence of default among the issues that came late in that period are reviewed by Grant [1987]. Feldstein [1987] sets forth guidelines and lists some red flags for the investor in looking at municipal bonds, while Spiotto [1987] discusses the risk of municipal bankruptcies.

Volcker [1987] offers his perspective on innovative securities and the international debt crisis. Cumming [1987] reviews the packaging of generally illiquid assets (obligations) for sale in securities form, including certain developments that have encouraged this trend. Sullivan, Collins, and Smilow [1987] review the guarantee arrangements and the special problems of estimating the pattern of cash flows on mortgage pass-through securities.

Of potential interest to taxable investors is a review of the U.S. federal income tax treatment of fixed-income securities by Fabozzi [1987]. A comprehensive review of the factors involved in the analysis of corporate and municipal securities can be found in Maginn and Andersen [1985].

Equity Expectational Inputs

Interesting thoughts on linking traditional methods with newer approaches are provided by Hagin [1988], who discusses engineered investment strategies, and by Fogler [1988], who discusses integration of security analysis and the use of dividend discount models. Sharpe [1984] describes factor models in general, as well as the two most influential examples—the capital asset pricing model (CAPM) and arbitrage pricing theory (APT). Berry, Burmeister, and McElroy [1988] discuss sorting out risks by using known APT factors.

Amihud and Mendelson [1986] perceive relative liquidity as a special risk factor and provide some documentation of its impact on stock returns. Sorensen [1988] notes the desirability of having a measure of equity duration and neatly pinpoints the problem in its use (i.e., that there are elements of duration in both the growth factor and the discount rate).

An efficient summary of a relatively new method for valuing common stocks, the T-Model, is provided by its creator, Estep [1985], while Michaud [1985] talks about bridging the gap between top-down investment information and bottom-up forecasts. Estep [1987] shows how estimates of financial results are used to develop return forecasts.

Background information on foreign equity returns is available in Ibbotson and Brinson [1987]. The relative valuation of international equity markets, with a special focus on Japan, is discussed by Aron [1988]. Pictet [1984] shares his perspective on how to balance the currency, country, industry, and company factors in the global market, with a special focus on Continental Europe.

Jacobs and Levy [1988] share some of their efforts to better understand the anomalies that have generated reward for bearing unsystematic risk, while McClay [1978] provides a continuing reminder of the penalties that are often experienced in assuming such risk. Cottle, Murray, and Block [1988] discuss traditional stock market sector analysis and document the return experience of particular homogeneous groups. A helpful review of the CAPM, its study and testing by many researchers, and some of the more notable anomalies, such as firm size, seasonal effects, and P/E ratio size, was done by Keim [1986].

Relating to the consideration of how to achieve foreign equity exposure, Jacquillat and Solnik [1978] determined that U.S. multinationals are a poor tool for such purposes. Separately, Solnik [1988] provides a review of concepts and techniques that should be helpful in selecting foreign equities, while Fisher [1984] discusses global investment research, with particular emphasis on industry analysis and the special considerations in Japan.

Because convertible securities represent an equity/fixed-income hybrid, the valuation of them by McCowin [1988] should help bridge the gap.

Modifying Expectations With Futures and Options

Fairly detailed background information on futures and options contract provisions and valuation principles are provided by Kolb and Gay [1985] as well as Kopprasch [1984] and Hansen [1984].

Telser [1986] develops an interesting perspective on the parallels between a futures contract and its underlying asset with money and real goods. Pashigian [1986] reviews the role of politics in the regulation of the futures markets. The performance of market index futures contracts is reviewed by Zeckhauser and Niederhoffer [1983].

The modern day seminal work on the pricing of options appeared in Black and Scholes [1973]. Some helpful insights on how to estimate the variance of returns that is essential to the use of the model is provided by Latanē and Rendleman [1976]. Trading costs for listed options are addressed by Phillips and Smith [1980].

Garber [1987] reviews the income tax treatment of interest rate futures and debt options.

BIBLIOGRAPHY

Altman, Edward I. "Measuring Corporate Bond Mortality and Performance." *The Journal of Finance*, September 1989.

Altman, Edward I., and Scott A. Nammacher. "The Default Rate Experience on High Yield Corporate Debt." *Financial Analysts Journal*, July/August 1985.

Amihud, Yakov, and Haim Mendelson. "Liquidity and Stock Returns." *Financial Analysts Journal*, May/June 1986.

The Appraisal of Real Estate, 6th and 7th eds. Chicago: American Institute of Real Estate Appraisers, 1973 and 1978.

Aron, Paul H. "Relative Valuation of International Equity Markets: The Japanese Example," in Katrina F. Sherrerd, ed. *Equity Markets and Valuation Methods*. Seminar Proceedings. Charlottesville, Va.: The Institute of Chartered Financial Analysts, 1988.

Asquith, Paul, David Mullins, Jr., and Eric Wolf. "Original Issue High Yield Bonds: Aging Analysis of Defaults, Exchanges, and Calls." Working paper, March 1989.

Berry, Michael A., Edwin Burmeister, and Marjorie B. McElroy. "Sorting Out Risks Using Known APT Factors." *Financial Analysts Journal*, March/April 1988.

Berry, Michael A., and Katrina F. Sherrerd, eds. "Introduction," in *Readings in Derivative Securities*. Charlottesville, Va.: The Institute of Chartered Financial Analysts, 1988.

Black, Fischer, and Myron Scholes. "The Pricing of Options and Corporate Liabilities." *Journal of Political Economy*, May/June 1973.

Carr, Richard C. "The Rationale for Investing in International Bonds and Currencies—Historical Returns, Risk, and Diversification," in Richard W. McEnally, ed. *International Bonds and Currencies*. Seminar Proceedings, The Institute of Chartered Financial Analysts. Homewood, Ill.: Dow Jones-Irwin, 1986.

Cornish, William A. "Sector and Individual Asset Expectations: The Micro Factors," in J.L. Maginn and D.L. Tuttle, eds. *Managing Investment Portfolios*, 1st ed. Boston: Warren, Gorham & Lamont, Inc., 1983.

Cottle, Sidney, Roger E. Murray, and Frank E. Block. "Stock Market Sector Analysis" (Ch. 7), and "Analysis of Financial Statements" (Part 2). *Security Analysis*, 5th ed. New York: McGraw-Hill Book Company, 1988.

Cumming, Christine. "The Economics of Securitization." *Quarterly Review*, Federal Reserve Bank of New York, Autumn 1987.

Dornbusch, Rudiger W. "The Dollar: How Much Further Depreciation Do We Need?" *Economic Review*, Federal Reserve Bank of Atlanta, September/October 1987.

Dunetz, Mark L., and James M. Mahoney. "Using Duration and Convexity in the Analysis of Callable Bonds." *Financial Analysts Journal*, May/June 1988.

Emmer, Edward Z. "Understanding the Instruments and Analyzing the Credits," in Richard W. McEnally, ed. *International Bonds and Currencies*, Seminar Proceedings, The Institute of Chartered Financial Analysts. Homewood, Ill.: Dow Jones-Irwin, 1986.

Estep, Preston W. "A New Method for Valuing Common Stocks." *Financial Analysts Journal*, November/December 1985.

———. "Security Analysis and Stock Selection: Turning Financial Information Into Return Forecasts." *Financial Analysis Journal*, July/August 1987.

Fabozzi, Frank J. "Federal Income Tax Treatment of Fixed Income Securities" (Ch. 3), in F.J. Fabozzi and S. Pollack, eds. *The Handbook of Fixed Income Securities*. Homewood, Ill.: Dow Jones-Irwin, 1987.

Farrell, James L. "Homogeneous Stock Groupings—Implications for Portfolio Management." *Financial Analysts Journal*, May/June 1975.

Feldstein, Sylvan G. "Guidelines in the Credit Analysis of General Obligation and Revenue Municipal Bonds" (Ch. 24), in F.J. Fabozzi and S. Pollack, eds. *The Handbook of Fixed Income Securities*. Homewood, Ill.: Dow Jones-Irwin, 1987.

Fisher, David I. "International Investing: Global Investment Research/Management (I)," in James R. Vertin, ed. *International Equity Investing*. Seminar Proceedings, The Institute of Chartered Financial Analysts. Homewood, Ill.: Dow Jones-Irwin, 1984.

Fisher, Lawrence, and James H. Lorie. "Some Studies of Variability of Returns on Investments in Common Stocks." *Journal of Business*, April 1970.

Fogler, Russell H. "Security Analysis, DDMs, and Probability," in Katrina F. Sherrerd, ed. *Equity Markets and Valuation Methods*. Seminar Proceedings. Charlottesville, Va.: The Institute of Chartered Financial Analysts, 1988.

Garber, Lawrence A. "Income Tax Treatment of Interest Rate Futures and Debt Options" (Ch. 47), in F.J. Fabozzi and S. Pollack, eds. *The Handbook of Fixed Income Securities*. Homewood, Ill.: Dow Jones-Irwin, 1987.

Gordon, Myron J. *The Investment, Financing, and Valuation of the Corporation*. Homewood, Ill.: Richard D. Irwin, 1962.

Grant, James. "The High-Yield Bond Market," in Richard W. McEnally, ed. *In-

novations in Fixed-Income Instruments and Markets. Seminar Proceedings. Charlottesville, Va.: The Institute of Chartered Financial Analysts, 1987.

Gray, William S. "Developing a Long-Term Outlook for the U.S. Economy and Stock Market." *Financial Analysts Journal*, July/August 1979.

Hagin, Robert L. "Engineered Investment Strategies: Problems and Solutions," in Katrina F. Sherrerd, ed. *Equity Markets and Valuation Methods*, Seminar Proceedings. Charlottesville, Va.: The Institute of Chartered Financial Analysts, 1988.

Hansen, Nicholas H. "Options and Futures: Strategic Tools for Portfolio Management (Part II)," in Donald E. Fischer, ed. *Options and Futures: New Route to Risk/Return Management*. Seminar Proceedings, The Institute of Chartered Financial Analysts. Homewood, Ill.: Dow Jones-Irwin, 1984.

Historical Default Rates of Corporate Bond Issues 1970–1988. New York: Moody's Special Reports, July 1989.

Howe, Jane Tripp. "Credit Analysis for Corporate Bonds" (Ch. 22), in F.J. Fabozzi and S. Pollack, eds. *The Handbook of Fixed Income Securities*. Homewood, Ill.: Dow Jones-Irwin, 1987.

Ibbotson Associates, Inc. *Stocks, Bonds, Bills, and Inflation, Yearbook 1988.* Chicago: Ibbotson Associates, Inc., 1988.

Ibbotson, Roger G., and Gary P. Brinson. "Foreign Equity Returns" (Ch. 7), and "The U.S. and International Bond Markets" (Ch. 10). *Investment Markets*. New York: McGraw-Hill Book Company, 1987.

Ibbotson, Roger G., Lawrence B. Siegel, and Kathryn S. Love. "World Wealth: Market Values and Returns." *The Journal of Portfolio Management*, Fall 1985.

Jacobs, Bruce I., and Kenneth N. Levy. "Disentangling Equity Return Regularities." *Financial Analysts Journal*, May/June 1988.

Jacquillat, Bertrand, and Bruno Solnik. "Multinationals Are Poor Tools for Diversification." *The Journal of Portfolio Management*, Winter 1978.

Keim, Donald B. "The CAPM and Equity Return Regularities." *Financial Analysts Journal*, May/June 1986.

Kolb, Robert W., and Gerald D. Gay. *Interest Rate and Stock Index Futures and Options*. Charlottesville, Va.: Financial Analysts Research Foundation, 1985.

Kopprasch, Robert W. "Options and Futures: Strategic Tools for Portfolio Management (Part I)," in Donald E. Fischer, ed. *Options and Futures: New Route to Risk-Return Management*. Seminar Proceedings, The Institute of Chartered Financial Analysts. Homewood, Ill.: Dow Jones-Irwin, 1984.

———. "Valuation of Futures and Options Contracts" (Ch. 17), in J.L. Maginn and D.L. Tuttle, eds. *Managing Investment Portfolios 1985–1986 Update*. Boston: Warren, Gorham & Lamont, Inc., 1985.

———. "Understanding Duration and Volatility" (Ch. 5), in F.J. Fabozzi and S. Pollack, eds. *The Handbook of Fixed Income Securities*. Homewood, Ill.: Dow Jones-Irwin, 1987.

Latané, Henry A., and Richard Rendleman. "Standard Deviations of Stock Price Ratios Implied in Options Prices." *The Journal of Finance*, May 1976.

Leibowitz, Martin L. "Analysis of Yield Curves" (Ch. 30), in F.J. Fabozzi and S. Pollack, eds. *The Handbook of Fixed Income Securities*. Homewood, Ill.: Dow Jones-Irwin, 1987.

Lillard, John S. "Overview of the Real Estate Market," in Susan Hudson-Wilson, ed. *Real Estate: Valuation Techniques and Portfolio Management*. Seminar Proceedings. Charlottesville, Va.: The Institute of Chartered Financial Analysts, 1989.

Maginn, John L., and Marvin D. Andersen. "The Fixed-Income Analysis Process: Return and Risk Analysis" (Ch. 7B), in J.L. Maginn and D.L. Tuttle, eds. *Managing Investment Portfolios 1985–1986 Update*. Boston: Warren, Gorham & Lamont, Inc., 1985.

Maginn, John L., and Donald L. Tuttle, eds. *Managing Investment Portfolios*. Boston: Warren, Gorham & Lamont, Inc., 1983.

————. *Managing Investment Portfolios 1985–1986 Update*. Boston: Warren, Gorham & Lamont, Inc., 1985.

McClay, Marvin. "The Penalties of Incurring Unsystematic Risk." *The Journal of Portfolio Management*, Spring 1978.

McCowin, Michael L. "Valuation of Convertibles," in Katrina F. Sherrerd, ed. *Equity Markets and Valuation Methods*. Seminar Proceedings. Charlottesville, Va.: The Institute of Chartered Financial Analysts, 1988.

McEnally, Richard W. "The Term Structure of Interest Rates" (Ch. 53), in F.J. Fabozzi and S. Pollack, eds. *The Handbook of Fixed Income Securities*. Homewood, Ill.: Dow Jones-Irwin, 1987.

Melton, William C. "Fedwatching and the Federal Funds Market" (Ch. 55), in F.J. Fabozzi and S. Pollack, eds. *The Handbook of Fixed Income Securities*. Homewood, Ill.: Dow Jones-Irwin, 1987.

Merton, Robert C. "Option Pricing When Underlying Stock Returns Are Discontinuous," in Michael A. Berry and Katrina F. Sherrerd, eds. *CFA Readings in Derivative Securities*. Charlottesville, Va.: The Institute of Chartered Financial Analysts, 1988.

Michaud, Richard O. "A Scenario Dependent Dividend Discount Model: Bridging the Gap Between Top-Down Investment Information and Bottom-Up Forecasts." *Financial Analysts Journal*, November/December 1985.

Morrison, David. "Forecasting Currency Changes and Interest Rates in Non-U.S. Markets," in Richard W. McEnally, ed. *International Bonds and Currencies*. Seminar Proceedings, The Institute of Chartered Financial Analysts. Homewood, Ill.: Dow Jones-Irwin, 1986.

Pashigian, B. Peter. "The Political Economy of Futures Market Regulation." *Journal of Business*, April 1986.

Phillips, Susan M., and Clifford W. Smith, Jr. "Trading Costs for Listed Options." *Journal of Financial Economics*, September 1980.

Pictet, Ivan. "Global Investment Portfolios: Continental Europe," in James R. Vertin, ed. *International Equity Investing*. Seminar Proceedings, The Institute of Chartered Financial Analysts. Homewood, Ill.: Dow Jones-Irwin, 1984.

Porter, Michael E. "The Structural Analysis of Industries" (Ch. 1), and "A Framework for Competitor Analysis" (Ch. 3). *Competitive Strategy*. New York: The Free Press, 1980.

Reinganum, Marc R. *Selecting Superior Securities*. Charlottesville, Va.: The Research Foundation of the Institute of Chartered Financial Analysts, 1988.

Roll, Richard. "An Analytical Valuation Formula for Unprotected American Call Options on Stocks With Known Dividends," in M.A. Berry and K.F. Sherrerd, eds. *CFA Readings in Derivative Securities*. Charlottesville, Va.: The Institute of Chartered Financial Analysts, 1988a.

————. "The International Crash of October 1987." *Financial Analysts Journal*, September/October 1988b.

Ross, Stephen A. "The Arbitrage Pricing Theory of Capital Asset Pricing." *Journal of Economic Theory*, December 1976.

Sharpe, William F. "Factor Models, CAPMs, and the APT." *The Journal of Portfolio Management*, Fall 1984.

Solnik, Bruno. "Equity: Concepts and Techniques" (Ch. 5), and "Bonds: Concepts and Techniques" (Ch. 7). *International Investments*. Reading, Mass.: Addison-Wesley Publishing Co., 1988.

Sorensen, Eric H. "Equity Duration," in Katrina F. Sherrerd, ed. *Equity Markets and Valuation Methods*. Seminar Proceedings. Charlottesville, Va.: The Institute of Chartered Financial Analysts, 1988.

Spiotto, James E. "The Risk of Municipal Bankruptcies," in Terry D. Trim, ed. *The Municipal Bond Market: New Rules, New Opportunities and New Strategies*. Seminar Proceedings. Charlottesville, Va.: The Institute of Chartered Financial Analysts, 1987.

Sullivan, Kenneth H., and Timothy B. Kiggins. "Convexity: The Name Is New But You Always Knew What It Was," in Frank J. Fabozzi, ed. *The Institutional Investor Focus on Investment Management*. Cambridge, Mass.: Ballinger Publishing Company, 1988.

Sullivan, Kenneth H., Bruce M. Collins, and Davis A. Smilow. "Mortgage Pass-Through Securities" (Ch. 16), in F.J. Fabozzi and S. Pollack, eds. *The Handbook of Fixed Income Securities*. Homewood, Ill.: Dow Jones-Irwin, 1987.

Telser, Lester G. "Futures and Actual Markets: How They Are Related." *Journal of Business*, April 1986.

Treneer, Paula. "A Practitioner's View: The Claims versus the Evidence," in Richard W. McEnally, ed. *International Bonds and Currencies*. Seminar Proceedings, The Institute of Chartered Financial Analysts. Homewood, Ill.: Dow Jones-Irwin, 1986.

Volcker, Paul A. "Innovative Securities and the International Debt Crisis," in Richard W. McEnally, ed. *Innovations in Fixed-Income Instruments and Markets*. Seminar Proceedings. Charlottesville, Va.: The Institute of Chartered Financial Analysts, 1987.

Whaley, Robert E. "On the Valuation of American Call Options on Stocks With Known Dividends," in M.A. Berry and K.F. Sherrerd, eds. *CFA Readings in Derivative Securities*. Charlottesville, Va.: The Institute of Chartered Financial Analysts, 1988.

Wilson, Jack W., and Charles P. Jones. "A Comparison of Annual Common Stock Returns: 1871–1925 With 1926–1985." *Journal of Business*, 1987.

Wilson, Richard S. "Domestic Floating-Rate and Adjustable Rate Debt Securities" (Ch. 14), in F.J. Fabozzi and S. Pollack, eds. *The Handbook of Fixed Income Securities*. Homewood, Ill.: Dow Jones-Irwin, 1987.

Woolford, W. David. "Forecasting Interest Rates" (Ch. 56), in F.J. Fabozzi and S. Pollack, eds. *The Handbook of Fixed Income Securities*. Homewood, Ill.: Dow Jones-Irwin, 1987.

Zeckhauser, Richard, and Victor Niederhoffer. "The Performance of Market Index Futures Contracts." *Financial Analysts Journal*, January/February 1983.

Part IV

Integration of Portfolio Policies and Expectational Factors

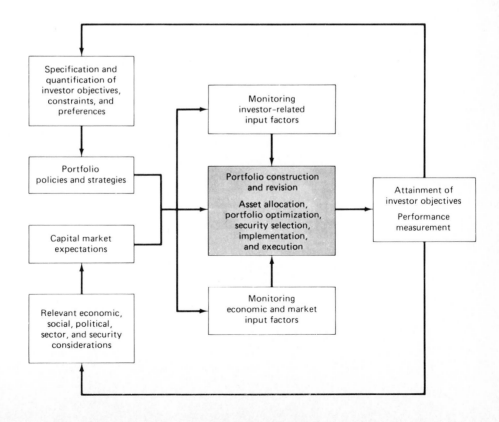

Specification and quantification of investor objectives, constraints, and preferences

Portfolio policies and strategies

Capital market expectations

Relevant economic, social, political, sector, and security considerations

Monitoring investor-related input factors

Portfolio construction and revision

Asset allocation, portfolio optimization, security selection, implementation, and execution

Monitoring economic and market input factors

Attainment of investor objectives

Performance measurement

CHAPTER 7

Asset Allocation

William F. Sharpe

THE ROLE OF ASSET ALLOCATION

Up to this point in the portfolio management process, everything has been preparatory. Having a good grasp of the investment basics (Chapter 2), the objectives and constraints leading to investment policies have been reviewed for the two major categories of investors: individual investors (Chapter 3) and institutional investors (Chapter 4). Similarly, the economic and financial characteristics of the capital market environment leading to return and risk estimates have been explored at two levels: the macro level (Chapter 5) and the micro level (Chapter 6). Given this groundwork, the actual portfolio building process is ready to begin. It starts with the asset allocation decision, discussed in this chapter, and continues to (1) individual asset class optimization for fixed income, equities, and real estate assets (and, as well, futures and options instruments), (2) execution, (3) portfolio monitoring and revision, and (4) performance evaluation. All of these are discussed in succeeding chapters.

Investment as a Multiple Stage Process

In a world in which information were freely available to all, it would make sense to approach the investment decision in a single stage. Estimates of risks, expected returns, and correlations would be made for all securities. All aspects of an investor's preferences and circumstances would be considered. Given these inputs, an optimal combination of securities (portfolio) would be selected.

In the real world, such a comprehensive analysis and optimization is rarely (if ever) done. Many organizations specialize in the analysis of only parts of the security market. Such specialists are reluctant to sell the information they obtain directly, because it may be difficult to insure that the buyer of the information does not sell or give it away to a third party. Moreover, the value of such information typically increases with the amount of money that is invested on the basis of the information. Thus, the specialist who obtains information seeks more revenue from those who use the information for investing large amounts of money than from those who use it for investing small amounts. Thus, to receive an appropriate amount of the value they add, information specialists typically organize as investment managers, and charge fees based on the amount of money under management for each client.[1]

If specialized managers are to be used, the investor or a person or persons acting as an agent for the investor must choose an appropriate mix of such investment managers. In many cases an agent must act on behalf of more than one individual who is ultimately affected by the investment performance of a pool of assets. Such agents bear fiduciary responsibility for the overall fund. A particularly important case arises when a corporation or governmental unit sponsors a pension plan. The sponsor and the pension fund officer must act as agents for the beneficiaries, while keeping in mind the possible effects of investment decisions on other interested parties (such as shareholders and taxpayers). In the United States, the provisions of the Employee Retirement Income Security Act of 1974 are especially strict in this regard: A fiduciary must "discharge his duties with respect to a plan solely in the interest of the participants and beneficiaries."[2]

To avoid circumlocution, this chapter uses the term *investor* to refer to the individual (or group) that makes the top-level decisions concerning a pool of assets. Some individual investors do this for themselves. Others use agents such as bank trust officers. Most pension funds are run by one or more officers of the sponsoring corporation or government under the supervision of a committee appointed by the board of directors or an elected official. Some unique problems faced by pension fund fiduciaries are discussed in later sections, after more general aspects are covered.

Many individual investors and some institutional investors approach the investment decision in two stages. Asset allocation is the top or first stage. Here, decisions are made concerning (1) the key asset classes in which funds can be invested and (2) the amount of money to be invested in each class. Security selection is the bottom stage. Within each asset class decisions are made concerning (1) the securities that belong in the class and (2) the amount of money to be invested in each one.

Some individual investors and many institutional investors use three stages. Asset allocation is the first stage. The second stage deals with manager selection. For each asset class, decisions are made concerning (1) the managers that can provide portfolios of securities within the class and (2) the amount of money (if any) to be invested by each one. The third stage

---

[1] For discussions of these and other aspects of decentralized investment management, see Rosenberg [1977], Sharpe [1981], and Pfleiderer and Bhattacharya [1985].

[2] See especially Section 404(a)(1) of the Act.

involves security selection. Here each of the managers selected in stage 2 chooses securities meeting the objectives specified at the outset.

Often the investment decision process is approached in even more stages. Asset allocation may focus on relatively broad classes (e.g., stocks or bonds), leaving to a second stage decisions concerning narrower groups (e.g., corporate versus government bonds or value stocks versus growth stocks). Manager selection and security selection then follow.

Any multiple-stage process can, in principle, be approached from (1) top down, (2) bottom up, or (3) a combination of the two. In practice, almost all investors mix aspects of top-down and bottom-up decision-making. Managers choose *investment styles* based partly on perceived needs of investors for satisfactory vehicles representing asset classes. Investors often take into account their assessments of managers' abilities when making asset allocation decisions. While formal procedures may conform more to a top-down approach in which asset allocation is done first, followed, in sequence, by lower-level stages, feedback from one period's results to the next period's decisions provides the essence of a mixed approach.

The Importance of Asset Allocation

Different investors approach asset allocation in different ways. Thus generalizations about its importance are difficult to make. Moreover, there are alternative ways of measuring the importance of most investment decisions, including the asset allocation decision. Despite these complications, it is generally agreed by theoreticians and practitioners alike that the asset allocation decision is by far the most important one made by an investor.

A study performed by Brinson, Hood, and Beebower [1986] measured the importance of "three-way" asset allocation for a group of 91 large pension funds from 1974 through 1983. At the beginning of each quarter, each fund's asset mix was broken into four components: cash equivalents, bonds, stocks, and "other." Then a *shadow asset mix* was created, consisting only of cash equivalents, bonds, and stocks, in the same proportions as were present in the fund. The return for this mix over the subsequent quarter was measured using returns on three indexes—each representing the asset class as a whole. For example, if a fund had 10 percent in cash equivalents, 30 percent in bonds, 40 percent in stocks, and 20 percent in "other," the return on the shadow asset mix corresponded to that of a fund with 12.5 percent (10/80) invested in a cash fund, 37.5 percent (30/80) invested in a passive bond market fund, and 50 percent (40/80) invested in a passive stock market fund.

For each fund in the sample, Brinson, Hood, and Beebower compared the actual return on the fund with that of the shadow mix for each quarter. Because the shadow mix involved only market-wide indexes, its return re-

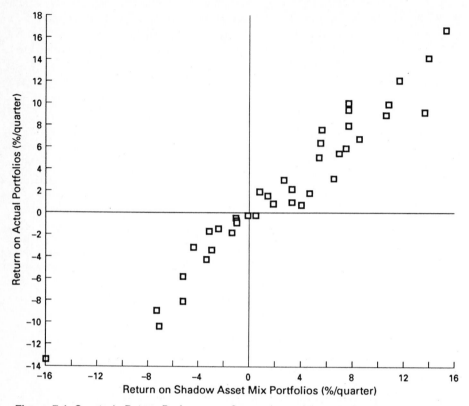

Figure 7-1. Quarterly Return Performance Comparison of Actual With Shadow Asset Mix Portfolios for a Representative Large Pension Fund, 1974–1983. SOURCE: Brinson, Hood, and Beebower [1986].

flected no security selection. Also, because it was not changed during the quarter, its return reflected no intraquarter shifts in asset mix. After 40 pairs of such quarterly returns were obtained, they were cross-plotted in the manner illustrated in Figure 7-1. To measure the "goodness-of-fit," the authors used the R-squared value associated with a regression line fitted through the points. In the illustrative case shown in Figure 7-1, that value is approximately 0.95, indicating that 95 percent of the variance in the returns on the fund could be attributed to changes in the returns on the shadow asset mixes.

This procedure was repeated for each of the funds studied. For some, the R-squared value was higher than 0.95; for others it was lower. The *average* value was 0.953 (95.3 percent). In terms of this measure, asset allocation was very important indeed, because less than 5 percent of the variance in returns from quarter to quarter was explained by non-asset allocation decisions—for example, those concerning security selection.

In the Brinson, Hood, and Beebower study, three-way asset allocation accounted for 95.3 percent of the variance in quarterly returns for a typical large pension fund. Had allocation across more classes been considered, the percentage would in all likelihood have been even larger.

APPROACHING THE ASSET MIX DECISION

Different asset mixes provide alternative combinations of risk and return. Different combinations of risk and return provide alternative levels of utility or satisfaction for an investor. The overall asset mix decision must take both the investment opportunities and the investor preferences into account.

Some investors approach the asset allocation decision informally; others use formal quantitative analysis. The key aspects are the same whether decisions are made quantitatively or qualitatively. Hence, it is important to understand the central concepts involved.

Investment Opportunities

One of the key steps in assessing investment opportunities is the determination of a *goal*—that is, the most important measure of the future outcome. For some investors, this measure is the value of total assets in a fund or, equivalently, the rate of return on current assets. For others it is the difference between the value of the assets and the value of liabilities to be covered by the fund.

Whatever the goal may be, it is unlikely that one can predict with certainty its future value. Estimates of likely outcomes must take into account the degree of uncertainty associated with each possible asset mix; this can be accomplished by summarizing the future prospects for a given asset mix with two measures, one indicating an expected outcome, the other indicating the range around that expected value within which the actual outcome is likely to lie.

For example, assume that the goal is to maximize the rate of return on the pool of assets. In principle, the first measure takes into account every possible return that might be obtained, then weights each possible outcome by its probability to determine the expected return.[3] In practice, the expected return for the overall mix is usually determined by taking a weighted average

---

[3] This and the other concepts in this section are based on statistical measures.

of the expected returns for the component assets, as discussed in Chapter 2.[4]

The likely range of outcomes is usually measured by the standard deviation. Assuming that the probabilities follow a normal ("bell-shaped") curve, the odds are roughly two out of three that the actual outcome will lie within one standard deviation of the expected outcome. Thus, if an asset mix has an expected return of 11 percent and a standard deviation of 10 percent, there are two chances out of three that the actual return will be between one percent (11 − 10) and 21 percent (11 + 10).

In principle, the standard deviation of an asset mix is determined by (1) calculating every possible deviation of an actual outcome from the expected outcome, (2) squaring each such deviation, (3) weighting each of the resulting values by its probability of occurrence, then (4) taking the square root of the sum of all such products. In practice, the standard deviation of an asset mix is usually computed using estimates of the standard deviations of the component assets and of the correlations among them, as also discussed in Chapter 2.[5]

The correlation between two outcomes measures the extent to which they are likely to "go together." Positive values indicate that better-than-expected outcomes for one are likely to be accompanied by better-than-expected outcomes for the other. Negative values indicate that better-than-expected outcomes for one are likely to be accompanied by worse-than-

----

[4] The formula for portfolio expected return is:

$$E(R_M) = \sum_{i=1,n} X_i E(R_i)$$

where:

n = the number of securities
$E(R_M)$ = the expected return for the asset mix, not to be confused with the expected return on the market (index) used elsewhere in this book
X_i = the proportion of the overall fund invested in asset i
$E(R_i)$ = the expected return for asset i

[5] The formula for portfolio variance is:

$$\sigma_M{}^2 = \sum_{i=1,n} \sum_{j=1,n} X_i X_j \rho_{ij} \sigma_i \sigma_j$$

where:

$\sigma_M{}^2$ = the variance of the return on the mix
σ_M = the standard deviation of the asset mix
X_i = the proportion of the overall fund invested in asset i
X_j = the proportion of the overall fund invested in asset j
ρ_{ij} = the correlation between asset i and asset j
σ_i = the standard deviation of asset i
σ_j = the standard deviation of asset j

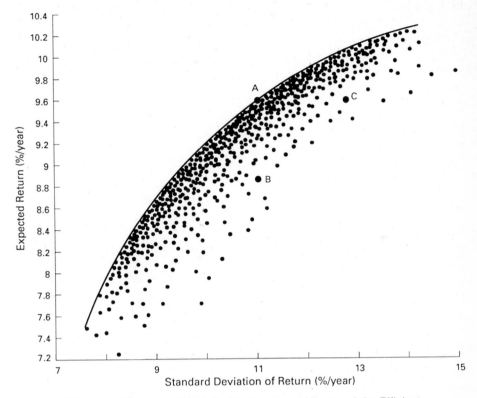

Figure 7-2. Expected Return and Risk for Various Asset Mixes and the Efficient Investment Opportunities Border.

expected outcomes for the other. A zero value indicates that the outcome for one is uncorrelated with that of the other. The largest possible value is +1.0, indicating perfect positive correlation, while the smallest possible value is −1.0, indicating perfect negative correlation.

Later sections discuss procedures for predicting asset class expected returns, standard deviations, and correlations. Collectively, these measures describe the current capital market conditions.

Given conditions in the capital markets, the formulas for portfolio expected return and portfolio variance can be used to compute the expected return and the associated standard deviation for any asset mix. If the process is repeated for a great many alternative mixes, a diagram such as that shown in Figure 7-2 is obtained.

Each point in Figure 7-2 shows the prospects associated with a particular asset mix. Those points lying below the upper left-hand curvilinear border are generally considered *inefficient*. For example, the mix plotting at point *A* provides (1) a better expected return and (2) the same range of returns as that plotting at point B. For any investor who prefers higher expected returns, A *dominates* B. Note also that the mix plotting at point A provides (1) the same expected return and (2) a narrower range of returns than that plotting at point C. For any investor who prefers narrower ranges of returns, A dominates C. An inefficient mix is one (such as B or C) that is dominated by some other mix. An *efficient* mix is one (such as A) that is not dominated by any other mix.

When making asset allocation decisions, most investors prefer (1) greater expected returns (all else equal) and (2) smaller ranges of returns (all else equal). For such investors, only efficient asset mixes are of interest. All the dots lying below the upper left-hand curve are inefficient, and thus to be avoided.

The shaded area in Figure 7-2 represents investment opportunities. The upper left-hand border represents *efficient investment opportunities*. Determining the locations of all the points requires detailed predictions of capital market conditions—that is, the expected returns, risks, and correlations for all asset classes. If liabilities (such as those of some pension funds) are also to be considered, similar estimates need to be made concerning their future values.

Investor Preferences

Capital market conditions represent only half of the ingredients required for an optimal asset mix decision. The investor's preferences and any relevant constraints represent the other half. A formal representation of the preferences of a given investor can be provided by Figure 7-3.

The investor's goal determines the items plotted. If asset return is of interest, the axes show expected return and standard deviation of return, as in this case. If the future value of a pension fund's surplus of assets over liabilities is of interest, the axes would show the expected value of future surplus and the standard deviation of future surplus. In general, if the investor's goal is to maximize X, the vertical axes in diagrams such as those in *both* Figures 7-2 and 7-3 plot "expected value of X" while the horizontal axes plot "standard deviation of X."

Once the axes have been chosen, an investor's preferences can (in principle) be represented by a set of *indifference curves* such as those shown in Figure 7-3. The investor is assumed to be indifferent among all combinations lying on a given curve. The investor portrayed in Figure 7-3 considers the combination of expected return and standard deviation of outcome shown by point A to be as desirable as that shown by point B (or, for that matter, any other point on the curve on which A and B lie). He or she prefers point C to point A. Indeed, this investor prefers any point on the curve on which C lies to any point on the curve on which A lies.

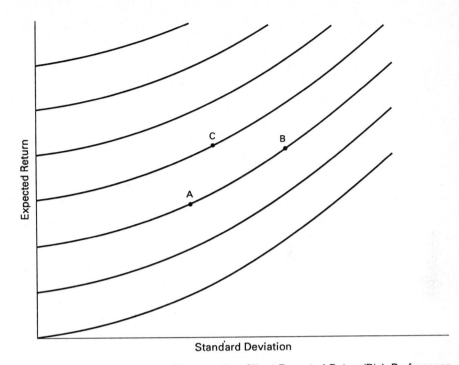

Expected Return

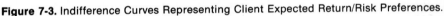

Standard Deviation

Figure 7-3. Indifference Curves Representing Client Expected Return/Risk Preferences.

Investor preferences usually display the characteristics plotted in Figure 7-3. Higher expected returns are preferred, as are smaller ranges; thus the curves are upward-sloping. Moreover, the slopes of the curves increase at an increasing rate. This means, for example, that as risk (measured by standard deviation) increases, the expected return must increase at an increasingly greater rate to adequately compensate the investor.

A particularly useful measure of an investor's willingness to take on added risk to achieve added expected return is termed *risk tolerance*. Formally, risk tolerance is the added variance (standard deviation squared) that just offsets a unit of added expected return, providing the same *expected utility* for the investor in question.

This relationship can be shown succinctly in a formula:

$$U_{Mk} = E(R_M) - \frac{\sigma_M{}^2}{t_k}$$

where:

U_{MK} = the expected utility of asset mix M for investor k
$E(R_M)$ = the expected return for mix M

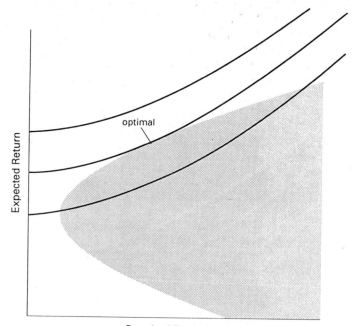

Figure 7-4. Combining Investor Return/Risk Preferences and Market Opportunities to Select an Optimal Portfolio.

σ_M = the standard deviation for mix M (σ_M^2 = variance)
t_k = investor k's risk tolerance

The final term in the equation (σ_M^2/t_k) can be considered a *risk penalty*. This term is greater, the greater the standard deviation of the asset mix and the smaller the risk tolerance of the investor. Correspondingly, the expected utility can be considered a *risk-adjusted expected return*, because it equals the expected return minus a penalty for the associated risk. This risk penalty is greater, the greater is investment risk (σ_M) and the smaller is the investor's risk tolerance (t_k). For investors who are extremely risk-averse, t_k is small and the risk penalty is large, leading to a smaller value of U_{Mk}. For investors who are less risk-averse, t_k is larger and the risk penalty is smaller, leading to a larger value of U_{Mk}.

The goal of an investor is to select the asset mix with the greatest expected utility (taking any required constraints into account.) The formal solution is shown in Figure 7-4. The optimal asset mix lies at the point at which an indifference curve is tangent to (i.e., touches but does intersect) the curve along which the efficient investment opportunities lie. Only at the point of tangency is the investor on the highest indifference curve that is attainable.

Taking Opportunities and Preferences Into Account

To find the optimal investment mix for a given investor requires both (1) knowledge of opportunities in the capital markets and (2) a full understanding of the investor's circumstances and preferences.

In the formal structure given earlier, the investor's circumstances and preferences determine the labels for the axes in a diagram such as Figure 7-4, as well as the shape of the indifference curves in the diagram.

Capital market opportunities play a key role in determining the opportunity set in a diagram such as that shown in Figure 7-4, but the investor's preferences and circumstances are also relevant. His or her goal determines the labels on the axes, and constraints on holdings may rule out some asset mixes. Moreover, if the investor's goal incorporates the future values of both assets and liabilities, risks and returns associated with the latter must also be taken into account.

To find the best possible asset mix, information about an investor and information about capital markets must be brought together. Some investors attempt to do the entire job themselves. Others rely on division of labor to exploit the comparative advantages that result from specialization.

Investment Manager Discretion. One solution delegates all investment decisions to an investment manager or counselor. This individual or organization specializes in knowledge of the capital markets and perhaps of other specialized investment management organizations but also devotes considerable time and attention to understanding the circumstances and preferences of each of its investors. When an investor relies on a single investment counselor, broker, or investment manager in this manner, it is incumbent on the investment professional, acting as a fiduciary for his or her client, to understand as fully as possible the investor's goal, circumstances, and risk tolerance.

In some situations a fiduciary must act on behalf of two or more parties, as is often the case when a trustee is appointed under a testamentary trust. The deceased may have provided that one party receives current income from a fund, with the remainder going to another party on the former's death. By "tilting" the asset mix toward high or low income securities, the trustee can favor either party at the expense of the other. Also, the trustee may have authority to "invade principal" to increase payments to the income beneficiary. In either case, the objectives, circumstances, and risk tolerances of all parties must be considered, and Solomon-like decisions must be made concerning the balance to be struck between potentially competing interests.

Investor Choice. A different approach leaves the ultimate investment decision to the investor. Here, one or more investment professionals may provide estimates of capital market opportunities and narrow the choice to a set of asset mixes that are efficient in terms of the investor's goal. That is, they lie on the upper left-hand border in a diagram such as that shown in Figure 7-2. The prospects for such mixes are then communicated to the investor who makes a final selection based on his or her ultimate preferences.

Investment professionals following this approach often perform additional analysis to state the likely ranges of outcomes for various mixes in terms that are especially meaningful to the investor in question. Thus, an individual investor may be shown ranges of likely retirement annuity values beginning at age 65, stated in terms of constant purchasing power, a pension sponsor may be shown ranges of likely coverage of liabilities 10 years hence, and the like.

Mixed Approaches. In many cases, some parties in the investment process play no direct role in the asset allocation process, while others share some of the ultimate responsibility for this decision. For example, an investment manager may define a particular strategy, announce its characteristics, then invite any investor who finds it suitable to place some or all of his or her funds accordingly. This approach is followed by most mutual funds. A number of organizations provide *families* of mutual funds, each with a different set of objectives. The investor, or his or her counselor, can then choose a mix of the funds to provide the best asset allocation.

Institutional investors often follow a similar strategy. *Pension fund consultants* provide lists of investment management firms prepared to follow a particular "style" (e.g., value stock investing). Working with the sponsor of a fund, the consultants recommend (1) a particular allocation of funds among such categories and (2) a preferred allocation of funds within each category among specific managers.

A manager who has selected an investment strategy, such as a growth stock strategy, then invited investors to provide funds to be managed following it, can be considered to have created a "black box" with a particular level of risk, expected return, and correlations that can be compared with black boxes created by other managers. The investor, advisor, or consultant takes the characteristics of such investment strategies as given. The key task is to estimate the expected return and risk of each strategy as well as all the relevant correlations, then find the *mix* of such strategies that is most suitable, given the investor's circumstances and risk tolerance.

To help in this process, individual investors can take advantage of the skills of investment counselors, securities brokers, or trustees. Institutional investors can use traditional pension consultants. Either can also seek the services of *asset allocation consultants,* who specialize in the asset allocation decision itself, using either passive investment strategies within asset classes or leaving the task of choosing active managers within each class to others.[6]

ASSET ALLOCATION AS EXPOSURES TO KEY FACTORS

Choosing Asset Classes

Underlying any asset allocation analysis are two prior sets of decisions: the *choices* of asset classes and their *definitions*. How many classes are to be used? Which securities are assigned to each class?

While practice varies widely, the major principle that should guide such decisions can be stated relatively easily. Parsimony is one goal: Asset classes should be few in number and broad in content. On the other hand, the exposures of a fund to the enumerated asset classes should account for most of any changes in its value. To accomplish both goals, one must enumerate a relatively small number of variables that represent the key factors that lead to changes in asset or security values. An understanding of the general characteristics of *return factor models* is required to make this statement more precise.

Return Factor Models

A return factor model breaks the return on a security or portfolio into a series of components. One set of such components represents the *factor-related* portion of return. The last component represents the *non-factor-related* portion (also known as the *idiosyncratic* or *residual* return).

Each of the factor-related portions of return is the product of (1) the security or portfolio's *exposure* to a factor and (2) the *actual value* of that factor. The former is represented by a "*b*-value." Thus b_{i1} represents the exposure to factor 1, b_{i2} the exposure to factor 2, and so on.[7]

---

[6] At least one plan sponsor experimented with an alternative approach in which the plan's investment managers served as a team offering advice on the overall asset mix of the fund.

[7] Letting f represent the number of factors, a standard representation is:

$$R_i = b_{i1}F_1 + b_{i2}F_2 + \cdots + b_{if}F_f + e_i$$

where:

R_i = the return on security or portfolio i
b_{i1} = the sensitivity of i's return to factor 1
F_1 = the value of factor 1
b_{i2} = the sensitivity of i's return to factor 2

Desirable Return Factor Model Characteristics. A good return factor model should have three characteristics. First, the non-factor-related return[8] should be uncorrelated with the values of the factors. Otherwise, some of the influences of the factors may be erroneously attributed to other effects.

Second, the factor-related components of return should account for most of the return. How much is accounted for is usually formalized by comparing the variance of the non-factor-related return with that of the security or portfolio. The difference between these two values, expressed as a percentage of the variance of the security or portfolio, can be interpreted as a measure of the portion of the latter collectively "explained by" the factors. If the first condition is met, this value is precisely the value of "R^2"—a standard statistical measure[9] of the portion of one variable explained by one or more other variables:[10]

$$R^2 = \frac{\text{Variance } (R_i) - \text{Variance } (e_i)}{\text{Variance } (R_i)}$$

The goal is to select a relatively small number of factors that nonetheless provide a large value of R^2 for most securities or portfolios.

The third characteristic concerns the relationship of one security's or portfolio's return to that of another. Common influences should be captured, to the greatest extent possible, by the selected factors. Equivalently, the non-factor-related return for one security or portfolio should not be correlated with that of another (because, if they are, some additional factor has been overlooked).

The Effects of Diversification. If a factor model accounts well for the returns on individual securities or portfolios and has the three characteristics given above, it accounts even more effectively for the returns on *combinations* of those securities or portfolios. The return on a combination of

---

$F_2 = $ the value of factor 2
$b_{if} = $ the sensitivity of i's return to factor f
$F_f = $ the value of factor f
$e_i = $ i's non-factor-related return

As noted in the text, e_i is sometimes termed the residual part of i's return, because it is the portion not attributable to the various factors. When making predictions about returns in a future period, only the values of $b_{i1}, b_{i2}, \ldots, b_{if}$ are known. The values of $R_i, F_1, F_2, \ldots, F_f$, and e_i are uncertain.

[8] That is, e_i.

[9] The term R^2 should not be confused with R_i, the measure of return.

[10] Even in cases in which the first condition may not be met precisely, the R^2 value generally constitutes a useful measure of the power of a factor model.

securities equals, of course, a weighted average of the returns on its components, using the relative market values as weights.[11]

Not surprisingly, the sensitivity of any mix of securities or portfolios to changes in any given factor also equals a weighted average of the sensitivities of its components to that factor, again using the relative market values as weights.[12] Similarly, the actual non-factor-related return for the mix is a market-value-weighted average of the non-factor-related returns of its components.[13]

When making predictions about future returns, the values of the non-factor-related components of return are unknown. However, if these values are uncorrelated across components, the uncertainty associated with the non-factor-related portion of the return for the mix typically is considerably less than that of a typical component. This result stems from the fact that one security's or portfolio's positive non-factor-related return is likely to be offset by another's negative non-factor-related return.[14]

---

[11] If X_i represents the proportion of overall funds invested in security or portfolio i and there are n such components, then the return on the overall mix is:

$$R_M = \sum_{i=1,n} X_i R_i$$

[12] If each component's return conforms to a factor model with f factors, the right-hand side of the factor model equation can be substituted for R_i in the equation given in the previous footnote. Doing so and simplifying gives:

$$R_M = b_{M1}F_1 + b_{M2}F_2 + \cdots + b_{Mf}F_f + e_M$$

where:

R_M = the return on the mix of assets
b_{M1} = the sensitivity of the mix's return to factor 1
F_1 = the value of factor 1
b_{M2} = the sensitivity of the mix's return to factor 2
F_2 = the value of factor 2
b_{Mf} = the sensitivity of the mix's return to factor f
F_f = the value of factor f
e_M = the mix's non-factor-related return

In fact, the sensitivity of the mix to a given factor, b_{Mk}, is a value-weighted average of the sensitivities of its components to that factor:

$$b_{Mk} = \sum_{i=1,n} X_i b_{ik}$$

[13] That is:

$$e_M = \sum_{i=1,n} X_i e_i$$

[14] Under such conditions:

$$\text{Variance}(e_M) = \sum_{i=1,n} X_i^2 \text{Variance}(e_i)$$

As long as the non-factor related returns of the components of a mix are uncorrelated, the uncertainty due to non-factor related effects is considerably smaller for the mix than it is for a typical component. This is a familiar result of diversification: When one component's non-factor-related return is larger than expected, that of another is likely to be smaller than expected, keeping the return of the overall mix near its factor-related value.

Because of this type of diversification, the R^2 value for a *mix* is likely to be considerably larger than that for a typical *component*. Thus, if only highly diversified mixes are to be considered, a factor model with relatively low R^2 values for individual components may prove quite acceptable because the "explanatory power" of the factors for the kinds of mixes that are being considered is the relevant test.

Asset Class Return Factor Models. Return factor models have been used with considerable success to explain returns on individual common stocks and combinations thereof (stock portfolios). Other models have been employed to good effect to explain the returns on individual bonds and combinations thereof (bond portfolios). For asset allocation, an *asset class return factor model* is needed.

The concepts behind such a model are straightforward. Each factor represents the return on an asset class. Each b-value represents a sensitivity of the return on the overall mix to the return on an asset class.

For asset allocation purposes, the components (i's) are usually fixed portfolios of securities (e.g., a unit trust of government bonds) or a "black box" representing the style of a particular manager (e.g., a growth stock mutual fund). For simplicity, the term *manager* is used to represent such a component. Thus, manager i can be characterized in terms of his or her b_{ij} sensitivities, that is, b_{i1}, the sensitivity of manager i's return to that of asset class 1, b_{i2}, the sensitivity of manager i's return to that of asset class 2, and so on through b_{if}, the sensitivity of manager i's return to that of asset class f.

Fortunately, a much more intuitive interpretation can be given to these values. Consider a manager who invests 25 percent of his or her money in an index fund representing asset class 1 and 75 percent in an index fund representing asset class 3. The resulting return is:

Thus if 10 components, each with a non-factor-related risk (variance of e_i) of Z were combined in equal portions:

$$\text{Variance}(e_M) = \sum_{i=1,10} (0.1)^2 Z$$

which would equal $\frac{1}{10}$ of Z.

$$R_i = 0.25F_1 + 0F_2 + 0.75F_3$$

where the F values are the returns on asset classes 1, 2, and 3, respectively.

In this case, b_{i1} equals 0.25, b_{i2} equals 0, and b_{i3} equals 0.75. Thus, the b_{ij} coefficients now represent the manager's exposures to the asset classes. That is, b_{i1} is manager i's exposure to asset class 1, b_{i2} is the manager's exposure to asset class 2, and so on through b_{if}, which is the manager's exposure to asset class f.

Typically, asset exposures are less direct than in this case. To cover implicit as well as explicit relationships of this sort, the term *effective asset exposure* can be employed. Thus, b_{ij} is manager i's effective exposure to asset class j, where j can represent any asset class (1 through f).

The set of such exposures can be termed the manager's *effective asset mix*. Substituting $R_{a1}, R_{a2}, \ldots, R_{af}$ for $F_1, F_2, \ldots, F_f$:

$$R_i = b_{i1}R_{a1} + b_{i2}R_{a2} + \cdots + b_{if}R_{af} + e_i$$

where R_{aj} is the return on asset class j.

The sum of the first f components on the right-hand side constitutes manager i's *asset-class-related return*. The last component can be considered the manager's *security-specific return*, or the return associated with idiosyncratic aspects of securities within asset classes.

The sum of the first f terms also equals the return on a *benchmark mix* invested solely in fully diversified portfolios representing the asset classes, using the same proportions as those in the manager's effective asset mix. The last component equals the difference between the manager's actual return and that of this benchmark mix. Before the fact this last component will generally be uncertain. In an asset allocation context, its expected value is often called the manager's *alpha value*, while its standard deviation or variance is termed the *security-specific risk*.[15]

Desirable Asset Class Characteristics

The characteristics of a good asset class return factor model are also desirable characteristics for a set of asset classes. The chosen factors (asset classes) should be relatively few in number and yet explain a substantial proportion of the variance in most components' (managers') returns. Non-factor-related (security-specific) portions of one component's (manager's) returns should be relatively uncorrelated with those of another. Moreover,

---

[15] Formally:

Expected(e_i) = manager i's alpha value

Variance(e_i) = manager i's security-specific risk squared

it should be possible to measure each component's (manager's) effective asset mix (*b*-values) with reasonable accuracy.

To facilitate implementation, and to help determine reasonable estimates of risks and expected returns, several other characteristics also are desirable. Returns on the asset classes should be easily measurable. It should be possible to form an effective index fund at low cost that will provide returns equal to those of each class—such a fund can serve as a relevant benchmark and offer an economic means of investment. It should also be possible to represent the overall set of securities held by a group of investors (e.g., citizens of the United States) with a combination of the asset classes— that is, the "parts" (asset classes) should be constructed so the "whole" (all outstanding securities) can be considered the sum of the parts.

These desired characteristics provide answers to the questions on which classes of assets are to be used and which securities are to be used in each class. While not all of these characteristics can be met completely, and trade-offs among them are usually required, asset classes should be chosen with them in mind. If an explicit factor model is to be used, the efficacy of a particular set of asset classes can be measured using measures such as manager R^2 values—other things equal, the greater the R^2 value obtained for a typical manager, the better the model. If an explicit model is not used, the analyst must rely on more intuitive notions. In either event, the goal is to identify a few key factors that are well reflected in the returns on asset classes—classes in which investments can be made efficiently if and when desired.

Choosing an Effective Asset Mix

Once a set of asset classes has been chosen, the asset allocation decision becomes a matter of selecting an optimal set of exposures to returns of those asset classes (in the terminology introduced earlier, choosing an effective asset mix). As the remainder of this chapter shows, this decision is complex.

MAJOR STEPS IN ASSET ALLOCATION

Asset allocation may be analyzed episodically or on a continuing basis. Most organizations conduct an *asset allocation review* relatively frequently. In conducting a review, a number of steps should be followed. This section outlines the review process. The next section describes three special cases in which one or more of the steps is omitted.[16]

---

[16] Portions of this and the next section are taken from Sharpe [1987b]. The steps laid out in Figure 7-5 are roughly akin to the portfolio construction, monitoring, and

For completeness, in the procedure outlined, liabilities such as those of pension funds (discussed in Chapter 4) are integrated into the analysis. Situations in which an "asset only" analysis is to be performed can be considered special cases in which liabilities equal zero.

Figure 7-5 shows the major steps. Boxes on the left are concerned primarily with the capital markets. Those on the right are specific to an investor. Those in the middle bring together aspects of the capital markets and the investor's circumstances to determine the investor's asset mix and its performance. Each review process begins at the top of the diagram and proceeds downward. Then it begins all over again.

Box $I1$ shows the things that matter to an investor—the current values of assets and (if applicable) liabilities. The investor's goal may be assumed to be the maximization of net worth. If only assets are of interest, net worth can be considered to equal asset value. If liabilities are also relevant, net worth can be defined (conventionally) as assets minus liabilities. An individual investor's net worth is his or her wealth; a defined benefit pension fund's net worth is the plan surplus.

Net worth generally determines an investor's current tolerance for risk, shown in box $I3$. The relationship between the investor's circumstances (box $I1$) and risk tolerance (box $I3$) can be portrayed by a *risk tolerance function*. It is shown in box $I2$ and can be thought of as the nature of the investor's aversion to risk over various levels of portfolio outcomes. Box $I3$ can be interpreted as containing an investment policy statement that clearly indicates the investor's current preferences for return vis-à-vis risk.

Box $C1$ shows the current state of the capital markets. Included are such things as current and historic levels of stock and bond indexes, past and projected dividends and earnings, current interest rates and inflation projections, and real estate values, as discussed in Chapter 5. Such information provides major inputs for predictions of the expected returns and risks of various asset classes and the correlations among their returns (shown in box $C3$). If liabilities are relevant, their risks, expected future values, and correlations with various asset classes must also be predicted. Some *prediction procedure* must be used to translate capital market conditions (box $C1$) into these estimates of asset and liability returns (box $C3$); it is shown in box $C2$.

Given an investor's risk tolerance (box $I3$) and predictions concerning expected returns, risks, and correlations (box $C3$), an *optimizer* can be employed to determine the most appropriate asset mix (box $M2$). Depending

revision process laid out in Figure 1-1 in Chapter 1. The process in Figure 7-5 is truncated, however, because it terminates with the asset allocation decision, implementation, and evaluation rather than proceeding to the optimization of each of the subportfolios (e.g., of fixed income, equity, real estate, and so on). Also, the monitoring/rebalancing feature is missing because for the all-important asset allocation decision the entire process needs to be repeated at each review period.

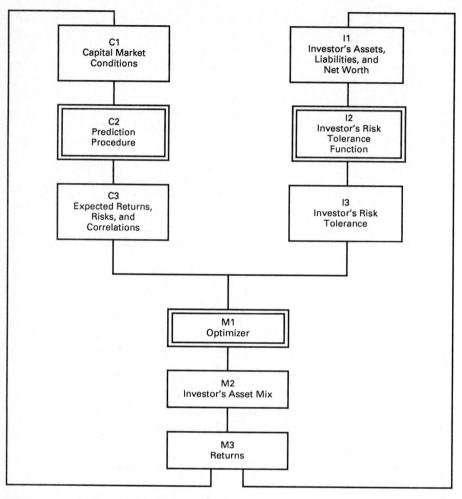

Figure 7-5. Major Steps in Asset Allocation.

on such things as the number of assets, the optimizer (shown in box *M1*) could be a simple rule of thumb, a mathematical function, or a full-scale quadratic program.

Box *M3* shows actual returns. Given the investor's asset mix at the *beginning* of a period (box *M2*), the asset returns during the period (box *M3*) plus any cash contributions and minus any cash withdrawals determine the values of the investor's assets at the beginning of the *next* period. New accruals of liabilities and pay-downs of old liabilities must also be taken into account. Changes in capital markets (including returns on fixed-income obligations) are likely to affect the values of the liabilities as well. Returns in one period thus influence the investor's assets, liabilities, and net worth at the beginning of the next period, as shown by the "feedback loop" from box *M3* to box *I1*. Returns during a period also constitute part of the overall capital market conditions at the beginning of the next period. This relationship is shown by the feedback loop from box *M3* to box *C1*. These loops illustrate that the process is a continuing one, with decisions and outcomes in one review period affecting the decisions in the next one.

From period to period, any (or all) of the items in boxes *C1, C3, I1, I3, M2,* and *M3* may change. However, the items in boxes *C2, I2,* and *M1* should remain fixed, because they contain *decision rules* (procedures). Thus the investor's risk tolerance (box *I3*) may change, but the risk tolerance *function* (box *I2*) should not. Predictions concerning returns (box *C3*) may change, but not the *procedure* (box *C2*) for making such predictions. The optimal asset mix (box *M2*) may change, but not the *optimizer* (box *M1*) that determines it. To emphasize the relative permanence of the contents of these boxes, they have been drawn with double lines.

Many investors make some or all of the decisions shown in boxes *I2, C2,* and *M1* "by hand" (and/or heuristically). However, in an increasing number of organizations some or all of these procedures have been automated, with decision rules specified in advance, then followed routinely. As the next section shows, procedures often described as "portfolio insurance" strategies fall clearly in this category, as do certain approaches described as "tactical asset allocation" methods.

INTEGRATED, STRATEGIC, TACTICAL, AND INSURED ASSET ALLOCATION

Integrated Asset Allocation

When all the steps discussed in the previous section are performed with careful analysis (formal or informal), the process may be termed *integrated asset allocation*. This term is intended to indicate that all major aspects have been included in a consistent manner. If liabilities are relevant, they are integrated into the analysis. If they are not, the procedure still integrates aspects of capital markets, the investor's circumstances and preferences, and the like. Moreover, each review is based on conditions at the time—those in the capital markets and those of the investor. Thus, the process is *dynamic* as well as integrated.

For some purposes it may be efficient to "shortcut" some of the steps. A number of specialized approaches to asset allocation do so. Key among them are strategic, tactical, and insured asset allocation procedures.

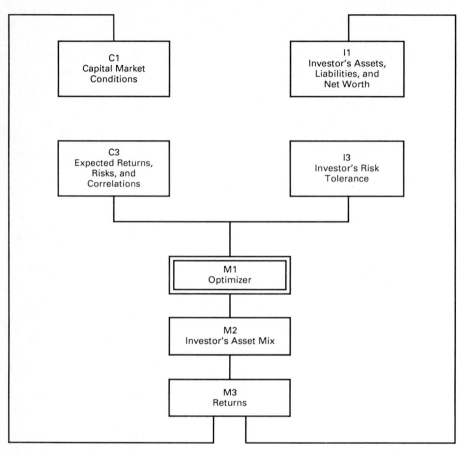

Figure 7-6. Strategic Asset Allocation.

Strategic Asset Allocation

Figure 7-6 portrays a typical *strategic asset allocation analysis* (sometimes also called *policy asset allocation analysis*) in terms comparable to those used earlier. Strategic asset allocation studies are usually done episodically (e.g., once every three years). Relatively few asset mixes are considered (e.g., bond/stock combinations with 0, 10, 20, . . . , 100 percent invested in stocks). An analysis (generally using Monte Carlo procedures of the type described in a later section) is performed to determine the likely range of outcomes associated with each mix. Typical outcomes analyzed for individual investors are annuity values on retirement, value of savings five years hence, and the like. Typical outcomes analyzed for institutional investors are required pension contributions over the next five years, attainable annual spending rates from an endowment fund, pension surplus five years hence, and so on.

When the analysis is complete, the investor is asked to examine the ranges of outcomes associated with each of the mixes, then choose the preferred one. This constitutes the policy, long-run, or strategic asset mix.

In the vast majority of such analyses, each mix is expressed in terms of the percentage of total value invested in each asset class. Such an approach can be termed a *constant mix strategy*. It differs from a *buy-and-hold strategy,* because transactions are required to rebalance the mix periodically after market moves change relative asset values. Although liabilities may be included, no explicit attempt is made to alter the asset mix to take the nature of the liabilities into account.

Strategic studies almost always employ "long-run" capital market conditions. In particular, asset expected returns, risks, and correlations remain constant throughout the simulation. This situation is portrayed by the absence of a connection between boxes *C1* and *C3* in Figure 7-6. Changing capital market conditions from period to period do not influence predictions concerning asset returns. Therefore, there is no need for a *C2* procedure box because the return, risk, and correlation inputs to the *M1* optimizer are long-run or strategic inputs not affected by short-run changes in market conditions.

For each set of simulations in a strategic study, the percentage asset mix is held constant. With constant capital market conditions, a constant asset mix can only be optimal if the investor's risk tolerance is unchanged.[17] This situation is portrayed by the absence of a connection between boxes *I1* and *I3* in Figure 7-6. Changing circumstances from period to period do not influence the investor's attitude toward risk. Therefore, there is no need for an *I2* function box because the investor's risk tolerance inputs to the *M1* optimizer are long-run/strategic inputs not affected by short-term changes in investor circumstances.

Each of the possible strategies considered in a policy study can be represented by a different level of risk tolerance. The smaller the tolerance for risk, the more conservative the asset mix. The analysis is framed in terms of asset mix. However, by selecting one of the constant asset mixes, the investor provides important information about his or her risk tolerance.

Strategic asset allocation provides an important set of benchmarks for an investor. It indicates the appropriate asset mix to be held under "normal" conditions. It also suggests the investor's long-run, or "average" level of risk tolerance. As conditions change, however, alterations in asset mix should be considered. Thus, strategic asset allocation should serve as the first step in a continuing process.

---

[17] For a more rigorous discussion, see Sharpe [1987b].

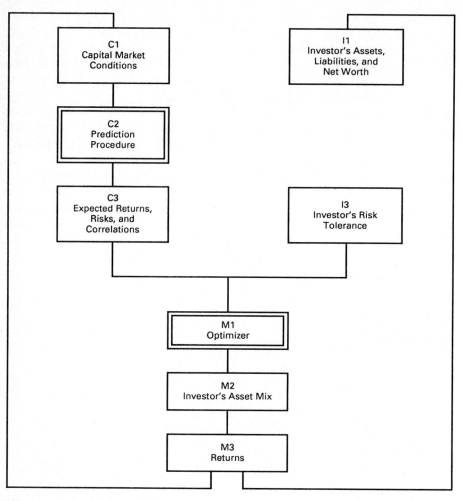

Figure 7-7. Tactical Asset Allocation.

Tactical Asset Allocation

Tactical asset allocation analysis is typically performed routinely, as part of continuing asset management. Its goal is to take advantage of perceived inefficiencies in the relative prices of securities in different asset classes. Early tactical asset allocators switched funds between bonds and stocks. Many now use bonds, stocks, and cash equivalents, and some employ even more asset classes. Figure 7-7 portrays a typical tactical asset allocation analysis in terms comparable to those used earlier.

Explicitly or implicitly, tactical procedures assume that the investor's risk tolerance is unaffected by changes in his or her circumstances. In the figure, this assumption is portrayed by the absence of a connection between boxes *I1* and *I3*. That is, there is no need for an *I2* function box, because in tactical asset allocation the investor's risk tolerance is held constant; the focus is entirely on the changing outputs from the *C2* prediction procedure box.

Tactical changes in asset mix are driven by changes in predictions concerning asset returns. In simpler systems, only predictions of expected returns on stocks and bonds change. In more complex systems, predicted expected returns, risks, and even correlations change.

In practice, tactical asset allocation systems are often *contrarian* in nature. Typically, the expected return on stocks is based on the relationship between the current level of a stock market index and justified price or intrinsic value based on projections of dividends or earnings for its component stocks. Variations in values based on projected dividends and earnings are usually smaller than the corresponding variations in stock prices. Thus, expected returns tend to fall when prices rise and values change little, if at all, leading to a tactical asset allocation decrease in stock holdings; expected returns rise when prices fall and values fall less, leading to a tactical asset allocation increase in stock holdings.

Changes in asset expected returns, risks, and correlations would take place in even the most efficient security markets. However, tactical asset allocation procedures sometimes operate on the assumption that markets overreact to information. In such cases, decisions are based on *deviant beliefs,* rather than those of the consensus of investors. Investors following such approaches believe that their predictions (1) diverge from those of other investors and (2) are superior.

Tactical asset allocation procedures can take into account changes in expected returns, risks, and correlations. And such changes do occur. On the other hand, tactical asset allocation typically does not consider possible changes in the investor's risk tolerance. Thus, it may provide only a partial solution to the overall asset allocation problem.

Insured Asset Allocation

Like tactical asset allocation, *insured asset allocation analysis* procedures are generally applied routinely, as part of continuing asset management. Insured asset allocation analysis procedures differ considerably, however, in both motivation and execution. In principle these procedures are intended to better adapt long-run results to an investor's objectives, without attempting to "time" the market (although, in practice, they are sometimes used for "closet" market timing). Figure 7-8 portrays an insured asset allocation procedure in the terms used earlier.

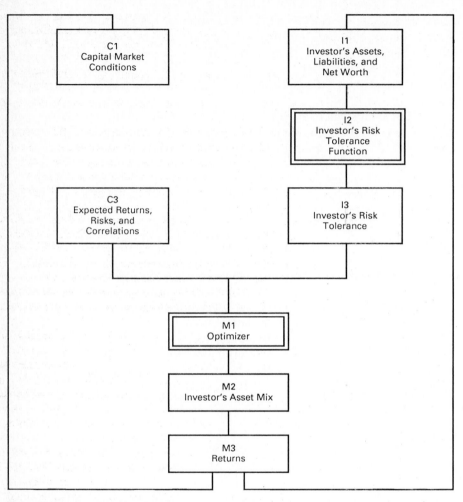

Figure 7-8. Insured Asset Allocation.

Most portfolio insurance strategies allocate assets between two major classes (e.g., stocks and Treasury bills). In essence, such an approach provides a rule that relates the appropriate asset mix to the excess of the current value of a set of assets (or the investor's net worth) over a desired minimum value or *floor*. The greater is the current value of the "cushion" of asset value or net worth over this floor, the greater the amount invested in the risky asset. If at any time the asset (or net worth) value falls to the level of the floor, nothing is invested in the risky asset, "insuring" that the floor will not be violated.

The formal analyses on which portfolio insurance strategies are based assume that expected returns, risks, and correlations remain the same over the period during which the insurance is "in force" (although some ad hoc procedures have been developed to deal with unexpected changes in risk). This assumption is portrayed by the absence of a connection between boxes *C1* and *C3* in the figure. That is, there is no need for a *C2* procedure box because revising return, risk, and correlation estimates on the basis of new market information is not the focus of the insurance process.

Explicitly or implicitly, insured asset allocation assumes that the investor's risk tolerance is highly sensitive to the level of his or her assets or net worth. The greater this value, the larger is his or her risk tolerance, leading to a more aggressive asset mix. The smaller the value, the smaller is risk tolerance and hence the less aggressive the asset mix. If the value falls to the floor, risk tolerance becomes zero, making the least risky asset mix available the optimal choice. Thus, box *I2* plays the key role in an insured asset allocation procedure.

Unlike tactical asset allocation, portfolio insurance does take into account possible changes in investor risk tolerance. However, it fails to account for changes in capital market prospects. To do both requires a fully integrated asset allocation analysis.

INVESTOR OBJECTIVES AND CONSTRAINTS

Defining the Objective

Before asset allocation can proceed, the *goal* of the investor must be determined. Many investors wish to obtain the greatest possible nominal asset value in the future. For others, the greatest real future asset value (i.e., value measured in terms of constant purchasing power) is more relevant. For yet others, the future difference between the value of assets and a measure of liabilities is crucial.

In this context, the goal constitutes a measure of the success or failure of the asset allocation *after the fact*. Before the fact, its level can rarely be known with certainty. Instead, its expected return and likely range (standard deviation) must be assessed.

The *objective* of an asset allocation analysis should be to find the asset mix that provides the best feasible combination of expected value and standard deviation of the investor's goal. The best combination is the one that best suits the investor's preferences, that is, the one that maximizes his or her expected utility. A combination is *feasible* if it meets all the constraints that are relevant in the situation.

The most important measure of an investor's preferences is his or her risk tolerance. This measure indicates the added risk (variance) the investor is willing to take on to obtain an additional unit of expected value. Both risk and expected return must, of course, be stated in terms of the investor's goal.

An investor's risk tolerance depends on a great many factors, and it is likely to change over time, as his or her circumstances (including asset values) change. Unless the investor is to make the ultimate choice among efficient asset allocations, his or her advisor or investment manager must carefully assess the investor's current risk tolerance before choosing or revising an asset mix.

Constraints and Other Aspects

Risk and return may be the most important measures of the prospects for an asset mix, but there are often other aspects to be considered.

Many investors are concerned as well with *liquidity*. Although measures differ, there is general agreement that some assets (e.g., Treasury bills) offer considerably more liquidity than others (e.g., real estate). Such differences can be accommodated either through *constraints* or by expanding the list of objectives. In the former case, only asset mixes providing a minimum amount of liquidity are considered. In the latter, the investor's expected utility can be composed of three elements: the expected value of the goal, a penalty for the associated risk, and a measure of the desirability of the liquidity of the mix. The latter measure incorporates both a measure of the liquidity of the mix and a measure indicating the investor's degree of preference for liquidity vis-à-vis expected return.

If the investor is concerned with real return, all values should be deflated by an appropriate price index (such as the Consumer Price Index or the gross national product deflator) before performing the analysis. If after-tax return is relevant, all values can be stated net of relevant taxes.

Legal and other constraints may also prove relevant. Many investors are constrained from taking short positions in securities. Others choose to avoid such positions because of the added costs and/or risks of potentially large losses. As a result, many asset allocation analyses restrict positions to nonnegative values (i.e., no short positions) for most, if not all, classes.

Upper limits on positions are often used. An investor may be unwilling or legally unable to hold more than a given amount of a particular asset class. In some cases, such limits are included to cover situations in which the investor fears that his or her agent may be influenced by an excessively bullish forecast for one or more asset classes. The imposition of upper limits on asset holdings by institutional investors is very common.

Individual Investors

As indicated in Chapter 3, individual investors are generally assumed to be concerned with future asset value. Increasingly, analysts are focusing on future real asset value on an after-tax basis. For strategic analysis, lifetime patterns of investment may be taken into account, with outcomes stated in terms of levels of retirement income.

A great many individual investors rely on mutual funds as vehicles for asset allocation. In some cases a single fund is used. In other cases, the investor (possibly with the assistance or advice of an investment professional) invests in two or more funds.

Mutual and Other Commingled Funds

Many mutual funds explicitly choose an "investment style" that is too specialized to serve as any investor's total fund. This is certainly the case for specialized industry funds (e.g., those holding only electronics stocks), but most practitioners would argue that it is also the case for many other types (e.g., funds specializing only in growth stocks).

A specialized fund can, in effect, choose any objective and set of constraints. The choice must be well defined and adhered to. Otherwise, the contents of the resulting black box may change without its users' knowledge, leading the ultimate investors to inappropriate asset allocations.

A number of mutual funds attempt to cover a sufficiently wide set of investments to provide at least some investors a "one-stop" investment fund. Most are called *balanced funds*, indicating the inclusion of both bonds and stocks. Here, too, almost any objective and set of constraints may be adopted. And here, too, it is crucial that the choice be well-defined and adhered to.

Bank trust departments often set up a series of commingled funds to serve as investment alternatives for their trust officers. Like mutual funds, these may be specialized or balanced. Again, objectives should be clearly stated and maintained over time.

Defined Contribution Pension Plans

Many companies and some public agencies provide employees with *defined contribution pension plans*. Each year the sponsoring organization adds some amount to each employee's retirement account. The amount may depend on the firm's overall profitability, the employee's salary, his years of service, and the like. It does not depend on the investment performance of the funds placed in the account previously. In such a situation, the investor bears the investment risk and enjoys the investment return.

In some plans, the employee may invest in a wide variety of investment vehicles (e.g., any or all of the mutual funds in a large "family of funds"). In others, the employer limits the choice to a relatively few vehicles provided through the firm or an outside agency. In addition, the employer may place restrictions on the amounts invested in certain vehicles, and/or the employ-ee's ability to move funds from one vehicle to another. In many cases, an employer places all employees' funds in a single investment pool controlled by the firm.

The greater the limits placed on investment alternatives by the sponsor of a defined contribution plan, the greater the role played by those respon-sible for the management of those investment alternatives. The most extreme case arises when there is a single pool of assets. Here the pension fund officer must select a single asset allocation for every employee of the firm. Because employees' circumstances, risk tolerances, and outside investments are likely to vary considerably, the task involves the balancing of many potentially conflicting objectives. Even when several investment vehicles are provided, the differing objectives of employees must be considered when selecting specific ones.

When setting up a defined contribution pension plan, the sponsor must deal with the issue of investor (employee) education. The greater the number of alternatives, the greater the opportunity for a well-informed employee to obtain an asset allocation that is best for him or her. But more vehicles also increase the probability that a poorly informed employee will make a bad asset allocation decision. Some employers offer employees free investment counseling, which approaches the comprehensive and individualized ser-vices available on a for-fee basis from independent advisors. Others rely on employees to make appropriate decisions (with or without the advice of others).

Defined Benefit Pension Plans

As pointed out in Chapter 4, another type of pension plan that is an important source of savings is the *defined benefit pension plan.* In this type of plan, the employer provides each employee with a promised set of benefits be-ginning at retirement. The amount paid at that time may depend on the employee's final salary, years of service, and many other factors. However, it does not depend on the investment performance of any funds that the employer has put aside to help defray the associated costs. In principle, in such a situation the employee neither bears the investment risk nor enjoys the investment return. Those who do participate in investment results may include a firm's officers and shareholders, a government unit's taxpayers, the Pension Benefit Guaranty Corporation, and others.

In practice, the situation is rarely this simple. Superior investment per-formance may result in increased benefits. Bankruptcy of a sponsoring cor-poration coupled with an underfunded pension plan may reduce the benefits of some employees (e.g., those whose benefits are not fully insured by the

Pension Benefit Guaranty Corporation). Thus, even a defined benefit plan may implicitly have some characteristics of a defined contribution plan.

Despite these qualifications, it is helpful to view a defined benefit pension plan as a type of financial institution owned by the sponsoring organization. Like any other such institution, it has assets (the pension fund), liabilities (the present value of benefits to be paid in the future), and a net worth (equal to assets minus liabilities). The latter is typically called the *pension surplus*.

In this view, the goal of asset allocation analysis should be stated in terms of pension surplus. The objective is to maximize the risk-adjusted future value of the surplus. Formally, this amount equals (1) the expected future surplus value minus (2) a risk penalty equal to the variance of that surplus value divided by a measure of risk tolerance.

If a formal optimization procedure is used, it is convenient to state the objective in units similar to those used for asset-only optimization. In the latter, outcomes are expressed in terms of return, measured as:

$$\text{Asset return} = \frac{\text{Change in asset value}}{\text{Initial asset value}}$$

A comparable notion in a "surplus optimization" analysis is:

$$\text{Surplus return} = \frac{\text{Change in surplus value}}{\text{Initial asset value}}$$

$$= \frac{\text{Change in asset value} - \text{Change in liability value}}{\text{Initial asset value}}$$

The expected value of this surplus return may be termed the *surplus expected return* and its standard deviation the *surplus risk*. The associated objective function can then be written as:

$$U_{Mk} = E(SR_M) - \frac{\sigma(SR_M)^2}{t_k}$$

where:

$$U_{Mk} = \text{the expected utility of asset mix } M \text{ for investor } k$$
$$E(SR_M) = \text{the expected surplus return for mix } M$$
$$\sigma(SR_M) = \text{the standard deviation of surplus return for mix } M$$
$$t_k = \text{investor } k\text{'s risk tolerance}$$

When the objective is to maximize utility, so defined, the resulting analysis is often termed an *asset/liability optimization* or *surplus optimization*.

Liability Returns

An asset's return is defined as the change in its value (including any intra-period cash flows) divided by its initial value. A comparable measure can be computed for a liability. Thus,

$$\text{Liability return} = \frac{\text{Change in liability value}}{\text{Initial liability value}}$$

Surplus return (as previously defined) is related to both asset and liability returns. The surplus return equals the sum of the weighted asset returns net of the weighted liability return, where the weight for each asset is the proportion of total assets invested in that class and the weight for the liability is the ratio of its value to the value of the assets.[18]

Measures of Pension Liabilities

Pension surplus equals assets minus liabilities. To compute it, an appropriate measure of pension liabilities is needed. Many have been proposed. Ulti-

---

[18] Let:

A_i = the initial value of asset class i

$A = \sum\limits_{i=1,n} A_i$ = the initial value of all assets

ΔA_i = the change in value of asset class i

Then surplus return equals:

$$SR = \frac{\sum\limits_{i=1,n} \Delta A_i}{A} - \frac{\Delta L}{A}$$

or:

$$SR = \sum\limits_{i=1,n} \frac{\Delta A_i}{A_i} \times \frac{A_i}{A} - \frac{\Delta L}{L} \times \frac{L}{A}$$

As can be seen, this involves both returns and relative values. Rewriting:

$$SR = \sum\limits_{i=1,n} R_i X_i - R_L X_L$$

where:

R_i = the return on asset class i

X_i = the proportion of total assets invested in asset class i

R_L = the return on the liabilities

X_L = the ratio of the liability value to the value of the assets

mately, the analyst must choose the measure that best reflects the objectives that are most relevant for purposes of allocating the assets of the fund.

The most straightforward measure is the *accumulated benefit obligation* (ABO). The measure takes into account cash flows that will be required in the future to meet obligations based on past service and past and current salaries. Using estimates of mortality and other measures, an actuary can estimate the set of such cash flows, year by year. An actuary, accountant, or financial analyst can then determine the present value of the set of cash flows, using an appropriate set of interest rates. For asset allocation purposes, it is important that the interest rate assumptions used in the present value calculations be consistent with current market conditions, so that liability values will be commensurate with the market-based asset values typically used in such an analysis. At the very least, some sort of measure of current market interest rates should be substituted for the rate used by the actuary or accountant when the most recent estimate of the ABO was determined, because only this will provide a current, relevant estimate of the ABO.

ABO values are produced (usually annually) for most private corporate plans and many government plans. Provisions of the Financial Accounting Standards Board's Financial Accounting Standard No. 87 (FAS 87) require private corporations to report shortfalls of asset values relative to ABO values on their balance sheets. Moreover, a liability value similar to the ABO plays a role in limits placed on private corporations vis-à-vis tax favored contributions to pension funds.

Actuaries and accountants routinely produce another measure of pension liability—the *projected benefit obligation* (PBO). For a plan in which benefits are tied explicitly to salaries, the PBO includes all the liabilities in the ABO plus additional benefits related to projected increases in salaries. These incremental liabilities depend, to a major extent, on the assumed future rate of increase in salaries. Often, salaries are assumed to increase by an amount equal to inflation plus a fixed real increment. If so, a portion of the cash flows associated with these incremental benefits is inflation-related.

Under FAS 87, changes in PBO values are used (in part) to compute the pension expense reported on a corporation's income statement. Most governmental agencies report a measure similar to the PBO as their primary estimate of pension liabilities.

Few private pension plans contain explicit provisions for postretirement increases in benefits in the event of high rates of inflation. Many public plans are indexed, but the rate of increase in benefits is usually "capped" at a relatively low rate (e.g., 2 or 3 percent per year). Nonetheless, many large private corporations and a great many public pension plans have chosen to increase benefits for those in pay status (i.e., receiving benefits) when inflation is especially high. De facto, such plans offer *implicit indexing* of benefits. A typical degree of such implicit indexing for a large private plan is 50 percent, while that of a typical state pension plan is close to 100 percent.

To reflect this type of implicit objective, many analysts compute measures of liabilities that include at least some postretirement indexing, in addition to the preretirement indexing implicit in the salary-related portion of the projected benefit obligation. While there is no standard procedure, such a measure can be termed an *indexed benefit obligation* (IBO). The greater the degree of assumed postretirement indexing, the larger the cash flows needed, and the more sensitive those cash flows are to the degree of inflation. (Note that "indexing" as used here does not mean putting a pension fund in an index of securities but refers to tying pension benefits to an index of inflation.)

The Effects of Indexing on Asset Allocation

An ABO value is equivalent to the present value of a portfolio of zero coupon bonds of various maturities, ranging from 1 year to 70 or 80 years (when the last current employee is assumed to die). Clearly this value is highly sensitive to changes in interest rates. Equally clearly, any surplus optimization in which the objective function deals with the *ABO surplus* (Assets − ABO) tends to favor long bonds, at least to some extent, because of their ability to provide a *hedge* against the risk of changes in the ABO value. Thus, when interest rates fall, the value of the liabilities rises. If long bonds are held, the value of the assets rises too. If not, the asset value may rise or fall, depending on conditions at the time. When asset values move in concert with those of liabilities, the assets are said to provide a hedge against changes in the value of the liabilities.

At the other extreme lies an optimization in which benefits are assumed to be completely indexed (both preretirement and postretirement). While the predicted *cash flows* associated with an IBO are highly sensitive to the degree of predicted inflation, its present value is considerably less so. An IBO value can be computed by (1) increasing the cash flows to reflect predicted future inflation, then (2) discounting these cash flows using the current term structure of interest rates. When predicted inflation increases, interest rates are also likely to rise. Thus, the new IBO value is based on *larger cash flows more deeply discounted*. The net effect could result in a larger, smaller, or similar value as before.

As a general rule, fully indexed benefit obligations are (1) high in value, but (2) low in risk. On the other hand, obligations based on cash flows that are not inflation-sensitive at all are (1) lower in value, but (2) high in risk—in particular, interest rate risk. Thus, a change in interest rates has a major effect (in the opposite direction) on the value of the fixed cash flows associated with an ABO. Conversely, a change in interest rates accompanied (as is usually the case) by a similar change in projected inflation (1) changes the cash flows associated with an IBO in the same direction and (2) changes the discount rates by a similar amount, also in the same direction. With both cash flows (in the numerator of each present value term) and discount rates (in the denominator) changed, the overall effect on the present value (i.e., the IBO) is minimal.

Surplus optimization in which the goal focuses on a fully indexed IBO surplus may lead to an asset allocation that differs relatively little from that resulting from an asset-only optimization. If the IBO value is not likely to change by very much (at least in the near future), there is little liability risk to hedge, and the presence of such a liability plays a relatively small role in the optimization. Hence, the similarity of the results in the two cases.

On the other hand, the presence of a substantial set of benefits sensitive to changes in interest rates is likely to have an important effect in an optimization analysis. In fact, experience shows that the optimal asset allocation is often fairly similar when either ABO surplus or PBO surplus is of interest.

While these generalizations provide some guidance, there is no substitute for careful analysis of the obligations of a particular plan and thoughtful decisions concerning the ultimate objectives of the sponsor. The appropriate measure of liabilities to be used for asset allocation should be approached in terms of the ultimate goal of the sponsoring organization and/or the beneficiaries. Accounting and actuarial calculations may prove helpful, but they should not be governing.

CAPITAL MARKET FORECASTS

Needed Estimates

An asset-only optimization requires estimates of the expected return of each asset, the risk (standard deviation of return) of each asset, and the correlations of each asset's return with that of each of the other assets.

For a surplus (asset/liability) optimization, all of these estimates are required plus the following measures relating to the liability return: the expected liability return, the liability risk (standard deviation of return), and the correlations of the liability return with that of each of the assets.

Some investment organizations and plan administrators approach the task of determining estimates in an informal manner. Thus, analysts' "best guesses" may be used for expected returns and their feelings about "likely ranges" for standard deviations. Other organizations use formal procedures (such as those described below) designed to produce numerical estimates for every item.

Extrapolation of Historic Results

Although it is always perilous to assume that the future will be like the past, it is at least instructive to find out what the past was like. The first step in the process involves the computation of returns over some historic period. A common choice uses 60 monthly total returns. The goal is to obtain as many data points (periods) as possible, while avoiding data from periods that are so distant as to be of limited relevance for predicting the future.

Asset returns are typically computed using the return on a value-weighted portfolio of securities representing a large portion of the class in question. Value weighting—weighting each security by its market value relative to the total market value of all securities in the portfolio—is more appropriate than equal weighting because a representative set of investments within a class conforms more to relative values than to equal values. Brokerage firms and others routinely prepare measures of total return on value-weighted indexes that can serve well as representatives for major asset classes.

Computation of historic liability returns is more difficult. If possible, estimates should be made of the values that a plan's currently accumulated benefits would have had at various times in the past. The associated relative changes from period to period may then be used to compute the liability returns. To do so, estimates of past market interest rates and inflation projections (e.g., at the end of each of the prior 60 months) are needed, along with the relevant cash flows and degree of indexing for the current level of benefits. Some investment organizations and plan administrators follow this procedure in complete detail. Others use approximations. Thus, the returns on a portfolio of very long duration bonds may be used as a surrogate for a plan's ABO liability returns, or the liability returns on a "representative" plan's PBO may be used in lieu of those of a specific firm.

Once historic returns have been computed, standard statistical procedures can be used to compute:

- Each asset's average return,
- Each asset's standard deviation of return,
- The correlations of each asset's returns with those of each of the other assets,

and, where relevant:

- The average return on the liability,
- The standard deviation of return for the liability, and
- The correlations of the liability's returns with those of each of the assets.

If the analyst is convinced that the historic results are in every way representative of future prospects, they may be used directly. That is:

- Expected returns can be assumed to equal historic average returns,
- Future risks can be assumed to equal historic standard deviations, and
- Future correlations can be assumed to equal historic correlations.

Evidence suggests that simple extrapolation of history in this manner can lead to highly concentrated investment strategies (i.e., with all or most of the assets invested in one class). While results vary from asset class to asset class and from time period to time period, experience suggests that for predicting future values, historic data appear to be quite useful with respect to standard deviations, reasonably useful for correlations, and virtually useless for expected returns. For the latter, at least, other approaches are a must.

Scenario Approaches

As explained in Chapter 5, instead of relying on historic data, some investment organizations make explicit judgmental forecasts (although historic data may be used to help form their judgments.) A few key *scenarios* (typically three to seven) are enumerated, then an estimate is made concerning the performance of each asset class for each scenario. A table such as the following may be used.

Scenario	Bills	Bonds	Stocks	Real Estate	Mortgages
Recession					
Stagflation					
Growth					
Inflation					

For example, the entry in the "inflation/stocks" box might be 10 percent—indicating that the analyst predicts that stocks will return 10 percent if there is inflation.

In some cases, such a set of predictions is all that is needed. The analyst considers the overall returns from different asset mixes in the various scenarios and then chooses one that appears best suited for the investor in question. A formal procedure that takes this approach is described in the next section.

In most cases, however, *probabilities* are assigned to indicate the likelihoods of the various scenarios, as illustrated in the following table.

Scenario	Probability
Recession	.10
Stagflation	.25
Growth	.40
Inflation	.25

Given these estimates, it is possible to compute the expected return and standard deviation of return for each asset and all the correlations among their returns.[19]

Scenario Approach Problems. Certain dangers are associated with scenario approaches of this type. First, there is a well-known tendency for the resulting estimates of asset risks (standard deviations) to be small by historic standards. This tendency appears to result from a behavioral regularity that makes people reluctant to forecast explicitly low-probability events in which extreme outcomes (e.g., 50 percent declines in value) would occur.

A second problem concerns the extent to which estimates are consistent with rudimentary notions of market efficiency. In many applications, the number of asset classes exceeds the number of scenarios. In such cases, it is highly likely that the analyst's estimates imply that some combination of asset classes (usually involving both long and short positions) could provide an *infinite* return in *all* scenarios. While the preclusion of short positions removes this possibility, it is still likely that some feasible combination will provide more return in every scenario than a riskless security. Such situations point up the dangers associated with representation of the myriad of conceivable actual "scenarios" with a limited number of possibilities.

A middle ground proposed by Markowitz and Perold [1981] utilizes the notion of a set of scenarios, but explicitly acknowledges that *within* a scenario, uncertainty remains. Thus, each cell in the scenario table may contain two numbers: an expected return and a standard deviation of return. For example:

---

[19] The standard formulas for making the computations are given in Chapter 5 of this book and in Sharpe [1985].

Scenario	Stocks
Inflation	.10 ± .04

This indicates that if an inflation scenario occurs, there are two chances out of three that stocks will have a return between 6 and 14 percent (i.e., one standard deviation below and one above the forecasted mean return). A related approach has been described by Fong and Fabozzi [1988]. While little used in practice at present, such procedures are far less likely to fall into the traps associated with traditional scenario analyses, because such approaches explicitly acknowledge that the few scenarios selected for analysis are insufficient to account for all of the actual uncertainty associated with security returns.

Risk and Correlation Models

As mentioned earlier, historic data can provide useful information concerning future asset risks and correlations. However, there is a well-known tendency for near-term future risks and correlations to be more like those of the recent past than like those of the distant past. Unless estimates are to be used for very long-range planning, it is important to take this fact into account.

A popular procedure to account for this tendency uses a limited historical period. For example, 60 monthly returns are analyzed, with each accorded equal importance. More sophisticated approaches examine the time-series behavior of risks and correlations to find a procedure that uses historic returns in the most efficient manner—that is, produces the best estimates of risks and correlations over the future period of interest (e.g., the next year).

In some cases the analyst alters correlations obtained via a risk model (whether sophisticated or simple), based on his or her judgment concerning changed conditions. It may be exceedingly difficult to do this in a manner that assures consistency among the estimates. Obviously, the correlation between asset classes A and C is related to (1) that between classes A and B and (2) that between classes B and C. To avoid serious inconsistencies, many analysts refrain from making judgmental forecasts of correlations or even altering those obtained using historical data.

A method for estimating risks that allows for the inclusion of judgment and assures consistency combines aspects of the scenario approach and the use of historic data. Each time interval (e.g., month, quarter, or year) from an historic period is treated as a scenario. Instead of assigning equal probabilities to these scenarios (as does the traditional historic procedure) or econometrically determined probabilities (as do more sophisticated risk models), the analyst selects probabilities judgmentally. For example, the analyst may estimate the probability that next year will be like 1938, the probability that it will be like 1939, and so on. Using these probabilities and the standard formulas for computing forward-looking standard deviations and correlations, the analyst can then obtain measures of risk and correlations for all the asset classes.

Equilibrium Expected Returns

While fairly recent historic data can provide useful estimates of asset risks and correlations, recent history is typically of little (if any) use when predicting expected returns. Instead, the analyst must both (1) rely on experience over very long periods and (2) take into account reasonable relationships among expected returns, risks, and correlations.

Two considerations provide the necessary structure for approaching this issue. First, in a given market at a given time there is a specific *risk premium,* equal to (1) the expected return on a portfolio of all marketable securities less (2) the riskless rate of interest. Second, in such a market, each security is priced so that the total amount investors are willing to hold equals the amount available. This second consideration is true not only for individual securities, but also for each asset class.

The optimal asset mix for any given investor depends on his or her (1) estimates of asset risks and correlations, (2) estimates of asset expected returns, and (3) risk tolerance. At any given time, some investors have a high level of risk tolerance, while others have a low one. Key to understanding the nature of an efficient capital market is the notion of *societal risk tolerance,* which is simply a weighted average of the current risk tolerances of all investors, with the amounts invested used as weights. In a sense, it equals the risk tolerance of a "typical" investor where "typical" is defined to take into account the fact that big investors play a greater role than small investors in determining values in capital markets.

It is useful to focus first on the overall market. *The market mix includes each asset class in proportion to the amounts held by the investors in the market in question.* For example, the "U.S. Mix" includes marketable securities held by investors based in the United States.[20] A straightforward relationship exists among (1) the risk premium for this mix (denoted $E(R_M) - r$), (2) its total risk (denoted $S(R_M)^2$), and (3) the societal risk tolerance for investors in the country in question (denoted τ). In words, *the premium*

---

[20] It is important that foreign securities be taken into account in this calculation if a truly international view of asset allocation is to be maintained. For a discussion of such a global approach, see Brinson [1986]. For analysis of the role of currency hedging in asset allocation, see Perold and Shulman [1988].

per unit of variance is inversely proportional to societal risk tolerance. In equation form:[21]

---

[21] Consider an investor choosing between (1) a market mix with an expected return of $E(R_M)$ and standard deviation of $S(R_M)$ and (2) a security with a riskless return of r. The problem is to choose X, the proportion of overall funds to be placed in the market mix. The objective is to maximize expected return minus a risk penalty based on the investor's risk tolerance t. In this case, the expected return equals X times the expected return on the market mix plus $(1 - X)$ times the riskless rate:

$$E = XE(R_M) + (1 - X)r$$

Similarly, the standard deviation equals X times that of the market mix:

$$S = XS(R_M)$$

The objective is to choose X to maximize:

$$E - \frac{S^2}{t}$$

which equals:

$$XE(R_M) + (1 - X)r - \frac{X^2 S(R_M)^2}{t}$$

To find the optimal value of X, the derivative of this equation relative to X is set equal to zero. This gives the desired value, which is:

$$X = \frac{E(R_M) - r}{2S(R_M)^2} \times t$$

Investors with high risk tolerance place more of their money "at risk." Those with low risk tolerance place less. If each side of the equation for a given investor is multiplied by his or her portion of total invested wealth, then a sum is taken over the equations for all the investors, the following result is obtained:

$$\overline{X} = \frac{E(R_M) - r}{2S(R_M)^2} \times \tau$$

where τ represents the societal risk tolerance, and $\overline{X}$ represents the value-weighted average proportion placed in the market mix.

For markets to clear, $\overline{X}$ must equal 1. Otherwise investors would not collectively wish to hold the available securities. Thus equilibrium requires that:

$$1 = \frac{E(R_M) - r}{2S(R_M)^2} \times \tau$$

or:

$$\frac{E(R_M) - r}{S(R_M)^2} = \frac{2}{\tau}$$

which is the relationship described in the text.

$$\frac{E(R_M) - r}{S(R_M)^2} = \frac{2}{\tau}$$

Some investment organizations assume (explicitly or implicitly) that all three components of this relationship (the market risk, the market risk premium, and the societal risk tolerance) remain constant over time. Others estimate changing values, as described in the next section.

Whatever assumptions are used, once two of the three components have been estimated, equilibrium considerations imply that the third should be estimated using the equation above. For example, if τ and $S(R_M)$ have been estimated, the value of $E(R_M) - r$ follows directly. Because r is easily observed, this implies the current value of $E(R_M)$. It remains to determine the expected returns on each of the asset classes, given an estimate of the expected return on the market mix.

For markets to clear, the mix chosen by any investor whose personal risk tolerance happens to equal that of the society (τ) must contain all asset classes, each in proportion to its outstanding total value. More precisely, *the market mix must be the optimal combination of asset classes for an investor with the societal risk tolerance.*

If this were not the case, investors' choices would not be *macroconsistent*—the chosen mixes would not "add up" to the market mix. In turn, pressure would be placed on the prices of some asset classes, leading to a new situation closer to that required for market clearing. Eventually, prices adjust until the *equilibrium condition* specified above obtains. [22]

For the market mix to be optimal for an investor with a risk tolerance of τ there must be a special relationship among (1) asset risks and correlations and (2) asset expected returns. Given a set of risk and correlation estimates, it is possible to find a set of expected returns that make the market mix optimal for risk tolerance τ. These returns may be considered *equilibrium expected returns.* [23]

Societal Risk Tolerance

If societal risk tolerance is assumed to be constant over time, it can be estimated using the long-run average excess return on the market mix as a surrogate for $E(R_M) - r$ and the long-run variance as a surrogate for $S(R_M)^2$. Since:

---

[22] This holds as long as either (1) short positions in asset classes are possible or (2) investors do not differ substantially in risk tolerance.

[23] The required set of expected returns is given by:

$$E(R_i) = r + \frac{2 \sum_j C_{ij}}{\tau}$$

where i and j indicate asset classes and C_{ij} is the covariance between classes i and j.

$$\frac{E(R_M) - r}{S(R_M)^2} = \frac{2}{\tau}$$

then:

$$\tau = \frac{2S(R_M)^2}{E(R_M) - r}$$

For example, over the past 50 or 60 years, the excess return on the U.S. mix (over short-term Treasury bills) has averaged approximately 4 percent per year with a standard deviation of approximately 10 percent per year. Substituting these numbers in the formula gives:

$$\tau = \frac{2 \times 10^2}{4} = \frac{200}{4} = 50$$

While this sort of approach may be acceptable for strategic asset allocation studies, it can be improved upon for dynamic strategies. An increasing body of evidence indicates societal risk tolerance changes over time.[24] When investors obtain better-than-expected performance, τ tends to rise; when they obtain poorer-than-expected performance, it tends to fall. By incorporating such effects in continuing asset allocation analyses, estimates of expected returns can be improved significantly.

Asset Alphas

Equilibrium expected returns of the type derived in the manner described earlier can reflect the views of the "typical" investor.[25] While they may be formally viewed as expected returns, it is more instructive to consider them *net expected returns* in the sense suggested by Ibbotson, Diermeier, and Siegel [1984]. To the extent that investors (on average) like some non-return aspect of an asset class, they may evaluate it on the basis of its true expected return plus a premium. If they dislike some aspect, they may evaluate it on the basis of its true expected return minus a penalty.

As an example of a penalty, true expected returns may be reduced to reflect relative degrees of illiquidity. For example, if the true expected returns for large- and small-capitalization stocks are, respectively, 12 percent and 15 percent, then investors may act as if the expected returns were 11.5 percent and 13 percent instead. It is these latter numbers that are obtained

---

[24] For evidence that can be interpreted as consistent with this assertion, see Grossman and Shiller [1981], Poterba and Summers [1988], and Fama and French [1987].

[25] In this context, "typical" refers to a value-weighted average of investors' tastes.

when equilibrium expected returns are inferred from current holdings (i.e., the market mix) in the manner described earlier.

If an investor's views concerning such "other" aspects (i.e., other than risk) are similar to those of the typical investor, the expected returns obtained in this way can be used "as is." If, however, such is not the case, appropriate alterations should be made. For example, illiquidity may be of no concern to a long-term investor. If so, 12 percent and 15 percent are better estimates than 11.5 percent and 13.5 percent in the previous example.

Such alterations can be accomplished by choosing *asset alphas*. The investor sets the expected return for asset class *i* equal to:

$$E(R_i) = E(R_i)^c + \alpha_i$$

where:

$E(R_i)^c$ = the consensus (equilibrium) expected return
α_i = the investor's chosen adjustment to $E(R_i)^c$

Some investors assign asset alphas that remain the same from month to month. Doing so may reflect a permanent difference of *circumstance* between the investor and the typical investor, as in the previous example, or it may represent a permanent difference of *opinion* concerning asset class (or manager) performance. In the latter case the investor can be considered to be making a permanent *bet* against the market (i.e., other investors). For example, an investor who believes that others continually underestimate the prospects for foreign stocks may assign a positive alpha to the corresponding asset class at all times.

Many investors explicitly or implicitly adopt values of asset alphas that vary over time. Such choices typically reflect opinions that markets are "out of line" from time to time. Asset classes that appear to be underpriced are assigned positive alphas; those that appear to be overpriced are assigned negative alphas. Those that appear to be priced correctly are assigned zero alphas. Investors using alphas in this manner can be said to have *deviant beliefs* and to be undertaking *active asset allocation*. As in other areas in which people bet against one another, those who make good bets are rewarded while those who do not are punished.

SELECTION TECHNIQUES

Linear Programming Approaches

Many business problems can be solved using a technique known as *linear programming*. A linear programming problem consists of an objective function that is to be either maximized or minimized subject to a set of relevant constraints, at least some of which involve upper or lower limits on variables or combinations of variables.[26]

A problem can be solved by linear programming methods as long as (1) the objective to be maximized or minimized is a linear function of the decision variables; (2) each constraint requires that a linear function of the decision variables be (a) less than or equal, (b) greater than or equal, or (c) exactly equal to a constant; and (3) at least one constraint (explicit or implicit) involves an inequality (i.e., uses a $\geq$ or $\leq$ sign).

Linear programming approaches are sometimes employed in conjunction with scenario methods to find optimal asset allocations. This use arises naturally, because the return of an asset mix for any given scenario is a linear function of the proportions of the overall fund invested in the various asset classes.

For example, an investor may wish to maximize return in a "growth" scenario subject to a constraint that return be at least 5 percent in every other possible scenario. Alternatively, an investor may wish to maximize the minimum outcome. Such a *maximin* strategy is designed to provide the best possible "floor" on overall return (regardless of any upside potential lost). Note that neither of these approaches requires the assignment of probabilities to the various scenarios.

Other linear programming approaches do use probability assessments. Because the expected return of an asset mix is a linear function of the proportions invested in the various asset classes, it may be included either as an objective function (to be maximized) or as a constraint (to guarantee a specified minimum value). Thus, for example, a linear programming procedure may be used to find the asset mix that provides the maximum possible expected return, subject to the constraint that return exceed a specified floor in every scenario.

The results obtained with any optimization procedure are only as good

---

[26] One way of writing such a problem is the following:

Maximize $c_1X_1 + c_2X_2 + \cdots + c_NX_N$

Subject to:

$$a_{11}X_1 + a_{12}X_2 + \cdots + a_{1N}X_N \leq b_1$$
$$a_{21}X_1 + a_{22}X_2 + \cdots + a_{2N}X_N \leq b_2$$
$$\cdots$$
$$a_{M1}X_1 + a_{M2}X_2 + \cdots + a_{MN}X_N \leq b_M$$

Simple transformations can be made to cover cases in which the *objective function* $(c_1X_1 + c_2X_2 + \cdots + c_NX_N)$ is to be minimized rather than maximized, and in which one or more *constraints* uses a greater than or equal to ($\geq$) or equal to ($=$) sign instead of a less than or equal to ($\leq$) sign. Usually, all the *decision variables* $(X_1, X_2, \ldots, X_N)$ are implicitly constrained to have nonnegative values.

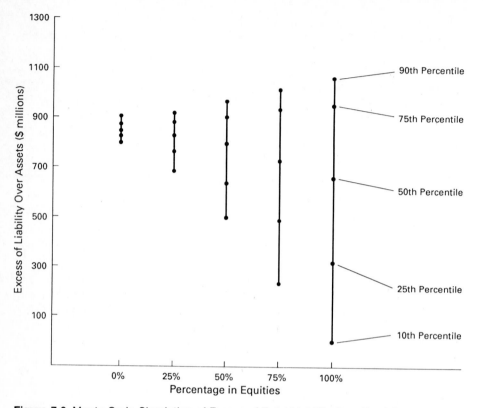

Figure 7-9. Monte Carlo Simulation of Excess of Total Liability Over Total Assets for a Defined Benefit Pension Plan in the Tenth Year, Assuming Various Percentage Exposures to Equities. SOURCE: McLaughlin [1975].

as the inputs used. As indicated earlier, scenario approaches are subject to certain limitations. In fact, a linear programming analysis of scenario-based predictions can often be used to identify any problems implicit in a set of scenario estimates.

Monte Carlo Simulation

Because most predictions of asset returns involve probability assessments, it is possible to derive the implied probabilities associated with various outcomes if a particular asset mix (or series of asset mixes) is chosen. Repeating the analysis can provide an investor with information concerning likely results for a set of alternative investment strategies. The investor can then choose from these alternatives the one he or she prefers.

Figure 7-9 shows a typical set of results from such an analysis. Five different stock/bond mixes were analyzed. For each one, the *probability distribution* of the excess of pension liability over assets 10 years hence was estimated, taking into account likely investment results, the effects of actuarial funding requirements, and the like. This excess of pension liability over assets corresponds to a *pension deficit*—that is, a negative pension surplus. In the figure, five *percentile* values are shown for each asset allocation. For example, if the entire fund is invested in equities, there is a 90 percent chance that the actual deficit will be less than $1.1 billion, a 75 percent chance that it will be less than $950 million, and so forth. Note how the range of values shrinks nonsymmetrically as the percentage invested in equities declines from 100 percent to zero percent.

Three questions arise in connection with such an approach. First, what outcomes should be presented? Second, which asset mixes (or strategies for changing asset mixes over time) should be analyzed? Third, what procedures should be used to determine the probabilities that various outcomes will be obtained with a specified asset mix or strategy?

Ultimately, the first question must be answered on the basis of the investor's needs and his or her ability to relate to characterizations of various investment outcomes. The second question is equally difficult. Because relatively few asset mixes can be analyzed in such an approach, it is essential that good ones not be missed. Often an explicit optimization method (e.g., linear or quadratic programming) is first used to select a few efficient mixes (i.e., mixes that provide the maximum expected outcome for a given level of risk). These mixes are then subjected to detailed analysis of this type.

The third issue is more amenable to formal procedures. In most cases, results many periods in the future are of interest. Such *projection* requires the analysis of repeated "draws" from a set of probability distributions. In some cases the distributions are assumed to remain the same from period to period; in others, they are assumed to change in a prespecified manner. In some analyses, the asset mix associated with a given strategy is assumed to remain constant (usually in percentage terms). In others, decision rules are provided to indicate the manner in which the asset mix is to change with relevant outcomes.

In some simple cases, *analytic* methods (i.e., formulas) can be used to make such projections. For example, if (1) a constant asset mix (by relative value) is assumed to be maintained, (2) the joint probability distribution of asset returns is assumed to remain constant, (3) returns in one period are assumed to be uncorrelated with those in preceding periods, and (4) no money is to be withdrawn from or added to the fund over the projection period, the end-of-period value may be readily approximated analytically.[27]

While analytic formulas are widely used for projecting long-term results

---

[27] Under these conditions V_P, the value at the end of P periods, is related to

from various types of asset allocation, they can be applied only in relatively simple cases. If changing probability distributions and/or more realistic decision rules are to be assessed, Monte Carlo procedures are required.

The Monte Carlo Approach. A Monte Carlo analysis involves "spinning the wheel" to simulate the results obtained when values are determined probabilistically. For example, assume that monthly stock returns are assumed to follow a normal distribution with an expected return of one percent (per month) and a standard deviation of 4 percent (per month), while one-month Treasury bill rates are assumed to remain constant at 0.5 percent (per month). How much will a $100 investment today be worth in five years if a strategy of rebalancing the mix every 12 months, to make stock and bill components equal in value, is followed?

---

the returns in each of the periods as follows:

$$V_P = (1 + r_1)(1 + r_2) \ldots (1 + r_P)$$

Taking the logarithm of both sides:

$$\ln(V_P) = \ln[(1 + r_1)(1 + r_2) \ldots (1 + r_P)]$$

or:

$$\ln(V_P) = \ln(1 + r_1) + \ln(1 + r_2) + \cdots + \ln(1 + r_P)$$

As long as returns are uncorrelated from period to period, the law of large numbers insures that the distribution of the sum on the right-hand side approaches normality as P gets larger and larger. If, further, each return is drawn from the same distribution:

$$E[\ln(V_P)] = P \times E[\ln(1 + r)]$$

and:

$$\text{Var}[\ln(V_P)] = P \times \text{Var}[\ln(1 + r)]$$

where $E[\ln(1 + r)]$ and $\text{Var}[\ln(1 + r)]$ are the expected value and variance, respectively, of $\ln(1 + r)$.

To utilize such a calculation, the expected value and variance of the logarithm of one-period return must be estimated. This is easily done using standard relationships between the (1) expected return and standard deviation of r and (2) the expected return and standard deviation of $\ln(1 + r)$. For details, see Sharpe [1987c].

Note that in this formulation, the logarithm of end-of-period value is assumed to be normally distributed. Equivalently, the end-of-period value itself is *lognormally distributed*. Lognormal distributions tend to have long right-hand tails and short left-hand tails. Moreover, the longer the projection period, the more pronounced is this tendency. This characteristic of lognormal distributions makes good sense, because "downside risk" for most asset mixes is limited to an ending value of zero, while the "upside potential" can be very large if returns are compounded over a sufficiently long period.

To answer the question, a computer program is needed that includes a procedure for simulating a random draw from a normal probability distribution that, in standard statistical terms, is assumed to have a mean of zero and a standard deviation of 1.0. Using this procedure, a set of instructions can produce a possible five-year history. First, a stock return for month 1 is produced by making a random drawing from the distribution, multiplying it by 4.0 (the assumed standard deviation), and adding 1.0 (the assumed expected return). This procedure is used to determine the value of stocks at the end of month 1. The value of bills is then increased, using the assumed bill return. Next, this procedure is repeated for month 2, then month 3, and so on, up to month 12. At this point, the decision rule is invoked and any required rebalancing is performed. The simulation then continues in a similar manner until month 60 is reached. At this point *one* possible outcome (value in five years) is obtained.

The entire process is repeated many times, thereby producing numerous (e.g., 1,000) possible results. The resultant set of 1,000 ending values provides an approximate probability distribution for the aspect of interest (here, value in five years).

Changing probability distributions and complex decision rules can be analyzed relatively straightforwardly using Monte Carlo methods. The more complex the assumptions, the larger the number of simulated histories should be to assure that the set of outcomes obtained is representative.

Utility Function Evaluation

Whether Monte Carlo or analytic methods are used to determine the probability distribution of relevant outcomes associated with each of a set of selected asset mixes (or strategies), some procedure must be invoked to choose the "best" among them. One approach leaves this choice to the investor. He or she is presented with one or more representations of the alternative probability distributions, then asked to choose the preferred one.

An alternative used by several financial institutions evaluates each distribution using an assumed *utility function*. The *expected utility* of each distribution is then calculated. The preferred asset mix is the one providing the greatest expected utility.

Figure 7-10 shows a typical function of this type. Utility is plotted on the vertical axis and the outcome (here, compound return over a 10-year period) on the horizontal axis. The utility function is composed of three straight-line segments. The investor is required to specify three key variables: two threshold returns that represent levels at which the attitude toward return changes and a "risk ratio" that specifies the utility of returns below the lower threshold (numerator) to returns above the upper threshold (denominator). For returns below a floor or minimum level such as 8 percent

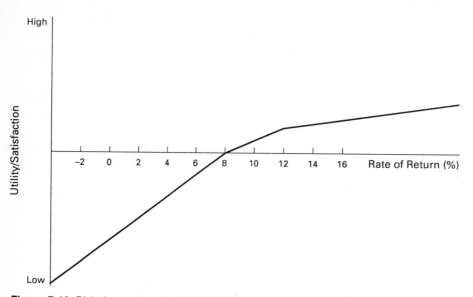

Figure 7-10. Risk Averse Investor's Utility Function. SOURCE: Wells Fargo Investment Advisors.

(e.g., the actuarially assumed rate of return for a defined benefit pension plan), utility is highly sensitive to return. For returns between 8 percent and 12 percent, it is somewhat less sensitive. For returns above 12 percent, it is even less sensitive. This decline in sensitivity reflects the assumption that while more return is always preferred, the utility added by a 100 basis point increase in return is greater when one is poor (return is low) than when one is well off (return is high).

To calculate the expected utility associated with a given probability distribution, the utility for each possible outcome is multiplied by its probability, and the results are totaled. Equivalently, *the expected utility associated with an asset mix is a weighted average of the utilities associated with the outcomes it can provide, using the associated probabilities as weights.*

Table 7-1 shows the results obtained when this method was applied to a set of predictions. In this example, stocks are assumed to have an expected return of 18.2 percent per year with a standard deviation of 18.0 percent. Bonds are assumed to have an expected return of 15.0 percent with a standard deviation of 8.0 percent. The correlation between stock and bond returns is assumed to equal +0.5.

This analysis focuses on compounded returns over a five-year period. The investor's utility function is assumed to have "kinks" at the points corresponding to a lower threshold return of 12 percent per year and an upper threshold return of 16 percent per year. Finally, the utility function

TABLE 7-1. Utility Rankings for Selected Asset Mixes, Five-Year Time Horizon

Assumptions

	Expected Return	Standard Deviation
Stocks	18.2%	18.0%
Bonds	15.0	8.0
Correlation	+0.5	

Utility function
Lower threshold: 12%
Upper threshold: 16%
Risk ratio: 5/1

Results

Asset Mix Stocks	Bonds	Mean Return	Standard Deviation	Utility Ranking
100.0%	0.0%	18.2%	7.9%	11
90.0	10.0	17.9	7.3	9
80.0	20.0	17.6	6.8	8
70.0	30.0	17.2	6.2	6
60.0	40.0	16.9	5.6	5
50.0	50.0	16.6	5.1	3
40.0	60.0	16.3	4.7	1
30.0	70.0	16.0	4.2	2
20.0	80.0	15.6	3.9	4
10.0	90.0	15.3	3.7	7
0.0	100.0	15.0	3.6	10

SOURCE: Wells Fargo Investment Advisors [1981].

is constructed so its risk ratio is 5/1; that is, the left-hand portion has a slope five times as great as that of the right-hand portion.

The table shows the relative rankings of 11 bond/stock mixes based on the calculated expected utility of each one. From this analysis, the conclusion is reached that an asset mix invested 40 percent in stocks and 60 percent in bonds is optimal for the investor in question.

Quadratic Programming Approaches

While the expected utility approach described in the previous section has many favorable attributes, it suffers from two limitations. First, a utility function represented by three straight-line segments of different slopes is somewhat crude—a smooth curve with ever-decreasing slope appears to capture better the typical investor's attitudes concerning investment results.

Second, only a limited number of asset mixes or strategies can be evaluated using such a procedure. A method that could (in principle) identify the very best (highest expected utility) mix of all is preferable.

These objectives can be readily met. The idea is to focus on "one-period" (e.g., monthly) return, on the grounds that sensible selection of an optimal asset mix *each* period can lead to a preferred set of such mixes over many periods. Although interactions between returns in adjacent periods, transaction costs, and the like make it impossible to argue formally that such a "one step at a time" approach guarantees a fully optimal multiperiod strategy, this approach appears to be a pragmatic one to an essentially intractable problem.[28]

If it is assumed that one-period returns are normally distributed and an investor's utility function can be represented by a particular type of smooth curve, the expected utility of an asset mix is, in fact, equal to that shown earlier in this chapter:[29]

$$U_{Mk} = E(R_M) - \frac{\sigma(R_M)^2}{t_k}$$

where:

U_{Mk} = the expected utility of mix M for investor k
$E(R_M)$ = the expected return for mix M
$\sigma(R_M)^2$ = the variance (standard deviation squared) for mix M
t_k = investor k's risk tolerance

As noted earlier, expected utility is equivalent to the expected return of the mix minus a risk penalty. The risk penalty is, in turn, equal to the risk (expressed as variance) of the asset mix divided by the investor's risk tolerance. This view leads some to interpret U_{Mk} as a *risk-adjusted expected return*.[30]

Consider an asset mix with an expected return of 12 percent and a standard deviation of 10 percent. For an investor with a risk tolerance of 50:

$$U_{Mk} = 12 - \frac{100}{50}$$

$$= 10$$

---

[28] While a multiperiod problem can be formalized as one of dynamic programming, actual solutions are well beyond present capabilities.

[29] For details, see the appendix in Sharpe [1987b].

[30] Risk-adjusted expected return, an *ex ante* measure, should not be confused with *ex post* measures of risk-adjusted return used in performance measurement.

For this investor the mix has an expected utility of 10 percent, equal to its expected return (12 percent) less a penalty of 2 percent, reflecting both the magnitude of risk involved and the investor's current tolerance for bearing such risk.

Such an asset mix is as desirable for this investor as one offering 10 percent for certain. To see this, apply the formula to such a "sure thing":

$$U_{Mk} = 10 - \frac{0}{50}$$

which also equals 10 percent. This latter view leads some to interpret U_{Mk} as a *certainty-equivalent return.*

Whether U_{Mk} is called expected utility, risk adjusted expected return, or certainty equivalent return, finding the mix that provides the maximum possible value at any given time is relatively straightforward. Doing so involves solving a *quadratic programming problem.*

Like linear programming problems, quadratic programming problems involve linear constraints, at least one of which must be represented by an inequality sign. The difference lies in the objective function. In a quadratic programming problem, the objective is to maximize or minimize a *quadratic function* of one or more of the decision variables (i.e., a function involving terms in which a variable value is squared and/or the product of two of the variables is required). This situation arises naturally in asset allocation problems, because the risk of an asset mix is, in fact, related in this manner to its composition (i.e., the variance of a portfolio is the sum of terms involving the products of portfolio weights in pairs of assets).

Here, the goal is to maximize:

$$U_{Mk} = E(R_M) - \frac{\sigma(R_M)^2}{t_k}$$

But, as shown earlier:

$$\sigma(R_M)^2 = \sum_{i=1,n} \sum_{j=1,n} X_i X_j \rho_{ij} \sigma_i \sigma_j$$

and:

$$E(R_M) = \sum_{i=1,n} X_i E_i$$

Because U_{Mk} involves terms with both X_i and $X_i X_j$ values, it is a quadratic function of the decision variables (the X_i values).

The objective function in such an optimization is U_{Mk}. Constraints on asset holdings may be implicit (e.g., all values of X_i greater than or equal to zero) or explicit (e.g., X_1 no less than 0.05 and no greater than 0.25). The X_i values must also be constrained to sum to 1.0. In addition, other limitations may be imposed and transaction costs may be included.

A number of algorithms have been developed to solve problems of this type. One used in many software packages designed for asset allocation is described in Sharpe [1987a].

Quadratic programming approaches are widely used for asset allocation. Unlike most other approaches, they can deal effectively with the fact that risk depends on *interactions* among security holdings.

DYNAMIC STRATEGIES

Dynamic and Strategic Approaches to Asset Allocation

In principle, a *dynamic strategy* can be formulated as a decision rule that indicates precisely how an asset mix is to be altered as a function of relevant outcomes. Many "policy studies" designed to determine a "strategic asset mix" implicitly evaluate alternative dynamic strategies. For example, a "60/40" stock/bond mix strategy requires that stocks be sold whenever their relative value exceeds 60 percent of the value of the total fund and be purchased whenever their relative value falls below 60 percent.

In practice, however, the term *dynamic asset allocation* strategy is generally reserved for an approach that involves major changes designed to alter the relative values of various asset classes as market conditions and/or investor circumstances change.

A dynamic approach to asset allocation may be based on changes in investor risk tolerance, changes in capital market conditions, or both.

Changes in Investor Risk Tolerance

A particularly popular form of dynamic asset allocation in the mid-1980s was that termed *portfolio insurance*. As indicated earlier, such procedures were designed to respond to assumed changes in investor risk tolerance brought about by changes in the overall value of an "insured portfolio." Often this portfolio consisted of just one asset class. However, the procedure can be applied to "insure" the value of an asset mix (or, for that matter, a pension surplus). The key idea involves dynamic allocation between (1) a risky asset mix and (2) a riskless one, where risk is measured in terms of the aspect of interest (e.g., asset value or surplus value).

The earliest forms of portfolio insurance involved dynamic changes in asset allocation designed to replicate effects obtainable with certain option positions. For example, a program could be designed to replicate the outcomes obtained by holding a portfolio of risky assets plus a one-year put option written on that portfolio. Equivalently, a program could replicate the outcomes obtained by holding a one-year Treasury bill plus a one-year call option on the risky portfolio. Both strategies are described in detail in Chapter 11, In either case, the striking price of the option—the guaranteed price at which the option holder can buy or sell the underlying security—represents a *floor* below which the value of the investor's assets at the specified horizon date should not fall. Such an approach can be termed *option-based portfolio insurance*.

Early option-based portfolio insurance strategies required the amount invested in the risky asset portfolio to be a function of both the current value of the asset *cushion* (i.e., value above the floor) and the time remaining before a specified *horizon* (i.e., the option's expiration date). As the horizon date approached, the investment position became more and more concentrated until all the assets were invested in either the risky portfolio or the riskless asset, depending on whether assets were above the floor or on it.

Since the optimal mix of risky and riskless positions depends on the time left before the horizon is reached, option-based portfolio insurance strategies are *time variant*. Many clients objected to this feature. In particular, such a characteristic seems inappropriate for an ongoing pension fund with a very long (or infinite) horizon.

In the late 1980s, attention turned to *time-invariant* approaches to portfolio insurance. With such a procedure no horizon date is specified, so the asset mix is not a function of time per se.

An important example of a time-invariant approach is *constant proportion portfolio insurance* (CPPI).[31] CPPI uses a simple rule of the type shown in Figure 7-11: The dollar amount invested in the risky asset mix should equal a constant times the size of the cushion (asset value minus floor value), with the constant having a value greater than 1.0.

For example, assuming that all values are in millions of U.S. dollars, an investor with assets currently worth 100 might specify a floor of 80. Thus, at present the cushion is 20. The CPPI strategy may call for an amount equal to 3 times the cushion to be placed in stocks, with the remainder invested in Treasury bills. At present, then, 60 (3 times 20) is invested in stocks and 40 (100 minus 60) in Treasury bills. If the value of the mix rises to 110, the stock portion is increased to 90 (3 times the new cushion of 30). If the value falls to 90, the stock portion is decreased to 30 (3 times the new cushion of 10). And if the value falls to 80, the entire amount is placed in Treasury bills (because the formula calls for a stock portion equal to 3 times the cushion of zero).

---

[31] For details, see Black and Jones [1987]. The foundation on which the approach is based was provided in Merton [1971]. An excellent description with important extensions is provided in Perold [1986].

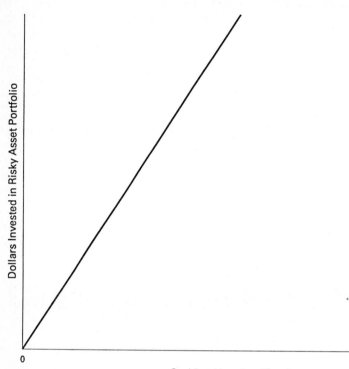

Figure 7-11. Risky Asset Investment in a Constant Proportion Insured Portfolio as the Cushion Changes.

While portfolio insurance strategies are normally *analyzed* in terms of a relationship such as that shown in Figure 7-11, they are *motivated* by a relationship of the type shown in Figure 7-12. As before, the horizontal axis plots the level of the asset cushion, but the vertical axis now indicates the investor's *risk tolerance*—defined earlier as his or her willingness to take on added risk to obtain added expected return. Risk tolerance is zero when assets reach the minimum value at which the floor can be assured. As asset value increases, so does the investor's risk tolerance. This process of adjustment forms the *risk tolerance function* in the diagram for insured asset allocation shown in Figure 7-12. As the value of the investor's assets changes, his or her risk tolerance changes accordingly. As this information is processed (e.g., by an optimizer using a quadratic programming approach), the asset mix changes in the manner shown in Figure 7-11.[32]

Different portfolio insurance approaches imply different relationships of the type shown in Figure 7-12. Some are time variant; some are not. Some

----

[32] For details, see Sharpe [1987b].

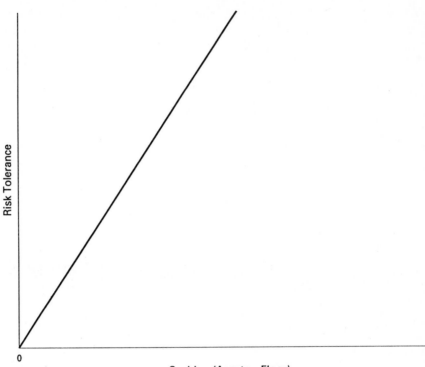

Figure 7-12. Risk Tolerance in a Constant Proportion Insured Portfolio as the Cushion Changes.

give linear relationships; some do not. However, all can be viewed as implicit specifications of the investor's *risk tolerance function*. For details of some of these relationships, see Perold and Sharpe [1988].

Changes in Market Conditions: Tactical Allocation

A very different type of dynamic asset allocation strategy is that usually termed *tactical asset allocation*. As indicated earlier, it responds to changes in estimated capital market conditions rather than variations in investor risk tolerance. In fact, formal procedures for tactical asset allocation usually assume that the investor's risk tolerance remains constant over time.

Tactical asset allocation procedures tend to focus on relatively few assets. Early versions were "two-way"—moving funds between either stocks and bills or stocks and bonds. Most tactical asset allocation procedures are now at least "three-way"—using stocks, bonds, and bills—although some include as many as 10 asset classes.

In practice, most attention is given to estimating expected returns. While yield-to-maturity may be used as a proxy for the expected return on bonds, and the current yield on bills for the expected return on short-term investments, detailed processing of analysts' predictions of future earnings and dividends is typically used to estimate the expected return on stocks.

Analysts usually forecast a stock's dividends and earnings over the next two years, then estimate payout ratios and earnings growth over some subsequent period. By combining such estimates with an assumption about long-term growth, it is possible to determine an *internal rate of return* for a security, given its current price. For example, assume that dividends have been projected for five years (D_1, D_2, D_3, D_4, D_5), along with earnings in year 5 (E_5), and a "normal" price/earnings ratio expected to hold in year 5 (*PEN*). If today's price is P_0, then the internal rate of return is the value of r that satisfies the following equation:

$$P_0 = \frac{D_1}{(1 + r)} + \frac{D_2}{(1 + r)^2} + \frac{D_3}{(1 + r)^3} + \frac{D_4}{(1 + r)^4} + \frac{D_5}{(1 + r)^5} + \frac{E_5 \times PEN}{(1 + r)^5}$$

The resultant internal rate of return can be used as a proxy for the stock's expected return. By repeating the process for many stocks (e.g., all those in Standard and Poor's 500 stock index), then taking a value-weighted average of the resulting expected returns, the expected return on stocks as a whole can be estimated.

Several tactical asset allocators use this type of "bottom-up" approach to determine the expected return on stocks. Others approach the task "top-down," treating a stock index as if it were a single stock. Aggregate dividends and/or earnings are estimated, then combined with the current aggregate value of the stocks in the index to find the overall internal rate of return.

Predictions made by analysts in brokerage firms are typically used for near-term dividends and/or earnings, with the tactical asset allocation organization estimating long-term conditions (e.g., "normal" price/earnings ratios five years hence). In practice, the latter estimates are usually changed relatively infrequently.

While in theory there is no reason for procedures of this type to produce expected returns that vary in any simple way with market prices, experience shows that there is an inverse relationship. The predictions of dividends, earnings, and long-term relationships used to compute the internal rates of return typically move in the same direction as security prices, but such changes tend to be slow and smaller in magnitude than actual changes in prices. The net result is a tendency for expected returns to increase when prices fall and to decrease when prices rise. This in turn leads to a strong tendency for *contrarian behavior*—that is, buying stocks after market declines and selling them after market rises—when the resulting predictions are used for asset allocation.

Many tactical asset allocators assume that asset risks and correlations change seldom, if at all. Almost all the "action" is caused by changes in the spreads between expected returns on the included asset classes.

Some tactical asset allocation procedures of this type have provided superior risk-adjusted returns.[33] These superior returns may have resulted from an ability to identify and exploit periods when relative returns on asset classes were "out of line." If so, more investors can be expected to adopt such approaches. As they do, the efficacy of the procedures can be expected to diminish. However, there are reasons (discussed in the next section) to believe that at least some of the superior performance obtained by these procedures may continue into the future.

Individual vs. Societal Risk Tolerance

In a fully integrated dynamic asset allocation strategy, changes in both capital market conditions and investor risk tolerances are taken into account. While many aspects affect the overall result, a key determinant concerns the relationship between the investor's risk tolerance and that of the society as a whole.

The point can best be seen in a simple context in which an investor is choosing between the "market mix" and a riskless security. As shown earlier, in such a situation, the optimal proportion for the investor to place in the market mix is:

$$X = \frac{E(R_M) - r}{2S(R_M)^2} \times t$$

where t is the investor's current risk tolerance.

For there to be equilibrium in the capital markets, the premium per unit of variance must be related to the societal risk tolerance in the manner shown earlier:

$$\frac{E(R_M) - r}{S(R_M)^2} = \frac{2}{\tau}$$

where τ is the current level of societal risk tolerance. Combining these two equations and simplifying gives:

$$X = \frac{t}{\tau}$$

The optimal level of aggressiveness thus depends on the investor's risk

---

[33] See, e.g., Evnine and Henriksson [1987].

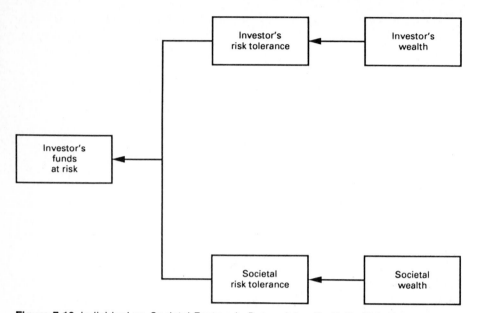

Figure 7-13. Individual vs. Societal Factors in Determining Portfolio Risk Exposure.

tolerance (t) relative to that of the society as a whole (τ). The investor's risk tolerance generally depends on the level of a measure of wealth that is relevant to him or her (e.g., personal wealth, pension surplus, and the like). As described earlier, societal risk tolerance depends significantly on the level of wealth of investors as a whole. Figure 7-13 summarizes all these relationships.

In this context, under what conditions should an investor "buy and hold"? One case clearly calls for such a policy: If the investor holds the market mix and has a risk tolerance function that is precisely equal to that of the society as a whole (i.e., the average investor), full investment in the market mix continues to be the optimal strategy and no changes are required. There are other cases, but they involve improbable combinations of changes in the key components shown in the diagram.

Under what conditions should an investor buy portfolio insurance— that is, place *less* funds "at risk" as his or her wealth falls? A clear case arises when the investor's risk tolerance is more sensitive to wealth than is that of the average investor and the investor's wealth moves as much or more as does that of the market as a whole when values change. Most cases are not this clear, however, and the situation must be reassessed at each portfolio review.

Under what conditions should an investor act in a contrarian manner— that is, place *more* funds at risk when the market falls? A clear case arises when the investor's risk tolerance is constant, no matter what happens to his or her wealth. Recall that societal risk tolerance moves significantly with the level of the overall market, and in the same direction. For example, as wealth falls, the average investor becomes less tolerant of risk, causing the risk premium to rise. After a market fall, then, an investor with constant risk tolerance should take more risk to take advantage of the resulting higher risk premium. In terms of the formula: With t unchanged, X increases as τ falls.

These interrelations show why tactical asset allocation strategies may produce superior risk-adjusted returns in the future, even after their characteristics become more widely known. An investor with constant risk tolerance is abnormal. He or she is just as willing to bear risk when others are least willing to do so as when they are most willing to do so. When times are bad (e.g., after the market has fallen severely, lowering average wealth positions), "normal" investors are willing to pay the tactical asset allocator well (via a high risk premium) to bear a disproportionate amount of the total risk to be borne. When times are good (e.g., after a sustained bull market), normal investors are not willing to pay very much in terms of the market risk premium. The tactical asset allocator thus performs a valuable social service—bearing more risk in bad times and less in good times—for which he or she can expect to be rewarded over the long run.[34]

Even in a highly simplified setting the nature of an optimal dynamic strategy is not simple. In a more realistic analysis taking into account multiple asset classes, transaction costs, and so forth, the relationships become even more complex. Thus, it is crucial to integrate as many aspects as possible in the overall process used for asset allocation.

IMPLEMENTATION: THEORY VS. REALITY

As the preceding sections indicate, successful asset allocation is difficult in theory. In practice, it is even harder. To implement it efficiently, several important aspects of reality must be confronted.

---

[34] Tactical asset allocation procedures do not operate in only this manner. In practice, such approaches have a tendency to operate as if the investor's risk tolerance actually increases when the market falls, leading to an even more "contrarian" type of behavior. This tendency results from the failure to estimate adequately changes in market risk. When markets fall, they tend to do so rapidly. Thus, after a major market fall, both risk and the risk premium tend to increase. Tactical procedures that ignore the increase in risk react more than those that incorporate it in the analysis. The resulting tactical asset allocation is thus similar to that obtained if the increased risk is taken into account and risk tolerance increased.

Balancing Costs and Benefits

The asset mix that provides the maximum utility for an investor typically differs from that currently held. The reallocation of assets needed to obtain the new mix typically incurs *transaction costs*—both explicit (e.g., brokerage commissions) and implicit (via any impacts on prices when trades are made). Clearly, it is foolish to make a change if the benefits do not exceed these costs.

The trade-off is not easily measured. A better asset mix can offer improved expected utility over many periods, but transaction costs are incurred only when changes are made. To compare a change in expected utility (expressed in terms of percentage return per period) with a transaction cost (expressed frequently in terms of a percentage cost per execution), the latter must be *amortized* over some suitable likely holding period. Assume, for example, that asset mix changes are expected to remain in place for two years on average. Thus, utility must increase by at least half the transaction costs each year to provide sufficient cumulative benefit before a new transaction changes the asset mix. In such a case, 50 percent of the transaction costs can be deducted from U_{Mk} to obtain a measure of *net expected utility*.

Procedures for maximizing such a measure of utility net of amortized transaction costs are included in some commercially available asset allocation programs.[35] Such methods recommend changes only up to the point at which the marginal benefit (in increased utility) falls below the marginal cost (in added amortized transaction costs). Chapter 12 discusses transaction costs in considerable detail, and Chapter 13 discusses the marginal cost versus marginal benefit of rebalancing a portfolio.

Rapidly Changing Market Conditions

Most asset allocation analyses make assumptions about both present and future market conditions. For some procedures, the accuracy of such predictions can be crucial. For others, it is of less importance.

In this context, a particularly important case is that of portfolio insurance. If a specified floor on value is to be insured, it is crucial that risky assets can be sold in time and at appropriate prices as the market falls. Insurance procedures designed to replicate option positions depend heavily on an ability to make such trades. Indeed, most of the early portfolio insurance models assumed that markets would move smoothly from one level to another, and that trades could be made with little or no price impact at any point along those smooth paths.

---

[35] For an algorithm designed to deal with transaction costs, see Sharpe [1987a]. For an implementation and further discussion of this procedure, see Sharpe [1987c].

The October 1987 Crash. The Black Monday (October 19, 1987) stock market crash showed that reality can be wildly inconsistent with such an assumption. Prices moved suddenly and by large amounts, making it impossible to execute trades in the manner called for by some of the strategies. Moreover, many stocks did not trade at all for more than an hour at a time, making even the current level of "the market" subject to great uncertainty. Under such conditions, some portfolio insurers assumed that the rapidly falling prices of stock index futures best represented the true level of the market, while others assumed that the lagging indexes based on prior prices of individual stocks did so. The former approach sold more risky assets than did the latter, thereby (in the particular instance) coming closer to their goal of insuring specific floor values.

Investors with "real time" systems are, of course, able to react more quickly than those with less frequent review periods. When markets move rapidly and frantically in ways that fail to conform to the assumptions of the model used, rapid reaction may prove especially valuable. During the events of October 1987, this appears to have been the case.

Some have estimated that in early October 1987 between $60 and $80 billion U.S. dollars were invested using mechanized portfolio insurance strategies, while only $15 to $20 billion were invested using mechanized tactical asset allocation strategies. Because the latter tend to be natural trading partners for the former, this disparity left an "overhang" or imbalance of $40 to $65 billion poised to sell into a falling market. The presence of this force, with its potential for at least temporarily exacerbating any market decline, should have led those following such strategies to modify their models of market dynamics. Apparently few did.

In the months immediately following October 1987, the forces of equilibrium functioned well. The amount of money invested using portfolio insurance techniques fell, while that invested following tactical asset allocation methods increased. In late 1989, the two dynamic strategies appeared to be of roughly equal importance.

This traumatic experience points to the importance of carefully assessing not only the current risks and expected returns of various asset classes but also the ways in which those risks and returns can change. It is also important to remember that if a strategy becomes sufficiently popular, that strategy may affect the very process that it is intended to exploit. In effect, the actors can become part of the drama.

Determining an Effective Asset Mix

As indicated earlier, an investor's *effective asset mix* can be described by the sensitivities of the returns on his or her fund to returns on major asset classes. Using the previous notation:

$$R_M = b_{M1}R_{a1} + b_{M2}R_{a2} + \cdots + b_{Mf}R_{af} + e_M$$

where:

R_M = the return on the asset mix
b_{M1} = the sensitivity of the mix's return to the return on asset class 1
b_{M2} = the sensitivity of the mix's return to the return on asset class 2
$\vdots$

b_{Mf} = the sensitivity of the mix's return to the return on asset class f
R_{a1} = the return on asset class 1
R_{a2} = the return on asset class 2
$\vdots$

R_{af} = the return on asset class f
e_M = the component of return not due to asset allocation

When multiple managers are employed, the sensitivity of the overall fund to an asset class is a weighted average of the corresponding values for the managers' portfolios:

$$b_{Mk} = \sum_j X_j b_{jk}$$

where:

b_{Mk} = the sensitivity of the fund's return to the return on asset k
X_j = the proportion of the fund invested by manager j
b_{jk} = the sensitivity of manager j's return to the return on asset k

Note that the b_{jk} values for a given manager (j) represent his or her effective asset mix. Thus, the exposure of the overall mix to an asset class (b_{Mk}) depends on the exposure of each of the managers to that class (b_{1k}, b_{2k}, . . .) and the relative amounts of money invested by each manager (X_1, X_2, . . .).

To find the effective asset mix of a *fund* (b_{M1}, b_{M2}, . . . , b_{Mf}), the effective asset mix of each of its managers (b_{j1}, b_{j2}, . . . , b_{jf}) must be estimated.

Regression Approach. One possible method to help determine the effective asset mix of each manager uses multiple regression analysis. The goal is to find values of b_{j1}, b_{j2}, . . . , b_{jf} that "best explain" a given manager's actual returns over time. More precisely, assume that the manager's historic returns period by period (e.g., monthly) are summarized as shown in the following table.

Period	Manager Return R_j	Asset Class 1 Return R_{a1}	Asset Class 2 Return R_{a2}	...	Asset Class f Return R_{af}
1					
2					
⋮					

The goal is to "fit" the following equation to the data:

$$R_j = b_{j1}R_{a1} + b_{j2}R_{a2} + \cdots + b_{jf}R_{af} + e_j$$

Multiple regression procedures can do this. The manager's returns become the dependent variable (R_j) and the asset class returns become the f independent variables $(R_{a1}, R_{a2}, \ldots, R_{af})$, with each period's values forming one observation. By design, such a procedure finds the set of regression coefficients $(b_{j1}, b_{j2}, \ldots, b_{jf})$ that minimize the variance of the residual (e_j).

While seemingly ideal in principle, such an approach does not appear to be particularly efficient in practice. The b_{jk} values obtained often turn out to be extreme (e.g., much greater than 1.0 or significantly negative). Because a value greater than 1.0 corresponds to an investment of more than 100 percent of the manager's funds in an asset class (e.g., via margined positions), this value may be inappropriate. Similarly, because a negative value corresponds to a negative holding (short position), such a value is also likely to be inappropriate. While margined or short positions are sometimes taken either explicitly or implicitly, they are considerably more rare than suggested by such results.

In this context, regression procedures apparently are too likely to respond to "noise" (unrelated events with effects that happened to coincide with particular returns on asset classes), incorrectly attributing to asset classes transitory elements of return caused by other influences. To minimize such problems and allow the true "signal" (manager asset exposures) to be obtained, constraints reflecting prior knowledge of actual investment practices can be added.

Quadratic Programming Approach. A natural procedure simply requires that all b_{jk} values be nonnegative.[36] This problem lends itself to qua-

---

[36] Formally, the objective is to minimize Var(e_j), subject to f constraints: $b_{j1} \geq 0, b_{j2} \geq 0, \ldots, b_{jf} \geq 0$.

dratic programming and can be solved using standard or specialized procedures designed for such purposes.

Experience shows that this formulation is extremely useful for determining the effective asset mix of a portfolio maintained by a typical money management organization.[37] When such estimates are aggregated across multiple managers employed by a single investor, highly accurate estimates of the overall effective asset mix can be obtained.

Reallocating Assets

Style analysis of the type described in the previous section can help determine an investor's *current* effective asset mix. Analysis of the type described in the earlier sections of this chapter can help determine the *optimal* effective asset mix. But how should the investor move from one to the other?

Two different extreme approaches may be taken. Funds can be moved from one or more active (traditional) managers to one or more other active managers. Or, funds may be moved among passive (index) funds designed to provide "pure asset plays." The next subsection discusses the first approach; the following one discusses the second. Combinations of the two are also possible; they are discussed in the section "Asset Allocation Accounts."

Allocating Assets Among Active Managers. Assume that an investor wishes to change his or her effective asset mix by transferring $100 million from value stocks to growth stocks. Assume also that the most highly growth-oriented manager is $G1$, whose effective asset mix is shown in the following table, while the most highly value-oriented manager is $V1$, whose effective asset mix is also shown below. Note that neither follows a "pure" strategy; this is not atypical. Many "growth" managers tend to favor growth stocks, but retain some exposure to movements in the value stock sector. The opposite tends to be true for many "value" managers.

Manager	Value	Growth
G1	0.25	0.75
V1	0.75	0.25

If $100 million is transferred from $V1$ to $G1$, the effective decrease in exposure to value stocks equals only $50 million, as does the effective increase in exposure to growth stocks. This result follows because the transfer

---

[37] For details, see Sharpe [1988].

removes $75 million from the value category via $V1$ and adds $25 million via $G1$, for a net decrease of $50 million. Correspondingly, the growth exposure is reduced by $25 million and increased by $75 million, providing a net increase of $50 million. Clearly, to accomplish an effective move of $100 million, a total of $200 million has to be reallocated, thereby doubling the associated transaction costs.

An even worse situation is reflected in the example for the same desired transfer shown in the following table.

Manager	Value	Growth	Small
G2	0.20	0.70	0.10
V2	0.75	0.25	0.00

Here, manager $G2$ has some exposure to small stocks. If $100 million is transferred from $V2$ to $G2$, growth stock exposure increases by $45 million ($100 million times $(0.70 - 0.25)$), value stock exposure decreases by $55 million ($100 million times $(0.20 - 0.75)$), and small stock exposure increases by $10 million ($100 million times $(0.10 - 0.00)$). To accomplish the original objective, other money must be transferred simultaneously (e.g., from a small stock manager to one with a growth stock emphasis).[38]

Yet a third problem can arise. In practice, active managers' effective asset exposures are not known with certainty. A more representative situation may be as indicated in the following table.

Manager	Value	Growth
G3	0.20 to 0.30	0.80 to 0.70
V3	0.70 to 0.80	0.30 to 0.20

If $100 million is transferred from $V3$ to $G3$, the increased exposure to growth stocks could be any amount between $40 million (if $V3$ actually had an exposure of 0.30 and $G3$ an exposure of 0.70) and $60 million (if $V3$ had an exposure of 0.20 and $G3$ an exposure of 0.80). There is thus no way to insure that an effective increase of $100 million is obtained.[39]

---

[38] In fact, to meet the original goal, a linear programming problem might have to be solved. It is entirely possible that there would be no feasible solution.

[39] This kind of situation can be exacerbated when equity managers are allowed to hold cash, but the actual amount held at any time is not known by the pension fund sponsor.

Allocating Assets Among Pure Asset Plays. All the problems illustrated in the previous section can be avoided if assets are allocated among "pure asset plays." Such a play involves either an index fund, a "basket of securities," an index futures position, or an index option as a passive means of investing in a specific asset class. Thus, if G4 and V4 represent a growth stock index fund and a value stock index fund, respectively, the situation can be summarized as shown in the following table. None of the problems described earlier need arise.

Manager	Value	Growth
G4	0.00	1.00
V4	1.00	0.00

Such an approach has an additional advantage and one potential disadvantage. Transaction costs (both commissions and price impacts) are smaller, because securities can be traded passively rather than actively. On the other hand, passive management cannot provide alpha values from superior security selection. Investors who believe that they can pick active managers able to beat their peers in this game (after costs) may be reluctant to give up the associated rewards.

Asset Allocation Accounts

An investor need not choose one or the other of the two approaches described in the previous sections. It is possible to use active managers and pure asset plays, thus obtaining the attributes of both.

The idea is simple in concept, although not quite as simple in execution. One portion of the investor's funds (e.g., 85 percent) is invested using an appropriate mix of active and passive managers. The remainder is placed in various "pure asset plays" (index funds, security baskets, futures, or options) in an *asset allocation account* (sometimes called a *shift account* or *swing account*). When a shift in overall asset allocation is desired, it is accomplished (to the extent possible) by moving funds among the pure asset plays in this account.[40] This tactic minimizes the associated costs and maximizes the likelihood that the desired shifts are in fact made.

While many subtle issues arise in connection with such a strategy, it offers the possibility that an investor can do business as usual with a sub-

---

[40] For a discussion of one group's experience with this approach, see Good [1986].

stantial part of his or her funds while still adjusting overall asset allocation effectively as market conditions and/or his or her circumstances change.

SUMMARY

Successful asset allocation requires a great deal of information, sophisticated analysis, and economical implementation. However, its overwhelming importance decrees that it be accorded the required resources. While many experts can and should provide help, the decisions in this crucial area ultimately should be made by those who have fiduciary responsibility.

During the decade of the 1980s, attention increasingly focused on the asset allocation process. New strategies and methods were developed and tested. Some were found wanting and are now little used. Others are undergoing additional testing. Yet others have become an important part of the investment processes of many organizations. Only with the close of the decade is the sorting out process with respect to strategies—such as integrated, strategic, tactical, and insured—and techniques—such as linear programming, Monte Carlo analysis, investor utility preferences, and quadratic programming—beginning to gel.

Methods used for asset allocation will change, but its central role will not. In most environments, asset allocation is the most important part of the investment decision process.

FURTHER READING

For an overall discussion of the major steps in the asset allocation process, see Sharpe [1987b]. Alternatives to the standard scenario forecasting approach for estimating return and risk can be found in Markowitz and Perold [1981] and Fong and Fabozzi [1988].

The international aspects of asset allocation are discussed in Brinson [1986], Ibbotson and Brinson [1987], Perold and Shulman [1988], and Solnik [1988].

As to asset allocation selection techniques, further elaboration on Monte Carlo techniques can be found in Sharpe [1987c]; on utility function evaluation, in Wells Fargo Investment Advisors [1981]; and on quadratic programming approaches, in Sharpe [1987b].

Discussion of constant proportion portfolio insurance is contained in Merton [1971], Black and Jones [1987], and Perold [1986].

How changing market conditions are taken into account in tactical asset allocation schemes to produce superior risk-adjusted returns is discussed in Evnine and Henriksson [1987].

Dealing with transaction costs in implementing asset allocation strategies is covered in Sharpe [1987a, 1987c]. The effectiveness of quadratic programming is discussed in Sharpe [1988]. The use of portfolio swing accounts in implementing asset allocation is discussed in Good [1986].

BIBLIOGRAPHY

Black, Fischer, and Robert Jones. "Simplifying Portfolio Insurance." *The Journal of Portfolio Management,* Fall 1987.

Brinson, Gary P. "Implementing and Managing the Asset Allocation Process—Part I," in M.D. Joehnk, ed. *Asset Allocation for Institutional Portfolios.* Seminar proceedings, Institute of Chartered Financial Analysts. Homewood, Ill.: Dow Jones-Irwin, 1986.

Brinson, Gary P., L. Randolph Hood, and Gilbert L. Beebower. "Determinants of Portfolio Performance." *Financial Analysts Journal,* July/August 1986.

Evnine, J., and R. Henriksson. "Asset Allocation and Options." *The Journal of Portfolio Management,* Fall 1987.

Fama, Eugene F., and Kenneth R. French. "Forecasting Returns on Corporate Bonds and Common Stocks." Working Paper 220, Graduate School of Business, University of Chicago, Dec. 1987.

Fong, H. Gifford, and Frank J. Fabozzi. "Asset Allocation Optimization Models," in Robert D. Arnott and Frank J. Fabozzi, eds. *Asset Allocation: A Handbook of Portfolio Policies, Strategies & Tactics.* Chicago: Probus, 1988.

Good, Walter R. "Implementing and Managing the Asset Allocation Process—Part IV," in M.D. Joehnk, ed. *Asset Allocation for Institutional Portfolios.* Seminar Proceedings, Institute of Chartered Financial Analysts. Homewood, Ill.: Dow Jones-Irwin, 1986.

Grossman, S.J., and R.J. Shiller. "The Determinants of the Variability of Stock Market Prices." *American Economic Review,* May 1981.

Ibbotson, Roger G., Jeffrey J. Diermeier, and Laurence B. Siegel. "The Demand for Capital Market Returns: A New Equilibrium Theory." *Financial Analysts Journal,* January/February 1984.

Ibbotson, Roger G., and Gary P. Brinson. *Investment Markets.* New York: McGraw-Hill Book Co., 1987.

Markowitz, Harry, and Andrē F. Perold. "Portfolio Analysis With Factors and Scenarios." *The Journal of Finance,* September 1981.

McLaughlin, Frank C. "Using Simulation to Chart the Way." *Pension World,* September 1975.

Merton, Robert C. "Optimum Consumption and Portfolio Rules in a Continuous Time Model." *Journal of Economic Theory,* June 1971.

Perold, Andrē F. "Constant Proportion Portfolio Insurance." Working paper, Harvard Business School, August 1986.

Perold, Andrē F., and William F. Sharpe. "Dynamic Strategies for Asset Allocation." *Financial Analysts Journal,* January/February 1988.

Perold, Andrē F., and Evan C. Shulman. "The Free Lunch in Currency Hedging: Implications for Investment Policy and Performance Standards." *Financial Analysts Journal,* May/June 1988.

Pfleiderer, Paul, and Sudipto Bhattacharya. "Delegated Portfolio Management." *Journal of Economic Theory,* June 1985.

Poterba, James M., and Lawrence H. Summers. "Mean Reversion in Stock Prices: Evidence and Implications." Working paper, 1988.

Rosenberg, Barr. "Institutional Investment Management With Multiple Portfolio Managers." Working Paper 65, University of California at Berkeley, Institute of Business and Economic Research, October 1977.

Sharpe, William F. "Decentralized Investment Management." *The Journal of Finance,* May 1981.

———. *Investments,* 3d ed. Englewood Cliffs, N.J.: Prentice-Hall, Inc., 1985.

———. "An Algorithm for Portfolio Improvement," in Kenneth D. Lawrence, John B. Guerard, Jr., and Gary D. Reeves. *Advances in Mathematical Programming and Financial Planning,* Vol. 1. Greenwich, Conn.: JAI Press, 1987a.

———. "Integrated Asset Allocation." *Financial Analysts Journal,* September/October 1987b.

———. *Asset Allocation Tools,* 2d ed. Redwood City, Cal.: The Scientific Press, 1987c.

———. "Determining a Fund's Effective Asset Mix." *Investment Management Review,* November/December 1988.

Solnik, Bruno. *International Investments.* Reading, Mass.: Addison-Wesley Publishing Co., 1988.

Wells Fargo Investment Advisors. *Institutional Counsel Service Newsletter,* November 1981.

CHAPTER

Portfolio Construction: Fixed Income

H. Gifford Fong

OVERVIEW

Given the establishment of an asset mix for the overall portfolio, the next problem becomes the process of selecting specific portfolios of the asset classes chosen. The emphasis is on identifying, measuring, and controlling the return and risk characteristics of the alternative portfolios available. These then can be most effectively matched to best serve the previously defined needs and objectives of the investor. In its broadest terms this is what modern portfolio management is concerned with.

Fixed-income portfolios can be considered unique in that they provide an investment asset class bridging the return and risk characteristics between cash equivalents and stocks, while offering special features not found in either of the other two. Properly constructed fixed-income portfolios can provide a wide range of return and risk characteristics. This permits a continuum of asset choice and also a potential synergistic blending of asset type—a dual dimension that makes fixed-income portfolio management both rewarding and challenging.

This chapter begins with a reveiw of the role of the fixed-income portfolio. This section includes a review of the return and risk characteristics of fixed-income securities and the portfolios that can be constructed from them. There follows a discussion of alternative portfolio strategies spanning the range from passive buy-and-hold approaches through combinations of active/passive strategies to fully active strategies. Variants of the major strategies are also discussed.

ROLES OF THE FIXED-INCOME PORTFOLIO

The fixed-income portfolio represents one of a number of asset categories that may be part of the total portfolio. Whether this category belongs in the

8-1

overall portfolio, and in what proportion, should be related to the investment objectives of the investor and investment policies commensurate with those objectives. That is, the return and risk characteristics of fixed-income portfolios should be directly related to the objectives and constraints of the investor. The problem from a bond portfolio construction standpoint is to select fixed-income assets such that the total return is the highest for a desired level of risk; or, alternatively, a specified return is achieved with the lowest level of risk.

Return and Risk Characteristics Including Time Horizon Factor

The dominant source of fixed-income portfolio return and risk arises from the effect of interest rates. Although fixed-income securities derive return from their yield (coupon payments and/or amortization of discount or premium price), for typical management time horizons of up to two years, the most important source of return and risk impact arises from the change in interest rates over the horizon or holding period. Therefore, it is not only the level of rates but the change in rates over typical management horizons that are the dominant determinants of risk and return. As the horizon lengthens, however, the reinvestment return becomes the most important return source. That is, for horizons greater than about two years, reinvestment return will replace the level and change in rates as the controlling source of risk and return.

Yield Curves. A popular indicator of the level and changes in interest rates is the yield curve for U.S. Treasury securities, where the percentage yield is plotted as a function of maturity. Any change in rates across the maturity spectrum can be observed by comparing the position and shape of the curve for different periods.

Yield curves may be used in many ways. Consider, for example, the change in rates between two points in time, as illustrated in Figure 8-1. At the starting time, a plot of Treasury bond yields versus term to maturity results in the curve labeled "Yield curve 1". The yield of a specific (not necessarily Treasury) bond at this time is shown at point A_1. At a later time, Treasury rates have moved to the new curve labeled "Yield curve 2," and the specific bond we are considering has shortened in maturity and increased in yield to point B_1. We can use this basic illustration to identify the three major and one additional minor sources of the return from this bond over the period between the two yield curves. They are:

1. The return due to the yield level as the bond moves closer to maturity from point A_1 to point B_3. That is, if there is no change in either the slope or level of the market yield curve—represented

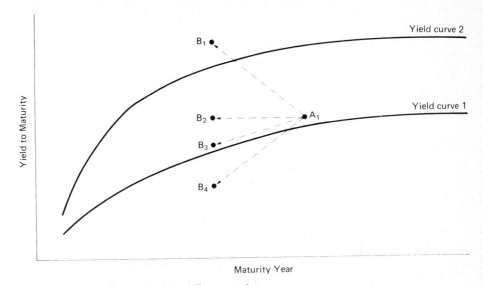

Figure 8-1. Yield Curve Analytical Framework.

by curve 1—or in the bond's valuation relative to the market, this bond will "ride the yield curve" from A_1 to B_3.

This return source has also been called the return from the impact of time because it is based on no change in interest rates and merely the effect of the passage of time.

2. The impact of changes in the slope and/or level of interest rates, such as from curve 1 to curve 2. This is illustrated by the movement from A_1 to B_1.

3. The return implied by the yield curve position when a cash flow arises for reinvestment. For example, suppose a coupon is paid at A_1. The return of position A_1 would be the reinvestment yield for that cash flow if reinvested in the same type of investment; or, if the coupon were to be held in cash equivalents, the relevant yield would be a point on the short maturity portion of yield curve 1.

4. The impact of changes in market valuation that arise from the characteristics of the bond itself. This is illustrated by the movement from A_1 to B_4 as the yield to maturity changes from a premium relative to the market—again represented by curve 1—to a discount with the consequent increase in market value relative to the market. A widening of the yield premium and the consequent lower valuation relative to the market are reflected in the movement from A_1 to B_2.

Figure 8-2 further illustrates a current and projected yield curve as of June 30, 1988. The current yield curve was obtained from a term structure analysis of outstanding Treasury securities. The projected yield curve was

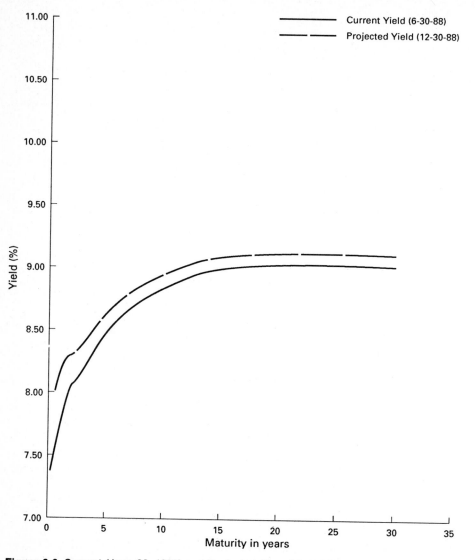

Figure 8-2. Current (June 30, 1988) and Projected (Dec. 30, 1988) Yield Curves, U. S. Treasury Issues. SOURCE: Gifford Fong Associates.

derived from assuming no change in the forward rates of the current term structure where the projected spot rates result from rolling along the current forward rate series. Both the capital changes and the reinvestment return of fixed-income assets will be directly affected by changes in interest rate levels.

Interest rate changes can be characterized by various yield curve shifts,

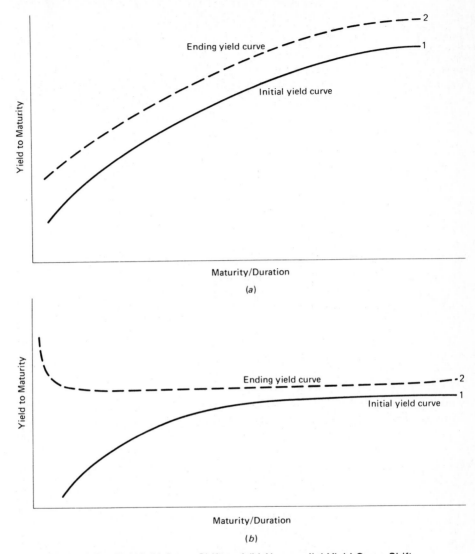

Figure 8-3. (a) Parallel Yield Curve Shift and (b) Nonparallel Yield Curve Shift.

as shown in Figure 8-3. Parallel changes are those having equal basis point moves across all maturities; nonparallel changes are exemplified by unequal basis point shifts.

Term Structure Analysis. The term structure of interest rates is a collection of data that describes the dependence of interest rates, generally of U.S. Treasury issues, on their term to maturity date. These data may be expressed in different forms, as described in Fong and Vasicek [1982], probably the most useful being spot rates. A spot rate may be defined as the yield on a pure discount (zero coupon) security. The term structure, then, may be expressed as a series of such rates for each maturity within the range of maturities of a homogeneous universe of bonds. In its most common form, the universe would be made up of default-free U.S. Treasury issues. These interest rates are, in effect, yields that have been adjusted to remove the complicating effects of coupons and default risk. The term structure also may be expressed in terms of forward rates: interest rates appropriate to the period between two future dates. Commonly, forward rates are expressed over regular intervals of time: a day, month, or year.

As shown in Fong and Vasicek [1982], all of the theoretically pure spot rates located on the spot rate curve can be converted mathematically into a set of one-period spot forward rates based on the *expectations theory*. That is, the *n*-period spot rate in the term structure is equal to the compound average (*n*th root) of the current one-period spot rate times all the successive one-period forward rates out to the maturity of the *n*-period spot rate. For example, the five-year maturity spot rate would be equal to the compound average (geometric mean) of the current one-year spot rate and each of the four succeeding one-year forward rates, or the 5th root of the product of these five rates.

In effect, each of the spot rates and, taken together, all of the spot rates in the total term structure imply a continuum of one-period future reinvestment rates that are expected at each future maturity date *if* the term structure created is assumed to remain constant. When compounded, this continuum of forward rates or expected return yields on pure discount zero coupon bonds provides the bond investor with a basic market implicit return *regardless of maturity*. That is, it is the equilibrium scenario compound rate of return for the entire term structure such that no maturities or payment schedules are *ex ante* (before the fact) preferred to any others. Why? Because it encompasses all that the market is currently requiring in the way of return across the entire spectrum of future maturities.

The question then remains of how the market implicit rate so derived can be most effectively used. It has not been an accurate estimator of future rates in an absolute sense. A prime benefit of market implicit forecasts is to provide a most likely scenario in a probabilistic decision making framework. This scenario is then bracketed by less probable optimistic and pessimistic rate forecasts to produce a probability distribution of returns. The approach can also be used in simulations where sensitivity analysis is done and the effect of "what if" changes in assumed rates are measured. Hence, this use of the term structure should provide a more comprehensive perspective of potential rate changes and can serve as a basic building block for much further analysis, such as for bond performance analysis as discussed in Fong, Pearson, and Vasicek [1981].

The fourth source of return and risk identified earlier in the discussion of Figure 8-1 is the yield differences attributable to sector and individual security effects. Sectors are segments of the bond market classified on the basis of some common characteristic(s) such as industry, maturity, issuer, or combinations thereof. Because the yield differential or "spread" (as measured by the number of basis points from a comparable U.S. Treasury security) changes over time, this has been a source of incremental return and risk for fixed-income portfolios. The return/risk component associated with yield spread changes can occur over holding periods ranging from several days to perhaps a few months.

PASSIVE BUY-AND-HOLD STRATEGY

There are four principal portfolio management strategies pursued by fixed-income investors: (1) buy and hold, (2) indexation, (3) immunization, and (4) active.

A buy-and-hold strategy essentially means purchasing and holding a security to maturity or redemption (e.g., by the issuer via a call provision) and then reinvesting cash proceeds in similar securities. Ongoing cash inflows, as well as outflows, are generally present from coupon income being received and reinvested. The emphasis is on minimizing the expectational inputs (i.e., expected return and risk usually based on assumptions about the future direction and level of interest rates). By holding securities to maturity, any capital change resulting from interest rate change is neutralized or ignored (by holding to maturity, the par amount of the bond will be received). Portfolio return, therefore, is controlled by coupon payments and reinvestment proceeds. While interest rate forecasting is largely ignored, analysis is important to minimize the risk of default on the securities held.

Income-Maximizing Investors

The buy-and-hold strategy is used primarily by income-maximizing investors interested in the largest coupon income over a desired horizon, such as endowment funds, some bond mutual funds, insurance companies seeking maximum yield over an extended period of time, or other large pools of money where the size of the fund and large cash inflow make portfolio turnover difficult because of possible market impact. Typically, this strategy has been adopted by investors who viewed fixed-income securities as safe assets with predictable cash flows and low price volatility. In the context of a long-term perspective, their objective is a return in excess of inflation with interest rate risk minimized. This is a classic example of a willingness to accept less than maximum return to avoid the inherent risk associated with a higher possible return, a strategy consistent with many investment objectives, constraints, and attendant policies.

Techniques, Vehicles, and Costs

Because this strategy seeks to minimize the requirement of expectational input and will hold securities to maturity or refunding, only default-free or very high quality securities should be held. Moreover, securities with *embedded options*, such as mortgage-backed securities, will introduce uncertain cash flows and are, therefore, less appropriate. Government and high quality, noncallable straight corporate securities would be the main securities employed. Callable and puttable bonds are less desirable, too, because the exercise of their embedded options drastically alters their cash flows. The call feature of a bond is an option that allows the issuer to buy back the bond at a particular price and time; a put is an option that allows the bond holder to sell the bond to the issuer at a specified price and time.

A further application of the strategy is for those investors seeking to lock in a rate of return through the purchase of zero coupon securities with a maturity at the date the proceeds are required (this is, in reality, an immunized strategy, which will be explained in a later section). Funds for college tuition or retirement are examples of this application.

The inability to enhance return because of restrictions on (1) the use of less-than-highest-quality instruments, (2) the use of embedded option securities, and (3) trading in the face of market volatility are significant handicaps to the return potential of this strategy. On the other hand, transaction costs are minimized and, if the strategy is implemented astutely, it can be highly productive. For example, when interest rates are high, and expected to remain high for some time, allocation of funds to bonds to be held to maturity may be particularly effective.

QUASI-PASSIVE INDEXATION STRATEGIES

The passive strategy called indexation is less restrictive than a buy-and-hold strategy. Here, the objective is to replicate the characteristics of the bond market using a proxy that is frequently a designated index. Typically, either the Salomon Brothers Broad Index or the Shearson Lehman Hutton Government/Corporate Bond Index is used. Consistent with a buy-and-hold strategy, minimization of expectational inputs is stressed. Indexation will be discussed in greater detail in the following section.

Market-Return-Replication Investors

For those investors who have investment objectives that call for market-related returns or require a fixed-income strategy with known risk characteristics (as may have been assumed in the overall portfolio asset allocation), indexation may be the answer. Although the return achieved may be less than the highest achievable, the indexation process assures that it will be closely related to a recognized benchmark: the chosen index.

Techniques, Vehicles, and Costs

There is a trade-off between practical considerations and the desire to replicate the market as a whole. Because the fixed-income market is both larger in size and broader in security type than the equity market, an all-inclusive replication tends to be unwieldy. For example, although the Shearson Lehman Hutton Corporate Bond Index has over 4,000 securities, it still represents only high quality corporate bond issues. The breadth of the fixed-income market is such that a compromise must be made when selecting among the popular indexes. Comprehensive coverage and a manageable market representation are competing trade-offs. Moreover, the strategy of buying every bond in an index in proportion to its weighting in the index (as is popularly done for stocks) is not a practical one. However, a relevant segment or segments of the bond market can usually be identified as an acceptable substitute index or *bogey*. The basic assumption is that the segment or segments are representative of what is sought from an investment objectives standpoint and will provide the relevant return with acceptable risk. Just as the S&P 500 Index does not represent the entire stock market but is still a useful benchmark, a narrower bond index can serve a similar function.

Alternative Vehicles. Two alternative approaches may be followed in indexation. In a sampling approach, the securities to be held are selected randomly from the universe of bonds making up the chosen index. Alternatively, in a stratified approach, the index is segmented into components from which individual securities are selected.

It is important to point out that, when applying the concept of an index fund to a bond portfolio, management of the fund cannot be totally passive. The first decision that must be made is the selection of the target bond market index or bogey. Once a target is selected, the portfolio manager must decide whether to replicate the target market index exactly (purchasing all securities with the same weighting as in the index), or to select only a sample of issues. With either approach, there will be transaction costs associated with (1) purchase of the issues used to construct the index, (2) reinvestment of cash proceeds from coupon interest payments and principal repayment (at maturity or early redemption), and (3) rebalancing of the portfolio if the composition of the issues in the target index changes.

Although the full replication approach will track the index exactly, practical considerations (such as transaction costs and the large number of issues), generally preclude this approach. If the stratified approach is adopted, portfolio management is simplified. However, transaction costs will be incurred to rebalance the fund over time in order to mirror the target index. With the stratified approach, the number of issues to be included must be determined. The manager must evaluate the costs and benefits associated with portfolios of larger versus smaller sizes.

In addition, transaction costs and management fees will result in a divergence between the return on the target index and the constructed index fund. The role of the portfolio manager in an index fund also involves minimizing this discrepancy and perhaps even including an attempt to add enough value to beat the index. Strategies for this purpose are described later in this chapter in the sections on bond valuation and swapping.

Sampling Approach. McEnally and Boardman [1979] have shown how diversification of bonds varies with portfolio size. It appears that the effect of portfolio size parallels closely the relationship found in common stock portfolios. This suggests that once an index is selected, it can be closely replicated with a manageable number of securities, probably fewer than 40. Table 8-1 provides the relationships between portfolio size and the mean and standard deviation of returns, both empirically observed as well as theoretically expected.

These findings provide support for the general principle of the sampling approach to indexation for long holding periods. When considering indexes that contain a diversity of security types, such as some of the broader indexes (e.g., the Salomon Brothers Broad Investment Grade Index) or when close tracking over shorter time frames is desirable (such as monthly or quarterly), a more refined approach to indexation is appropriate.

Stratified Approach. It is clear that even if it were possible to buy the whole universe of bonds that is used in the calculation of the index to be duplicated, practical considerations argue that an indexed portfolio should be limited to a much smaller number of securities. Moreover, the portfolio must be rebalanced periodically to reinvest cash flows and to reflect changes in the index composition. This cannot be accomplished in practice if the portfolio is too large. The question, then, is how to construct and maintain an actual portfolio that will replicate the index as closely as possible under realistic operating conditions.

An example of one approach consists of three steps. The first step is to define the classes in which the index universe securities are to be held in the portfolio. Each class should be as homogeneous as possible. This

TABLE 8-1. Return Variance of Randomly Generated Portfolios of Corporate Bonds of All Quality Classes, January 1973 to June 1976 ($\times$ 10^4)

Number of Bonds in Portfolio	Mean[a] (Standard Deviation) of V_{Pn}	Theoretical[a] V_{Pn}
1	9.367 (7.471)	9.257
2	7.469 (3.972)	7.148
4	6.004 (2.102)	6.094
6	5.782 (1.701)	5.742
8	5.591 (1.469)	5.566
10	5.376 (1.327)	5.461
12	5.401 (1.220)	5.391
14	5.341 (1.098)	5.340
16	5.299 (1.035)	5.303
18	5.266 (0.973)	5.273
20	5.274 (0.902)	5.250
40	5.155 (0.633)	5.144

SOURCE: McEnally and Boardman [1979].

[a] Variable V_{Pn} is the expected value of the variance of returns of portfolios constructed by investing $1/n$ of the portfolio in each of n randomly selected securities.

could be accomplished by dividing the universe into classes by issuing sector/ quality (Treasury, Aaa Industrial, Baa Financial, and so forth), maturity range, and coupon range.

For example, suppose that the objective is to track the Shearson Lehman Hutton Government Index with a portfolio of 40 or fewer bonds. The classes can be defined by distinguishing between Treasuries and agencies, breaking the maturity range into 10 intervals (for example, 1–2, 2–3, 3–4, 4–6, 6–8, 8–10, 10–12, 12–15, 15–20, and 20–30 years to maturity), and separating the securities with coupons of 10 percent or less from those with coupons over 10 percent. The total number of classes will then be 40 (2 $\times$ 10 $\times$ 2). Each class is reasonably homogeneous because it contains only one type of security in a narrow maturity range and with similar coupon levels.

The second step is the selection of securities. On the initial date, as well as on each rebalancing date (typically monthly), one security is chosen from each class for inclusion in the investment portfolio. The methodology places no requirements on the selection of the security from the class. This gives the portfolio manager freedom to exercise some judgment. The portfolio manager may review the list of bonds in the class and select the one that has the most appeal in terms of valuation, availability, liquidity, and the like. To keep turnover down, the portfolio manager will probably choose a security that is already held in the portfolio (if any), unless there are reasons to prefer a new security within the class. Basing the selection on a valuation model that ranks the securities in the class from the most underpriced to the most overpriced is a particularly attractive approach. It may contribute to overcoming or even exceeding the negative effect of transaction costs.

The third and final step is the determination of the amount to be held in each security selected. This step does not involve any judgmental input and may be done by a quadratic programming algorithm that accomplishes the following:

1. Insures that the duration of the portfolio is equal to that of the index. (See Chapter 6 for a discussion of duration.)
2. Insures that the distribution of maturities in the portfolio is equal to that of the index (control of convexity).[1]
3. Insures that the amount held in each of the selected securities is as close to being proportional to the total weight of its class in the index as is possible given the above constraints.

The first condition insures similar responsiveness of the portfolio to the index regarding parallel term structure shifts, while the second insures similar responsiveness of the portfolio to the index regarding nonparallel shifts or a twisting of the term structure. The last condition minimizes the differences that might arise from sector effects (see section on Sector and Security Strategies).

Provision for round lot and minimum/maximum size trade requirements are also typically made a part of the optimization procedure.

Stratification Example. As an illustration of the application of this approach, Table 8-2 summarizes the results of replicating the Shearson Leh-

---

[1] Convexity can be interpreted as a measure of the rate of change of duration as a function of interest rate change or as a measure of cash flow dispersion of a stream of payments or liabilities. Alternatively, convexity is the amount of price change on a bond for (large) changes in interest rates that are not accounted for by duration. As interest rate changes increase from 100 to 200 to 300 basis points, the typical bond's price change not explained by duration will expand disproportionately or in accelerated fashion. See Chapter 6 for a more complete discussion of convexity.

TABLE 8-2. Portfolio Characteristics Comparison of a Tracking Portfolio With the Shearson Lehman Hutton Full Treasury Index
(Evaluation Date 6-30-88)

PORTFOLIO COMPOSITION

	Number of Issues	Average Coupon (%)	Average Maturity (years)	Average Duration (years)	Convexity (yr/(%/yr))	Yield to Effective Maturity (%)	Average Quality Ratings
		(Par Value Weighted)			*(Market Weighted Average Value)*		
PORTFOLIO:	16	8.585	8.55	4.552	.168	8.445	AAA
INDEX:	160	9.223	8.65	4.555	.168	8.467	AAA

	Maturity Composition (% Bonds and Cash)			Sector Composition (% Bonds Only)				
	Cash Value	Short (0–5) yrs	Intermediate (5–10) yrs	Long (10–50) yrs	U.S. Treasury	U.S. Agency	Industrial	Utility	Finance	Other Sectors
PORTFOLIO:	.0	52.3	14.2	33.4	100.0	.0	.0	.0	.0	.0
INDEX:	.0	52.3	21.6	26.1	100.0	.0	.0	.0	.0	.0

SOURCE: Gifford Fong Associates.

man Hutton Treasury Index. It was assumed the initial portfolio would be $100 million in size and the portfolio structure would be similar to the specifications of the Shearson Lehman Hutton Government Index except that there would be no need to provide for agencies, because they are not included in the Treasury Index.

Table 8-3 lists the securities chosen along with the amount, concentration, and other descriptive information for each security chosen. The securities selected by the bond manager are weighted by the optimizer to match the duration and convexity of the portfolio to those of the index and to match the concentration of desired market sectors. Using this stratified sampling technique one can replicate the interest rate sensitivity of the entire universe of 160 bonds with a portfolio of only 16 bonds and still allow the portfolio manager the freedom to select the bonds used, within some limits.

SEMIACTIVE MANAGEMENT: IMMUNIZATION

Immunization, a hybrid strategy having both active and passive elements, is a strategy that was originally formulated by Macaulay [1938] and Redington [1952]. A number of advances that extend their analyses will be discussed.

Accumulation-Maximizing Investors

Accumulation-maximizing investors, who require a high degree of assurance of compound return over their investment time horizon, use this semiactive bond management approach. By accepting a more modest return than the highest that can be expected, they achieve a greater likelihood of realizing an assured return. This is another example of the classic trade-off between return and risk.

Techniques and Vehicles

Classical immunization may be defined as the process by which a fixed-income portfolio is created having an assured return for a specified time horizon irrespective of interest rate change. In a more concise form, the following are the important characteristics:

- Specific time horizon
- Assured rate of return to a fixed horizon date
- Insulation from the effects of potential adverse interest rate change on portfolio value

TABLE 8-3. Security Listing for a Shearson Lehman Hutton Treasury Index Tracking Portfolio (Evaluation Date 6-30-88)

Index Portfolio

Bond No.	Face Value ($000)	Conc. (%)	CUSIP Number	Issuer Name	Quality	Coupon Rate (%)	Stated Maturity Date	Price (% Par)	Yield to Effective Maturity (%)	Duration (yrs)	Market Value ($000)
57	15200.	15.2	912827TP	U.S. TREASURY NOTES	AAA	6.875	5 15 89	99.281	7.726	.8	15221.
64	14800.	15.0	912827TX	U.S. TREASURY NOTES	AAA	6.625	8 15 89	98.750	7.796	1.0	14983.
119	11400.	11.1	912827UH	U.S. TREASURY NOTES	AAA	6.625	2 15 92	94.813	8.307	3.1	11092.
147	5700.	5.5	912827UL	U.S. TREASURY NOTES	AAA	7.000	1 15 94	93.281	8.546	4.3	5500.
168	5200.	4.8	912827TQ	U.S. TREASURY NOTES	AAA	7.375	5 15 96	92.094	8.784	5.7	4837.
170	3300.	3.3	912827UW	U.S. TREASURY NOTES	AAA	8.500	5 15 97	97.969	8.832	6.0	3268.
215	12800.	14.0	912810DT	U.S. TREASURY BONDS	AAA	9.875	11 15 15	108.313	9.048	9.8	14022.
122	3000.	3.4	912827SB	U.S. TREASURY NOTES	AAA	11.750	4 15 92	110.781	8.364	3.0	3397.
125	3900.	4.4	912827SL	U.S. TREASURY NOTES	AAA	10.375	7 15 92	106.750	8.370	3.1	4349.
164	500.	.6	912827SP	U.S. TREASURY NOTES	AAA	10.500	8 15 95	109.344	8.708	4.9	566.
186	3500.	4.1	912810DC	U.S. TREASURY BONDS	AAA	10.750	2 15 03	113.531	9.059	7.5	4115.
187	3400.	3.9	912810DD	U.S. TREASURY BONDS	AAA	10.750	5 15 03	113.563	9.069	7.7	3907.
195	3400.	4.0	912810DR	U.S. TREASURY BONDS	AAA	10.750	8 15 05	113.969	9.120	8.0	4012.
114	2900.	3.3	912827RG	U.S. TREASURY NOTES	AAA	12.250	10 15 91	111.250	8.266	2.7	3300.
184	2700.	4.0	912810CZ	U.S. TREASURY BONDS	AAA	14.250	2 15 02	141.031	8.969	6.9	3952.
205	2600.	3.4	912810CS	U.S. TREASURY BONDS a	AAA	12.750	11 15 10(11/05)	130.688	8.907C	8.1	3439.

TOTAL PORTFOLIO MARKET VALUE 99960.

INITIAL CASH BALANCE ($000)		INITIAL MARKET VALUE ($000)		FINAL MARKET VALUE ($000)		FINAL CASH BALANCE ($000)		TRANSACTION COST ($000)
100000.	+	0.	=	99960.	+	40.	+	0.

SOURCE: Gifford Fong Associates.

a Bond No. 205, the U.S. Treasury 12¾s of November 2010, is callable in November 2005. The yield to maturity of 8.907 percent is the yield to the call date.

Potential users include life insurance companies, some pension funds, and some banks for their own investment portfolios. Life insurance companies can use immunization to invest the proceeds from their guaranteed investment contracts (GICs) and fixed annuities. GICs provide for a lump sum payment at a prespecified time in the future at some rate of return guaranteed by the insurance company. Annuities provide for a series of payments for a predetermined period (sometimes to death). These are investment vehicles that have a specified required payment at or until some specified future date. The difference between the promised return on the contract or annuity and the realized portfolio return would be revenue available for expenses and profit. The ability to fund specified liabilities on a timely basis also makes immunization attractive. Pension funds seeking to fund their retired lives liability and seeking an alternative to a GIC have also used immunization strategies. This application represents an asset alternative that can fill an investment need customized for the fund sponsor. Use by banks and other savings institutions involves structuring the assets of the investment portfolio to match the liabilities of the balance sheet. A further application is the use of an immunization portfolio for portfolio protection strategies (see Fong and Tang [1988]).

In all of these applications, the important principle is the ability to define future liabilities with certainty such that the duration of liabilities can be calculated. Without this characteristic, one of the fundamental requirements of immunization analysis cannot be met and, hence, the objectives of the investor are frustrated.

The fundamental mechanism underlying immunization is a portfolio structure that balances the portfolio capital changes (from interest rate change) with the return from reinvestment of portfolio cash flows (coupon and principal payments). In other words, if rates rise, the higher reinvestment return will offset the decrease in portfolio value caused by such a rise; conversely, as rates decline, the increase in portfolio value will offset a lower reinvestment return. To accomplish this balancing requires the use of the concept of duration (see discussion of duration in Chapter 6).

Duration. As noted in Chapter 6, duration can be defined as a measure of the average life of a security or, more precisely, the average time (in years) necessary to receive the present value of all future payments (coupon plus principal repayment), where each cash flow is discounted by the security's yield to maturity. This has been called Macaulay's duration to distinguish it from a number of alternative measures such as those described in Bierwag, Kaufman, Schweitzer, and Toevs [1980]. The Macaulay measure is the one most commonly used and tested for immunization purposes (see, for example, Fisher and Weil [1971]). By setting the duration of the portfolio equal to the desired time horizon, the balance between capital changes and reinvestment return is achieved. This is *the* necessary condition for *classical immunization* and a necessary condition for *modern immunization*.

Classical immunization was premised upon the assumptions that (1) the term structure was flat (i.e., no yield difference as a function of maturity); (2) only parallel shifts in the term structure would occur (equal basis point shifts throughout the maturity range); and (3) if there were an interest rate change, it would be an instantaneous and one-time shift. The evolution to modern immunization approaches seeks to address the limiting nature of these assumptions.

Target Rate of Return. Based on the beginning of the time horizon term structure of interest rates or yield curve existing at the beginning of the horizon period, the assured rate of return of immunization can be determined. Theoretically, it is defined as the total return of the portfolio assuming no change in the term structure. This will always differ from the portfolio's present yield to maturity unless the term structure is described by a flat line, because by virtue of the passage of time there will be a return effect as the portfolio moves (matures) along the yield curve. That is, for an upward sloping yield curve such as the curve in Figure 8-8, the yield to maturity of a portfolio would be quite different from its immunization rate of return, whereas for a flat yield curve the yield to maturity would roughly approximate the assured return. In general, for an upward sloping yield curve the immunization target rate of return will be less than the yield to maturity because of the lower reinvestment return; and, conversely, a negative or downward sloping yield curve would have the immunization target rate of return greater than the yield to maturity because of the higher reinvestment return.

Alternative measures of the immunization rate of return include the yield implied by a zero coupon bond of comparable quality and duration as the portfolio, or a simulation where the initial portfolio is rebalanced given scenarios of interest rate change. Granito [1984] has suggested the duration weighted yield to maturity as a proxy that can be calculated directly from the initial portfolio holdings.

Time Horizon. The range of time horizons is controlled by the ability to match the investor's desired time horizon with the weighted average duration of the portfolio. In principle, duration matching is straightforward: portfolio duration is equal to a weighted average of the individual security durations where the weights are the relative amounts or percentages invested in each. The most typical immunized time horizon is five years; it is a common planning period for GICs and allows flexibility in security selection because there is a fairly large population of securities to create the necessary portfolio duration. In addition, the type of security in the portfolio should be limited to high quality, very liquid instruments, because portfolio rebal-

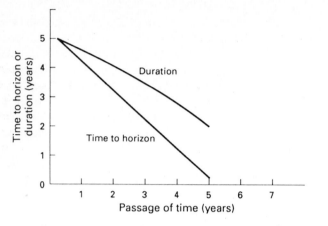

Figure 8-4. Duration vs. Time to Horizon With the Passage of Time.

ancing is required to keep the portfolio duration synchronized with the horizon date. In other words, as the portfolio matures, the portfolio duration must be kept equal to the remaining time to the horizon.

In any interest rate environment different from a flat term structure the duration will change at a different rate than time. Hence, starting with a portfolio duration of 5 for a 5-year GIC, at the end of one year the portfolio duration will be greater (less) than four years if the term structure is upward sloping (downward sloping). Figure 8-4 illustrates the difference in the rate of change for time and duration. The top line traces the change in duration over the life of a 5-year immunized portfolio; the bottom line depicts the behavior of time-to-horizon over the same 5-year horizon. As can be seen, the duration of the portfolio shortens more slowly than time-to-horizon and the vertical distance between the two lines represents the risk of not rebalancing. Therefore, to maintain proper duration control, rebalancing of the portfolio duration is necessary if for no other reason than the passage of time. Figure 8-5 provides another reason for rebalancing over time. Three lines are shown representing a 12 percent coupon bond of different maturities. The change in duration for a range of yield changes is displayed. The longer the maturity of the bond, the greater the change in duration with changes in interest rates. In any case, ongoing monitoring of the portfolio is appropriate.

Interest Rate Shifts. Perhaps the most critical assumption of classical immunization techniques concerns the type of interest rate change anticipated. Specifically, the yield curve is assumed always to move in a one-time parallel fashion during the portfolio time horizon, that is, interest rates either move up or move down by the same amount for all maturities. This would appear to be an unrealistic assumption, because such behavior is rarely, if

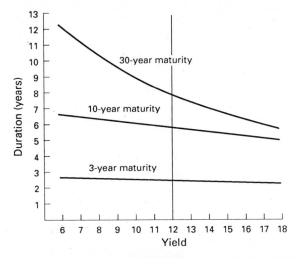

Figure 8-5. Durations vs. Yield Change for Various Maturity 12 Percent Coupon Bonds.

ever, experienced in reality. According to the theory, if there is a change in interest rates that does not correspond to this *shape preserving shift*, matching the duration of the portfolio to the investor's desired time horizon no longer assures immunization. For a more complete discussion of these issues, see Cox, Ingersol, and Ross [1979].

Figure 8-6 illustrates the nature of portfolio value of an immunized port-

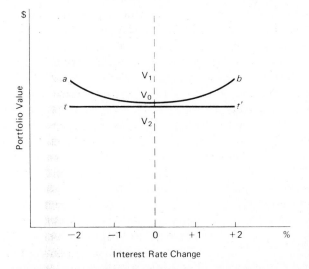

Figure 8-6. Changes in Portfolio Value via Parallel Interest Rate Changes for an Immunized Portfolio.

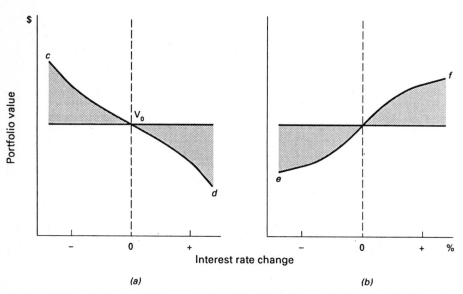

Figure 8-7. Two Patterns of Changes in Portfolio Value Caused by Nonparallel Interest Rate Shifts for an Immunized Portfolio.

folio following a parallel shift in rates. The curve *ab* represents the behavior of the portfolio value for various changes in rates, ranging from a decline to an increase as shown on the horizontal axis. Point V_O (or line *tt'*) is the level of portfolio value assuming no change in rates. It can be seen that an immunized portfolio subjected to parallel shifts in the yield curve will actually provide a greater portfolio value, following a parallel shift in rates, than the assured target value under the no change in interest rate assumption. This target value therefore will become the portfolio's minimum value. If interest rates move in a parallel fashion, either up or down, the portfolio return will be greater than the target return.

For example, if interest rates rise, the increased return from reinvestment will more than offset the negative return from portfolio value changes. Conversely, if interest rates decline, the return from portfolio value increases will more than offset the diminished return from reinvestment.

Figure 8-7 illustrates the same relationship when interest rates do not shift in a parallel fashion. It indicates the possibility of a portfolio value less than the target. Depending on the shape of the nonparallel shift, either the (*a*) or the (*b*) relationship will occur. The important point is that merely matching the duration of the portfolio with the portfolio time horizon may not prevent significant undesirable deviations from the target rate of return.

Maturity Variance. To handle the problem of nonparallel shifts in interest rates, the concept of *maturity variance* has been introduced by Fong and Vasicek [1980]. Assuming the proper portfolio duration, the greater the dispersion of expected cash flows about the liabilities being funded, the greater the immunization risk. Immunization risk is defined as the potential dispersion of return (standard deviation) around the target return. The matching of portfolio duration to the remaining time to the horizon takes care of the risk of parallel shifts of the term structure. By the proper control of portfolio maturity variance, immunization risk from nonparallel term structure shifts can be controlled. In the special case of portfolios constructed from a universe of *pure discount* or *zero coupon securities*, holding securities with the same maturities as the horizon date would eliminate immunization risk. At the other extreme, high coupon securities with maturities that are "laddered" over the portfolio time horizon would result in very high immunization risk. A laddered portfolio is one constructed with securities having regularly spaced maturities (the rungs or steps of the ladder being each maturity). This type of portfolio would have a part of the portfolio regularly maturing and subject to reinvestment. Because of the wide range of maturities and the requirement for frequent principal reinvestment, there is high exposure to reinvestment risk and, therefore, to immunization risk. Such a portfolio would have high sensitivity to nonparallel changes in interest rates. Therefore, for a single period liability, such as one represented by a GIC, the best minimum risk portfolio would be one holding securities that most closely resemble pure discount securities maturing at the horizon.

Quantification of immunization risk can be achieved by calculating the expected standard deviation of the target rate of return (Fong and Vasicek [1980]) or by simulation where the portfolio is subject to alternative scenarios of interest rate change (Nemerever [1983]).

SEMIACTIVE MANAGEMENT: DEDICATED PORTFOLIOS

Where there are a number of specific liabilities to fund over a period of time, a *dedicated portfolio* approach may be appropriate. This is a portfolio with a structure designed to fund a schedule of liabilities from coupon payments and asset values, with the portfolio's value diminishing to zero after payment of the last liability. Two approaches to a dedicated portfolio are available.

Methodology

Immunization Approach. The first approach uses immunization. For a multiperiod situation, where there is a series of liabilities over the portfolio time horizon, the following two conditions must exist: (1) The (composite) duration of the portfolio assets equals the (composite) duration of the liabilities and (2) the distribution of the durations of portfolio assets has a wider range than the distribution of durations of the liabilities.

The first condition can be achieved by having the weighted average duration of assets equal the weighted average duration of liabilities; the second requires that the portfolio payments be more dispersed in time than the liabilities. That is, there must be an asset with a duration equal to or less than the duration of the shortest duration liability, and there must be an asset with a duration equal to or greater than the longest duration liability. This *bracketing* of shortest and longest duration liabilities with even shorter and longer duration assets ensures the balancing of changes in portfolio value with changes in reinvestment return. If both of these conditions are met, then by minimizing maturity variance, the portfolio can be structured to generate the necessary cash flows on a timely basis at minimum immunization risk.

In all of these applications the important principle is the ability to define future liabilities with certainty such that the duration of liabilties may be calculated. Without this ability, one of the fundamental requirements of immunization analysis cannot be met.

Cash Flow Matching. A procedure called *cash flow matching* is an alternative to multiple-period (liability) immunization. This method can be described intuitively as follows. A bond is selected with a maturity that matches the last liability. An amount of principal equal to the amount of the last liability is then invested in this bond. The remaining elements of the liability stream are then reduced by the coupon payments on this bond, and another bond is chosen for the next to last liability, adjusted for any coupon payments of the first bond selected. Going backward in time, this sequence is continued until all liabilities have been matched by payments on the securities selected for the portfolio.

Table 8-4 displays a portfolio chosen to match a sequence of liability payments shown in the second to last column of Table 8-5. These bonds range in maturity from cash (shortest) to just before the date of the longest liability. (Table 8-4 also includes a number of descriptive statistics of the individual securities held and the portfolio as a whole.) Table 8-5 provides a cash flow analysis of sources and application of funds. The last column in the table shows the excess funds remaining at each period that are reinvested at the assumed 6 percent reinvestment rate supplied by the user. The greater the excess cash the greater the risk of the strategy.

In the special case where all of the liability flows were perfectly matched by the asset flows of the portfolio, the resulting portfolio would have no reinvestment risk and, therefore, no immunization or cash flow match risk. However, given typical liability schedules and bonds available for cash flow matching, perfect matching is unlikely. Under such conditions, a minimum immunization risk approach would, at worst, be equal to cash flow matching

TABLE 8-4. Characteristics of a Sample Universe for Cash Flow Matching (Evaluation Date 6-30-88)

PRICE SCAN

FORWARD RATES DATE: 6-30-88
LONG RATE: 8.964%
SHORT RATE: 6.395%
INTEREST RATE MODEL:
  SPEED OF REVERSION: 0.890
  VOLATILITY PARAMETER: 0.200 ((YR)** -3/2)
ANALYSIS INCLUDES ACCRUED INTEREST

Bond No.	Par Value ($)	% of Total	CUSIP	Issuer Name	Quality	Coupon (%)	Effective Maturity Date	Price ($)	Adj. Y-T-M (%)	Adj. Duration (yrs)
17	$2800.	10.2%	912794QD	BILL	AAA	.000%	12/22/88	$ 96.709	7.117%	.463
19	153.	.6	888888ZZ	CASH	UNRTD	.000	12/31/88	100.000	6.862	.487
1	1600.	6.3	313586NB	FEDERAL NATL MTG ASSN	AAA	11.300	12/11/89	104.344	8.052	1.317
2	1700.	6.4	313388PF	FEDERAL HOME LN BKS	AAA	8.700	12/26/90	100.656	8.402	2.197
3	1700.	7.0	313388MU	FEDERAL HOME LN BKS	AAA	11.400	12/26/91	108.594	8.501	2.873
6	1600.	6.5	795498AD	SALOMON INC	A1	10.700	8/ 1/92	103.152	9.741	3.135
4	100.	.4	313388KR	FEDERAL HOME LN BKS	AAA	11.100	11/25/92	108.375	8.761	3.451
13	2500.	10.2	002824AD	ABBOTT LABS	AA1	11.000	2/ 1/93	103.771	9.951	3.415
18	1200.	5.2	912827RM	UNITED STATES TREAS NTS	AAA	11.625	11/15/94	114.500	8.617	4.544
16	1800.	6.6	958118AA	WESTERN ELEC INC	AAA	8.375	10/ 1/95	95.933	8.709	3.794
10	500.	1.8	462506AU	IOWA PWR & LT CO	AA3	8.250	7/ 1/96	91.584	9.639	5.011
14	1400.	5.0	239753AN	DAYTON HUDSON CORP	AA3	8.375	10/ 1/96	92.036	9.641	5.204
12	1800.	5.5	744567AX	PUBLIC SVC ELEC & GAS CO	A1	6.250	6/ 1/97	80.214	9.576	6.282
7	400.	1.4	441812CC	HOUSEHOLD FIN CORP	A1	8.250	3/ 1/98	88.725	10.003	5.833
5	1500.	4.8	341081AX	FLORIDA PWR & LT CO	AA3	7.000	10/ 1/98	83.969	9.411	6.766
8	1700.	5.6	441812AU	HOUSEHOLD FIN CORP	A1	7.750	10/ 1/99	85.581	9.843	6.682
15	1800.	5.1	812387AL	SEARS ROEBUCK & CO	AA2	6.000	5/ 1/00	74.750	9.617	7.596
11	1700.	5.7	665772AV	NORTHN STS PWR CO MINN	AA1	8.250	6/ 1/01	88.602	9.765	7.218
9	1700.	5.8	066365AE	BANKERS TRUST NY CORP	A1	8.625	11/ 1/02	88.929	10.029	7.297

PORTFOLIO TOTALS

AVERAGE ADJUSTED DURATION (YRS)	4.221
AVERAGE ADJUSTED YIELD (%)	9.057
DUR. WTD. AVG YIELD (%)	9.449
AVERAGE COUPON (%)	7.976
AVERAGE EFFECTIVE MATURITY	1-30-95
AVG TIME TO MATURITY (YRS)	6.585
AVERAGE QUALITY	AA2
TOTAL PAR VALUE ($000)	27652.870
TOTAL MARKET VALUE ($000)	26581.790
TOTAL PRINCIPAL VALUE ($000)	26164.470
TOTAL ACCRUED INTEREST ($)	417.328
NUMBER OF ISSUES	19

SOURCE: Gifford Fong Associates.

TABLE 8-5. Cash Flow Analysis of a Sample Universe for Cash Flow Matching: Reinvestment Rate—6 Percent (Evaluation Date 6-30-88)

CASH FLOW ANALYSIS

Date	Prev. Cash Balance ($000)	+	Interest on Balance ($000)	+	Principal Payments ($000)	+	Coupon Payments ($000)	+	Reinvestment of Payments ($000)	−	Liability Due ($000)	=	New Cash Balance ($000)
12-31-88	$ .0		$ .0		$2960.2		$1102.8		$ 14.8		$4038.0		$ 39.804
12-31-89	39.8		2.4		1600.0		2205.7		63.9		3900.0		11.851
12-31-90	11.9		.7		1700.0		2024.9		56.8		3762.0		32.272
12-31-91	32.3		2.0		1700.0		1877.0		54.5		3624.0		41.690
12-31-92	41.7		2.5		1700.0		1683.2		90.4		3474.0		43.813
12-31-93	43.8		2.7		2500.0		1363.4		178.5		3330.0		758.402
12-31-94	758.4		46.2		1200.0		1225.9		40.9		3174.0		97.317
12-31-95	97.3		5.9		1800.0		1086.4		55.3		3012.0		32.952
12-31-96	33.0		2.0		1900.0		935.6		59.8		2850.0		80.422
12-31-97	80.4		4.9		1800.0		720.9		81.5		2682.0		5.670
12-31-98	5.7		.3		1900.0		648.1		43.6		2514.0		83.765
12-31-99	83.8		5.1		1700.0		526.6		38.4		2346.0		7.894
12-31-00	7.9		.5		1800.0		340.9		80.9		2178.0		52.198
12-31-01	52.2		3.2		1700.0		216.8		65.7		2004.0		33.854
12-31-02	33.9		2.1		1700.0		146.6		20.5		1900.0		2.996

SOURCE: Gifford Fong Associates.

and would probably be better, because an immunization strategy would require less money to fund liabilities. This is due to two factors. First, a relatively conservative rate of return assumption for short-term cash, which may be occasionally substantial, must be made throughout the life of the plan in cash flow matching, whereas an immunized portfolio is essentially fully invested at the remaining horizon duration. Second, funds from a cash flow matched portfolio must be available when each liability is due and, because of the difficulty in perfect matching, usually before. An immunized portfolio need only have sufficient *value* on the date of each liability because funding is achieved by a rebalancing of the portfolio. Because the reinvestment assumption for excess cash for cash flow matching is for many years into the future, a conservative assumption is appropriate. Thus, even with the sophisticated linear programming techniques used in cash flow matching, in most cases it will be technically inferior to immunization. However, cash flow matching is easier to understand, and this has occasionally led to its selection over an immunized strategy for multiperiod problems.

Universe Considerations. In the actual process leading to the construction of a dedicated portfolio, the selection of the universe is extremely important. The lower the quality of the securities considered, the higher the potential return and risk. Dedication assumes there will be no defaults and immunization theory further assumes securities will be responsive only to overall changes in interest rates. The lower the quality, the greater the possibility that these assumptions will not be met. Further, securities with embedded options such as call features or mortgage-backed prepayments complicate and may even prevent the accurate measure of cash flow and hence duration, frustrating the basic requirements of immunization and cash flow matching. Finally, liquidity is a consideration for immunized portfolios because they must be rebalanced over time.

Optimization. Optimization procedures can be used for the construction of dedicated portfolios. For an immunized portfolio this typically takes the form of minimizing maturity variance subject to the constraints of duration and necessary duration dispersion (in multiple-liability immunization). Typically, cash flow matching takes the form of minimizing the initial portfolio cost subject to the constraint of having sufficient cash at the time a liability arises. Further considerations such as average quality, minimum and maximum concentration constraints, and, perhaps, issuer constraints may be included. Throughout this process the need to establish realistic guidelines and objectives is critical. In addition, because the optimization is very sensitive to the pricing of the universe being considered, accurate pricing and the interface of an experienced trader are valuable. Because of the many inputs and variations that are typically available, the optimization process should be approached in an iterative manner where the final solution is the result of a number of trials.

Monitoring. Finally, the ongoing monitoring of a dedicated portfolio can be facilitated by periodic performance measurement. For a bullet portfolio (single horizon date), performance monitoring may take the form of regular observations of the return to date linked with the current target return and annualized. This return should fluctuate with small amplitude about the original target return.

The performance of a multiple-liability immunized plan can most easily be monitored by making periodic comparisons of the current market value of the assets and comparing this with the present value of the remaining liabilities. (In determining this present value, use can be made of the current internal rate of return on the immunized portfolio to discount the remaining liabilities.) These two quantities should track one another closely. It may also be useful to monitor the estimated standard deviation of the terminal value of the fund to make sure that it falls more or less uniformly to zero as the horizon date approaches.

ACTIVE STRATEGIES

Total Return-Maximizing Investors

For those seeking the highest return possible, active strategies offer the greatest opportunity (and the greatest risk). These are used primarily by total return-maximizing investors, either in single- or multiple-holding-period frameworks. The objective is to maximize return, whether it be from capital changes or income or a combination thereof.

Many pension funds and closed-end mutual funds embrace this approach because they are willing to make assumptions about the future. The greater the accuracy of those assumptions, the greater the return. Active strategies, which are dominated by interest rate anticipation and sector/security strategies, actually span a fairly wide range of possibilities. Indeed, the increased volatility of the bond market has stimulated the development of active management techniques because there are larger payoffs possible from correctly forecasting interest rate and yield spread changes.

Techniques and Vehicles

The objective in interest rate anticipation is to take advantage of expectations of interest rate change by managing the duration of the portfolio. As has been discussed in Chapter 6, interest rate change is the dominant source of marginal total return. As interest rates change there will be a direct effect on the price of a security. Rising rates will decrease the price (to adjust the yield to the higher rate level), and declining rates will increase the price (to adjust the yield to the lower rate level). As long as there are changes in rates, this will exist. How to manage this effect is the key to active management.

Interest Rate Anticipation Strategies

As an active management technique, interest rate anticipation should be concerned with three dimensions: direction of the change in rates, magnitude of the change across maturities, and the timing of the change. If interest rates drop, the price of the bond will rise to reflect the new yield level and vice versa if rates increase. The amount of price increase or decrease will usually be directly related to the security's duration.

Therefore, the maturity should be lengthened or, more precisely, duration should be increased when rates are expected to drop and the opposite action taken when rates are expected to rise. The greater the shift of the duration prior to the change in rates, the greater the incremental return. Where along the maturity spectrum to position the portfolio should be guided by the shape of the expected yield curve change. Expectations of nonparallel interest rate shifts would dictate positioning the duration in the region where rates are expected to rise least or fall most. Finally, the timing of the expected rate change will be important in evaluating the relative importance of rate change, coupon return, and reinvestment return.

Premature positioning of the portfolio duration may compromise the reinvestment return. This would occur in an environment of a downward sloping yield curve where the expectation is for interest rates to decline. Positioning the portfolio too soon with a long duration will give up the high short duration reinvestment return. The point is that the total rate of return is due to the contribution of all three factors, and trade-offs between the three may have to be made.

Analysis of interest rate anticipation strategies seeks to recognize and assess the role of interest rate changes on the total return of a portfolio over a specified time horizon. Generation of the required interest rate forecast will not be covered (see Chapter 5 for this discussion). Rather, the emphasis will be on harnessing the forecasts once they are determined. To assess the impact and implications of interest rate change, it is useful to apply the forecasts of interest rate change to a portfolio and compute the expected return of each bond held or considered (see, for example, Fong [1980]).

Scenario Analysis. Table 8-6 summarizes inputs suitable for simulating the effect of interest rate change. The particular values of the inputs are

TABLE 8-6. Return Simulation Example of Bond Portfolio Analysis

PORTFOLIO: MODEL PORTFOLIO—U.S. TREASURY

INTEREST RATE PROJECTION: 6-30-88 to 6-30-89

SCENARIO 1 (33.33% PROBABILITY): FALLING RATES, 36-YEAR HISTORICAL VOLATILITY
  BASIS (5-52 TO 6-88)
    REINVESTMENT RATE IS CALCULATED FOR EACH BOND.

SCENARIO 2 (33.33% PROBABILITY): MARKET IMPLICIT FORECAST
    REINVESTMENT RATE IS CALCULATED FOR EACH BOND.

SCENARIO 3 (33.33% PROBABILITY): RISING RATES, 36-YEAR HISTORICAL VOLATILITY
  BASIS (5-52 TO 6-88)
    REINVESTMENT RATE IS CALCULATED FOR EACH BOND.

INTEREST RATE PROJECTION:

Maturity (Yrs)	Present YTM (%)	Scenario:	Forecast Yield (Percent)		
			1	2	3
.250	6.985%		4.911%	8.261%	10.410%
.500	7.394		5.643	8.338	9.667
1.000	7.683		5.559	8.398	11.114
2.000	8.026		6.040	8.403	10.851
3.000	8.143		6.358	8.533	10.438
4.000	8.294		6.657	8.672	10.315
5.000	8.441		6.878	8.773	10.302
10.000	8.821		7.492	9.049	10.182
20.000	9.040		7.887	9.193	10.281
30.000	9.045		7.911	9.179	10.302

SOURCE: Gifford Fong Associates.

for purposes of illustration. The maximum benefit of this kind of analysis arises from the manager's own inputs; moreover, by subjecting a portfolio to at least two divergent scenarios (optimistic and pessimistic) a form of *sensitivity analysis* is achieved.

A time frame of one year has been chosen, but this would vary according to one's own expectations and planning horizon. Three scenarios of interest rate change are shown. These have been derived from historical interest rate change tendencies over the past 36 years, where the standard deviation of change has been measured at various points along the yield curve. There is a bullish scenario, a market implicit forecast, and a bearish scenario. The bullish and bearish scenarios are derived by projecting one standard deviation of interest rate change at various points along the yield curve based on historical data. The market implicit forecast is derived from a term structure analysis and represents a scenario of interest rate change where the forward rates are assumed to be unchanged.

Multiscenario approaches recognize the uncertainty associated with interest rate forecasting and, accordingly, they allow a form of sensitivity analysis. In the example, these forecasts include a most likely (market implicit) case, an optimistic (declining rates) case, and a pessimistic (rising rates) case. The manager's own forecast would be, of course, a fourth alternative or a substitute for one or more of the scenarios. Each scenario is described along with its associated probability. The forecast yield for each scenario and the present yield to maturity for each maturity shown are presented in Table 8-6.

Table 8-7 exemplifies the result of translating interest rate change into expected rates of return for individual securities. In this example, a hypothetical U.S. Treasury bond portfolio is analyzed. The columns are largely self-explanatory, but those of particular importance are described in the footnotes for the table.

Clearly, the returns of each bond make it easy to identify the bullish and bearish scenarios. The sensitivity of the returns to rate change will be observed to increase with duration, as is expected. Also note an important property of Scenario 2, the market implicit scenario: The returns of all bonds that survive through the projection period are almost exactly equal.

The foregoing analysis may be extremely helpful in executing an effective active management strategy. Analytical insights are achieved by further partitioning the total return into its components. For example, the effect on reinvestment return as the time horizon is altered can be evaluated. Moreover, this analysis permits further analysis which will now be described.

Relative Return Value Analysis. An example of the analytical insight that can be derived from the return simulation process is illustrated in Figure 8-8. Duration is on the horizontal axis and on the vertical axis is the composite expected return, which is the probability-weighted average of each of the three scenario returns. Within the diagram is a regression line (upward sloping series of dashed lines), individual security representations (asterisks), the portfolio average return/duration (identified by the letter T), and bond identification numbers (far right-hand margin). The regression line represents the average relationship between return and duration exhibited by the individual securities making up the portfolio. Bonds above the line are those with greater expected return per unit of duration than the average relationship. Bonds below the line have less return per unit of duration. For example, the best bond for the total expected return and duration optimizer appears to be Bond 2, which has a duration of about 1.4 years and a composite return of about 8.0 percent. The worst bond appears to be Bond 10, with a duration of about 10.0 years and a composite return of about 9.2 percent. Referring back to Table 8-7, the return components of Securities 2 and 3 can be evaluated and compared. The large negative impact (-4.1) on return that occurred for Security 3 because of the security's sensitivity to the adverse interest rate change of Scenario 3 did not occur for Security

TABLE 8-7. Bond Portfolio Analysis of High Coupon U.S. Treasury Bonds: Three Scenario Interest Rate Forecast
(Current Date: 6-30-88; Projection Date: 6-30-89)

Bond Description	Price ($)	Yield to Effective Maturity (%)	Components of Return (%)						Total Return (%)	Effective Maturity	Duration[a] (Yrs)	Note
			Yield Curve[a]	Time[b]	Spread Change[c]	Earned Interest[d]	Mat./Call[e]	Reinv.[f]				
1 888888AA												
CASH EQUIVALENTS												
0.0000% 10-06-88 TR AAA CURR:	$ 98.265	6.63% MAT	.0	.0	.0	.0				10-6-88	.27	
SCEN 1:	100.000	.00 MAT	.0	.0	.0	.0	1.8	4.6	6.3	10-6-88	.00	MATURE
SCEN 2:	100.000	.00 MAT	.0	.0	.0	.0	1.8	5.2	7.0	10-6-88	.00	MATURE
SCEN 3:	100.000	.00 MAT	.0	.0	.0	.0	1.8	5.6	7.4	10-6-88	.00	MATURE
COMP:	100.000	.00 MAT	.0	.0	.0	.0	1.8	5.1	6.9	10-6-88	.00	
2 888888AB												
1.0–2.0 YR U.S. TREASURIES												
8.5214% 1-2-90 TR AAA CURR:	100.876	7.89 MAT								1-2-90	1.45	
SCEN 1:	101.610	5.28 MAT	1.0	-.3	.0	8.4	.0	.1	9.3	1-2-90	.51	
SCEN 2:	100.075	8.37 MAT	-.5	-.3	.0	8.4	.0	.1	7.8	1-2-90	.51	
SCEN 3:	98.896	10.81 MAT	-1.7	-.3	.0	8.4	.0	.2	6.6	1-2-90	.51	
COMP:	100.194	8.15 MAT	-.4	-.3	.0	8.4	.0	.1	7.9	1-2-90	.51	
3 888888AC												
2.0–3.0 YR U.S. TREASURIES												
9.1007% 12-24-90 TR AAA CURR:	102.161	8.12 MAT								12-24-90	2.28	
SCEN 1:	104.586	5.83 MAT	2.9	-.5	.0	8.9	.0	.2	11.4	12-24-90	1.42	
SCEN 2:	100.904	8.44 MAT	-.7	-.5	.0	8.9	.0	.2	7.9	12-24-90	1.42	
SCEN 3:	97.427	11.03 MAT	-4.1	-.5	.0	8.9	.0	.2	4.5	12-24-90	1.42	
COMP:	100.972	8.43 MAT	-.7	-.5	.0	8.9	.0	.2	7.9	12-24-90	1.42	
4 888888AD												
3.0–4.0 YR U.S. TREASURIES												
10.2111% 1-1-92 TR AAA CURR:	105.777	8.28 MAT								1- 1-92	3.05	
SCEN 1:	109.034	6.26 MAT	4.2	-1.1	.0	9.7	.0	.1	12.9	1- 1-92	2.29	
SCEN 2:	103.726	8.53 MAT	-.8	-1.1	.0	9.7	.0	.2	7.9	1- 1-92	2.28	
SCEN 3:	98.946	10.70 MAT	-5.3	-1.1	.0	9.7	.0	.2	3.4	1- 1-92	2.27	
COMP:	103.902	8.50 MAT	-.7	-1.1	.0	9.7	.0	.2	8.0	1- 1-92	2.28	
5 888888AE												
4.0–5.0 YR U.S. TREASURIES												
8.9142% 12-23-92 TR AAA CURR:	101.945	8.39% MAT								12-23-92	3.80	
SCEN 1:	107.348	6.52 MAT	5.2	.1	.0	8.7	.0	.2	14.2	12-23-92	3.09	
SCEN 2:	100.869	8.62 MAT	-1.1	.1	.0	8.7	.0	.2	7.9	12-23-92	3.07	
SCEN 3:	95.753	10.40 MAT	-6.1	.1	.0	8.7	.0	.2	2.9	12-23-92	3.06	
COMP:	101.323	8.51 MAT	-.7	.1	.0	8.7	.0	.2	8.3	12-23-92	3.07	

SOURCE: Gifford Fong Associates.

[a] Return due to changes in the nominal yield curve.
[b] Return assuming the initial yield curve remains constant over the projection horizon.
[c] Return attributable to spread change and volatility effects that are assumed to be zero for Treasury issues.
[d] Interest accrued over the projection period.
[e] Change in principal value for securities projected to be called or to mature.
[f] Interest on interest earned over the projection period.
[g] First figure in column is current duration; remaining figures are the durations at the end of the assumed holding period for the particular scenario.

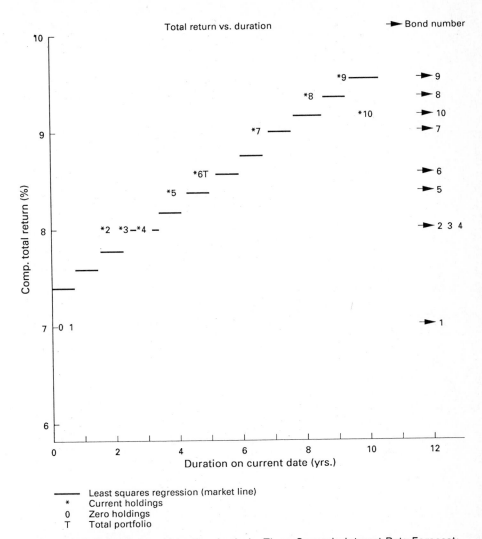

Total return vs. duration

━━▶ Bond number

	Least squares regression (market line)
*	Current holdings
0	Zero holdings
T	Total portfolio

Figure 8-8. Relative Return Valuation Analysis. Three Scenario Interest Rate Forecast: Model Portfolio—High Coupon U.S. Treasury (June 30, 1988 to June 30, 1989). SOURCE: Gifford Fong Associates.

2 (it was only − 1.7), largely because of the smaller duration (shorter maturity, smaller coupon) for Security 2.

Strategic Frontier Analysis. Figure 8-9 illustrates another display useful for analytical insight. The total return of the best case (Scenario 1) is measured along the vertical axis and the total return of the worst case (Scenario 3) as a risk proxy, is measured along the horizontal axis. Each security

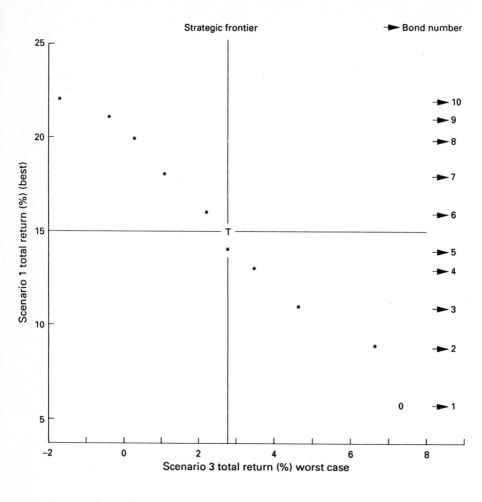

*   Current holdings
0   Zero holdings
T   Total portfolio

Figure 8-9. Strategic Frontier Analysis. Three Scenario Interest Rate Forecast: Model Portfolio—High Coupon U.S. Treasury (June 30, 1988 to June 30, 1989). SOURCE: Gifford Fong Associates.

is represented within the diagram (asterisks) and identified by bond number (right-hand margin). Cash (equivalents) is identified by the number 0. The portfolio average (letter T) is at the origin, or center, of the quadrants.

The upper left-hand quadrant of the figure represents securities having *aggressive* qualities. That is, if the best case scenario (rate decline) materializes, these securities will achieve high returns, but if the worst case scenario (rate rise) occurs then they will do relatively poorly. Securities 10, 9, 8, 7, and 6 are aggressive. Securities in the upper right-hand quadrant are *superior* securities because, regardless of the scenario outcome, the portfolio average return (letter T) will be enhanced. There are no securities in this quadrant, but if there were, these would be the purchase candidates regardless of scenario expectation. The lower right quadrant has securities with *defensive* characteristics; if the worst case materializes they will do well, but if the best case occurs they will do relatively poorly. Bonds 5, 4, 3, 2, and 1 are defensive. The lower left quadrant would be those securities that are *inferior* because, regardless of scenario outcome, they would pull down the return of the portfolio. There are no securities in the inferior quadrant, but if there were, they would be sell candidates, regardless of scenario expectation.

Both of the analyses just described provide examples of extensions to the return simulation process. Using a multiscenario approach, the return and risk characteristics of individual bonds as well as the portfolio can be evaluated.

Normally, there would be a distribution of securities such that most would fall into the upper left and lower right quadrants with a few securities in the lower left and upper right quadrants. Because the analysis was based on model securities, the normal distribution is not observed, but the basic principle is still demonstrated.

Timing

The timing of active strategies can be important. Over a given planning horizon, judgment is necessary to determine when a strategy is to be implemented. Figure 8-10 illustrates two common yield curve shapes. When the first curve (positively sloped) exists, and if it is interpreted as a forecast of higher future interest rates, the strategy taken must be carefully timed. To benefit from an ensuing rate increase, a shortening of maturity (duration) is called for. However, by moving to the left of the curve, a lower yield to maturity must be accepted. Premature rate anticipation under these circumstances would result in a lower realized return for the period before rates increase; if the increase never materializes or materializes only after a prolonged wait, significant return give-up and a negative impact on portfolio results may be experienced.

Conversely, if the second curve (negatively sloped) prevails and rates are expected to decrease, timing is important because a premature lengthening of maturity results in a lower yield to maturity and total return along with a much riskier longer maturity (duration) portfolio. The conclusion is that effective timing of rate anticipation is a necessary and important consideration.

Moreover, rate anticipation should not be considered complete after the initial timing issue is resolved. The point at which the manager should reverse

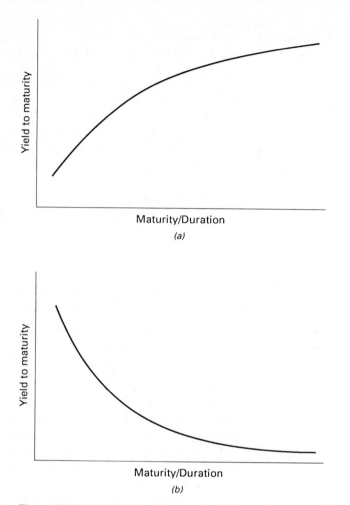

Figure 8-10. (*a*) Positive or Upward Sloping Yield Curve; (*b*) Negative or Downward Sloping Yield Curve.

or modify the strategy must be continually considered. The return component interactions originally estimated will be constantly in flux, and the manager must continually balance anticipated capital changes against current yield and reinvestment return effects. This makes the "round-trip" character of successful rate anticipation apparent. That is, the rate anticipation efforts of the manager cannot be judged to be successful until the move taken in anticipation of any given rate increase (decrease) is reversed with a timely opposite move when rates are expected to decrease (increase). In fact, this is an ongoing process of continuing to analyze and manage in the face of changing expectations.

Bond Feature Effects. The terms of individual securities, such as the effects of refunding terms, should also be analyzed. For example, suppose that in a scenario of rising rates the prepayment experience of Government National Mortgage Association (GNMA) or Ginnie Mae securities is expected to decline because mortgage holders tend to hold on to lower interest rate mortgages. Conversely, if rates decline, there is an incentive to refinance, with the result that higher refunding and therefore shorter-lived Ginnie Maes can be expected. Forearmed with knowledge of the anticipated average life of a GNMA security under various interest rate scenarios, the manager can decide whether to use or avoid these securities.

As another example, the call feature of a bond tends to be unused by its issuer if rates rise because the issuer will not want to retire or refinance bonds issued at rates lower than current rates. As a result, callability is not of concern to the manager when rising rates are forecast. The opposite is true when rates are expected to fall; the issuer will then have an incentive to retire callable bonds and refinance at lower rates.

Fortunately, all of these considerations can be integrated into the return simulation analysis described. This allows the manager to focus attention on the most important dimensions of direction, shape, and timing of interest rate changes.

Interest rate forecasting is a difficult challenge because of highly efficient markets. Wide distribution of information, low transaction costs, and many intelligent participants contribute to the difficulty of consistently and correctly forecasting the direction of interest rate changes. This does not say that some people cannot do it well, but it does suggest that success is extremely difficult to consistently achieve. However, the rewards of being right are great, not only in terms of realized returns, but also in terms of the amount of investment management business that one can attract. Unfortunately, the converse is also true. Using the previously described techniques can contribute to the desired outcome.

Sector and Security Strategies

Beyond rate anticipation, there is the possibility of enhancing returns by evaluating individual securities and subgroups of securities. This takes three basic forms: credit analysis, spread analysis, and bond valuation.

Credit Analysis. Credit analysis is concerned with the assessment of default risk—the probability that the issuer will be unable to meet all contractual obligations fully and in a timely manner. Default risk is important for two reasons: The first is the chance of loss due to actual acts of default; the second is the likelihood of adverse bond price changes that are precipitated by any increased probability of default, typically from the downgrading of a bond's quality by the rating agencies, even though no act of default actually takes place. The popularity of *leveraged buyouts* in the late 1980s spawned the notion of *event risk*, where previously high credit rated securities become downgraded (and hence lose value) because of the change in leverage associated with takeover activity of the issuer.

Default risk has both systematic and unsystematic elements. For a variety of reasons, individual bond issuers may experience difficulty in meeting their obligations from time to time. If these are isolated acts of default, they may be diversified away or be eliminated by effective credit analysis. More worrisome is the possibility of adverse general business conditions, such as occurred during the 1930s, the mid-1970s, and in the early 1980s, that are associated with significant increases in the frequency of defaults and with widespread price declines due to concern over credit quality. These concerns require more macro-oriented analysis, such as found in Chapter 5.

As indicated previously, risk of default is often quantified by quality ratings provided by Duff & Phelps, Fitch's, Moody's, and Standard & Poor's. Historically, such ratings have proved to be valid, but they are not foolproof indicators of risk. They also appear to be closely related to other traditional measures of credit quality, such as relative debt burden, interest or fixed charges expense coverage (by earnings before deduction of interest and tax expenses), and variability in earnings streams. However, many fixed-income investors complement the evaluations of the rating agencies with their own credit analysis (see Chapter 6). Reasons cited include more accurate, comprehensive, and timely analyses and recommendations.

Spread Analysis. Spread analysis involves anticipating changes in sectoral relationships. It may be possible to identify subclasses of fixed-income securities that tend to behave in a highly similar manner. For example, prices and yields on lower investment grade bonds tend to move together, as do yields on utility bonds. Such identifiable classes of securities are referred to as sectors. (In this sense, maturity ranges are also sectors, but the influence of maturity on total return is so dramatic that yield/maturity analysis is usually treated separately.) Relative prices or yields among sectors may change due to (1) altered perceptions of the creditworthiness of a sector or of the market's sensitivity to default risk; (2) changes in the market's valuation of some attribute or characteristic of the securities in the sector, such as a zero coupon feature; or (3) changes in supply and demand conditions.

Analysis of relative sectoral relationships, if coupled with appropriate management response, can be rewarding in fixed-income portfolio management. The objective, obviously, is to be heavily invested in the sector or sectors that will display the strongest relative price movements. In monitoring such sectoral relationships, it is customary to concentrate on spreads (i.e., the difference, usually measured in basis points, in yield between two yield series that are broadly representative of the securities in the sector).

A number of brokerage firms maintain such yield series on an historical basis so that a normal framework of analysis can be identified. These firms are usually able to conduct specialized analyses for clients, such as measurement of the historical average, maximum, and minimum spread among sectors. Such analysis plus consideration of other relevant factors (such as duration effects) leads to what is, in effect, a relative valuation of a sector's worth. If the relative values are enough out of line, one could pursue arbitrage-like sector swapping to achieve gains or minimize losses before sector yields return to more normal relationships.

In both credit analysis and spread analysis the potential for return enhancement, although dominated by gains from proper rate anticipation, still holds the promise of a significant contribution to portfolio performance. Potential drawbacks include the need to do many trades for the contribution to be meaningful, the possibility of poor timing, and the danger that overall changes in interest rates will dwarf these efforts.

Valuation Analysis. From the estimated term structure of pure discount zero coupon bonds, the value of default-free securities such as U.S. Treasuries can be estimated; or, for other types of securities, their default-free equivalent values can be estimated. Other characteristics of a bond can then be valued by using a form of multiple factor regression analysis. This analysis allows one to quantify the values attributable to the quality rating, coupon effect, sector effect, call provision, and sinking fund features of the bond. From these yield premia components, the total premium over the default-free equivalent of the issue can be calculated. Once the current market valuation of the various bond attributes has been estimated, the value of any given bond can be determined by adding the yield premium for each of the bond's characteristics to the appropriate default-free yield. The valuation model may be used for a number of purposes, including:

1. *Yield Component Analysis.* By identifying the components of yield, the model may contribute to an understanding of the structure of the yield of the bond.
2. *Identification of Mispriced Securities.* The price fitted by the model, as discussed below in connection with Table 8-8, may be compared to an actual quoted price to show the extent of price deviation. The T-statistic (T-stat), illustrated in a tabular example later, provides a statistical test of the price differential.
3. *Pricing of Private Placements.* The fitted price may be used as a price estimate in the valuation of issues for which market values are not readily available, such as inactive securities or private placements.
4. *Performance Measurement.* Prices fitted by the model may be used in historical valuation of securities and portfolios, a

necessary step in performance measurement when infrequently traded bonds are in the portfolio.

5. *Active Bond Management*. Quantifying the yield differential available for various bond characteristics permits the analysis of the trade-off between higher yield and attendant risk.

Table 8-8 details the components evaluated in arriving at a fitted value for a group of agency and corporate bonds. Let us look at the third bond, Canadian National Railway Co. (15 percent coupon, 06/01/06 maturity). The sector/quality code, C2, indicates that this is a non-U.S., U.S. dollar-pay, AA2 rated bond.). Based on analysis of the term structure of U.S. Treasuries for June 30, 1988, the default-free value of this bond, without embedded options, would be 140.882 (8.595 percent yield to maturity).

Canadian National Railway is a corporation. The cash flows are not guaranteed. The marketplace accounts for this risk by charging a risk premium. Based on a cross sectional multiple regression analysis of approximately 3,500 corporate bonds, the sector premium (for a non-U.S. issuer) is evaluated at 73.6 basis points (bp) and the quality premium at 13.2 bp (versus an AAA credit in this sector).

Relative to the default-free valuation, which is based solely on the term structure spot rates, a premium of 27.2 bp is also associated with a "coupon effect." At one time this effect could be associated with the differing U.S. tax treatment between capital appreciation and interest income. However, even with the elimination of the tax differential there still persists a yield premium based on coupon.

Finally there is the "option effect." The option effect is evaluated as the price difference between the bond without any embedded options and the bond with an embedded option.

There are several items to recognize in valuing an option. First, the option is evaluated to the bond's *maturity*. In the past, bonds with embedded options were frequently evaluated on a "yield to worst case" scenario. The maturity of the worst case scenario was substituted for the maturity of the bond. Hence the yield to worst case represented the yield to a date shorter than the actual maturity of the bond. Using options valuation, the yield on the bond is measured to the final *maturity* of the bond (although the duration and effective maturity of the bond are adjusted to reflect the option effect). Because the option changes the duration and effective maturity of the bond, it is not relevant to talk about the yield spread associated with the option.

The price resulting from the sum of these effects is the fitted value. (The "Issue Effect" is an adjustment entered by the user to account for special situations other than the four effects described previously: sector, quality, coupon, and the embedded option. Often, the embedded option is zero.)

The T-stat measures the significance of the difference between the fitted

TABLE 8-8. Bond Valuation Computer Program Output

VALUATION DATE: 6/30/88
YIELD PREMIA COEFFICIENTS FROM: 6/30/88
CALL SOURCE: PORTFOLIO

Bond Description		Default Free	Sector Effect	Quality Effect	Coupon Effect	Option Effect	Issue Effect	Fitted Value	Actual Value	T-Stat	Adj Dur
1 313311QA											
FEDERAL FARM CREDIT BANK	PRICE($)	99.881	-.295	.000	-.161	.000	.000	99.425	99.470	-.112	.87
7.350% 6-1-89 AG AAA	YIELD(%)	7.476	.339	.000	.184		.000	7.999	7.948		
2 313311JB											
FEDERAL FARM CREDIT BANK	PRICE($)	105.630	-.723	.000	-.536	.000	.000	104.372	104.625	-.261	2.00
10.600% 10-22-90 AG AAA	YIELD(%)	7.876	.339	.000	.250		.000	8.465	8.346		
3 136375AQ											
CANADIAN NATL RY CO (C,S)	PRICE($)	140.882	-5.805	-.999	-2.248	-12.229	.000	119.602	120.981	-.967	2.71
15.000% 6-1-06 C2 AA2	YIELD(%)	8.595	.736	.132	.272		.000	9.303	8.862		
Callable/Sink	Y-T-EffMat	(6-1-91)							10.737		
4 669827DD											
PROVINCE OF NOVA SCOTIA	PRICE($)	106.059	-3.634	-.335	-1.130	.000	.000	100.960	101.696	-.333	4.56
9.625% 1-1-95 C3 A2	YIELD(%)	8.397	.736	.069	.222		.000	9.424	9.272		
5 010392BJ											
ALABAMA POWER CO (C)	PRICE($)	100.495	-9.962	1.567	-1.950	-.279	.000	89.872	92.278	-.716	7.93
8.875% 3-1-06 E3 A1	YIELD(%)	8.817	1.248	-.210	.222		.000	10.067	9.740		
Callable	Y-T-EffMat	(3-1-06)							9.800		
6 008140AB											
AETNA LIFE & CAS CO (C,S)	PRICE($)	93.130	-5.414	.000	-1.727	-.016	.000	85.974	83.230	.856	7.89
8.000% 1-15-17 F1 AAA	YIELD(%)	8.793	.714	.000	.214		.000	9.719	10.110		
Callable/Sink	Y-T-EffMat	(7-16-06)							10.112		
7 140186AJ											
CAPITAL HOLDINGS (C,S)	PRICE($)	99.564	-5.833	-2.402	-1.906	-.036	.000	89.386	85.542	1.180	7.73
8.750% 1-15-17 F3 A1	YIELD(%)	8.798	.714	.315	.219		.000	10.043	10.582		
Callable/Sink	Y-T-EffMat	(7-16-07)							10.585		

SOURCE: Gifford Fong Associates.

value and the actual value. The difference is divided by the variance calculated in the original price estimation process.

The analysis in Table 8-8 helps one analyze the components of yield evaluation and provides a comparison of fitted value to actual value. The over- or undervaluation provides a starting point for evaluating whether a bond is "rich" or "cheap." The portfolio manager must consider whether there are missing elements in this analysis before acting on such a rich/cheap analysis, such as some event risk missing from the analysis or a market anticipation of an upgrade.

The table estimates that Canadian National Railway is rich by approximately 1.4 points. The same report estimates that the Aetna bond (bond no. 6) is cheap by some 2.7 points. Should the Aetna bond be purchased and the Canadian National Railway bond be sold? Unfortunately, swaps cannot and should not be evaluated this easily. In other parts of this chapter we have discussed portfolio construction techniques such as immunization and indexation. Purchase and sale decisions should be made relative to the portfolio objectives.

For instance, the duration of the Canadian Railway bond is 2.71 years; the duration of the Aetna bond is 7.89 years. A swap between these two bonds would significantly lengthen the relative duration, and this may be undesirable in the context of portfolio objectives.

Optimization

Variance/Covariance Approach. The objective of portfolio optimization is to maximize expected return at a given level of risk or to minimize risk at a given level of expected return. Two alternative methods of optimization can be identified. How to quantify ex ante risk (or risk before it is actually experienced) of a bond portfolio is the main difference between the two methods.

In most equity optimization approaches, the standard deviation or variance of portfolio returns has been used as the risk objective to be minimized. The process for equities involves creating a covariance matrix that, along with expectations of stock returns, is then optimized by a quadratic optimization program. Including such things as turnover, concentration, and dividend yield constraints, a minimum risk portfolio for a given level of return is produced. The problem is tractable because the covariance matrix can always be estimated based on historical return experience.

In bond analysis, however, no such convention is available. Because of the finite life of a fixed-income security, its covariance characteristic with other bonds changes with time, if for no other reason than because the maturity of each bond becomes shorter with time. Moreover, with a given rate change, there can be yield curve shape changes as well as direction changes. The latter can alter, and in some cases reverse, the covariance relationship between securities. The problem thus becomes one of estimation. Indeed, if a covariance matrix could be created, then the optimization process would parallel the analysis for stocks.

Worst Case Approach. An alternative approach defines risk as the worst case interest rate scenario or the outcome given the most adverse change (increase) in interest rates. The objective becomes to maximize bond portfolio expected return with risk defined as the level of return under the worst case interest rate scenario, constrained to some minimum level. Risk is specified in terms of minimally acceptable return levels that in turn are a direct result of the worst case interest rate scenario expectations. Because the analytical procedure is linear, a linear programming optimization algorithm may be used.

Other Active Strategies or Tactics

In addition to the active strategies already discussed, a number of other approaches can be identified. These emphasize the individual sector or security rather than the portfolio as a whole. Their potential impact on total portfolio return may not be as great but they still may make a significant contribution to overall returns.

Pure Yield Pickup Trade or Exchange. Switching to a security having a higher yield is called a pure yield trade or exchange. The transaction may be made to achieve either a higher coupon yield or a larger yield to maturity. It would appear that such transactions would always be done as long as there is no significant shift in risk level (or liquidity). However, accounting rules or regulatory mandates constrain some investors from yield pickup trades that create a loss, usually unless offset by a gain elsewhere in the portfolio, even though a portfolio benefit would result.

Substitution Trade or Exchange. This transaction involves substituting one security for another that has a higher yield to maturity but is otherwise identical in terms of maturity, coupon, and quality. This type of trade depends on a capital market imperfection. That is, the portfolio manager expects the yields to maturity on the two securities to reestablish a normal yield spread relationship, resulting in a price increase and hence capital appreciation for the holder of the higher yielding issue. The workout period (time for the expected realignment in yields to occur) can be critical, because the sooner it occurs, the greater the return on an annualized basis; if the workout period is extensive, such as having to hold the security several years until it matures, the realized additional annual return may be marginal.

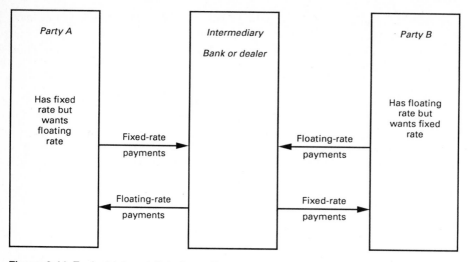

Figure 8-11. Typical Interest Rate Swap Transaction.

Intermarket or Sector Spread Trade or Exchange. Based on the expected normal yield relationship between two different sectors of the bond market, trades may be made when there is a perceived misalignment. This may involve switching to the higher yielding security when the yield spread is too wide and is expected to narrow, or to the lower yielding security when the spread is too narrow and is expected to widen. The risk, especially of the latter switch (because it will be into a lower yielding security), is that the anticipated adjustment will not be made, resulting in a reduced portfolio yield.

Interest Rate Swaps. In the 1980s, the swap market developed to allow borrowers and lenders to exchange specified interest rate payment streams without exchanging the underlying debt. These payment streams are considered to be interest payments on a specified principal amount. The latter is defined as *notional principal* because no transfer of principal actually takes place between the parties to an interest rate swap.

In a typical interest rate swap, party A makes fixed-rate payments to party B who in turn makes floating-rate payments to party A or vice versa. The interest rates on which the swap is based reflect current capital and money market levels. The typical term of a swap ranges from one to twelve years and the typical minimum notional principal amount is $5 million.

Most often, a swap is arranged through an intermediary such as a merchant bank or investment bank that serves as a principal and thus is a full *counterparty* in the transaction, as illustrated in Figure 8-11. The creditworthiness of the counterparty is an important consideration for those participating in a swap since the integrity of the transaction depends on the willingness and ability of the counterparty to maintain the agreed upon stream of fixed or floating rate payments.

The motivation for an interest rate swap is based on certain structural differences within or between markets that relate to the characteristics of:

1. *Borrower vs. Lender.* One counterparty may have a comparative advantage borrowing or lending at fixed rates versus floating rates. For example, in the United States, banks and thrift institutions have a unique ability to attract low cost, short-term demand or time deposits because of the federal insurance that protects such deposits up to $100,000 per account.

2. *Short End vs. Long End of the Market.* One counterparty may have a comparative advantage in terms of interest rates paid or received from funds borrowed or lent that have a very short maturity (e.g., a bank loan) as compared with a much longer maturity (e.g., a mortgage loan).

3. *Domestic vs. International Markets.* One counterparty may have a comparative advantage in one market versus another, such as borrowing at a floating rate in the Euromarket.

In effect, swap opportunities are created out of the yield spread differentials that arise from these structural and comparative differences.

Quite often, interest rate swaps are used as duration management tools by financial institutions. In fact, they are considered by many as a substitute for interest rate futures in many cases, especially where the hedging horizon is longer than the maturity of the typical futures contract. However, interest rate swaps are generally less liquid than futures and are dependent on the creditworthiness of the counterparty. In effect, the portfolio manager can use cash, futures, or swap transactions to correct duration gaps between assets and liabilities.

For example, a portfolio manager for a life insurance company may want to shorten the duration of the assets in a segment of the portfolio to reduce or eliminate an asset/liability mismatch. Longer term assets could be sold and shorter term assets acquired with the proceeds but these transactions have liquidity, tax, and return differential implications that must be considered. By using an interest rate swap with a creditworthy counterparty, the portfolio manager could agree to make semiannual fixed-rate payments and receive semiannual floating-rate payments tied to a key interest rate series, such as the London Interbank Offered Rate (LIBOR), and adjusted every six months. The duration of the floating rate payments will now be six months. In effect, the portfolio manager has converted the duration of the notional amount invested from longer term to six months over the life of the swap agreement.

Table 8-9 provides an illustration of the yield differentials that result from interest rate swap transactions. As shown in the table, swaps tend to

TABLE 8-9. An Example of Yield Levels and Spread Relationships for Interest Rate Swaps

| Maturity | U.S. Treasury Yield Level | Spreads | |
		Interest Rate Swap vs. Treasury	A-Rated Industrial Bonds vs. Treasury
6 months	9.60%	+70 basis points	+35 basis points
1 year	10.10	+70	+35
2 years	10.95	+75	+35
3 years	11.15	+75	+35
5 years	11.60	+55	+40
7 years	11.75	+50	+45
10 years	11.85	+45	+45
20 years	11.90	—	+60

SOURCE: Platt [1986].

provide the greatest yield advantage in the shorter maturities. It is this ability to generate additional returns, because of the structural and comparative differences noted earlier, that has enabled the swap market to grow to a several hundred billion dollar market in a few short years. As the size suggests, the swap market has evolved rapidly to a level of complexity and sophistication that is beyond the scope of this chapter.

In addition to duration management, there are several other common uses of interest rate swaps.

1. *Managing gaps* by using swaps to match fixed-rate assets with fixed-rate liabilities or floating-rate assets with floating-rate liabilities.
2. *Reducing the cost of capital* because credit risk differentials are much narrower in the short-term market, which tends to be a floating-rate market, as compared with the longer term, fixed-rate market.
3. *Restructuring debt* by using swaps to, in essence, convert long-term debt into a short-term debt structure.
4. *Managing basis risk* by seeking to arrange swaps such that changes in interest rates, especially floating rates, move parallel to rates on the underlying asset or liability that is being modified by the swap transaction.

Interest rate swap transactions can be modified by *caps* and *collars*. A cap transaction is one where no payments are made unless the floating rate exceeds a specified level. A collar transaction is one where no payments are made unless the floating rate exceeds a specified level or falls below a specified level. Caps and collars are essentially *contingent swaps* that can be created on a stand-alone basis or can be applied to interest rate swap transactions.

This market is continuing to evolve and, as it becomes more standardized, the potential exists for a secondary trading market to develop. For now, the swap market should be described as an effective but relatively illiquid means of expanding the portfolio manager's options for modifying the underlying portfolio's characteristics.

Currency Swaps. Managers of internationally diversified portfolios may want to consider currency swaps, which are essentially packages of forward currency contracts. These swaps are used to provide borrowers or lenders with the opportunity to make or receive payments in the currency of their choice. A foreign company may wish to borrow U.S. dollars but lacks market recognition among U.S. lenders. In this case, the foreign company would be better off borrowing in its domestic market. Through an intermediary, it could arrange to swap its payments for those of a U.S. company that wants to borrow in the currency of the foreign company's country.

A U.S. portfolio manager can use these currency swaps to seek incremental risk-adjusted returns by converting the interest and principal payments to be received from a foreign bond investment into U.S. dollars, thus eliminating currency risk. As an example, for a few months during the 1980s, it was possible for a U.S. portfolio manager to purchase intermediate term U.K. Gilt securities and enter into currency swaps to convert the semiannual interest payments and the principal payment on the Gilts into U.S. currency and realize a yield advantage of 70 basis points over the comparable U.S. Treasury security. The currency swap involved was a series of forward contracts, one for each of the interest payments and one for the ultimate principal payment.

Currency Interest Rate Swaps. Currency swaps predate interest rate swaps and played a major role in spawning fixed-rate/floating-rate swaps. Thus, it is not surprising that the two types of swaps can be integrated to provide for the exchange of types of payments—fixed versus floating—when more than one currency is involved.

Maturity-Spacing Strategies. Alternative portfolio maturity structures may be used as a source of potential extra return. These include a balanced or laddered maturity strategy with equal spacing of maturities held; an all short or all long maturity strategy; or a barbell maturity structure, where bond holdings are concentrated in both short maturities and long maturities, with few, if any, intermediates. The rationale for an equal maturity strategy is to provide the portfolio with some reinvestment risk protection, spreading reinvestment out over the full interest rate cycle. That is, there will be a relatively continuous cash flow over time from maturity *laddering*, and these funds can be reinvested at the then current rates. The effects of overall interest rate change will tend to be averaged, and the extremes of return and risk will be truncated.

An all short or all long maturity portfolio strategy is frequently a temporary strategy adopted as a result of rate (change) anticipation. For those who stay with an all short portfolio there is usually either a preference for high liquidity or an extreme aversion to principal risk. A barbell approach anticipates that the best return/risk reward is achieved by balancing the defensive qualities of short-term securities with the aggressive qualities of long-term securities and avoiding the intermediates. A temporary barbell strategy is appropriate when short rates are expected to be rising and long rates are forecast to be relatively stable, that is, *twisting* in the yield curve is anticipated.

Comparing the laddered to the barbell approach as a constant strategy has not shown one to be superior to the other (see, e.g., Fogler, Groves, and Richardson [1976] and Fogler and Groves [1976]).

Contingent Claims Analysis. Fixed-income securities may have cash flows that are dependent on the future direction of interest rates because of embedded option features. How to evaluate these options is the objective of contingent claims analysis.

A callable bond is perhaps the best known example of a security with an embedded option (i.e., a contingent claim). Depending on the future direction of interest rates, the cash flow, and hence also the duration, yield to effective maturity, and convexity of the security may change.

Traditionally, a *yield to worst case assumption* was used to estimate cash flows, where the callable bond would assume the characteristics of the lower of the yield to maturity or yield to the call date of the security. Of course, if one uses a single (most likely) scenario of interest rate change, then the cash flow would be deterministic. It is the uncertainty associated with the future direction of rates that gives rise to the notion of contingent claims analysis—the valuation of the embedded option given uncertain interest rates. The critical element in contingent claims analysis is to evaluate the stochastic nature of interest rate change *without* having to predict the direction of rates.

The two main analytical solutions, explained more completely in most textbook treatments of option valuation, include the *binomial approach* and the *continuous time approach* (where a partial differential equation is solved). The binomial approach values the embedded option based on specific scenarios of interest rate change. The continuous time approach typically will depend on the following assumptions:

1. The value of the security depends only on current and future interest rates.

2. The term structure is described by a stochastic process (e.g.,
   driven by the short rate).
3. No profitable riskless arbitrage is possible.

These assumptions make possible the analysis of the risk characteristics,
duration, convexity, and value of embedded options.

The value of an interest rate dependent security is determined by mar-
ketwide assumptions about future interest rate behavior. The continuous
time models of interest rate behavior that have been developed typically
assume that interest rates move in a random but continuous fashion around
some long-term average level. They assume that these fluctuations tend to
move toward the long-term average level with a strength that increases as
the amount of the deviation from the long-term average increases. The fluctuations and their central tendency are usually expressed by a stochastic
differential equation.

These models also typically assume that the market is efficient in the
sense that riskless arbitrage is prohibited. For example, suppose a portfolio
can be theoretically constructed such that its instantaneous return (or return
over a very short period of time) is not dependent on interest rates, perhaps
by mixing long and short securities positions. The instantaneous return on
this portfolio should not differ from the shortest-term spot rate, which is the
rate that one would pay for funds borrowed to purchase the portfolio.

Under all of the above assumptions the price of a bond, based on the
spot rates that hold over its term to maturity, is subject to a partial differential
equation. This equation expresses the total value of the security as a function
of interest rates and time, other model parameters that characterize the
stochastic, or random, behavior of interest rates, and the parameters that
describe the security's cash flow and option characteristics.

The cash flow specification simply describes the contractual payments
on the security. For example, the cash flows of a callable bond are just its
coupon payments for as long as the bond survives without being called and
zero after the bond has been called or matures. Boundary conditions are
necessary if a unique solution to the differential equation is to be obtained.
The boundary conditions specify the value of the security at maturity and
at extreme rate levels. For example, a callable bond's value at maturity is
its face amount. Its value should interest rates become infinitely high is
extremely small.

The options are specified by comparing the value of the security at any
date on which an option may be executed with its value immediately after-
wards, assuming that the option is not exercised. For a callable bond, the
value on any call date is the smaller of the call price and the value of the
bond if not called.

For a callable bond, for example, even though all of these relationships
are easy to specify, a thorny mathematical problem remains: how to obtain

the solution to the partial differential equation. These equations are always solved numerically (i.e., on a computer). (The Black-Sholes option pricing formula for stock options is a special case in which an analytical solution can be found. No calculable analytic solutions have been discovered for embedded bond options.) The solution technique usually involves taking tiny steps backward in time from the maturity date (when the price is known) and computing the price for different interest rate levels at each step via use of the partial differential equation while simultaneously keeping track of the option relationships.

This is a tedious and rather slow process even for a computer. One of the solution techniques requires the assumption that rates move only up by a specified amount or down by a specified amount over each time interval. This is a binomial model. Another approach involves a continuous model. This type of model allows the imposition of prohibitions against profitable, riskless arbitrage and a detailed description of the stochastic process of interest rates. Variations of this stochastic process lead to the progressively more complex models. In the simplest case, but one which leads to very useful results, interest rates at all maturities are assumed to be dependent on the random level of the short-term rate. A more complex model assumes that interest rates at all maturities are dependent on random short-term and long-term rates. Unfortunately, as these models are made more and more realistic, they become more and more difficult to solve computationally. It is fortunate, then, that useful results have been obtained by using all of the preceding models. The valuations they provide differ somewhat, of course, since they all embody slightly different assumptions.

Effects of Call Option Valuation. Consider three examples of the way call option valuation can alter the analysis of a callable bond. Each of these relationships has been derived based on the characteristics of the same security. It has a coupon of $11\frac{1}{8}$ percent, matures on 6/15/10, is currently (as of 6/30/89) callable at 107.33, and has successively lower call prices (above par) each year until it becomes callable at par on 6/15/09. In each case specified, the relationship of a single parameter of this bond to the bond's yield is examined. The meaning of yield to maturity, when there are interest rate contingent cash flows, must be reconsidered, but this question is outside the scope of this chapter. Instead, it is assumed that yield has been acceptably defined by the theory of contingent claims, and the objective is to examine how the use of this theory alters established notions of the basic bond relationships.

First, consider the relationship of price and yield as shown in Figure 8-12. It is clear that the effect of the call option is to prevent the continued increase of the price of a bond as its yield decreases. This is what produces the difference between the price of an equivalent noncallable security and that of the callable bond. However, note how much more of a "ceiling effect"

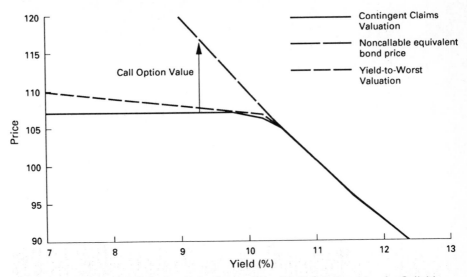

Figure 8-12. Effect of Call Option Valuation on Price/Yield Relationship of a Callable Bond: Commonwealth Edison 11⅛s of 6/15/10 Evaluated on 6/30/89.

(reduction in yield, but no increase in price) there is when the contingent nature of the call option is fully evaluated (solid line). This is partly due to the fact that the traditional yield-to-worst (case assumption) measure ignores the out-of-the-money nature of the current call feature (in the lowest yield region, where the contingent claims price curve is essentially flat).

More importantly, however, in the intermediate region, price overestimations of as much as 1.0 percent or more at a given yield are routinely made by using the traditional yield-to-worst relationship. This is because the assumption used in the yield-to-worst case is that the ultimate date of the exercise of the call option is one of the future bond call dates and is determinable based on the current price. In reality, it is entirely unknown when the option will be exercised, if at all. All that is known is that it will be exercised to the disadvantage of the bondholder. This means that the *true* yield of a bond at a given price is lower than its yield to *any* call date or maturity date.

In passing, note that the value of the call option may be identified graphically in Figure 8-12. It is simply the distance from the price of the callable bond to the price of its noncallable equivalent. This provides a reminder that the value of a security with an option attached is just the value the security would have had if there had been no option less (or plus, depending on who owns the option) the value of the option.

Figure 8-13 displays the (modified) duration of the callable bond as a function of its yield. The duration of the noncallable equivalent increases continuously as the yield decreases. In reality, the duration must fall sig-

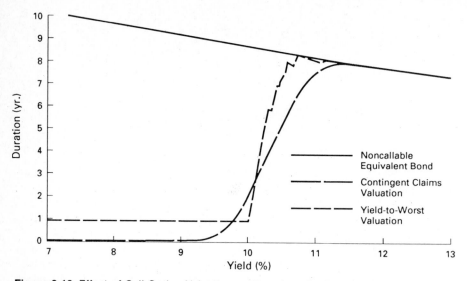

Figure 8-13. Effect of Call Option Valuation on Duration of a Callable Bond: Commonwealth Edison 11⅛s of 6/15/10 Evaluated on 6/30/89.

nificantly as yield decreases because the bond would likely be called at lower yield levels. However, note again how significantly the yield-to-worst technique misestimates the duration relative to the contingent claims techniques in the intermediate region. It misses it too in the very low yield region, but that is because this technique ignores the fact that the security is immediately callable should the price rise above its current call price. This latter problem is less serious because it can be dealt with by simply calculating the yield to the current effective maturity date that will cause the bond price to exceed the current call price.

The contingent claims analysis, on the other hand, shows that the true, or effective, duration of the security in the intermediate region is much less (i.e., 1 or 2 years) than that estimated by using the yield-to-worst approximation. It also shows that the duration declines smoothly to zero as the yield falls until, at about 9.5 percent, it reaches zero, indicating that the bond's price would then exceed the current call price, and the bond would be called.

Finally, Figure 8-14 shows a similar situation with respect to the relationship of yield and the measured effective maturity of a callable bond. The yield-to-worst-case model predicts a stair step behavior for this function, moving from the stated maturity at high yields to the time to the first future call date for low yield levels. Note, though, how erroneous the estimated time to maturity is in the 10 to 12 percent range of yields (e.g., as much as 5 years for a 19-year bond) when compared with the estimation provided by the contingent claims model.

The contingent claims estimation of effective maturity is a probability-

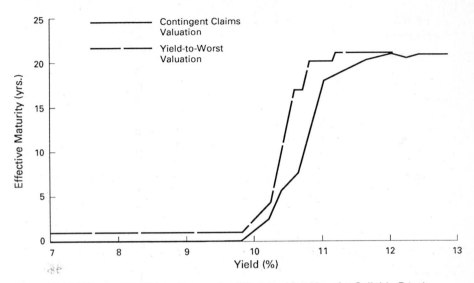

Figure 8-14. Effect of Call Valuation on the Effective Maturity of a Callable Bond: Commonwealth Edison 11⅛s of 6/15/10 Evaluated on 6/30/89.

weighted average of all possible redemption dates. The probabilities are based on the assumptions of the model of future interest rate behavior.

This type of analysis has been extended to mortgage-backed securities, as reported in Chung, Fong, and Tang [1988]. Similar analysis may be applied to contingent liabilities and other fixed-income embedded options. While the application of this type of analysis is still developing, its potential for valuation without the need for interest rate forecasting is exciting and compelling.

COMBINATION STRATEGIES

A number of basic portfolio strategies have already been reviewed. It should be kept in mind, however, that the range of portfolio strategies is really a continuum. At various phases during an interest rate cycle, particular strategies may be most appropriate, but more often than not, a blending of alternatives is best for part or all of the cycle. The determination of what is optimal may be made by the investor or pension plan sponsor or, alternatively, by the portfolio manager.

Under conditions of high conviction, a one strategy approach may be optimal; in the more customary situation of large uncertainty, strategy combinations may be best in a return/risk trade-off sense. This might result, for example, in a portion of the portfolio return and risk being tied to some baseline portfolio, the performance of which over the long term should provide satisfactory results, with the remaining portion being actively managed. By retaining an active component, the opportunity for superior performance is retained. How best to determine the proportion to be allocated to each strategy could follow the same general procedure as that for asset allocation discussed in Chapter 7. This, in effect, would be an allocation among strategies within the fixed-income asset category.

It is not uncommon for managers to be selected on the basis of their expertise in specific strategies. This specialization can be in any of the continuum of strategies available and is particularly attractive in the multimanager situation typical of large pension plan sponsors.

Recent developments in option valuation theory have provided an additional capability for not only enhancing particular strategy types, but also creating combinations of strategies. Again, a continuum of applications is possible ranging from changing the duration of an actively managed fixed-income portfolio to allocating assets between passive and active strategies. In a later section on multiple asset performance (MAP), an example of this approach can be found.

Active/Passive Combination

Two of the most popular combination strategies are active/passive and active/immunization combinations. An active/passive combination consists of a core component of the portfolio allocated to a passive strategy, with the balance allocated to an active component. The passive strategy would replicate an index or some sector of the market. In the active portion, the manager would be free to pursue a return maximization (for some given level of risk) strategy. A large pension fund may have a large allocation to a core strategy, consisting of an indexed portfolio, with additional active strategies chosen on the margin to enhance overall portfolio returns.

Active/Immunization Combination

Similarly, an active/immunization combination consists of two components. The immunized portfolio provides an assured return over the planning horizon and the balance of the portfolio is applied to an active high return/high risk strategy. Instead of a core component being tied to the return of an index (if the core strategy was an indexed portfolio), the immunization component would provide a guaranteed absolute return source. A *surplus protection strategy*, where the surplus of a pension fund is allocated to an active strategy and the liabilities allocated to an immunized portfolio, is an example of a possible application.

Contingent Immunization. Two specific forms of active/immunization combinations have been suggested. Leibowitz and Weinberger [1981] have called one version *contingent immunization*. Contingent immunization allows active management of the portfolio as long as the portfolio return exceeds a *safety net return*. If it falls to the safety net level, the portfolio is then immunized and active management cannot be resumed.

Three considerations are especially important in pursuing this strategy. The first is identification of the safety net return or minimum satisfactory level of return, which is smaller than the available immunization return. If the safety net level is set too close to (i.e., just below) the immunization return there will be a limited opportunity to manage the portfolio actively. The second consideration is the choice of time horizon. The longer the horizon, the greater the opportunity to manage the portfolio actively. Finally, policy considerations applied to the active strategy, such as minimum or maximum duration constraints, can also affect the potential return.

The manager can continue to pursue an active strategy until an adverse investment experience drives the then available combined active (from actual past experience) and immunized (from expected future experience) return down to the safety net level; at such time, the manager would be obligated to immunize the entire portfolio and lock in the safety net return. As long as this safety net is not reached, the manager can continue to manage the portfolio actively. The key considerations include establishing accurate immunized initial and ongoing available target returns, identifying a suitable and immunizable safety net return level, and implementing an effective monitoring procedure to ensure that the safety net return is not violated. An example of a monitoring analysis is shown in Tables 8-10 through 8-12.

Table 8-10 provides a summary description of a contingently managed portfolio and the return status of the portfolio relative to the inception date, present date, and horizon date. In the return analysis section of the table, the *Return to Date* is the return actually achieved by active management since the inception date. The *Present Immunization Target Return* is the return that could be earned between the present and horizon dates from current immunization of the portfolio (i.e., without any active management component). The *Return Achievable With Immunization Strategy* is a combination of the actual return from active management from inception to the present date and the anticipated return from immunization between the present and horizon dates. Finally, the *Required Return on Assets* is the safety net or minimum assured return. The *Achievable Excess Return* is the difference or cushion between these last two returns. In the example shown, there is a positive cushion of 1.96 percent per year, indicating that active relative to immunized management has been successful thus far, and continued active management is warranted.

Table 8-11 evaluates the current portfolio for interest rate change sensitivity. The various scenarios of interest rate change are parallel shifts of the amounts shown in the second column of the table. Under sensitivity

TABLE 8-10. Summary Description of a Contingently Immunized Portfolio

Performance Monitoring

	Actual Asset Values ($000)	Required Asset Values ($000)
Inception Date	6-30-85	
Present Date	6-30-88	
Horizon Date	6-30-91	
	$18110.	
	26582.	$23762.
		30712.
Time to Horizon	3.00 Yr.	
Actual Portfolio Duration	4.61 Yr.	

Asset Value Analysis

Present Actual Asset Value	$26582.	Achievable Terminal Asset Value	$34357.
Present Required Asset Value	23762.	Required Terminal Asset Value	30712.
Present Excess Asset Value	$ 2820.	Achievable Excess Terminal Asset Value	$ 3645.

Return Analysis

Return to Date	13.21%/Yr	6-30-85 to 6-30-88
Present Immunization Target Return	8.74%/Yr	6-30-88 to 6-30-91
Return Achievable with Immunization Strategy	10.96%/Yr	6-30-85 to 6-30-91
Required Return on Assets	9.00%/Yr	6-30-85 to 6-30-91
Achievable Excess Return (Cushion)	1.96%/Yr	6-30-85 to 6-30-91

SOURCE: Gifford Fong Associates.

TABLE 8-11. Sensitivity Analysis of a Contingently Immunized Portfolio

Sensitivity of Achievable Portfolio Performance to Present Interest Rates

Interest Rate Scenario	Yield Curve Change (Parallel Shift)	Asset Value Analysis				Return Analysis			
		Simulated Asset Value ($000)	Required Asset Value ($000)	Excess Asset Value ($000)	Scenario Modified Return to Date (%/Yr)	Estimated Immunization Target Return[a] (%/Yr)	Return Achievable With Immunization Strategy (%/Yr)	Required Return (%/Yr)	Achievable Excess Return (%/Yr)
CURRENT	NO CHANGE	$26582.	$23762.	$2820.	13.21%	8.74%	10.96%	9.00%	1.96%
2	200 UP	25023.	22434.	2589.	11.07	10.75	10.91	9.00	1.91
3	100 UP	25925.	23088.	2836.	12.32	9.74	11.03	9.00	2.03
4	100 DOWN	27910.	24446.	3464.	14.95	7.75	11.32	9.00	2.32
5	200 DOWN	29002.	25161.	3842.	16.33	6.76	11.49	9.00	2.49

SOURCE: Gifford Fong Associates.

[a] Duration weighted average yield of portfolio immunized to the horizon date.

relative to asset value analysis, the column titled *Simulated Asset Value* shows the actual market value of the bond portfolio as of the present date under each interest rate scenario assumed, diminishing (from the current value) with higher rates and increasing with lower rates. The column titled *Required Asset Value* provides the amounts needed (also as of the present date) such that the portfolio, if immunized, would achieve the safety net return. The third column in this group indicates the excess of column 1 over column 2 for each interest rate scenario. With respect to the *Return Analysis* section of the table, the *Current* figures were derived in Table 8-10 and the other figures in this table would be calculated similarly. Finally, Table 8-12 summarizes the characteristics of the optimal immunized portfolio. This is the portfolio, immunized to the horizon date, whose *Estimated Target Return* (8.74 percent) is used to determine the current *Achievable Excess Return* (1.96 percent). Its duration (2.99 years) is matched to the horizon date (3.00 years), and it has been constructed from a universe of higher quality (AAA vs. AA2) securities to further increase the certainty that the target return would be achieved were it necessary to immunize now.

An accurate immunization target is critical in determining not only the basis for the initial problem set-up (e.g., the safety net return will usually be a certain basis point difference from the target over a specified period), but also in determining what immunization levels are available during the management horizon. Again, a safety net set too close to the initial target return makes triggering the immunization process highly likely, while too low a safety net defeats the purpose of the process because a very low satisfactory minimum return would probably trigger immunization only in the event of an active management disaster. Finally, without an adequate monitoring procedure, the benefits of the strategy may be lost because of an inability to know when immunization action is appropriate.

Figure 8-15 graphically illustrates the potential rewards and risks involved with contingent immunization as of a single point in time. The figure assumes an active manager has purchased a 30-year portfolio that could have been classically immunized to produce a 12 percent return. However, because the manager hopes to achieve a return larger than 12 percent, principally from an expected fall in long-term interest rates, active management is undertaken instead. If the expected rate change occurs, the portfolio return will move up as yields fall, as shown in the left half of the figure. However, if rates trend up instead of down, returns will be less than expected. If they fall to a point where the combination of active return to date and future immunized return is only 11 percent, immunization will be triggered as shown in the right half of the diagram, thus precluding even lower return generation.

By contrast, Figure 8-16 shows the pattern of potential returns for successful and unsuccessful active management, with the latter involving immunization when the 11 percent safety net return is reached.

TABLE 8-12. Characteristics of Optimal Portfolio Under Contingent Immunization

Selection Criterion: Risk Minimization

Portfolio	No. of Issues	Par Value ($000)	Market Value ($000)	Accrued Interest ($000)	=	Principal Value ($000)	Yield to Maturity (%) Mkt. Val. Weighted	Yield to Maturity (%) Duration Weighted	Average Coupon (%)	Average Quality Rating	Average Duration (Yr.)
CURRENT	19	$27653.	$26581.795	$417.328	=	$26164.	9.112%	9.512%	8.154%	AA2	4.608
OPTIMAL	14	26296.	26533.229	470.849		26062.	8.696	8.738	8.368	AAA	2.991
TRANSACTION SUMMARY											
BOUGHT	10	18796.	18541.667	285.849		18256	8.471	8.477	7.434	AAA	2.941
SOLD	15	20153.	18590.233	232.327		18358.	9.065	9.562	7.130	AA2	5.253
HELD	5	7500.	7991.561	185.000		7807.	9.219	9.313	10.536	AA1	3.108

ESTIMATED STANDARD DEVIATION OF TERMINAL VALUE ($000): 64.

ESTIMATED STANDARD DEVIATION OF TARGET RETURN: 6. B.P./Yr.

ESTIMATED RETURN AT CONFIDENCE LEVEL OF:

90% = 8.66%
95% = 8.63%
99% = 8.59%

SOURCE: Gifford Fong Associates.

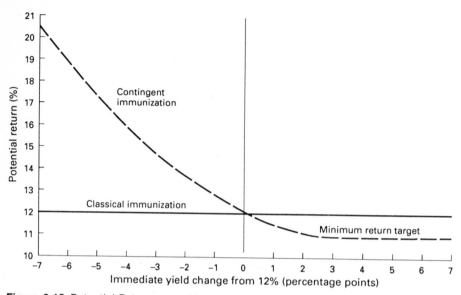

Figure 8-15. Potential Returns on a 30-year Bond Portfolio Under 12 Percent Classical Immunization and 11 Percent Contingent Immunization for Various Yield Change Assumptions. SOURCE: Salomon Brothers, Inc.

Combination by Formula. Another example of a strategy where active and immunization approaches are combined has been described by Gifford Fong Associates [1981]. In contrast to contingent immunization, this procedure allocates a portion of the initial portfolio to active management, with the balance being immunized according to the following relationship, which assumes that the immunization target return is greater than either the minimum or the expected worst case active returns:

$$\frac{\text{Active}}{\text{Component}} = \frac{\text{immunization target return} - \text{minimum return}}{\text{immunization target return} - \text{worst case active return}}$$

As an example, assuming that the available immunization target is 10 percent per year, the minimum return acceptable to the fund sponsor is 7 percent, and the worst case return for the actively managed portion of the portfolio is anticipated to be 4 percent, then the percentage in the active portion of the portfolio would be $(10 - 7)/(10 - 4) = 50$ percent. An examination of the formula shows that for any given immunization target return, the smaller the minimum acceptable return and the larger the expected active return, the larger will be the percentage of the portfolio under active management. Note that the numbers assumed for the example change over time in an interactive, dynamic sense; it is the portfolio manager's responsibility to monitor these factors constantly, adjusting the portfolio and rebalancing the portfolio as appropriate.

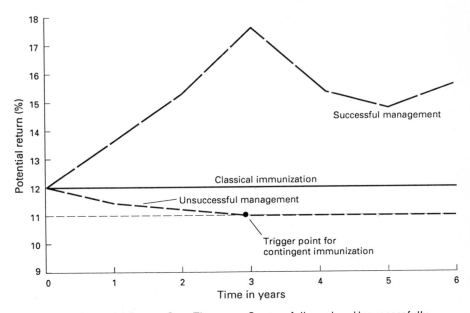

Figure 8-16. Potential Return Over Time on a Successfully and an Unsuccessfully Actively Managed 30-Year Bond Portfolio With Contingent Immunization. SOURCE: Salomon Brothers, Inc.

As long as the worst case scenario is not violated—that is, as long as the actual return experienced does not drop below the expected active return—the desired minimum return will be achieved.

Multiple Asset Performance. Multiple Asset Performance (MAP) is an option valuation-based approach to fixed-income asset allocation. The objective of the MAP strategy is to achieve a return on the total portfolio equal to the return of the best performing of the various fixed-income asset classes held in the portfolio, *less a predetermined strategy cost*. Consider, for example, a portfolio allocated between U.S., Japanese, and U.K. Government bonds. If U.S. bonds happen to perform the best of the three, the return of the strategy will be that of the U.S. Treasury bond market less the precalculated cost.

The strategy is equivalent to purchasing an option that allows the buyer to choose the asset to call or buy at a guaranteed price. However, the essence of the strategy is to create the option synthetically by an active asset allocation among the assets in the portfolio. The simplest example is a portfolio insurance technique involving the creation of a synthetic call by the appropriate allocation between cash and index futures, using a Black-Scholes option valuation model.

The cost of this synthetic option will depend on the number of assets chosen, their associated risk (standard deviation of returns and correlations), and the length of the horizon period. Because all of these can be estimated at the beginning of the horizon period, an estimate of the cost of the strategy can be determined at the outset. For example, the approximate option cost for a portfolio of two fixed-income assets is about 4 percent per year. Although this figure will vary somewhat from year to year, the MAP returns for any year will be those of the best performing of the assets, whichever is greater, less about 4 percent. Conceptually, this return differential may be thought of as the opportunity cost of not being 100 percent in the best performing asset class. The initial asset allocation will be based on the same determinants as the synthetic option cost, so the final portfolio return will never equal the return of the best performing asset but will be that return less the option cost.

Importantly, no return forecast is required in this approach. The only inputs are those typically required by option valuation equations. These include the expected standard deviation of the return of each asset and the correlation estimate between all pairs of assets, all of which may be estimated based on historical experience. The allocation can also be between particular securities (such as long and short bonds) or between strategies (such as an immunized and an actively managed portfolio).

One such approach is to include a "safety" asset in the allocation. The safety asset must maintain a duration in years equal to the plan's remaining time to horizon and have a defined return over the investment horizon. It can be an immunized bond portfolio or a zero coupon bond. The safety asset can ensure that a minimum or floor return is achieved for the portfolio. That is, the portfolio is invested in a way such that, if all other assets selected perform poorly, the portfolio will achieve the return of the safety asset, minus the cost associated with inclusion of the safety asset. Because the return of this safety asset and the MAP costs associated with the strategy are known in advance, this strategy can create an assured minimum rate of return for the portfolio. In addition, it has more flexibility than other active/passive combinations because a shift back to the other assets (or to active management) can be made if desired.

Another application of the MAP strategy is to protect a surplus of assets relative to liabilities in a pension fund. This can be achieved by making one of the assets in the portfolio a bond portfolio immunized to the liabilities. Remaining assets can then be other asset classes such as stocks, other bonds, and so forth. If the higher expected return assets perform well, more and more of the portfolio will be shifted to these assets. Conversely, if these assets perform badly the portfolio will be shifted to the immunized portfolio and, because the liabilities have already been immunized, adequate funding will continue.

Table 8-13 summarizes a simulation study applied to the Shearson Leh-

TABLE 8-13. Annual Returns for Simulated Multiple Asset Protection Portfolio Compared With Returns on Three Fixed-Income Indexes, 1978–1987

Year	SLGT	USTB	SLGC	MAP	MAP ATC
1978	−1.44%	6.85%	1.19%	4.06%	3.89%
1979	−0.53	10.10	2.30	7.31	7.18
1980	−2.94	11.75	3.06	5.32	4.98
1981	0.37	16.10	7.26	10.40	10.21
1982	41.76	12.70	31.09	34.87	34.64
1983	1.99	9.17	8.00	4.98	4.80
1984	14.79	10.99	15.02	10.29	10.03
1985	31.56	8.35	21.30	24.58	24.30
1986	24.10	6.69	15.62	16.69	16.50
1987	−2.67	6.41	2.29	1.93	1.77
Geometric mean	9.68	9.87	10.33	11.63	11.42
Standard deviation	15.55	2.93	9.38	9.95	9.93

Key: SLGT   = Shearson Lehman Hutton Long Treasury Bond Index
       USTB   = Three-Month U.S. Treasury Bill Index
       SLGC   = Shearson Lehman Hutton Government/Corporate Bond Index
       MAP   = Best return of SLGT or USTB net of predetermined strategy cost
       MAP ATC = MAP's returns after transaction costs

SOURCE: Gifford Fong Associates.

man Hutton Long Treasury Bond Index and a three-month U.S. Treasury Bill Index, during the period January 1, 1978 to December 31, 1987. The objective is to achieve the return of the best performing of these two assets each year less the predetermined cost.

In the simulations, the risk parameters were estimated with historical data from the three years prior to the analysis date. Thus, the volatility estimates, return differentials, and the initial portfolio allocation were computed only with information available at the inception of each plan.

Over the 10-year horizon, the return on the Shearson Lehman Hutton Long Treasury Index varied between −2.94 and 41.76 percent, with a geometric mean return of 9.68 percent and a standard deviation of 15.55 percent. The MAP portfolio returns ranged from 1.93 to 34.87 percent with an annual return of 11.63 percent and a standard deviation of 9.95 percent. Also included for comparison purposes are the annual returns of the Shearson Lehman Hutton Government/Corporate Index. Significantly, even though no return forecast was required or used for the period evaluated, relatively good returns were achieved as compared to the returns on the Shearson Lehman Hutton Government/Corporate Bond Index.

INTERNATIONAL STRATEGIES

International fixed-income investing involves the effects of currency changes in addition to the impact of interest rates as the major determinants of return. Consideration of interest rate levels, as well as prospective changes in the term structure, remain appropriate for each respective country in international strategies. However, currency fluctuations relative to the base currency, which have historically been a major determinant of total return, must also be given consideration. There is, therefore, an additional source of return contribution, beyond those described earlier, that must be considered in international fixed-income management. See Table 8-14 for a comparison of returns in local currency terms of various non-U.S. bonds versus returns in U.S. dollars.

Rationale for International Investing

The rationale for investing in bonds internationally include:

1. *Size of the market.* As can be seen in Table 8-15, the value of the U.S. bond market as of the end of 1987 represented less than half of the value of the markets listed. This suggests that investment opportunities beyond the domestic market are significant and, by implication, the potential for benefit is worth pursuing.

2. *Active management potential.* With the additional return component of currency effect as part of total return, another dimension of active management is present. From Table 8-14, it can be seen that the year-to-date (YTD) column for the U.S. dollar government bond market shows a return of 8.1 percent for calendar year 1988. In local currency terms, the Canadian dollar government bond market had a 10.1 percent return, but in U.S. dollar terms, the return was 20.0 percent. This contrasts with the return of the Swiss franc government bond market in local currency terms of 3.3 percent versus a return of -12.5 percent in U.S. dollar terms. These examples of wide return differentials because of the currency effect illustrate the potential for successful currency management.

3. *Return and diversification potential.* As with other international assets, the benefits of a broader range of return and diversification alternatives are increased with the use of international bonds.

While a full range of management strategies may be pursued, a distinction between *specific country* and *global* (across country) *strategies* must be made. For example, indexing to some comprehensive world index or within a given country is a frequently used vehicle. Immunization within a country is appropriate; however, immunization with internationally diversified bonds is not possible because of the need to relate the effect of interest rate changes to respective security country term structures. In general, when there is a direct incorporation of interest rate effects, then a country specific application is necessary. Where there is no direct dependence on an interest rate assumption, then a mixed country portfolio strategy is possible.

International Investment Considerations

There are a number of factors that must be considered in the international investing of bonds. These include:

1. *Taxes*. There are domestic issues, instruments issued by domestic entities overseas (e.g., Eurodollar bonds), and foreign entities issuing bonds in another country (e.g., Yankee bonds from foreign issuers denominated in yen), all of which have potentially different tax treatments. For example, many domestic issues are subject to withholding tax by the issuing country when bought by foreigners. Although treaty provisions may (as in the current U.S./Canada case) alleviate the problem, careful consideration is warranted because nonrecoverable taxes represent a direct reduction of return.

2. *Security characteristics*. Since different conventions for calculating yield are used abroad, comparability may be a problem. For example, there are perpetual bonds (i.e., no maturity date) in the United Kingdom, and interest in Australia is paid annually rather than semiannually. Reconciliation of such differences is necessary if comparative analysis is to be meaningful.

3. *Information availability*. Since there are many differences in the regulation and maturity of the various markets, the availability and significance of information for analysis is uneven.

4. *Liquidity*. Marketability varies widely among countries and even within a given country, depending on sector.

5. *Custody*. While a number of banks can provide global custodial support, service features and their costs can differ considerably from similar domestic services.

6. *Controls on foreigners*. The regulation of both foreign exchange transfers and access to specific markets can be obstacles. For example, Korea currently restricts foreign participation in its markets.

7. *Execution and settlement*. Because of time zone differences and local customs, attention to the costs, effectiveness of trading, and financial details of settlement must be more or less continuous.

(*text continued on 8-68*)

TABLE 8-14. Salomon Brothers International Bond Market Performance Indexes: December 30, 1988 (Total rates of return, remaining maturities of at least five years)

	Avg. Mat. (Yrs.)	Avg. Dur. (Yrs.)	Local Currency Terms					U.S. Dollar Terms				
			Index[a]	Percentage Change				Index[a]	Percentage Change			
				1 Mo.	3 Mo.	12 Mo.	YTD		1 Mo.	3 Mo.	12 Mo.	YTD
U.S. Dollar												
Government	15.6	7.6	272.0	0.6%	1.2	8.1%	8.1%	272.0	0.6%	1.2%	8.1%	8.1%
Foreign (Yankee)	16.1	7.5	298.3	0.0	1.2	10.4	10.4	298.3	0.0	1.2	10.4	10.4
Euro$ Str.	7.1	5.0	286.7	0.4	0.6	9.1	9.1	286.7	0.4	0.6	9.1	9.1
Euro$ Str. 5 Yr.	5.0	4.0	297.6	0.2	0.3	7.8	7.8	297.6	0.2	0.3	7.8	7.8
Euro$ 10 Yr.	10.0	6.3	295.9	1.4	1.1	11.5	11.5	295.9	1.4	1.1	11.5	11.5
Euro$ FRN	10.2[b]	NA	326.8	0.8	2.4	9.1	9.1	326.8	0.8	2.4	9.1	9.1
Euro$ Zero[c]	9.7	9.7	303.3	1.3	2.6	15.7	15.7	303.3	1.3	2.6	15.7	15.7
Canadian Dollar												
Government	11.9	6.5	295.0	0.2	1.8	10.1	10.1	270.5	-0.2	3.8	20.0	20.0
Euro-C$	6.7	4.8	306.6	0.6	2.5	12.2	12.2	281.1	0.2	4.5	22.3	22.3
Deutschemark												
Government	8.2	6.3	215.5	-0.1	1.5	5.7	5.7	254.4	-2.4	7.1	-6.3	-6.3
Euro-DM	8.1	6.4	221.7	0.2	2.1	7.0	7.0	261.7	-2.1	7.7	-5.1	-5.1
Japanese Yen												
Government	8.8	6.8	241.0	0.2	4.3	7.4	7.4	460.7	-2.5	11.6	4.2	4.2
Samurai	7.2	5.6	219.3	0.5	1.9	7.2	7.2	419.2	-2.2	9.1	4.0	4.0
Euroyen	7.3	5.9	217.6	0.5	3.1	6.2	6.2	415.9	-2.3	10.3	3.1	3.1
U.K. Sterling												
Government	12.1[b]	6.7	351.9	1.0	1.0	7.2	7.2	331.1	-1.3	8.1	2.9	2.9
Euro-£	9.8	5.9	329.0	1.2	0.9	6.5	6.5	309.5	-1.1	7.9	2.2	2.2

				0.3%	1.1%	3.3%	3.3%		-3.1%	6.8%	-12.5%	-12.5%
Swiss Franc												
Government	9.0	7.2	156.1	0.3	1.0	5.3	5.3	206.1	-3.1	6.8	-12.5	-12.5
Foreign Sfr	8.7	6.8	167.4	0.4	1.0	5.3	5.3	221.1	-3.0	6.7	-10.8	-10.8
Dutch Guilder												
Government	6.9 b,d	5.5	246.4	0.0	1.0	6.3	6.3	278.8	-2.4	6.5	-6.1	-6.1
Foreign	6.9 d	5.2	263.2	-0.3	1.4	7.5	7.5	297.8	-2.7	6.8	-5.1	-5.1
Euro-Dfl	3.0	2.8	256.2	0.1	1.8	5.8	5.8	289.9	-2.3	7.2	-6.5	-6.5
French Franc												
Government	9.1	5.9	351.7	1.5	3.6	17.8	17.8	271.2	-0.9	9.0	3.7	3.7
Euro-Ffr	7.0	5.2	356.6	0.7	2.8	16.3	16.3	274.9	-1.6	8.1	2.4	2.4
Australian Dollar												
Government e	8.2	5.1	170.5	-1.0	-1.3	10.3	10.3	174.8	-3.6	7.5	30.3	30.3
European Currency Unit												
Euro-ECU e	6.2	4.9	156.9	0.2	1.8	9.6	9.6	247.5	-1.8	7.3	-2.6	-2.6
World Bond Index												
Weighted	11.6 b	6.7	271.8	0.5	1.8	8.2	8.2	315.0	-0.7	4.9	5.9	5.9

SOURCE: Salomon Brothers, Inc.

a 30 Dec. 1977 = 100.

b Excludes a small number of perpetual issues in calculation of average maturity.

c Base: 26 Feb. 1982 = 100.0.

d Average remaining life of sample, rather than average final maturity.

e Base: 28 Sept. 1984 = 100.0.

TABLE 8-15. Size of Major Bond Markets at Year-End 1987 (Nominal value outstanding, billions of U.S. dollars equivalent) [a]

Bond Market	Total Publicly Issued	As Percentage of Public Issues in All Markets	Central Govt.	Central Government Agency & Govt. Guar.	State and Local Government	Corporate (Including Convertibles)	Other Domestic Publicly Issued	International Bonds [b] Foreign Bonds	International Bonds [b] Euro-bonds	Private Placement Unclassified
U.S. dollar	$4,165.7	44.3%	$1,335.2	$945.1	$776.3	$658.5	$16.0	$55.1	$379.5	$364.8
Japanese yen	2,120.6	22.6	1,236.2	153.5	54.0	157.3	412.7	41.0	65.9	346.9
Deutschemark	811.5	8.6	191.7	34.6	23.6	1.6	456.0	104.0		328.4 [c]
Italian lira	540.1	5.7	415.5	24.6	—	5.4	91.3	1.8	1.5	—
French franc	336.8	3.6	98.9	160.5	3.6	62.8	—	3.1	7.9	—
U.K. sterling	332.7	3.5	258.6	—	0.2	19.4	—	6.6	47.9	—
Belgian franc	196.8	2.1	97.0	60.4	—	7.6	27.0	4.4	0.4	—
Canadian dollar	192.9	2.1	78.4	0.1	63.4	31.3	0.7	0.8	18.2	—
Swiss franc	171.7	1.8	9.1	—	10.5	35.2	36.4	80.5	—	58.1
Danish krone	171.2	1.8	49.8	—	—	—	117.9	—	3.5	—

Swedish krona	$ 160.6	1.7%	$ 68.7	—	$ 2.4	$ 12.8	$ 76.6	—	$ 0.1	—
Dutch guilder	128.4	1.4	77.3	—	3.9	29.8	—	12.1	5.3	92.2[c]
Australian dollar	73.6	0.8	28.5	13.8	—	12.9	—	—	18.4	25.9
Total	$9,402.6[d]		$3,944.9	$1,392.6	$937.9	$1,034.6	$1,234.6	$858.0[d]		$1,216.3[c]
Sector as percentage of public issues in all markets	100.0%		42.0%	14.8%	10.0%	11.0%	13.1%	9.1%		

SOURCE: Salomon Brothers, Inc.

[a] Exchange rates prevailing as of December 31, 1987: ¥121.025/U.S.$, DM1.5698/U.S.$, Lit1,172.0/U.S.$, Ffr5.322/U.S.$, £0.5301/U.S.$, Bfr32.997/U.S.$, C$1.299/U.S.$, Sfr1.2905/U.S.$, Dkr6.051/U.S.$, Skr5.754/U.S.$, Dfl 1.7662/U.S.$, A$1.3889/U.S.$, and ECU 0.762/U.S.$.

[b] Includes straight convertible, and floating rate debt.

[c] In addition, there exists an unspecificable amount of privately placed issues of the private sector.

[d] In addition, there was $33.8 billion of outstanding ECU-denominated Eurobonds at year-end 1987.

International Diversification

The following discussion describes the important elements of fixed-income international diversification. While the framework employed may be modified by the use of expectational judgments, it does outline the usual decision steps leading to the formation of a portfolio.

The most straightforward strategy is to hold government bonds for each included country in proportion to the capitalization of each market, denominated in the base currency. This approach produces a portfolio that has a structure akin to a worldwide governments index such as the Salomon Brothers World Government Index. Without exception, the greatest liquidity will be found in this sector for each country. The need to take positions of institutional significance encourages careful analysis of which countries offer sufficient liquidity, first in the government market, then in the nongovernment sectors. This leads, then, to the desirability of a brief checklist for developing an international fixed-income portfolio strategy.

International Strategy Checklist

Country selection
Sector selection
Security selection
Weighting decision
Currency hedging

As a representative checklist for investing internationally, the above list provides some guidance. The first decision is in which countries to invest. Aside from valuation considerations, attention should be devoted to the capitalization available. Sector selection basically involves a decision to employ either governments or nongovernments beyond the U.S. market. A lack of liquidity, as well as the specialized analysis required to participate effectively in nongovernments in many markets, makes a government only approach attractive. Security selection is most conveniently achieved based on membership in a popular fixed-income index.

The weighting decision may be based on the weighting of the desired international benchmark or index, which is usually based on capitalization; alternatively, it could be based on another weighting scheme, such as Gross National Product (GNP). Finally, the issue of currency hedging must be dealt with. Recent analysis has suggested that there are distinct benefits to currency hedging (see Perold and Schulman [1988]); however, if a passive approach to international diversification is desired as in indexing, hedging is usually not used.

Any one of these activities may be overridden by imposing a judgment. For example, ongoing country valuation can be used to control the weighting decision.

Suffice it to say, international fixed-income investing adds another dimension to the range of alternative opportunities. Both in terms of potential return and prospective risk reduction, there have been and will be opportunities. (See Chapter 9 for a discussion of risk reduction and potential return enhancement via international equity diversification.) Taken in the context of the growing globalization of capital markets and the increasing interrelationships of the world's economies, the issue is not whether to engage in international investing, but to what degree.

SUMMARY

Two dominant themes may be identified in this chapter. The first involves the investment characteristics of fixed-income securities; and the second, the procedures for harnessing these characteristics in a portfolio.

The range of investment return/risk combinations is wide for fixed-income securities. Because fixed-income securities have an assured cash flow and a specified maturity, a number of policy and strategy objectives are made possible. Alternatives range from nonexpectational passive strategies, to quasi-passive indexation strategies, to semiactive immunization and dedicated portfolio strategies, to highly expectational active strategies. Each has distinguishing levels of required judgment and commensurate associated risk. How to pursue these strategies within an analytical framework is of central interest.

Application of option valuation theory has introduced new techniques that have found usefulness in contingent claims analysis and in risk-control-and-return-augmentation strategies. These offer a new dimension in analysis with the requirement for expectations minimized.

Finally, the increasing importance of international investing can draw upon the same structure of strategies previously discussed, along with the additional benefits and associated risk unique to foreign investment.

The topics covered convey a perspective of continuing importance, as well as evolution, for fixed-income portfolios. How best to harness this diverse potential in the context of specific investment objectives and policies continues to be the challenge.

FURTHER READING

Fixed-income portfolio management is as diverse as the securities used. Further, the associated complexity and subtlety for many topics require much more treatment than is possible in this chapter. To help fill the gap, the following discussion reviews some further reading which, while not exhaustive, is representative of additional sources.

An overview of fixed-income portfolio management, including a review of important concepts and definitions, may be found in Sharpe [1985]. A more detailed treatment of fixed-income strategies for the practitioner is included in Homer and Leibowitz [1972], Leibowitz [1979], Fong [1980, 1985], and Fabozzi and Fong [1987]. For a collection of articles on various topics, Fabozzi and Pollack [1987] provides perspectives from a number of practitioners. The sources of return are described in Bierwag [1987], Brennan and Schwartz [1982], and Kaufman [1981].

Two studies that report on the effectiveness of various spaced-maturity bond portfolio management strategies are Fogler, Groves, and Richardson [1976] and Fogler and Groves [1976]. For an interesting rationale for the use of bonds for pension funds to make use of attractive current tax treatment, see Black and Dewhurst [1981]. A description of duration and a theoretical discussion of its uses and limitations is included in Cox, Ingersoll, and Ross [1979] and Bierwag et al. [1983]. For a review of alternative measures of duration and empirical results of immunization as a fixed percentage income strategy, see Bierwag et al. [1980].

A number of articles describe the earliest theoretical derivation of the immunization concept. See Macaulay [1938] and Redington [1952]. Another extension of classical immunization strategy, including the provision for active management, is described in Leibowitz and Weinberger [1981] and Fong and Tang [1988]. Extending immunization to include all types of interest rate changes, an explicit risk measure, a multiperiod risk measure, and multiperiod capability can be found in Fong and Vasicek [1980]. A further overview can be found in Nemerever [1983]. For a review of the relative merits of immunization and cash flow matching from the standpoint of the funding requirements of the respective strategies, see Gifford Fong Associates [1981], and Leibowitz [1980, 1981, 1984, 1985].

Contingent immunization is described in detail in Leibowitz and Weinberger [1981, 1982, 1983] and a more general description can be found in Tuttle [1983].

Individual security analysis may be found in Fabozzi and Fong [1987], and the use of financial ratios for quality analysis of issuing firms is described in Murphy and Osborne [1979].

A detailed decomposition of realized returns is described for the portfolio as well as for individual securities in Fong, Pearson, and Vasicek [1981].

The theory and analysis appropriate for determining the term structure of interest rates is contained in Fong and Vasicek [1982].

Contingent claims analysis is discussed in Chung, Fong, and Tang [1988] and Boyce, Koenigsberg, and Tatevossian [1987].

The multiple asset performance analysis is discussed in Fong and Vasicek [1988] and Vasicek [1988].

International fixed-income portfolio management is an emerging area with many facets that must be addressed. Jorion [1987] reviews some of the reasons why and Perold and Schulman [1988] address the important question of currency hedging. For a practitioner perspective, McEnally [1985] provides insights from a number of international investment participants.

COMPUTER APPLICATIONS

The use of the computer to assist in fixed-income analysis can take a number of forms. Listed below is a generic description of analysis by functional type which can serve as an overview of the types of analyses available.

Individual Security Analysis

Swap systems	Allows comparison of individual securities with the objective of identifying historical price (or basis point spread) relationships.
Term structure analysis	Evaluates the current level of yields by producing spot, discount, and forward rate structures, as well as market implicit forecasts of interest rates.
Bond valuation model	Develops a normative value for corporate and mortgage-backed securities based on the evaluation of those characteristics of the security that contribute to overall price.
Contingent claims model	Evaluates the embedded option in a security without forecasting interest rates.

Active Management Systems

Return simulation	Predicts bond and portfolio behavior given alternative interest rate scenario projections.
Optimization	Constructs an optimal portfolio given desired portfolio requirements.

Dedication Strategies

Immunization model	Creates and maintains a portfolio that will have an assured return over a specified horizon irrespective of interest rate change.
Cash flow matching model	Creates and maintains a portfolio that will have cash flows (principal payments, coupon payments, and reinvestment income) required to fund a series of liabilities.

Passive Strategies

Indexing system	Creates a portfolio that will track the performance of a given bond index with a manageable set of securities.

Other

Performance measurement system	Calculates the total return for a bond portfolio and attributes the return to its sources.
Risk analysis report	Calculates option-adjusted average duration, convexity, and yield for a portfolio.

BIBLIOGRAPHY

Bierwag, G.O., G.G. Kaufman, R. Schweitzer, and A. Toevs. "Risk and Return for Active and Passive Bond Portfolio Management: Theory and Evidence." Unpublished paper, Center for Capital Market Research, University of Oregon, October 1980.

————. *Innovations in Bond Portfolio Management: Duration Analysis and Immunization.* Greenwich, Conn.: JAI Press, 1983.

————. "Duration Analysis: Managing Interest Rate Risk." *The Journal of Finance,* 1987.

Black, Fischer, and Morey P. Dewhurst. "A New Investment Strategy for Pension Funds." *The Journal of Portfolio Management,* Summer 1981.

Boyce, William M., Mark Koenigsberg, and Armand Tatevossian. "The Effective Duration of Callable Bonds: The Salomon Brothers Term Structure-Based Option Pricing Model." Salomon Brothers Inc., April 1987.

Brennan, Michael J., and Eduardo S. Schwartz. "Bond Pricing and Market Efficiency." *Financial Analysts Journal,* September/October 1982.

Chung, Ki-Young, H. Gifford Fong, and Eric M.P. Tang. "The Valuation of Mortgage-Backed Securities: A Contingent Claims Approach," in Frank J. Fabozzi, ed. *The Handbook of Mortgage-Backed Securities,* 2d ed. Chicago: Probus, 1988.

Cox, John C., John E. Ingersoll, Jr., and Stephen A. Ross. "Duration and the Measurement of Basis Risk." *Journal of Business,* 1979.

Fabozzi, Frank J. "Return Enhancement for Portfolios of Treasuries Using a Naive Expectations Approach," in Frank J. Fabozzi, ed. *The Handbook of Treasury Securities.* Chicago: Probus, 1987.

————. "Asset Allocation Optimization Models," in Robert Arnott and Frank J. Fabozzi, eds. *Asset Allocation: A Handbook of Portfolio Policies, Strategies and Tactics.* Chicago: Probus, 1988.

Fabozzi, Frank J., and H. Gifford Fong. "Overview of Fixed Income Portfolio Management," in Frank J. Fabozzi and Irving M. Pollack, eds. *The Handbook of Fixed Income Securities,* 2d ed. Homewood, Ill.: Dow Jones-Irwin, 1987.

Fabozzi, Frank J., and Irving M. Pollack, eds. *The Handbook of Fixed Income Securities.* Homewood, Ill.: Dow Jones-Irwin, 1987.

Fisher, Lawrence, and R. Weil. "Coping With Risk of Interest Rate Fluctuations: Return to Bondholders From Naive and Optimal Strategies." *Journal of Business,* October 1971.

Fogler, H. Russell, and William A. Groves. "How Much Can Active Bond Management Raise Returns?" *The Journal of Portfolio Management,* Fall 1976.

Fogler, H. Russell, William A. Groves, and James G. Richardson. "Managing Bonds: Are 'Dumbbells' Smart?" *The Journal of Portfolio Management,* Winter 1976.

Foldessy, Edward P. "Companies Facing Severe Problems Because of Rising Short-Term Debt." *The Wall Street Journal,* October 26, 1981.

Fong, H. Gifford. *Bond Portfolio Analysis.* Monograph No. 11. Charlottesville, Va.: The Financial Analysts Research Foundation, 1980.

Fong, H. Gifford, and Frank J. Fabozzi. *Fixed Income Portfolio Management.* Homewood, Ill.: Dow Jones-Irwin, 1985.

Fong, H. Gifford, Charles J. Pearson, and Oldrich A. Vasicek. "Bond Performance Analysis." New York: Institute for Quantitative Research in Finance, 1981.

Fong, H. Gifford, and Eric M.P. Tang. "Immunized Bond Portfolios in Portfolio Protection." *The Journal of Portfolio Management,* Winter 1988.

Fong, H. Gifford, and Oldrich A. Vasicek. "A Risk Minimizing Strategy for Multiple

Liability Immunization." New York: Institute for Quantitative Research in Finance, 1980.

———. "Term Structure Modeling Using Third Order Exponential Splines." *The Journal of Finance*, May 1982.

———. "Forecast Free International Asset Allocation." *Financial Analysts Journal*, March/April 1989.

———. "Achieving the Best Return in Asset Allocation Without Forecasting," in Robert Arnott and Frank J. Fabozzi, eds. *Asset Allocation: A Handbook of Portfolio Policies, Strategies and Tactics*. Chicago: Probus, 1988.

Gifford Fong Associates. "The Costs of Cashflow Matching." Unpublished paper, 1981.

Granito, Michael R. *Bond Portfolio Immunization*. Lexington, Mass.: Lexington Books, 1984.

Homer, Sidney, and Martin L. Leibowitz. *Inside the Yield Book: New Tools for Bond Market Strategy*. Englewood Cliffs, N.J.: Prentice-Hall, 1972.

Ibbotson, Roger G., and Rex A. Sinquefield. *Stocks, Bonds, Bills and Inflation: The Past and the Future*. Charlottesville, Va.: The Financial Analysts Research Foundation, 1982.

Jorion, Philippe. "Why Buy International Bonds?" *Investment Management Review*, September/October 1987.

Kaufman, Henry. "The Many Faces and Implications of the Yield Curve." Speech given at the 32d Annual Investment Seminar, New York State Bankers Association, November 30, 1981. New York: Salomon Brothers, Inc., 1981.

Leibowitz, Martin L. "Goal Oriented Bond Portfolio Management." *The Journal of Portfolio Management*, Summer 1979.

———. *Matched Funding Techniques: The Dedicated Bond Portfolio in Pension Funds*. New York: Salomon Brothers, Inc., 1985.

———. *Pros and Cons of Immunization*. New York: Salomon Brothers, Inc., 1980.

———. "Trends in Bond Portfolio Management," in *The Investment Manager's Handbook*. Homewood, Ill.: Dow Jones-Irwin, 1979.

Leibowitz, Martin L., Thomas E. Klaffky, Steven Mandel, and Alfred Weinberger. "Horizon Matching: A New Approach to Dedicated Portfolios." *The Journal of Portfolio Management*, Fall 1984.

Leibowitz, Martin L., and Alfred Weinberger. *Contingent Immunization: A New Procedure for Structured Active Management*. New York: Salomon Brothers, Inc., 1981.

———. "Contingent Immunization—Part I: Problem Areas." *Financial Analysts Journal*, November/December 1982.

———. "Contingent Immunization—Part II: Risk Control Procedures." *Financial Analysts Journal*, January/February 1983.

———. *Optimal Cash Flow Matching: Minimum Risk Bond Portfolios for Fulfilling Prescribed Schedules of Liabilities*. New York: Salomon Brothers, Inc., 1981.

———. *Risk Control Procedures Under Contingent Immunization*. New York: Salomon Brothers, Inc., 1982.

———. "The Uses of Contingent Immunization." *The Journal of Portfolio Management*, Fall 1981.

Macaulay, Frederick R. *Some Theoretical Problems Suggested by the Movement of*

Interest Rates, Bond Yields and Stock Prices in the United States Since 1856. New York: National Bureau of Economic Research, 1938.

McEnally, Richard W., ed. *International Bonds and Currencies.* Charlottesville, Va.: The Institute of Chartered Financial Analysts, 1985.

McEnally, Richard W., and Calvin M. Boardman. "Aspects of Corporate Bond Portfolio Diversification." *The Journal of Financial Research*, Spring 1979.

Murphy, Joseph E., Jr., and M.F.M. Osborne. "Games of Chance and the Probability of Corporate Profit or Loss." *Financial Management*, Summer 1979.

Nemerever, William L. "Managing Bond Portfolios Through Immunization Strategies," in D.L. Tuttle, ed. *The Revolution in Techniques for Managing Bond Portfolios.* Charlottesville, Va.: The Institute of Chartered Financial Analysts, 1983.

Perold, Andre F., and Evan C. Schulman. "The Free Lunch in Currency Hedging: Implications for Investment Policy and Performance Standards." *Financial Analysts Journal*, May/June 1988.

Platt, Robert B. *Controlling Interest Rate Risk.* New York: John Wiley & Sons, 1986.

Redington, F.M. "Review of the Principle of Life Office Valuations." *Journal of the Institute of Actuaries*, 78:1952.

Sharpe, William F. *Investments*, 3d ed. Englewood Cliffs, N.J.: Prentice-Hall, 1985.

Tuttle, Donald L., ed. *The Revolution in Techniques for Managing Investment Portfolios.* Charlottesville, Va.: The Institute of Chartered Financial Analysts, 1983.

Vasicek, Oldrich A. "The Best-Return Strategy," in Donald L. Luskin, ed. *Portfolio Insurance: A Guide to Dynamic Hedging.* New York: John Wiley & Sons, 1988.

CHAPTER **9**

Equity Portfolio Management

Kathleen A. Condon, CFA

OVERVIEW

Structuring the equity portfolio for an individual or institutional investor is the second major portfolio optimization decision following the asset allocation decision. For long-term investors, this stage of the process is a large and important component of the total process. Traditionally, it has been largely an active management process because of the large potential excess returns from superior stock selection and weighting. But in the late 1980s, especially for large institutional equity funds, passive management became an increasingly important factor. These two management approaches, as well as combinations of the two, are discussed and critiqued in this chapter.

ROLE OF THE EQUITY PORTFOLIO

Domestic equities have long been a major component of most institutional portfolios. *Pensions & Investment Age* reported that as of September 1988, the top 200 employee benefit funds, with assets totaling $1.2 trillion, had 42.8 percent of their assets invested in equities (see Burr [1989]). The level of this commitment is to a large extent a function of historic performance. For the 63-year period ending in December 1988, total returns on U.S. stocks as represented by the S&P 500 compounded at 10.0 percent per year. This compares with returns of 5.0 percent per year for long bonds and 3.5 percent per year for cash equivalents.

Over the same period, stocks demonstrated significantly higher volatility, with a standard deviation of 20.3 percent versus 6.9 percent for long bonds and 0.9 percent for cash equivalents. In the late 1980s, however, the standard deviation for stocks was lower than its 63-year record, while that for long bonds was higher than its long-term level. For the five years ending

December 1988, the standard deviation for stocks was 18.4 percent, while for bonds it was 9.9 percent.

In any case, the volatility of stocks in a multiasset portfolio is mitigated by the low correlation between stocks and either bonds or cash equivalents. Again, over the 63-year period ending in December 1988, the correlation between stocks and bonds was +0.21, while the correlation between stocks and cash was −0.02. These low correlations mean that stocks can be combined with bonds and cash equivalents, as discussed in Chapter 7, to create a portfolio with acceptable volatility.

The other reason why stocks have long been a dominant asset in institutional funds is that these funds, especially defined benefit pension plans, are generally regarded as being long-term in their investment perspective; that is, they can bear short-term risk in the expectation of higher long-term returns.

International Equities

In the late 1980s, international equities grew significantly in popularity. Of the largest 200 employee benefit plans, 87 had investments overseas with assets totaling over $21 billion as of September 1988. International equities are attractive for much the same reason as are domestic equities—attractive returns—but with the additional benefit of reduced volatility from the additional portfolio diversification that they offer. Over the 15-year period ending in December 1988, the Morgan Stanley Capital International Europe, Australia, and Far East (EAFE) Index compounded at 18.8 percent per year in dollar terms versus a return of 12.2 percent for the S&P 500. In some years in the late 1980s, the return differential was even more pronounced. For the three-year period ending in December 1988, the EAFE returned 39.8 percent versus a return of 13.3 percent for the S&P 500.

The volatility of the EAFE has been similar to that of the S&P 500. In fact, the standard deviation was identical at 16.9 percent for the 15 years ending in December 1988. Over the same period, the correlation between the two indexes was +0.50. So holding foreign securities did lower the volatility of an overall U.S.-international combination portfolio. This is depicted clearly in Figure 9-1, which plots the return and standard deviation for a variety of portfolios over 10-year periods ending in the years 1978 through 1988. For each curved arrow, the dot farthest to the right represents a commitment of 100 percent to the S&P 500. As one moves to the left on each curve, the dots indicate a 10 percent movement from the S&P 500 into the EAFE: 90/10 for the first dot, 80/20 for the second, and 70/30 for the last (at the arrowhead). It is interesting to note that for most of these 10-year periods, a commitment to international equities increased the return of the portfolios. In all periods, however, a commitment to international equities decreased the volatility of the portfolio.

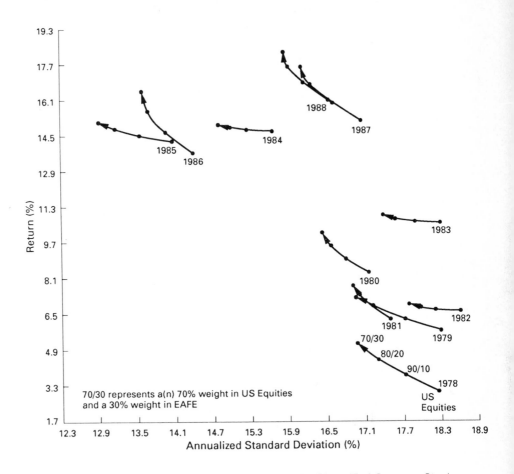

Figure 9-1. Comparison of Return/Risk Performance for Diversified Common Stock Portfolio Invested in Combinations of U.S. Domestic Stocks and EAFE Stocks for 10-Year Periods Ending in the Years 1978–1988. (Dots represent 100/0%, 90/10%, 80/20%, and 70/30% U.S./EAFE combinations reading right to left.) SOURCE: Frank Russell Company.

Domestic equities are an extremely important asset class, and international equities have become increasingly important. Both asset classes are managed by using a variety of strategies. This chapter reviews these strategies, examining the spectrum from passive through active management.

EFFICIENT MARKETS

Before getting into a discussion on management styles, it is helpful to review the efficient markets hypothesis (EMH) or random walk theory, and its implications for money management. The concept of efficient markets is often used as an argument against active money management. In fact, as noted in Chapter 2, there are three versions of the theory: weak, semistrong, and strong.

The weak form of the theory holds that the historic price movement of a stock provides no information on the direction or magnitude of future price movements. In other words, technical analysis has no value. The semistrong form argues that publicly available information is useless in selecting securities because once information is publicly available, it is immediately reflected in a security's price. Therefore, it is impossible to benefit from this information. The strong form of the argument says that no information, whether known or knowable, about a company's prospects can benefit the security analyst. If information is known, it is embedded in a security's price. If information is predictable, it is embedded in a security's price. If information is unpredictable, it will be random in its appearance and impact. If one believes in the strong form of the EMH, one would not engage in any form of active management. Belief in the weak or semistrong form does not necessarily have the same implication.

PASSIVE STRATEGIES

What distinguishes passive from active management? Unlike passive managers, an active equity manager attempts to add value through one (or more) of three strategies. The first strategy can be called *market timing*. Basically, this is the decision to move funds in or out of the equity market in an attempt to enhance returns. In reality, it is as much an asset allocation strategy as it is an equity strategy because it calls for shifting funds to another asset category.

The second strategy can be thought of as *theme selection*. On the domestic front, this could be choosing to emphasize small capitalization rather than large capitalization securities, to overweight specific industries or sectors versus others that are underweighted, or to emphasize factors such as growth or yield. For international portfolios, a good example of theme selection is the selection and over- or underweighting of countries.

The final strategy is to add value through the *selection of individual stocks*.

A portfolio that does not engage in stock selection and does not engage actively in market timing or theme selection can be thought of as *passive*. Passive management is a strategy of holding a portfolio of generic securities, without attempting to outperform other investors through superior market forecasting or superior ability to find mispriced securities. Often, although not always, a passively managed equity portfolio is well diversified.

The simplest type of passive portfolio is an *index fund*. An index fund is a fund designed to mirror the performance of a published benchmark. The most popular benchmark for domestic equity index funds continues to be the S&P 500, while for the international index funds it is the EAFE.

Index Funds

Index funds were first introduced in the United States in the early 1970s. Several factors influenced their development. On the academic front, there was significant interest being generated in the area of portfolio theory, specifically in the efficient markets hypothesis. Proponents of passive management argued that if the markets are truly efficient, the best estimate of a security's value is its existing price. One should not attempt to add value to a portfolio through security selection; rather, one should simply buy the market. Even Benjamin Graham was quoted by Malkiel [1985] as follows:

> I am no longer an advocate of elaborate techniques of security analysis in order to find superior value opportunities. This was a rewarding activity, say 40 years ago, when Graham and Dodd was first published; but the situation has changed . . . [Today] I doubt whether such extensive efforts will generate sufficiently superior selections to justify their cost . . . I'm on the side of the "efficient market" school of thought. . . .

In the investment community, another factor influencing the development of index funds was the growing interest in performance measurement. As discussed in Chapter 14, in 1968 the Bank Administration Institute (BAI) developed a formula for calculating time-weighted rates of return. Investment managers began calculating performance using the BAI standards. Performance began to be calculated consistently, which led naturally to performance comparisons. A.G. Becker (later SEI Corp.) introduced its universe comparisons, and, for the first time, plan sponsors had the ability to evaluate their managers versus both the market and other managers. What they saw was not encouraging.

Table 9-1 depicts annual performance numbers for the median equity portfolio among those in the SEI universe along with comparable numbers for the S&P 500. One can readily see that while the market declined sharply from 1973 through 1974, the median equity portfolio in the SEI universe did far worse. Furthermore, managers continued to lag behind the market as it rebounded from 1975 through 1976 and, once again, underperformed in the decline of 1977.

Nonetheless, indexing grew slowly through most of the 1970s. Fierce opposition within the investment community was certainly a factor. So too was performance; in 1978, active managers again began outperforming the S&P 500.

The pendulum swung once again in 1983, with the index proving to be

TABLE 9-1. Annual Return Performance of the SEI Universe Median Equity Portfolio and the S&P 500 Composite Stock Index, 1966–1988

Year	Annual Returns	
	Median Equity Portfolio	S&P 500
1988	16.80%	16.8%
1987	2.98	5.1
1986	18.06	18.7
1985	32.89	31.9
1984	1.25	6.1
1983	21.40	22.2
1982	21.95	21.7
1981	(5.03)	(4.8)
1980	32.65	32.5
1979	21.17	18.6
1978	7.15	6.6
1977	(7.81)	(7.1)
1976	19.11	23.8
1975	33.14	37.3
1974	(31.60)	(26.4)
1973	(22.22)	(14.8)
1972	18.15	19.0
1971	20.07	14.3
1970	(3.75)	3.9
1969	(6.93)	(8.4)
1968	11.11	11.1
1967	21.49	23.9
1966	(7.78)	(10.0)

SOURCE: SEI Corp. and Bankers Trust Company.

TABLE 9-2. Annual Return Percentile Ranking of the S&P 500 Index Among Portfolios in the TUCS Managed Equity Universe, 1984–1988

Year	S&P 500 Percentile Ranking
1984	28
1985	29
1986	36
1987	41
1988	52
5 Years: 1984–1988	38

SOURCE: Bankers Trust Company.

a difficult bogey for active managers. Table 9-2 depicts the results of another popular universe comparison service, the Trust Universe Comparison Service (TUCS). Performance for the S&P 500 is ranked along with the performance results for managed equity portfolios. The lower the percentile, the better the relative performance of the S&P 500 Index. Despite their relatively strong performance in 1988, the period from 1984 through 1988 was a difficult one for active managers, with 62 percent of them underperforming the S&P 500.

The performance gap is even greater if one takes fees into account. In the late 1980s, fees for actively managed portfolios averaged 35 basis points (0.35 percent) or more, while fees for index funds averaged 10 basis points or less. The result was that performance, coupled with an increased focus on cost, led to a tremendous influx of assets into index funds in the early to middle 1980s. By September 1988, 105 of the 200 largest pension funds had some funds in equity index funds, and the total in these funds was estimated at $114 billion, up from approximately $9 billion in 1980.

Domestic and Global Indexes. As mentioned previously, index funds are funds designed to mirror the performance of published indexes. In the United States, the S&P 500 continues to be the benchmark for the majority of index funds; however, in the late 1980s other benchmarks such as the Wilshire 5000 and the Russell 1000, 2000, and 3000 were gaining market share. On the international front, the EAFE continues to dominate, but other, more recently introduced indexes include the Financial Times Goldman Sachs Index and the Salomon Russell Index. Regardless of the index chosen, a fund can be constructed that will replicate its performance quite closely.

In discussing index fund performance, the term *tracking error* is commonly used. This is a measure of the deviation of fund performance from index performance. A fund with a tracking error of 20 basis points will earn the index return, plus or minus 20 basis points, 67 percent of the time (one standard deviation).

Construction Techniques. There are several techniques used in building index funds. These techniques fall into three categories: full replication, sampling, and optimization. *Full replication* is the most straightforward approach because, as its name implies, all of the securities in the benchmark are purchased in the index fund in their proportionate weightings. An S&P 500 Index fund that is created by using full replication will hold positions in all, or nearly all, of the 500 securities in amounts proportionate to their value relative to the market value of all stocks in the Index. Proponents of this approach argue that only by holding all of the securities in an index can one ensure close tracking of the actual index.

Funds can also be constructed using a *sampling approach*. A fund constructed in such a way usually holds positions in all of the larger securities in the benchmark, but samples the smaller companies such that the characteristics of the fund closely match those of the benchmark. A simple approach to constructing an S&P 500 Index fund would be to buy the larger names in their exact proportions while sampling the smaller ones such that the industry breakdown of the portfolio mirrors that of the Index. If one believes that securities within given industries tend to move in a similar manner, then controlling for industry diversification should lead to good tracking. In practice, the criteria for sampling can be far more complex than this, and one can control for any number of factors such as industry breakdown, market capitalization, yield, growth orientation, and the like. Proponents of sampling argue that if one can create a portfolio that captures the essential characteristics of a benchmark, without holding positions in each and every security, one can approximate the performance of the benchmark quite closely while keeping administrative and trading costs down.

The other approach to constructing index funds is to use a *quadratic optimization model*. Given data on securities, such a model attempts to create a portfolio with the minimum possible residual risk vis-à-vis the selected benchmark (i.e., return variability not explained by the benchmark itself). The attraction of this approach is that a portfolio can be constructed with fewer names than one would use in full replication or even sampling, and with a very low prospective tracking error. A potential problem, however, is that the data used to drive this type of model are historic in nature, and if the future does not replicate the past as is usually the case, the prospective tracking error on these funds can differ significantly from the actual tracking error realized.

Trading. Index funds gained tremendous popularity in the late 1980s, in part because of the competitive performance that they have provided and in part because of lower costs. A major component of these cost savings comes in the area of trading or transactions costs.

Trading costs incurred by index funds are typically lower than those for actively managed portfolios for two primary reasons: lower turnover and lower costs on the trades actually executed. Because no effort is made to trade securities in pursuit of excess return, turnover occurs only when there is cash flow into or out of the portfolio, when dividend income needs to be invested, or when there are changes in the index. Index fund vendors have long claimed that what trading they need to do can be executed at very low cost because these trades are by nature informationless. By "informationless," they mean that they are not buying or selling because of some insight into the future market performance of the stock. Rather, they are trading simply to bring their funds in line with the index. This trading to rebalance index portfolios is also discussed in Chapters 12 and 13.

Index fund managers trade in a variety of ways, and these differ significantly from the approaches used by most active equity managers. One popular way to trade is to *cross* securities with another index fund. If one fund needs to add to its position in a security while another is overweighted and needs to reduce its position, the security is simply crossed; that is, buy and sell needs/orders are matched, generally at a cost of one cent per share or less. Because crosses are frequently done at the market close, one can argue that there is no market impact. Index fund vendors place a premium on the ability to cross, and increasingly they cross or match buy and sell orders not only within their own shops but with other passive managers through computerized trading networks such as Instinet and Posit.

Package Trades. Another popular approach to trading index funds is to use *package trades*. A package trade is simply the bundling of a number of orders for simultaneous or nearly simultaneous execution in the market. Generally, one trades in an index fund because there is cash to be invested. Even where index sampling is used, this cash must generally be spread over a large number of securities. The goal of the fund manager is to get the money invested as quickly and as inexpensively as possible; hence, the advent of package trading.

Historically, when one did a package trade, one looked to the broker to guaranatee the transaction cost. Such a guarantee might work in the following way. The manager would contact a broker and outline the specifications of a package that he wished to do. The broker would be told whether it was a buy or sell package, the size, number of securities, and some information about the characteristics of the securities. He would not generally be given the specific names included in the package. The broker in turn would bid on the package, quoting a commission to be charged as well as a *maximum* market impact cost to be incurred by the fund. For example, the broker might quote a $0.05 per share commission plus a one-eighth market impact. Once the market had closed, the broker would be given the actual package to be traded. He would then trade the next day with a maximum cost to the plan of $0.175 ($0.125 market impact and a $0.05 commission). If the broker were able to trade the package for less than this, the plan would benefit, but in no event would the cost exceed this.

A *guaranteed price program trade* such as that described in the previous paragraph presents a risk to the broker. It must be assumed that his pricing reflects that risk. To the extent that the plan can hedge its risk by using index futures, using them is an attractive alternative. Such a trading strategy works as follows. A fund has money to invest in the market. Rather than immediately buying the equities, the manager invests in (i.e., takes a long position in) stock index futures contracts. These are generally liquid and have very low transaction costs. The fund gains immediate market exposure. The money is then invested in common stocks. This can be done immediately through a package trade or more gradually through individual security pur-

chases. As stocks are purchased, futures are sold. If, as stocks are purchased, prices are driven up, these transaction costs in the form of market
impact should be offset by a concurrent upward move in the price of the
futures contracts. The result is lower true transaction costs. Elaboration on
this can be found in Chapter 11.

Arbitrage. Using index futures to facilitate trading in index funds became increasingly popular in the late 1980s. Another use of futures in conjunction with index funds is *index arbitrage*. Index arbitrage is a strategy
through which one attempts to add value over and above the benchmark
return by moving assets between stocks (the cash instruments) and futures.
Futures can be used as a substitute for stock. The key difference is that
investors in stocks receive dividends, while investors in futures contracts
receive interest on the underlying fixed-income investments—the instruments that, in addition to their margined futures position, round out their
asset holdings. Accordingly, the futures should be priced in a fixed relation
to the stock index. As discussed in Chapter 6, this relation is as follows:

$$P_f = P_s(1 + i - y)$$

where:

P_f = Fair value of futures
P_s = Current stock index price
i = Interest cost, based on the yield received on highest quality fixed-income
investments
y = Dividend yield received on stocks in the index

Transposing the above equation, the result is as follows:

$$P_f - P_s = P_s (i - y)$$

and $P_f - P_s$ is commonly referred to as the *basis*.

One can readily see that if the yield on the fixed-income securities underlying the futures exceeds the dividend yield on the stock, the futures
should trade at a higher price than the stocks.

If futures are trading at a discount to this fair value, then the return on
the futures between the present time and expiration will exceed that for the
stock index. If, on the other hand, futures are trading at a premium to fair
value, return over the period to expiration will be lower than that for the
index. Index arbitrage is simply the movement of funds between the cash
instrument and futures in order to take advantage of these disequilibrium or
mispriced situations. When futures are trading at a discount to fair value,
stock will be sold and futures purchased. When futures trade at a premium
over fair value, the futures will be sold and stock purchased. Such trades

are only done when it is determined that value can be added over and above the transaction costs incurred.

Following the October 1987 stock market crash, index arbitrage trading was severely criticized by segments of the press as well as by some in the investment community. Critics in the media argued that arbitrage trading increased market volatility. They argued this despite the fact that Sanford Grossman [1987], in research undertaken for the Katzenbach study on program trading, found "no relationship between any measure of volatility and any measure of program trading intensity."

In reality, arbitrage trading adds liquidity to the marketplace and provides a link between the futures and cash markets that promotes market efficiency. The Presidential Task Force on Market Mechanisms, familiarly known as the Brady Commission, called for the recognition of the cash and futures markets as one overall market and recommended strengthened links between them. Arbitrage is the primary link.

In fact, the Brady Commission Report, or Report of the Presidential Task Force [1988], cites a lack of arbitrage activity as a factor contributing to the steep market decline on the afternoon of October 19, 1987. The study noted that during the morning and early afternoon on that date,

> index arbitrage had succeeded in transmitting futures selling pressure back to the stock market. After about 2:00 P.M., index arbitrage slowed because of concerns about delays in DOT (Designated Order Turnaround System). With some index arbitrageurs unwilling to sell stock through DOT, they also withdrew from the futures side of their trading, denying buying support to the futures market, allowing it to fall to a discount of 20 index points. In addition, the appearance of this dysfunctionally large discount inhibited buyers in the stock market. With these stock buyers gone, the Dow sank almost three hundred points in the last hour and one quarter of stock trading, to close at 1738.

Customized Funds

An "index fund" has been defined as a fund designed to mirror the characteristics and performance of a published benchmark. One can also construct a passive portfolio in which the benchmark is a customized, rather than a published, index. There are a variety of reasons why one might wish to create a customized benchmark. An obvious reason is that it places constraints on allowable securities. This is particularly an issue with public pension funds in the United States, where frequently these funds are restricted by statute regarding securities that can be held. It is not uncommon, for example, for funds to be able to hold only those securities that have paid dividends in previous years, are domiciled in the United States, and the like. In the late 1980s, it became fairly common for public funds to exclude stocks of companies doing business in South Africa. Because these stocks represent a sizable subset of the S&P 500 universe, funds imposing these restrictions oftentimes have found it necessary to go to a customized universe.

Completeness Funds. Yet another reason for creating a customized benchmark is the desire on the part of a plan sponsor to use the passive portfolio to complement, or complete, the array of active managers. Such a portfolio is familiarly known as a *completeness fund*. The intent is to create a specialized index fund to provide adequate portfolio diversification, rather than the entire market index, by excluding those segments of the market in which active managers have been hired to operate. If, for example, one has an active manager pursuing a small capitalization strategy, then there may be no need to include small capitalization stocks in the passive benchmark unless the fund under his managerment underrepresents the small capitalization sector. The passive benchmark used to create this specialized index fund is then defined as those segments of the market in which the active manager will never operate. Hence, the name "completeness fund." Figure 9-2 provides a graphic sequence of how a completeness fund is created.

This approach can be adapted to the international arena. Typically, the reference benchmark for an international equity portfolio is the EAFE, which is dominated by Japanese stocks. The plan sponsor might allocate his Japanese stock exposure to active managers, thereby hoping to gain some incremental return over and above the Japanese benchmark. The other 17 countries could be indexed. This index fund would be a type of completeness fund because its benchmark would be a universe in which the active managers would never operate. The combination—active plus index—provides the plan with a diversified international portfolio that holds the possibility of outperforming the benchmark.

Factor/Style Funds. An increasingly popular type of passive portfolio is the *factor*, or *style*, *fund* that uses the factor model approach discussed in Chapter 7. Rather than replicating the market as a whole, this type of fund replicates a benchmark geared to mimic the performance of a given common stock factor such as growth, small capitalization, or high yield. Funds can also be specialized or *tilted* toward specific sectors or industries such as the energy sector. These types of funds gained popularity in the late 1980s because they represented a low cost, viable alternative to active management. When selecting an active manager, most plan sponsors select within style guidelines. Consultants generally categorize managers by style, with growth and value being two of the more popular management styles. Plan sponsors who have had experience with index funds have come to realize that they can pursue a given style, but do it passively. In so doing, they minimize the costs of gaining exposure to the style.

Although growth and value can be defined in various ways, growth generally refers to a portfolio emphasizing securities with higher-than-av-

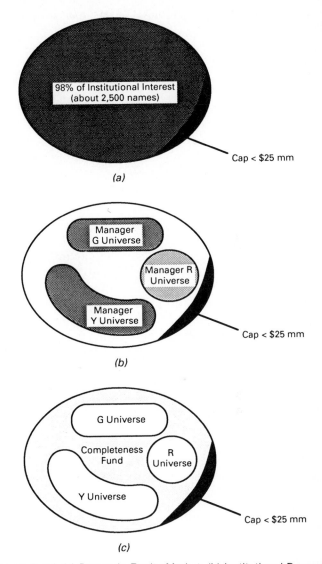

(a)

(b)

(c)

Figure 9-2. Completeness Fund. (a) Domestic Equity Market, (b) Institutional Domestic Equity Market Coverage Provided by Managers, (c) Institutional Domestic Equity Market Coverage Provided by Completeness Fund.

erage historic growth in earnings per share. Ancillary characteristics often include higher than average price/earnings (P/E) ratios and low dividend yields. Value portfolios are usually characterized as having lower-than-average price/book ratios. Low P/E ratios and high yields are other characteristics.

TABLE 9-3. Characteristics of a Typical Customized Growth Portfolio vs. the S&P 500 Index Portfolio

Portfolio Characteristic	Custom Index	S&P 500
Number of stocks	298	500
Capitalization range		
Largest	$21 billion	$71 billion
Smallest	$36 million	$36 million
Beta	1.11	1.00
P/E ratio	14.7×	12.1×
Price/book ratio	2.35×	1.86×
Dividend yield	2.0%	3.6%
Return on equity	20.0%	18.0%
5-Year growth of earnings per share	12.5%	10.2%

SOURCE: Bankers Trust Company.

A growth fund might be constructed as follows. Assume that the objective is to create a fund with a significantly higher exposure to growth than that of the S&P 500. A benchmark is constructed from companies with above average historic growth. Furthermore, it is constructed in such a way that its growth orientation is maximized, subject to meeting certain other desired criteria. For example, some diversification is critical. To expand the potential universe, securities not in the S&P 500 can be included, but portfolio characteristics are controlled relative to the S&P 500.

A comparison of the characteristics of this style fund versus the S&P 500 is shown in Table 9-3. This fund provides a client with passive exposure to stocks with above average historic growth and should do well in a market in which growth stocks are doing well.

HYBRID PRODUCTS

As discussed previously, one can distinguish active from passive strategies by analyzing what the portfolio is constructed to do. A passive portfolio is constructed to replicate the performance of a benchmark, and an active portfolio is designed to add value over and above that benchmark. The three primary ways in which an active manager attempts to add value are market timing, theme rotation, and stock selection.

Active/Passive Combinations

In the late 1980s, money managers introduced a number of *hybrid products*. These are products that combine active decisions with passive technology. A key to understanding hybrid products is to realize that these are products in which a manager takes risk *selectively*. The manager believes that he has skill in certain areas and is willing to take risk in those areas in pursuit of excess return. In all other ways, the portfolio is managed passively. The development of performance attribution models has given us the necessary tools to create this type of equity portfolio management approach.

As discussed in Chapter 14, performance attribution is simply the decomposition of performance. It allows an investor, such as a pension fund, to analyze the risks a manager is taking and how these risks relate to the returns generated in the portfolio. For example, one can see whether a manager's primary bets are based on sector/industry over- or underweightings vis-à-vis the benchmark, on specific factor tilts such as an emphasis on growth stocks, on individual stock selection, or on other bases. If attribution analysis shows that a manager is consistently invested in small capitalization securities, but is adding no extra return from stock selection, one can question whether value is being added. A small capitalization passive portfolio could be created that would give the fund the same exposure to the return of small-capitalization securities. If the stock selection is not adding any value, this is at least as attractive a return alternative and certainly is less expensive in terms of management fees and transaction costs.

Integrating Active With Passive

If the manager reorients the portfolio periodically, moving in and out of various sectors and/or factor tilts, and in so doing adds value to the portfolio, then he is truly earning his fee as an active manager. An example of a product in this area is an international portfolio in which the country weightings are actively managed, while the stock selection within countries is done passively via country specific index funds. This was a relatively new product in the late 1980s marketplace that garnered some attention. While it has been true that most international index funds have country weightings in line with the relative market capitalizations of the various countries, many plan sponsors intuitively have felt that a manager can add value by altering these passive country weightings. This belief is at least in part a response to the high valuation, and therefore high index percentage weighting, of certain national stock markets that periodically occur and persist over time, and the belief that the overvaluations will be corrected. For example, in mid-1988, Japanese stocks represented an unusually large percentage (more than 60 percent) of the EAFE largely because of the high valuation of Japanese corporate earnings.

In point of fact, very few managers have been able to equal the performance of the EAFE. Intersec Research Corporation, which maintains statistics on international investment managers, found that for the 5-year period ending in 1987, none of the 62 active managers in its universe was able to outperform the EAFE. Over that 5-year period, EAFE compounded at 40.6 percent, while the median active manager returned 21.9 percent. For the year 1987, for example, only 5 of 100 active international equity managers outperformed the EAFE, and again their median return significantly lagged that of the Index—11.3 percent versus 24.9 percent.

One reason for this shortfall was that many managers underweighted Japan, which was the top-performing market in 1987. However, the data indicate that the return from stock selection has been negative as well: -5.0 percent for 1987 and -4.5 percent over the three-year period ending in 1987 relative to the appropriate benchmark portfolios. The results show that if stocks had been selected passively rather than actively over these two periods, the managers would have had significantly better performance.

ACTIVE STRATEGIES

The Appeal of Active Management

Despite the performance problems of active managers and the strong growth of passive portfolios notwithstanding, active management continues to have strong appeal for many plan sponsors. The majority of equity assets continue to be actively managed. Plan sponsors continue to believe that they can find and hire managers with the ability to add value over and above passive benchmarks. In fact, there are active managers, pursuing a variety of styles, who have achieved strong long-term records. What, if any, common characteristics do they share?

Styles

Successful active managers generally have styles to which they adhere. A manager may feel that he has a talent for selecting undervalued securities or perhaps he feels that he has skill in selecting sectors of the market that will do well. Whatever the skill or style, successful managers are certain what it is and are consistent in adhering to it.

Warren Buffett, an extraordinarily successful investor, demonstrates this well. As related by Train [1980], Buffett, as manager of a family partnership in the 1960s, wrote the following promise to his co-investors each year: "I cannot promise results to partners, but I can and do promise this. (1) Our investments will be chosen on the basis of value, not popularity. (2) Our patterns of operations will attempt to reduce permanent capital loss, not short-term quotational (paper) loss, to a minimum." Buffett adhered to this philosophy throughout most of the 1960s with outstanding results. By

1969, however, it was difficult to find bargains in a booming market. As a result, he sent another letter to his partners:

> I am out of step with present conditions. When the game is no longer played your way, it is only human to say the new approach is all wrong, bound to lead to trouble, and so on. . . . On one point, however, I am clear. I will not abandon a previous approach whose logic I understand (although I find it difficult to apply) even through it may mean foregoing large, and apparently easy, profits to embrace an approach which I don't fully understand, have not practiced successfully, and which possibly could lead to substantial permanent loss of capital.

By the end of 1969, he folded the partnership.

Managers recognize that all styles go in and out of favor. A manager who is hired to manage a small capitalization portfolio may in fact be adding value in that sector of the market, yet he may be lagging the broad market indexes. He has skill, but that skill may not be obvious unless performance is evaluated properly. Again, performance attribution models, discussed in Chapter 14, can be invaluable in this regard.

Normal Portfolios. A trend in the market has been to have active managers define their *normal portfolios* and use these as specialized benchmarks for performance evaluation. A normal portfolio defines the market in which the manager will operate. Depending on the manager's style, it could be all domestic large capitalization companies, only companies with market capitalizations of less than a certain size, all companies with demonstrated growth of some specified amount, companies with price/book values of no greater than a predetermined level, and so forth. Whatever the specification, the normal portfolio defines the world in which the manager operates and the standard against which he is attempting to add value.

Because styles do go in and out of favor, it is important to evaluate the active equity manager against his particular normal portfolio. Assume that a manager is hired to run a small capitalization portfolio. It is unfair to penalize that manager because small capitalization stocks as a whole underperform the broad market indexes if he is adding value vis-à-vis the small capitalization sector. Conversely, one would not want to reward a small capitalization manager for performance if small capitalization stocks are doing well but if he in fact is adding no value through his stock selection.

Table 9-4 demonstrates the importance of using an appropriate benchmark. The Russell 1000 Stock Index is divided into two subindexes: a growth-oriented index and a value- or price-oriented index. Return information is provided for each. Comparable data are shown for the median growth-oriented and value-oriented managers from the TUCS Universe. Taking 1988 as an example, one can see that although the median value manager outperformed the S&P 500, he lagged the Russell Price Index. Conversely, the

TABLE 9-4. Performance of Russell and TUCS Style Indexes Relative to the S&P 500 Index, 1984–1988

Year	S&P 500	Russell Growth	TUCS Growth Median	Russell Price	TUCS Value Median
1984	6.1%	(1.0)%	(0.4)%	10.1%	9.6%
1985	32.0	32.9	31.4	31.5	29.7
1986	18.6	15.4	17.3	20.0	19.2
1987	5.2	5.3	5.7	0.5	0.9
1988	16.8	11.3	12.5	23.2	23.0
3 Years (1986–1988)	13.4	10.6	12.4	14.1	14.2
5 Years (1984–1988)	15.3	12.2	14.0	16.6	16.4

SOURCE: Bankers Trust Company.

median growth manager underperformed the S&P 500 but outperformed the Russell Growth Index. Assuming that the Russell indexes are appropriate benchmarks, one has a very different impression of manager performance based on the use of those indexes rather than the S&P 500.

Short-Term Performance Pressures. A problem that active managers encounter is the pressure for short-term performance. This is exacerbated by the existence of competitive universes that rank managers on a quarterly basis. The manager can be adding value versus his normal portfolio but look very poor in a broad universe of actively managed portfolios. A couple of quarters of poor performance have been known to lead to manager terminations. Hence, these types of comparisons may encourage a manager to abandon his style, when in fact he should be encouraged to stay with it.

Trading vs. Investing. A good case can be made for concluding that comparative universes have led to increased volatility in the equity market. Because a manager wants to look good in the short-term comparisons, he cannot afford to sit with stocks that are not performing, even if he is confident that they will do well over the long term. Hence, trading is encouraged. Increased trading means increased transaction costs, which translate into a drag on performance.

Bob Kirby [1984] addressed this issue a few years ago in an article titled "The Coffee Can Portfolio":

Are we traders, or are we really investors? Most good money managers are probably investors deep down inside. But quotrons, news services, and computers that churn out daily investment results make them act like traders. They start with sound research that identifies attractive companies in promising industries on a longer-term time horizon. Then, they trade those stocks two or three times a year based on month-to-month news developments and rumors of all shapes and sizes.

Although I cannot prove this, I believe there are many money managers in today's world who produce transaction costs that reach, or exceed, 2 percent of those assets per year. A. G. Becker data for the past five years shows a median turnover in institutional portfolios of 74 percent.

One half of the funds did more! In many cases, current transaction costs are running somewhere close to the hoped-for 2 percent return premium above a passive portfolio. It is fascinating to realize that you could virtually double the premium return that active management is in existence to obtain—if you could eliminate the transaction costs.

Limiting Portfolio Turnover. What is Kirby's solution to the turnover and transactions costs problem? Structure a diversified portfolio using the best research available, bury it in a coffee can in the back yard, and leave it alone for 10 years. Relieved of the burden of transaction costs, he is confident that such a portfolio would outperform the market indexes.

Warren Buffett takes much the same position when he lists *patience* as one of the six qualities needed to succeed as an investor. He feels that one should buy a stock only if one would be happy with it in the event that the stock exchange closed for 10 years.

He argues that investors should be issued lifetime punch cards with a very limited number of punches. Any significant decision would be a punch and would mean that the investor had one fewer punch to make in the future. His argument is that if investors take a long-term perspective and trade only when they have an overwhelming conviction that the trade will benefit the portfolio, returns will be much enhanced.

Unfortunately, many active managers seem to feel that the term "active" implies active trading. Arnold Wood [1988] undertook a survey of money managers to determine why they invested clients' money differently from their own. He concluded that most managers "are consumed with a 'do something,' Calvinist-like compulsion. . . . Activity for activity's sake, no matter how counter-productive, according to the survey, is clearly an outstanding feature of money management."

Structuring an Active Portfolio

To produce incremental returns, an active manager must take risks vis-à-vis his benchmark. The challenge is to take only appropriate risks and to add value by so doing. The manager must have opinions regarding which securities in his universe will do well and which will do poorly. These opinions can be formed in an endless number of ways. What is important is not how these opinions are formed, but rather how they are integrated into the design of a portfolio. Risk models are widely available and can be extremely helpful in this regard.

Factor Models. A popular type of risk model is the multifactor model or, more simply, *factor model*. Factor models decompose the risks of a stock into a variety of systematic factors—beta, size, growth orientation, leverage, foreign exposure, industry, and the like. Risk, other than that captured by one of the systematic factors, is labeled *unsystematic risk* or *specific risk*. Exposure to these various factors can be aggregated across the portfolio, enabling the manager to see the amount of risk he is taking vis-à-vis his benchmark and in what areas. For example, a manager might think that he is taking little risk vis-à-vis his benchmark, with the exception of a bet on chemical stocks, only to discover through a risk model analysis that he is actually making a significant bet on small companies. The latter may be desirable or undesirable, but at least the manager knows it exists.

Quadratic vs. Linear Programming Techniques. One could go a step further and use a *quadratic optimization model* to construct the portfolio. Such a model determines the best or "optimal " trade-off between a manager's return expectations and the risk estimated (i.e., to maximize return per unit of risk). This can be helpful to a manager in a number of ways, not the least of which is that it provides a framework for the efficient use of investment information. Nonetheless, optimizers are infrequently used by money managers, and, as Michaud [1989] points out, perhaps with good reason. Quadratic optimizers are sometimes referred to as "error maximizers." These models rely on the manager's risk and return estimates, estimates that are clearly subject to error. Securities with high estimates of return and low estimates of risk will be overweighted, and vice versa. These outlier estimates are precisely those most likely to be wrong.

Michaud suggests using a *linear programming model* as an alternative approach. These models are more intuitive for the average portfolio manager and allow him to construct a portfolio that maximizes expected return, subject to constraints he chooses to impose. Such constraints could include position size, industry diversification, yield, transaction costs, and so on.

Strategies

As mentioned previously, active managers pursue a variety of styles. In discussing managers, certain stylistic terms tend to be applied. Managers use processes that are usually categorized as either *top-down* or *bottom-up*. Styles are often generalized as *core*, *specialized*, or *quantitative*.

Top-Down. Managers are commonly referred to as top-down if their emphasis is on sector, industry, or theme bets as opposed to individual stock selection. Stocks are actively selected, but they are chosen in large part to flesh out a theme. An example is a manager who wants to emphasize companies with a high component of foreign earnings to benefit from his belief that the dollar will weaken. He then looks for companies with that characteristic.

An international manager pursuing a top-down approach might structure his process as follows:

1. Identify broad global themes that will influence world markets.
2. Incorporate those themes into specific economic and market forecasts for each country.
3. Factor in currency forecasts.
4. Use an asset allocation–type model to determine optimal country allocations
4. Given economic forecasts, determine sector weightings for each country.
6. Select stocks within these weightings.

The process is depicted in Figure 9-3.

Bottom-Up. A bottom-up manager takes the opposite tack from the top-down manager. His emphasis is on selecting attractive securities. Industries, sectors, and countries (in international portfolios) are incidental considerations.

An example of this approach is the $11 billion–plus Magellan Fund, which is managed by Peter Lynch. As related in *Institutional Investor* [1987], Lynch feels that a good way to lose money is to have a view on the economy. "We don't make economic judgments," he says flatly. "We don't have somebody here saying we're going to have a recession, so you can't buy electronic stocks, or we're going to have a boom, so you should buy Colgate-Palmolive."

Historically, the 1,800 stocks in the Magellan portfolio have included growth stocks, value stocks, special situations, and so forth. Sector weightings have been ignored. Lynch states:

> A lot of [investment] firms won't listen to a lot of ideas. . . . They'll buy only growth companies. They'll buy only companies without unions or companies in a growing industry. Or they won't buy foreign companies or bankrupt companies or companies that start with the letter "R." I mean, we'll just buy anything. We'll look at textile companies, we'll look at supermarkets. One of my best stocks of all time is a funeral company, Service Corp. International. It's been one of my top 50 positions and has gone up ten or fifteenfold since I bought it.

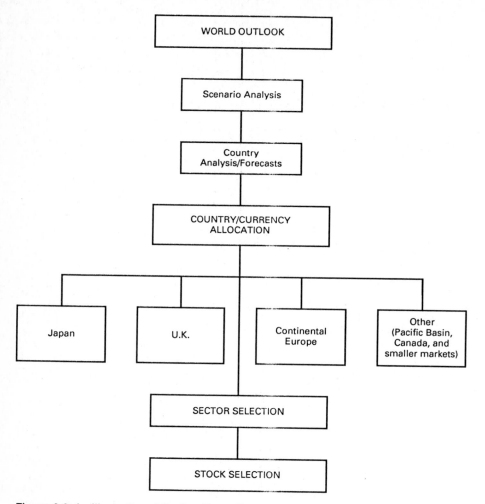

Figure 9-3. An Illustration of the Top-Down Equity Portfolio Investment Process.

Core Management. A core manager is one who is hired to manage a diversified portfolio. His benchmark would most likely be the S&P 500 or some other broad market index. He is hired because it is believed that he can add value over and above that available from a passive portfolio. Return objectives would be modest, reflecting the broad diversification character-istic of this approach. These managers do not "swing for the fences"; rather, they are hired with the hope that they will consistently add value vis-à-vis the market. They are the bedrock foundation, or central core, of active equity portfolio management on which a superstructure of other specialized, more dynamic management is built.

Specialized. A specialized manager is one who is hired to operate in a specific subset of the market. Common specialties include small capitalization managers, growth managers, and value managers. These managers are sometimes referred to as *boutique managers*, and they are generally hired in the expectation that they can add considerable value vis-à-vis their normal portfolios.

An example of a value manager is Dreman Value Management. The firm focuses on large capitalization stocks, screening the universes for companies with P/E multiples lower than the mean of the market and growth in both earnings and dividends of 10 percent or more over the previous five years. The number of securities in Dreman portfolios is small, averaging 20 to 30 stocks in each, but these stocks are spread widely across industries.

Quantitative. Some managers rely heavily on computer simulations in devising strategies. Robert Hagin [1988] refers to quantitative strategies as "engineered investment strategies" and defines them as

> having at least three characteristics: (1) the strategy is based on a sound theory— a reason why it has worked in the past and, most important, why it should work in the future; (2) there is an explicit 'quantified' statement of the strategy; (3) there is a precise determination of how the strategy would have worked in the past.

An example of a quantitative approach is a strategy that sells winners and buys losers. One could construct a portfolio with sector diversification in line with that of the S&P 500. Within sectors, however, rules are established for systematically selling the better performing stocks and investing the proceeds in poorer performing stocks. Such an approach meets Hagin's criteria for a quantitative strategy: A theoretical justification can be found in the concept of mean reversion, and the strategy can be quantified and backtested.

COMBINING ACTIVE AND PASSIVE

Most large funds have a number of equity managers. Almost all employ active managers of one style or another, and the majority have passive managers as well. The question then arises, How can the active and passive components of a portfolio best be combined? That is, what role is best served by active and what by passive?

Active/Core Portfolios

Passive funds are typically used as core portfolios. In this framework, an index fund is created to track a broad market index, most commonly the

S&P 500 but increasingly a broader index such as the Wilshire 5000 or the Russell 3000. The plan sponsor, having a broadly diversified core that he knows will perform in line with the market, then feels free to hire specialist managers in an attempt to add value to the total package. If the core fund is indexed to the S&P 500, an active specialist in the small capitalization area might be hired to get coverage of an important area of the equity market judged not to be adequately represented in the index. Frequently, several active speciality managers are hired to pursue a variety of styles, while the passive core is maintained to lock in market returns on a substantial portion of the assets.

Active/Completeness Fund Portfolios

Alternatively, the passive portfolio may be structured as a completeness fund. Proponents of the completeness fund concept argue that passive portfolios can be created to replicate any benchmark desired by the plan sponsor. Accordingly, it makes sense to decide first on the active managers to be hired. If an active manager seems to have the ability to add value in a market segment, he is hired to operate in that segment. Indeed, the plan sponsor hires whichever managers he thinks can add value. Once they are in place, he then can aggregate their normal portfolios and judge where "holes"— lack of equity market coverage—might exist. The passive fund is then created to fill in these holes, thus completing the desired coverage.

An example of how this might work follows. A fund has five active managers that when aggregated have characteristics quite similar to those of the S&P 500, with the exception that the aggregate normal portfolio has less exposure than the S&P 500 to growth stocks. In this instance, a passive portfolio with an orientation toward smaller capitalization, higher growth stocks is created. The goal is to create a fund that, when combined with the active normal portfolios, produces a composite portfolio with characteristics in line with those of the broad U.S. stock market.

The key to understanding the difference between these two approaches is that when the index fund is considered to be the core portfolio, active managers are hired to supplement and add value around that core. When the passive portfolio is used as a completeness fund, the initial focus is on hiring active managers and the passive fund is then customized to ensure that market segments are not systematically ignored.

SUMMARY

Like other aspects of the investment process, management of equity portfolios is an area experiencing rapid change. Prior to the early 1970s, all money was actively managed, much of it by active core managers. As we move into the 1990s, passive strategies are widely employed, frequently in conjunction with specialty active managers. Quantitative strategies have been developed, and hybrid products are an area of growth.

The introduction of passive technology has placed a burden of proof on the active money manager; to justify his existence he must be able to demonstrate that he can add value over and above that which is available from passive portfolios. One can think about various styles of portfolio management as lying along a spectrum of risk taking, with all managers along that spectrum having defined benchmarks. The passive manager takes little if any risk vis-à-vis that benchmark. His sole objective is to equal the return of the benchmark. The active manager, on the other hand, does take risk because only by taking risk can he hope to add incremental return. Models exist to help managers understand and measure the risk that they are taking. As more hybrid products are introduced, the gap in the spectrum between active and passive management will narrow.

FURTHER READING

This chapter builds on the excellent counterpart chapter on the same subject by Bill Gray in the first edition of this book. Many of the active versus passive strategy issues and the various styles employed by managers discussed in this chapter were initially treated there.

For an interesting treatise on strategies and methods that have met with significant success in the marketplace over time, see Lynch [1989].

A chronicle of the problems associated with index arbitrage and other program trading activities in the major market break of October 1987 can be found in the Report of the Presidential Task Force [1988].

For a discussion of a number of successful styles in equity management, see Train [1980]. One such style, the quantitative style, is covered in straightforward fashion in Hagin [1988]. Kirby [1984] provides some sobering observations on styles that involve heavy rebalancing and associated transaction costs.

BIBLIOGRAPHY

Burr, Barry B. "Funds Reduce Stocks." *Pensions & Investment Age*, January 23, 1989.

Grossman, Sanford J. "Report on Program Trading, an Analysis of Interday Relationships." Financial Research Center Memorandum No. 87, Princeton University, December 1987.

Hagin, Robert L. "Engineered Investment Strategies: Problems and Solutions," in K.F. Sherrerd, ed. *Equity Markets and Valuation Methods*. Charlottesville, Va.: The Institute of Chartered Financial Analysts, 1988.

Kirby, Robert G. "The Coffee Can Portfolio." *The Journal of Portfolio Management*, Fall 1984.

Lynch, Peter. *One Up on Wall Street*. New York: Simon & Schuster, 1989.

Malkiel, Burton G. *A Random Walk Down Wall Street*, 4th ed. New York: W.W. Norton & Company, 1985.

Michaud, Richard O. "The Markowitz Optimization Enigma: Is 'Optimized' Optimal?" *Financial Analysts Journal*, January/February 1989.

Report of the Presidential Task Force on Market Mechanisms. Washington, D.C.: U.S. Government Printing Office, January 1988.

Ring, Trudy. "Funds Keeping Options Open." *Pensions & Investments Age*, January 23, 1989.

Rohrer, Julie. "The Master of Magellan." *Institutional Investor*, September 1987.

———. "The Day of the Contrarian." *Institutional Investor*, October 1987.

Train, John. *The Money Masters*. New York: Harper & Row, 1980.

Wood, Arnold W. "Manager vs. Client: What's the Difference?" *The Journal of Portfolio Management*, Summer 1988.

CHAPTER 10

Real Estate Portfolio Management

_____ **Randall C. Zisler**

OVERVIEW

The optimization of the fixed-income and common stock components of a portfolio were covered in Chapters 8 and 9. This chapter covers the optimization of real estate, the third major asset class to be discussed, in terms of how properties are formed into efficient subportfolios.

REAL ESTATE IN A PORTFOLIO CONTEXT

Although the real estate market predates the securities market by centuries, the portfolio approach to real estate is a recent phenomenon.[1] Traditionally, equity real estate (also referred to as "property") has been regarded as an inefficient market in which the ability to select and negotiate an individual deal is the secret of success. Institutional buyers of property tend to stress the opportunistic nature of real estate acquisitions with little regard for the equally important issue of how an individual property fits the overall portfolio of investments and what, if any, contribution the transaction makes to portfolio risk and return.

In this chapter, some of the tools of modern portfolio theory are used to show ways in which portfolios of real estate can be structured rationally. These tools are applied every day in the management of large portfolios of stocks and bonds. In fact, it is difficult to imagine how these multibillion dollar portfolios could be structured and managed without the new portfolio management tools. The selection of asset sectors in which to invest is likely

_____

[1] This chapter is partially adapted from Firstenberg, Ross, and Zisler [1988]. The technical assistance of John Bruestle and James Love of Russell-Zisler, Inc., and Will Goetzmann of Yale University is gratefully acknowledged, as is the significant editorial assistance of John Maginn and Donald Tuttle. Any errors in this chapter are the responsibility of the author.

to be more important in managing stock and bond portfolios, especially the large ones, than the selection of individual investments. The same is true for real estate. The overall asset allocation decision is likely to be more critical for portfolio performance than a few good "opportunistic" bets.

The purpose of this chapter is neither to dismiss the traditional tools of real estate investing nor to present a cookbook or mechanistic "black box" approach to real estate portfolio management. Quite the contrary. The aim instead is to supplement the analysis of individual properties and markets with a full analysis of property's contribution to portfolio performance. This is not to say, however, that the analytical portfolio approach can simply be grafted to the traditional way institutional real estate investments are managed. Rather, the intention is to provide some portfolio management tools that respond to real estate's special characteristics. The portfolio approach not only introduces a discipline that is often missing in traditional asset management; it also forces all phases of property selection into a structure that is consistent with overall portfolio objectives, constraints, and strategies.

Real estate is a unique asset that requires specialized analytic tools. Properties do not trade in an auction market. Acquiring divisible shares in any property, however large or small, is costly and often beyond the reach of many investors.

Information flow in real estate markets is very complex. Fundamental real estate research is quite valuable at the margin. By contrast, stock and bond markets are well researched. Hence, it is difficult to add value to our understanding of IBM share price, for instance, with additional research.

Thus, good real estate judgment is extremely valuable, because even if an institutional investor relied solely on the judgment of real estate entrepreneurs or real estate money managers to acquire a portfolio of properties, the burden of creating an efficient or optimal portfolio of real estate investments would remain with the investor. The task of constructing efficient real estate portfolios is the subject of this chapter.

Current State of Affairs

Compared to the current practice and technology of managing stock and bond portfolios, real estate portfolio management is primitive. There are, of course, good reasons. One is that, unlike stocks and bonds, real estate is an asset class that generally does not trade in public markets. Real estate is still a private placement business, although even this is changing.

Second, as discussed in Hartzell [1986], institutional investors, primarily private and public pension funds, still have minor commitments to real estate equity. This is illustrated in Figure 10-1. Real estate equity constitutes less than 4 percent of total pension fund assets. The public pension

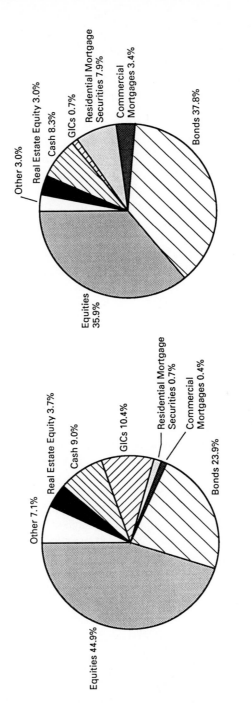

Figure 10-1. Estimated U.S. Corporate and Public Pension Fund Percentage Asset Allocation, June 30, 1988. SOURCE: Money Market Directory of Pension Funds [1989].

fund allocation to commercial mortgages, 3.4 percent, and residential mortgage securities, 7.9 percent, exceeds by a significant margin corporate pension fund investments in these instruments, 0.4 percent and 0.7 percent respectively. Mortgage loans, which are typically treated by institutional investors as fixed income and not real estate, and bonds both receive higher allocations by public funds.

The relatively small equity real estate holdings of institutional portfolios contrasts sharply with the estimated outstanding value of investment grade real estate in absolute dollars and relative to stocks and bonds, as shown in Figure 10-2. Unleveraged commercial equity real estate (office, retail, warehouse, and hotel properties), as of December 31, 1987, was estimated by Salomon Brothers to be about $2.5 trillion, which is slightly less than the outstanding capitalization of U.S. corporate equity.

Third, real estate as an asset class is not well understood by investors, even though there has been an increasing volume of research produced by academics and practitioners. The quality of the early equity real estate research published by brokers and real estate investment managers has varied in terms of its merit and rigor. More exceptions have emerged recently, particularly from Wall Street. However, the most innovative and scholarly real estate research that appeared in the late 1980s focused primarily on residential mortgage instruments.

A fourth reason why the portfolio approach to real estate investment is underdeveloped relative to stock and bond management is that the vast majority of real estate transactions are infrequent and small. Most commercial properties fall within a range of value of $100,000 to several million dollars. The megamillion dollar transactions are the province of large institutional players, such as life insurance companies, private real estate investment managers, Wall Street, and, of course, selected offshore investors such as the Japanese.

Fifth, real estate is not researched by cadres of research analysts, as are stocks and bonds. Real estate is so heterogeneous, infrequently traded, illiquid, and dominated by small properties that extensive research coverage of real estate has not been practical, especially for properties that are owned and traded in the traditional format. Furthermore, real estate data that are relevant to pricing a property accurately are costly, valuable to prospective buyers and tenants, and usually held in strictest confidence. By contrast, the market for public securities is regulated to encourage public disclosure of information that is material to efficient pricing, and acting on inside information is actively discouraged, whereas real estate is perhaps one of the last bastions where the use of inside information is both socially and legally sanctioned.

As a result, the lack of standardized accounting for real estate performance is not surprising. A growing need for credible performance data and useful reporting standards has generated industry efforts to remedy the con-

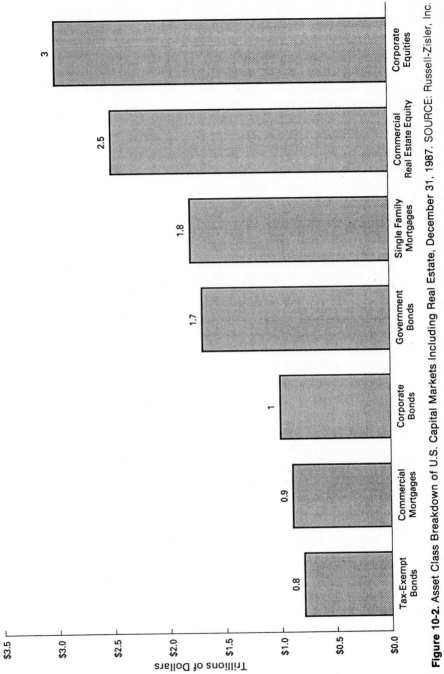

Figure 10-2. Asset Class Breakdown of U.S. Capital Markets Including Real Estate, December 31, 1987. SOURCE: Russell-Zisler, Inc.

fusion. The establishment of the National Council of Real Estate Investment Fiduciaries (NCREIF) and the creation of the Frank Russell Company Property Index are two examples of the effort being made to make equity real estate a respectable and viable asset class for institutional investment.

The securitization of real estate equity and debt, a process that has evolved more slowly for commercial than for residential properties, permits the trading of fractional interests in real estate in an entirely new format, one that provides investors with unique financial benefits not obtained with other assets. The portfolio approach to real estate will become more widespread with the securitization of real estate, an increase in real estate's asset allocation, the development of new real estate vehicles, more research and systems for monitoring and evaluating real estate performance, and the development of real estate portfolio analytics.

Need for a Portfolio Approach

What is wrong with institutional portfolio management today? Real estate portfolio discipline and management are often weak or nonexistent. Individual property or asset management is often disguised as portfolio management. Neither the portfolio benefits nor the limitations of real estate are fully appreciated or well articulated. Where the portfolio approach is preached, it is stated in macro and theoretical terms far removed from the daily practice of real estate asset management.

Real estate marketing (i.e., raising money) generally attracts the brightest and best compensated professionals, whereas ongoing property management is often entrusted to second best talent. This is particularly surprising because the operating, renovating, and particularly the leasing of properties are critical elements in effective portfolio management. Certain leasing terms may be points of indifference to a leasing broker. However, lease terms casually negotiated and improperly structured with little attention to their portfolio impact can introduce unanticipated risks and can significantly affect property values.

In practice, most attempts to diversify real estate portfolios have been well intentioned, but, in portfolio management terms, they have been naive. The covariance of historical or expected returns is either ignored or treated superficially. The market does not reward investors for risks that can be eliminated, such as unsystematic or diversifiable risks. By contrast, above-market returns can be achieved by assuming greater systematic risk. To the extent that real estate portfolios are poorly diversified, investors are assuming uncompensated risks or equivalently sacrificing risk-adjusted return, as noted in Firstenberg, Ross, and Zisler [1988].

Need for Well-Defined Strategies. An important problem with real estate portfolio management is that too often real estate strategies are poorly defined, ill conceived, or simply nonexistent. Consultants and managers have done a poor job developing meaningful guidelines based on portfolio measures that have financial relevance. For example, some managers of real estate closed-end funds, as well as many of the consultants who advise pension clients on appropriate managers and investment vehicles, are frequently unaware of the onerous business implications of the redemption and termination provisions of group trust agreements. That is, there has been greater emphasis on the general property type, geography, and manager "style" than on the intrinsic financial characteristics that shape investment performance. Only recently have investors demanded more portfolio analytics.

That the portfolio is "50 percent invested in office properties" fails to recognize the diversity of financial structures, underlying leases, geographic markets, embedded options, and risk sensitivities that affect portfolio performance. While asset allocation is the most important factor affecting real estate portfolio performance, its execution is often naive. In large part this is because the language of real estate often fails to convey the effective financial characteristics of real estate within the portfolio context.

The casual and anecdotal treatment of real estate risk contrasts sharply with risk analysis in fixed-income and equity securities. Real estate investors simply do not appreciate the sensitivities of their portfolios to risk factors, such as unanticipated inflation, changes in investor confidence, shifts in the yield curve, and the movements of the business cycle.

Need for Better Data. If real estate portfolio management is to gain a solid foothold, then investors need the correct information. Now, real estate investors typically receive too much information that is irrelevant, too technical, too superficial, or just incorrect. Manager reporting systems focus on asset management and tend to ignore factors that are critical at the portfolio level. Compared to stock and bond investors, real estate investors (and particularly plan sponsors) have little of the basic data necessary to make portfolio decisions. The data are generally retained by managers who do not have the mandate, inclination, or perspective to share data. It is not unusual to hear a manager proclaim indignantly to the pension client that the detailed lease-by-lease data pertaining to the client's buildings are proprietary (i.e., the property of the manager).

The next section compares real estate performance with that of stocks and bonds. The nature of real estate markets and their information flows introduce special statistical problems.

REAL ESTATE AND THE PROBLEM OF RETURN MEASUREMENT

Total Return

Real estate, unlike stocks and bonds, does not trade in a continuous auction market, and the costs of real estate transactions and performance measurement are significant. Consequently, it is misleading and incorrect to compare raw real estate performance with stock and bond return data.

Typically, investment managers focus on total returns which include both income and changes in market value. It is often accepted that "cash is cash" and that the investor is indifferent between an investment with a total return of 15 percent, all of which is appreciation, or all of which is cash income. After all, by selling a sufficient amount of the investment that has appreciated, the investor can realize the same cash as the all income investment provides. This is, of course, a simplification of the real world. Some investors have a preference for cash and others prefer to forego cash returns in favor of appreciation. Growth in income as well as growth in value is an attractive characteristic of equity real estate.

The high costs associated with a real estate transaction are an important reason why a real estate investor might have an income *as well as* a total return objective. Some investors with significant current cash requirements, particularly those holding a substantial percentage of their portfolio assets in properties in countries and locations within countries where capital gains and real estate taxes are onerous, may place as much emphasis on maintaining minimum income rates of return as on total return. This chapter does not address methods of managing the income objective. However, this is not a serious omission because income rates of return for property are *relatively* stable over time compared to appreciation rates of return. Differences in income rates of return do not seriously affect the asset allocation decision across the property sector for most large real estate funds.

Real Estate Markets

Total return consists of an income and an appreciation component. While income is relatively straightforward, price appreciation is much more difficult to determine. Unlike stocks and bonds, real estate does not trade in a continuous auction market, which means that cheap and frequent price quotes are not available. In fact, properties trade infrequently. Whereas the time between trades of IBM stock is measured in seconds, decades may pass before a building is sold. This does not mean that a property lacks a market value. Rather, market value is more difficult to estimate. For institutional investors who must report property returns quarterly, appraisals are the most important source of property valuations. However, the use of appraisal data in performance analysis raises some important theoretical and practical problems, one of which is the tendency of the appraisal process to smooth or reduce the variance of returns. Return smoothing tends to distort performance comparisons of real estate with fixed-income, equity, and cash securities. Furthermore, appraisal-based performance data have obvious practical importance, particularly where a real estate portfolio manager's compensation is based on the value of total assets under management.

Appraisals and Returns

Most publicly available property return data are based on appraisals. As discussed in Chapter 6, appraisals generally rely on one or all of three approaches to the estimation of market value: (1) cost or replacement, (2) market comparables, and (3) income approach to value which capitalizes future cash flows. The choice of method is dictated by factors that include the property type and market characteristics. Each approach has its own limitations. All approaches are interrelated and all require painstaking market analysis.

None of these methods can be as accurate as an actual market price. Are there inherent biases? Probably there are, but it is not at all clear what the nature of these biases really are. There are few carefully crafted statistical studies of appraisal bias. In the long run, appraisals are probably unbiased. Even if the appraisals are biased, as long as the bias is constant over time, the calculated rate of appreciation will not be biased.[2]

Comparison of Returns

The concern regarding bias is fueled by the sluggishness, or *high positive serial correlation*, of appraisal-based return data. The volatility of real estate return data is far less than other risky assets' return series, a situation that Shulman [1986] explores in an attempt to properly compare stock and property returns. Is the low volatility of unleveraged real estate return series a true characteristic of the real estate itself or the process by which real estate values are determined? The answer is not known for sure.

Real Estate Indexes. The Frank Russell Company Property Index (FRC Index) is a quarterly time series of equity returns extending from 1978 to the present. It is broken down by income and appreciation and also by region and property type. The FRC data base has approximately 1,000 prop-

---

[2] For a critical treatment of appraisals, see Cole, Guilkey, and Miles [1986a, 1986b], Gilberto [1987], and Guan and Quigley [1987].

TABLE 10-1. Comparison of Real Estate Returns and Standard Deviations With Securities, 2Q1978–2Q1988

Index	Total Return	Standard Deviation
Real estate		
FRC	12.02%	2.89%
FRC (cap-adjusted)	10.21	9.56
EREIT	18.06	13.48
Other assets		
S&P 500 stocks	17.01	16.42
Small stocks	20.61	23.83
Corporate bonds	10.53	15.52
Government bonds	10.47	16.15
Treasury bills	8.78	1.30
Inflation	5.98	2.23
Risk premium		
(Spread over Treasury bills)		
FRC	3.24	
FRC (cap-adjusted)	1.43	
S&P 500 stocks	8.23	
Small stocks	11.83	

SOURCE: Russell-Zisler, Inc.

erties owned in *institutional* real estate portfolios with an average value of about $10 million per property. The selection of properties is dependent on the choice of real estate money managers. Consequently, the FRC Index may not be representative of a value-weighted total U.S. real estate index. Important property types, particularly apartments and hotels, are under-represented. FRC properties are owned by institutional investors and are usually unleveraged. Leverage is typically associated with real estate and most property is not institutionally owned. It is not known what small sample biases exist in the FRC Index because a broader based index is not available for comparison.

Three real estate indexes are reported in Table 10-1: (1) the raw FRC Index; (2) an FRC Index capitalization rate adjusted (cap-adjusted FRC Index) for possible sluggishness due to appraisal bias; and (3) an equity Real Estate Investment Trust (EREIT) Index based on data from the National Association of Real Estate Investment Trusts (NAREIT).

Table 10-1 shows that for the period 1978 through 1988 the standard deviation of stocks and bonds was over five times greater than that of real estate as measured by the FRC Index.

FRC Cap-Adjusted Index. The cap-adjusted series, in attempting to correct for sluggishness in appraisal-based return data, estimates appreciation from a discounted cash flow model. Changes in current income are indicators of changes in market value.[3] While there are a number of problems with this approach, it is based on known data, and a similar procedure applied to stock market data produces estimates that approximate the true value for volatility. See Firstenberg, Ross, and Zisler [1988]. The result is a cap-adjusted FRC Index standard deviation of nearly 10 percent versus 3 percent without the adjustment.

Figure 10-3 shows a 10-year history of the raw FRC Property Index, the S&P 500 stock index and U.S. Government long bonds.

The unadjusted property series is much less volatile than either stocks or bonds. However, the cap-adjusted series, compared to the raw return data, has significantly greater volatility, as shown in Figure 10-4.[4]

The equity REIT index has an average total return and volatility similar to stocks and greater than the FRC Index, both raw and cap-adjusted (see Figure 10-5). Reconciling the differences between EREIT and FRC property returns is not easy. Clearly, the EREIT index follows the stock market more closely than it does the FRC index.

Correlation Characteristics. The unsystematic or diversifiable risks associated with property, or for that matter any asset, are uncorrelated. Assets that have low correlations with a portfolio can be included to reduce portfolio risk without sacrificing return.

Table 10-2 shows the correlation coefficients among real estate, stocks, bonds, Treasury bills, and inflation. Real estate measures include both the raw and the cap-adjusted FRC Index as well as equity REITs. The raw FRC index is negatively correlated with EREITs, stocks, and U.S. Government bonds and positively correlated with inflation. The cap-adjusted series is positively correlated with stocks, bonds, EREITs, and inflation. However, unlike the FRC Index, equity REITs are negatively correlated with inflation. Stocks, as well as equity REITs, have historically been poor inflation hedges. If the true unleveraged real estate return index behaves more like the FRC Index, then real estate performed like an inflation hedge from 1978 to 1988. However, if the cap-adjusted FRC Index or the equity REIT index best

---

[3] The capitalization rate adjustment procedure, while deficient in a number of respects, is based on net operating income, which is not only directly observable but typically used in property valuation. For a detailed description of the methodology, see Firstenberg, Ross, and Zisler [1988]. An alternative method of correcting for appraisal sluggishness is found in Ross and Zisler [1987]. This recursive correction models appraisal returns as a weighted average of past t ue returns and estimates the standard deviation of the FRC Property Index in the 9 percent to 13 percent range, comparable to the estimated volatility of the cap-adjusted FRC Index but somewhat less than the standard deviation of U.S. Government bonds and U.S. stocks.

[4] It is interesting to note that the cap-rate-adjusted total return appears more volatile from 1984 through 1986, a period of dramatically rising office vacancy rates and robust retail property performance.

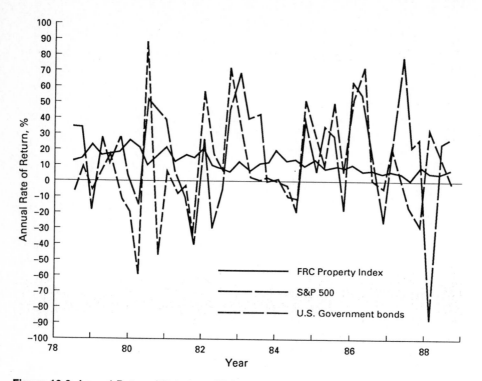

Figure 10-3. Annual Rates of Return on FRC Property Index, S&P 500, and U.S. Government Bonds, 2Q1978–2Q1988. SOURCE: Russell-Zisler, Inc.

describes unleveraged property returns, then real estate performed more like stocks or bonds.

It is not likely that the returns on equity REITs are a good proxy for the returns of the underlying asset. Equity REIT returns reflect as much the market's view of the EREIT management as they do the performance of the underlying asset. The lesson of the closed-end mutual stock funds is that they often sell at unexplained discounts as well as premiums from their net asset values. If that can happen for funds whose holdings of stocks are traded and readily valued, then these discrepancies must be even greater for EREITs.

Real estate is no more homogeneous than stocks and bonds. Consequently, real estate, depending on many factors that will be subsequently discussed, may behave with respect to inflation and interest rates like bonds,

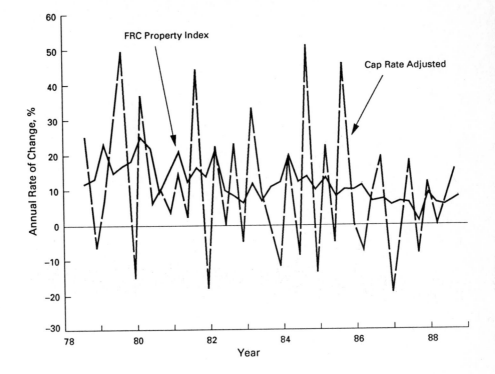

Figure 10-4. Annual Rates of Change for FRC Property Index With and Without Cap Rate Adjustment, 2Q1978–2Q1988. SOURCE: Russell-Zisler, Inc.

stocks, or like something not even resembling stocks or bonds. Not surprisingly, reality is complex.

Effect of Leverage. Neither the equity REIT index nor the unadjusted FRC Index are adequate measures of the return or the riskiness of unleveraged equity real estate. The true volatility probably lies somewhere between 3 percent and 13.5 percent, a very wide range. It is possible that the low volatility of real estate is not entirely illusory. While the FRC Index is unleveraged, companies whose stock trades on exchanges are leveraged. Most real estate, as it has been noted already, is held with some leverage. However, leveraging the FRC Index to the same extent that the companies in the S&P 500 are leveraged, as reported by Gyourko and Linneman [1988], results in return variances that are still much less than common stock equity.

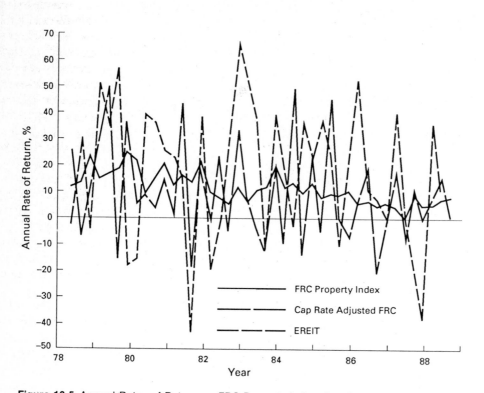

Figure 10-5. Annual Rates of Return on FRC Property Index, Cap Rate Adjusted FRC Index, and EREIT Index, 2Q1978–2Q1988. SOURCE: Russell-Zisler, Inc.

TABLE 10-2. Correlations Among Asset Class Index Returns, 2Q1978–2Q1988

Index	FRC	FRC Cap-Adjusted	EREIT	S&P 500	U.S. Government Bonds	Treasury Bills	Inflation
FRC	1.00						
FRC, cap-adjusted	0.32	1.00					
EREIT	−0.02	0.13	1.00				
S&P 500	−0.15	0.10	0.75	1.00			
U.S. Govt. bonds	−0.29	0.05	0.42	0.35	1.00		
Treasury bills	0.58	0.16	−0.09	−0.23	−0.06	1.00	
Inflation	0.54	0.11	−0.16	−0.13	−0.37	0.55	1.00

SOURCE: Russell-Zisler, Inc.

Accordingly, the FRC Property Index would have to be leveraged 70 to 80 percent for return variances to equal those of long-term bonds or stocks.

Return Variance. Even if appraisals were not biased, unleveraged real estate returns might still have variances lower than stocks. Properties with high occupancy rates tend to have income flows that are very stable compared to the income of tenants. Property should have a lower return variance than bonds because bond coupons are in fixed dollars whereas most leases have expense escalation clauses that at least partially index rental income for inflation. Thus, property is particularly attractive compared to bonds during times of unexpected inflation and accompanying volatile interest rates.

If real estate volatility, expressed as a percentage of total returns, is so much lower than stock and bond volatility, then why do institutional investors own so little real estate, given its average return? If the liabilities of pension funds are long-term, then why should pension funds hold so much more liquid than illiquid assets? If real estate is such a good deal on a risk-adjusted basis, then why do not institutions arbitrage or take advantage of the free ride? Perhaps some insight can be obtained from an analysis of real estate's unique characteristics.

COMMERCIAL REAL ESTATE: A UNIQUE ASSET CLASS

Fixed-Income and Equity Characteristics

Not only is there is no asset class quite like real estate, but there is no such thing as "pure" real estate other than raw land. Even a multitenanted office building that is owned free and clear of any debt is far from pure equity. Instead, such an investment is really a portfolio of leases with different maturities and bond-like cash flows. In that sense, an income property consist of bond equivalents, called *leases*, and a *call option* on the residual equity. Most real estate practitioners do not look at real estate investments in this way. Real estate and its components are usually analyzed outside the mainstream of modern finance.

Real estate returns are shaped by the interaction among several investment characteristics: location, type of property, lease structure, financial structure, replacement cost and building obsolescence, and property enhancement. Location has historically been emphasized as one of the key determinants of value. It is ironic, however, that in practice much attention has been paid to the neighborhood characteristics of location at the expense of metropolitan and regional factors. Where regional and metropolitan economic factors are addressed by appraisers and investors, the analysis is usually superficial. The relationship between investment underwriting assumptions and the broader economic factors that affect property performance is poorly understood and hence not well articulated.

Regional and metropolitan differences in the supply and demand for space probably explain more of the inter-city variation in property returns than do the differences in a building's physical and neighborhood characteristics. This is particularly important because real estate asset pricing is based on a stream of expected returns, which are shaped by disequilibrium in leasing markets and the rate of return on capital assets of equivalent risk.

Leasing market disequilibrium (i.e., the difference in supply and demand at prevailing effective rental rates) is a complicated process due to the durability of property, the high transaction costs typically associated with tenant relocation and expansion and with contract negotiation, valuation, and the like. The subtle differences in property characteristics, some of which are crucial but difficult to assess and others which are easy to measure but trivial, make real estate complex in its heterogeneity and elusive in its valuation.

As a result of real estate's heterogeneity, the broad asset class "real estate" is too vague to be meaningful for purposes of managing real estate portfolios or devising real estate strategies. The development of real estate performance data bases, a recent endeavor, suffers as well from the traditional and too simplistic view of real estate. The data are typically reported using conventional categories that may not have direct relevance to the underlying financial characteristics of property.

REAL ESTATE RISK ANALYSIS

Expected return is related to systematic risk. Just how many risk factors explain returns is still a matter of debate among researchers. However, there is evidence that multifactor models perform better than single factor models in explaining security returns. This seems reasonable. After all, to what extent can a single measure of risk capture the effects of unanticipated changes in inflation, interest rates, and so forth? In addition, the multifactor approach can illuminate the unique characteristics of real estate.

Systematic Risk

Real estate is a unique asset class with a risk profile all its own. That is why real estate can play an important role in portfolio diversification. However, very little is known about the sensitivity of real estate returns to specific risk factors that are common to all assets, that is, systematic risk factors. There is no more consensus about which factors explain the systematic risk of real estate than there is of stocks and bonds. Much work in this area

TABLE 10-3. Sensitivity of Real Estate Returns to Macroeconomic Factors, 2Q1978–2Q1988

Raw FRC Index	Macroeconomic Factors					
	A	B	C	D	E	R^2
Total	0.195	−0.273	−0.078	−0.221	0.466	
t-statistic	0.582	−2.125	−2.368	−1.997	1.033	0.27
Office	0.396	−0.439	−0.126	−0.382	0.625	
t-statistic	0.631	−1.818	−2.020	−1.833	0.738	0.22
Retail	−0.571	−0.033	−0.039	0.053	−0.011	
t-statistic	−2.201	−0.327	−1.532	0.617	−0.032	0.17
Research & dev.	−0.247	−0.085	−0.100	−0.109	−0.216	
t-statistic	−0.501	−0.451	−2.048	−0.667	−0.325	0.12
Warehouse	0.077	−0.240	−0.057	−0.134	0.232	
t-statistic	0.288	−2.348	−2.164	−1.521	0.647	0.24
East	0.446	−0.260	−0.155	−0.079	−0.272	
t-statistic	0.853	−1.300	−2.997	−0.455	−0.386	0.31
Midwest	−0.571	−0.033	−0.040	0.053	−0.011	
t-statistic	−2.201	−0.327	−1.532	0.617	−0.032	0.17
South	−0.247	−0.085	−0.100	−0.109	−0.216	
t-statistic	−0.501	−0.451	−2.048	−0.667	−0.325	0.12
West	0.077	−0.240	−0.057	−0.134	0.232	
t-statistic	0.288	−2.348	−2.164	−1.521	0.647	0.24

Key:
A = Unanticipated inflation
B = Investor confidence or risk premium (Aaa yield − Baa yield)
C = Long-run expected inflation (U.S. Government long bond returns − Treasury bill rate)
D = Strength of the economy (monthly industrial production)
E = Strength of the economy (per capita consumption growth)

SOURCE: Russell-Zisler, Inc.

remains to be done. The analyses and insights in the following paragraphs are preliminary and reflect the combined effort of the author and Stephen Ross to adapt a multifactor model to real estate.

Tables 10-3, 10-4, and 10-5 report some initial findings regarding the sensitivity of real estate and other securities to these factors. The analysis is not rigorous. In fact, much work remains with regard to econometric specification, selection of appropriate factors, statistical tests of signifi-cance, and the like. However, even in its preliminary form, these results are suggestive of determinants that may differentiate the financial charac-teristics of real estate from other asset classes.

The Model. This multifactor approach is intended to measure, in a multivariate context, how real estate returns vary with changes in certain macroeconomic factors. The sensitivities that are calculated can then be

TABLE 10-4. Sensitivity of Asset Returns to Macroeconomic Factors, 2Q1978–2Q1988

Securities	Macroeconomic Factors					
	A	B	C	D	E	R^2
S&P 500 stocks	3.848	0.142	0.778	−0.218	7.995	
t-statistic	2.306	0.222	4.715	−0.395	3.555	0.46
Small stocks	4.203	0.329	0.827	−0.423	10.269	
t-statistic	1.534	0.312	3.054	−0.465	2.781	0.29
U.S. corporate bonds	−0.556	0.995	0.947	−0.004	−1.386	
t-statistic	−2.247	10.459	38.685	−0.044	−4.154	0.99
U.S. Government bonds	−0.555	−0.005	0.947	−0.004	−1.385	
t-statistic	−2.242	−0.058	38.685	−0.045	−4.150	0.99
Treasury bills	0.107	−0.090	−0.029	−0.134	−0.153	
t-statistic	0.727	−1.595	−1.986	−2.739	−0.770	0.31
Equity REITs	0.668	0.563	0.556	0.021	4.272	
t-statistic	0.446	0.978	3.757	0.043	2.117	0.35

Key:
A = Unanticipated inflation
B = Investor confidence or risk premium (Aaa yield − Baa yield)
C = Long-run expected inflation (U.S. Government long bond returns − Treasury bill rate)
D = Strength of the economy (monthly industrial production)
E = Strength of the economy (per capita consumption growth)

SOURCE: Russell-Zisler, Inc.

used to evaluate the risk and return of real estate investments with respect to the risks inherent in various economic scenarios.

The model, which was estimated for various asset classes using ordinary least squares, is specified as follows:[5]

$$R = A + B_a X_{at} + B_b X_{bt} + B_c X_{ct} + B_d X_{dt} + B_e X_{et} + e_t$$

where A is the unique part of total return, the various Bs are regression coefficients and e_t, an error term, is unsystematic risk. The systematic risk factors are as follows:

X_a = *Unanticipated inflation*—the difference between actual inflation and predicted inflation based on an autoregressive model of past inflation.

X_b = *Investor confidence*—the spread between the return on corporate and U.S. Government bonds.

---

[5] The source of property return data in the model testing is the FRC Property Index, which begins in 1978. Because of its relatively recent starting date, the data exclude many of the important post-World War II economic cycles and produce a sample of relatively small size. The small sample size as well as multicollinearity may explain the rather low calculated t-statistics reported.

TABLE 10-5. Sensitivity of Real Estate Returns to Macroeconomic Factors, 2Q1978–2Q1988

Cap-Adjusted FRC Index	Macroeconomic Factors					
	A	B	C	D	E	R^2
Total	1.035	−0.465	0.022	−0.606	1.992	
t-statistic	0.818	−0.957	0.173	−1.446	1.168	0.09
Office	−1.613	−1.285	−0.268	−1.590	4.479	
t-statistic	−0.650	−1.350	−1.092	−1.935	1.341	0.18
Retail	−0.564	−0.706	0.105	−0.073	0.478	
t-statistic	−0.317	−1.036	0.595	−0.124	0.200	0.08
R&D	1.587	−0.133	0.114	−0.371	1.155	
t-statistic	1.211	−0.264	0.876	−0.855	0.654	0.07
Warehouse	0.572	0.159	−0.011	−0.065	−0.829	
t-statistic	0.414	0.298	−0.082	−0.141	−0.444	0.02
East	5.236	−1.277	0.288	−1.461	10.109	
t-statistic	1.502	−0.917	0.835	−1.265	2.152	0.16
Midwest	−0.564	−0.706	0.105	−0.073	0.478	
t-statistic	−0.317	−1.036	0.595	−0.124	0.200	0.08
South	1.587	−0.133	0.114	−0.371	1.155	
t-statistic	1.211	−0.264	0.876	−0.855	0.654	0.07
West	0.572	0.159	−0.011	−0.065	−0.829	
t-statistic	0.414	0.298	−0.082	−0.141	−0.444	0.02

Key:
A = Unanticipated inflation
B = Investor confidence or risk premium (Aaa yield − Baa yield)
C = Long-run expected inflation (U.S. Government long bond returns − Treasury bill rate)
D = Strength of the economy (monthly industrial production)
E = Strength of the economy (per capita consumption growth)

SOURCE: Russell-Zisler, Inc.

X_c = *Long-run expected inflation*—the spread between U.S. Government long maturity bond returns and Treasury bill rates.

X_d = *Monthly industrial production*

X_e = *Per capita consumption growth*

One benefit of this approach is the ability to examine the effects on return of each risk factor while holding other factors constant. In principle, this sounds terrific. However, in practice the factors are not completely independent. After all, we would be surprised were there not even a weak relationship between production or consumption and inflation. We also are not certain whether there are omitted variables. Consequently, it is not known to what extent the associated tests of significance of coefficient estimates may be biased.

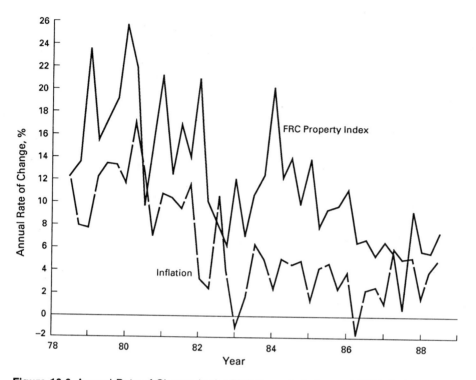

Figure 10-6. Annual Rate of Change in the FRC Property Index and CPI Inflation, 2Q1978–2Q1988. SOURCE: Frank Russell Co.

Unanticipated Inflation

Inflation risk derives from inflation that is unanticipated and therefore not considered in the pricing of assets. We measured unanticipated inflation by taking the difference between anticipated and current inflation. Anticipated inflation cannot be directly observed, so we estimated it using an autoregressive model of past inflation.

How have property returns responded to inflation? A simple comparison of the unadjusted FRC total return index and inflation, as shown in Figure 10-6, suggests a lagged positive but weak response. The relationship was stronger in the early 1980s than it has been since 1985. The reason is that fluctuations in excess demand for space and real estate assets are not perfectly correlated with aggregate excess demand for the overall economy. This lack of synchronization across markets also explains some of the estimated coefficient signs in the tables. More importantly, it suggests that the relationship between property performance and inflation is complex. In addition, a simplistic two-variable comparison of asset returns with inflation without holding other sources of variation constant can mask the true and often richer economic characteristics of the asset class. In addition, such a comparison does not distinguish between expected and unexpected inflation.

As long as leases contain effective escalation provisions, then unanticipated price increases affecting building operating expenses can be practically shifted to the tenants (although even well-crafted inflation pass-through clauses will shift inflation-based expense increases with a lag). Inflation protection is only one of many issues that tenants and landlords must address. In fact, the price of this protection as well as the price of other lease terms is established in the leasing market. How efficiently the market prices these terms is a separate but related issue of considerable importance.

Lease terms, such as usable space occupied by tenants, periods of free or abated rent, building-provided improvements, renewal options, specified rent increases, termination options, sublease and assignment options, and expense escalations, define a bundle of attributes that the tenant hopes to realize over the term of occupancy. Lease negotiation is the process by which these attributes are priced in the market. Some attributes are complements while others are substitutes.

An important issue is whether the optimum set of attributes for the building still constitutes an optimum for the portfolio. Without an appreciation of the portfolio's sensitivity to variations in any one of these factors, it is difficult for the lease negotiator to determine the risk and return implications of any one attribute and the price that ought to be paid for its inclusion in the lease.

The market trade-offs or rates of substitution between attributes will therefore vary by location and type of property. Not surprisingly, the extent to which a property's value is sensitive to inflationary or other shocks will depend on the complex interaction among the attributes of the lease, the relative pricing of attributes, the conditions of the local leasing market, and the return on alternative assets, especially bonds.

The estimated sensitivities to unanticipated inflation in Table 10-3 are generally consistent with this view. Based on the t-statistic, the sensitivity of the total FRC property index is not statistically distinguishable from zero. Transitory changes in inflation are only partially hedged by lease escalation provisions. Base rents do not respond to one-time increases or decreases in inflation. The story is much the same for property when it is disaggregated. Property in the South and Midwest, two relatively weak regions in the late 1970s and 1980s, were poor unexpected inflation hedges. The regions' coefficients are negative. However, only the Midwest is significantly different from zero. (Note that the t-statistics may be biased downward because of multicollinearity.) The South may be weakly negative because property returns exhibited strong upward trends during the early 1980s. The East and West point estimates are positive but they are not significant.

The inflation sensitivities for various property types indicate that office and warehouse properties were weak inflation hedges. Somewhat surprising is retail's negative, and statistically significant, sensitivity to unanticipated inflation. Retail, it should be noted, performed poorly during the late 1970s and early 1980s, an inflationary period. It was only after the end of the early 1980s recession and with the consumer-led recovery that retail performed well, just at a time when inflation was falling. While the estimates do not support the widely held claim that retail is a good inflation hedge, retail in *well-balanced leasing markets* in fact might be an excellent hedge owing to the *percentage leases* that are typical of many retail centers. These leases specify a base rent and additional rent calculated as a percentage of retail sales above a given level of sales. That the retail property market tightened while inflation was falling does not negate the inflation hedging character- istics of retail property. It does imply, however, that inflation protection does not work in all economic environments. A respecification of the factor model should statistically control for disequilibrium in local leasing markets and for percentage leases.

Table 10-4 displays the estimated sensitivities for other securities' re- turns for the period 2Q1978 to 2Q1988. Common stock and equity REIT securities, holding other factors constant, responded positively to unanti- cipated inflation. This is at first a bit surprising, especially because the same model estimated for the 1969 through 1986 period indicates a negative re- lationship between returns on both the S&P 500 and equity REIT returns and unexpected inflation. However, the period 1986 through 1988 was an unusual one. The stock market rose dramatically while inflation declined. U.S. Government and corporate bonds, by contrast, responded in the ex- pected fashion. When inflation is unexpectedly high, lenders forfeit real in- come and principal.

Table 10-5 repeats the analysis for property using the cap-adjusted re- turn series. Some of the estimated coefficients are statistically weaker. It is not clear whether these results are generated by the data adjustment pro- cedure or whether they reflect real estate's inherent risk characteristics.

Investor Confidence. The risk premium, the spread between the re- turn on U.S. Government and corporate bonds, is used as a measure of general economy-wide investor confidence. Table 10-3 suggests that as investors become more uncertain, or as confidence erodes, with other factors held constant, real estate returns increase. The results are quite consistently negative for the overall FRC Property Index and as well for region and property types. While real estate is a good hedge against economic uncer- tainty, stocks, equity REITs, and especially corporate bonds respond negatively to uncertainty, as shown in Table 10-4. These results are consistent with the notion that in times of trouble, investors take flight to hard assets.

Long-Run Expected Inflation. Table 10-4 indicates that increases in long-run *expected* inflation, with other factors held constant, result in higher nominal bond returns (although the opposite is true of Treasury bills). Equity REIT and common stock returns exhibit much the same positive relationship. It is noteworthy that the sensitivity of equity REITs is not as strong as the S&P 500, possibly reflecting the peculiar nature of the underlying real estate and its sensitivity to expected long-run inflation. The S&P 500 is not quite as sensitive as bonds, either. All coefficient estimates are significant.

Real estate reacts quite differently, even perversely. As long-run inflationary trends continue, long-term leases already in place prevent a full inflationary adjustment of the base rent. If expense escalation provisions that are favorable to the landlord have been written in tight leasing markets, then expense pass-throughs adjust with a lag to nominal increases in expenses. In addition, property discount rates, which are a function of bond yields and a risk premium, rise as long as long-run inflationary trends continue. The lags in adjustment of base rents, due to the typical lease maturities of 3 to 10 years, accounts for the negative measured relationship between continuing expected inflation and realized property returns. The estimated coefficients for property are statistically significant but much less so than for other securities. Theory suggests that nominal property returns should be positively correlated with long-term inflation expectations. The character of the leases embedded in the property data and the lack of return data spanning several inflationary cycles indicate that these empirical results should be interpreted and used with caution.

Business Cycles. Real estate responds differently than either stocks or bonds to economic fundamentals. In Tables 10-3 and 10-5, monthly industrial production and per capita consumption growth, two interdependent factors, were used to measure real estate's sensitivity to the business cycle. In runs with data from 1978 through 1986, dropping one of these two variables reduced the t-statistic of the other variable. Therefore, it was determined that both variables should be included when evaluating the sensitivity of returns to the business cycle.

The response of stocks (and particularly equity REITs) to rising consumption is strongly positive, as shown in Table 10-4. However, the sensitivity of bonds is negative. As economic activity strengthens, the economy approaches capacity utilization, thus placing upward pressure on prices, wages, and interest rates. Although a rising economy is beneficial, an overheated economy increases default risk and duration or interest rate risk for creditors. The impact on real estate equity is mixed. Rising industrial production depresses the FRC Property Index while increased consumption stimulates property returns. The impact on real estate is no more conclusive for the region or property type. These conclusions may be attributed either to noise in the data or to one of the important characteristics of equity real estate: its combined bond-like and equity-like features.

The similarity, with certain exceptions, of real estate's sensitivity across all regions and property types to these five factors suggests that these risk factors are systematic and cannot be hedged with 100 percent of one's assets committed to real estate. However, real estate's unique risk and return characteristics make it an attractive asset within a portfolio of stocks and bonds precisely because it responds differently to these risk factors than do stocks and bonds.

Tax Factors

This chapter abstracts from the impact of taxation on real estate portfolio management. Taxation is a controversial and complex subject, deserving careful treatment by nontaxable as well as taxable investors. This may seem surprising because taxation is customarily regarded to be the exclusive province of the taxable investor. In fact, tax-exempt investors that neglect tax benefits potentially usable by taxable investors may fail to realize the full value of their real estate investment. In the United States, the 1986 tax reform severely limited or eliminated so-called tax loopholes or tax shelter opportunities. Still, certain investors may still be able to generate and effectively use tax losses while generating positive cash flow. Increasing awareness of the tax laws by taxable and tax-exempt investors has led to the creation of innovative equity and debt financing structures that more efficiently allocate cash, appreciation, and tax benefits to various investor classes. In fact, economists consider tax-motivated financial structuring as an important way in which the capital markets shift the burden of the tax.

Tax-exempt investors, such as pension funds, have also been affected by the price distortion that is typically associated with taxation. Taxes typically affect relative, as well as absolute, prices. The price impact of taxes on property varies by property type, size, and use. Properties that are typically owned by taxable investors tend to be priced on a before and after tax basis quite differently than properties in the portfolios of tax-exempt investors.

How much did tax incentives stimulate the U.S. building boom of the 1980s? There are various estimates but little consensus other than that taxes played a large role. Whatever the answer, to the extent that overbuilding is tax-induced, weak or negative property appreciation in some markets affects tax-exempt as well as taxable investors.

Government as a Partner. A taxable investor in commercial property typically deals with several coinvestors, each with different claims on the property's income and appreciation. The U.S. Government is an important partner. It not only shares in the profits as well as the losses, but its claim on taxes is senior to the claim of any equity investor or creditor. The government may be an unwelcome partner. However, it also shares in the risks of ownership, especially when marginal tax rates are high.

An investor in a commercial mortgage loan that is collateralized by the property and the income from the property's leases has a claim that is senior to the equity but junior to the government. The equity holders in effect own a call option on the property assets. The option's exercise price is the value of the outstanding debt.

Convertible Mortgages. Some mortgage instruments have equity and debt characteristics. These hybrid debt instruments are often attractive to taxable borrowers as well as taxable and tax-exempt investors. Healey and Ewald [1988], for example, examine scenarios under which convertible debt is more attractive than refinancing a property, a nontaxable transaction, or selling the property and hence creating a taxable event. In the 1980s, the elimination of preferential rates on U.S. capital gains and the rise in interest rates made convertible mortgages, as an alternative to conventional debt, attractive to borrowers and investors.

Convertible mortgages provide an interesting way to examine the symbiotic relationship between taxable and tax-exempt investors in the real estate capital markets and the way in which tax benefits can be shifted. For example, the terms of a typical convertible mortgage may call for a 10- to 12-year term, a fixed interest rate of 7.5 percent, a participating interest of 30 percent in the property's net operating income, a loan-to-value ratio of 70 percent, and an option to convert the outstanding debt into 70 percent of the equity in the seventh year. In U.S. property markets where the combined federal, state, and local income and transfer taxes are high, this refinancing alternative provides for tax deferral. The value of the tax deferral can be shared by tax-exempt as well as taxable investors. The conversion and participation options are valuable. If the income stream and property value increases sufficiently, the conversion options will be in the money. In return for the conversion option, the investor, or lender, may accept a higher loan-to-value ratio and a lower interest rate compared to conventional financing. In effect, the taxable borrower passes along some of the tax benefits to the tax-exempt investor. The combination of equity and debt features not only provides the investor with downside protection but also offers him an inflation hedge in a balanced leasing market. A crucial issue for both investor and borrower is that the tax authorities determine that the convertible mortgage is entirely debt, rather than part equity or total equity. Investors in convertible issues have traditionally been life insurance companies and pension funds. As Shulman [1989] has noted, foreign investors, particularly the

Japanese, are increasingly attracted to the convertible mortgage because of its downside protection.

In sum, when investing in real estate, tax-exempt *as well as* taxable investors must carefully consider the tax ramifications of every transaction.

Unsystematic Risk

This chapter has already examined systematic risk. Well-diversified portfolios have only systematic risk. Poorly diversified portfolios contain considerable amounts of unsystematic risk, which is risk that is specific to an individual security or property. Distinguishing between risk factors that are systematic and unsystematic may be difficult in practice. For example, a tenant may default on its lease because its employees embezzle funds. On the other hand, many tenants may default because of a national recession. Houston provides a good example of how distinctions are made. Oil is a systematic risk factor for a Houston portfolio. However, it may be mostly unsystematic with regard to a global real estate portfolio.

Although this section on unsystematic risk focuses on lease structure and leasing markets, both could have been treated from the perspective of systematic risk because both are affected by risk factors that are commonly considered to be systematic.

Lease Structure. Lease structure, along with location and property type, affect real estate's unsystematic or unique risk attributes and its potential for diversification. The contractual nature of the cash flows from leases gives real estate the characteristics of debt, while the long-term correlation of rents with replacement costs provides real estate with the attributes of equity.

Leases can be short-term or long-term and fully indexed, partially indexed, or not indexed at all. Indexation is an important feature of longer-term leases. Fully indexed leases permit full pass-through of expense increases related to inflation or other factors. Extremely short-term leases, like short-term bonds, can be rolled over frequently to release space at new rates. (Technically, for example, hotels renew their leases every day.) However, owners have minimal protection against falling effective rents when lease maturities are short. Short-term leases tend to have greater *releasing risk*, which is analogous to reinvestment rate risk for bonds.

In contrast, properties with long-term leases have more stable occupancy rates and rental revenues. However, long-term leases face three types of risk. The first is *tenant default risk*. The second relates to the bond-like quality of long-term leases, namely *interest rate* or *duration risk*. The third risk, *inflation risk*, is associated with the extent to which the lease is indexed to pass through inflationary expense increases, thus preserving net operating income. Some leases are even indexed to reflect increases in prevailing market rent.

In rising rental rate markets, long-term leases are usually a drag on property performance, whereas properties with short average lease maturities in strong rental markets sell at higher multiples of net operating income. However, in weak or falling rental rate markets, buildings with long-term leases containing efficient expense escalation clauses protect real rental income as well as nominal revenues. Periodic rent adjustments to market rates, if they are stipulated by the lease, are usually upward only.

Lease Simulations. The importance of lease structure for performance can be seen easily with the help of lease simulations. Panels A through D of Figure 10-7 decompose the total rate of return in any period to its component parts. These are current appreciation and income from *lease tranches* of various maturities. Net operating income from leases that are signed, say, in 1990 and expire in 1997, is expressed in any one year as a percentage of current market value. Market value is determined using the typical parameters used by a broker or appraiser in pricing or appraising a property. Property value is marked to market in each year.

Lease rental income, like interest income from bonds, has cash flow and duration characteristics that affect the market value of the property. As just noted, the duration characteristics of the leases for a particular property determine the "reinvestment" or "releasing" risk for a property. Rental rate changes can occur when leases are renewed, lease escalation clauses are triggered, or new tenants replace old ones. Releasing risk is modified by the fact that, with the exception of periods of severe recession or oversupply of leasable space, lease rental rates tend to be less volatile than interest rates.

Panels A and B in Figure 10-7 are return simulations for two buildings, each with a different maturity structure and thus different lease durations. Both are in a low real rental growth market with fixed rental rates. For purposes of this illustration, all leases are assumed to have had an original term of seven years. Other important lease characteristics, such as free rent, tenant improvements, and elapsed time required to release vacated space are ignored for the purposes of the example.

The important points illustrated by Panels A through D are related to the configuration and relative importance of the *components* of total return, rather than the *levels* of the hypothetical total returns.

The building in Panel A of Figure 10-7 has fewer near-term lease expirations than the building in Panel B. The lease expirations scheduled for the building in Panel A occur mostly after three years. The bondlike quality of the building in Panel A is indicated by the large share of total current return over time that is attributable to leases currently in place.

The building in Panel B illustrates the impact of substantial near-term

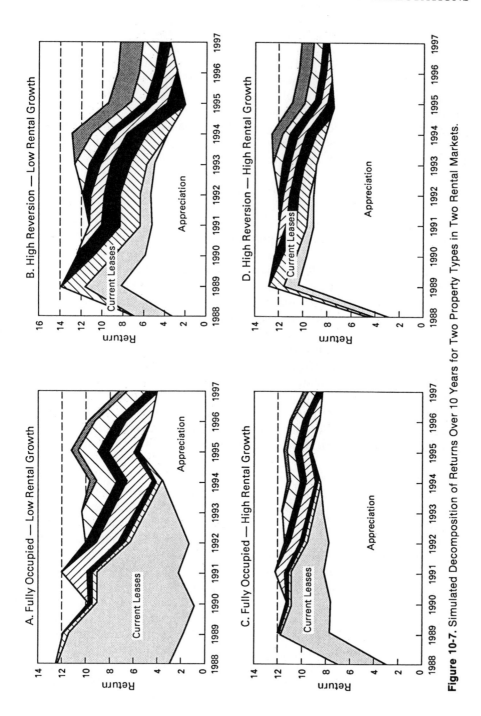

Figure 10-7. Simulated Decomposition of Returns Over 10 Years for Two Property Types in Two Rental Markets.

lease expirations, holding constant the rental growth rate and lease term to maturity. Current return constitutes a smaller share of total return than does the property in Panel A.

Releasing risk increases (1) the shorter the average term to maturity, (2) the lower the quality of the tenant, and (3) the closer that the market rental rate at expiration is in relation to the lease contract rental rate (because being close leaves less room for a lease rental rate increase). Near-term lease expirations, whatever the average lease term to maturity, move the releasing risk closer to the present so that in a present value sense the property is riskier than an otherwise identical building with later lease expirations.

Panels C and D of Figure 10-7 contrast a fully occupied building with few near-term lease rollovers with a property whose leases roll in the first few years. Both properties are located in a high rental growth market. Because of this fact, in contrast to Panels A and B, appreciation constitutes a larger share of total return in both the C and D cases. The bondlike characteristic of the leases is offset to a greater extent in Panels C and D by the higher rate of appreciation. The higher rate of appreciation stems from the expectation of greater rental rate increases when leases expire. In practice, high market rental growth rates are associated with shorter intervals of time between leases as well as with smaller tenant concessions. These tenant concessions can include subsidized tenant improvements, periods of free rent, and less inflation indexation of base rents.

Effect of Interest Rate Changes. Changes in the long-term bond rate affect not only the value of bonds but the value of leases too. A fall in interest rates, depending on the cause, can be beneficial or neutral. (If declining nominal interest rates are associated with a general recession, then rental rates may decline faster than nominal expenses.) If the overall economy is operating at or close to full capacity, then an increase in interest rates is generally associated with an increase in the overall price index or inflation. Nominal default-free interest rates reflect a real rate of interest plus an inflation premium. The effect of higher interest rates on property value depends on the degree to which the property market is in equilibrium as well as on the degree to which a property's leases accommodate inflation increases.

The overall economy may be operating at or close to capacity, while the leasing market may be characterized by an excess supply of space. But the opposite condition is also possible; that is, the market for space may be tight even if the economy is growing at a slow rate or declining. Nominal rents may increase because of an increase in real rents, or an increase in the rate of economywide inflation. If the supply of space exceeds demand, then real rental rates will decline. This decline in real rents will offset partially (or completely) any increase in the rate of inflation. Conversely, in a low inflation economy, low vacancy rate (or high rental growth rate) markets may generate real rental growth rates that exceed the inflation rate.

When inflation increases, nominal interest rates generally rise. However, real interest rates may not increase just because nominal interest rates and inflation increase.

If a property is characterized by leases of infinitesimal term to maturity, by way of example, then in a balanced leasing market, where supply equals demand, nominal rents and expenses increase by the rate of inflation. It can be shown that nominal property prices rise by the rate of inflation, even with an increase in nominal interest rates. Thus, real quantities are preserved.

What happens if vacancy rates are high and real rental rates are falling? If real rental rates are falling, then nominal rental rates cannot increase at a sufficiently high rate to match inflationary increases in expenses or interest rates. Therefore, nominal property prices may actually decrease while nominal interest rates rise.

However, even in a balanced leasing market, nominal property prices may not increase at the rate of inflation. Leases may not allow prices to rise with nominal interest rates and inflation. Leases that do not permit continuous inflation indexing of rents cause nominal property prices to rise at a slower rate than either expenses or nominal discount rates. Sticky nominal rents are due to long-term fixed leases, infrequently adjusting leases, or partially adjusting leases.

It is well known that distant events are more important in a present value sense when interest rates (i.e., discount rates) decline. In low interest rate environments, distant lease rollovers have a greater impact on property value. The expiration of long-term leases in the distant future will have a greater impact on property value if leases do not permit periodic rental adjustments throughout the lease term, if the lease contract rent does not match the market rent at expiration, or if the long-term interest rate declines.

What happens in a falling rental market when the rate of inflation increases? Expenses and nominal discount rates rise to reflect the increase in the overall price index, and property prices fall. The shorter the lease term is, the quicker the decline in contract rents to match market rents. The longer-term lease, especially a 25-year U.K.-type lease with upward-only rent reviews every 5 years, protects better against releasing risk, but, much like a bond, it is more sensitive to interest rate or duration risk.

Clearly the relationship between interest rate changes and property prices is complex. A number of factors intervene. These include the characteristics of a property's underlying leases, the market for rental space, and the relationship between the rate of inflation and nominal interest rates. Lease characteristics, such as the degree to which contract rental rates are permitted to increase (or decrease) in response to changes in market rental rates and the rate of inflation, or the term maturity of each lease, have a subtle impact on property values and their sensitivity to changes in interest rates.

Leases in practice are very complicated. Without a thorough understanding of the financial characteristics of leases and how they affect property values, it is difficult or impossible to assess the sensitivity of property returns to various macroeconomic risk factors. For example, a real estate portfolio's average remaining years to lease maturity may change over time. Likewise, real rental rates fluctuate during the business cycle in response to imbalances in the market for space. Thus a real estate portfolio's inherent financial characteristics, including the duration of leases, may change in subtle but important ways. Hence, in the absence of conscious rebalancing, an investor's real estate asset allocation, while initially optimal, may drift over time at the cost of lost return and added risk.

Credit or Default Risk

Credit or default risk pertaining to leases is not well understood. Most of the work on default has been directed to commercial property owner/developer or residential mortgage default. There are a number of studies that address this topic. With regard to tenant default, relevant research addresses the determinants of corporate bankruptcy. Unfortunately, many tenants are not public companies and therefore ratings of their debt are not available. The few attempts to measure default risk or at least diversify its potential consequence have focused on identifying the tenant's Standard Industrial Classification (SIC) code in the hope that there is some correlation between tenant default and SIC code. However, the SIC coding system does not discriminate between establishments that are subsidiaries of larger companies and establishments that are not. Even though a tenant may be a subsidiary of a financially healthy parent whose SIC code represents a thriving industry, an unprofitable subsidiary may be instructed by the parent to default on its lease. If the parent has accepted no liability for lease payments, then the property owner may have little recourse against the parent.

While a credit check is often made by the owner or his leasing broker before a lease is signed, there is usually no attempt to analyze the likelihood of tenant default at the property, much less at the portfolio, level once the lease is signed. Usually the tenant is under no obligation to supply additional financial information as long as the rent payments are not delinquent. In weak leasing markets, the emphasis is more on filling the building. The quality of lease underwriting varies by market conditions, leasing broker, asset manager, and owner.

Even if a tenant enjoys an excellent credit rating, the lease may contain termination options that are quite favorable to that tenant. Such options are sometimes negotiated by aggressive leasing agents in weak markets. The lease therefore may not be "bankable" in the sense that a lender might disregard the lease for purposes of collateral. Thus, no matter how low his or her default risk, a tenant that can move with little penalty can have the same impact on a property's cash flow as if he or she had defaulted. As a result, the tenant's option to terminate may be undervalued by the owner.

How important is tenant default at the portfolio level? It is difficult to say with any precision. Its importance is probably overshadowed by other risk factors. Far more important may be the concentration of lease rollovers or the sensitivity of the present value of leases to interest rate risk. Moreover, unsystematic risk factors associated with default may be effectively reduced with less cost by carefully selecting a well-diversified portfolio of cities, property types, and tenant sizes and types. A portfolio containing many leases may have little unsystematic risk attributable to tenant default. However, this is, at best, informed speculation.

Role of Fundamental Analysis. Why be concerned with fundamental property analysis? Why not assume that property prices impound all available information, much like stock prices?

There is anecdotal and some statistical evidence that real estate markets are not efficient. Ross and Zisler [1987a and 1987b] have shown that there is significant serial correlation between property returns, thus indicating that one can predict tomorrow's return just by knowing today's property performance. If this is indeed true, then fundamental analysis of property performance may be profitable at the margin. Knowledgeable buyers and sellers can make money by exploiting these inefficiencies.

A concern about much real estate market research today is that it does not sufficiently distinguish between information that is already incorporated, or discounted, in property prices and information that is not. Furthermore, retail and office property fundamentals differ substantially. The differences are what create the low return correlations between property returns of various types.

Portfolio managers who are responsible for managing stocks, bonds, and real estate often lack an appreciation of the subtle relationships among the inventory of commercial space, the demand for space, changes in long-term bond yields and risk premiums, and property performance. The following sections describe the relationship between the retail and office leasing and asset markets since 1976. Appreciation rates of return closely track leasing market fundamentals, such as vacancy rates and changes in effective rental income. Beckeman [1987] has shown that office appreciation returns have a high negative correlation with the current relative vacancy rate.

Office Property Leasing Fundamentals. Total office property return consists of income and appreciation. Figure 10-8 shows that the FRC income rate of return is quite stable compared with total return. In fact, the rate of

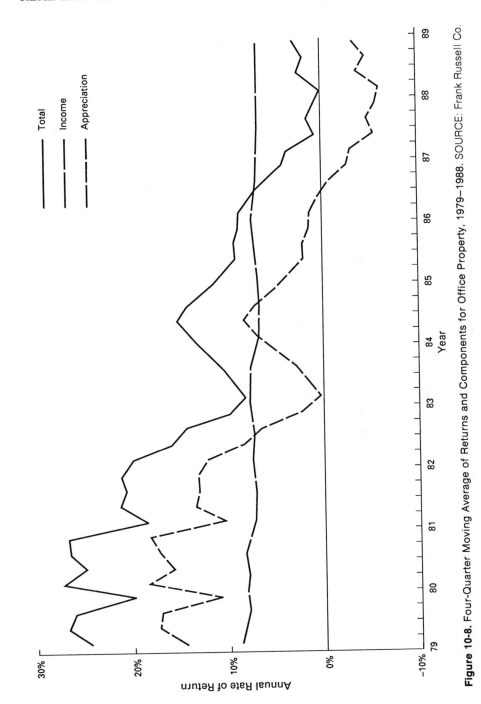

Figure 10-8. Four-Quarter Moving Average of Returns and Components for Office Property, 1979–1988. SOURCE: Frank Russell Co.

appreciation shows more variability in relationship to its mean than does total return. The variability in appreciation is closely related to disequilibrium in the leasing markets or equivalently the excess supply (or demand) for space by tenants.

Office property rates of appreciation peaked in the late 1970s and rallied briefly during 1984, two unusual periods. During the 1979 to 1981 period, office vacancy rates in the United States hit a cyclical low, as shown in Figure 10-9, while the rate of total employment growth increased. The excess demand for space was caused by depressed construction starts during the late 1970s, as shown in Figure 10-10, following two recessions in the United States during the period 1973 to 1975 and in 1979, the REIT debacle, and a resurgence in the demand for commercial space. Growth in demand was fueled by low space per worker and absolute increases in white collar employment, and particularly in the finance, insurance, and real estate (FIRE) industries, large users of office space as indicated in Figure 10-11.

Note that the Coldwell Banker suburban vacancy rate index, which starts in 1983 in Figure 10-9, exceeds the downtown rate by 5 to 7 percentage points. There are a number of explanations that include the technology, labor market, land use constraint, and building cost differences between suburban and downtown office buildings.

The rate of appreciation for office property was high over a long period during the 1970s, but it was not sustainable over the long term. The high expected risk-adjusted return to office property investment in the early 1980s stimulated history's greatest office building boom. The construction boom paused briefly in 1983, following an extended recession. The rate of appreciation fell to essentially zero in 1983, only to be lifted by a dramatic recovery in the number of FIRE-industry workers. Appreciation increased despite rapidly climbing vacancy rates across the nation. During the 1980s in the United States, construction starts remained high despite rising national aggregate vacancy rates. Successive cities were overbuilt as development moved from the Southwest and South to the Midwest and Northeast. In other words, although it is not feasible to move the excess space (in 1989) in Houston to Boston, it is quite easy for developers to identify and exploit low vacancy rate cities.

In 1983, the majority of property in the FRC Index was located in large urban centers. Thus, while suburban vacancy rates by 1982 exceeded 15 percent, downtown vacancy rates were much less, but increasing. The rapid and sustained business recovery following 1983 resuscitated office building construction just as the rate of FIRE employment growth began declining. After 1984, nominal rates of office property appreciation deteriorated so badly that total return in 1988 was negative.

Retail Property Leasing Fundamentals. In the late 1970s and early 1980s, the performance of U.S. retail property lagged the performance of

(*text continues on page 10-39*)

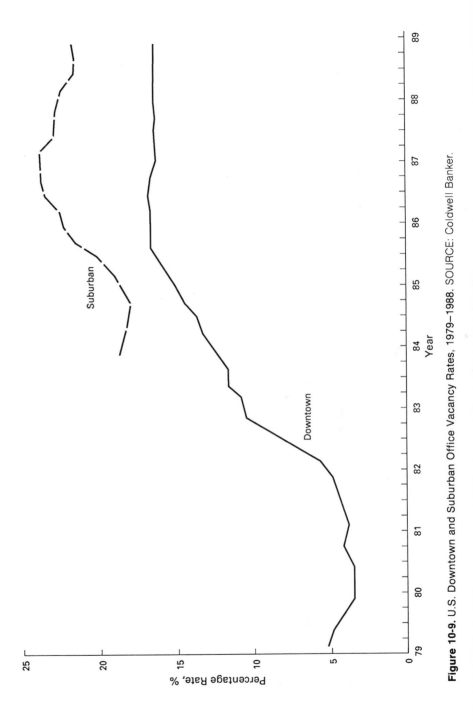

Figure 10-9. U.S. Downtown and Suburban Office Vacancy Rates, 1979–1988. SOURCE: Coldwell Banker.

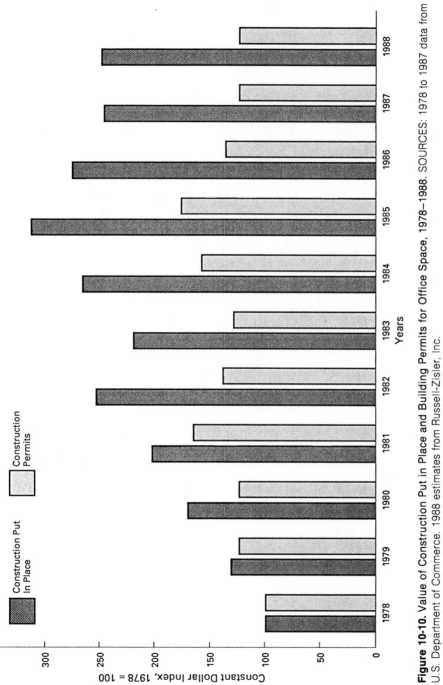

Figure 10-10. Value of Construction Put in Place and Building Permits for Office Space, 1978–1988. SOURCES: 1978 to 1987 data from U.S. Department of Commerce. 1988 estimates from Russell-Zisler, Inc.

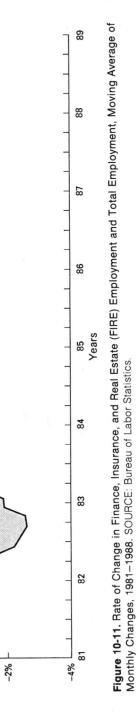

Figure 10-11. Rate of Change in Finance, Insurance, and Real Estate (FIRE) Employment and Total Employment, Moving Average of Monthly Changes, 1981–1988. SOURCE: Bureau of Labor Statistics.

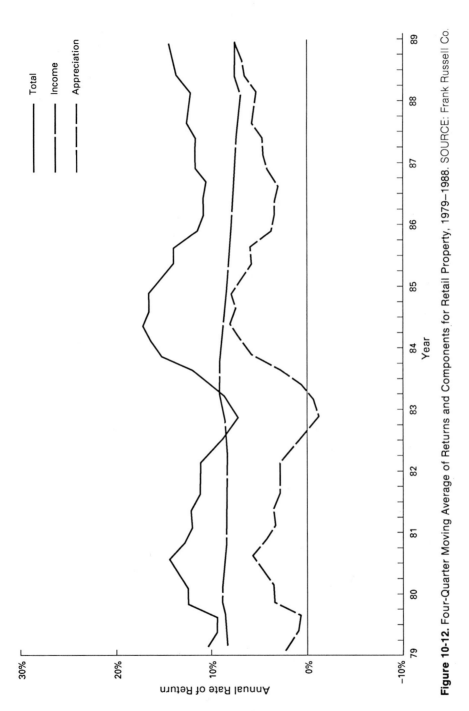

Figure 10-12. Four-Quarter Moving Average of Returns and Components for Retail Property, 1979–1988. SOURCE: Frank Russell Co.

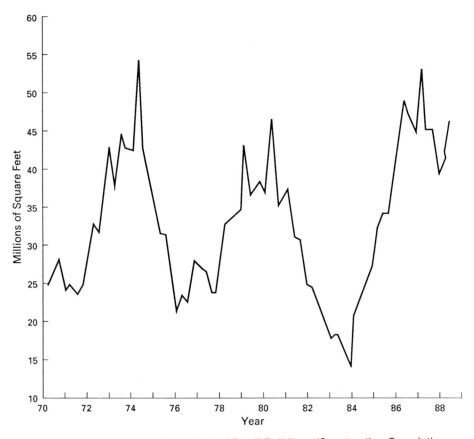

Figure 10-13. Net Increase in the Stock of Retail Buildings (Construction Completions Minus Depreciation), 1970–1988. SOURCE: F.W. Dodge Co.

office property. See Figure 10-12. The FRC Retail Property Index is heavily weighted by mid-size shopping centers and not by large regional malls, which outperformed the smaller centers during the 1979 to 1988 period. Retail property appreciation was briefly negative in early 1983 in the aftermath of the recession. Retail construction completions for centers of all sizes hit a 20-year low by late 1983, as shown in Figure 10-13. However, retail property sales as well as starts picked up dramatically in 1983 and, by 1984, so had appreciation. Completions followed with a lag of at least 18 months.

Retail leases often have provisions for base rent and additional rent based on retail sales. Consequently, net operating income closely reflects the prosperity of tenants. Figure 10-14 shows an estimate of real retail sales (less automobiles) in relation to the inventory of U.S. retail space.

This index, which closely tracks retail property appreciation, reflects the fundamentals of the retail leasing market. Retail property returns re-

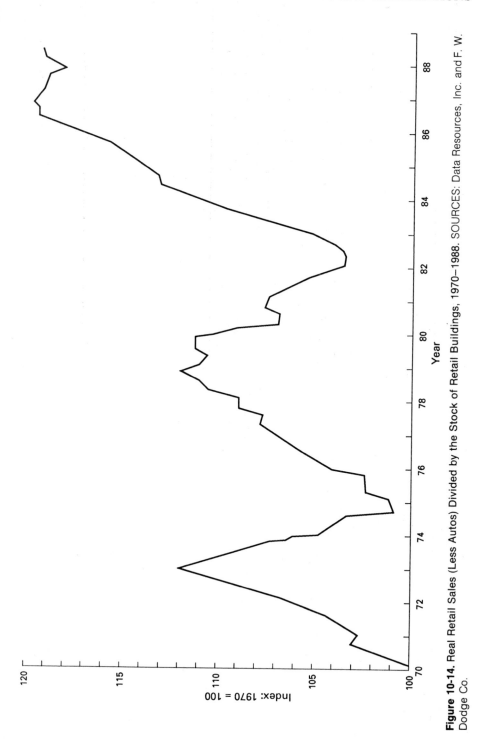

Figure 10-14. Real Retail Sales (Less Autos) Divided by the Stock of Retail Buildings, 1970–1988. SOURCES: Data Resources, Inc. and F. W. Dodge Co.

mained strong in 1988. Still robust retail sales and weak office property markets supported strong rates of retail appreciation and declining current retail property income yields (or increasing price to net operating income ratios). It is not clear to what extent the shift in capital from office to retail property has been partially the product of a speculative bubble, similar to what might have driven the demand for office property during the early 1980s, or whether indeed the new pricing for office and retail properties fairly represents the new fundamentals. Questions such as these pervade the property markets. Thus, it will not be surprising if fundamental analysis of property markets assumes new importance. Whether it adds value, and for whom, remains to be seen.

REAL ESTATE PORTFOLIO DIVERSIFICATION

Diversification is the most critical of all portfolio management principles, and yet until recently it has been neglected in all but its most naive forms by most real estate managers. A large, well-diversified portfolio has negligible unsystematic risk. Because the market only compensates the investor for bearing systematic or nondiversifiable risk, it pays the investor to diversify. Diversification is not costless, particularly for real estate. Consequently, it is important to balance the costs of diversification with the benefits. The nature of these costs may determine which dimensions of diversification (e.g., geographic, property type, or the like) are the most practical means of reducing unsystematic risk. Furthermore, it is probable that money managers will devise investment vehicles that enable investors to alter real estate asset allocations with negligible costs.

It is not unusual to hear protests from managers with regard to this point. They correctly point out that real estate has traditionally been an illiquid asset. However, the market will reward those managers who devise low cost ways of reducing traditional real estate transactions costs. The recent trend toward securitization of commercial as well as residential real estate equity and debt may be promising in this regard.

The next section identifies the types of diversification available in the real estate markets and the relative return and risk relationship that result.

Geographic Diversification

Geographic diversification not only matters, but it may be more important than property diversification. However, most real estate portfolios do not systematically exploit the low covariance between different regions and cities. This is noteworthy, especially because economic cycles differ by location in their timing, intensity, and underlying economic fundamentals.

TABLE 10-6. Commercial Building Inventory for 1970, 1984, and 1990 and 1970–1990 Percentage Growth for the 10 Largest U.S. States

State	Commercial Building Inventory (Billions of Square Feet)			Percentage Growth
	1970	1984	1990[a]	1970–1990[a]
California	1.8	2.8	3.4	3.3%
New York	1.7	1.7	1.8	0.4
Ohio	1.2	1.4	1.5	1.1
Texas	1.1	2.0	2.6	4.2
New Jersey	1.1	1.2	1.3	0.9
Illinois	1.0	1.3	1.4	1.6
Pennsylvania	1.0	1.2	1.2	0.9
Michigan	0.7	0.9	0.9	1.5
Florida	0.6	1.2	1.7	5.2
Massachusetts	0.5	0.6	0.7	1.1

SOURCE: F.W. Dodge/DRI Construction and Real Estate Information Services.
[a] Projected.

Furthermore, no one city or state dominates the national real estate market. California, for example, accounts for approximately 10 percent of U.S. commercial property. Table 10-6 lists the top 10 states with respect to their commercial building inventory on three dates: 1970, 1984, and 1990. As the table indicates, commercial space has not grown at uniform rates across states any more than population has. Of the largest states, the inventories of Florida, Texas, and California have grown the fastest for the period 1970 to 1990 according to F. W. Dodge. If the property markets of cities, states, and regions have low covariance, then the United States real estate market offers opportunities for diversification not found within most countries. In fact, the only other opportunity for geographic diversification worth exploring may be international property diversification, an issue that is treated later in this chapter.

The risk-return trade-off achieved from geographic diversification is evident in Figure 10-15, which shows the efficient frontiers when the FRC Property Index, raw and cap-adjusted, respectively, is divided into four regions, the East, Midwest, South, and West.

The efficient frontier shows all the possible combinations of return and risk available from holdings of property across different regions. The performance of a portfolio under the curve can be enhanced through diversification. That is, total portfolio risk can be reduced without sacrificing return. Conversely, risk can be lowered by diversifying away unsystematic risk without forfeiting return. The return of efficient portfolios, those portfolios on the efficient frontier, can only be increased by assuming more risk.

Regional Risk and Return Characteristics. Table 10-7 shows the mean returns and standard deviations, as well as the regional correlation

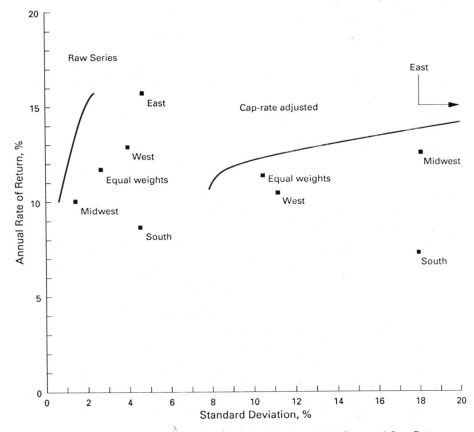

Figure 10-15. Comparison of Risk and Return by Region of the Raw and Cap-Rate-Adjusted FRC Property Index, 2Q1978–2Q1988. SOURCE: Russell-Zisler, Inc.

matrix for the raw and cap-adjusted FRC data. Regional property returns are not perfectly correlated. In fact, some regions, such as the South and Midwest, have extremely low correlations owing partially to their very different economic bases.

The capitalization rate adjustment, which corrects for appraisal smoothing, increases the regional standard deviations while the impact on mean return is mixed. Adjusting the data for smoothing increases the measured correlation between the FRC returns for the four regions. It is not clear whether this is an artifact of the regional division or of the property type weighting within each region.

Figure 10-15 shows that the cap-adjusted frontier is shifted to the right relative to the unadjusted frontier in return/risk space. Figure 10-15 illustrates the four pure regional portfolios. The East dominates all other regions

TABLE 10-7. Annualized Mean Returns, Standard Deviations, and Correlations of the Raw and Cap-Adjusted FRC Property Indexes by Region, 2Q1978 to 2Q1988

Region	Raw Series		Cap-Adjusted Series	
	Mean Return	Standard Deviation	Mean Return	Standard Deviation
East	15.7%	4.7%	15.3%	27.3%
Midwest	10.0	1.5	12.7	18.1
South	8.7	4.6	7.5	17.9
West	12.9	4.0	10.7	11.2

Regional Correlation Matrix
(Raw Series)

	East	Midwest	South	West
East	1.00			
Midwest	0.39	1.00		
South	−0.03	−0.24	1.00	
West	−0.01	−0.24	0.34	1.00

Regional Correlation Matrix
(Cap-Adjusted Series)

	East	Midwest	South	West
East	1.00			
Midwest	0.30	1.00		
South	0.37	0.16	1.00	
West	0.39	0.22	0.54	1.00

SOURCE: Russell-Zisler, Inc.

whether the adjusted or unadjusted portfolio is used. However, the capitalization adjustment affects the regional portfolio mix at lower portfolio risk levels. In Table 10-8, the raw return numbers generate a low risk portfolio in which the Midwest accounts for a 93 percent share versus a 53 percent share for the West in the cap-adjusted low risk portfolio. A portfolio whose assets are concentrated in any region may be unnecessarily risky.

Table 10-8 shows that only the 100 percent eastern property portfolio, with a cap-adjusted return of 15.3 percent and a standard deviation of 27.3 percent, is located on the efficient frontier. This apparent market anomaly is an ex post result, like a downward-sloping capital market line, that occurs relatively infrequently for a particular period.

As noted above, the lowest risk raw FRC portfolio is largely composed of Midwest properties. (Although the 100 percent East portfolio was efficient, given the regional definitions employed in this analysis, there is no assurance that the East will perform in a similar fashion during the next decade.) It is easy to show, using either the raw or cap-adjusted series, that

TABLE 10-8. Percentage Allocation Among Regions, Returns, and Risk for Efficient Portfolio Mixes by Region Based on Raw and Cap-Adjusted FRC Index Series, 2Q1978 to 2Q1988

	(a) Raw Series Risk Tolerance			
	1	2	3	4
Allocation	Lowest			Highest
East	0.0%	50.7%	85.9%	100.0%
Midwest	93.0	27.4	0.0	0.0
South	3.2	0.0	0.0	0.0
West	3.8	21.9	14.1	0.0
Return	10.1	13.6	15.3	15.7
Risk (standard deviation)	0.7	1.5	2.1	2.3

	(b) Cap-Adjusted Series Risk Tolerance							
	1	2	3	4	5	6	7	8
Allocation	Lowest							Highest
East	1.3%	4.7%	11.1%	17.7%	30.8%	47.8%	67.5%	100.0%
Midwest	30.0	30.2	30.4	30.5	30.7	30.9	31.2	0.0
South	15.5	8.7	0.0	0.0	0.0	0.0	0.0	0.0
West	53.2	56.4	58.4	51.8	38.5	21.3	1.3	0.0
Return	10.9	11.2	11.8	12.1	12.8	13.5	14.5	15.3
Risk (std. deviation)	7.9	8.1	8.8	9.6	12.0	16.0	21.3	27.3

SOURCE: Russell-Zisler, Inc.

a pure regional portfolio, with the exception of the East, for high risk aversion investors can be substantially improved through regional diversification. The efficient frontier is approximately 600 basis points above the pure southern portfolio, indicating that a significant amount of total risk associated with southern properties is unsystematic or diversifiable risk. Moreover, a portfolio with a 100 percent allocation to property in the West dominates the pure southern portfolio. See Hartzell, Shulman, and Wurtzebach [1987] for an analysis of regional diversification by segmenting the nation's commercial property market into contiguous regions that are based on similar economic bases.

Naive Diversification. Naive diversification often produces results that are inefficient. Industry practice adopts a number of rules of thumb for diversification. One such rule is to construct a real estate portfolio that contains one quarter of its holdings in each region. Figure 10-15, which shows

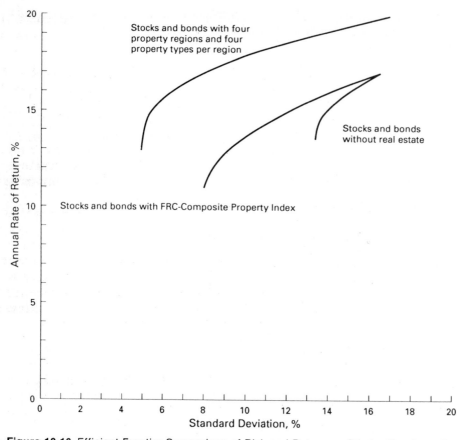

Figure 10-16. Efficient Frontier Comparison of Risk and Return on Stocks, Bonds, and Real Estate Using Cap-Rate-Adjusted FRC Real Estate Index, 2Q1978–2Q1988. SOURCE: Russell-Zisler, Inc.

the equally weighted portfolio for the raw and cap-adjusted frontiers, suggests that, especially in the case of the raw series, this strategy may be costly. The equally weighted portfolio is almost 400 basis points lower than the efficient frontier based on the raw data. However, this performance gap is less dramatic using the cap-adjusted series.

Defining Regional Markets. How critical is the method used to define property markets by regions? The results, of course, may be sensitive to the method. However, it may be highly critical to the extent that performance differences between cities, even within regions, are significant. Disaggregation minimizes the likelihood that arbitrary regional definitions constrain the optimal selection of locations. Thus, more regional disaggregation moves the efficient frontier northwest in return/risk space. Figure 10-16 shows the impact of regional disaggregation of the property return data on a portfolio of property, stocks, and bonds. All efficient frontiers in the figure contain stocks and bonds. The middle curve combines stocks and bonds with one real estate asset—the FRC Index—whereas the highest curve combines stocks and bonds with several real estate assets grouped geographically and by property type.

The results indicate that unbundling real estate by location may achieve as much as a 400 basis point reduction in unsystematic risk for portfolios with total returns of 13 to 14 percent. Recent research indicates that increasing the number of regions from four to eight lowers interregional correlation coefficients. Thus, disaggregation may allow more efficient portfolio diversification.

Regions should be defined such that property returns within regions have a high correlation and returns across regions have a low correlation, holding other factors such as property type constant. Moreover, regions should be economically cohesive. Regions are generally defined as contiguous states and their cities. However, a functional approach to geographic diversification should define clusters of cities in which each cluster contains economically similar property sectors. Regional clusters for offices may differ from retail or hotel clusters. Moreover, clusters may contain cities that are separated by great distances (e.g., financial centers or state capitals).

Regional disaggregation is severely limited by the return sample size. Carefully constructed return series for all of the U.S. metropolitan areas as well as for the major property types at the national level and for all cities are lacking. The absence of highly disaggregate locational return data is disturbing because *regional diversification appears to generate greater diversification benefits than diversification by property type alone.* One way to deal with the absence of return data for all U.S. cities is to construct return proxies that reflect the local fundamentals determining net operating income flows and risk premiums.

Real estate investment acquisitions typically are made with little if any appreciation of the opportunities for reducing portfolio risk without sacrificing return. Even a rudimentary attempt to discriminate between cities and to define regions on a sound functional basis would be an important step toward enhancing overall portfolio performance.

Property Type Diversification

Table 10-9 reports the mean returns, standard deviations, and correlations for the raw and cap-adjusted FRC series. Adjusting the data increases the variability substantially and reduces mean returns slightly. Correlations between property returns are higher for the raw series than for the cap-adjusted data. This is quite different from the correlations for the overall and regional

TABLE 10-9. Annualized Mean Returns, Standard Deviations, and Correlations of the Raw and Cap-Adjusted FRC Property Indexes by Property Type, 2Q1978–2Q1988

Property Type	Raw Series		Cap-Adjusted Series	
	Mean Return	Standard Deviation	Mean Return	Standard Deviation
Office	12.4%	5.2%	10.4%	19.8%
Retail	11.4	2.1	11.3	13.6
Research & dev.	13.2	3.9	11.5	9.8
Warehouse	12.4	2.2	12.1	10.3

Property Type Correlation Matrix
(Raw Series)

	Office	Retail	R&D	Warehouse
Office	1.00			
Retail	0.17	1.00		
Research & dev.	0.52	0.31	1.00	
Warehouse	0.66	0.46	0.41	1.00

Property Type Correlation Matrix
(Cap-Adjusted Series)

	Office	Retail	R&D	Warehouse
Office	1.00			
Retail	0.28	1.00		
Research & dev.	−0.11	−0.00	1.00	
Warehouse	−0.02	0.06	0.16	1.00

SOURCE: Russell-Zisler, Inc.

FRC Indexes. For the overall indexes, as shown in Table 10-2, the correlation between the cap-adjusted FRC Index and the S&P 500 is .10. That is, the cap adjustment produces a correlation that is less negative.

Similarly, for the regional FRC Indexes in Table 10-7, the cap adjustment made 5 out of 6 of the correlations, between regions, less negative. By contrast, for property types in Table 10-9, the cap adjustment produced 5 out of 6 correlations, between property types, that were *more* negative. Thus, the effect of the cap rate adjustment procedure on the correlations for the three comparisons—real estate with the S&P 500, real estate by region, and real estate by property type—are quite different. There is no obvious reason why the cap adjustment should have a positive or negative impact on the correlations.

Figure 10-17 indicates the trade-off between risk and return obtained in a portfolio of assets distinguished only by property type. The cap-adjusted

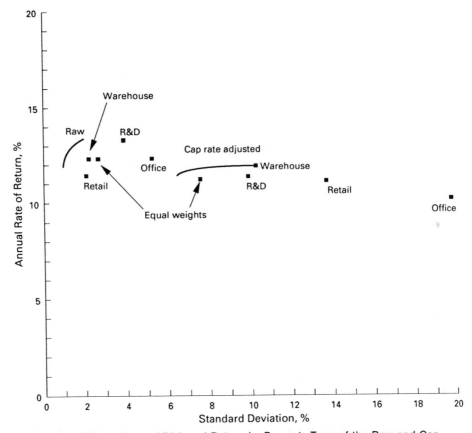

Figure 10-17. Comparison of Risk and Return by Property Type of the Raw and Cap-Rate-Adjusted FRC Property Index, 2Q1978–2Q1988. SOURCE: Russell-Zisler, Inc.

efficient property type frontier has a smaller slope, indicating that increased return is purchased at the cost of substantially higher risk.

The minimum variance portfolio is dominated by R&D (office/warehouse) and warehouse properties. Office and retail dominate the riskiest portfolios. A pure office and, to a lesser degree, a pure retail portfolio are substantially riskier than any portfolio found on the efficient frontier. Only a pure warehouse portfolio is efficient. For most of the efficient frontier, some diversification is appropriate.

There are a number of problems with this analysis. First, important properties are excluded from the analysis: apartments and hotels. Although the missing property types are represented within the FRC Index, their sample sizes within the index are too small to be useful. Second, it is not clear to what extent the results are an artifact of the regional weightings of each property type. How much do the statistical correlations reflect regional disequilibria associated with the particular period? This is a problem that affects the regional diversification analysis as well.

International Diversification

As noted in Chapter 4, U.S. pension funds have dramatically increased their asset allocations to international stock and bond investments. The dollar commitment, particularly by large plans, has grown substantially since 1974. The reasons for this expansion of offshore investments include (1) the growth of total pension assets, (2) more companies making initial commitments, and (3) plan sponsors increasing the allocation to international, even though the commitment remains low as a percentage of total assets.

Recently there has been some interest expressed by plan sponsors and their money managers in learning more about investing in international real estate. Their interest has been stimulated by a weakening U.S. property market and the prospects of lackluster returns in the late 1980s, strong commercial property performance in Europe at the same time, and the prospect of reducing unsystematic risk through international diversification. Additionally, offshore property with "upward-only" rent adjustments and long-term (e.g., 25-year) leases, along with severe limits on foreign new construction, has made these properties attractive to U.S. investors.

Data Limitations. International property return data are not collected with the same exacting standards to which the FRC Property Index adheres. The best property return data are collected in the U.K. and the United States, although indexes are currently being developed or refined in other countries. Consequently, this section uses only U.S. and U.K. annual data from 1981 through 1987. Other countries with substantial inventories of investment grade real estate are excluded. Canadian data have been published by local brokers and it is difficult to assess their quality. Japan's property sector, which has one of the largest inventories of commercial space, is unique. Properties seldom trade because of onerous capital gains taxes, and property performance is held in strictest confidence by owners. It is expected that the institutionalization and globalization of property investment will encourage the development of high quality performance data. In the meantime, analysts will be challenged to develop clever statistical techniques for handling less than ideal performance data.

Even the U.K. data present severe data limitations for several reasons. Although U.K. institutions have established larger allocations to the property sector than have their U.S. counterparts, they have not made their performance data public even in aggregate form. Their real estate money managers, the chartered surveyor firms, devoted resources to performance analysis long before most U.S. real estate money managers. However, until

TABLE 10-10. Mean Return, Standard Deviations, and Correlation Coefficients for U.K. vs. U.S. Stock, Bond, and Property Investments, 1981–1987

Asset Class	United Kingdom		United States	
	Mean Return	Standard Deviation	Mean Return	Standard Deviation
Stocks	21.46%	8.28%	14.45%	12.71%
Bonds	15.87	14.50	15.77	16.79
Property	11.51	5.92	10.57	4.09

Correlations

	United Kingdom			United States		
	Stocks	Bonds	Property	Stocks	Bonds	Property
U.K.						
Stocks	1.00					
Bonds	0.32	1.00				
Property	−0.90	−0.24	1.00			
U.S.						
Stocks	0.55	0.37	−0.63	1.00		
Bonds	0.55	0.57	−0.64	0.62	1.00	
Property	0.10	−0.31	−0.29	−0.35	−0.26	1.00

SOURCE: Russell-Zisler, Inc.

recently, each U.K. surveyor firm published its own performance indexes, calculated using methods that vary substantially across firms. As a result, standardized performance data collected across the major institutional property investors are only a recent phenomenon even in the United Kingdom.

The lack of good international property performance data for countries with substantial inventories of investment grade property restricts careful analysis of international real estate strategies. Aside from the data problems, there still remain a host of difficult issues regarding transactions costs, exchange rate hedging, taxation, land use regulations, property management, local business customs, and so on. These issues, which should not be dismissed casually, are not addressed in this section. Rather, the purpose is to highlight the potential benefits of international property investments. Whether it makes sense on a risk-adjusted basis for U.S. institutions to invest in property abroad remains to be seen. However, a first cut analysis suggests that the benefits may be more real than illusory.

Table 10-10 shows average total returns and standard deviations as well as correlation coefficients for stocks, bonds, and property in both the United Kingdom and the United States from 1981 to 1987. The U.K. property data, compiled by Investment Property Databank (IPD) of the U.K., consist of return data for 8,330 properties with a value in 1987 exceeding £16 billion. Although the FRC Property Index is reported quarterly, the U.K. property data are only published annually. Hence, the data set is very small. The results, therefore, are not robust and may differ depending on the sample period. Nevertheless, the results suggest that there may be substantial benefits, gross of transactions and management fees, from international property diversification.

The structure of stock, bond, and property returns and volatilities are different in the United Kingdom. U.S. and U.K. property both have experienced very low volatilities in relation to their mean return. However, at least for the 1981 through 1987 period, U.K. stock returns were about double U.K. property returns, and stock volatility, calculated on an annual basis, was much less than twice property's volatility.

Property was negatively correlated with stocks and bonds in both countries. The negative correlation between U.K. property and U.K. stocks was quite strong, much stronger than the negative relationship between U.S. property and U.S. stocks. Cross-country correlations indicate that U.K. and U.S. property exhibited negative correlations, suggesting benefits from adding unleveraged U.K. property investments to U.S. property portfolios. However, the negative correlation between U.S. property, on the one hand, and either U.K. property or U.S. bonds, is comparable in magnitude, indicating similar diversification attributes, although the return/risk characteristics of these two asset classes are quite different.

Diversification Benefits. How important is international diversification? Figure 10-18, which shows three efficient frontiers, and Table 10-11, which describes the actual allocations for different risk levels and portfolio strategies, suggests that the benefits do in fact exist. Adding U.K. property to a portfolio of U.S. properties, stocks, and bonds—Panel (c) versus Panel (b) of the table—can reduce the volatility of the minimum variance portfolio by approximately 200 basis points. This is determined by comparing the risk levels of the lower risk tolerance portfolios in the two panels. The total real estate allocation remains about the same, only split between U.K. and U.S. property in these low risk tolerance portfolios. Bonds constitute less than 20 percent in these same portfolios. Property allocations decline to zero as portfolio risk is increased. U.K. property dominates U.S. property allocations at intermediate risk levels. U.S. bonds dominate all other assets at higher risk tolerances, again, for the 1981 through 1987 period.

Adding U.K. stocks and bonds to the available choices reduces U.S. property and bonds but increases U.K. stock allocations in the minimum variance portfolio. Total returns are substantially increased. U.S. property is present at low risk tolerances while U.K. property is present in all but the riskiest portfolios.

If these results are indicative of true property performance, then there may be a strong argument for international property diversification. Much additional work awaits larger and carefully constructed data sets.

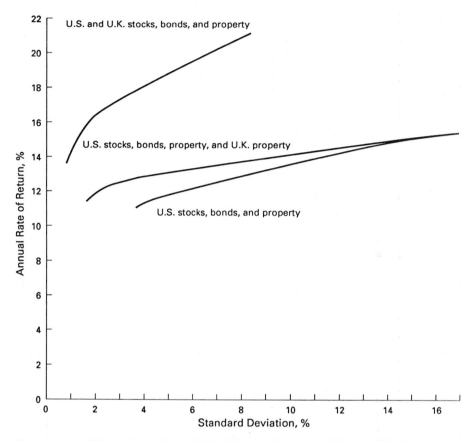

Figure 10-18. Efficient Portfolios of U.S., U.K., and Combined U.S. and U.K. Stocks, Bonds, and Property, Annual Data, 1981–1987. SOURCE: Russell-Zisler, Inc.

Diversified Portfolio of Stocks, Bonds, and Real Estate

This section shows the impact on portfolio risk and return from adding real estate to a stock and bond portfolio. Real estate is treated in two ways. Earlier, in Figure 10-16, the efficient frontier labeled "with one property type" consisted of stocks, bonds, and property, with the latter represented by the cap-adjusted FRC property index. The minimum variance portfolio has a lower return but even much less risk than the pure stock and bond portfolio. Thus, property contributes considerable diversification benefits, particularly at lower levels of risk.

Disaggregating the property sector by type and region will affect the location and shape of the efficient frontier, as shown in Figure 10-16. The efficient frontier constructed using four property types within each of the four regions (16 property asset classes in all) as well as stocks and bonds

(*text continues on page 10-56*)

TABLE 10-11. Efficient Mixes of Stock, Bond, and Property Asset Classes for the United Kingdom and United States, 1981–1987

(a) U.K. and U.S. Asset Classes

Allocation	1 Lowest	2	3	4	5	6	7 Highest
				Risk Tolerance			
U.K. stocks	22.82%	34.84%	46.00%	59.53%	80.34%	93.34%	100.0%
U.K. bonds	0.00	0.00	0.00	0.00	0.00	0.00	0.00
U.K. property	46.25	50.33	53.54	40.47	19.66	6.66	0.00
U.S. stocks	0.00	0.00	0.00	0.00	0.00	0.00	0.00
U.S. bonds	6.02	3.18	0.46	0.00	0.00	0.00	0.00
U.S. property	24.92	11.65	0.00	0.00	0.00	0.00	0.00
Return	13.80	15.00	16.11	17.43	19.50	20.80	21.46
Risk	0.78	1.10	1.68	2.95	5.61	7.36	8.26

(b) U.S. Asset Classes

Allocation	1 Lowest	2	3	4	5	6	7 Highest
				Risk Tolerance			
U.S. stocks	0.00%	0.00%	8.86%	55.46%	28.40%	10.03%	0.00%
U.S. bonds	10.37	18.13	29.75	44.07	71.60	89.97	100.00
U.S. property	89.63	81.87	61.39	0.47	0.00	0.00	0.00
Return	11.11	11.51	12.46	15.01	15.40	15.64	15.77
Risk	3.62	3.89	5.91	13.00	14.53	15.93	16.79

(c) U.S. Asset Classes and U.K. Property

Allocation	Risk Tolerance						
	1 Lowest	2	3	4	5	6	7 Highest
U.K. property	40.36%	48.76%	56.48%	62.24%	8.36%	0.00%	0.00%
U.S. stocks	0.00	4.91	12.35	19.87	31.71	19.21	0.00
U.S. bonds	12.97	16.00	16.30	17.89	59.92	80.79	100.00
U.S. property	46.66	30.33	14.86	0.00	0.00	0.00	0.00
Return	11.62	12.05	12.43	12.86	15.00	15.52	15.77
Risk	1.62	2.02	2.67	3.53	12.61	15.20	16.79

SOURCE: Russell-Zisler, Inc.

substantially improves return at all risk levels without increasing volatility. The minimum variance portfolio, constructed using data for 16 property asset classes portfolio, is less risky than portfolios containing property defined solely by region or property type. Bonds are present only in the minimum variance portfolio, as shown in Table 10-12. Stock allocation increases with higher risk tolerances. Aggregate property comprises about 80 percent of low-risk portfolios in which all property types are represented. Retail and R&D in the West receive a disproportionately large allocation. The higher risk efficient portfolios are dominated by stocks, R&D in the West, retail in the East, and offices in the East and Midwest. At extreme levels of risk, R&D and warehouses drop out, Midwest and East offices comprise 50 percent of the entire portfolio, and the remainder is split between stocks and retail property in the East.

Figure 10-19 aggregates the region-property type allocations and compares them with stocks and bonds. Bonds play a minor role at all levels of risk. It is conceivable that property dominates bonds because of the bond-like nature of leases. Property also dominates stocks. An important caveat here relates to the data problems for real estate and the effects of inflation on real estate returns versus stocks and bonds. If these results even remotely reflect the true risk/return trade-off among property, stocks, and bonds, then property is indeed very underweighted. While the author is not prepared to argue that, in practice, mixed asset portfolios should contain even as much as 70 percent property, it is tempting to conclude that current property allocations, on the order of 15 percent (or less) in the case of some pension funds, are far too low.

How large should the allocation to property be? Whatever the answer, it should be determined as much by pragmatic as by purely quantitative methods. The data are not sufficiently plentiful to make fine distinctions among property types. After all, some properties perform as though they are near substitutes for bonds. Furthermore, the data exclude information on leasing structure. Such data would be helpful in classifying property. Property asset classifications should be constructed to reflect the underlying fundamentals that distinguish asset classes. Unfortunately, property performance data are not collected in ways that recognize these differences.

However, even if the riskiness of real estate is understated, the lack of strong positive correlation between property and other assets makes property an important asset in a well-diversified portfolio. It would not be surprising to find that, assuming sufficient data were available and properly evaluated, property's share of a well-diversified portfolio eventually expands to as much as 30 to 50 percent. The implications for the entire money management and real estate industries, if this be the case, are no doubt revolutionary. Even a 25 percent share would tax the current acquisition, property, and portfolio management capabilities of most real estate money managers.

TABLE 10-12. Efficient U.S. Portfolio Mixes by Region, Property Type, Stocks, and Bonds, 2Q1978–2Q1988

Property Type	Region	Risk Tolerance							
		1 Lowest	2	3	4	5	6	7	8 Highest
Office:	East	0.0%	1.6%	4.4%	7.5%	12.0%	15.6%	17.5%	21.8%
	Midwest	3.1	4.1	5.2	6.4	9.1	16.6	21.4	33.7
	South	3.6	0.0	0.0	0.0	0.0	0.0	0.0	0.0
	West	7.0	4.0	0.2	0.0	0.0	0.0	0.	0.0
Retail:	East	0.0	0.0	0.0	0.4	3.6	9.3	12.9	21.0
	Midwest	0.0	0.0	0.0	0.3	0.0	0.0	0.0	0.0
	South	6.4	8.8	5.1	0.6	0.0	0.0	0.0	0.0
	West	18.9	18.5	11.9	5.0	0.0	0.0	0.0	0.0
R&D	East	1.4	0.0	0.0	0.0	0.0	0.0	0.0	0.0
	Midwest	0.7	0.0	0.0	0.0	0.0	0.0	0.0	0.0
	South	3.5	4.2	4.4	3.1	0.0	0.0	0.0	0.0
	West	19.4	24.5	30.9	37.8	43.8	28.7	15.7	0.0
Warehouse:	East	3.5	0.0	0.0	0.0	0.0	0.0	0.0	0.0
	Midwest	6.7	7.2	7.7	7.8	5.2	0.0	0.0	0.0
	South	0.0	0.0	0.0	0.0	0.0	0.0	0.0	0.0
	West	9.4	10.3	10.0	8.2	0.0	0.0	0.0	0.0
S&P 500		10.3	16.9	20.2	22.7	26.3	29.8	32.5	23.6
U.S. Government Bonds		6.1	0.0	0.0	0.0	0.0	0.0	0.0	0.0
Return		13.0	14.8	15.7	16.6	17.9	19.9	21.1	23.8
Risk		5.0	5.4	6.2	7.5	10.1	16.4	21.3	33.0

SOURCE: Russell-Zisler, Inc.

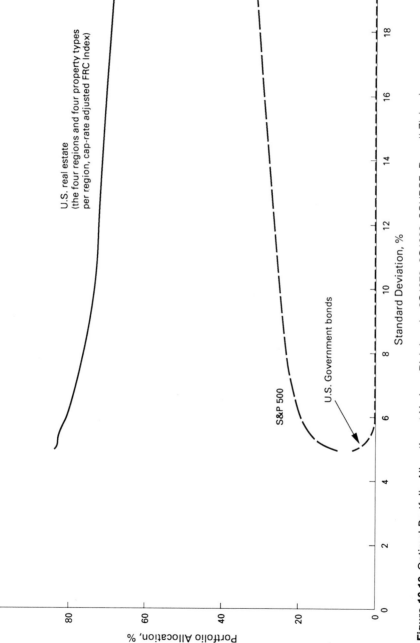

Figure 10-19. Optimal Portfolio Allocation at Various Risk Levels, 2Q1978–2Q1988. SOURCE: Russell-Zisler, Inc.

SUMMARY AND IMPLICATIONS FOR
PORTFOLIO MANAGEMENT

This chapter has demonstrated the rich complexity of real estate. While it is not the homogeneous asset class implied by the graphs of efficient frontiers presented in this chapter, it is nevertheless clear that real estate offers investors important diversification benefits. Some implications are these:

1. There is a trade-off between the riskiness of a portfolio containing real estate and other assets and the total expected return it generates. Additional return is generally achieved by assuming additional risk. In the case of adding real estate to a portfolio, additional returns are possible and risk can be reduced.

2. The market does not reward diversifiable or unsystematic risk. That is why it is so important to include property in portfolios of stocks and bonds that are not fully diversified across all asset classes including real estate.

3. Diversification across properties with noncovariant returns reduces portfolio risk but potentially without sacrificing return. Assets should be selected based on their return volatilities and return correlations with other asset classes, as well as on their expected returns.

4. Fundamental analysis in real estate is valuable. However, unless the investor has a consistently excellent ability to acquire and manage properties with diverse characteristics, lack of diversification introduces additional risks. For most investors a strict diversification approach, coupled with sound asset management, probably makes the most sense.

5. Another portfolio management approach involves dividing the portfolio into a strictly diversified component (a core portfolio) and a higher risk portfolio (an opportunistic portfolio). The opportunistic portfolio will reflect strategic as well as tactical bets based on forecasts of risk and return associated with different property classes. For example, investors with special skills in retail mall management may have great confidence in their ability to spot under- as well as over-priced properties, and to implement innovative renovation and management strategies. The core portfolio would be selected and managed in a more standard, orthodox return/risk trade-off manner.

6. The portfolio approach should apply with equal force to sell as well as buy decisions. In fact, portfolio management should not be separated out from ongoing asset management. Overvalued properties that are not likely to make solid risk-reducing diversification contributions to the portfolio should be sold.

7. Articulating and adopting a portfolio strategy brings important collateral benefits. Assumptions and strategies should be explicit

and not implied. A serious commitment to portfolio management requires continual dedication to a process and not to a static asset allocation. As market conditions evolve, so must portfolio allocations be reexamined and investment programs adjusted.

8. Still lacking are the proper complement of data and theoretical tools for thinking clearly about property in the portfolio context. The analysis in this chapter is intended for pedagogical purposes. However, the benefits of portfolio management are real. The art of portfolio management must be pragmatic, not theoretical. Ironically, the practice of portfolio management will evolve only as the data and theoretical tools improve.

FURTHER READING

The following is a selective list of texts and articles for those who seek additional real estate information.

Real Estate Finance and Investment Principles

For an introduction to the basic principles of real estate finance, see Sirmans and Jaffe [1984] and Fisher [1983]. Kau and Sirmans [1985] and Follain [1986] provide treatments of real estate tax issues without the usual accounting and legal jargon. The former is designed for practitioners, while the latter is more suited for those with background in economics, especially public finance. Miles [1984] is a special edition of the *Journal of the American Real Estate & Urban Economics Association* dedicated to institutional real estate investment. Of particular relevance among this diverse collection are the articles by Ibbotson and Siegel [1984], Brueggeman, Chen, and Thibodeau [1984], Miles and McCue [1984], and Jaffee and Sirmans [1984]. In the same volume, the Melnikoff article is a valuable personal reflection on the growth of pension investing by one of the pioneers. Downs [1985] is a nontechnical treatment of the many institutional and economic changes buffeting the real estate markets. Dramatic changes have occurred since this book was published.

Real estate portfolio issues are now receiving greater attention in the literature. Firstenberg, Ross, and Zisler [1988] provides a nontheoretical introduction to real estate portfolio theory designed for experienced investors. Ross and Zisler [1987a, 1987b] are more technical articles that are best read in conjunction with Firstenberg, Ross, and Zisler [1988]. Harzell [1986], Hartzell, Heckman, and Miles [1986], Hartzell, Shulman, and Wurtzebach [1987], Beckeman [1987], and Grissom, Kuhle, and Walter [1987] focus on diversification issues. The ICFA seminar proceeding edited by Hudson-Wilson [1989] provides a broad review of real estate analysis and portfolio management issues.

Appraisals

The proper evaluation of real estate performance is crucial to portfolio analysis. Appraisals are the source of most commercial real estate performance data. The American Institute of Real Estate Appraisers published *The Appraisal of Real Estate* [1983]. Although it is not written from the perspective of modern financial or economic theory, it does represent the approach to real estate analysis adopted by the largest professional appraisal society in the nation. Thoughtful empirical analyses of the reliability of the appraisal process can be found in Cole, Guilkey, and Miles [1986a and 1986b]. More theoretical critical treatments include Gilberto [1987], Guan and Quigley [1987], and Gyourko and Linneman [1988].

Real Estate and Urban Economics

Most treatments of real estate finance gloss over the market forces that generate property income and prices. The basic references on the economic structure and functioning of urban areas are found in Mills [1980]. Muth [1969] and Mieszkowski and Straszheim [1979] offer theoretical treatments of land use economics, including the determination of urban land pricing and rents. The reader derives an appreciation for the general equilibrium context in which real estate prices are determined and hopefully concludes that the standard appraisal analysis of prices is but a special case of the more general theoretical models used by urban economic theorists.

BIBLIOGRAPHY

The Appraisal of Real Estate. Chicago: American Institute of Real Estate Appraisers, 1983.

Beckeman, W.J. "The Effect of Geographical Diversification on Real Estate Portfolio Risk." Master's Thesis, Massachusetts Institute of Technology, 1987.

Brueggeman, W.E., A.H. Chen, and T.G. Thibodeau. "Real Estate Investment Funds: Performance and Portfolio Consideration." *AREUEA Journal*, Fall 1984.

Chen, Nai-Fu, Richard Roll, and Stephen Ross. "Economic Forces and the Stock Market." *Journal of Business*, July 1986.

Clapp, J. *Handbook for Real Estate Market Analysis*. Englewood Cliffs, N.J.: Prentice-Hall, 1987.

Cole, R., D. Guilkey, and Mike Miles. "Appraisals, Unit Values and Investor Confidence in Real Estate Portfolios." Working paper, University of North Carolina, March 1986a.

———. "Toward an Assessment of the Reliability of Commercial Appraisals." Working paper, University of North Carolina, March 1986b.

Diermeier, Jeffrey J., J. Kurt Freundlich, and Gary G. Schlarbaum. "The Role of Real Estate in a Multi-Asset Portfolio." Appendix to Tom S. Sale, ed. *Real Estate Investing*. Seminar Proceeding. Charlottesville, Va.: The Institute of Chartered Financial Analysts, 1986.

Downs, A. *The Revolution in Real Estate Finance.* Washington, D.C.: The Brookings Institution, 1985.

Firstenberg, Paul M., Stephen A. Ross, and Randall C. Zisler. "Real Estate: The Whole Story." *The Journal of Portfolio Management,* Spring 1988.

Fisher, Jeffrey D. "Portfolio Construction: Real Estate," in J.L. Maginn and D.L. Tuttle, eds. *Managing Investment Portfolios,* 1st ed. Boston: Warren, Gorham & Lamont, Inc., 1983.

Follain, J.R. ed. *Tax Reform and Real Estate.* Washington, D.C.: Urban Institute, 1986.

Frank Russell Company. *FRC Property Index—FRC Hybrid Mortgage Index,* Third Quarter, 1988.

Gilberto, S. Michael. "The Use of Appraisal Data in Indexes of Performance Measurement." Working Paper, Southern Methodist University, May 1987.

Grissom, Terry V., James L. Kuhle, and Carl H. Walter. "Diversification Works in Real Estate, Too." *The Journal of Portfolio Management,* Winter 1987.

Guan, Daniel C. and John M. Quigley. "The Micro Foundation of Real Estate Returns and Appraisal: Statics and Dynamics." Working Paper, Center for Real Estate and Urban Economics, December 1987.

Gyourko, Joseph and Peter Linneman. "Analyzing the Risk of Income-Producing Real Estate: A New Perspective." Working Paper, Wharton Real Estate Center, February 1988.

Hartzell, David J. *Real Estate in the Portfolio.* New York: Salomon Brothers Inc., August 27, 1986.

Hartzell, D.J., J. Hekman, and Mike Miles. "Diversification Categories in Investment Real Estate." *American Real Estate and Urban Economics Association Journal,* Summer 1986.

Hartzell, David J., A. Lepcio, J. Fernald, and S. Jordan. *Commercial Mortgage-Backed Securities: An Investor's Primer.* New York: Salomon Brothers Inc., May 1987.

Hartzell, David J., David G. Shulman, Terence C. Langetieg, and Martin L. Leibowitz. *A Look at Real Estate Duration.* New York: Salomon Brothers Inc., December 1987.

Hartzell, David, David G. Shulman, and Charles H. Wurtzebach. "Refining the Analysis of Regional Diversification for Income-Producing Real Estate." *The Journal of Real Estate Research,* Winter 1987.

Healey, Thomas J. and Charles R. Ewald. "The Convertible Mortgage Alternative." *The Real Estate Finance Journal,* Summer 1988.

Healey, Thomas J. and Frank J. Walter. "Financing Corporate Properties with Rated Mortgage Debt." *The Real Estate Finance Journal,* Fall 1988.

Hoag, James. "Toward Indices of Real Estate Value and Return." *The Journal of Finance,* May 1980.

Hopkins, Robert E., and David Shulman. *Ranking Metropolitan Growth: A Real Estate Tool to Be Used With Caution.* New York: Salomon Brothers, Inc., June 1987.

Hudson-Wilson, Susan, ed. *Real Estate: Valuation Techniques and Portfolio Management.* Seminar Proceeding. Charlottesville, Va.: The Institute of Chartered Financial Analysts, 1989.

Ibbotson, R., and L.B. Siegel. "Real Estate Returns: A Comparison With Other

Investments." *American Real Estate and Urban Economics Association Journal*, Fall 1984.

Jaffee, Austin J., and C.F. Sirmans. "The Theory and Evidence on Real Estate Financial Decision: A Review of the Issues." *AREUEA Journal*, Fall 1984.

Kau, J.B. and C.F. Sirmans. *Tax Planning for Real Estate Investment*. Englewood Cliffs, N.J.: Prentice-Hall, 1985.

Kroll, Cynthia A., and Sam Taff. "The Measurement of Effective Rent." Working Paper, Center for Real Estate and Urban Economics, March 1988.

Mieszkowski, P., and M. Straszheim, eds. *Current Issues in Urban Economics*. Baltimore: Johns Hopkins Press, 1979.

Miles, M., ed. *Journal of the American Real Estate and Urban Economics Association*, Fall 1984.

Miles, Mike, and T. McCue. "Commercial Real Estate Returns." *Journal of the American Real Estate and Urban Economics Association*, Fall 1984.

Mills, E. *Urban Economics*. Glenview, Ill.: Scott, Foresman and Co., 1980.

Muth, R.F. *Cities and Housing*. Chicago: University of Chicago Press, 1969.

Ross, Stephen A., and Randolph W. Westerfield. *Corporate Finance*. St. Louis: Times Mirror/Mosby College Publishing, 1988.

Ross, Stephen A., and Randall C. Zisler. *Managing Real Estate Portfolios—Part 2: Risk and Return in Real Estate*. New York: Goldman Sachs & Co., November 1987.

———. *Managing Real Estate Portfolios—Part 3: A Close Look at Equity Real Estate Risk*. New York: Goldman Sachs & Co., November 1987.

Sirmans, C.F., and A. Jaffee. *The Complete Real Estate Handbook*. Englewood Cliffs, N.J.: Spectrum, 1984.

Shulman, David G. *The Relative Risks of Equity Real Estate and Common Stocks: A New View*. New York: Salomon Brothers Inc., June 1986.

Smith, Laurence B. *Adjustment Mechanisms in Real Estate Markets*. New York: Salomon Brothers Inc., June 1987.

Zerbst, Robert H. and Barbara Cambon. "Historical Returns on Real Estate Investments." *The Journal of Portfolio Management*, Spring 1984.

Zisler, Randall C. and Stephen A. Ross. *Stock and Bond Market Volatility and Real Estate's Allocation*. New York: Goldman Sachs & Co., November 1987.

Zisler, Randall C. "Toward the Discipline of Real Estate Portfolio Management." *Institutional Investor*, September 1988.

CHAPTER 11

Futures and Options Strategies in Portfolio Management

David M. Dunford, CFA

INTRODUCTION

Futures and options contracts share many similarities, including trading mechanics and margin requirements. Futures and options are also similarly based on the same underlying investment instruments—primarily stocks and bonds, which is why they are called *derivative securities*. Both types of contracts, especially in terms of large-volume, regularized trading, are relatively new. Futures and options contracts, however, are fundamentally and substantially dissimilar in their impact on a portfolio of assets. Because futures and options are distinctly different, their respective strategic uses in portfolio management are different.

MODIFYING PORTFOLIO RISK

The important distinction between a futures contract and an options contract is that the futures contract is an *obligation*. The investor who purchases or sells a futures contract has an obligation to accept or deliver the underlying commodity on the expiration date. For the bond, stock index, and currency futures contracts reviewed in this chapter, that underlying commodity is either the appropriate bond, the cash settlement equivalent to the value of the stock index, or the appropriate currency. In contrast, the buyer of an option contract is not *obligated* to accept or deliver the underlying commodity, but instead has the *right*, or choice, to accept or deliver the underlying commodity at any time during the life of the contract. The difference between an obligation and a right has an important effect on the risk faced by a futures contract buyer or seller as compared to an option contract buyer or seller.

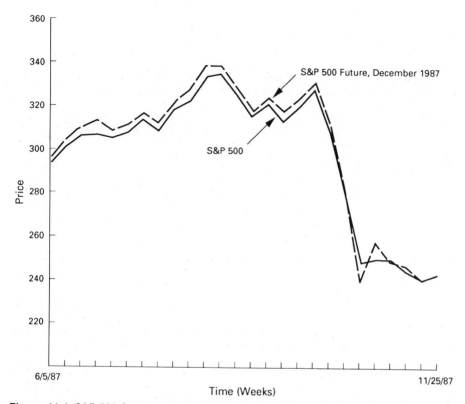

Figure 11-1. S&P 500 Stock Index vs. S&P 500 Index Futures Contract, June–November 1987. SOURCE: The Travelers Investment Management Co.

Risk Modification With Futures Contracts

Futures and options modify a portfolio's risk in different ways. Buying or selling a futures contract has an impact on a portfolio's upside risk or volatility and downside risk or volatility by a similar magnitude. Some literature has referred to this as *symmetrical impact*. The price of a futures contract varies directly with the price of the underlying bond or stock index, both as that price moves up and as it falls.

Figure 11-1 offers a view of the Standard & Poor's 500 Composite Stock Price Index (S&P 500), as it moved during the time period from June 1987 through November 1987, versus the price of the December S&P 500 futures contract. The figure indicates how close the prices of the two instruments have been to each other on both the upside and the downside. The area between the lines represents the difference between the absolute S&P 500 price and the price of the future.

On average, it can be expected that the futures price will be a very close

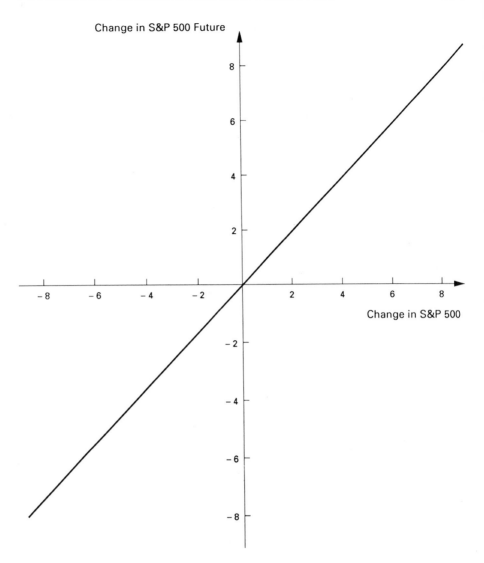

Figure 11-2. Index Futures Price Sensitivity.

approximation of the S&P 500 Index price. Owning (or shorting) one is essentially equivalent to owning (or shorting) the other.

Figure 11-2 displays the fair value price action of an S&P 500 futures contract versus a given change in the S&P 500. The x-axis of the figure represents a dollar value change in the S&P 500 at an instantaneous point in time. The y-axis represents the dollar change that will occur in the futures contract. The 45-degree diagonal straight line on the chart indicates that there is a dollar-for-dollar relationship in the price change of the S&P 500 and the price change of the S&P 500 future. As discussed in Chapter 2, in capital asset pricing model terms, the beta of either asset relative to the other is 1.0. This dollar-for-dollar relationship holds both on positive, or upside, changes in the index and on negative, or downside, changes in the index. For example, assume that the S&P 500 is selling at a price of 260. Also assume that the S&P 500 futures contract is selling at 265. Should the S&P 500 rise to a level of 262, the futures contract price will simultaneously increase from 265 to 267, assuming that the contract price stays at fair valuation. Because the value of a one-point move in this contract is $500, the value of the contract increases by $1,000 (2 × $500). Should the S&P 500 fall from 260 to 258, or 2 points, the price of the futures contract will simultaneously fall 2 points, from 265 to 263, again assuming the maintenance of fair value. The exception to this process occurs when the futures contract nears expiration as its price converges toward the level of the S&P 500.

The risk modification impact of a futures contract on an equity portfolio is displayed in Figures 11-3, 11-4, and 11-5. Figure 11-3 is the return distribution of an equity portfolio over a one-year period, assuming that the underlying equity portfolio is the market portfolio and has a market value of $130 million. If it is assumed that the expected return on the S&P 500, $E(R_{S\&P500})$, is 16 percent over a one-year period, with a standard deviation of that return, $\sigma_{S\&P500}$, of 20 percent over that one year, then Figure 11-3 indicates the possible distribution, or dispersion, of actual returns that could occur in that portfolio. Assume also that the risk-free rate of return (R_f) for the one-year holding period is 10 percent. The probability values on the y-axis of Figures 11-3, 11-4, and 11-5 were determined by calculating the probability of the portfolio return falling within a 2 percent interval (i.e., plus or minus one percent) around the x-axis return value. Different interval assumptions would result in different derived probability values, but the basic shape of the distribution would remain the same.

Selling or buying stock index futures contracts does not change the general bell shape of this return distribution. Selling or buying futures contracts expands or contracts this distribution, or the risk exposure of the portfolio, in a way that is similar to increasing or decreasing cash (equivalents) in a portfolio.

Selling Futures Contracts. Figure 11-4 displays the risk characteristics of the portfolio, assuming that the manager has *sold* stock index futures contracts to reduce the overall portfolio risk. The example assumes that stock index futures equivalent to one-half of the market value of the portfolio, or $65 million, have been sold. At an index value of 260, that figure requires the sale of 500 contracts. Because selling or buying a stock index futures contract is equivalent to selling or buying the same amount of stock exposure in the actual stock market, this action has the effect of selling one-half of the stock exposure of this portfolio. The sale of 500 futures contracts has

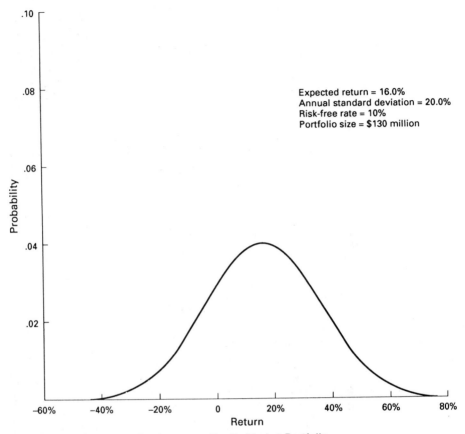

Figure 11-3. Return Distribution on an Equity Market Portfolio.

created a portfolio equivalent to a $130 million portfolio that is 50 percent invested in stocks and 50 percent invested in risk-free cash instruments. The expected return of the resulting portfolio, $E(R_p)$, is:

$$E(R_p) = E(R_{S\&P500}) \times \text{stock weighting} + R_f \times \text{cash weighting}$$
$$= 16\% \times .5 + 10\% \times .5$$
$$= 13\%$$

The standard deviation of the resulting portfolio, (σ_p), in which cash has a zero standard deviation or risk, is:

$$\sigma_p = \sigma_{S\&P500} \times \text{stock weighting}$$
$$= 20\% \times .5$$
$$= 10\%$$

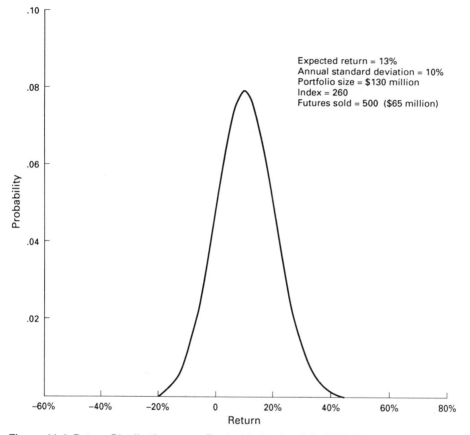

Figure 11-4. Return Distribution on an Equity Market Portfolio With Futures Sold Equal to One-Half the Portfolio.

The resulting portfolio has an expected return of 13 percent, with a standard deviation of 10 percent over the one-year period. Figure 11-4 displays the return distribution corresponding to this portfolio. The basic shape of the risk pattern of the portfolio has been maintained. Selling futures has narrowed the distribution, or dispersion, of possible returns, and lowered the risk level of the portfolio. See Hill-Schneeweis [1984] for further discussion.

Buying Futures Contracts. Figure 11-5 displays the opposite activity. The example assumes that stock index futures contracts have been *purchased* in an amount equivalent to one-half of the market value of the portfolio, or $65 million. At an index price of 260, a total of 500 S&P 500 futures contracts have been purchased. The effect is *equivalent to borrowing on*

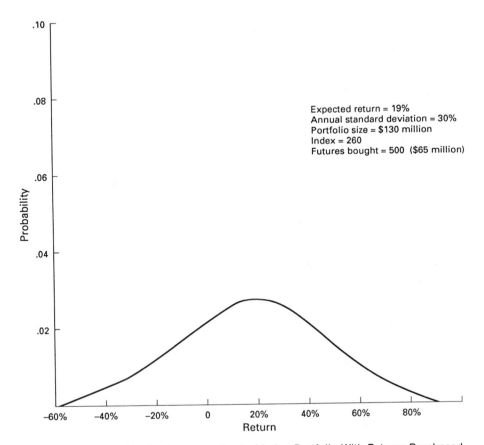

Expected return = 19%
Annual standard deviation = 30%
Portfolio size = $130 million
Index = 260
Futures bought = 500 ($65 million)

Figure 11-5. Return Distribution on an Equity Market Portfolio With Futures Purchased Equal to One-Half the Portfolio.

margin, at the risk-free rate, an amount of cash equal to one-half of the value of the portfolio and reinvesting the borrowed proceeds in stock. By buying stock index futures contracts, the equity portfolio has been significantly leveraged to the point where the portfolio weighting in stocks is 150 percent, while cash is weighted minus 50 percent. The expected return of the portfolio of 19 percent over the one-year time period and standard deviation, or risk level, of 30 percent can be derived by using the previously stated formulas.

In summary, buying or selling futures contracts produces symmetrical effects on the risk exposure of a portfolio. Buying or selling a future is exactly equivalent to subtracting or adding cash from that portfolio. In fact, through the purchase of futures, cash may be "subtracted" to such an extent that the underlying portfolio becomes substantially leveraged, depending on the investor's aversion to risk and regulations on maximum margin borrowing.

Risk Modification With Options Contracts

The addition of a call or put option to a portfolio does not have a similar impact on upside portfolio risk and downside portfolio risk. Unlike futures contracts, the impact of options on the risk profile of a portfolio of assets is not symmetrical. In terms of risk modification, the distinction between options and futures is seen in the definitions of a call option and a put option. The owner of an American call option on an individual stock has the right to *buy* shares of that individual stock at the agreed-upon contract price, or strike price, at any time during the life of that contract. The owner of a call option is not faced with the risk of having to pay more for that stock. The terms of the contract state that the owner can buy stock at the strike price and that the seller of the call option must sell the stock at that strike price. In contrast, the owner of an American put has the right to *sell* shares of that stock at the agreed upon strike price at any time during the life of the contract. Should the actual price of the individual stock fall below the strike price, the owner of the put option still may receive that strike price upon exercising the put option. European call and put options are similar in all ways to American options, except that they are exercisable only at expiration.

Buying Call Options. The price, or premium, of a call option on an individual stock varies directly with the price of that stock as the stock's price advances, as long as the stock's price is above the option's strike price (i.e., the option is *in the money*). The price of the call, however, will not vary directly with the price of the stock should the stock price be below the option's strike price (i.e., the option is *out of the money*). The call price cannot fall below zero.

Figure 11-6 displays the price action of IBM stock and the price of the IBM call option with a strike price of 110 and expiration in July 1988. The figure covers the period from March through June in 1988. The price of the call option moved fairly responsively with the price of IBM stock when the option was in the money at the beginning and at the end of the time period, but much less responsively relative to the IBM stock when the option was out of the money during the middle part of the period. Unlike a futures contract, a call option contract is not an exact equivalent to owning the underlying security, which in this case is the individual stock of IBM. There is essentially unit elasticity between the call option and the underlying stock when the option is in the money, but less than unit elasticity when the price relation changes in such a way that the option becomes out of the money.

Figure 11-7 displays the relationship between the price of the underlying stock and the fair price of the call option on the stock, based on the option pricing model described in Black and Scholes [1973]. The example assumes that IBM is selling at $120 per share and the call option is at the money (i.e.,

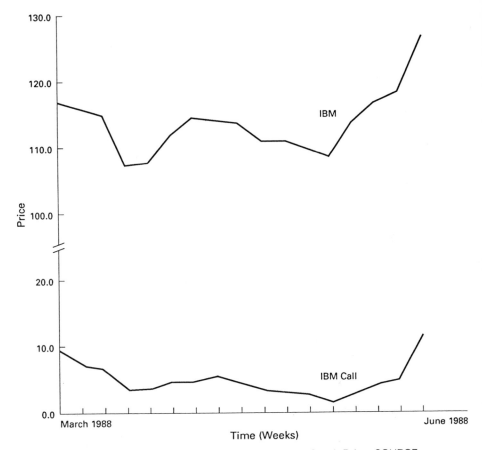

Figure 11-6. IBM 115 July 1988 Call Option Price vs. IBM Stock Price. SOURCE: Travelers Investment Management Co.

the market price is equal to the strike price) with a strike price of 120 and six months to maturity. The x-axis is the price of a share of IBM stock while the y-axis is the price of the call option. Should the share price of IBM increase from 120 to 125, the price of the call option will increase from 8½ to about 11¾. The diagonal line in the upper-right quadrant indicates that there is a one-to-one relationship between the price of the underlying stock and the intrinsic value of the call as the call becomes in the money. Should the price of the IBM stock fall five points, from 120 to 115, and become out of the money, the fair price of the call will fall only 2¾ points, to a price of 5¾. Should the IBM stock price fall 10 points, from 120 to 110, then the call will fall to only 3⅝. Any further decline in the price of the IBM stock is reflected in only a minimal decline in the price of the call option because, while it is out of the money and therefore has no *intrinsic value*, the option

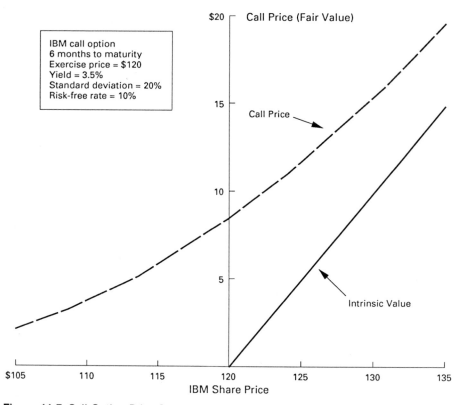

Figure 11-7. Call Option Price Sensitivity. SOURCE: Travelers Investment Management Co.

still has an ever-diminishing *time value* reflecting the chances of the stock's market price to rise above the strike price in the time remaining until expiration of the option contract. The call option cannot have a value of less than zero. The price of the call option does not move symmetrically with the price of the underlying asset, which in this case is a share of IBM.

Owning a call option is like owning an insurance policy on the underlying stock. A premium for the insurance is paid in terms of the price of the call. Paying the premium allows the call option owner to participate in the upside action of the stock, with limited participation in any downside movement.

Buying or selling option contracts in a portfolio of assets changes the shape of the return distribution and provides a significant skewness to the risk profile of the portfolio. For example, options truncate upside price potential or downside price risk, depending on whether the investor is selling a call or buying a put option within the portfolio. The numerical examples in the following sections display the impact that different option contracts have on the risk profile of the portfolios.

Buying Calls Plus Cash Equivalents. Figure 11-8 displays a specific example of the risk profile of a portfolio that contains call options plus cash equivalents as compared to a portfolio that contains only stocks. One strategy is a single stock portfolio strategy, in which one share of stock is bought at $50 and no dividends are expected. The other strategy involves buying one call on the same stock, with the funds not invested in the call option held in cash equivalents. It is assumed that for a six-month call at a $50 strike price or exercise price, the premium (or price) of the call is $6. Then $44 is invested in cash equivalents, such as Treasury bills, at 10 percent interest per year. For both portfolios, the total assets involved are $50.

The table in the center of Figure 11-8 shows the returns on each of these two portfolios, given a change in the price of the underlying stock. If the stock price falls at the end of six months to 35, then there is a loss of $15 on that share of stock. This loss results in a return on Portfolio 1, which includes just the stock, of minus 30 percent. In Portfolio 2, for which a call option and Treasury bills have been bought, the call option falls to a price of approximately zero, given a $15 decline in the stock, while the remaining $44 in Treasury bills earns 5 percent, or $2.20, for the six-month period. Portfolio 2 then has a value of $46.20, or $50.00 minus $6 lost on the call plus $2.20 interest. The net loss in the portfolio is $3.80, for a portfolio return of minus 7.6 percent.

Should the price of the stock increase to a level of 65, the gain in Portfolio 1 will then be $15, for a return of 30 percent. In Portfolio 2, the call option at the end of six months will have a value of $15, which is the difference between the price of the stock and the exercise price of the option. The total value of the portfolio at the end of the six-month period would then be $50 plus the $15 value of the call option minus $6 paid for the call option plus $2.20 interest on the Treasury bills, for a total portfolio value of $61.20. This represents a gain of $11.20, for a portfolio return of 22.4 percent.

The difference in the risk profile between the stock-only Portfolio 1 and Portfolio 2, containing the call option, is visibly displayed at the bottom of Figure 11-8. The portfolio containing the call option moves with the stock-only portfolio as the stock's price advances and lags only by an amount equal to the premium paid for the call option minus the return on the Treasury bills. The portfolio return of the portfolio containing the call and Treasury bills is truncated at minus 7.6 percent, while the return of the stock-only portfolio continues to fall with the decline in the stock's price.

The risk modification characteristics of buying a call option contract in conjunction with holding cash equivalents can be viewed in terms of their impact on the risk profile, or forecasted return distribution, of the underlying portfolio. As with the example in Figure 11-3, assume that the underlying portfolio is the stock market as represented by a stock market index such as the S&P 500. Again, assume that the expected risk-free rate of return is

Compare two strategies:

1. Buy stock at $50/share, no dividends
2. Buy one call on same stock, with the balance in bills
   - $6 for six-month call ($50 exercise price)
   - $44 in Treasury bills at 10% annual interest
     Total = $50 in assets

At the end of six months (maturity of call):

Stock Price	Gain (Loss)	Portfolio Return	Buy Call Buy Bill	Gain (Loss)	Portfolio Return
$35	$ − 15	− 30%	$46.20	$ − 3.80	− 7.6%
40	− 10	− 20	46.20	− 3.80	− 7.6
45	− 5	− 10	46.20	− 3.80	− 7.6
50	0	0	46.20	− 3.80	− 7.6
55	+ 5	10	51.20	+ 1.20	2.4
60	+ 10	20	56.20	+ 6.20	12.4
65	+ 15	30	61.20	+ 11.20	22.4

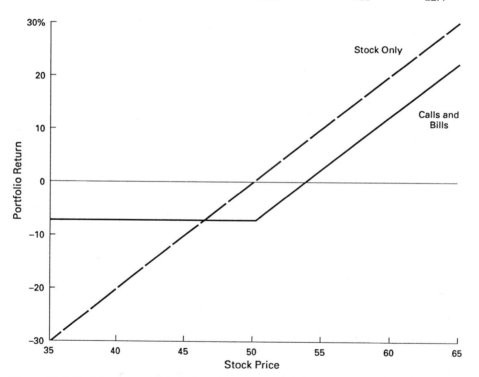

Figure 11-8. Performance of Call Option and Cash Portfolio vs. Underlying Common Stock Portfolio. SOURCE: Travelers Investment Management Co.

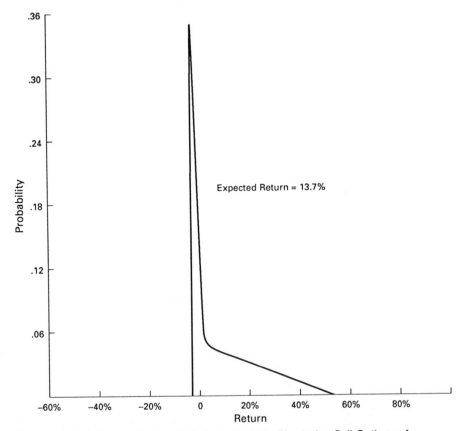

Figure 11-9. Return Distribution of Cash Equivalents Plus Index Call Options of Equivalent Market Exposure.

10 percent and that the expected return on the underlying portfolio of the stock market over a one-year holding period is 16 percent, with an annual standard deviation of 20 percent. Figure 11-3 shows the risk profile, or projected return distribution, of the underlying portfolio over a one-year period.

Figure 11-9 displays the forecasted return distribution of a portfolio that includes cash (equivalents) and call options on the market index. The portfolio has the same upside market value exposure as the stock market portfolio displayed in Figure 11-3. The index call options purchased are one-year at-the-money calls priced at the fair value as determined by the Black-Scholes model. The model input assumptions are an annual standard deviation of the index of 20 percent, a risk-free rate of 10 percent, and a dividend yield of 4.5 percent. The resulting fair price of the call option is $10.20. The cash plus index call option portfolio is then 89.8 percent invested in cash and 10.2 percent invested in call options.

The return distribution is truncated at a minimum loss level of approximately minus one percent. The truncation occurs at the point at which the call options have fallen to a price or value of zero. The cash equivalents held in the portfolio remain and are assumed to earn the risk-free rate of return. Buying the call option has created this skewed risk profile, in which insurance against participation in adverse price outcomes has been obtained at a cost equal to the price of the call option.

Figure 11-9 indicates that the expected return of the cash plus call option portfolio (13.7 percent) is moderately less than the expected return of the all stock portfolio (16.0 percent) displayed in Figure 11-3, the difference being the premium paid for the insurance protection.

Writing Covered Call Options. Figure 11-10 displays the return and risk modification from selling a call option on a stock held in a portfolio. The exhibit compares the portfolio strategies of owning only the stock and owning the stock with a call option sold or written against that stock. Assume that the first portfolio involves buying one share of stock at a price of $50 with no dividends over the time period. Assume that the second portfolio involves buying one share of the stock at a price of $50 and selling for $6 one six-month at-the-money call option with an exercise price of $50. The total assets in each of the two portfolios again equals $50.

The table in the center of Figure 11-10 displays the returns generated on each of these two portfolios, given different changes in the stock's price. If the stock's price falls to $35, Portfolio 1, containing just the stock, has a loss of $15, for a portfolio return of minus 30 percent. In Portfolio 2, which contains the stock plus the sold call option, the stock has fallen by $15, for a loss of $15, while the call option, which was originally sold for $6, falls to zero, for a gain of $6. The net value of the portfolio, then, is $50 minus the $15 loss on the stock plus the $6 gain on the call option, or $41. The net loss is $9, for a portfolio return of minus 18 percent.

Should the stock price instead increase to 65, Portfolio 1 will experience a $15 gain over the six-month period, for a portfolio return of 30 percent. In Portfolio 2, the stock will increase by $15 and the call option will increase to a value of $15, for a loss on the sold call option position of $9. The net gain on the portfolio will then be $15 minus the $9 loss on the call option, or $6, for a total portfolio value of $56. This represents a portfolio return of 12 percent, which is demonstrated in the table to be the maximum return achievable. The portfolio return distribution for Portfolio 2 is truncated on the positive return side at plus 12 percent. The return can never be any higher, no matter how much the price of the underlying stock increases or decreases.

In summary, selling a call option on a stock portfolio has the opposite effect on the portfolio's risk profile of buying a call option plus holding cash equivalents. When a call option is sold, a portfolio's return distribution is

Compare two strategies:

1. Buy stock at $50/share, no dividends
2. Buy stock at $50/share, no dividends
   Sell one call on same stock
   - $6 for six-month call
   - $50 exercise price

At the end of six months (maturity of call):

Stock Price	Gain (Loss)	Portfolio Return	Buy Stock Sell Call	Gain (Loss)	Portfolio Return
$35	$ − 15	− 30%	$41.00	$ − 9.00	− 18%
40	− 10	− 20	46.00	− 4.00	− 8
45	− 5	− 10	51.00	1.00	2
50	0	0	56.00	6.00	12
55	+ 5	10	56.00	6.00	12
60	+ 10	20	56.00	6.00	12
65	+ 15	30	56.00	6.00	12

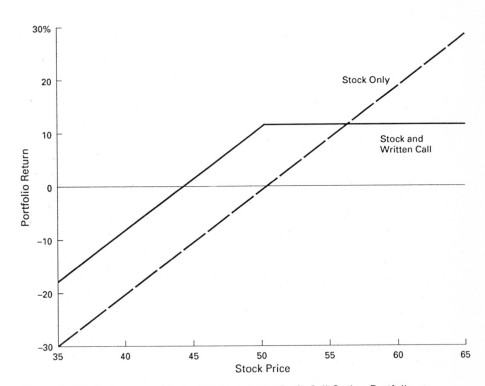

Figure 11-10. Performance of Stock With Written (Sold) Call Option Portfolio vs. Underlying Common Stock Portfolio. SOURCE: Travelers Investment Management Co.

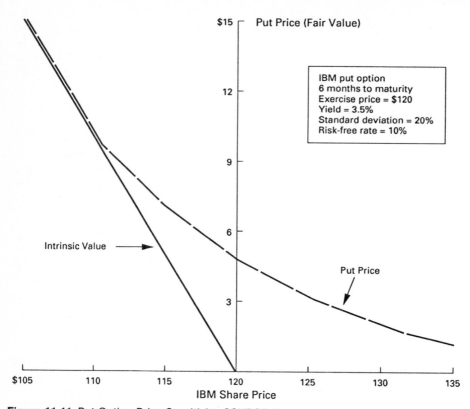

Figure 11-11. Put Option Price Sensitivity. SOURCE: Travelers Investment Management Co.

skewed to the downside, with the upside portfolio potential being truncated at a specific, positive percentage return. The downside portfolio returns are cushioned by the amount of the call premium received when the call option is sold. This downside cushion is achieved only at the expense of some participation on the upside. By contrast, a calls plus bills portfolio results in the portfolio's return distribution being skewed to the upside with the downside portfolio potential being truncated at a specific, usually modest, negative percentage return.

Buying Put Options. In terms of return and risk modification, buying or selling a put option produces a counterpart to buying or selling a call option. Figure 11-11 displays the fair price of a put option versus the price of the underlying stock. As in Figure 11-7, the example assumes that IBM is selling at a price of $120 per share. The put option is at the money, with a strike price of 120 and six months to maturity. The x-axis represents the price of a share of IBM stock, while the y-axis is the price of the put option. An increase in the price of IBM from 120 to 125 results in a reduction of the put option's Black-Scholes fair price from $4\frac{7}{8}$ to $3\frac{1}{4}$. As the price of the stock continues to rise, the price of the put option falls toward zero. On the other hand, should the price of IBM fall from 120 to 115, the fair price of the put option would increase from $4\frac{7}{8}$ to $7\frac{1}{8}$. As the price of IBM continues to fall, the price of the put option moves up as the price of the stock declines on an approximate one-for-one basis. The diagonal solid line in the upper-left quadrant indicates this relationship.

Figure 11-12 displays a numerical example that compares a stock-only portfolio with a portfolio containing both the stock and a put option on the stock. Portfolio 1 includes just a share of stock, assumed to be purchased at $70 per share with a semiannual dividend of $2. Portfolio 2 includes the share of stock having a dividend of $2 and a six-month put that has a strike price of 70 and was purchased for $5. The table in the center of Figure 11-12 displays the returns on each of these two portfolios, given changes in the price of the underlying stock. If the price of the stock falls to 55, the loss incurred in Portfolio 1 is a $15 capital loss plus a $2 dividend, or a net loss of $13, for a portfolio return of minus 18.6 percent. In Portfolio 2, which contains the stock with a put option, the value of the portfolio is $55 for the share of stock plus $15 for the value of the put option minus the cost of the put option of $5, plus the $2 dividend, for a total portfolio value of $67. This represents a net loss of $3, for a portfolio return of minus 4 percent. By contrast, if the stock price increases to 85, Portfolio 1 will have a total gain of $15 plus $2, or $17, for a return of 24.3 percent. Portfolio 2, which contains the stock and put option, has a total value of stock of $85 minus the $5 cost of the put plus $2 in dividends, for a total of $82. The net gain is $12, for a portfolio return of 16 percent.

The return and risk profiles of the two portfolios are displayed at the bottom of Figure 11-12. In this example, the downside risk exposure of the portfolio containing the put option is limited to minus 4 percent. The put option in Portfolio 2 has modified the return/risk profile of the stock portfolio to the extent that participation in the downside is limited and some upside participation is maintained.

Option Spread Strategies. Call and put options can be purchased or sold in many different combinations to achieve the desired risk profiles for portfolios. In particular forecasted market environments, such strategies are often implemented to achieve an increment to portfolio return. These strategies are often called *spread strategies* because they involve buying or selling options at different strike prices or expiration dates.

One example is one type of *bull spread*, in which a portfolio manager sells an out-of-the-money call option on a stock and purchases an in-the-money or at-the-money call option on the same stock with the same expiration date. The portfolio will gain incremental return should the stock price rise (a "bull" move) to the strike price of the short or sold option. Should

Compare two strategies:

1. Buy stock at $70/share, $2 dividends
2. Buy same stock and six-month put with $70 exercise price for $5

At the end of six months (maturity of put):

Stock Price	Gain (Loss)	Portfolio Return	Buy Stock Buy Put	Gain (Loss)	Portfolio Return
$55	$ – 13	– 18.6%	$67.00	$ – 3.00	– 4.0%
60	– 8	– 11.4	67.00	– 3.00	– 4.0
65	– 3	– 4.3	67.00	– 3.00	– 4.0
70	+ 2	2.9	67.00	– 3.00	– 4.0
75	+ 7	10.0	72.00	+ 2.00	2.7
80	+ 12	17.1	77.00	+ 7.00	9.3
85	+ 17	24.3	82.00	+ 12.00	16.0

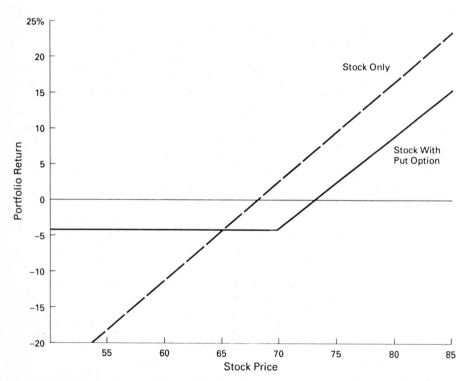

Figure 11-12. Performance of Stock With Put Option vs. Underlying Common Stock Portfolio. SOURCE: Travelers Investment Management Co.

TABLE 11-1. Return and Risk Measures for Historical Simulations for Four Investment Strategies for Six-Month Holding Periods From July 1963 to June 1977 Employing the 30 Dow Jones Industrial Stocks in the Underlying Stock Portfolio (in percent)

	Dow Jones Industrial Stocks	Stocks Plus Fully Covered Call Writing	Call and Commercial Paper Buying	Stocks Plus Protective Put Buying
Average rate of return	4.6%	3.15%	5.4%	4.5%
Standard deviation	13.7	6.1	10.4	7.9
Highest return	49.1	16.0	34.4	35.1
Lowest return	−16.4	−9.2	−5.7	−1.8
Average compound return	3.7	2.9	4.9	4.2

SOURCE: Merton, Scholes, and Gladstein [1982].

the stock price fall below the strike price of the purchased option, the cost to the portfolio will be limited to the difference between the premium paid on the purchased option and the premium received on the short option.

A second example is one type of *bear spread*, in which the opposite transactions occur. A manager buys an out-of-the money call option and sells an at- or in-the-money call option with the same expiration. The portfolio will gain the difference between the premium received and the premium paid should the stock price fall (a "bear" move). Should the stock price rise, the adverse portfolio impact will be limited because the gain in the purchased call will offset the loss in the short call.

A more complete summary of different option spread strategies can be found in Cox and Rubinstein [1985] and Yates [1987].

Results of Empirical Studies. Merton, Scholes, and Gladstein [1982] conducted a number of simulations using historical data on portfolios containing these and other combinations of stocks and put and call options. Their results confirm the hypothesized impact that options have on modifying the return/risk profile of a portfolio.

Table 11-1 presents a brief summary of some results of the study. Historical simulation data are provided for the Dow Jones 30 industrial stocks portfolio and for three option strategies: selling calls on all the stocks in a portfolio, maintaining a portfolio that is 10 percent invested in call options and 90 percent invested in commercial paper, and buying puts on all the portfolio's stocks. The simulation covered 28 six-month periods from July 1, 1963 through June 30, 1977. For each strategy, the stock portfolio was assumed to be an equal-weighted portfolio of the 30 Dow Jones industrial stocks. The weightings were rebalanced every six months. The fair value option prices were calculated by using the Black-Scholes model for calls and the Merton model for puts.

The results in Table 11-1 assume the purchase or sale of at-the-money puts and calls with six months to maturity. The options were purchased or sold at the beginning of each six-month period and held to maturity. The inputs to the option-pricing model were as follows:

- The price of the stock at the beginning of the period
- The risk-free rate of return on six-month prime commercial paper
- The stock's dividend yield
- The option exercise price equal to the current stock price
- The stock's return variance, which was assumed to be equal to the variance of the previous six-month period

The results in Table 11-1 verify the risk modification characteristics of option strategies. The stock-only portfolio containing the 30 Dow Jones industrial stocks exhibited a range of six-month returns from minus 16.4 percent to plus 49.1 percent. A portfolio in which covered calls were written on all 30 stocks in the portfolio produced returns ranging from minus 9.2 percent to plus 16.0 percent. Upside stock price movements were truncated, while the downside moves were cushioned. A portfolio containing (purchased) call options on all 30 stocks plus cash equivalents in the form of six-month commercial paper exhibited returns that ranged from minus 5.7 percent to plus 34.4 percent. Either the risk-free rate or the upside stock price movement was reduced by the cost of the insurance. Finally, a portfolio containing stocks plus (purchased) put options on each of the stocks exhibited returns from minus 1.8 percent to plus 35.1 percent. The downside stock price movement was truncated at the expense of some upside movement. The historical simulations confirm the risk modification patterns for these three option strategies, which are exhibited in Figures 11-8, 11-10, and 11-12, respectively.

MODIFYING SYSTEMATIC RISK

The various futures and options contracts can be used to modify or control both the systematic and unsystematic risks in a portfolio. Systematic risk in a portfolio relates to the risk or volatility of the stock or bond market as a whole. Unsystematic risk in a portfolio is the sum of the risk or volatility of market subgroups plus the risk or volatility specific to any individual security. Futures contracts on Treasury bonds and stock market indexes, options on high-quality bonds and bond futures, and options on stock indexes and stock index futures all can be used to modify the systematic risk exposure of bond and stock portfolios.

TABLE 11-2. An Example of Systematic Risk (Duration) Modification Using Fixed-Income Futures

Portfolio: $90 million
Portfolio duration: 8.0
Treasury bond price: 90
Futures value: $90,000/contract

Treasury Bond Futures Contracts Transaction	Portfolio Duration
Sell 100 contracts	7.2
200	6.4
300	5.6
Buy 100 contracts	8.8
200	9.6
300	10.4

Fixed-Income Portfolios

Systematic risk in a fixed-income portfolio can be thought of as the risk of changes in interest rates. The exposure of a fixed-income portfolio to systematic risk can be measured by the duration of the portfolio. Futures contracts on Treasury bonds or other Treasury securities can increase or decrease the exposure to interest rate risk by the altering of the duration of the portfolio (a measure of bond price volatility, explored in Chapter 6), which is accomplished through buying or selling bond futures.

Table 11-2 presents an example of modifying the systematic risk, or duration, of a fixed-income portfolio by buying or selling futures contracts. The table assumes an initial portfolio of $90 million invested in Treasury bonds. The portfolio has a duration of 8.0. If the Treasury bond is assumed to sell at a price of 90, then the sale of one Treasury bond futures contract is equivalent to the sale of $90,000 of Treasury bonds. Selling 100 Treasury bond futures contracts is equivalent to selling $9 million of Treasury bonds, or one-tenth of the portfolio. Selling 100 futures contracts reduces the portfolio's duration proportionately, or by 10 percent, from 8.0 to 7.2. Selling 200 futures contracts reduces the duration of the portfolio to 6.4. Buying 100 futures contracts increases the systematic risk or duration of the portfolio from 8.0 to 8.8, and buying 200 futures contracts increases the duration to 9.6. Alteration of bond portfolio duration is discussed in greater detail elsewhere in this chapter.

Options on fixed-income instruments can be used to modify the systematic risk exposure of the fixed-income portfolio in a nonsymmetric manner. Table 11-3 assumes that put options are bought on the $90 million portfolio using additional funds. These put options are assumed to be six-month at-the-money options on Treasury bond futures with a strike price of 90. The table shows the duration of the $90 million portfolio for different amounts

TABLE 11-3. Systematic Risk (Duration) Modification Using Put Options on Treasury Bond Futures

Portfolio: $90 million
Portfolio duration: 8
Treasury bond price: 90
Put option on bond future: Strike price 90 with six months to maturity
Risk-free rate: 10%

Bond Price	Portfolio Duration, Given the Percentage of Total Portfolio Assets Protected by Put Options				
	20%	40%	60%	80%	100%
100	8.0	8.0	7.9	7.9	7.9
95	7.9	7.8	7.7	7.5	7.4
90	7.6	7.2	6.8	6.4	6.0
85	7.1	6.2	5.3	4.5	3.6
80	6.7	5.3	4.0	2.6	1.3

of put protection and for different instantaneous changes in the price level. The variation in duration shown in the table is a direct result of the skewed impact that options contracts have on the risk profile of a portfolio. At different put protection levels the exposure to risk in the portfolio varies substantially for any particular price change of the underlying bond. Duration changes little in response to bond price changes in a 20 percent put-protected portfolio, but it changes significantly in a 100 percent protected portfolio.

Equity Portfolios

In an equity or common stock portfolio, the systematic risk portion of the total portfolio risk arises from the movement of the overall market and can be measured by the portfolio's beta. Stock index futures contracts may be used to alter the beta of a portfolio in a way similar to the fixed-income duration example in Table 11-2.

Table 11-4 presents a numerical example of the use of stock index futures in altering the systematic risk exposure of stock portfolios. The initial portfolio is assumed to be worth $130 million and the S&P 500 is assumed to be at 260. Buying or selling one future is equivalent to buying or selling $130,000 worth of common stock (260 × $500 = $130,000). It is assumed that the beta of the $130 million portfolio, as measured against the S&P 500, is 1.0. If 100 S&P 500 futures contracts are sold, equity exposure is reduced by $13 million, and beta is reduced from 1.0 to 0.9. If 200 contracts are sold, beta is reduced to 0.8. If 100 S&P 500 futures contracts are bought, beta is increased from 1.0 to 1.1; if 200 contracts are bought, beta is increased to 1.2.

TABLE 11-4. Systematic Risk (Beta) Modification Using Stock Index Futures

Portfolio: $130 million
Portfolio beta: 1.0
S&P 500: 260
Index futures value: $130,000/contract

S&P 500 Futures Contracts Transaction	Portfolio Beta
Sell 100 contracts	0.9
200	0.8
300	0.7
Buy 100 contracts	1.1
200	1.2
300	1.3

Buying a put option on the $130 million portfolio has a similar impact on modifying the systematic risk profile of the portfolio. Table 11-5 assumes that additional funds are used to purchase at-the-money put options on $130 million of the S&P 500 with a strike price of 260. The table presents the beta or systematic risk exposure of the portfolio, given different percentages of portfolio put protection and an instantaneous change in price of the underlying portfolio, which is the S&P 500. For example, when a portfolio holds stocks with a beta of 1.0 and put options with the characteristics listed in Table 11-5 that are sufficient to put-protect 60 percent of the total market value of the portfolio, it exhibits a beta of 0.76 at an index price of 260. Should the price of the index rise to 270, the put options will move out of

TABLE 11-5. Systematic Risk (Beta) Modification Using S&P 500 Put Options

Portfolio: $130 million
Portfolio beta: 1.0
S&P 500: 260
S&P 500 put option: Strike price of 260, with six months to maturity
Yield: 3.0%
Risk-free rate: 10%
S&P 500 annual standard deviation: 20%

	Portfolio Beta, Given the Percentage of Total Portfolio Assets Protected by Put Options				
Index Price	20%	40%	60%	80%	100%
280	0.96	0.92	0.88	0.84	0.79
270	0.94	0.88	0.82	0.77	0.71
260	0.92	0.84	0.76	0.68	0.60
250	0.90	0.80	0.69	0.59	0.49
240	0.87	0.75	0.62	0.50	0.37

the money, where their price will be less responsive to changes in the price of the index because the put has no intrinsic value, and the portfolio beta will increase to 0.82. Should the price of the index fall to 250, the options will move in the money, where the price of the put option will become more responsive to changes in the index's price, and the portfolio's beta will fall to 0.69. As with duration, beta varies as the S&P 500 changes because of the nonsymmetrical impact that options have on the systematic risk profile of the portfolio.

MODIFYING UNSYSTEMATIC RISK

The ability of futures and options contracts to modify unsystematic risk is more limited. In a fixed-income portfolio, unsystematic risk is the sum of any sector spread volatility plus any default risk on individual issues. Yield spreads of various bond market sectors against Treasury bonds have considerable variability and can produce considerable unsystematic risk. Fixed-income futures and options, however, cannot be used to modify unsystematic risk, because substantially all of these contracts are based on Treasury bonds and Treasury yields. Treasury derivatives can only hedge the interest rate risk of Treasury securities or, alternatively, movements and changes in the shape of the Treasury yield curve. Futures and options contracts on Treasury bonds cannot modify the risk of sector yield spreads. Therefore, there are only a very limited number of contracts among the new instruments that allow for modification and control of unsystematic risk in a bond portfolio. However, there is relatively little unsystematic risk for investment-grade bonds as compared to common stocks, making the need for such derivative instruments less acute. This topic is more fully discussed in the fixed-income sections later in this chapter.

In an equity portfolio, unsystematic risk, or residual risk, relates to portfolio volatility that does not result from movement in the underlying market as represented by a stock market index. For a diversified portfolio, as much as 95 percent of the total portfolio risk may be the result of systematic risk. As indicated previously, this systematic risk can be modified and controlled through the use of futures contracts on stock indexes. The remaining 5 percent of portfolio risk, the unsystematic risk, can be only minimally affected through the use of stock index futures or options on those futures contracts. On the other hand, options on market subgroups and options on individual stocks can be used to impact significantly the unsystematic risk of a portfolio. These options can be used to change the risk profile of a portfolio's unsystematic risk through the buying or selling of insurance on the portfolio's exposure to individual stocks and stock subgroups.

ASSET ALLOCATION

As indicated in Chapter 7, the decision about *asset allocation*—how much of a portfolio's assets should be placed in broad asset classes such as stock, bonds, real estate, and cash equivalents—ultimately has more impact on the performance of the portfolio than any other investment decision. The active control of asset allocation, whether derived passively or as the result of an active judgment, is a key element in maximizing portfolio return and risk trade-offs.

Futures and option contracts offer a means to control a portfolio's risk exposure in the asset allocation decision and maximize the benefits of that decision in terms of incremental returns for the level of portfolio risk chosen. The strategic use of futures and options in the control of the asset allocation of a portfolio is perhaps the most effective and fundamental use of these new instruments. The uses of futures and options contracts in asset allocation are discussed in the following section.

Futures in Asset Allocation

Financial futures can play a very important role in portfolio construction by facilitating decisions about asset allocation. Once it is decided how much of a portfolio's assets should be in stocks and how much should be in bonds, this decision has to be implemented, a process that is not without cost. Nevertheless, the contribution that asset allocation makes to portfolio return must be viewed net of execution costs. Because the potential returns from active asset allocation can be substantially diluted by execution costs, many institutional investors limit asset allocation decisions to strategic rather than tactical judgments.

The asset allocation decision may be executed in a portfolio by using futures instead of transacting in the underlying securities. Futures offer an alternative to actually buying or selling stocks and bonds to increase or decrease stock or bond exposure. A review of the costs incurred in executing the asset allocation decision indicates the strategic role that stock index futures and Treasury bond futures, for example, can play in portfolio management.

Execution Costs. The four costs that could be incurred during the execution phase—commissions, market impact, time, and disruption—are best illustrated by a simple example. Assume that the goal is an increase of a portfolio's exposure to common stock by $40 million. This increase may be accomplished by buying either $40 million of common stock in the stock market or $40 million of equivalent stock exposure through stock index futures. Assume that the S&P 500 future is currently selling at 260. One futures contract is therefore equivalent to $130,000 of common stock exposure (260 × $500 = $130,000).

Brokerage Commission. The first cost is *commissions*. If the average price per share of a common stock is assumed to be $40, a purchase of $40 million of stock under the first method involves buying one million shares of that stock. At a commission rate of $0.05 a share, a rate lower than the average for all institutional trades in early 1989, that method would involve total commissions of $50,000. The alternative is to buy $40 million of stock exposure by purchasing futures. If each future were equivalent to $130,000, then 308 futures contracts would be needed. The commission to buy 308 contracts is one-half the round trip commission of approximately $25 per contract, or $12.50 times 308 contracts, for a total commission of $3,850. In this example, utilizing futures has reduced commissions by about 92 percent.

Market Impact. A second cost is *market impact*. A stock purchase of $40 million can be expected to have an adverse impact on the price level of the shares. A portfolio manager may have to pay up an eighth or a quarter of a point to transact. The market impact of buying 308 S&P 500 futures contracts can be expected to be less because of the greater relative liquidity currently observable in the futures markets and because of the commonality of that single contract, the S&P 500 future. The purchase of 308 contracts is likely to occur at or near the current market price.

Transaction Time. A third execution cost is *time*. It can take time to buy $40 million of stock, especially if market impact is considered large. During that time, strategic opportunity may erode and the portfolio may be at an investment risk level different from the one that was targeted. Given the relatively greater liquidity of the futures market, it would take less time to purchase futures contracts than to buy the stock outright.

Disruption. The fourth important cost, and perhaps the least observable of all, is the *cost of disruption*. If the first execution method of actually buying common stock is chosen, the $40 million must be obtained by reallocating funds from various sources. Perhaps it will come from a portfolio run by another manager or from a balanced portfolio. A large transfer from one source to another will cause significant overall portfolio imbalance for some time period, during which the judgments of the investment managers will not be reflected accurately. The result could be the loss of at least a portion of the incremental return expected from undertaking the asset allocation change. Execution using futures does not require the movement of funds of such magnitude. The margin deposit required for futures typically is much less than the amount of funds involved in the purchase of the actual

TABLE 11-6. Asset Allocation Application of Treasury Bond and S&P 500 Futures Contracts

Fund size = $400 million

Asset	Actual Mix	Target Mix	Net Change
Stocks	60% ($240 million)	50% ($200 million)	−$40 million
Bonds	40% ($160 million)	50% ($200 million)	+$40 million

Action to be taken:
  Sell 308 S&P 500 futures contracts
  Buy 444 Treasury bond futures contracts

instrument. Potential disruption and the loss of incremental return is accordingly minimized.

The four costs just described may be significant drains on portfolio performance. Futures offer an alternative for strategy execution and cost minimization. This topic is covered in more detail in Chapter 12.

Example of an Asset Mix Change With Futures. Table 11-6 presents an example of how futures are used to execute an asset allocation decision. Assume that the manager of a large portfolio wishes to change the stock/bond mix to reflect new investment judgments. Assume that the mix of this $400 million portfolio or pension fund is 60 percent in stocks, or $240 million, and 40 percent in bonds, or $160 million. Assume also that the manager's judgment calls for lowering stock exposure and raising bond exposure by 10 percent of total value, or $40 million, in each asset category. To achieve the new target of 50 percent in stocks and 50 percent in bonds, $40 million of stocks has to be sold and $40 million of bonds has to be bought.

There are two ways of executing this strategy. The traditional way would be to sell $40 million in stocks and buy $40 million in bonds. The alternative would be to use futures. A portfolio manager could sell the equivalent of $40 million of stock exposure by selling stock index futures and buy the equivalent of $40 million of bond exposure by purchasing Treasury bond futures. If it is assumed that one stock index future is equivalent to $130,000 of stock exposure and one Treasury bond future is equivalent to $90,000 of bond exposure, these actions would involve the sale of 308 S&P 500 futures contracts and the purchase of 444 Treasury bond futures contracts.

In addition to the advantages of lower transaction costs, quicker execution, and minimal portfolio disruption, the asset mix can be altered using less money because of the leveraged nature of a futures contract. Assume that the manager of a $400 million fund may alter the stock/bond mix within a 10 percent range around some long-term normal mix, such as a 60/40 mix. Asset allocation changes of this degree could be accomplished, using the futures approach, with approximately $8 to $10 million of cash for margin requirements, whereas $80 million would be required to buy and sell the stocks and bonds. With this approach, more funds remain available to the specific security selectors to generate superior returns.

There has been considerable discussion of how much incremental portfolio return is generated through tactical asset allocation. Much of the skepticism about the value of tactical asset allocation is based on some studies that have shown that actual incremental portfolio returns attributed to this type of asset allocation appear to be small or nonexistent. Small returns are mainly the result of an inability to quickly and cheaply execute the tactical asset allocation decision. The utilization of financial futures offers a technique for capturing the maximum benefit from an asset allocation decision and for minimizing its dilution.

Advantages in a Multiple-Manager Environment. The use of financial futures to execute an asset allocation decision is particularly attractive in a multiple-manager structure. A common investment structure used in medium- to large-size pension funds involves the hiring of a number of external money managers, each specializing in either stocks or bonds. As a result, the asset allocation of the fund commonly is the sum of the individual pieces. Often control of the stock/bond mix on the aggregate level is not attempted, because controlling the actual mix is difficult. Traditionally, the methods used to control the stock/bond mix on the aggregate level have involved either redirecting the contributions flow to the appropriate managers—a very time-consuming process—or reallocating funds from one set of managers to another. Reallocating funds can be both time-consuming and disruptive to the managers involved.

In a multiple-manager environment, using financial futures to achieve the target stock/bond mix on the aggregate level avoids this loss of time and portfolio disruption. The individual investment managers specializing in their markets or market subgroups need not even know that the futures activity is occurring. The aggregate fund can gain incremental return by benefiting from both the alpha or superior-return judgments of the investment managers on individual stocks and the asset allocation decision concerning stocks and bonds made at the aggregate level.

Country Allocation in International Portfolios

The technique of using futures contracts to implement asset allocation decisions may also be applied to the decision to change country weightings in an international portfolio. The growth of futures contracts on international stock markets in the 1980s has allowed the use of this technique in international portfolios. Many of the major stock markets around the world have

TABLE 11-7. Country Allocation Application of S&P 500 and Japanese Nikkei 225 Index Futures Contracts

Fund size: U.S.$60 million
Exchange rate: ¥1 = U.S.$0.0067
S&P 500: 260
Nikkei 225 Index: 30,000

Stocks	Actual Mix	Target Mix	Net Change
United States	50% ($30 million)	60% ($36 million)	+$6 million
Japan (U.S.$)	50% ($30 million)	40% ($24 million)	−$6 million
(¥)	(¥4.5 billion)	(¥3.6 billion)	−¥900 million

Action to be taken:
  Buy 46 S&P 500 futures contracts
  Sell 600 Nikkei 225 Index futures contracts

futures contracts that apply to their major price indexes and more have been proposed by local regulatory authorities. New exchanges for the trading of these instruments have also been proposed.

One of the early stock index futures on a non-U.S. stock market was the Nikkei 225 index futures. The Nikkei index, traded on the Singapore International Monetary Exchange, is a measure of the price activity of the Japanese stock market. Table 11-7 provides an example of using two very popular stock index futures, the S&P 500 and the Nikkei 225, to implement a country allocation decision in an international portfolio.

Assume that a fund totals $60 million in assets in U.S. dollars. Also assume that the portfolio currently has representation in two markets, the U.S. stock market and the Japanese stock market, and that the current mix is 50 percent, or $30 million, invested in U.S. stocks and 50 percent invested in the Japanese stock market. At an assumed exchange rate of ¥1 equaling $0.0067 (or ¥150 to $1), $30 million of Japanese exposure equates to ¥4.5 billion.

Assume that investment judgment calls for an increase in the weighting of U.S. stocks to 60 percent, or $36 million, and a decrease in the weighting in the Japanese stocks to 40 percent, or $24 million. Such a move would result in a reduction in Japanese exposure from ¥4.5 billion to ¥3.6 billion. To accomplish this new target country allocation, the investment manager must increase U.S. stocks by $6 million and decrease Japanese stock exposure by $6 million, which in local currency would be equivalent to selling ¥900 million at the assumed exchange rate. This desired strategic change in the portfolio can be implemented by buying $6 million exposure of S&P 500 futures contracts and selling $6 million exposure of the Nikkei 225 index futures contracts. If the S&P 500 were at 260, this would call for buying 46 S&P 500 futures contracts. With a currency exchange rate of ¥1 equal to

$0.0067 and the Nikkei 225 at 30,000, then the Japanese stock exposure can be reduced by ¥900 million by selling 60 Nikkei 225 futures contracts. The market value equivalent of the Nikkei 225 future is similar in specification to the S&P 500 future in that one Nikkei 225 future is equivalent to 500 times the index value of the Nikkei 225, in this case 500 times 30,000, or ¥15 million. At this equivalent market value, 60 Nikkei 225 futures contracts are equivalent to ¥900 million of Japanese stock market exposure.

All of the advantages of using futures contracts for asset allocation are valid for this international portfolio. As the scope of capital markets becomes more global, futures markets will continue to be created and continue to grow to satisfy the demands of portfolio managers, who can use them to implement investment decisions in a timely, cost-effective manner.

Options in Asset Allocation

Options contracts help to structure the optimal asset mix for a portfolio. The discussions in Chapter 7 indicate the importance of the interaction of capital market expectations, along with their implications for expected returns and risk, with the risk tolerance, or utility function, of the portfolio owner or the client in determining the appropriate asset allocation. Much of the analysis applied to asset allocation requires willingness to accept a key simplifying assumption, which is that investors or portfolio owners have a utility function or risk preference function based solely on the mean or expected return and the variance (or its square root, the standard deviation) of the return distribution. The expected return is viewed as having positive utility, while variance is viewed as having negative utility. A greater variance indicates more portfolio risk and, other considerations aside, diminishes utility to the investor. However, restricting an investor's utility function to mean and variance underpinnings implies that insurance, or the skewness of a risk profile, has no value. But as the discussion of portfolio insurance strategies in asset allocation in Chapter 7 indicates, the ability to reshape return distributions can be extremely valuable to some investors.

Skewness Preference Strategies. With the frequent introduction and rapid growth of options contracts, it is becoming increasingly common to find fund sponsors who invest a fraction of their assets in option instruments. Incorporating options contracts into a portfolio changes the underlying return distribution of the portfolio. As has been previously demonstrated, the resulting portfolio will have a sharply changed distribution skewness, or risk profile. Managers employ three main strategies in which skewness preference plays a role in portfolio selection.

Writing Call Options. Some fund managers prefer to write call options against the underlying stocks in their portfolios, which has the effect of modestly increasing the portfolio's return when the stock returns are flat or negative and limiting it when the stock returns are up sharply. This strategy limits the portfolio's upside potential and is indicative of either an irrational lack of preference for positive skewness or, more likely, a strong probabilistic belief that returns will be flat or negative.

Buying Protective Put Options. A second strategy is to buy put options on the underlying stocks in a portfolio to protect the portfolio against large negative stock returns. The puts reduce return when the stock returns are flat or increasing, but they protect the portfolio against large losses. This strategy is an indication of a preference for positive skewness and is compatible with rational investor risk aversion.

Buying Bills and Call Options. A third strategy, similar in effect to the protective put strategy, is to invest a large portion of the portfolio, typically 90 percent, in Treasury bills and to purchase call options with the remaining 10 percent. This strategy gives the investor upside potential if stocks perform well while sharply reducing downside exposure if stocks decline significantly. Use of this strategy is also an indication of a preference for positive skewness. The objective of this strategy, at a minimum, is to earn the risk-free return less the cost of the calls while maintaining the potential for large returns if the stock market does well. The size of those returns will be determined by such factors as the beta of the underlying stocks, whether in-, at-, or out-of-the-money calls are used, and the exact percentage split of the portfolio between calls and bills.

Example of an Asset Mix Change With Options. Buying or selling risk insurance or modifying the risk profile of a portfolio with options is an attractive portfolio management technique. Table 11-8 and Figures 11-13 and 11-14 demonstrate how including stock options in a multiasset portfolio effectively alters the portfolio's asset allocation and changes the return distribution to match more closely a fund sponsor's desired risk profile.

Assume that a fund sponsor must choose an optimal portfolio from the following five asset classes: U.S. stocks, U.S. long-term corporate bonds, equity real estate, non-U.S. stocks, and Treasury bills. Also assume that the sponsor prefers a more positively skewed distribution than any combination of these assets allows. By adding a portfolio of 30 purchased call options to the list of asset classes, a more positively skewed return distribution, or risk profile, can be achieved in this multiasset portfolio. The first step is to determine the fund sponsor's optimal portfolio from all combinations of the five basic asset classes.

An efficient frontier of optimal portfolios, including all asset groups except the options portfolio, can be derived. Table 11-8 presents the asset

TABLE 11-8. Capital Market Assumptions About Five Major Asset Classes

Asset Class	Expected Annual Return	Portfolio Representation Upper Bound	Annual Standard Deviation
U.S. equities	16.0%	100%	20.0%
U.S. corporate bonds	11.8	100	10.0
Real estate	13.5	20	12.0
International equities	16.5	15	21.0
Treasury bills	10.0	100	0.0

Correlation Matrix

Asset Class	U.S. Equities	Corporate Bonds	Real Estate	International Equities	U.S. Treasury Bills
U.S. equities	1.0				
U.S. corporate bonds	0.4	1.0			
Real estate	0.1	0.4	1.0		
International equities	0.65	0.1	0.2	1.0	
Treasury bills	0.0	0.0	0.0	0.0	1.0

SOURCE: Nadbielny and Dunford [1984].

class assumptions used for the purpose of this example. The top part of the table lists the annual expected return on each of the five asset classes, the upper bound of the asset class representation in the portfolio, and the annual standard deviation of the expected return. The bottom half of the table presents the correlation matrix for the five asset classes.

Following the analytical techniques discussed in Chapter 7, the efficient frontier of portfolios across the risk/variance spectrum can be derived. Assume that the fund sponsor chooses the optimal portfolio at the plan's desired risk or variance level, producing an investment mix composed of 42 percent U.S. equities, 23 percent U.S. corporate bonds, 20 percent equity real estate, 15 percent international equities, and no cash.

Figure 11-13 displays the probability distribution of expected returns on the five-asset-class portfolio (called Portfolio A) for a one-year holding period. The probability distribution is based on a simulation involving 1,000 trials. The return distribution for the fund sponsor's optimal portfolio is approximately symmetrical around the annual expected return of 14.6 percent, with a standard deviation of 12.4 percent.

Adding 30 purchased call options to this portfolio alters the risk profile and obtains the desired positive skewness by redirecting a portion of the portfolio's funds out of the five-asset-class optimal mix, in proportion to their original weightings, and into the calls. Assume that the calls are all at the money, with six months to maturity, and are priced at fair value. They are all equally weighted and held to maturity.

Figure 11-14 displays the probability distribution, or risk profile, of a

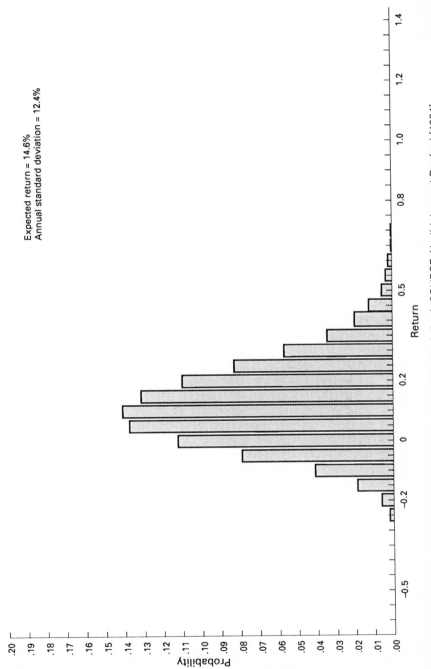

Figure 11-13. Probability Distribution of Returns on 100% Portfolio A. SOURCE: Nadbielny and Dunford [1984].

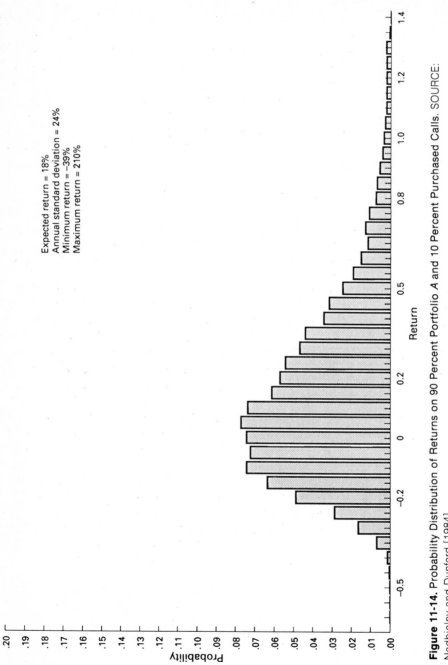

Expected return = 18%
Annual standard deviation = 24%
Minimum return = –39%
Maximum return = 210%

Figure 11-14. Probability Distribution of Returns on 90 Percent Portfolio A and 10 Percent Purchased Calls. SOURCE: Nadbielny and Dunford [1984].

new portfolio comprising 90 percent of the five-asset-class optimal portfolio, all with their original *relative* weightings, and 10 percent invested in the purchased call option portfolio. The resulting probability distribution, derived from 1,000 simulations, displays a marked positive skewness. The expected return of this multiasset portfolio containing call options is 18 percent, with a standard deviation of 24.1 percent. Both of these parameters are considerably higher than the former optimal portfolio of five asset classes because of the higher risk nature of the call options. For the 1,000 simulations, however, the minimum return achieved was a loss of approximately 39 percent, while the maximum return was a gain of 210 percent on the portfolio over the one-year period.

The probability distribution is no longer symmetrical around the expected return. The addition of call options to the portfolio containing multiasset classes can alter the risk profile to fit more closely the fund sponsor's desired risk tolerance, measured now in three, rather than two, key dimensions.

In summary, both futures and options contracts can play an important role in asset allocation. Futures contracts offer a means to execute a portfolio asset allocation decision in a timely, cost-effective manner, with the result that more of the potential benefits than can be derived from the asset allocation decision can actually be achieved. Through their insurance characteristics, options contracts offer a way to alter the risk profile of a multiasset portfolio so that it reflects more closely an enhanced and enriched definition of the desired risk patterns of the portfolio owner or plan sponsor.

DERIVATIVE INSTRUMENTS IN EQUITY PORTFOLIO MANAGEMENT

There are a number of ways that futures or options can be used to control risk, minimize costs, or add incremental return in managing common stock portfolios. While some techniques, such as hedging timing differences, are generally applicable to all equity managers, others are used primarily by either passive (or index fund), active, or semiactive managers (such as completeness fund managers), as discussed in Chapter 9.

General Equity Portfolio Management

A few activities of equity portfolio managers, such as deposits and withdrawals, are generally of concern to all managers. Deposits and withdrawals may occur in any portfolio at any time. Futures and options can play very important roles in these primary portfolio activities. A cash contribution or a large deposit is a common occurrence in equity portfolio management.

Buying additional common stock with a sudden, large cash inflow may take time—time during which the portfolio is exposed to significant market moves. For example, any portfolios that were started with cash in the last quarter of 1982 or early in the first half of 1983 most likely underperformed the market, perhaps significantly, because in the rising market it took time to invest the entire cash contribution. Stock index futures offer an attractive alternative.

Hedging a Cash Contribution. As an example of utilizing stock index futures to hedge a large deposit into an equity portfolio, assume that on Day 1 there is a $50 million deposit to the portfolio. This deposit could immediately be invested in the stock market. The desired stock market exposure could be achieved by buying $50 million worth of futures contracts with the initial margin deposit, with the balance of the $50 million above that deposit invested in cash equivalents. If you assume that the S&P 500 is selling at 260, then one S&P 500 futures contract is equivalent to $130,000 of common stock exposure (260 × $500 = $130,000). Buying $50 million worth of stock market exposure could be accomplished by buying 385 contracts. These contracts may then be sold off as desired individual issues are purchased for the portfolio.

Assume, as in the preceding example, that such stock purchases occur evenly over a 10-day period from Day 2 through Day 11. *On each of these days*, a portfolio manager buys $5 million worth of attractive stocks and sells one-tenth of the futures contract position, or approximately 39 contracts. The desired stock market exposure of the portfolio is maintained at all times. The important point illustrated in this application is that futures offer a significant means to control the risk level of a portfolio and reduce exposure to unintended risks and unintended investment judgments. For example, the manager's investment strategy may have been to be 95 percent invested in stocks over a certain time period. Because of the large deposit and the time it might have taken to invest it in attractive stocks, the portfolio might actually have been only 80 percent invested. An important penalty to incremental return would have been incurred that could have been avoided through using futures contracts.

Hedging a Cash Withdrawal. Futures contracts can also be used to manage portfolio withdrawals, although in the opposite way. Assume that 11 days from now a portfolio will have a large withdrawal of $50 million demanded in cash. In portfolio management, the traditional way to accommodate this large cash withdrawal is to gradually sell $50 million worth of stocks over 10 days and to fund the $50 million withdrawal on Day 11. If the stock sales occur evenly over the 10-day sale period, then for that 10-day period the portfolio will have, on average, a $25 million cash position, a position that may cause the portfolio's risk exposure to be significantly less than intended. In a period of a rising market, the portfolio would incur a penalty to incremental return because of this unintended risk posture.

Here is a numerical example of the use of stock index futures to hedge the risks of a large portfolio withdrawal. Assume that on Day 11 there will be a $50 million withdrawal from the portfolio. Again, assume that one S&P 500 futures contract is equivalent to $130,000 of stock market exposure and that $50 million in market value is equivalent to 385 futures contracts. The desired risk, or market exposure, level of the portfolio can be maintained and stock disruption can be minimized by evenly selling $50 million in stocks over a 10-day period from Day 1 through Day 10. On each of these days, a portfolio manager sells $5 million worth of the least attractive stocks and buys one-tenth of the total futures contract position, or approximately 39 contracts. By the end of Day 10, $50 million in cash has been raised through the sale of stocks, while the portfolio maintains $50 million of common stock exposure by owning 385 contracts. On Day 11, the withdrawal of $50 million in cash can occur and the futures contracts can immediately be sold. Portfolio risk, or market exposure, has been controlled at the desired level by using stock index futures to facilitate the withdrawal.

An alternative method of using futures to manage a portfolio withdrawal involves selling 385 contracts on Day 1 and then selling the stock and buying back the futures on Days 2 through 11. While this method of managing withdrawals may appear attractive, the desired risk level of the portfolio is not in fact maintained. This approach immediately reduces portfolio risk below desired levels on Day 1 by reducing stock exposure by $50 million.

Stock index futures can be purchased when the timing and amount of net future portfolio contributions or deposits can be accurately estimated. Such a purchase is known as a *long hedge*. A hedge in which stock index futures are gradually purchased as stocks are sold and then liquidated on the day of withdrawal could be used when future cash withdrawals are predictable.

Options Hedges for Contributions and Withdrawals. Options contracts can also be used to hedge the portfolio risks of deposits and withdrawals. In the case of a $50 million deposit in a portfolio, a portfolio manager could buy $50 million of stock market exposure by buying call options instead of buying $50 million of equivalent market exposure with stock index futures. Assume that the S&P 500 is selling at 260 and assume that an in-the-money call option on the S&P 500 index futures contract has a strike price of 255, with a call premium of $6. Assume that this in-the-money call option will move point-for-point with the S&P 500. One call option at an index price of 260 will be the equivalent of $130,000 of stock market exposure (260 × $500 = $130,000). The cost of this call option is the premium of $3,000 (6 × $500 = $3,000). To hedge the $50 million deposit immediately, 385 options contracts could be bought with funds from the portfolio. The cost of these contracts would be $1,155,000 (385 × $3,000 = $1,155,000). As in the futures examples, these call option contracts could be sold when attractive stocks are identified and actually purchased. The desired risk exposure to the market is maintained.

Passive Equity Portfolio Management

The applications of futures contracts and options contracts in passively managed portfolios or index funds are limited because of the emphasis on full equity diversification, minimal portfolio activity, and minimal use of investment judgment or expectational inputs. However, these contracts do have some important uses.

Offsetting Cash Inflows. Cash inflows into an equity index fund cause specific portfolio problems. Because the goal of an index fund is to match as closely as possible the return on the index over every time period, any amount of cash held in the portfolio will cause greater tracking error of the index fund versus the index.

Stock index futures can be used to minimize this risk. As cash inflows or common stock dividends are accumulated in a portfolio, an equivalent amount of stock index futures can be purchased. This process continues until enough cash is accumulated so that the index fund can be rebalanced with minimal transaction costs. During the rebalancing, the equivalent amount of stock index futures can be sold. Cash inflows are a problem or risk common to the management of all index funds. Utilizing stock index futures helps to hedge this risk.

Utilizing options contracts can also be helpful when rebalancing an index fund. An index fund can move out of balance in terms of individual stock representation or subgroup representation when either a cash rebalancing is less than perfect or a deposit into an index fund is made in stock instead of in cash. When an individual stock, such as IBM, or an industry or subgroup, such as the oil and gas industry, is overweighted in an index fund relative to the benchmark index, then call options on IBM stock or on the oil and gas subgroup index can be sold in the proper numbers as an alternative to selling actual securities. The call options can then be repurchased as the underlying securities are sold. Should futures on market subgroups become available, they could similarly be used to rebalance a subgroup overweighting or underweighting.

Enhanced Index Fund Construction. Stock index futures may be used to construct an enhanced index fund. These funds have a risk level similar to the index, with the potential for positive incremental return. A numerical example illustrates the construction mechanics. Assume that a client wishes to structure an index fund of $100 million and that the current price of the S&P 500 is 260. Each contract is therefore equivalent to a common stock exposure of $130,000 (260 × $500 = $130,000). To gain the equivalent exposure of $100 million in common stocks, one could easily and quickly purchase 769 S&P 500 futures contracts, or $100 million divided by $130,000.

There are many advantages to such an approach. The benefits of lower transaction costs have been mentioned. The low commission rate on futures trades and the high level of liquidity in the futures market offer the potential for significant cost savings. Portfolio construction via futures contracts offers the advantage of actually buying the index. When index futures are purchased, a manager also purchases exposure to all 500 stocks in the index. The exposure is weighted by each stock's market value relative to the aggregate market value of all 500 stocks. Also, because buying a futures contract is equivalent to buying the index at all points in time, the portfolio is no longer exposed to changes in the names of the 500 stocks included in the index. The change in the composition of the S&P 500 because of the AT&T breakup illustrates that such changes may be significant. Another important advantage is that, because the futures approach does not involve the receipt of dividends, periodic rebalancing of the index fund to adjust for cash dividends is not required. Dividends are already priced within the futures contract. A fourth advantage is that maintenance of portfolio flexibility favors the creative investing of the cash equivalents for a rate of return higher than that from Treasury bills or the equivalent.

Mispricing Strategies. An index fund can also be constructed with stock index futures contracts to take advantage of the misvaluation of futures contracts. An index fund of stocks can be actively arbitraged with an equivalent number of stock index futures, depending on the undervaluation or overvaluation of the futures contract, because the price of the future must converge to the index price at expiration. When the futures contracts are undervalued, the index fund can be constructed with cash equivalents and futures. When the futures contracts are overvalued, the cash and futures can be swapped into the underlying stock index fund. The result should be a portfolio with a risk or volatility equivalent to the S&P 500 and a return somewhat higher than the S&P 500 over time, depending on the frequency and magnitude of mispricing.

In addition to the uses already discussed, options contracts may also be used in an index fund portfolio through the selling of call options against individual securities or groups of securities when the call option is believed to be overpriced. While some upside movement of the stock index fund could be truncated, the increased portfolio income from the sale of misvalued call options most likely will lead to an incremental return above the S&P 500 over the long term.

TABLE 11-9. Beta Control Application of Stock Index Futures

Portfolio size	$20 million
Portfolio target beta	1.2
Stock-only beta	1.1
Stock/cash ratio	95:5
Contracts purchased	31

Active Equity Portfolio Management

Actively managed equity portfolios can also benefit from the strategic use of futures and options contracts to hedge the risk of deposits and withdrawals. In actively managed portfolios, the use of futures and options contracts can be split between applications that manage systematic risk and applications that impact unsystematic risk.

Control of Systematic Risk. Investment managers in general and market timers in particular can use stock index futures and options on index futures to control a portfolio's beta level or systematic risk exposure level. For example, assume that a portfolio manager has a positive outlook for the stock market and wishes to raise the exposure of the portfolio to the market by raising the portfolio's beta.

Table 11-9 illustrates alternative methods of implementing the strategic systematic risk decision. Assume that the manager has a $20 million portfolio with a target beta of 1.2. Assume also that the beta of the present stock component is 1.1. Stocks currently represent 95 percent of the portfolio, with the remaining 5 percent being in cash. One way to move the portfolio to the beta target of 1.2 is to sell a number of the lower-beta stocks and buy an equivalent amount of higher-beta stocks. This procedure maintains the stocks at 95 percent of the portfolio but raises the beta of the stock portion of the portfolio to about 1.25. The result would be a portfolio with an overall beta of 1.2. Implementation by this method could be a long and costly process, and significant turnover would be likely. The alternative approach is to raise the beta by buying an appropriate number of stock index futures. Assuming that one S&P 500 futures contract is equivalent to $130,000 of underlying market exposure, one would need to purchase only 31 futures contracts. The appropriate number of futures to purchase is calculated in the following equation:

$$\$19 \text{ million} \times 1.1 + \$130,000 \times \text{Number of index contracts} = \$20 \text{ million} \times 1.2$$

In these circumstances, the advantages of controlling beta by using stock index futures are the following:

1. The target beta of 1.2 could be achieved almost immediately, and the portfolio would then be constructed to reflect the desired investment judgments.
2. The transaction costs would be considerably lower, in part because turnover could be very high in trading the lower-beta stocks for the higher-beta stocks.
3. The optimal stock mix would be maintained.

This last advantage is extremely important. Presumably the stock component with the beta of 1.1 represents the optimal mix of stocks—the one with the highest alpha or superior return potential. By selling low-beta stocks and buying high-beta stocks, the portfolio manager most likely is adding stocks with lower alpha expectations to the portfolio. The manager may be reducing the expected alpha of the stock component and giving up the potential incremental return from the stock selection judgments. This loss of incremental return is avoided by achieving the portfolio target beta through buying S&P 500 futures.

Stock index futures can also be used to eliminate completely the systematic risk of a portfolio. The example illustrated in Table 11-9 presents a $20 million portfolio that is 95 percent invested in stocks and 5 percent invested in cash. The beta of the stock component is 1.1. The beta of the portfolio could be reduced to zero by selling 161 S&P 500 futures contracts, using the same pricing assumptions. The appropriate number of contracts is derived by using the following equation:

$$\$19 \text{ million} \times 1.1 - \$130,000 \times \text{Number of index contracts} = \$20 \text{ million} \times 0$$

Through the selling of 161 futures contracts, systematic risk has been reduced to zero. The unsystematic risk of the stock component remains untouched. The reward expected for incurring this unsystematic risk, portfolio alpha, remains intact. The resulting portfolio would then exhibit an expected return of the expected risk-free rate plus the expected alpha return on the stocks. Such a strategic application of futures contracts might be appropriate for an investment manager who wishes to emphasize stock selection capabilities while minimizing any impact from systematic return.

Control of Unsystematic Risk. Because futures on stocks are only available on indexes or on systematic risk proxies, options contracts are the only instruments available that can be used to manage unsystematic risk in an actively managed equity portfolio. Unsystematic risk in a portfolio is composed of the risk of group or industry movement plus the risk of variability of individual stocks. Investment managers who are group rotators could use market subgroup index options to hedge against, or lower the risk of, unexpected adverse sector or industry movements and decrease unsys-

TABLE 11-10. Subindex Options as a Strategy Tool to Alter Portfolio Unsystematic Risk

Portfolio size	$100 million
Oil and gas industry holdings	$12 million (12%)
Oil and gas index	100
Oil and gas put option price	$5
Oil and gas put option value	$10,000

Goal: Reduce oil and gas industry exposure by $6 million.
Strategy: Buy 600 put options.

tematic risk exposure. These managers could also leverage or increase exposure to an expected positive sector price movement.

Table 11-10 presents an example of this application of options contracts. Assume that an investment manager is managing a portfolio of $100 million that has an exposure in the oil and gas industry of $12 million, or 12 percent of the portfolio. Assume also that the investment manager likes the oil companies that are held in the portfolio on a specific company-by-company basis, but he does not want such a high portfolio exposure to the oil and gas industry overall. Assume that an oil and gas subgroup in-the-money put option is selling at a price of $5 and that each option is equivalent to a market value or exposure in that subgroup of $10,000. If the investment manager wished to reduce the portfolio oil and gas industry exposure by half, he could buy $6 million worth of oil and gas subgroup put options, or 600 contracts, with funds from the portfolio. In this example, using options contracts offers the unique ability to maintain the portfolio's exposure to the desired specific risk of the individual oil companies while reducing and controlling the risk of the oil companies as a group. The maximum cost in terms of return reduction would be the cost of the put option.

Finally, options on individual stocks can be used to control a portfolio's exposure to the unsystematic risk of individual stock holdings. Table 11-11 presents an example of this application. Again assume that a portfolio man-

TABLE 11-11. Options on Individual Stocks as a Strategy Tool to Alter Portfolio Unsystematic Risk

Portfolio size	$100 million
Desired position in *XYZ* stock	$5 million (5%)
XYZ stock price	$50
XYZ call option price	$6
Call option value	$5,000

Goal: Purchase a $5 million exposure in *XYZ* stock
Strategy: Buy 1,000 call options on *XYZ* stock

ager is managing a $100 million portfolio. Assume also that the manager wants a $5 million position in an attractive $50 stock. If portfolio cash is not available to buy that stock, an equivalent $5 million position can be constructed by buying an appropriate number of calls. Assume that the call option on stock *XYZ* has a strike price of $45 with a premium of $6, and assume also that the in-the-money call option will move point for point with the stock. If each call option is equivalent to 100 shares of stock, then each call option is equivalent to $5,000 of equivalent exposure in the stock of company *XYZ*. To obtain a 5 percent, or $5 million, portfolio position, 1,000 calls have to be bought. At a premium of $6 per call, this can be done for $600,000. This position can be established immediately by buying call options with portfolio funds. The call options can be sold as cash is generated in the portfolio and the shares of stock *A* are actually purchased. This example also models a way to hedge timing differences with individual stock options.

Altering Risk Exposure

Pension fund managers and institutional asset holders are increasingly investing a greater proportion of their assets in foreign stocks and bonds. The increasing globalization of the world economies, the increasing communications between the capital markets around the world, and the rapid growth of foreign capital markets—including stocks, bonds, futures, and options— are creating an environment that favors increased investment in these types of securities by U.S. asset holders.

A portfolio investment in international securities presents the risk of currency fluctuations. The return in U.S. dollars to a U.S. based asset holder of international equities or bonds is the return of those equities or bonds in the local currency after adjusting for any currency gains or losses incurred over the time period. Over the short term, currency fluctuations can greatly add to or detract from the overall investment return on the portfolio. Portfolio managers are increasingly making active judgments on currency, judgments that involve the identification of undervalued and overvalued currencies.

If a portfolio manager believes that the currency in which a portfolio has invested is overvalued, then the traditional approach has been to sell those securities and not to accept the currency risk. However, doing so may involve giving up some fairly attractive returns generated in local currency terms.

An alternative method of controlling currency exposure in an international equity portfolio is to use currency futures. A number of currency futures are traded in the U.S. markets, primarily in the International Monetary Market (IMM) on the Chicago Mercantile Exchange.

Table 11-12 provides an example of how currency futures may be ef-

TABLE 11-12. Currency Futures as a Strategy Tool to Alter Portfolio Currency Exposure

Changing currency exposure

£1 = $1.80	Can$1 = U.S.$0.80

U.S. portfolio size	$20 million
Current currency exposure	U.S.$, 30%; Can$, 30%; £, 40%
Target currency exposure	U.S.$, 30%; Can$, 45%; £, 25%

Buy 38 Canadian dollar futures (IMM)
Sell 67 British pound futures (IMM)

fectively used to alter the currency exposure of an international equity portfolio to reflect active currency judgments on the part of portfolio managers. Assume that a portfolio of equities is composed of U.S.$20 million and that the mixture of actual equities held results in a 30 percent exposure to the U.S. dollar, a 30 percent exposure to the Canadian dollar, and a 40 percent exposure to the British pound. Also assume that the investment manager has an active relative valuation judgment on these currencies. This judgment is that the Canadian dollar is undervalued, while the British pound is overvalued and will decline over the near to intermediate term. Thus the portfolio manager wishes to move the currency exposure of the portfolio to a target exposure of 30 percent in the U.S. dollar, 45 percent in the Canadian dollar, and 25 percent in the British pound. The manager therefore wishes to increase exposure in the Canadian dollar by 15 percent and decrease exposure in the British pound by 15 percent.

The traditional approach would be to sell British securities and buy Canadian securities, a process that could take time and result in considerable transaction costs. An alternative is to implement the decision through the use of currency futures. Assume that the pound is currently equivalent to U.S.$1.80 and that the British pound futures contract on the IMM is equivalent to £25,000 of exposure. Therefore, at an exchange rate of U.S.$1.80 equals £1, the contract is equivalent to $44,000 worth of U.S. currency exposure. Selling one British pound future would be equivalent to selling U.S.$44,000 worth of British pound exposure.

The Canadian dollar future on the IMM is equivalent to Can$100,000 in terms of contract size. At an exchange rate of Can$1.00 equals U.S.$0.80, each Canadian dollar future is equivalent to U.S.$80,000. Buying one Canadian future in a portfolio is equivalent to increasing the exposure in the Canadian dollar by U.S.$80,000.

To achieve the target currency exposure, the manager wishes to increase Canadian dollar exposure by 15 percent, or U.S.$3 million, and to decrease British pound exposure by 15 percent, or U.S.$3 million. This can be achieved by buying 38 Canadian dollar futures, or U.S.$3 million divided by U.S.$80,000 per contract, and by selling 67 British pound futures contracts, or U.S.$3 million divided by U.S.$44,000 per British pound futures contract. The currency exposure in the portfolio will immediately be shifted to the target of 30 percent U.S. dollar, 45 percent Canadian dollar, and 25 percent British pound.

The advantage of using the currency futures approach is threefold:

1. The disruption in the portfolio is minimized because the potential heavy selling and buying of securities is avoided.
2. Transaction costs are lower, which is particularly significant because the transaction costs observed on a number of overseas exchanges are considerably higher than those observed in the United States.
3. The attractive stocks held by the manager in the overseas markets are maintained.

This last advantage is particularly important. Those stocks that are viewed as having high alpha potential within their respective markets are maintained in the portfolio, and the return of the portfolio can be expected to benefit accordingly.

The market for currency options is also fairly liquid. This same change in currency exposure could be accomplished through the purchase of Canadian dollar call option contracts and the sale of British pound call option contracts. This could effectively be accomplished by transacting in well-in-the-money call options. The effect on the portfolio would be virtually the same, but with some risk skewness characteristics.

Active/Passive Equity Portfolio Management

The applications of stock futures contracts and stock options contracts in an active/passive portfolio structure are similar to those discussed previously. Within the passive part of the portfolio of such a structure, futures may be used to hedge the risk of deposits and withdrawals. Futures may be used in two additional ways:

1. To construct an enhanced passive part of the portfolio by buying an equivalent amount of futures and creatively investing the cash.
2. To arbitrage the misvaluation of futures by swapping the futures contracts for a portfolio of stocks that is indexed at the appropriate times.

Options contracts can be used within the active part of the portfolio structure to manage and control unsystematic risk in terms of both sector representation and the representation of individual securities. Long or short positions in market subgroup options contracts or options on individual securities can be established to accumulate or liquidate positions quickly and efficiently in the nonpassive or actively managed portion of the equity portfolio.

In Chapter 9, the concept and construction of a semiactive completeness fund was discussed. A completeness fund is constructed by first noting and accumulating the positions of the various active stock managers. Sector and within-sector industry underweightings are observed. The completeness fund is then constructed to adjust the weightings of those sectors or industries that are either underweighted or overweighted in the active portfolios to their appropriate weightings in the overall market index. A situation may occur in which an active investment manager specializing in one sector or industry subgroup is replaced by another manager who has a different specialty. For example, if a manager with a constant overweighting in technology stocks is replaced with a manager whose universe and portfolios are dominated by utilities, the overall fund will then be exposed to a systematic underweighting in the technology area. The appropriate representation in the completeness fund to rebalance this underweighting in the technology industry could be implemented quickly and efficiently by buying the appropriate equivalent number of technology subindex call options. The application and the mathematics are similar to the examples given in Tables 11-10 and 11-11.

Creation and Use of Synthetic Equity Securities

Stock index futures and stock options may also be used in portfolios to create synthetic securities or instruments. That is, futures and options may be combined with equity or debt instruments in a number of ways to duplicate or facilitate the duplication of other security types. For example, a noncallable convertible bond may be viewed as a straight bond plus a call option on the stock shares. As the price of the stock increases above conversion parity, the call option becomes in the money and the price of the convertible bond increases. Similar return patterns can be produced and a convertible bond can be synthetically approximated by purchasing any straight bond and an appropriate number of call options on the bond issuer's stock.

Two specific applications of stock index futures contracts highlight the portfolio creation of synthetic securities: the use of futures to synthetically create cash equivalents and the use of futures to facilitate the creation of synthetic put-protected portfolios through a dynamic hedging strategy.

Cash Equivalents. A cash equivalent can be synthetically produced by constructing a fully diversified portfolio of stocks and completely hedging away the systematic risk by selling the appropriate number of stock index

TABLE 11-13. Tax-Advantaged Cash Equivalent

Assumptions:	
Portfolio	$100 million
Expected risk-free rate	10%
Corporate tax rates	34% net income
	70% dividend exclusion
	34% long-term capital gains
Portfolio 1	
$100 million in cash equivalents	
Pretax expected return	10% ($10 million)
After-tax expected return	6.6% ($6.6 million)
Portfolio 2	
$100 million in S&P Index fund hedged with S&P 500 futures	
Yield	4%
Pretax expected return	10% ($10 million)
After-tax expected return	7.552% ($7.552 million)

futures. The resulting pretax expected return of this synthetic cash portfolio should be the expected risk-free of return if the futures are fairly valued when sold. For a taxable entity such as a corporation, this synthetic cash portfolio provides a superior after-tax return as compared to owning cash equivalents outright. Because common stock dividends are a large part of the return on this synthetic cash portfolio, and because dividends are 70 percent excluded for tax purposes, the after-tax returns on the synthetic cash portfolio are superior.

Table 11-13 presents an example of the relative returns achievable from the two cash management strategies over a one-year period. Assume that the expected risk-free rate of return is 10 percent. Portfolio 1, which includes $100 million of cash equivalents, would be expected to earn 10 percent, or $10 million, before taxes. If the corporation is paying taxes at a 34 percent tax rate, then the after-tax return to the corporation is 66 percent of $10 million, or $6.6 million. Portfolio 2 is a $100 million portfolio that is fully invested in an index fund, or a highly diversified group of stocks, and is completely hedged with the sale of futures. The portfolio is assumed to have a dividend yield of 4 percent. Over the one-year period, the portfolio is also expected to generate a total return equal to the risk-free rate of return of 10 percent, or $10 million, of which $4 million is derived from dividend income and $6 million is derived from capital gains, either from the short futures positions or the stock holdings.

If the overly simplified but arithmetically convenient assumptions are made that the tax treatment of the stock capital gains and losses is similar to the treatment of futures gains and losses, and that the capital gain is long-term, then the after-tax return to the corporation of Portfolio 2 is the sum of the capital gains multiplied by one minus the capital gain tax rate, plus the nontaxable dividends received, plus the taxable dividends received multiplied by one minus the corporate tax rate. Because the capital gain is $6 million and the capital gain is taxed at 34 percent, the after-tax capital gain is $6 million × (1 − 0.34) = $3,960,000. If 70 percent of the $4 million in dividends received are excluded from taxation, then the nontaxable dividends are $4 million × 0.70 = $2,800,000. If the remaining 30 percent of the $4 million in dividends is taxed at the corporate tax rate of 34 percent, then the taxable dividends retained are 30% × ($4 million × (1 − 0.34)) = $792,000. The total after-tax expected return for Portfolio 2 is the sum of the three components, or $7,552,000. The after-tax return to a taxable corporation of this synthetic cash instrument using stock index futures is superior.

Because tax laws are constantly being reviewed, portfolio managers should consult the current tax laws to determine the appropriateness and viability of this strategy.

Dynamic Hedging. Stock index futures may also be used to facilitate a dynamic hedging strategy. The dynamic hedging strategy or dynamic portfolio insurance program seeks to synthetically alter the return profile of a stock portfolio to that of a stock with put option portfolio without using actual put option contracts. The return profile of a stock with put option portfolio is shown in Figure 11-12. As in buying put options on a stock portfolio, the objective of dynamic hedging for portfolio insurance is to assure a floor asset value of minimum return without placing a cap on the upside performance.

The discussions accompanying Figures 11-11 and 11-12 indicate that as the aggregate price of a stock portfolio falls, a put option on that stock portfolio will become more in the money to the extent that, for every one point move in the price of the stock portfolio, the price of the put option will move one point in the opposite direction. When the put option is substantially in the money, the stock plus put option portfolio as a whole will be insensitive to changes in the aggregate price of the stocks. The portfolio will effectively be out of stocks and earning the risk-free cash equivalents return. Under these circumstances, the price sensitivity hedge ratio of the stock portfolio plus put option is zero.

As the aggregate price of the stocks increases and the put option moves out of the money, the opposite occurs. For every one point change in the price of the stock-only positions, the price of the put changes very little. The stocks plus put option portfolio essentially moves with changes in the price of the stock holdings and effectively is 100 percent invested in the stocks. Under these circumstances, the price sensitivity hedge ratio of the stock portfolio plus put option is 1.0.

At any point during the life of a dynamic hedging program, the hedge ratio targets depend on the primary inputs to an option valuation model. In particular, these inputs are the time horizon remaining in the program, the

TABLE 11-14. Historical Simulation Data Using Portfolio Insurance, 1970–1986

Time horizon: One year
Minimum return: −5%
One-way transaction cost: 30 basis points

Year	Insured Portfolio	S&P 500	Cash
1970	−1.62%	4.01%	6.76%
1971	10.09	14.31	4.35
1972	15.28	18.77	4.06
1973	−4.85	−14.81	6.96
1974	−5.01	−26.44	9.56
1975	31.77	37.24	6.36
1976	19.62	23.67	5.49
1977	−4.04	−7.32	4.94
1978	2.97	6.55	7.84
1979	17.00	18.52	11.12
1980	29.83	32.34	13.10
1981	−4.01	−5.01	17.18
1982	15.33	21.49	13.10
1983	18.77	22.18	9.12
1984	5.64	6.07	10.49
1985	28.29	31.47	8.10
1986	14.58	18.08	6.75
Cumulative returns	445.16	440.12	299.69
Geometric returns	10.48	10.42	8.49

volatility assumptions of the stock market, the level of interest rates, and the minimum return level desired during the life of the replicated put option.

The dynamic hedging strategy duplicates the return profile of a stock plus put option portfolio by replicating the price sensitivity hedge ratio with stocks and cash. As the aggregate price of a stocks-only position falls, the synthetic put option moves in the money and the ratio falls. Such an effect can be duplicated in a stock and cash portfolio by selling the appropriate proportion of stocks. As the stock component increases in price, the effect is to increase the ratio by buying more stocks. By frequently adjusting the stock and cash proportions to reflect the appropriate put option price sensitivity hedge ratio, the return profile of a stock plus put option portfolio can be synthetically duplicated by a portfolio containing only stocks and cash. An article by Rubinstein and Leland [1981] more fully explains the process of dynamic hedging and the theory behind it.

Simulation of Dynamic Hedging. A historical simulation, conducted with a proprietary option-based computer model, demonstrates the dynamic hedging strategy and its comparative returns. The results of the analysis are presented in Table 11-14. The study, done over the 17-year period from 1970 through 1986, assumed that at the beginning of January each year, a 1-year, moderately out-of-the-money put option was purchased on the S&P 500 through dynamic hedging replication. The strike price of this replicated put option was set to assure a −5 percent minimum return on the dynamically hedged S&P 500 portfolio. The put option valuation model was used to determine target stock/cash proportions. The previous period's standard deviation of the S&P 500 was used as the S&P 500 volatility input. For this analysis, it was assumed that transactions would occur only when a portfolio shift in the S&P 500 proportion of greater than 5 percent was required. Transaction costs were assumed to be 30 basis points on both the buy and sell transactions. The results, summarized in Table 11-14, demonstrate the effect of dynamic hedging. The minimum floor of −5 percent was maintained in each of the 17 years, a fact that is particularly noteworthy in the significant down markets of 1973 and 1974. The insured portfolio did lag in stronger uptrends in the market, demonstrating the cost of the put option.

Over the 17 years, the dynamically hedged insurance portfolio achieved a compound annual return of 10.48 percent, slightly higher than the 10.42 percent return of the S&P 500. This compares with a cash return of 8.5 percent compounded annually over the same period. The insured portfolio outperformed the S&P 500 primarily because the put option was particularly valuable in 1973 and 1974.

Table 11-14 presents one example of one particular put option. For a particular client, the stock plus put option portfolio to be replicated by dynamic hedging may vary. The optimal strategy appropriate for an investor is a function of the investor's time horizon, the desired level of protection, and the cost of the dynamic hedging. By determining these three parameters, the appropriate put option can be specified and hedge ratios can be calculated by noting the time to expiration of the put option (time horizon), the strike price of the option (desired level of protection), an estimate of stock volatility, and the observed level of interest rates. The benefits of the dynamically hedged portfolio can then be viewed in relation to the cost, or put premium, required to design and assure the desired level of protection.

Cost of Dynamic Hedging. A major difference between replicating the stock plus put option through dynamic hedging and actually buying put options on stocks is in the cost, or premium, of the option. The costs of buying put options are known in advance. In dynamic hedging, the cost of the insurance is not known until after the put option has expired. There are four primary determinants of the cost of the insurance:

1. The time horizon
2. The level of interest rates
3. The volatility of the market
4. The minimum desired level of the return

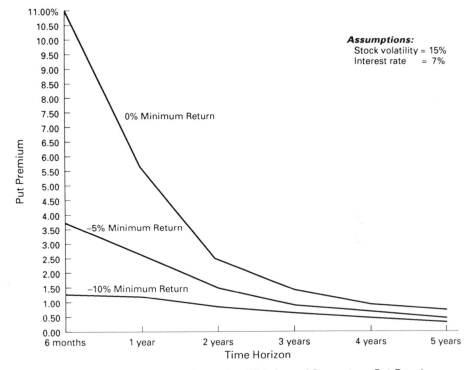

Figure 11-15. Portfolio Insurance Simulation With Annual Percentage Put Premiums Internally Funded.

Three of these—the time horizon, interest rates, and minimum desired level of return—are known with a fair degree of certainty. Only the volatility of the market is uncertain; the level of volatility can be known with certainty only after the fact. It is the prime cause of the variability of the cost of dynamic hedging. A high level of volatility experienced over the life of the dynamic hedging program results in a high cost of insurance, determined by using the dynamic hedging technique. Low volatility results in a low cost of insurance.

When evaluating the dynamic hedging strategy and choosing the appropriate parameters for the put replication, estimates of cost can be made. The premium, or cost, for a specific level of protection in an option strategy can be estimated with a fair value model. The inputs to the model can be estimated and assumed. If this is done, the insurance premium can also be expressed as a percentage loss of upside capture. Using dynamic hedging, the ultimate cost of the insurance can be measured as the difference in the expected return in the underlying portfolio with and without intervention through dynamic hedging portfolio insurance.

Figure 11-15 displays the expected premiums, or costs, of different dynamic hedging strategies viewed over different time horizons, from six months to five years, and at different desired minimum return levels. The top line represents a minimum desired return of zero percent; the middle line represents a minimum return of −5 percent; and the bottom line represents a minimum return of −10 percent. In calculating these put premiums, it was assumed that the volatility of the stock market was 15 percent and interest rates were 7 percent.

As Figure 11-15 shows, the costs are higher over shorter time periods, the shortest being six months. On an *annual basis*, a zero percent minimum-return dynamic hedging strategy for six months would have an expected cost of 11 percent. A −5 percent minimum-return, six-month dynamic hedging strategy would have an annual cost of 3.7 percent, and a minus 10 percent minimum-return, six-month strategy would have a yearly cost of 1.3 percent.

As the time horizon of the program is extended, the annual expected put premiums converge to lower numbers. This type of analysis provides appropriate data for making the investment trade-offs between the desired put option to be replicated and the cost of that put option. An article by Singleton and Grieves [1984] offers a more complete analysis of the costs of synthetic put options, or dynamic hedging.

Dynamic Hedging Implementation. In choosing the appropriate implementation of a dynamic hedging program, three issues should be analyzed. They are:

1. *Filter Rules.* The trade-off between transaction costs and replication accuracy can be viewed in terms of how much the underlying stock portfolio can appreciate or depreciate (the filter size) before a transaction is triggered to move to the new appropriate hedge ratio.

2. *Cash vs. the Futures Markets.* The advantages of using futures contracts to increase or decrease stock market exposure have been listed. At any point a portfolio manager needs to analyze the trade-off between futures mispricing and the savings differential in trading costs and make a judgment about which of the instruments should be used to implement changes in market exposure.

3. *The Use of Listed Options.* An effective way to control costs within dynamic hedging is to use not only cash, stocks, and stock index futures but also listed options. Call options and put options can be blended in proportions that will achieve the target hedge ratio. The primary advantage of using the listed options is that the costs of these options are known in advance. This knowledge provides some protection against costs associated with unforeseen increases in the volatility of the markets.

PROGRAM TRADING TO HEDGE MARKET INEFFICIENCIES

As discussed in Chapter 9, *program trading* is a general term used to describe common stock trading activity in which a basket of stocks is traded at one time to increase or decrease general market exposure or systematic risk. The same approach can be taken in trading fixed-income securities, although it occurs much less frequently.

The term "program trading" generally refers to three types of activities:

1. *Portfolio insurance*, which involves buying or selling stocks or futures to raise or lower stock exposure to implement a dynamic hedge insurance strategy
2. *Index fund management*, which involves buying or selling a basket of securities that represents the systematic risk of the market
3. *Index arbitrage*, which involves hedging market and intermarket pricing inefficiencies and taking advantage of these inefficiencies to add incremental return to a portfolio at minimal risk

Index arbitrage refers to buying or selling index futures and options while simultaneously selling or buying a group of stocks in order to arbitrage price differentials. As an example, the S&P 500 futures contract may be below fair value as indicated by valuation procedures. A portfolio manager could add incremental return by arbitraging this price inefficiency, which could be done by simultaneously buying the S&P 500 futures and selling a basket of stocks with the risk characteristics of the S&P 500. The selected stocks could be either all 500 securities or an optimized subset of those securities. This activity would provide the portfolio manager an incremental return if the futures and stocks were held until the futures' expiration. It would serve to bring the markets closer together in terms of pricing efficiency.

Options may also be a part of index arbitrage. A common pricing efficiency relationship in the options market is the put/call parity theorem. This parity relationship is stated in the following equation:

$$\text{Stock} + \text{Put} = \text{Cash} + \text{Call}$$

A stock can be created by holding cash plus a call option minus a put option. If the S&P 500 appears overvalued as compared to its call and put options, a portfolio manager could arbitrage the price differential by selling the S&P 500 basket of securities, buying a call option on the S&P 500, and selling a put option while holding the cash differential.

A final example of index arbitrage is substituting an S&P 500 future for the stock. It has been previously noted that holding a future is virtually the same as holding an underlying stock. Therefore, program trading could also be used in arbitraging an index across the futures and options market. If a future is overvalued, one can sell a future and buy a basket of securities identical to the S&P 500 as noted previously, or one can sell an S&P 500 futures contract and, in addition, buy a call on the S&P 500 and sell a put on the S&P 500 at the same at-the-money expiration price.

These three types of program trading—index arbitrage, portfolio insurance, and index fund management—are also appropriate strategies for managing internationally based portfolios.

DERIVATIVE INSTRUMENTS IN FIXED-INCOME PORTFOLIO MANAGEMENT

A number of strategies that utilize futures or options offer transaction cost and portfolio risk control advantages that result in incremental portfolio returns. The strategic uses of fixed-income futures and options are similar to the uses in equity portfolio management described earlier in this chapter. While the strategies are similar, the specifications of the underlying instrument on fixed-income futures and options and the fixed-income securities in the portfolio are different from those used in equity portfolio management. As with equity portfolio management, the strategic uses of fixed-income futures and options can be separated into five categories:

1. General uses of fixed-income futures and options appropriate to all portfolio management activities, independent of the investment manager's style; these uses include hedging portfolio deposits, hedging portfolio withdrawals, and hedging the timing difference between the receipt of funds and the investment of the funds.
2. Uses in passively managed buy and hold, or index fund, portfolios.
3. Uses in actively managed portfolios; for example, controlling the duration or systematic exposure to interest rate risk in a fixed-income portfolio appropriate to investment judgment, and controlling the exposure of the portfolios to different fixed-income market sectors.
4. Uses in semiactive or passive/active portfolio structures; for example, altering the duration of a portfolio of assets to match more closely the duration of liabilities from which the assets arose, and altering the duration of an immunized portfolio when a mismatch between duration and time to horizon develops.
5. Uses in the creation of synthetic securities in a number of different portfolio configurations.

The discussions in this section focus primarily on the uses and applications of futures contracts. In general, options contracts perform the same or similar functions as futures in portfolios, as discussed earlier in terms of insurance skewness.

Hedging Using Fixed-Income Futures

The process of hedging fixed-income instruments with fixed-income futures contracts is similar to that of hedging equity securities with equity futures. The portfolio effects are similar. The differences arise primarily from the different specifications of the futures contract in fixed-income futures. The first characteristic is that most fixed-income futures contracts, including Treasury bond notes and futures contracts, are not cash settlement contracts. Should the contracts go to expiration, delivery is made in the actual underlying security. In the case of the Treasury bond future, the security is the Treasury bond. The second characteristic is that fixed-income instruments are generally not perpetual in nature, as are common stocks. Because the lives of fixed-income instruments are finite, the most deliverable underlying security to settle a future contract can change over time as actual fixed-income securities appear and replace others that have matured. This section explores the effect of these two characteristics.

Selection of the Hedge Vehicle. Hedging involves adding to a portfolio an investment instrument that will have price movements that are opposite in direction and approximately equal in magnitude to the price changes of the target security or portfolio of securities. This does not mean that the hedger must find a security whose price movements move dollar-for-dollar with the target security. The hedge vehicle can be weighted to achieve balanced price movements. It is most important in the debt market that the yield movements of the target and hedge vehicle be related; this relationship is an important criterion for selection of the hedge vehicle. Also, choosing a hedge vehicle that has a maturity close to the target security's maturity eliminates a source of hedging error caused by shifts in the slope of the yield curve. To achieve the opposite price movement necessary for hedging, the hedge vehicle must be capable of being sold short. This requirement eliminates some potential contenders. It is also necessary that the hedge vehicle have sufficient liquidity for the size of the hedge.

These criteria lead most often to the Treasury market as the source of the hedge vehicle, either by short sale, forward sale, futures transactions, or options. In setting up the hedge position, each is approached in the same way.

One final criterion for the hedge vehicle concerns its relative price. Hedging holdings of assets requires a short sale. If the hedge vehicle is viewed as being underpriced, the vehicle is not attractive for a short sale, because it would be unlikely to drop in price as much as the average security and would thereby produce a smaller gain on the short-futures position. Instead, a relatively "rich" (overpriced) security is attractive for a short sale.

The Underlying Security. The applications discussed in the remaining part of this section primarily use U.S. Treasury note and U.S. Treasury bond futures. The Treasury bond futures contract is based on the delivery of a nominal 8 percent Treasury bond with at least 15 years to maturity or first (earliest possible) call. Actual physical delivery is required of all the short positions not closed out prior to the end of trading. The actual bond that most closely matches the desired characteristics of the deliverable Treasury bond may change over time, depending on bond availability and the movement of interest rates. It is possible that during the life of a Treasury bond futures contract, the actual underlying Treasury bond that is most deliverable, and hence the one on which the price of the futures contract is based, may change a number of times. Treasury note futures contracts are based on the same pricing or deliverable mechanism as the bond contracts (i.e., an 8 percent nominal coupon rate on the bond). Other contract specifications are virtually identical, except that the allowable maturity ranges from 6.5 to 10 years on the underlying instrument instead of the minimum 15 years on the bond contract.

Basis Risk in Using Fixed-Income Futures. The ability of Treasury bond futures contracts to achieve the desired hedge in portfolios depends on two characteristics. The first is the *basis risk* inherent in the pricing of the Treasury bond future as compared to that of the most deliverable Treasury bond. The second characteristic is the basis risk inherent in the difference between the movements of Treasury bond fixed-income securities and those of the rest of the fixed-income securities in the bond market.

In terms of the first characteristic, during the life of any Treasury bond futures contract the price of that contract may at times vary from the price of the underlying deliverable Treasury bond instrument. Figure 11-16 shows the price differential of a Treasury bond future compared to the actual underlying deliverable Treasury bond. The squares represent the weekly price of the Treasury bond futures contract expiring in December 1987. The crosses represent the weekly price of the appropriate most deliverable, or cheapest-to-deliver, Treasury bond underlying the Treasury bond future at any point. The price of the bond is adjusted for the appropriate factors of equivalency as discussed in the next section. Figure 11-16 shows the relative price movement for the six months from May 1987 through the beginning of December 1987. At the beginning of the period the price of the future was a few points below the price of the actual bond. In the last three months of the period the price of the future and the price of the bond were very close

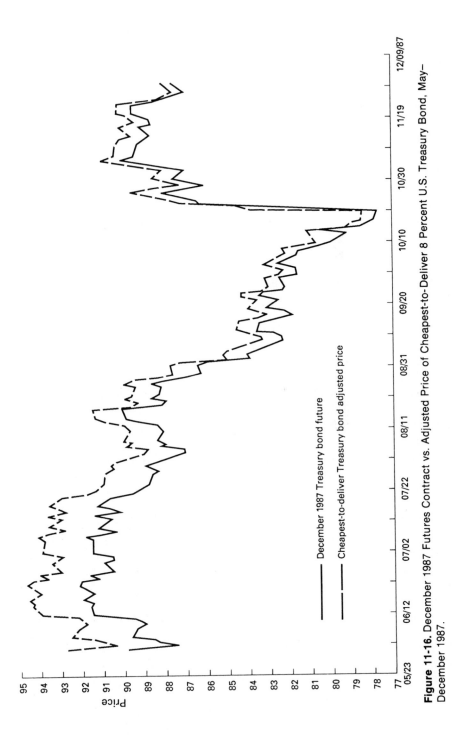

Figure 11-16. December 1987 Futures Contract vs. Adjusted Price of Cheapest-to-Deliver 8 Percent U.S. Treasury Bond, May–December 1987.

to each other. At some times the actual price of the bond in the market was above the fair value of the bond future. At other times the price was below fair value. Basis risk occurs from this source.

The second source of basis risk in hedging fixed income portfolios is illustrated in Figure 11-17. In general, the Treasury bond future closely hedges the longer Treasury bond securities. A fixed-income portfolio, however, generally includes other bonds in addition to Treasury bond instruments, including corporate bonds of various quality ratings. The prices of these non–Treasury bond securities do not always move with the Treasury bonds. Figure 11-17 shows how the spreads of Aa corporate bonds and Baa corporate bonds changed as compared to Treasury bonds over the four years ended May 1988. The spread relationships are volatile; yield spreads do change. At times the prices of the Baa securities and/or the Aa securities move in opposite directions from the Treasury securities. Treasury bond futures, because they are priced to the Treasury bond, cannot and do not hedge the price risk inherent in changing quality spreads and sector spreads in fixed-income portfolios. The remaining discussion in this section assumes that all portfolio holdings are Treasury bond securities and that Treasury bond futures are the hedging instruments. The discussion therefore assumes that a considerable portion of this basis risk does not exist.

The Hedge Ratio. Calculating the *hedge ratio*, or the appropriate number of futures contracts to buy or sell, is straightforward in an equity portfolio when using S&P 500 contracts. As the previous examples demonstrate, one can simply divide the market value by which one wishes to increase or decrease the portfolio exposure by the market value equivalent of S&P 500 futures contracts. The result gives the number of S&P 500 futures contracts appropriate to buy or sell to achieve the targeted portfolio risk level.

Calculating the appropriate number of Treasury bond futures contracts to buy or sell when altering the risk level of a fixed-income portfolio is more complicated and involves two additional steps, which can be demonstrated in a simple example. Assume that the portfolio to be hedged contains only Treasury fixed-income securities. Also assume that the yield curve is flat and that all shifts in the yield curve are parallel. Duration is then the appropriate measure of price change. In this example, the calculation involves three factors. In brief, the number of Treasury bond futures contracts to buy or sell equals the market value equivalent of the futures multiplied by a *conversion factor* multiplied by a *duration adjustment factor*.

The first factor is simply the market value equivalent of futures to be bought or sold. For example, assume that a portfolio manager wishes to buy the equivalent of $10 million of fixed-income exposure. Also assume that the Treasury bond futures contract has an equivalent market value of $90,000. On the basis of this first factor alone, the appropriate number of futures to buy is $10 million divided by $90,000, or 111 futures contracts.

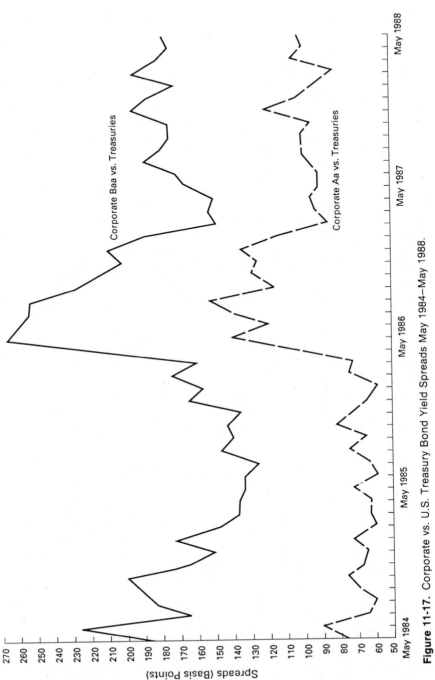

Figure 11-17. Corporate vs. U.S. Treasury Bond Yield Spreads May 1984–May 1988.

The second factor adjusts for the fact that the underlying cheapest-to-deliver Treasury bond must be adjusted, or converted, to the specifications of the Treasury bond futures contract (i.e., an 8 percent coupon bond with 15 years to maturity (the "reference" bond). This factor adjusts for the fact that $100,000 par value of the cheapest-to-deliver bond will not cost the same as $100,000 par value of the reference bond with the same yield. A table specifying these conversion factors, published by a number of financial institutions and futures exchanges, will take the two key differences between the cheapest-to-deliver bond and the contract specifications—yield and time to maturity—and note the appropriate conversion factor for contract equivalence.

The third factor adjusts for the fact that the portfolio may have a different duration level than the duration of the cheapest-to-deliver Treasury bond (adjusted for the conversion factor), on which the Treasury bond futures contract price is being based. An adjustment can be applied that will adjust for this duration differential. Duration will differ primarily in two cases: when a difference exists in coupon rate between the Treasury bond future specifications and the portfolio and when there is a difference in the time to maturity between the Treasury bond futures specifications and the portfolio. This factor can be viewed simply as the ratio of the duration of the portfolio to the duration of the Treasury bond future.

Multiplying these three factors together results in the appropriate number of Treasury bond futures to buy or sell to achieve the change in risk position desired in an all-Treasury fixed-income portfolio. An example illustrates the process. Assume that a manager wishes to completely hedge a $10 million portfolio of Treasury bonds. Also assume the following:

- The market equivalent of the Treasury bond futures contracts is $90,000 per contract.
- The conversion factor for converting the cheapest-to-deliver Treasury bond to the Treasury bond futures contract specifications is 1.2.
- The duration of the portfolio to be hedged is 80 percent of the duration of the Treasury bond future.

Therefore, the number of Treasury bond futures contracts that are appropriate to sell is calculated as follows: $10 million divided by $90,000 per contract, multiplied by the conversion factor of 1.2, multiplied by the relative duration adjustment of 0.80. This equals approximately 107 Treasury bond futures to sell.

This simplified example serves to illustrate the basic steps involved in determining hedge ratios. In the more realistic situation in which the portfolio to be hedged contains non-Treasury securities in which the yield curve shifts in a nonparallel manner, a common method for making this adjustment is to use regression analysis. Over a recent time period, regression analysis would examine the relationship between the movement in prices on the Treasury securities as compared with the movement in prices on the non-Treasury securities in the portfolio. A simple regression would result in a demonstration of how, on average, the prices of the non-Treasury securities could change as compared with the prices of the Treasury securities. A more complete discussion of this more rigorous method of calculation of the hedge ratio can be found in Kopprasch [1982].

For purposes of simplicity, the examples of applications of fixed-income futures and options discussed in the remaining parts of this section assume that no adjustments are necessary for a conversion factor or for non-Treasury securities. While it does perhaps oversimplify, this assumption allows for a clear illustration of the strategy and its implementation for each application. The preceding calculations and techniques can be used to determine more precisely the appropriate numbers of futures to buy or sell.

General Fixed-Income Portfolio Management

A few uses of the new instruments are very general in nature. These uses relate to the portfolio as an entity and are independent of the manner by which the specific securities are selected or for what purpose. Normal portfolio activity occurs in any group of assets, including stocks and bonds, brought together as a portfolio. Such activity includes deposits, withdrawals, managing the risk of the overall portfolio appropriate to the liabilities or cash flow needs of the portfolio owner, and finally, implementing strategic market judgments through trades of specific assets and groups of assets.

Here is an example of managing contributions into a fixed-income portfolio using Treasury bond futures. This example is similar to the situation discussed earlier with equities. Assume that on Day 1 $50 million is deposited into an existing portfolio. Three different approaches could be used to invest this money. The first alternative is to invest it gradually to minimize transaction costs. The risk in this alternative is that the portfolio has too much cash for the investment strategy being pursued. A second approach is to buy $50 million of bonds immediately. As with equities, this approach could move the market a number of $\frac{1}{32}$s and also incur other, related transaction costs.

A third and superior alternative is to use Treasury bond futures. On Day 1, the manager can buy the equivalent of $50 million of fixed-income market value by buying the appropriate number of Treasury bond futures. Assume that each Treasury bond future is equivalent to $90,000 of fixed-income market value exposure, as derived from the Treasury bond price of 90 multiplied by $1,000, which is the contract specification. Each future, therefore, is equivalent to $90,000 in market value. The manager can buy $50 million of equivalent Treasury bond fixed-income exposure by buying

TABLE 11-15. Enhanced Index Fund Application of Treasury Bond Futures

Fund size	$100 million
Duration of index	5.0
Duration of Treasury bond	8.0
Treasury bond price	90
Contract value	$90,000
Contracts purchased	695

$50 million of exposure divided by $90,000 per contract, or 555 Treasury bond futures contacts. The portfolio's risk level will be maintained at the desired level. Over the 10 days that follow, the manager can maintain the portfolio at the desired risk level by gradually selling the futures position and buying the bonds. For example, *on each of the 10 days*, the manager would buy $5 million worth of bonds and sell one-tenth, or 55, of the total number of Treasury bond futures contracts. By stretching the bond purchases over a longer time period, implicit transaction costs may be lowered.

The risk of the portfolio is managed and maintained over the time period by effectively using the Treasury bond futures. As with equity portfolios, the opposite activity can be performed by using Treasury bond futures contracts if a portfolio experiences a withdrawal. Instead of gradually raising cash to fund a withdrawal and altering portfolio risk levels to undesired levels, a manager could alternatively maintain risk levels by selling off some fixed-income securities to raise the cash for the withdrawal and buying an equivalent market value of Treasury bond futures. These actions can be taken over a period of time. The futures position can then be eliminated on the day of the withdrawal as the cash leaves the account. The advantage of this approach is that, once again, portfolio risk is controlled and managed effectively. Portfolio risk is maintained at the targeted level in a cost-effective manner.

Passive Fixed-Income Portfolio Management

Fixed-income futures can be used effectively in the management of passive bond portfolios. The successful management of an index fund requires very careful risk control to minimize any tracking variance in portfolio returns from the market index target. Proper management also requires the greatest possible minimization of transaction costs. Using fixed-income futures in the management of a fixed-income fund effectively achieves these two goals.

This approach illustrated in Table 11-15, which provides an example of an index fund of fixed-income securities. The portfolio manager must invest $100 million in the fund to match a targeted index with an assumed a duration of 5.0. One approach is to buy all the bonds in the index, or the subset of all of the bonds that most closely match the index. To buy $100 million of bonds would entail time and transaction costs that could lead to undesirable tracking variance.

An alternative approach is to use Treasury bond futures contracts. Assume that the duration of the Treasury bond futures is 8.0 and that the bond price for the Treasury bond is 90, resulting in a contract value of $90,000. To construct a $100 million index fund with a duration of 5.0, the manager would buy 695 Treasury bond futures. This number is derived from the following equation:

Fund size × Fund duration = Number of contracts to be purchased

× Contract value per contract × Duration of each contract

or,

$100,000 × 5 = Number of contracts purchased × $90,000 × 8

Through the use of Treasury bond futures, the passively managed fixed-income index fund has been constructed. Tracking error will be relatively small, assuming that the index to be matched is basically an index of Treasury bonds. In addition, transaction costs have been minimized because of the low transaction cost of each futures contract.

There is one other advantage in using the Treasury bond futures approach. It is possible to take advantage of the misvaluation of Treasury bond futures versus the underlying Treasury bonds to gain incremental return to this passively managed fund. The approach illustrated in Table 11-15 is even more beneficial when the Treasury bond futures are underpriced versus fair value. In addition to achieving cost efficiencies and tracking variance efficiency, the portfolio may also gain incremental return if the prices of the futures move more toward fair value. Should the prices of the Treasury bond futures be above fair value, however, the portfolio manager always has a choice of not using the futures at that point, but instead buying the bonds. The availability of Treasury bond futures provides considerable flexibility in controlling tracking variance, minimizing transaction costs, and potentially gaining incremental return for the portfolio.

In managing fixed-income index funds, unlike managing equity index funds, the opportunities to utilize options contracts are limited. Particularly useful in equity index funds to assist in rebalancing specific stock or market subsector overweightings or underweightings, options are more difficult to use in a fixed-income index. Because in the United States options on individual bonds do not exist, specific bond weightings cannot be effected by options on the individual bonds. Options on market subsectors are limited. The futures market for fixed-income securities has developed considerably faster than that for option instruments. Hence, there are limits on the ability to effectively use fixed-income options to manage the risk of index funds in achieving the goals of passive fund management.

Active Fixed-Income Portfolio Management

Fixed-income futures contracts can also be strategically used in actively managed bond portfolios to hedge the risk of deposits and withdrawals. Other uses of futures and options contracts can be viewed within applications that manage systematic risk and applications that manage unsystematic risk.

Control of Systematic Risk. As with equity portfolios, investment managers can use fixed-income Treasury and index futures and options on fixed-income instruments and fixed-income futures to control the duration level, or systematic risk exposure, of a fixed-income portfolio.

The following is an example in which a portfolio manager has a positive outlook for the fixed-income market and wishes to raise the systematic risk exposure of a fixed-income portfolio of $20 million by raising the portfolio's duration. Assume that the manager wishes to have a systematic risk exposure, or portfolio duration, of 6.0 and that the duration of the bond component of the portfolio is 5.0. Finally, assume that bonds represent 95 percent of the portfolio and cash represents the remaining 5 percent.

Two methods will achieve the portfolio target duration of 6.0. In a way that is similar to equity portfolio management, the portfolio manager may increase the portfolio's duration by selling lower duration bonds and buying higher duration bonds. This approach may take time and may incur high transaction costs. An alternative method is to raise the duration of the portfolio by buying an appropriate number of Treasury bond fixed-income futures contracts. Assume that one Treasury bond futures contract is equivalent to $90,000 of fixed-income market exposure and that the duration of the Treasury bond futures contract is 8.0. To raise the duration of the portfolio from 5.0 to 6.0, the manager need purchase only 35 Treasury bond futures contracts. The appropriate number of futures can be derived from the following equation:

$$\$19 \text{ million} \times 5 + \$90,000$$
$$\times \text{ Number of index contracts to be purchased} \times 8 = \$20 \text{ million} \times 6$$

As with equity portfolio management, the advantage of controlling duration in these circumstances by using fixed-income futures is threefold:

1. The target duration of 6.0 can be achieved quickly with the portfolio constructed to reflect the desired investment strategy.

2. The transaction cost would be lower because turnover could be high in trading lower duration bonds for higher duration bonds.
3. The optimal bond mix would be maintained.

The advantages of the last point are extremely important. The existing bond component with the duration of 5.0 may well be the optimal mix of bonds with the highest alpha, or excess return potential. By selling lower-duration bonds and buying higher-duration bonds, the manager may be moving away from this optimal bond portfolio. The manager may be reducing the expected alpha of the bond component and giving up this potential incremental return. This situation can be avoided by achieving the duration target through the use of Treasury bond fixed-income futures.

Treasury bond futures contracts may also be used to hedge completely the systematic risk or duration of the fixed-income portfolio. Given the preceding example, in which a $20 million portfolio is 95 percent invested in bonds and 5 percent invested in cash and has a bond component that has a duration of 5.0, the portfolio manager can reduce the duration of the portfolio to zero by selling 132 Treasury bond futures contracts, using similar pricing assumptions. The appropriate equation is as follows:

$19 million × 5 − $90,000 × Number of index contracts to be sold

$$\times 8 = \$20 \text{ million} \times 0$$

The sale of 132 futures contracts in the example has reduced the systematic risk in the portfolio to zero. The unsystematic risk remains as before, with the alpha expectation intact. The expected return on the portfolio would then be, as in the earlier equity portfolio example, the risk-free rate of return plus the expected alpha from the individual bond selection.

Control of Unsystematic Risk. Unsystematic risk in a fixed-income portfolio arises from exposure of the portfolio to subgroups in the market and to individual fixed-income holdings. Because there are very few futures or options contracts on individual bond securities, there is little that can be done to use these instruments to control unsystematic risk in a portfolio arising from individual bond selection.

There are, however, a greater number of futures contracts, and some options contracts, that cover fixed-income market subgroups or sectors such as Treasury bonds, mortgage-backed securities, and municipal bonds. There are also futures and options that cover different maturities of the yield curve, including Treasury bill futures, Treasury note futures, Eurodollar futures, and Treasury bond futures. The existence of these futures and options contracts allows a portfolio manager to raise or lower the unsystematic risk exposure to any of these market sectors or yield curve maturity exposures in ways that are appropriate to the investment strategy.

TABLE 11-16. Hedging Sector Risk Using Fixed-Income Futures

Portfolio size	$20 million
Actual municipal/corporate mix	50:50
Target municipal/corporate mix	35:65
Strategy: Sell 34 municipal index futures	
Buy 33 Treasury bond futures	

Table 11-16 presents a strategy for changing the unsystematic risk of the portfolio through fixed-income futures on market subgroups. Assume that the manager has a portfolio of $20 million and that the mix of the portfolio is currently 50 percent invested in municipal securities and 50 percent invested in corporate bonds. Also assume that the manager wishes to change the exposure to these market subgroups and has a target of 35 percent of the portfolio, or $7 million, for the municipal bond sector and 65 percent, or $13 million, for the corporate bond sector. The manager wishes to reduce exposure in the municipal bond sector by $3 million and increase exposure in the corporate bond sector by $3 million. If the portfolio manager assumes that the Treasury bond future is a close proxy to the corporate bond sector and that one Treasury bond future has a market value equivalent of $90,000, then 33 Treasury bond futures need to be purchased to increase exposure to the corporate bond sector in the portfolio by $3 million. If one municipal bond index future has the equivalent market value exposure of $88,250, then the exposure to the municipal bond sector can be reduced by $3 million by selling 34 municipal index futures. In this example, unsystematic risk has been effectively managed in a timely, cost-effective manner by using these available futures instruments to alter the municipal/corporate mix.

Yield curve management is a second way in which fixed-income futures contracts can be used to manage unsystematic risk exposure in a fixed-income portfolio. Assume that a portfolio of Treasury bonds has a duration of 5.0 and contains both medium maturity and longer maturity Treasury bonds. Also assume that the portfolio manager's investment strategy calls for the intermediate maturity part of the yield curve to increase in interest rate levels while the longer maturity part of the yield curve declines in interest rates. Assume that the manager wishes to maintain an overall duration in the portfolio of 5.0 but wants more exposure to the longer end of the yield curve and less exposure to the 5- to 10-year maturity portion of the yield curve.

Again, there are two methods to change this unsystematic risk exposure. The manager could sell some intermediate maturity Treasury notes and place the proceeds in long Treasury bonds and cash instruments appropriate to maintain the duration level of 5.0. This can be time-consuming and costly.

An alternative approach is to sell the appropriate number of Treasury note futures to reduce the exposure to the intermediate maturity Treasury notes and buy the appropriate smaller number of Treasury bond futures to bring the portfolio's systematic risk exposure back to the target of 5.0. By using this approach, the portfolio manager can quickly and at low cost alter the unsystematic risk exposure to the different parts of the yield curve in accordance with the investment strategy.

Active/Passive-Fixed-Income Portfolio Management

Futures contracts can be effectively used in managing fixed-income portfolios within an asset/liability management context. As noted in Chapter 4, most financial institutions are faced with the investment task of managing assets, mostly fixed-income assets, relative to the liability structure of the business. The liabilities are generally also fixed-income in nature. The use of futures contracts on fixed-income instruments facilitates asset/liability risk management through implementation of investment risk targets in a more timely, more cost-effective manner.

Asset/liability management is a form of active/passive portfolio management. The approach is to hedge the risks involved in the differential between the asset interest rate exposure and the liability interest rate exposure, which is a passive activity. The hedging, however, is conducted through active transactions. The use of futures contracts in asset/liability management is illustrated by three examples given in the sections that follow.

Matching Asset and Liability Durations. In the example, the asset manager wishes to control the duration of assets appropriate to the liabilities. Assume that the liabilities that back, or are appropriate to, the assets of the portfolio have a duration of 4.0. Also assume that the assets have a duration of 5.5 and that the size of the asset portfolio is $100 million. It is the portfolio manager's target to match the duration of the assets and liabilities by reducing the duration of the assets from 5.5 to 4.0.

There are two ways to achieve this goal. The first and more traditional way is to sell some of the higher-duration assets and reinvest the proceeds in lower-duration assets to reduce the duration to 4.0. The problem with this approach is that in many financial institutions, particularly in banks and insurance companies, assets have historically been very illiquid and difficult to sell. It may be that these assets are private placements or mortgages. Even with the ability to securitize many of these relatively illiquid securities and sell them in the market, liquidity is still hampered for these types of fixed-income investments. To reduce duration, considerable transaction costs may have to be paid. The assets of private placements and mortgages may have to be sold well below an appropriate market value. Also, it may take considerable time to structure these transactions.

An alternative approach is to reduce the duration of the assets to 4.0 by selling the appropriate number of Treasury bond futures. If the Treasury bond futures price is 90, each futures contract has a market value equivalent of $90,000. Assume that the duration of each Treasury bond future is 9.4. The duration of the assets can then be reduced from 5.5 to a level of 4.0 by selling 177 Treasury bond futures. This number of Treasury bond futures is derived from the following equation:

$100 million × 5.5 − Number of index contracts to sell

$$\times \ \$90{,}000 \ \times \ 9.4 \ = \ \$100 \ \text{million} \ \times \ 4.0$$

Through the use of this approach to reducing the duration of the assets, the mismatch between asset duration and liability duration can be quickly brought to zero and asset/liability risk eliminated. A financial institution may also benefit by retaining the investments in private placements or mortgage securities that gain incremental return.

Duration Adjustment in Immunized Portfolios. Another example of the use of futures in asset/liability management is found in a duration-immunized portfolio. As discussed in Chapter 8, an immunized fixed-income portfolio is a fixed-income portfolio management technique in which the duration of the portfolio matches a certain time horizon set when the investment strategy is first implemented. The duration of the portfolio must be adjusted constantly and lowered as time passes and the time horizon nears.

The purpose of this investment strategy in fixed-income portfolio management is to achieve a return that is insensitive to interest rates over the targeted time horizon. The strategy eliminates the systematic risk to the portfolio while exposing it to incremental return potential through the use of corporate and other non-Treasury, fixed-income instruments. Over the life of the immunized portfolio, the duration must be shortened. Fixed-income futures contracts offer an effective mechanism for shortening the duration. Instead of selling longer-duration bonds and reinvesting the proceeds in shorter-duration bonds, a manager can sell the appropriate number of fixed-income futures contracts at each point in time to reduce the duration of the assets to match the initially specified time horizon. This action maintains the goal of immunizing the assets from the interest rate risk desired at the initiation of the strategy, and transaction costs are minimized.

Hedging Timing Differences. A third example of the use of futures in asset/liability management arises from the goal of hedging timing differences. In a financial institution, an asset is often not purchased simultaneously with the placing of the liability on the balance sheet. There is considerable risk that an asset could be purchased well after a liability is incurred at a much different interest rate than that used to price the liability. For example, assume a liability is incurred at an interest rate of 10 percent. Before an appropriate asset can be purchased with the proceeds from the liability, interest rates fall to a level of 9 percent. The financial institution then has a 10 percent liability matched by a 9 percent asset. This results in a negative spread that could have an adverse impact on the institution's income.

For example, a common liability in the insurance industry is the guaranteed investment contract (GIC), in which the insurance company and the purchaser of the contract agree on a rate that the company will pay on funds deposited by the contract holder. The risk to the insurance company is that, if rates fall between the time the contract is initiated and the time an appropriate, attractive asset is identified and purchased to back the liability, a timing difference between the liability and the asset will arise.

Through the use of fixed-income futures, this timing difference can be effectively hedged. At the time the new GIC liability is incurred by the financial institution, the institution can immediately purchase the equivalent market value of fixed-income futures contracts. Should interest rates fall, the gains on the futures will offset the income losses that will be incurred when the actual asset is purchased at the lower interest rate. When an attractive asset is identified and purchased, the futures contracts can be sold. The financial institution will then have hedged the timing difference.

The timing difference in the opposite direction can also be hedged through the use of fixed-income futures. It may be that the financial institution has identified a highly attractive asset before a GIC is sold. The financial institution can purchase the asset and immediately hedge its interest rate exposure by selling an equivalent market value number of Treasury bond futures. The rate achieved by the asset can then be used to back an appropriate GIC liability. The risk inherent in the timing difference between the purchase of the asset and the sale of the liability contract is eliminated through the futures transaction. Through the purchase of the asset and the sale of the futures contract, price volatility protection is purchased. That is, gains or losses in the contract will offset losses or gains in the underlying asset and that value will be protected, thereby maintaining investment of the original principal amount in the new rate environment, in which a GIC can be structured and sold as an opportunity arises.

Creation of Synthetic Fixed-Income Instruments

Fixed-income futures and options contracts can be combined with various types of fixed-income instruments to create synthetic versions of other fixed-income instruments. The primary reasons for creating synthetic instruments are twofold. The first is to create a portfolio risk/return pattern that cannot

TABLE 11-17. Examples of Fixed-Income Synthetic Assets and the Portfolio Instruments and Futures Transactions Used in Their Creation

Portfolio Holding	Futures Transaction	Synthetic Asset
Money market instruments	Buy bond futures	Long-term bond
Long-term bonds	Sell bond futures	Money market instrument
Floating-rate note	Buy bill or Eurodollar strip futures	Fixed-rate note

be achieved through any other available investment. As with the use of options and futures in equity portfolio management, any desirable risk/return pattern can be created via the selection and combination of appropriate put and call options at different strike prices and expirations. The risk exposure can be effectively implemented in a timely, cost-effective manner by the use of futures.

The second reason to use futures and options in creating synthetic instruments relates to cost and value. Through the appropriate buying and selling of futures and options and the underlying fixed-income instruments, a synthetic instrument can be created at a lower cost than, and perhaps at a better price than, that of the equivalent actual debt instrument available in the fixed-income market. This situation can create opportunities for arbitrage between the synthetic instrument and the actual instrument available in the market. These arbitrage opportunities create the opportunity for incremental return for the portfolio.

Table 11-17 presents examples of fixed-income synthetic assets and the portfolio instruments and futures transactions used in their creation. Long bonds can be created by holding money market instruments and buying bond futures. Money market instruments can be created by holding long bonds and selling bond futures. Finally, floating rate notes can be combined with buying Treasury bill futures or Eurodollar futures to create a synthetic fixed-rate note.

Synthetic Long Bonds. As reviewed in the previous section on passive portfolio management, buying the appropriate number of Treasury bond futures while holding money market instruments allows one to create an equivalent exposure to duration or interest-rate sensitivity that is comparable to holding the long-term bond. The portfolio manager has the potential to add incremental return to a portfolio if bond futures can be purchased at a price below fair value. Incremental return can also be achieved in a portfolio by buying cash instruments and Treasury bond futures instead of the long-term bond if, at the time the long-term bond is desired, that bond is overvalued. The alternative of holding cash and buying fairly valued Treasury bond futures is superior and can be accomplished at a more attractive price.

Synthetic Money Market Securities. Money market instruments can also be synthetically created by holding bonds and selling Treasury bond futures. Here is an example of creating cash instruments in this way. This example is similar to the one given in the section on passive fund management. Assume that an investment manager is managing a $50 million portfolio and that the portfolio contains corporate bonds and has a duration of 5.0. Also assume that the duration of the Treasury bond future is 8.0 and that each Treasury bond futures contract has a market value equivalent of $90,000. The duration of the corporate bond portfolio can be reduced to zero and cash equivalents can be created by selling 347 Treasury bond futures contracts, a number derived from the following equation:

$$\$50 \text{ million} \times 5.0 - \$90,000 \times \text{Number of contracts to be sold}$$
$$\times 8.0 = \$50 \text{ million} \times 0$$

Synthetically creating cash equivalents through this approach provides the opportunity for the portfolio to gain incremental return above that available from cash equivalent instruments. The incremental return can come from two sources:

1. If the futures are selling at less than fair value, a manager can buy them when they are undervalued. Holding the futures to contract expiration allows the price to converge to fair value and therefore provides incremental return for the portfolio.
2. Holding a long-term bond and selling an appropriate number of bond futures or, alternatively, holding money market instruments and buying an appropriate number of bond futures, can create synthetic fixed-income instruments with any targeted duration along the yield curve and potentially provide incremental return to the portfolio. For example, assume that a portfolio is 100 percent invested in corporate bonds and that the portfolio manager is hedging the duration using Treasury bond futures. The sensitivity of the portfolio to interest rate changes can be hedged through the use of Treasury bond futures. However, the spread between corporate bonds and Treasury bonds is not hedged. Over time, this spread should add incremental return and provide a return in the portfolio in excess of that available from existing money market instruments.

Floating- to Fixed-Rate Conversions. The third application of futures in creating synthetic fixed-income instruments involves futures on short-term instruments. A portfolio holding of floating-rate notes can be transformed to a fixed-rate note through the purchase of an appropriate number of Treasury bill or Eurodollar strip futures. This application is discussed in more detail in Kopprasch and Pitts [1983] and Pitts and Kopprasch [1984].

Synthetic Mortgage-Backed Securities. Fixed-income options may also be used to create synthetic securities. A primary example is mortgages or mortgage-backed securities. Mortgage loans, both residential and commercial, are fixed-income instruments on which a call option has been sold to the mortgage borrower. Many grant the borrower the option to prepay the mortgage at any time. The incremental yield available to the mortgage lender from investing in mortgages and mortgage securities arises from granting this call feature. A comparable fixed-income instrument with similar risk and return patterns could be created by holding a corporate bond of a quality similar to that of any mortgage and selling a Treasury bond call option with an appropriately chosen strike price. The result is an increment to the yield of the underlying corporate bond from the premium received from selling a call option. By selling the call option, however, the portfolio manager truncates any potential to participate in an upward move in the market value of the corporate bonds should interest rates fall.

By buying a corporate bond and selling a Treasury bond call option, a synthetic security similar to a mortgage or mortgage-backed security is created. This synthetic security may well be a preferred investment if the mortgages or mortgage-backed securities are not available or if they are overvalued in the market. Alternatively, a corporate bond could be synthetically created by holding a mortgage security and buying a Treasury bond call option at the appropriate strike price. This purchase of a call option offsets the implied sale of the call option in the mortgage security itself. The risk pattern created by buying a mortgage and buying a fixed-income call option is similar to holding a straight corporate fixed-income instrument. Combining fixed-income options with fixed-income instruments of different durations and qualities can create a spectrum of synthetic fixed-income instruments from which a portfolio manager can choose at any time in order to gain incremental return to a fixed-income portfolio—sometimes without adding *proportionately* to the risk borne.

Rate Anticipation Trading

Active portfolio managers trade to achieve maximum performance within the risk constraints imposed on them. If no duration constraint is imposed, active managers trade various maturities on the yield curve based on their expectations of interest rate levels in the future. Options and futures allow these managers to implement rate anticipation strategies without having to disrupt their portfolios and pay large transaction costs. Futures and options can be used independently of the rest of the portfolio as speculative vehicles.

Call options and long futures positions can be used to capitalize on expectations of falling rates and rising prices. Similarly, put options and short futures positions can be used profitably if market prices fall.

The choice between options and futures is dependent on premium levels, or the cost of the options; the price of futures versus their fair value; and the manager's expectations and tolerance of risk. Options add another dimension to the possibilities by offering a choice of strike prices, with higher strike prices resulting in lower premiums for calls. To become profitable higher strike prices require a larger price move in the underlying fixed-income instrument, but once such a price move occurs, they can provide a dollar-for-dollar movement. After choosing options, or while still evaluating the choice between futures and options, a manager must consider this effect of the strike price on the ultimate profitability of the trade.

A short futures position or the purchase of puts can provide profits in a declining market. Once again, because the puts give the holder the right but not the obligation to sell the security, the put holder can lose no more than the premium. Puts, like calls, offer several strike prices and patterns of return that are similar to calls, except that they are reversed with respect to market direction.

SUMMARY

This chapter has focused on the impact that futures and options contracts have on portfolios of assets and on their strategic uses in portfolio management. These derivative instruments offer the means to structure and control portfolio risk in a timely, cost-effective manner. However, when creating a portfolio with optimum return/risk characteristics, managers should consider these instruments within the entire spectrum of investment vehicles available.

FURTHER READING

A number of investments textbooks contain discussions of strategic applications of futures and options contracts in portfolio management. Texts emphasizing option strategies include Jarrow and Rudd [1983], Bookstaber and Clarke [1983], and Cox and Rubinstein [1985]. Bibliographies within these texts are particularly extensive. A good summary of strategies using stock index futures can be found in Fabozzi and Kipnis [1984]. A discussion of the foundations of dynamic hedging can be found in Rubinstein and Leland [1981]. An excellent discussion of the use of futures contracts in building and maintaining immunized portfolios can be found in Yawitz and Marshall [1985]. An extensive and comprehensive compilation of important articles on futures and options, as well as an excellent bibliography, can be found in Berry and Sherrerd [1988]. An excellent discussion of the valuation of futures and options can be found in Kopprasch [1985].

BIBLIOGRAPHY

Belongia, Michael T., and G.J. Santoni. "Hedging Interest Rate Risk with Financial Futures: Some Basic Principles." *Federal Reserve Bank of St. Louis Review*, October 1984.

Berry, Michael A., and Katrina F. Sherrerd, eds. *CFA Readings in Derivative Securities*. Charlottesville, Va.: Institute of Chartered Financial Analysts, 1988.

Black, Fischer. "Fact and Fantasy in the Use of Options." *Financial Analysts Journal*, July/August 1975.

Black, Fischer, and Myron Scholes. "The Pricing of Options and Corporate Liabilities." *Journal of Political Economy*, May/June 1973.

Bookstaber, Richard M., and Roger G. Clarke. "Problems in Evaluating the Performance of Portfolios with Options." *Financial Analysts Journal*, January/February 1985.

———. "Option Portfolio Strategies: Measurement and Evaluation." *Journal of Business*, October 1984.

———. *Option Strategies for Institutional Investment Management*. Reading, Mass.: Addison-Wesley Publishing Co., 1983.

———. "An Algorithm to Calculate the Return Distribution of Portfolios with Option Positions." *Management Science*, April 1983.

———. "The Description and Evaluation of Option Portfolio Strategies." Unpublished paper, Institute of Business Management, Brigham Young University, 1983.

———. "Use of Options in Altering Portfolio Return Distribution." Library paper, Institute for Quantitative Research in Finance, Columbia University, 1982.

———. "Options Can Alter Portfolio Return Distributions." *The Journal of Portfolio Management*, Spring 1981.

Chambers, Donald R. "An Immunization Strategy for Futures Contracts on Government Securities." *The Journal of Futures Markets*, Summer 1984.

Chance, Don M. "An Immunized-Hedge Procedure for Bond Futures." *The Journal of Futures Markets*, Fall 1982.

Cox, John, and Mark Rubinstein. *Option Markets*. Englewood Cliffs, N.J.: Prentice-Hall, 1985.

Dattatreya, Ravi, and Mark A. Zurack. "Asset Allocation Using Futures Contracts." Stock Index Research, Goldman Sachs & Co., February 1985.

Dubofsky, David A. "Hedging Dividend Capture Strategies with Stock Index Futures." *The Journal of Futures Markets*, October 1987.

Evnine, Jeremy, and Andrew Rudd. "Option Portfolio Risk Analysis." *The Journal of Portfolio Management*, Winter 1984.

Fabozzi, Frank J., and Gregory M. Kipnis, eds. *Stock Index Futures*. Homewood, Ill.: Dow Jones-Irwin, 1984.

Figlewski, Stephen. "Hedging Performance and Basis Risk in Stock Index Futures." *The Journal of Finance*, July 1984.

Fisher, Donald E., ed. *Options and Futures: New Route to Risk/Return Management*. Sponsored by The Institute of Chartered Financial Analysts. Homewood, Ill.: Dow Jones-Irwin, 1984.

Gay, Gerald D., and Robert W. Kolb. "Interest Rate Futures as a Tool for Immunization." *The Journal of Portfolio Management*, Fall 1983.

Hegde, Shantaram P. "The Impact of Interest Rate Level and Volatility on the Performance of Interest Rate Hedges." *The Journal of Futures Markets*, Winter 1982.

Hill, Joanne M., and Thomas Schneeweis. "Reducing Volatility With Financial Futures." *Financial Analysts Journal*, November/December 1984.

————. "Risk Reduction Potential of Financial Futures for Corporate Bond Positions." *Interest Rate Futures: A Comprehensive Anthology*, ed. G. Gay and R.W. Kolb. Richmond, Va.: Robert F. Dame, 1983.

————. "An Analysis of the Impact of Variation Margin in Hedging Fixed Income Securities." *Review of Research in Futures Markets*, 1983.

Ibbotson, Roger G., and Rex A. Sinquefeld. *Stocks, Bonds, Bills and Inflation: The Past and the Future*. Charlottesville, Va.: The Financial Analysts Research Foundation, 1982.

Jarrow, Robert, and Andrew Rudd. *Option Pricing*. Homewood, Ill.: Dow Jones-Irwin, 1983.

Kane, Alex, and Alan J. Marcus. "Conversion Factor Risk and Hedging in the Treasury-Bond Futures Market." *The Journal of Futures Markets*, Spring 1984.

Kolb, Robert W. *Understanding Futures Markets*. Glenview, Ill.: Scott, Foresman and Co., 1985.

————. "Valuation of Futures and Options Contracts," in John L. Maginn and Donald L. Tuttle, eds. *Managing Investment Portfolios, 1985–1986 Update*. Boston: Warren, Gorham & Lamont, Inc., 1985.

Koppenhaver, G.D. "Bank Funding Risks, Risk Aversion, and the Choice of Futures Hedging Instrument." *The Journal of Finance*, March 1985.

Kopprasch, Robert W. "Introduction to Interest Rate Hedging." Salomon Brothers, Inc., November 1982.

Kopprasch, Robert W., and Mark Pitts. "Hedging Short-Term Liabilities With Interest Rate Futures." Salomon Brothers, Inc., April 1983.

Kuberek, Robert C., and Norman G. Pefley. "Hedging Corporate Debt With U.S. Treasury Bond Futures." *The Journal of Futures Markets*, Winter 1983.

McCabe, George M., and Charles T. Franckle. "The Effectiveness of Rolling the Hedge Forward in the Treasury Bill Futures Market." *Financial Management*, Summer 1983.

Merton, Robert C. "Theory of Rational Option Pricing." *The Bell Journal of Economics and Management Science*, Spring 1973.

Merton, Robert C., Myron S. Scholes, and Mathew L. Gladstein. "The Returns and Risk of Alternative Put Option Portfolio Investment Strategies." *Journal of Business*, 1982.

————. "The Returns and Risks of Alternative Call-Option Portfolio Investment Strategies." *Journal of Business*, April 1978.

Moriarity, Eugene, Susan Phillips, and Paula Tosini. "A Comparison of Options and Futures in the Management of Portfolio Risk." *Financial Analysts Journal*, January/February 1981.

Nadbielny, Thomas, and David Dunford. "Determining Optimal Asset Allocation Given a Skewness Constraint." Unpublished paper, Travelers Investment Management Company, May 1984.

Nordhauser, Fred. "Using Stock Index Futures to Reduce Market Risk." *The Journal of Portfolio Management*, Spring 1984.

Parker, Jack W., and Robert T. Daigler. "Hedging Money Market CDs With Treasury-Bill Futures." *The Journal of Futures Markets*, Winter 1981.

Peck, A.E., ed. *Selected Writings on Futures Markets: Exploration in Financial Futures Markets.* Book V, Readings in Futures Markets. Chicago: Chicago Board of Trade, 1985.

Pitts, Mark. "The Pricing of Options on Debt Securities." *The Journal of Portfolio Management*, Winter 1985.

————. "Options on Futures on Fixed-Income Securities." Salomon Brothers, Inc., December 1983.

Pitts, Mark, and Robert W. Kopprasch. "Reducing Inter-Temporal Risk in Financial Futures Hedging." *The Journal of Futures Markets*, Vol. 4, No. 1, 1984.

Presidential Task Force on Market Mechanisms (Nicholas F. Brady, Chairman). *Report of the Presidential Task Force on Market Mechanisms.* Washington, D.C.: Presidential Task Force on Market Mechanisms, January 1988.

Rebell, Arthur L., and Gail Gordon. *Financial Futures and Investment Strategy.* Homewood, Ill.: Dow Jones-Irwin, 1984.

Rendleman, Richard J., Jr., and Richard W. McEnally. "Assessing the Costs of Portfolio Insurance." *Financial Analysts Journal*, May/June 1987.

Rubinstein, Mark, and Hayne E. Leland. "Replicating Options With Positions in Stock and Cash." *Financial Analysts Journal*, July/August 1981.

Schaefer, Steven. "The Problem With Redemption Yields." *Financial Analysts Journal*, July/August 1977.

Senchack, Andrew J., Jr., and John C. Easterwood. "Cross Hedging CDs With Treasury Bill Futures." *The Journal of Futures Markets*, Winter 1983.

Singleton, J. Clay, and Robin Grieves. "Synthetic Puts and Portfolio Insurance Strategies." *The Journal of Portfolio Management*, Spring 1984.

Slivka, Ronald T. "Risk and Return for Options Investment Strategies." *Financial Analysts Journal*, September/October 1980.

Sweeney, Richard J. "Beating the Foreign Exchange Market." *The Journal of Finance*, March 1986.

Toevs, Alden L., and David P. Jacob. "Futures and Alternative Hedge Ratio Methodologies." *The Journal of Portfolio Management*, Spring 1986.

Trainer, Francis H., Jr. "The Uses of Treasury Bond Futures in Fixed-Income Portfolio Management." *Financial Analysts Journal*, January/February 1983.

Welch, William W. *Strategies for Put and Call Option Trading.* Cambridge, Mass.: Winthrop Publishers, 1982.

Yates, James W. *The Options Strategy Spectrum.* Homewood, Ill.: Dow Jones-Irwin, 1987.

Yates, James W., and Robert W. Kopprasch, Jr. "Writing Covered Call Options: Profits and Risks." *The Journal of Portfolio Management*, Fall 1980.

Yawitz, Jess B., and William J. Marshall. "The Use of Futures in Immunized Portfolios." *The Journal of Portfolio Management*, Winter 1985.

CHAPTER 12

Implementation of Portfolio Building: Execution

Jack L. Treynor
Wayne H. Wagner

OVERVIEW

At this point the portfolio building process is almost complete. Investment policy based on the preferences of and constraints on individual and institutional investors has been developed. Macro and micro expectational factors relevant to investing have been identified. Portfolio composition has been decided through the joint consideration of investment policy and expectational factors. Assets have been allocated and portfolios containing the various asset categories—bonds, common stocks, and real estate, along with futures and options modifiers—have been optimized.

The last step in the portfolio building process is to implement the optimally prescribed portfolios within asset categories by selling existing assets and buying desired assets in the optimal amount. This is the execution step. Without it the portfolio building process cannot be implemented. It is *not* a simple or costless step. The execution process is complex and often costly, and it can have an important effect on investment results. Therefore, it is important to have an understanding of the transacting process, the strategies used by the key players, the tactics used by the trading desk to effectively carry out these strategies, and some of the explicit costs, in terms of both time *and* money, that are involved.

Unfortunately, the way in which orders are communicated to the trading desk of investment organizations and the sophistication with which the performance of the trading function is monitored are regarded by most institutions as quasi-clerical functions. In reality, the trading desk is a vital link in the two-way information chain connecting the decision maker in the investment organization with exchange specialists, over-the-counter dealers, and block positioners who bring together buyers and sellers of securities, often with a time lag that necessitates some financial exposure on the part of those specialists, dealers, and positioners. The buy-side trader thus occupies a unique position in the execution process as someone who must thoroughly understand the motives, desires, and strategies of the portfolio manager who wishes to buy and sell as well as the motives, desires, and strategies of potential sellers and buyers with whom he may transact. The buy-side trader also needs to know how markets operate as well as all of the various vehicles, orders, and techniques to develop trading tactics that will meet his manager's needs in a cost-effective fashion.

In this chapter, Jack Treynor identifies the key transactors, describes their motives and deeds, discusses their strategies, develops the role of the dealer, and indicates who wins and loses and why. Wayne Wagner then lays out the buy-side trader's role, the trader's relationship with the portfolio manager, some of the explicit costs of trading, how key markets work, the types of trades available, a taxonomy of trading techniques showing the tradeoff between speed and cost of transacting, the notion of evaluating trading effectiveness, and some ethical considerations.

THE KEY PLAYERS

To succeed at the trading game, the investor needs to understand the nature of transacting, who the players are or are likely to be on *either* side of the transaction, what motives and needs drive the players to trade, and what strategies the players employ.

Securities transacting is different from normal business transacting in two fundamental ways. First, businessmen entering into a transaction often do so only if they understand the motives of the party on the other side. Curiously, in most securities transactions, not only the motives but even the identity of the other party are concealed.

The second important difference between securities transactions and most other business transactions is that a securities transaction is a zero-sum game. Both parties can gain from a business transaction, and both usually do. But aside from considerations of taxes and ability to bear risk, a security represents the same amount of future cash to the buyer as the seller. This means that the usual constructive motives for a business transaction are absent in most securities transactions. It tells us that if there is going to be a winner in a securities transaction, there is also going to be a loser.

If an active investor's position is long (short) relative to the market portfolio, the rest of the investing world has to be short (long) relative to the market portfolio. If the security's price goes up (down) more than (less than) the market, the investor gains relative to market performance. The rest of the investing world loses. On the other hand, passive investing is not a zero-sum game. Passive investors can all gain from their respective investments in the market portfolio. But active investing cannot help one investor without injuring the rest of the investors in the market. More to the point, the rest of the investing world cannot improve its performance by active investing unless it injures the particular investor competing with it. The result is that when investors trade securities, they are in the same position as the hunter on a safari who hears rustling in the bush. His unseen target may be a rare gazelle or a hungry tiger. If the hunter does not go after the prey, a magnificent gazelle may be lost. On the other hand, the hunter cannot contribute to the tiger's weight gain program without seriously jeopardizing his own. The more the hunter learns about both gazelles and hungry tigers, the more effective he can be in capitalizing on his opportunities. When the tall grass begins to rustle, however, it is too late to start that education.

Value-Based Transactors

Just as it is useful for a hunter to know which animals are carnivorous and which are merely flower munchers, a trader in the securities market needs to make a similar set of distinctions. When securities are traded, the two basic types of investment carnivores that are usually encountered are value-based and information-based transactors. The *value-based transactor* (VBT) compares the price at which other investors are trading with his assessment of value and trades when that difference is large enough. The VBT bases his assessment on public information and makes an absolute value judgment about the (probability distribution of) the justified price (JP_{VBT}) of a security, based on extensive fundamental analysis of all the macro and micro expectational factors that might affect value, such as those covered in Chapters 5 and 6. He is basically a bargain hunter looking to buy or sell securities that look cheap or expensive to him as compared to other securities. As Cottle, Murray, and Block [1988] point out, the essence of the VBT's research is *comparison*.

For practical reasons not pertinent to this discussion, most value-based investors prefer to hold long, rather than short, positions. But if they establish that stock A is a bargain as compared to stock B, there is only a 50 percent chance that A is underpriced, rather than B being overpriced. With a broader base of comparison of securities, of course, the problem diminishes rapidly. But a broad base of comparison, as a practical matter, must include the following:

- Enough analysts to cover many securities representing many industries

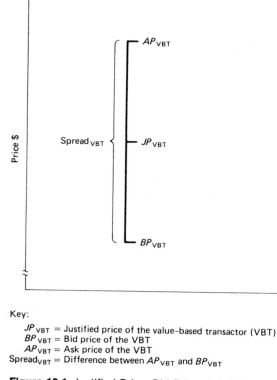

JP_{VBT} = Justified price of the value–based transactor (VBT)
BP_{VBT} = Bid price of the VBT
AP_{VBT} = Ask price of the VBT
Spread$_{VBT}$ = Difference between AP_{VBT} and BP_{VBT}

Figure 12-1. Justified Price, Bid Price, Ask Price, and Spread for a Value-Based Transactor.

- A common economic outlook
- A common valuation framework

Not surprisingly, value-based institutions tend to have large staffs, large amounts of assets under management, extensive supervision, and—to guarantee comparability—extensive monitoring. In short, they tend to be classic, highly disciplined, top-down organizations in which research and justified prices are frequently compared with those of others for reinforcement, consistency, and compatibility.

In terms of market activity, the value-based transactor, in effect, makes the market for a security, determining the spread between the respective prices at which one can buy and sell quickly. That is, the VBT considers the expected value of the probability distribution of justified price possibilities to be the best estimate of the true equilibrium value of the security and sets a bid price (BP_{VBT}) below JP_{VBT} and an ask price (AP_{VBT}) above JP_{VBT} as shown in Figure 12-1.

The spread shown in this figure between BP_{VBT} and AP_{VBT} is not so

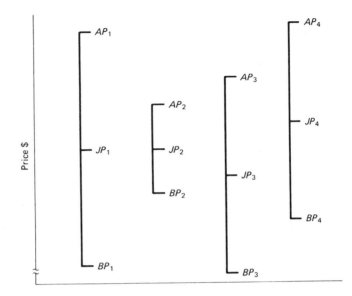

Figure 12-2. Examples of Justified Price, Bid Price, and Ask
Price for Four Value-Based Transactors.

wide as to attract additional VBTs who are willing to transact at narrower
spreads, nor is it so narrow as to inhibit trading by the primary transactor
on the other side of the market, the *information-based transactor* (IBT).

Spread Represents a Consensus

In actuality, the spread portrayed in the figure can be considered a consensus
of the spreads of thousands of VBTs, a few of whom are depicted in Figure
12-2. VBT_1, with a wider spread, will transact less, on average, because his
ask price is higher and his bid price lower than the consensus. VBT_2, however, will transact more because of his smaller spread, lower ask price, and
higher bid price. VBT_3 will get more sells but fewer buys, and VBT_4 will
get more buys but fewer sells.[1]

Hence, Figure 12-2 has implied in it the contents of Figure 12-3, in which
each of the three prices used by value-based transactors is portrayed as a
distribution of VBT-based prices in the marketplace. Note that unless the

---

[1] As Figure 12-2 might lead one to conclude, there should be distributions of
justified prices and distributions of bid and asked price spreads among transactors.
These are not necessarily interrelated. The mean of the justified price distributions
represents the judgments of the market participants about value, whereas the average
spread around that mean represents their risk judgment about the chances of getting
bagged by other transactors.

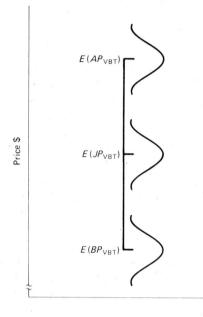

Key: $E(\ )$ = Expected value of a price variable

Figure 12-3. Probability Distributions of Justified Price, Bid Price, and Ask Price for a Value-Based Transactor.

distribution of ask prices *overlaps* that for bid prices, as in Figure 12-4, there will be *no* transactions in a marketplace consisting only of VBTs.

In sum, the value-based transactor is the anchor or base for the trading system. The VBT places no value on time. In a market with dealers, a subject to be considered later in this chapter, VBTs would place limit orders to buy and sell with a spread that encloses justified price and is wide enough to provide a cushion to offset losses from "getting bagged" by information-based traders. Ultimately, it is the VBT who establishes the framework within which dealers operate.

Information-Based Transactors

Information-based transactors are traders who come into possession of new information that will have a substantial effect on a security's price, information that is not yet accurately absorbed by value-based transactors.[2] Be-

---

[2] Only a small fraction of the broad spectrum of information available to investors, ranging from economic theories to ideological insights to insights relating to business strategy, is off limits to the IBT. The subject of what represents material

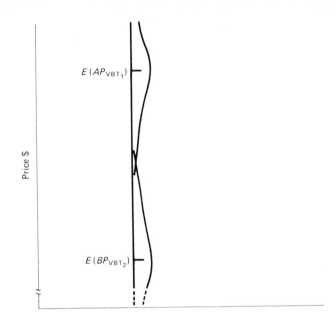

Key: $E(AP_{VBT_1})$ = Expected value of probability distribution of ask prices for value-based transactor 1.
$E(BP_{VBT_2})$ = Expected value of probability distribution of bid prices for value-based transactor 2.

Figure 12-4. Example of Overlapping Probability Distributions of Bid Price and Ask Price of Two Value-Based Transactors.

cause this information has value only as long as it has not been fully discounted in the security's price, time is of the essence. Since the VBT cares only about value-based analysis of available information relative to market price, his only concern is how much price movement toward the justified price will occur. The IBT, on the other hand, cares more about how long it will take for the market price to move up or down in response to the new information.

The situation for a market consisting only of VBTs and IBTs is shown diagrammatically in Figure 12-5. The VBT has ask, justified, and bid prices set as shown. The IBT comes into possession of adverse information on the security, indicating that a sharp drop should occur in all three of the VBT's

information under the antifraud statute, Rule 10b-5 of the Securities and Exchange Commission, has been written about extensively by many authors. Among the best is John Gillis, Esq., who wrote a series of articles published in the *Financial Analysts Journal* in the 1970s and 1980s.

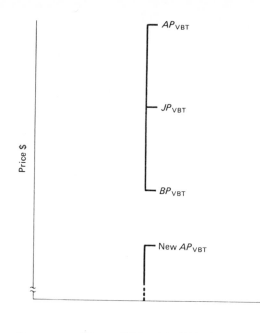

Key: BP_{VBT} = VBT's original bid price
          = IBT's short sale price
     New AP_{VBT} = VBT's new ask price
          = IBT's bid price to cover short sale
BP_{VBT} − New AP_{VBT} = Profit for IBT

Figure 12-5. Marketplace With Value-Based and
Information-Based Transactors Before and
After the Arrival of New Information.

prices. How far they will drop is not known and may only be roughly estimated by the IBT. All the IBT wants is a high degree of assurance that
the VBT's new ask price will drop substantially below the VBT's current
bid price. That being the case, the IBT will sell or sell short the security to
the VBT at the latter's bid price and will make a profit equal to the difference
between this price and the VBT's new ask price when the market vindicates
the IBT's beliefs about the value of the information.

Contrasting Analyses Used. Information-based transactors often use
not only fundamental security analysis, although on an incremental basis,
but also technical analysis, since timing is such a critical factor and since
price behavior reflecting the arrival of new information is so important. IBTs
tend to *investigate* rather than *analyze* a security in searching for undiscovered material information. They cannot, however, determine whether
fundamental analytical information is already impounded in the security's
price, because they do not assess the absolute value of the security. All that

they can do is assess the approximate marginal fundamental and technical factors' combined impact on the security's price.

In contrast to VBTs, IBTs use a bottom-up, undisciplined, unstructured asset-picking (such as stock-picking) approach. They are usually found in small institutions that manage small portfolios and emphasize speed in their trading.

Trading Between VBTs and IBTs

In a market made up entirely of value-based and information-based investors, value-based traders establish price, while information-based traders determine volume. The value-based trader does not care when he trades, as long as he gets his price. The information-based trader does not care what he pays to trade, as long as he trades quickly. One would consequently expect trades between these two contrasting types of investment carnivores to be very common. How a market made up of VBTs and IBTs actually works is shown in the trading array in Figure 12-6.

As shown in the array, transactions between two value-based transactors do not occur unless one of them is seriously in error, since neither trades in the absence of a discrepancy between price and value. Such a discrepancy cannot simultaneously be to the advantage of both buyer and seller. Transactions between an information-based buyer and an information-based seller occur only when their respective information has contrary implications for price and neither transactor is aware of the other's information. In that case, the transaction will be executed quickly and at a price that each transactor will consider a bargain.

On average, however, both transactors will be disappointed by an amount equal (ignoring brokerage commissions, transfer taxes, and dealer spread) to the security analysis research-based expectation of the transactor on the other side. If one defines the cost of trading as the difference between what a transactor expects, based on unbiased securities research, and what he gets, then the principal element in the average cost of trading is the gross research advantage motivating the transactor on the other side.

This holds equally true for transactions between an information-based buyer and a value-based seller (or vice versa). The information-based buyer wants to transact before his information gets impounded in the price, but the value-based transactor is unwilling to sell unless the price exceeds his estimate of the security's value. If the information-based buyer is willing to pay the price, there will be a quick transaction, but the information-based buyer will be paying a price concession for it. He is likely to be disappointed to the extent that the concession absorbs the trading advantage of this information.

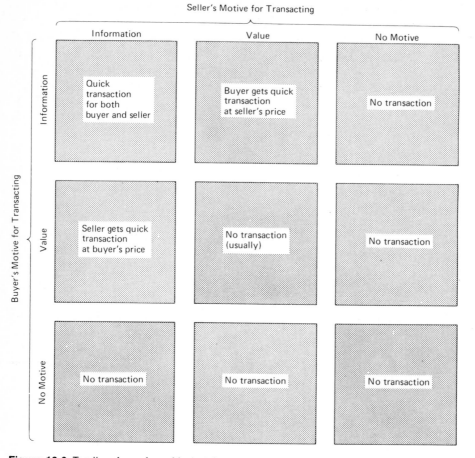

Figure 12-6. Trading Array for a Market Composed of Value-Based and Information-Based Transactors.

Trading Risk and Spread Size. As indicated earlier, the value-based seller will ultimately be disappointed if the information possessed by the buyer subsequently increases the value of the shares sold. "Getting bagged"—having price move in the direction inferred by the buying or selling activity and the research conclusions of the party on the other side of the transaction—is the principal business risk of the value-based transactor. But because the value-based transactor sets the price at which the transaction takes place, he can exact a premium for assuming this risk. The value-based transactor, in effect, makes the market in the security. He determines the spread between the price at which one can sell quickly and the price at which one can buy quickly.

This spread varies with the likelihood of large price moves in a security.

If a company has volatile sales, a high degree of operating and/or capital structure leverage, and a low degree of product diversification that combine to produce volatile earnings, the risk of getting bagged by trading in its shares will be great. In equilibrium, the spread on the stock expands until, on average, the discrepancy between its bid and ask prices and its justified price is just sufficient to compensate the value-based transactor for assuming the risk of taking a long or short position in the security. If the spread expands beyond this point, value-based transactors will be attracted to the stock, driving the spread back toward equilibrium. Conversely, if the spread shrinks, VBTs in the stock will withdraw. In equilibrium, therefore, the cost of trading on information is closely related to the cost of trading on value.

The Trading Paradox

Alas, equilibrium in real world markets cannot be as simple as described to this point. To see why, consider the information-based transactor. If the IBT knew the size of the value-based transactor's spread, the IBT would trade only if the value of his information exceeded the spread. But this implies that the information-based trader would trade only when it was to the value-based transactor's disadvantage. Therefore, no matter how large the value-based trader's spread is, it is never large enough to make value-based trading profitable if the information-based trader estimates the spread correctly. In effect, the IBT is playing a "heads I win, tails you lose" game with the VBT.

To be willing to trade, therefore, the value-based trader must believe that the transactor on the other side either:

1. Underestimates the worth of the value-based research used in determining the value-based trader's spread;
2. Overestimates the value of his own information; or
3. Is trading for reasons other than investment advantage.

Reasons 1 and 2 may seem to be errors that a competent information-based transactor is unlikely to make consistently. However, as later discussion of dealer markets in this chapter suggests, these errors are surprisingly easy to make.

Liquidity-Based Transactors

Many transactions entail no attempt to reap investment advantage. Securities are sold to make way for the purchase of other securities or bought to invest a cash contribution, for example. Thus, many transactors who have no information are not holding out for a transaction price more favorable than value; indeed, they may be willing to transact at an unfavorable price in order to transact quickly even if they lack information. They are the flower munchers alluded to earlier.

These informationless traders are called *liquidity-based transactors* (LBTs). Their role was originally described by Jack Treynor, then writing under the name Walter Bagehot [1971]. They are transactors who trade to obtain or divest cash or, equivalently, to rebalance portfolios that have gotten out of balance relative to original dollar allocations because of price movements (up or down) of some securities.

In a market consisting solely of value-based and liquidity-based transactors, trades take place quickly because of LBTs buying at VBT ask prices and LBTs selling at VBT bid prices. Hence, with a positive spread, the VBT consistently makes a profit in such a market equal to the difference between the two prices.[3]

Pseudo-Information-Based Transactors

A fourth type of trader is Bagehot's [1971] *pseudo-information-based transactor* (PIBT). This is the trader who either exaggerates the value of new information or believes his information has value, when in fact it has already been largely impounded in the price of the security. As such, the PIBT, like the LBT, is essentially an informationless transactor.

In the case of adverse information, for example, the justified price of the security falls little or not at all, and the PIBT is forced to cover at the VBT's ask price, incurring a loss equal to the VBT's spread.

Winners and Losers

Given the four categories of transactors—VBTs, IBTs, LBTs, and PIBTs— some preliminary statements about who wins and who loses in the zero-sum trading game can be made. Basically, the valued-based transactor always loses to information-based transactors. On the other hand, the VBT always wins in his transactions with liquidity-based and pseudo-information-based transactors. To the value-based transactor, however, information-motivated, liquidity-motivated, and pseudo-information-motivated traders are

---

[3] In the discussion of trading later in this chapter, the notion of a *passive trader* or *transactor* is introduced. The passive transactor is similar to the liquidity-based transactor in that he has cash to invest (or needs cash) for the passive or index fund he manages. However, the passive manager is distinguished from the LBT in that execution cost minimization is a critical factor in achieving performance as close to that of the index as possible. Hence, this transactor's execution behavior differs *significantly* (i.e., tends to be more pro-active as a price setter rather than as a price taker) from that of the LBT.

largely indistinguishable. In order for the VBT to survive and prosper, his combined gains from LBTs and PIBTs must exceed his losses to IBTs. The spread he sets between his bid and ask prices affects each.

If the value-based investor could distinguish between information-based and informationless traders, he could refuse to deal with the former and greatly reduce his spread to the latter. But, of course, information traders quickly learn to talk and act like informationless traders—like wolves in sheep's clothing—in order to deceive the value-based investor. It follows that the break-even spread for the value-based investor will be larger when the occurrence of information-based trades is more frequent and more damaging, and the break-even spread will be smaller when the volume of informationless trades is greater. In effect, informationless transactors such as LBTs and PIBTs will lose to information-based transactors, with the value-based investor serving as the conduit for these losses.

One might suppose that if an investor's research is worthless, the price of the security in question is as likely to go up as it is to go down subsequent to his transaction. It now should be clear that this thinking ignores the motive of the investor on the other side. If he is not motivated, he will not trade. If the investor's trade is executed successfully, the investor on the other side had to have a motive, and the odds are no longer even regarding the subsequent direction of price changes.

Regardless of whether investors trade on information or on value, they make certain assumptions about the *future* level of justified price. If investors trade on information, they measure their opportunity by the difference between the current justified price and that implied by their information. If investors trade on value, they measure their opportunity by the difference between the current trading price and the current justified price. But when investors trade on information, of course, they *actually* trade on a price different from the current justified price. When investors trade on value, they *actually* close out their position at a future justified price different from the current justified price.

The difference between the opportunity envisioned by the information-based trader and his actual gain is the opportunity envisioned by the value-based trader; the difference between the opportunity envisioned by the value-based trader and his actual gain is the opportunity envisioned by the information-based trader. Each investor's disappointment equals the other's opportunity. Put another way, each investor's shortfall is equal to what it takes to motivate the other to transact.

Each investor tends to focus on his own research opportunity, ignoring the research opportunity motivating the investor on the other side. But if one set of investors tends to see its own research opportunities as being large, is it reasonable to assume that the research opportunities of other sets of investors are small?

By contrast, in markets involving dealers, the spreads are usually a tiny fraction of the security's value. If trading is potentially so expensive, why is it that the cost does not show up in the round trip cost of trading with the dealer? The dealer is remarkably innocuous. His spread is small, and he has no damaging information. Indeed, he is equally willing to buy or sell. But the key is that the dealer does not plan to hold the position he acquires in accommodating a transaction. Lurking behind the dealer, with identity and transacting motives that are unknown, is the investor's true trading adversary. The dealer's spread serves to motivate only the dealer. Alas, an investor finds out only later what it took to motivate the transactor on the other side.

When a carnivorous investor such as a VBT or IBT wins, he wins only after a lag—after his information gets into the price in the case of an IBT, or after trade prices return to the justified price in the case of a VBT. But this means that whoever loses to the carnivore loses after the same lag. Thus, this element—the predominant element—in the cost of trading can never be measured by simply comparing the price of a particular trade with observed data, such as the closing or opening price, or calculated data, such as the average of the opening and closing prices.

In effect, an investor's transaction is not really over until the dealer's transaction with the other investor is completed. Only then will the first investor know whether the assumptions that motivated his end of the transaction were correct or, if his assumptions were erroneous, just how costly those errors were.

As discussed in the next section, the dealer manages his trading in such a way that the big costs generated by the carnivorous investor on one side are passed to the carnivorous investor on the other side. Therefore, in order for investors to clearly understand their own trading costs, it is necessary to understand exactly how the dealer shifts these costs from himself to them.

ROLE OF THE DEALER

Consider the plight of two anxious liquidity-based investors, one eager to buy and the other eager to sell. If they could transact with each other, there would be no need to motivate value-based investors to transact, and their transaction could take place at, or close to, justified price. In order to transact with each other, however, they must arrive at the market at exactly the same time. Otherwise, the first to arrive will end up transacting with the value-based investor on one side of the market (in bid-ask price dimensions) and the second will end up transacting with the value-based transactor on the other.

Unfortunately for both liquidity-based transactors, value-based investors do not trade unless the discrepancy between anticipated trade price and

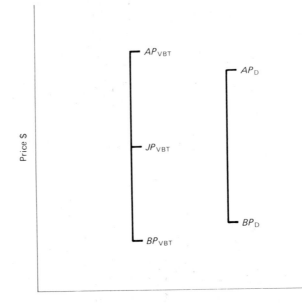

Figure 12-7. Bid and Ask Prices of a Dealer Relative to a
Value-Based Transactor.

justified price is large, perhaps 20 to 40 percent of justified price. The solution
is to find someone who can position the first eager transactor's trade until
the second transactor comes along, in effect enabling them to transact with
each other even though their arrivals in the market are not simultaneous.

That someone intermediating between eager buyers and sellers is, of
course, the *dealer*. Under this generic heading are included over-the-counter
dealers, block positioners, and exchange specialists. As shown in Figure 12-
7, the dealer preempts transacting by setting a bid and ask price inside the
prices set by value-based transactors thereby creating a smaller spread than
that of the VBT. By setting a bid price higher than the VBT's bid price and
setting an ask price lower than the VBT's ask price, the dealer causes all
transactors who would normally sell to and buy from a value-based transactor to sell to and buy from the dealer.

What results, then, is a marketplace with dealers and three of the four
types of transactors operating as shown in Figure 12-8. The resulting market
is a hard one in which to make consistent trading profits even though it is
obviously less than perfectly efficient. This market can be characterized as
follows:

- Assuming their information is substantiated by the market, IBTs
  win in their transaction with dealers by an amount exceeding what

they would have won against VBTs, unless the dealer's bid (or ask) price is close to the VBT's bid (or ask) price.

- Dealers consistently win against LBTs by an amount equal to their bid-ask spread.
- Dealers win against PIBTs, albeit possibly in a lesser amount.
- VBTs transact very little, except when the dealer lays off to or buys in from them. Legally usable new information tends to bag VBTs rather than the dealer.

Width of the Dealer's Spread

Garbade [1982] provides a systematic review of some additional factors that affect dealer spreads. These additional factors are summarized in the following subsections.

Time Rate of Transactions. The literature views the dealer as providing a liquidity-in-depth service for transactors that bridges the gaps between the arrival of buy and sell orders. Since greater liquidity service is provided by dealers with relatively long gaps between offsetting orders, dealers in low volume securities, other things being equal, set a larger bid-ask spread than do dealers in high volume securities. This inverse relationship between trading volume and spread has been documented by a number of researchers, among whom Demsetz [1968] was the earliest.

Price of the Security. Demsetz and others argue that, other things equal, the bid-ask spread on a security should be directly proportional to the price of the issue. However, several empirical studies on common stocks have demonstrated that spreads are less than directly proportional. Demsetz [1968] and Benston and Hagerman [1974] attribute this phenomenon to the size of commission costs involved in trading a given dollar amount of a stock; that is, lower priced stocks incur larger costs than do higher priced stocks. The result is a tendency of institutional investors to prefer higher priced stocks. With the larger volume thereby generated producing a faster rate of transactions, spreads are narrowed further.

Size of Trade. A third factor affecting the dealer's bid-ask spread is the size of individual transactions. The bid-ask spreads for standard sized lots of securities, which vary from one type of security to another, have been empirically observed to be smaller than those for larger and smaller transactions. Little or no explanation for this observation is available other than the hypothesis that the cost of the liquidity service provided by the dealer is greater in these circumstances.

For blocks of securities larger than the standard size, the arrival of

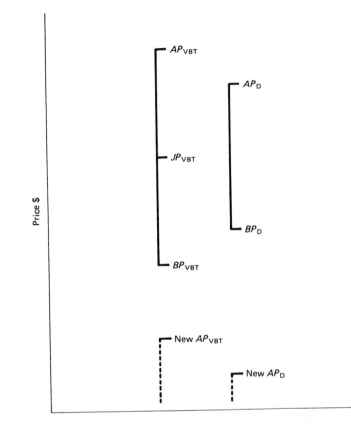

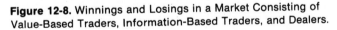

Key: $AP_D - BP_D$ = Dealer profit against LBT
BP_{VBT} — New AP_{VBT} = IBT profit against VBT
BP_D — New AP_D = IBT profit against dealer

Figure 12-8. Winnings and Losings in a Market Consisting of Value-Based Traders, Information-Based Traders, and Dealers.

market order blocks indicates an imbalance in supply and demand that serves as a proxy variable for relevant information unknown to the dealer, who then widens his spread to reduce the impact of getting bagged. For blocks of securities smaller than the standard size, the dealer has an assembly problem; that is, he needs to find enough additional non-standard-sized small blocks on the other side of the market before he gets bagged by the arrival of new information.

Insider Trading. Bagehot [1971] has pointed out the losing nature of dealer transactions with new information available to transactors. Benston and Hagerman [1974] and Barnea and Logue [1975] carried the investigation further by demonstrating that the size of dealer spreads depends on the importance of the information affecting the price of the security. They assumed that the importance could be measured by the security's specific risk as defined in Chapter 2. They found that variations in specific risk among securities explains a significant portion of observed variations in spread. The largest spreads tend to be those of nondiversified companies.

Dealer Layoffs and Buy-Ins

Under normal circumstances, the dealer is able to charge a relatively small spread. He can do so because he attracts relatively large trading volume and does not take large residual positions. As a result, he does not expect to be greatly exposed for any length of time. His holding period is measured in minutes or hours, as compared to weeks or months for VBTs, for example. He also expects that most of the securities he acquires in transactions with IBTs, LBTs, and the like who are selling will be dealt away in transactions with other IBTs and LBTs who are buying.

Unfortunately for the dealer, dealing is not as simple as depicted in this scenario. Instead of being followed by a buyer, a seller is as likely as not to be followed by another seller. The result is what statisticians call a "random walk" in the dealer's position. Random walks disturbingly have no natural bounds; once begun, trends are as likely to be continued as they are to be reversed. Sooner or later the dealer accumulates a long (or short) position large enough that prudence compels that it be *laid off* (or that it be offset by a *buy-in*).

In order to lay off or buy in securities, the dealer must be willing to transact at a price that is attractive to the transactors on the other side. These are, of course, the value-based transactors, since they are the only investors who respond to price relative to a security's absolute value. The threshold price at which VBTs respond is governed by their spread. Figure 12-9 depicts an example in which the dealer has acquired either (1) an excess inventory or long position, which causes him to lay off to a VBT, or (2) an excess short position, which causes him to buy in from a VBT to cover that short position.

As Figure 12-9 shows, at any given time the dealer has a desired inventory level (horizontal axis) at I_0. The VBT has a larger spread around the justified price (vertical axis) than does the dealer. Any buying, selling, or shorting activity that takes the dealer substantially away from his optimal inventory position increases the likelihood of his having to incur the cost of laying off at that spread. This in turn tends to cause the dealer to shift the level of his own bid and ask prices relative to the VBT's bid and ask prices to reflect the resulting change in the expected cost of accommodating information and liquidity motivated buyers and sellers. In Figure 12-9, assume

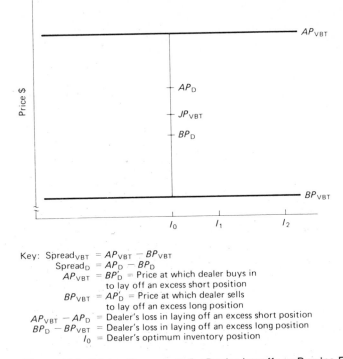

Key: $Spread_{VBT} = AP_{VBT} - BP_{VBT}$
$Spread_D = AP_D - BP_D$
$AP_{VBT} = BP'_D$ = Price at which dealer buys in
to lay off an excess short position
$BP_{VBT} = AP'_D$ = Price at which dealer sells
to lay off an excess long position
$AP_{VBT} - AP_D$ = Dealer's loss in laying off an excess short position
$BP_D - BP_{VBT}$ = Dealer's loss in laying off an excess long position
I_0 = Dealer's optimum inventory position

Figure 12-9. Pricing Framework for Dealer Layoffs or Buy-Ins From Value-Based Transactors Resulting From Excess or Deficient Securities Inventories.

that the dealer experiences an imbalance of sell orders, accumulating inventory to an undesired higher level I_1 relative to the optimum I_0. If sell orders net of buy orders continue to materialize, the dealer lowers both the justified price and bid and ask prices until, at inventory level I_2, he is able to sell (i.e., lay off) securities to the VBT. He is able to sell the securities at this point because, at this high inventory level, the dealer's ask price, AP'_D, equals the VBT's bid price, BP_{VBT}. The dealer's loss in laying off to the VBT is BP_D minus BP_{VBT}.

If the process goes in the opposite direction, with the dealer going more and more short, the dealer will finally be able to buy in from the VBT because at that point BP'_D will equal the VBT's ask price, AP_{VBT}. The dealer's loss in buying from the VBT is AP_{VBT} minus AP_D.

Location of Dealer Trades

Just how does the location of dealer trades trace out over the spectrum ranging from dealer layoffs to buy-ins? If the dealer is rational (and most dealers are very rational) the mean of his bid and ask prices will be very close to the value-based transactor's bid price when the dealer is overly long (i.e., has too much inventory) and is about to lay off, and very close to the value-based investor's ask price when the dealer is acutely short (i.e., lacks inventory) and is about to buy in. At positions just inside of the positions at which the dealer is about to lay off or buy in, what are the appropriate prices at which the dealer should accommodate customers? Certainly not at bid and ask prices near the justified price, because if that transaction then precipitated a layoff or buy-in, a huge loss would be incurred. Instead, bid and ask prices located just above the layoff (or VBT bid) price or just below the buy-in (or VBT ask) price would be appropriate. Proceeding with this logic, the dealer would establish mean and bid-ask prices for positions progressively closer to his neutral position, moving inward from the value-based transactor's bid and ask prices at the dealer's layoff and buy-in positions to a price approximately halfway between those prices—at the dealer's neutral inventory position—where the dealer is neither long nor short. Under fairly plausible conditions, the mean of the dealer's bid and ask prices varies as a straight line function of the dealer's position over the range between the extremes of laying off and buying in. Graphically, it is plotted as a diagonal straight line as in Figure 12-10. The slope of this line, which tells the dealer how to set his mean price as a function of his position, is completely determined by two things: the size of the maximum positions, long and short, that the dealer is able to tolerate and the spread between the value-based trader's bid and ask prices.

To recapitulate, the dealer enters into two fundamentally different kinds of transactions:

1. Transactions with investors in a hurry (e.g., liquidity-based) at times chosen by those investors
2. Transactions with value-based investors at times chosen by the dealer

Dealers commonly characterize themselves as *market makers*, referring to their special role in standing ready to accommodate other investors at times of the latter's choosing. In the first type of transaction, the dealer is clearly a market maker; he deals with investors who care more about time than about price. In the second type of transaction, however, the value-based investor, who cares more about price than about time, is the market maker accommodating the dealer. In the first type, the investor in a hurry accepts the dealer's price. In the second type, the dealer with inventory difficulties accepts the value-based investor's price.

Inside vs. Outside Spreads

In transactions with investors in a hurry at times chosen by the investor, the dealer profits at a rate determined by the difference between the prices

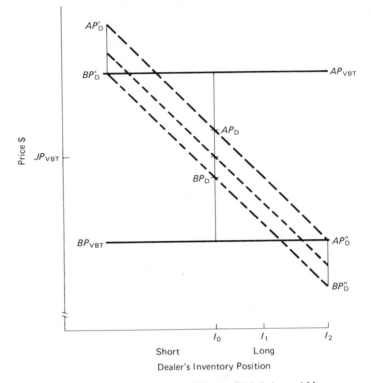

Figure 12-10. Potential Locuses of Dealer Bid, Ask, and Mean Prices Between Opposite Ends of His Layoff Spectrum.

at which he buys and sells (i.e., by the dealer's spread). In transactions with value-based investors at times chosen by the dealer, the dealer loses at a rate determined by the difference between the value-based investor's bid and ask prices (i.e., by the value-based investor's spread). For convenience, the first, the dealer spread, is called the *inside spread* and the second, the value-based trader's spread, is called the *outside spread*. The inside spread, levied on the dealer's customers, is determined by the outside spread borne by the dealer in the following way: Most of the position that the dealer accumulates in buying from customers eager to sell is offset by selling to other customers eager to buy. Thus the dealer needs to engage in layoff or buy-in transactions far less frequently than he accommodates his own customers. He breaks even (before ordinary business expenses such as rent and telephones) when his gross gains from the inside spread on transactions accommodating his customers just offset his gross losses on (far less frequent) transactions at the outside spread that are imposed by value-based investors.

Efficiency and Resiliency. The inside, or dealer, spread is what most observers have in mind when they talk about market *efficiency*. The steepness of the slope of the dealer's price-position line measures what most people have in mind when they talk about market *resiliency*. In fact, the greater the slope of this line, the less resilient is the market in question. The reason for this is that the steeper the line is, the greater is the price adjustment for a unit change in inventory position. [4]

Because the rational dealer always sets his price to a customer to reflect what he knows his position will be *after* the trade, trades large enough to significantly alter his position are priced to reflect both the inside spread and the slope of the dealer's price-position line (i.e., both the efficiency of the market in the conventional sense and its resiliency). It should be obvious, however, that since they affect the dealer's current position, previous trades as well as the current trade can have a big impact on dealer price. The price obtained by the dealer's customer depends to a large extent on how the customer is trading *relative to the crowd* (i.e., those who are trading in a hurry). Is the customer trading *against the crowd, with the crowd,* or *independently of the crowd*? This idea is developed in more detail later in the chapter.

The preceding discussion makes clear why the dealer can service or accommodate information-based investors, despite his small spread: As long as he lays off (or buys in) the position accumulated in these accommodations *before* the new information becomes embedded in the justified price, he cannot be damaged (i.e., "bagged") by the information. Instead, by quickly laying off or buying in, he shifts that risk to the value-based investor. He gets bagged only by information so concrete and obvious in its implications for value that it is embedded in the price before the dealer can lay off. In the inside information case law, such information, which is consequently damaging to the dealer, is called *material*.

Needless to say, information damaging to the dealer is a very small fraction of the information that ultimately alters the justified price. If, in response to this situation, trading on all information were to be outlawed, then trading on worthless information, which generates the bulk of the innocent trading volume on which market makers depend, would of necessity be outlawed. (Remember that investors trading on worthless information do not know it is worthless.)

Proscriptions against trading on information that gets into the consensus

---

[4] What most people have in mind when they talk about resiliency in connection with the stock market is the effect of trading pressure on market price. A security is said to be resilient when its market price is relatively stable in the face of stampeding buyers or stampeding sellers. If the dealer's price-position line is steep, small changes in the dealer's position result in large changes in dealer (i.e., market) price. Conversely, the slope of the price-position line for resilient securities is shallow, reflecting some combination of VBTs willing to trade at a small outside spread or dealers willing to take large positions before laying off or buying in, or both.

very quickly protect value-based investors as well as dealers. But such proscriptions give value-based investors no protection from more slowly prop-
agating information that gives the dealer time to lay off or buy in, because
value-based investors are the very investors that dealers lay off to or buy
in from.

Shifting Costs to Transactors. The dealer's practice of adjusting the
mean of his bid and ask prices continuously up his diagonal price-position
line from the outside bid price to the outside ask price as his position swings
from lay off to buy in (and vice versa) has the practical effect of shifting the
cost of these expensive transactions to those customers eager enough or
careless enough to trade with the crowd. That is, if a customer is buying a
security when many other customers are buying the same security, thus
forcing the dealer's inventory to a more and more short position, he can be
confident that, with or without his transaction, the dealer is trading close to
the outside ask price. If the outside spread is indeed many times the size of
the inside spread, then the difference between the dealer's price to his customer and the justified price will be many times the size of the inside spread.
In this fashion, the high cost of transacting at the VBT's ask price is transferred from the dealer to the dealer's customer. For example, the cost to
the information-based transactor trading with the crowd is large and is incurred by him rather than by the dealer. The following list summarizes the
important factors in determining trading costs:

1. The total, true cost of trading to whoever is transacting is the
   difference between justified price and the price of the trade.
2. Conventional measures of trading cost measure the inside spread.
3. Although the (mean) price of a trade is normally bracketed by the
   inside spread (i.e., by the dealer's bid and ask prices at the
   moment of the trade), the justified price is often higher or lower
   than that trade price.
4. The result of the difference between the trade price and the
   justified price is a hidden cost of trading that dwarfs the inside
   spread and hence badly distorts conventional measures of trading
   cost.
5. In order to know what his trade will really cost, the investor
   needs to know where the dealer's current mean price lies in
   relation to the justified price or, alternatively, the dealer's current
   inventory position relative to his desired inventory position.

Because liquidity-motivated investors arrive randomly with respect to
dealer position, they generate very little revenue for value-based investors.
Hence, the trading volume they generate is almost useless in reducing the
equilibrium level of the outside spread. But pseudo-information-based inves-

tors, most of whom are responding to published news in one form or another and consequently tending to trade with the crowd, force the dealer into layoffs and buy-ins and generate unintentionally innocent trading volume for the value-based investor. Thus, pseudo-information-based investors, unlike liquidity-motivated investors, tend to lower the equilibrium level of the outside spread by their trading. It follows that the volume of innocent trading relevant to the dealer's determination of the dealer spread is different from the volume relevant to determination of a value-based investor's, or outside, spread, although as noted previously the latter has some indirect bearing on the former.

Sophisticated Trading Strategies

In theory, it is the difference between the value based on new information and the existing justified price that drives the information-based investor. But he does not know what the new value is. Thus, the information-based transactor can easily find himself in the unhappy position of trading at the outside bid or ask price on information that is already fully impounded in the justified price and dealer price.

To avoid the resulting losses, the information-based investor needs to know whether his information is in the justified price and how far the dealer's price departs from that price. If he knows the approximate location of the outside bid and ask prices, he also knows the justified price because the justified price is approximately the mean of the two. One of the principal problems with attempting to determine from recent price history whether an adjustment for the information has already taken place is the "noise" imposed on the history by fluctuations in the dealer's position. A history of *justified* price is consequently far more trustworthy in arriving at this judgment than is a history of *dealer* price. Ongoing research on justified price histories has the potential for adding significantly to the knowledge needed for productive strategic decision making.

If the information-based transactor knows the dealer's layoff and buy-in prices, he knows the current cost of trading quickly because he can locate the current trade price (which is directly observable) relative to these prices. Is it close to the dealer's buy-in price? If so, then buying quickly will be very expensive—that is, the cost, measured relative to the justified price, will be many times the inside spread—and selling quickly will be cheap. Is the current trade price close to the dealer's layoff price? If so, then selling quickly will be very expensive, and buying quickly will be cheap.[5]

---

[5] Some authors have hypothesized that as the dealer's buy-in and layoff points are approached, the dealer's straight diagonal price-position line becomes curvilinear (curving upward at the buy-in point and downward at the layoff point) and the dealer's spread simultaneously widens. Both reflect the dealer's reaction to an extreme

Value-Based Transactors. As noted earlier, the big cost of trading for the value-based transactor arises from getting bagged. But he trades only when either pseudo or valid information drives the dealer to lay off or buy in. The more likely that pseudo information is the occasion for his trading opportunity, the less likely he is to get bagged. In particular, highly visible stories in the news media (encouraging the kind of pseudo-information trading the dealer is asking the value-based transactor to accommodate) reduce the likelihood of his getting bagged and hence his expected cost of trading.

On the other hand, if the value-based transactor knows the dealer's current layoff and buy-in prices, he can be virtually certain of participating in any layoff or buy-in he chooses because the current trade price (which the value-based transactor can directly observe) will equal the layoff or buy-in price only when the dealer is substantially trimming or adding to his position. Even though it would be contrary to the basic transacting philosophy of the VBT, the trading desk would simply enter limit orders on listed securities just inside the layoff or buy-in price.

These comments suggest that there are two fundamentally different ways for a value-based transactor to operate:

1. The VBT can trade whenever the difference between market price (i.e., dealer price) and the security analysis–based estimate of justified price exceeds his threshold.
2. The VBT can participate with other VBTs when the dealer is known to be laying off or buying in.

Here the analyst's contribution is to identify current influences on investor opinion from the media and Wall Street releases. The problem with the first approach is error in the value-based transactor's estimate of value. If the analyst is on the high side, the value-based investor will get layoffs at a smaller spread between the justified price and the VBT bid price than he intended, but no buy-ins. This occurs because the VBT's justified price estimate is high, which results in a higher ask price than that for most other VBTs (the buy-in price for the dealer) and a higher bid price than that for most other VBTs (the layoff price for the dealer). If the analyst is on the low side, the value-based investor will get buy-ins at a smaller spread between the VBT ask price and the justified price than he intended, but no layoffs. Here the VBT's ask price is attractively low, while his bid price, also low, is unattractive. If he increases his spread to counter the problem, only his largest valuation errors will lead to trades, which will continue to be unprofitable.

For this reason, the second approach is probably better, but it requires

---

disequilibrium inventory position, but there is little empirical evidence to support these contentions.

that the trading desk know the outside bid and ask data (i.e., the bid and ask prices imposed by *other* value-based transactors).

Passive Investors. The well-diversified proxy for the market portfolio in a passively managed portfolio gradually becomes less diversified as positive security-specific returns cause the weight of some securities in the proxy portfolio (relative to aggregate market portfolio value) to increase, while negative specific returns cause the relative weight of others to decrease. In order to get back to the original index weights, the remedy is to trim back positions in the former, and increase positions in the latter. But this requires trading.

On the other hand, this kind of *rebalancing* activity does *not* require trading quickly. Half of the troublesome price moves will subsequently be offset by price moves in the opposite direction because subsequent specific returns are as likely to offset previous returns as they are to extend them.[6] Furthermore, specific risk in the proxy portfolio is insensitive to small changes in the weights accorded to individual securities. In view of this situation, how should the trading desk handle such trades?

In the first place, the rebalancing should be undertaken to address changes in *justified* price, not changes in *dealer* price. Otherwise, the passive investor's trading desk will find itself unconsciously mimicking the trading of value-based investors, but without the necessary spread.[7]

In addition, the passive investor does not want to pay for unneeded trading speed. Thus, he will defer buying when the dealer is close to buying in (i.e., when the transaction price is high relative to the justified price) and selling when the dealer is close to laying off (i.e., when the transaction price is low relative to justified price).

At any give time the passive investor will have a number of securities that he wants to sell and a number of others that he wants to buy. To avoid having his buy and sell lists "cherry-picked" by information-based investors, he must take care not to offer to trade these securities via market orders or their equivalent. If he does, he will get bagged along with value-based inves-

---

[6] Random price moves cause a cumulative change in the value of a passive investor's holdings that causes it to diverge from the original optimally diversified value. On average, the divergence grows with the square root of time. The longer the manager defers rebalancing, the larger the manager's rebalancing trades tend to be in accordance with this square root rule. But the *frequency* of these trades is inversely related to the length of the rebalancing period. Thus, the amount of rebalancing trading *per unit of time* declines the longer the manager defers rebalancing, although at the cost of some increase in specific or unsystematic risk.

[7] Suppose, for example, that the dealer's accommodations significantly alter his position and hence his price while leaving justified price unchanged. If, in order to rebalance, a portfolio manager sells every time dealer price rises, he will be selling when the dealer's position is falling (algebraically) and hence when the dealer's information-based customers are buying.

tors, but without their VBT spread compensation.[8] A trading desk's objective must be to use the flexibility that rebalancing affords to trade only those securities that are as close to the desirable extremities of the outside spread as possible. It should offer securities for sale near the dealer's buy-in point and offer to purchase securities near the dealer's layoff point.

Liquidity-Based Investors. As noted, the liquidity-based investor has trading motives largely unrelated to those of other investors: Their cost of trading is sometimes high and sometimes low, or even negative, but their average cost for a round trip is the dealer's inside spread.[9]

If the liquidity-motivated investor has several securities from which to choose, then the one to sell (or buy) is the one about which there are cheery (or gloomy) stories in the current media and which the dealer is likely to be close to buying in (or laying off). Even in liquidity-based trades, both the security analysts and the trading desk have contributions to make. Here again the object is not to make money, but to avoid getting bagged without the compensation of the outside spread.

In sum, regardless of whether the investment organization that employs him is passive or active, and regardless of whether it is information-based or value-based, the most valuable thing that the buy-side trader can do is to locate the current outside bid and outside ask prices. He cannot avoid incurring (half) the inside spread on trades accommodated by the dealer, and probably he should not try to do so.

The next section discusses how the trading function, primarily in a buy-side organization, is organized and managed, what choices are available to traders and what they cost in time or money, and what tactics are employed in carrying out the strategies outlined in this section.

MANAGING THE TRADING FUNCTION

The investment process has been described as a three-legged stool, supported equally by securities research, portfolio management, and securities trading. Of the three, trading is the least understood and least appreciated.

---

[8] If the rebalancing manager offers to trade the securities he wants to buy and sell at the market price, information-based investors will oblige him on those securities for which they have information that would be valuable or damaging—and will forget the rest. Instead of being a random selection from his offerings, the securities that trade are the ones that the rebalancing manager will ultimately have reason to regret having traded.

[9] Note that from the public policy viewpoint, this is the crucial measure of trading costs because it is the cost of using the security in question as a store of value with which to meet unforeseen emergencies. If the inside spread is too high, only the richest investors can afford to hold such securities. Democratic capitalism requires dealer markets, which means that it requires healthy dealers.

Unlike securities analysis and portfolio management, trading has not been considered a formal profession. Trading is a learn-by-doing occupation. No one studies trading at Harvard Business School. No one takes trader certification exams to become a Chartered Securities Trader. Traders learn on the job. As they gain in proficiency, they progress from apprentice to journeyman to master. Knowledge, skill, adaptivity, relationships, and trust slowly build over a period of years.

The basic job of the institutional buy-side trader revolves around the daily orders generated by the portfolio manager. The job of the trader is to execute the desired trades quickly, without error, and at favorable prices. It is the final, critical step in the interlinked investment process. Yet in many institutions, the trader is only peripherally involved in the portfolio process.

Day-to-day, the buy-side trader spends most of his time in telephone contact with "street-side" or "sell-side" traders at selected brokerage firms. Sell-side traders tend to be more aggressive and better paid than are buy-side traders. Buy-side traders are little known outside their own organizations. Even in their own organizations, traders are often regarded as the least critical link in the decision-making chain from the securities analyst to the portfolio manager to the trader. In some buy-side organizations, the trader is little more than a clerk, carrying out instructions without questioning and without discretion. The sell-side trader determines the when, where, and how of order execution.

This limited view of the trader's contribution originates from one of three common ways of thinking about trading and transaction costs:

1. Trading is inexpensive and unimportant when contrasted to the benefits from securities research. This view prevailed through the 1950s, 1960s and into the 1970s. In the early days, institutional portfolio managers were highly dependent on Wall Street firms for investment intelligence and ideas. The traditional way to reward the broker was to channel the resultant trading activity through him. It is no exaggeration to state that professional investment management grew out of seeds planted by Wall Street firms.

Treynor, writing under the name Bagehot [1971], has pointed out how the New York Stock Exchange (NYSE) in those days was truly "the only game in town." Venerable traditions and well-tested procedures assured that all orders received equivalent execution. Most portfolios were run with a "search for undiscovered value" philosophy, and trades were small relative to NYSE capacity. A trader needed little knowledge and discretion.

In the early 1970s, several important trends converged to change buy-side trading forever. As pension fund assets grew, the prevailing fixed commission schedule created an unjustifiable bonanza for the exchange community. Investment managers and pension sponsors alike were pressured to bring commission charges more in line with the cost of providing the service. The result was a move to fully negotiated commissions, beginning May 1, 1975. As a result, different levels of execution services could be bought for different commission charges, presenting the buy-side trader with new choices.

In addition, the first practical applications of the efficient market hypothesis (EMH) came to life in the form of index funds. Index fund managers strongly disagree with the traditional view of trading as being "just a cost of doing business." Since index fund managers have no expectation of recovering trading costs through security selection, reducing trading costs is a paramount goal. Yet, like the traditional view, their view often attached limited value to the skills of the trader.

2. Stocks are fairly priced; as a result, trading is not worthwhile and trading costs are to be minimized. The quants who worked on Efficient Market Hypothesis measurements turned from portfolio composition studies to trading costs and methods. For the first time, trading processes were subject to analytical thinking. Costs were measured, and trading experiments led to different trading attributes. Trading tactics developed at that time were attuned to a specific investment decision process. These new techniques were applied repetitively, however. The trader's job required only rote skills.

During the 1980s, confidence in the efficient market notion eroded as more and more anomalies arose. In addition, institutional investors—pension fund sponsors in particular—became concerned that trading costs were too high and exacted too great a penalty on investment performance, thus leading to the evolution of a third, emerging view of transacting.

3. Trading is expensive, and trading tactics need to be carefully designed and tailored to the investment decision itself. The job of the trader has become much more complicated. In 1990, the buy-side trader has at his command alternative tactics to accomplish a given investment goal. A trader can go to an exchange, to the block houses, or to "meet" markets such as the crossing networks. He can gain equity exposure through equities, American Depositary Receipts, convertible bonds, warrants, options, or futures. The trader may work for an information-based manager who needs immediate liquidity and pays what is demanded. Conversely, he may work for a value-based transactor, and can lay back and hope to draw interest from a more anxious trader at a favorable price. Understanding and judging the available alternatives is the new challenge to the buy-side trader.

At last the buy-side trader is beginning to be viewed as a critical component of the investment management process. What the trader knows is becoming an integral part of the investment process.

THE PORTFOLIO MANAGER/TRADER RELATIONSHIP

Markets are organized to accommodate investors who wish to trade. Transacting tactics differ based on trading motivation, which is the domain of the

TABLE 12-1. Summary of Trading Motivations, Time Horizons, and Time vs. Price Preferences

Trader	Motivation	Time Horizon	Time vs. Price Preference
Value-based traders	Valuation error	Weeks to months	Price
Information-based traders	New information	Hours to days	Time
Pseudo-information-based traders	Seemingly new information	Hours to days	Time
Liquidity-based traders	Invest cash or divest securities	Hours to days	Time
Passive traders	Rebalancing[a]	Days to weeks	Price
Dealers	Accommodation	Minutes to hours	Indifferent

[a] Also concerned with investing cash or divesting securities.

portfolio manager. Trading motivations can be broadly categorized into the types identified earlier in this chapter. Table 12-1 describes the attitudes toward trading displayed by the various traders in the market.

Value-based traders act on absolute value judgments that are based on careful, sometimes painstaking research. They move quickly when the price moves into their value range. As explained earlier, they trade infrequently and are motivated only by price and value.

Information-based traders usually stress speed of execution. They are likely to use market orders and rely on market makers to accommodate their desire to trade quickly. They must *buy* time; that is, the information on which they are buying or selling has limited time value. The trading tactics for pseudo-information-based traders are the same because these traders believe they trade on information.

Information traders are more likely to trade in large blocks than are liquidity traders. Their information frequently concerns the prospects of one stock, and they seek to maximize the value of the information. Successful information-based traders are wary of acquiring a public reputation for astute trading because if they did, who would wish to trade against them? Accordingly, information traders often use deceptive actions to hide their intentions.

Liquidity-based traders, acting on behalf of liquidity-based managers, do not transact to reap an investment advantage for the securities involved. These transactions are not motivated by value or by information per se. Rather, liquidity-based transactions are a means to an end, which is the release of cash proceeds to facilitate purchase of another security, reduce market exposure, or fund a distribution. Liquidity-based traders tend not to be price sensitive, and some may not be trading cost sensitive.

Passive traders, acting on behalf of passive or index fund portfolio managers, similarly seek liquidity in their rebalancing transactions, but these sophisticated institutional buy-side traders are much more concerned with the cost of trading. They tend to use less time sensitive techniques in the hope of trading time indifference for lower cost execution. Passive traders have much flexibility to use different and, hopefully, lower cost trading techniques. In some respects, because of the types of orders and markets they use, these traders resemble dealers in the sense that they allow the opposing party to determine the timing of the trade in exchange for determining the price.

Thus, the keystone of the buy-side trader's choice of trading strategy is the urgency of the trade. Is the decision based upon fundamental value, valuable new information, or the need to rebalance? Will the value of completing the trade disappear or dissipate if it is not completed immediately?

From the portfolio manager's view, the key to effective trading is to realize that the portfolio decision is not complete until shares are bought or sold. This implies a continuing, two-way conversation with the trader that begins when the trade is first seriously contemplated: How sensitive is the stock to buying or selling pressure? How much volume can be accumulated without having the price move out of the desirable range? Are there any special considerations (e.g., news, rumors, or competing buyers) that make this a particularly good or particularly poor time to deal in this stock? In other words, how resilient is the market? Is the price being driven toward a dealer layoff or buy-in position? Armed with this data, the portfolio manager hones his interest in the security.

The trader can also begin to tune up his awareness, providing the portfolio manager with a stream of information on market conditions and stock trading behavior. The crucial function of the trading desk is to match the impending transaction's price-time trade-off with market circumstances. This trade-off may change rapidly because of market conditions, dealer inventories, and changes in the portfolio manager's desires.

THE BUY-SIDE/SELL-SIDE RELATIONSHIP

The model of the dealer presented earlier under the heading "Role of the Dealer" can be expanded in several practical dimensions that profoundly affect the tactics chosen by the buy-side trader. In addition to the dealer functions identified in that section of this chapter, buy-side traders interact with agency functions of the broker, who collects a commission for skillful representation of the trade to the dealers. The size of this commission often exceeds the cost of representing the order, creating a "soft dollar" environment in which commission allocation often dominates broker and market selection. Direction of the flow of orders rests with the buy-side trader.

This agency relationship via the broker or account representative contrasts with the adversarial nature of the dealer trading relationship. The dealer is an adversary dealing for his own account, while the agent is a trusted representative. Yet the distinctions between broker and dealer have long been blurry within many buy-side organizations. Bond markets and over-the-counter stock markets operate only as dealer markets, without explicit commissions, which adds to the confusion. The distinctions are further confused by buy-side pressures to reduce commissions, which cause broker-dealer firms to replace falling commission income with dealer profits.

Brokerage Commissions

Brokerage commissions are the most visible portion of trading costs. The dealer spreads and responses to market pressures detailed earlier are very difficult to gauge. The commissions, however, are printed on every ticket. For better or worse, efforts to reduce transaction costs focus first on commissions.

Conflicting interests are raging concerning the answer to the question, Whose commissions are they? The manager traditionally allocates brokerage business to buy research services that aid portfolio management. The broker thinks of commissions as payment for services rendered. The plan sponsor increasingly views commissions as being leakage out of the pension trust. All are contending for control of the commission dollar.

Commissions (or other trading costs) customarily buy two services: research and execution. The extensive security and economic research available through the brokerage industry is essential to most active managers. Even quantitative managers access analytical power and data through brokers.

Execution Services

When buying *execution*, services directly associated with trading through a broker-dealer are secured, including the following:

- **Finding the buyer.** The broker who spends time finding the other side of a trade expects (and deserves) compensation.
- **Immediacy.** The market will accommodate (for a price) someone who feels he must trade immediately. The broker-dealer does not bear risk without compensation. Depending on the dealer's inventory position, this service may come at a high cost.
- **Market Information.** Who is buying? Who is selling? How much buying or selling interest is showing on the exchange floor or nearby? This market intelligence, which can be provided by the broker, is very valuable to the buy-side trader when he considers his trading tactics.

- **Secrecy.** As noted previously, buy-side traders place great value on preserving the anonymity of their trading intentions. Notice, however, that such secrecy does not extend to the sell-side trader, whose stock in trade is the knowledge of where supply and demand exist. That an investor is willing to trade is a very valuable piece of information. It has been suggested—only a bit facetiously—that the broker ought to pay the investor for this valuable information.
- **Escrow.** Escrow guarantees the delivery and correct exchange of ownership.
- **Supporting the market mechanism.** Paying a commission indirectly assures the continuance of the needed market making facilities.

Because these services and information are critical to the trading decision, buy-side traders are strongly influenced by sell-side traders. The buy-side trader's internal contacts may be slim indeed. They might be simply a pile of tickets or a computer file of orders. In contrast, the sell-side trader is a constant verbal window on the world because he possesses information vital to the buy-side trader's job. Over the years, the buy-side trader builds up a reservoir of trust, friendship, comfort, and goodwill with his sell-side counterparts on Wall Street.

"My word is my honor" is the code of both the buy-side and the sell-side trader. Nonetheless, valuable information is the stock in trade of the markets, and the temptations are great. Morton [1988] has found that one of the side effects of the explosion of trading techniques and trading alternatives is that it is difficult to trace the uses to which information is put.

It is often necessary to rely on the sell side's reputation for integrity and its long-term desire to maintain relationships. The buy-side trader must balance trust and kinship with his sell-side counterpart against the need for control and prowess over this sometime adversary. The buy-side trader's first allegiance must always be to his firm's clients, for whom he acts in a fiduciary capacity.

THE COSTS OF TRADING

One of the consistently most troubling aspects of professional investment management is the repeated inability of active managers as a group to deliver stated performance goals. Table 12-2, based on data from *Business Week*, is typical: Year after year, most managers fail to beat the Standard & Poor's 500 Composite Stock Price Index. Note that the statistics for managers fired for poor performance are dropped from the data. Therefore, these figures almost certainly *overstate* manager performance.

Most who have searched for the source of this mysterious shortfall suspect transaction costs to be the most likely cause. Fund sponsors are

TABLE 12-2. Performance of Professional Managers

Period Ending 12/84	Percentage of Managers Underperforming the S&P 500 Stock Index
1 year	74%
3 years	68
5 years	55
10 years	56

increasingly aware that transaction costs play an important role in investment performance. In addition, pension fund sponsors recognize expanded fiduciary responsibilities concerning transaction costs. Legally, these trusts operate solely for the benefit of the beneficiaries. There is a clear fiduciary duty to spend funds wisely. The U.S. Department of Labor imposes a regulatory requirement for "best execution." But how is best execution measured? As discussed later in this chapter, traditional exchange practice leads to a homogenization of trading. If trades look alike, do they *all* qualify as being best executions, or has the problem merely been masked? On the other hand, if current trading practices lead to distinctive differences, there is a need for reliable trade cost measurement.

In theory, "transaction cost" is best defined as the difference between what the seller receives per share and what the ultimate and unknown buyer pays. In actual trading practice, one or more market intermediaries may separate the two parties. The presence and profitability of these intermediaries is difficult—or perhaps impossible—to discover. For the lack of a better alternative, most transaction studies have ignored the intermediaries and looked at the transaction process only as experienced by the buyer or the seller.

Trading Cost Categories

Trading costs can be divided into five subcategories, the first two of which are investigated in the first half of this chapter:

1. *"Inside" spreads*—Payments to dealers or other market functionaries for conducting the continuous market.
2. *Market impact*—Discounts on sells or premiums on buys that compensate for undesired changes in dealer inventories.
3. *Commissions*—Direct payments to brokers acting as agents.
4. *Administrative costs*—The cost of running a trade desk and clearing trades.

TABLE 12-3. Estimates of Explicit Transaction Costs[a]

Study	Round-Trip Cost
Demsetz [1968]	2.6%
Krause and Stoll [1972]	2.6
Cuneo and Wagner [1975]	
Information-motivated	2.6
Liquidity-motivated	0.9
Beebower and Priest [1974]	1.0
Condon [1981]	1.8
Loeb [1983]	
Large cap (greater than 5,000 shares and $1.5 billion in assets)	1.1
Small cap (less than 5,000 shares and $10 million in assets)	17.3
Wagner [1985] (program trades)	0.9
Berkowitz, Logue, and Noser [1988]	0.5
Hasbrouck and Schwartz [1988]	1.3
Fisher study, as reported in Chernoff [1988] (accommodative trades)	−0.015

[a] Some heroic interpretation and extension of the studies cited was necessary to develop these estimates. Any errors in this interpretation are the responsibility of the authors of this chapter, not that of the authors of the original studies.

5. *Opportunity costs*—The cost of failing to complete a desired trade before the price is driven out of the trading range. Opportunity costs show only as shortfalls in portfolio performance.

Think of transaction costs as an iceberg, with the commission being the tip above the surface. *The major parts of transaction costs are unobservable.* They do not appear in accounting statements, and they appear only indirectly in manager evaluations. Even formal studies cannot clearly gauge the size and relative importance of transaction cost components.

The high visibility of the commission component and the elusiveness of the other components have led sponsors to a misdirected assault on commissions. Commissions can be driven down by fiat; the danger is that this pressure will merely drive the other elements of total cost out of sight, rather than result in their overall true reduction.

A number of researchers have attempted to measure the explicit cost of transacting. Table 12-3 summarizes the results of several of the transaction cost studies completed over two decades. As shown in the table, most of the round trip costs average 1 to 2 percent, although there is some variability. A totally different approach to estimating the cost of transacting is taken by Wagner [1988b]:

The 1988 NYSE Fact Book reports that members earned commissions income of $8.249 billion and "trading and investment profits" of $10.987 billion. These figures (especially the trading and investment profits) include elements besides equity profits, but when added together and divided by the total value of dollars traded, they imply a 1.98 percent transaction cost.

The dispersion in these estimates is large enough to cast some doubt on the entire process of transaction cost measurement, yet certain factors can be identified that partially account for the variability:

- *Date of study*. The early studies by Demsetz [1968], Kraus and Stoll [1972], and Cuneo and Wagner [1975] were performed before fully negotiated commissions were mandated in 1975. The effect of negotiated commissions was to increase liquidity and decrease transaction costs.
- *Sample of trades*. Some studies, such as Beebower and Priest [1974] and Berkowitz, Logue, and Noser [1988] were broad-based, examining large volumes of accounting records of transactions. The trades were generated by managers with different investment styles and trading tactics. Other studies, such as Cuneo and Wagner [1975], Loeb [1983], and Fisher [1988] were more narrowly based and concentrated on a set of trades that were executed by a specific institution and designed to implement specific investment objectives.
- *Trading strategy*. Cuneo and Wagner [1975] studied passive trading, Loeb [1983] studied principal trades; Wagner studied program trades; and Fisher [1988] studied trades placed to provide liquidity to the market as a profit-making activity.
- *Methodology*. Numerous methodologies were applied by the various researchers. Cuneo and Wagner [1975] and Loeb [1983] evaluated trades relative to a previously determined execution price. Beebower and Priest [1974] used closing prices as a benchmark. Berkowitz, Logue, and Noser [1988] used the average price of the day as a standard. Hasbrouck and Schwartz [1988] derived a measure by examining the volatility of short-term price movements relative to long-term price movements. Each of these approaches has its own merits and shortcomings.

The clear implication of the divergent cost estimates highlights the need for thoughtful approaches to trading strategies. Poor trading involving inattentive, incorrect trading tactics leads to higher transaction costs. Conversely, good trading lowers transaction costs. Trading costs are variable and strongly influenced by the buy-side trader, who needs to ask two questions:

1. What is the right trading tactic for this particular trade?

2. What is the expected vs. experienced cost for this type of trading tactic?

Nonetheless, the dispersion of divergent cost estimates causes great confusion among plan sponsors anxious to manage the cost of transacting. Better insight into the true cost of trading is still an unsolved mystery, the solution to which is better models and more complete data.

HOW THE MARKET WORKS

Markets in the United States and around the world are organized differently to serve their clients. However, it is worthwhile to elaborate on the mechanisms of the New York Stock Exchange (NYSE) because more transactions have been executed there than anywhere else. Visitors to the floor of the NYSE inevitably hear a comment such as "This is the best of all possible markets." "Best" on the NYSE floor usually implies an ability to execute reasonably large trades without major impact, but it also implies an ability to rapidly adapt to changing market conditions, and improve mechanisms as new technologies and new investor demands arise.

The great advantage of market liquidity is that traders and investors can trade in reasonable volume without a major impact on stock price. Many factors contribute to making a market liquid:

- The continuous interaction of *many buyers and sellers* is both the cause and the effect of liquidity. Investors are more willing to hold shares that they can dispose of whenever they choose to do so.
- A *diversity of opinion, information,* and *investment needs* among market participants. A large pool of investors enhances the diversity of opinion.
- Convenience: A *readily accessible location,* either physical or electronic, *operating continuously* during convenient market hours, which implies that an assigned specialist or a group of market maker–dealers is present to maintain market continuity.
- A *reasonable cost of transacting,* so that investors can trade positions without excessive loss of value. High transaction costs destroy market liquidity. Without a reasonable cost of transacting, investors could not profitably trade except on information of great significance.
- Market *integrity*: Investors who receive fair and honest treatment in the exchange process will trade again.
- The *sanctity of the contract*: To ensure the certainty of trade completion, participating brokers guarantee the trade to both buyer and seller. Exchange members must pass standards of financial strength, knowledge, and integrity.

Value from liquidity also flows to the companies whose securities trade on the exchange. Investors will pay for securities that possess the valuable trait of liquidity. Higher stock prices enhance corporate value and lower the cost of equity capital.

Obviously, not all companies are large enough, or have a sufficient market for their securities, to support an extensive pool of buyers and sellers. Markets for thinly traded securities have little "natural liquidity"; they must be *made* liquid artificially. A need is thus created for a functionary to make the market (i.e., create liquidity). A market is made when a market maker stands ready to provide *bridge liquidity* by buying stock offered by a seller and holding it until a buyer arrives. This is also the mechanism that allows markets to operate continuously.

The need for bridge liquidity creates a liquidity cost; a market maker must be compensated for providing it. Like any merchant, he makes money by selling inventory for a higher price than the price for which he bought it. The seller takes a little less than the stock is worth; the buyer pays a little more for timely order fills. The difference, the inside spread, is the market maker's profit.

Large blocks of securities unbalance market makers' inventories and strain their capital. As a result, spreads widen and trade prices reflect dealer inventory shortages and surpluses as well as justified price. When commission levels come under pressure, trading costs shift to the less observable spreads and impact components.

The NYSE has evolved into an *agency auction with affirmative obligation*. "Agency" means that only NYSE members represent orders on the floor. "Auction" means that buyers compete by raising the price offered to attract sellers. The NYSE imposes an affirmative obligation on a specialist to maintain an "orderly market" by absorbing temporary trade imbalances into his personal account. This affirmative obligation is strictly monitored and enforced according to NYSE rules and regulations. Most of the time this mechanism provides the specialist with opportunities to earn market maker inventory profits. At times, however, the affirmative obligation forces a money-losing proposition onto the specialist. To balance occasional financial losses, the NYSE grants three valuable privileges to specialists:

1. A semimonopoly to function as the dealer in the assigned stocks.
2. The opportunity to collect a spread on orders from sellers and buyers.
3. Privileged access to valuable information concerning investor intentions.

Institutional size investing has considerably strained this venerable procedure. The personal capital available to any specialist is trivial when compared to institutional buying power. Thus, an informal support system has arisen to fill needs that are otherwise not well serviced by the specialist.

While it is convenient to equate the dealer function with the activities of the NYSE specialist, many parties can and do perform parts of the dealer function. The largest brokerage firms operate "upstairs" trading desks, committing dealer capital to support client trading desires. Equally important, investors can compete with dealers on or off the NYSE floor. Upstairs traders can reduce their trading costs by providing accommodative dealerlike services. These ancillary arrangements are vital to the survival of the major exchanges in their present form.

Even so, critics fault the system for not being adequately capitalized, accommodative, or accessible, particularly under times of strain. The system is designed to prevent markets in which orders are executed improperly or only with large price discontinuities. At times like the October 1987 stock market decline, when large, rapid market movements are unavoidable, the system becomes dangerously strained. Continuing change is surely in store for the trading process. For more discussion of how markets work, see Wagner [1989b].

TYPES OF TRADES

All trades go through the organized exchanges or the ancillary arrangements discussed in the preceding section. From a tactical standpoint, the buy-side trader must choose a specific order type that matches the trading or investment strategy under which he operates. In this section, the most common order types are defined. The next section shows how these order types are used to carry out different trading strategies. The following are 11 trade types:

1. The *market order* is the most common type of trading instruction. It instructs the broker to execute the transaction promptly in the public markets at the best price available. Little discretion is left to the broker.

2. A similar order, but one which gives the floor broker greater discretion, is the *market-not-held order*. "Not held" means that the broker is not required to trade at any specific price or at any time interval. Discretion is placed in the hands of an agent, called a floor broker, who represents the trade on the exchange floor. The agent may choose not to participate in the flow of orders on the exchange if he believes he will be able to improve the price in subsequent trading. Market-not-held orders are probably the most commonly used institutional exchange order.

3. The *best efforts order* gives the floor broker even more

discretion to work the order only when he judges market conditions to be propitious. Like the first two types of orders, some degree of immediacy is implied, but not immediacy at any price.

4. Some orders place even higher importance on the immediacy of execution. *Principal trades* require the broker to commit his own capital to complete the trade. A price concession is often needed as an incentive for the broker to function as a dealer. These orders are used most frequently when the trade is larger and/or more urgent than what can be accommodated within the normal ebb and flow of exchange trades.

5. *Program trades* are popular when many issues must be traded at once. Index fund transactions, security liquidations, major portfolio restructurings, and futures-related strategies are typical uses of program trades. Programs share many similar characteristics with principal trades, except that higher commissions often replace the price concessions.

6. *Participate (do not initiate) orders* are deliberately low key and are designed to allow the trader to wait for and respond to initiatives of more active traders. Participate orders serve a rudimentary dealer function. Buy-side traders who use them hope to capture the inside spread in exchange for letting the other side determine the timing of the trade.

7. Some types of orders are executed at specific times. *Market-on-open orders* are executed at the opening price, a time that many investors feel provides maximum liquidity.

8. Some orders are executed at specific prices. A *limit order* is executed only when the market price reaches the limit price specified by the trader. The timing of the trade is left to be determined by the ebb and flow of the market and the willingness of transactors on the other side to trade.

9. Some traders with very large orders advertise their intentions in advance to draw out the other side of the trade. Some of the terms applied to this order placement tactic are *secondary offerings* or *"sunshine" trades*.

10. Traders may avoid the exchange entirely and seek the other side directly in a dealerless, institution-to-institution market. These are called *third* or *fourth market trades*, a historic distinction that has blurred.

11. *Direct crosses* and *crossing networks* attempt to find the other side of the trade without the dealer services and without publicly revealing a trading interest. The costs of dealer services and information leakage are eliminated, but crossing participants cannot be guaranteed that their trades will find an opposing match.

Other kinds of orders exist, but they are used infrequently by institutional investors.

TRADING TACTICS

How does a trader decide which type of order to use? In the first part of this chapter, the strategic decision of the trade is identified as one of buying or selling time, deciding how much urgency to attach to trade completion. The worst trader errors are selling time too cheaply when executing value-based transactions and buying time too expensively when executing information-based transactions. A third error, and the most serious error for a liquidity trader, is to appear motivated by information, thus unnecessarily evoking self-protective responses from dealers and other market participants.

The tactical decision faced by buy-side traders concerns the type of order to be used. Few portfolio managers base their investment decisions solely on value, information, or liquidity. Most managers mix strategic goals in response to client agreements, manager perceptions, and market cycles. For example, clients may require full investment in equities at all times, regardless of whether superior investment alternatives are available. Accordingly, trading tactics may at times appear inconsistent with the stated long-term strategic investment thrusts. Thus, all buy-side traders need to understand, and occasionally use, alternative trading methods.

The subsections that follow develop a *taxonomy* or categorization of similarities and differences among various trading techniques. Table 12-4 summarizes the uses, costs, advantages, and weaknesses of these trading techniques.

Liquidity at Any Cost

Information traders who believe they need to trade with immediacy, usually in large size, use these trading techniques. The trader quickly secures a guaranteed execution at a guaranteed price. The major cost of these trades arises when the broker-dealer is placed at risk and must receive fair compensation for bearing that risk.

These trades also demand high liquidity on short notice. They may overwhelm the available liquidity in the market and cause prices to move when their presence is detected. Traders using these techniques usually recognize that these methods are expensive, but they pay the price in order to achieve the desired execution.

Of the orders that fall into this category, program trading, despite its roots in index fund trading, shares the aggressive trader characteristics of

TABLE 12-4. A Taxonomy of Trading Techniques

Primary Type of Trade/Order	Uses	Costs	Advantages	Weaknesses
Liquidity at Any Cost				
Principal trades	Immediate execution in institutional block size	Places broker at risk Creates impact	Guaranteed execution Guaranteed price	High potential for market impact
Program trades				
Costs Not Important				
Market orders	Certainty of execution Suited to simple trades	Pays the spread May create impact	Competitive price	Control of trade lost
Market-on-open orders				
Market-on-close orders				
Possible Hazards, Need Agent				
Best efforts trades	Larger-size trades, low-scale advertising	Higher commission Lower impact	May do better on price	Control of trade lost
Market-not-held orders				
Participate orders				
Advertised Orders				
Secondary offerings	Large size trades Advertising "Gravitational pull"	High operational and organizational costs	Competitive price	More difficult to administer
Sunshine trades				
Low Cost, Whatever the Liquidity				
Limit orders	Noninformational trading Indifferent to timing	High operational cost	Low commission No spread Low impact	Uncertainty of trading "Chasing" the stock
Third market trades				
Fourth market trades				
Direct crosses				

shifting risk to the broker-dealer and ignoring market liquidity. Program trades are also used to secure arbitrage profits between underlying equities and the futures or options markets. Here prices and execution costs are irrelevant; what counts is securing the spread between the markets. Any resultant increase in volatility is not important to the initiating trader.

Costs Not Important

Many investors seldom consider using anything other than market orders when trading securities. Market orders reflect the traditional view that trading costs are not significant. They work acceptably well for most mixes of investment strategies, in which it is difficult to assign pure information, value, or liquidity motivation. They also serve to mask trading intention, since all market orders look alike on the floor of the exchange.

Traders who use market orders trust the competitive market to generate a fair price. For many orders, fair market price is a reasonable assumption. Exchanges encourage market orders and set up elaborate procedures to assure that these orders receive fair "best execution" prices. Active control of the order is not required.

Market orders work best for smaller trades and more liquid stocks. They are sometimes called "no brainers" because they require little trading skill on the part of the buy-side trader or the broker. They often produce "soft dollar" commissions in exchange for broker-supplied services.

Traders who use these orders pay ordinary spreads and commissions to have their orders executed rapidly. Trade costs are accepted without question; indeed, they are seldom even considered.

The weakness of market orders is that all discretion is surrendered. The trader has no control of the trade, and the broker exercises only the most rudimentary cautions. The exchange processes are viewed as sufficient to assure fair treatment.

Possible Hazard, Need Agent

Buy-side traders often need to execute larger orders than the exchange can accommodate at any given moment, particularly when dealing with thinly traded issues. They recognize that their orders may create adverse impact if they are not handled carefully. Accordingly, they engage the services of a carefully selected floor broker to skillfully "work" the order by placing a best efforts, market-not-held, or participate order. The advantage of these trades is that they match trading desires to contra orders as they are brought into the market. Orders are usually completed through a series of partial trades. Obviously, immediate execution is not of primary importance, so such orders are less useful for information-based traders.

These orders are the epitome of the agency relationship. The trader passes control of the order to the broker, who then controls when and at what price the orders execute. The trader frequently does not know how much of an order was cleared until after the market closes.

The agent, however, may serve multiple masters, including other clients and even his own brokerage firm. The valuable information that a buyer or seller exists is revealed to the broker. It is difficult for the trader to know whether that information is used exclusively in his best interests.

Implied in these agency orders is an authorization to do some low level advertising on the exchange floor. Advertising lets the market know that a willing buyer or seller is around. That presence may exert a "gravitational pull" to draw out the other side of the trade. "Gravitational pull" is the term coined by Cohen, Maier, Schwartz, and Whitcombe [1986] to describe the effect of revealing a trading interest. As Cohen et al. describe it, "If a trader's price is close enough to a counterpart offer, he will 'jump' his price and transact with certainty via a market order."

Advertised Orders

Advertising is an explicit trade-enhancing technique used with secondary offerings and sunshine trades, which publicly display trading interests in advance. These orders draw attention (and trading interest) to themselves. If publicity attracts enough contra-side traders, the trade may execute with little or no market impact.

Low Cost, Whatever the Liquidity

Minimizing trading costs is the primary interest of buy-side traders who use these types of orders. There may not be a contra party to the trader's order who is willing to trade on the terms suggested. The trader takes the chance that the order may not be executed at all. It is best suited to passive and value-based trading situations.

The advantages of low cost trades are low commissions, low impact, and possibly the elimination of the market maker spread. The major weakness, of course, is the uncertainty of whether any trades will be made at all. Traders fear that they may end up "chasing the stock" if they are unable to find the other side in these "meet" markets.

TRADERS' ORDERS

All of the orders discussed in the subsections that follow are available to and used tactically by buy-side traders as market conditions and the motivations of the portfolio manager warrant.

Value-Motivated Traders

The value-motivated trader develops independent assessments of value and waits for market prices to move into the range of his assessment. Thus, the market maker comes to him with an excessive inventory problem and presents him with attractive opportunities.

The typical value-based trader uses limit orders, or their computerized institutional market equivalent, with which price is controlled but timing is not. All that is required is timely action at the attractive price. Even though the value transactor may act quickly, he is still accommodative and pays none of the penalties of anxious traders. Accordingly, all of the tactics described in the beginning of this section can be used to great advantage. Operating as "the dealer's dealer," the value-motivated trader buys stock when the market functionaries most want to sell stock.

Information-Motivated Traders

Information traders believe that they need to trade immediately, often in large quantities. Demands for high liquidity on short notice may overwhelm the ready supply of stock in the market and cause adverse price movements as the effect of their presence reverberates through the market. Information traders may use fast action principal trades or program trades. By transacting with a dealer, the buy-side trader quickly secures execution at a guaranteed price. The major cost of these trades arises because the dealer demands a concession away from the justifiable price to cover the risks undertaken. Information traders know this is costly, but they believe their information justifies the increased trading cost. Accordingly, information-motivated traders may not wish to display their anxious trading need. Wherever possible they use less obvious orders, such as market orders, to disguise their trading intentions. This behavior has led information traders to be called wolves in sheep's clothing.

Liquidity-Motivated Traders

The commitment or release of cash is the primary objective of liquidity-based traders. The types of orders used include market, market-not-held, best efforts, participate, principal trades, program trades, third and fourth market orders, and crossing networks. The advantage of the first five types of orders to the liquidity-based trader is timely, but not necessarily quick, execution with relatively small market impact. The advantages of the last three types of orders are low commissions and small impact. The major weakness of these last three order types is the uncertainty of whether trades will be completed on a timely basis.

Many liquidity-motivated traders believe that displaying their true liquidity-seeking nature works in their favor. When trading with an liquidity-based trader, dealers and other market participants can relax some of the protective measures that they use to keep from getting bagged.

Passive Traders

Low cost trading is a strong interest of passive traders, even though they are liquidity-motivated in their portfolio rebalancing operations. As a result, these traders tend to favor limit orders, third and fourth market orders, and crossing networks. The advantages, in addition to certainty of price, are low commissions, low impact, and the possible elimination of the inside spread. The major weakness is the uncertainty of whether trades will be completed within a reasonable time frame. There may not be a contra party willing to trade on the terms requested. These orders and markets are best suited to non- or low-information trading in which rebalancing needs are not acute; that is, either not large or not heavily concentrated in high-returns-correlated market sectors.

EVALUATING TRADING EFFECTIVENESS

Active traders intuitively perceive the difference between good and bad executions, but a systematic analysis often leads to deeper insights.

There are two ways of estimating trading costs. The macro approach is to total the profits made by the dealers and exchange specialists. The micro approach is to analyze specific trading activity. The macro approach yields rough estimates in the 1 to 2 percent range, but it is useless in evaluating the effectiveness of any particular trader or broker.

The second method attempts the impossible: a comparison of the actual trade record against the prices that would have prevailed *if this trader had not been present*. Since these "shadow" prices can never be observed, a surrogate is chosen. The two most popular surrogates are the closing price and the day's average price. Both methods have avid supporters, but it is beyond the scope of this chapter to contrast them.

Like the electronic signs that flash SUNNY or RAIN, today's trade evaluation systems give a rough idea of the magnitude and nature of trading expense. The details of evaluating trading effectiveness remain sketchy. Nonetheless, the exercise alerts trader, portfolio manager, client, and broker that execution costs are a matter of concern. At best these techniques look only at the effectiveness of the trader. A more comprehensive view would encompass the entire portfolio manager–trader relationship.

THE ETHICS OF THE TRADING COMMUNITY

"My word is my honor." The code of both the buy-side and sell-side trader is that verbal agreements will be honored. The code is self-enforcing: Any trader who does not adhere to it quickly finds that no one is willing to deal with him.

Nonetheless, as stated earlier in this chapter, valuable information is the stock and trade in the markets, and the temptations are great. One of the side effects of the explosion of trading techniques and trading alternatives is that it is difficult to trace the uses to which information is being put. It is often necessary to rely on the strength of a trader's reputation and his avid desire to maintain and build long-term relationships.

Nonetheless, trading can be looked at as a "zero-sum game" in which one trader's losses are another trader's gain. The disappearance of the brokerage commission has caused more trading costs to be less observable. Markets are becoming more adversarial and less agency-oriented, making it more difficult to align investor or buy-side interests with broker-dealer or sell-side interests.

In every case, the ethical focus for the institutional or buy-side trader must be the interests of his client. As previously mentioned, the buy-side trader acts in a fiduciary capacity, with access to the client's assets. Loyalties to his own firm and relationships with sell-side traders must be maintained within the confines of the fiduciary relationship.

SUMMARY

Different order types exist because they serve investors with different motives and trading needs. The ability of the exchange system to adapt and create solutions to investment requirements is impressive. In general, traders get the trading services they demand. In return, they pay a competitive price for the services provided by the broker-dealers and exchanges.

Technology has played a major role in reducing transaction costs and will continue to do so. Faster dissemination of information, improved public access, more sophisticated analysis, and eventually the replacement of exchange floor trading by electronic trading can be expected. These efficiencies will reduce the cost of running the exchange system, but they will not necessarily reduce the cost of dealer services provided. Nor will the pressure to reduce costs and improve portfolio performance diminish.

Because of the intensity of competition and the readiness to adapt and innovate, present levels of trading costs may be as low as they can be, unless, as suggested by Wagner [1986b], the nature of the services demanded changes. Buy-side traders who demand the facilities and conveniences now provided by the exchange community must pay the costs. To reduce trading costs, a better understanding of the trading process and the costs implied is needed. Sponsors and investment advisors may face make-or-buy decisions concerning future trading services. The ancillary research services now attached to the trading process need to be unbundled.

Investors and traders are accustomed to a market that handles the duties, costs, and risks of trading. In addition, the sell side delivers a plethora of valuable but sometimes dimly related services without additional charge. Such services do not come free. Buy-side traders are not accustomed to the thought that such a market is expensive to maintain. In the future, pension plan sponsors and other clients will demand that portfolio managers and traders make more informed choices that reconcile trade costs with benefits received. Sponsors or other clients pay the costs of trading and are entitled to—and are increasingly demanding—a clear accounting of benefits derived.

FURTHER READING

A further discussion of the economic principles of market making can be found in Bagehot [1971], Barnea and Logue [1975], Benston and Hagerman [1974], Demsetz [1968], Garbade [1982], and Treynor [1981].

Two prominent research contributions into the behavior of dealer pricing have been done. One involves the recognition of the two distinct elements of price changes occasioned by transactions: information and the dealer's cost of doing business. This research was developed by Lawrence Glosten in Glosten and Milgram [1985] and Glosten and Harris [1985]. A second involves the use of time series analysis to separate from the impact on actual market prices of changing equilibrium value the impact of dealers and other market participants by Richard Roll [1984]. Lawrence Harris [1985] has been successful in weaving together these two threads of investigation.

For a further discussion of explicit transactions costs and trading performance, see Beebower [1989], Beebower and Surz [1980], Berkowitz, Logue, and Noser [1988], Condon [1981], Loeb [1983], and Treynor [1981]. A comprehensive treatment of how markets work can be found in Wagner [1989b]. A categorization of orders used by traders and their uses, costs, advantages, and shortcomings can be found in Wagner [1988a]. For a more complete discussion of advertised orders, see Bodurtha [1989]. For more on ethics and trading, see Morton [1988].

BIBLIOGRAPHY

Amihud, Y., and H. Mendelson. "Trading Mechanisms and Stock Returns: An Empirical Investigation." *The Journal of Finance*, July 1987.
Amihud, Y., et al., eds. *Market Making and the Changing Structure of the Securities Industry*. Lexington, Mass.: Lexington-Heath, 1985.

Bagehot, Walter. "The Only Game in Town." *Financial Analysts Journal*, March/April 1971.

Barnea, A. "Performance Evaluation of New York Stock Exchange Specialists," *Journal of Financial and Quantitative Analysis*, September 1974.

Barnea, Amir, and Dennis Logue. "The Effect of Risk on the Market Maker's Spread." *Financial Analysts Journal*, November/December 1975.

Beebower, Gilbert. "Evaluating Transaction Costs," in W. Wagner, ed. *The Complete Guide to Securities Transactions*. New York: John Wiley & Sons, 1989.

Beebower, Gilbert, and William Priest. "The Tricks of the Trade." *Journal of Financial and Quantitative Analysis*, September 1974.

Beebower, Gilbert, and R. Surz. "Analysis of Equity Trading Execution Costs." Working Paper, Center for Research in Securities Prices, University of Chicago, November 1980.

Benston, George, and R. Hagerman. "Determinants of Bid-Ask Spreads in the Over-the-Counter Market." *Journal of Financial Economics*, December 1974.

Berkowitz, Stephen A., Dennis E. Logue, and Eugene A. Noser, Jr. "The Total Cost of Transactions on the NYSE." *The Journal of Finance*, March 1988.

Black, Fischer. "Noise." *The Journal of Finance*, July 1986.

Bodurtha, Steven. "Sunshine Trading," in W. Wagner, ed. *The Complete Guide to Securities Transactions*. New York: John Wiley & Sons, 1989.

Chernoff, Joel. "Trading Strategy a Boon for CREF." *Pensions & Investment Age*, July 25, 1988.

Cohen, K., S. Maier, R. Schwartz, and D. Whitcombe. "Transaction Costs, Order Placement Strategy and the Existence of the Bid-Ask Spread." *Journal of Political Economy*, April 1981.

Cohen, Kalman J., et al. *The Microstructure of Securities Markets.* Englewood Cliffs, N.J.: Prentice-Hall, 1986.

Condon, Kathleen A. "Measuring Equity Transaction Costs." *Financial Analysts Journal*, September/October 1981.

Copeland, T., and D. Galai. "Information Effects on the Bid-Ask Spread." *The Journal of Finance*, December 1983.

Cottle, S., Roger F. Murray, and Frank E. Block. *Graham and Dodd's Security Analysis*, 5th ed. New York: McGraw-Hill, 1988.

Cuneo, Larry J., and Wayne H. Wagner. "Reducing the Cost of Stock Trading." *Financial Analysts Journal*, November/December 1975.

Demsetz, Harold. "The Cost of Transacting." *Quarterly Journal of Economics*, February 1968.

Garbade, Kenneth. *Securities Markets.* New York: McGraw-Hill, 1982.

Glosten, L., and L. Harris. "Estimating the Components of the Bid-Ask Spread." Working Paper, October 1985.

Glosten, L., and P. Milgram. "Bid, Ask and Transaction Prices in a Specialist Market With Heterogeneously Informed Traders." *Journal of Financial Economics*, March 1985.

Harris, Lawrence. "Estimation of 'True' Stock Price Variances and Bid-Ask Spreads From Discrete Observations." Working Paper, July 1985.

Hasbrouck, Joel, and Robert A. Schwartz. "Liquidity and Execution Costs in Equity Markets." *The Journal of Portfolio Management*, April 1988.

Kraus, Allan, and Hans R. Stoll. "Price Impacts of Block Trading on the New York Stock Exchange." *The Journal of Finance*, July 1972.

Loeb, Thomas F. "Trading Cost: The Critical Link Between Investment Information and Results." *Financial Analysts Journal*, May/June 1983.

Morton, John J. "Ethical Issues in Trading," in K. Sherrerd, ed. *Trading Strategies and Execution Costs*. Seminar Proceeding. Charlottesville, Va.: The Institute of Chartered Financial Analysts, 1988.

Roll, Richard. "A Simple Measure of the Effective Bid-Ask Spread in an Efficient Market." *The Journal of Finance*, September 1984.

Schwartz, Robert A. *Transaction Costs and Institutional Investor Trading Strategies.* New York: Salomon Brothers Center for the Study of Financial Institutions, New York University, 1988.

Stoll, Hans R. *The Stock Exchange Specialist System: An Economic Analysis.* New York: Salomon Brothers Center for the Study of Financial Institutions, New York University, 1985.

Treynor, Jack L. "What Does It Take to Win the Trading Game?" *Financial Analysts Journal*, January/February 1981.

———. "Economics of the Dealer Function." *Financial Analysts Journal*, November/December 1987.

Wagner, Wayne H. "Package Trading." Proceedings of the Seminar on the Analysis of Securities Prices, Chicago, November 1985.

———. "A Taxonomy of Trading Techniques," in K. Sherrerd, ed. *Trading Strategies and Execution Costs*. Seminar Proceeding. Charlottesville, Va.: The Institute of Chartered Financial Analysts, 1988a.

———. "Buttonwood II." *Financial Analysts Journal*, March/April 1988b.

———. "Broker to the Floor: What Happens at the Exchange," in W. Wagner, ed. *The Complete Guide to Securities Transactions*. New York: John Wiley & Sons, 1989a.

———. *The Complete Guide to Securities Transactions*. New York: John Wiley & Sons, 1989b.

Part V

Managing the Investor's Portfolio

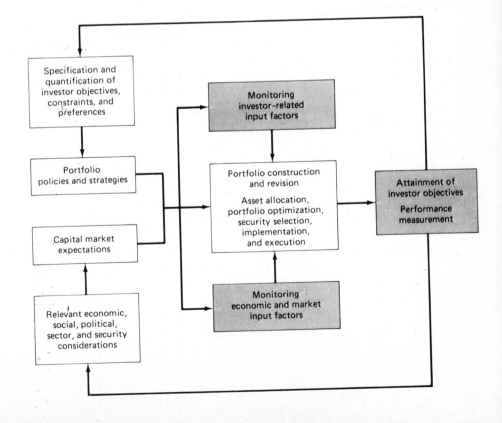

Monitoring and Rebalancing the Portfolio

Robert D. Arnott
Robert M. Lovell, Jr.

OVERVIEW

Do even carefully crafted portfolios run themselves? They do not. Investment managers are not architects, who erect an edifice then leave its denizens to their own devices. Instead, they reside with the client, making revisions when circumstances demand it. Portfolio structures that suited clients yesterday are already out of date, although the extent and even the direction of their move toward inefficiency is often hard to assess. Change is the only constant, working inexorably to alter client circumstances, market risk attributes, and securities' return prospects. The constant charge of the investment manager is to monitor these changes and respond by rebalancing portfolios to accommodate them.

Earlier chapters address portfolio construction. How does an investment manager assess the client's situation? What are the significant differences between individual investors and their institutional counterparts? What role do these differences play in shaping asset allocation policy, and what effect will the result have on risks and rewards? Which investments build efficient subportfolios and how can one transact to structure them? This chapter concerns itself with *day-to-day* portfolio management. How does the investment manager assure the portfolio remains appropriate to the ever-changing environment?

OBSERVATIONS ON PORTFOLIO REBALANCING

Portfolio rebalancing involves a simple trade-off: the cost of trading versus the cost of not trading. The cost of *not* trading affects clients in several ways.

It may mean holding an asset or a portfolio that has become overpriced, offering inferior future rewards. It may involve holdings that no longer fit the needs of the client. It may mean holding a poorly diversified portfolio, which is riskier than it needs to be. Trading exacts its own set of costs: commissions, the impact that a trade may have on the market, and the substantial cost of desirable trades that never occur. The essence of rebalancing, indeed that of portfolio management, lies in weighing and balancing these countervailing costs.

The cost of transacting can take nonfinancial forms. If a client grows uncomfortable with turnover he considers excessive, lost credibility may limit future trading. In short, even if trading is timely and likely to be profitable, it may impose subjective costs that are all too real. Finance theory recognizes these by directing managers to optimize client *utility* rather than maximizing *return*. Even the most profitable strategy or investment process is useless if the client abandons it. Its elegance is then wasted.

Not trading invariably imposes costs. After even one day, no portfolio is exactly optimal. On the other hand, the cost of transacting is real and it may be prohibitive. Hence, rebalancing may not make sense when there are only small differences between the current portfolio and the best possible one.

The Wrong Way to Revise Portfolios

There are pervasive misconceptions and ironic gaps between rebalancing theory and its practice. Some of these errors are so flagrant that they might amuse a thinking person if they were not so very costly. Some managers persist in rejuggling the asset mix and churning portfolios in response to their basic emotions and clouded thinking, often shrouding their actions with marketing glitz. Clients tend to hire managers after recent success and fire them after recent disappointment. This sorry drama is part of the human condition.

Straying From Established Roles. Diverging from established roles is a problem that can be characterized by a parody on a common adage: "If it ain't broken, *fix it*." Nature conditions us to feel that what has been working will continue to work and that failure heralds failure. This all too human model suggests that trees grow to the sky and that indisposition foreshadows extinction. Experience belies this notion. Consider investment managers who scramble to find a fix when their style is out of fashion. Often they (and their clients) change their approach as a period of disappointment ends, and just before results rebound.

Each of these costly errors stems from a quest for the comfort that the capital markets rarely reward. Investors, and most others, crave the solace that companionship affords. In this business, when one has too much company, success is improbable.

In 1984, Myra Drucker, in an unpublished work, reviewed historic performance data for the asset classes used in the pension fund of Xerox, then her employer. She tested two exactly opposite strategies: Shift just 5 percent of plan assets from last year's best performing asset class to last year's laggard or, alternatively, increase the bet on last year's winner in the more typical fashion. The contrary strategy dominated the more typical one by an astonishing 80 basis points annually *on the whole pension plan*. This difference would compound mightily over time. For a $1 billion portfolio growing at 10 percent per year, this 80 basis point advantage translates into almost $200 million after 10 years! What her research fails to reveal is how many sponsors mounted such a rebellion against convention and comfort and chose the contrary strategy. It is easy to guess.

Clashing Cultures. Successful corporations and winning investors are profoundly different. Corporations, known to be cooperative enterprises, prize teamwork and reward triumph while dismissing failure. The exceptional investor pursues an opposite course, staying distant from the crowd and seeking opportunities in the occasional excesses of the crowd. Securities, after all, stand apart from their owners. Owners, in turn, should resist viewing their holdings as either paragons or pariahs.

There is a subtle pattern in the trading of successful investors. They increase turnover when they are performing well and endure disappointment patiently. That behavior challenges both human nature and the culture of the typical business. When investments have performed poorly, instinct directs the investor to address the problem by changing the portfolio. If investments are doing well, the tendency is to coast with the winning strategy. This common pattern is a sure way to risk giving up market gains through complacency.

Traditional Portfolio Revision

Professional investment managers follow two dictates: "Know your client" and "know your markets." When this knowledge engenders effective action, portfolio managers discharge their responsibility. How could an investor muster the confidence to buy U.S. bonds after the 10-year bear market that concluded in 1981? How can an investor defend (even to himself) an investment style when his chosen game plan falls out of favor, attracting no players or customers? There is an overriding reason why investors sacrifice return by fleeing to comfort. For fashionable securities, investors appear to be willing to trade expected return for the comfort of being a part of the crowd. This type of investor is the celebrity investor discussed in Chapter 3.

A perfect world would hold investors to a demanding standard: If an investor or portfolio manager were to begin building a portfolio afresh today, would it mirror his existing portfolio? If not, he should consider changing his existing portfolio.

FACTORS SUGGESTING PORTFOLIO REBALANCING

A myriad of factors may suggest portfolio rebalancing. Important changes in client objectives demand that rebalancing be considered. Change in the markets' risk attributes or in return prospects for individual investments may lead a portfolio manager to act. When change warrants revision, portfolios are affected in three primary ways:

1. Most significantly, the portfolio manager may adjust asset mix by selling overpriced or overweighted classes and reinvesting in others. This procedure is described in Chapter 7. The impact of asset allocation can be considerable. But, as discussed below, tactical asset allocation inevitably introduces risk relative to the predetermined strategic or normal policy allocation.
2. An investor may alter investment emphasis within subportfolios. Two examples are changing duration in the fixed-income sector or adjusting the style of the equity portfolio.
3. Finally, an investor may trade an individual issue for one that seems to offer better value.

Changes Affecting the Client

The investment manager must remain sensitive to client needs and make every effort to anticipate events that might alter those needs. Each client is unique, precious to the enterprise, and worthy of constant concern. His or her circumstances may change for a host of reasons.

Change in Wealth. Unalloyed utility theory suggests that increased wealth allows investors to move out on the risk spectrum, accepting more systematic risk with its attendant reward. In reality, investors often behave contrarily. Concerned that newfound riches will dissipate, they may incur considerable opportunity costs to keep what they never expected to have. The portfolio manager should try to understand this psychology and work to restrain its excesses.

Changing Time Horizons. Time is one of life's certainties, advancing inexorably on mankind and its institutions. Individuals age and pension funds mature. In the abstract, reducing investment risk is advisable as the calendar runs its predictable course and time horizons shorten; bonds become more suitable investments as this occurs. For example, with luck, continuing generosity, and conservative spending rules, an endowment fund may avoid time's scythe, but even this is far from certain.

Occasionally, time horizons shift abruptly. When the last income beneficiary of a trust dies and the residue passes to the remaindermen, the *policy*, as well as the *portfolio*, should be adjusted promptly. Termination of an existing pension plan by providing annuities for retirees and vested employees should elicit a similar response. The successor pension fund, serving a younger population, should consider an aggressive policy, particularly in its early stage when assets are modest and the time horizon is long. Then, more time is available to make up for adverse outcomes, permitting a more aggressive stance, which in turn should lessen contributions over time.

Changing Liquidity Requirements. When the client needs money to spend, the portfolio manager should strive to provide it. Inevitably, the exigencies of the client's situation limit the available menu of suitable investments. Managers of trust accounts serve two masters, balancing the income requirements of life tenants and the growth expectations of the remaindermen. Money spent today, along with the return it would have earned over time, will be unavailable to meet future demands.

Tax Circumstances. Taxes are another of life's certainties. What is uncertain is the form they will take next year. Managers for taxable investors must assess the current situation and construct portfolios that deal with it. There are no lasting solutions, but other things being equal, managers should avoid taxes. The tactical niceties are client and location specific and thus lie beyond the scope of this chapter.

Laws and Regulations. In the United States, the Reagan years saw heralded changes in the tax laws, but the Administration's advertised fealty to deregulation produced mixed operating results for many segments of the economy. Pension managers, in particular, need to be aware of significant developments affecting their clients.

As noted in Chapter 4, accountants and legislators brought U.S. corporations the Financial Accounting Standards Board's Statement No. 87 (FAS 87) and the more recent Omnibus Budget Reconciliation Act of 1987 (OBRA), respectively. Keying on the ratio of assets to the actuarial accumulated benefit obligation, FAS 87 and OBRA draw critical attention to the natural volatility of the funding ratio, which affects pension expense. In simpler times, actuarial smoothing had hidden this volatility from corporate management.

OBRA's immediate impact on pension cash flow will concentrate corporate minds on volatility, as underfunded plans confront sharply accelerated contributions and increased Pension Benefits Guaranty Corporation insurance premiums. Simultaneously, OBRA blocks contributions to the most comfortably funded plans, gradually forcing their funding ratios into a range where the risk of underfunding becomes very real.

Thus, recent regulations, enacted for a host of persuasive reasons and for a benevolent purpose, subject pension managers and their clients to unintended consequences. All funds will face new pressures to adopt conservative policies, which will suboptimize long-term investment returns for most. Pension sponsors and their managers should plan strategies to resist those pressures.

Unique Circumstances/Preferences. The client's circumstances may change for many reasons, including extraneous political ones. For example, in recent years, distaste for the apartheid system in South Africa led to decisions in a number of cases to divest institutional holdings in companies doing business there. Endowments and public pension plans have been particularly likely to be involved in this change of investment attitude. Such changes in circumstances, when translated into investment action, incurred a series of costs, both explicit and subtle. Liquidation of proscribed holdings with reinvestment in approved alternatives produced transaction costs. Also, the portfolios' inability to participate in many large companies, disproportionately represented among those doing business in South Africa, introduced non-market-related risks and an unavoidable small capitalization stock bias. In the mid-1980s, when smaller stocks were demonstrating their usual return advantages over their larger brethren, this seemed a costless (even profitable) strategy. But the long run risks of such an imbalance or bias are sizable and cannot be ignored.

New Investment Alternatives

As noted in Chapter 11, the 1980s saw the growth and acceptance of derivative securities, which permit asset allocation shifts without transacting in individual securities. This development finally permitted investors to adjust asset mix without interfering with management of the underlying stock and bond portfolios. Surprisingly, many have ignored this new and efficient opportunity; this is unfortunate for both managers and their clients because these vehicles sharply expand their opportunity horizons. Derivative securities offer the most practical way to accomplish important tactical asset shifts in large portfolios expeditiously, as shown in Chapter 11 and later in this chapter.

At the same time, some old investment alternatives have virtually disappeared. For example, new income tax laws in the United States have greatly reduced the usefulness of tax-sheltered vehicles, which were previously encouraged by high marginal rates and favorable accounting rules.

TABLE 13-1. Correlations of Prior Period Standard Deviations With Subsequent One-Month Returns for a Key Bond and Stock Market Index, 1947–1986

Time Period and Asset Return	Prior 6 Mos. Std. Dev.		Prior 24 Mos. Std. Dev.	
	S&P 500	Treas. Bonds	S&P 500	Treas. Bonds
1946–1985:				
S&P 500 stocks	0.12[a]	0.04	0.07	0.03
20-year U.S. Treasury bonds	0.06	0.11[b]	0.07	0.14[a]
1966–1985:				
S&P 500 stocks	0.22[a]	0.11[c]	0.14[b]	0.10[c]
20-year U.S. Treasury bonds	0.07	0.08	0.08	0.13[b]

SOURCE: First Quadrant Corp.
[a] Significant at the 1% level.
[b] Significant at the 5% level.
[c] Significant at the 10% level.

Changes in Asset Risk Attributes

Market prices for all assets reflect consensus perceptions of risk and reward. Changes in those perceptions produce immediate gains or losses. Once again, comfortable investments are rarely profitable because market prices tend to reflect reduced regard for reward. Successful managers assess differences between actual risk and perceived risk of an investment and embrace that investment when the consensus view is unduly pessimistic.

Changes in risk present both opportunities and threats to investment professionals. Historically, increasing volatility has signaled opportunity more often than not. It provides buying opportunities when intuition prompts others to sell.

Investment theoreticians and practitioners have long recognized the risk/reward trade-off. Important incremental rewards are unattainable without incurring incremental risk. Conversely, some return must be sacrificed when seeking to minimize risk. Systematic risk, which diversification cannot eliminate, is most likely to promise reward according to the CAPM. While there is *some* linkage between systematic risk and return, it is less dominant than pure theory suggests. Table 13-1 shows a surprisingly stronger relationship than one would expect between *past* volatility and *future* return. Moreover, the relationship over the more recent 20-year period is stronger than that over the entire 40-year period in most cases.

In this table, stock return standard deviation measures stock market volatility over the preceding 6 or 24 months. This variable has been a useful indicator of future stock market performance in the United States.

The relationship travels well. Overseas, stock market return differen-

TABLE 13-2. Monthly Relative Returns on Stocks and Bonds vs. Prior Stock Market Volatility for 13 Countries, 1978–1987

| Country | Regression Coefficients Between 6-Month Stock Market Standard Deviations and Subsequent Relative Asset Class Performance | | |
	Stock/Bond	Stock/Cash	Bond/Cash
Australia	−0.33	0.77	1.01
Belgium	0.65[a]	0.88[b]	0.23[b]
Canada	2.00[a]	2.48[b]	0.47
Denmark	0.14	0.60	0.46
France	−0.47	−0.84	−0.37
Germany	0.22	0.44	0.22
Italy	0.36	0.37	0.02
Japan	1.00	1.13	0.13
Netherlands	0.73	1.04	0.32
Sweden	2.40	2.88[a]	0.48
Switzerland	0.25	0.28	0.04
United Kingdom	−0.18	−0.25	−0.11
United States	1.27[a]	1.83[b]	0.56
Average	0.62[a]	0.89[b]	0.27[b]

SOURCE: First Quadrant Corp.
[a] Significant at 5% level.
[b] Significant at 1% level.

tials calculated relative to bond and cash returns (called "relative returns" throughout this chapter) were positively related to past volatility in over three-quarters of the 13 countries examined. These results are shown in Table 13-2. Thus, past volatility has had global relevance.

Bull and Bear Markets. The markets' major swings present unusual opportunities to be either right or wrong. When things are going well, securities eventually perform too well; during economic weakness, assets decline excessively. Weakness engenders an environment that may foreshadow extraordinary profits, while ebullient markets provide unusual opportunities to sell, reinvesting elsewhere. Market veterans recall (often ruefully) the environment of late 1974 as an extraordinary opportunity. At one point the earnings yield of stocks was 600 basis points higher than bond yields, a difference not seen in over 20 years. Conversely, in 1980 and 1981, bond yields exceeded earnings yields by a wide margin. That presented another historic opportunity: to sell the stocks that had proven so comfortable and to buy the bonds that the investment world abhorred.

     Individual securities routinely show similar excesses. There are always securities whose issuers have received either such laudatory notices or suffered such unremitting adversity that their prices depart from reality. It is

difficult to isolate those securities and then to act; only those suitably prepared and armed with courage will accept the challenge.

Opportunistic investors must steel themselves against discomfort. Only
knowledge and discipline can give them the confidence needed to transact.
Indeed, even then, consideration for clients (or fears of their reactions) may
inhibit the profitable move. Who aggressively bought stocks in late 1974?
How many dared to buy long bonds in 1981? Who backed Lee Iacocca's
Chrysler with their buying in early 1982? These perceived speculations filled
most investors with fear at the time. Disciplined investment decision processes add value by providing an *objective* basis for confidence to pursue
the uncomfortable investment.

Central Bank Policy. As discussed in Chapter 5, Federal Reserve and
other central bank monetary policy retains its power in the capital markets
through its influence on liquidity. Figure 13-1 charts the course of the S&P
500, along with the Boston Company's proprietary Monetary Stock Market
Composite, which contains seven variables designed to reflect Federal Reserve monetary policy and resulting liquidity in the marketplace. This figure
argues strongly that money supply growth, and the policy that determines
it, in essence provides the funds for stock market demand. Monetary and
liquidity constraints eventually exact a toll on the stock market. Figure 13-
1 shows that the trend of the stock market flattened or declined on those
occasions when the Federal Reserve reduced liquidity.

Monetary policy also has an immediate impact on the money markets,
but it has less effect on long-term bond yields. This observation contradicts
conventional market wisdom. The Federal Reserve's influence on bond market *volatility*, on the other hand, is profound. In 1979, the Board, under Paul
Volcker, changed its focus from controlling interest rates to controlling monetary growth. Thus, the Board made adjustments to the discount rate in
response to movements in the money supply, while simultaneously trying
to manage that supply. Interest rates took a back seat in the Board's delib-
erations. The effect was dramatic. Volatility in the bond market exploded
from late 1979 into mid-1982, when policy was quietly reversed to combat
recession.

This unprecedented alteration in the Fed's traditional focus *may* have
made its intended contribution to reducing the rate of inflation in the early
1980s. It *unequivocally* magnified bond market volatility, spreading ripple
effects throughout the world. Greater volatility heralded greater risk and
investors demanded payment. Yields soared as bond prices plunged. High-
yielding bonds provided a compelling alternative to stocks, then affording
relatively low earnings yields. This unwanted competition put downward
pressure on stock prices until the summer of 1982, when rallying bond prices
and declining bond yields finally eased the pressure.

The lesson bears repetition. Fed policy matters and should not be ig-

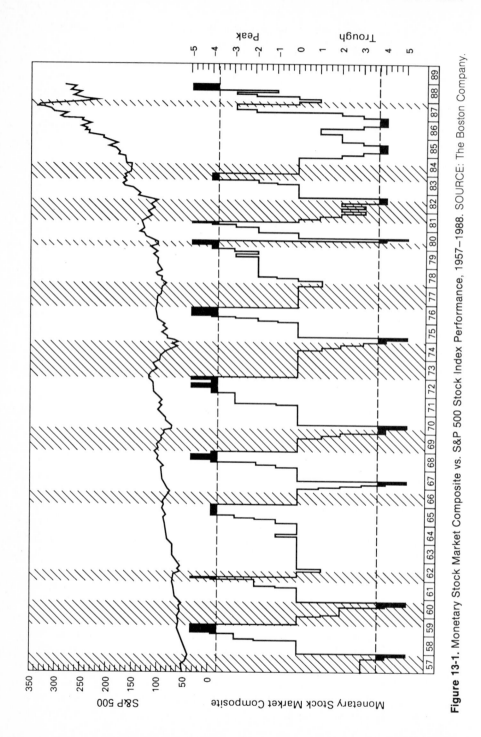

Figure 13-1. Monetary Stock Market Composite vs. S&P 500 Stock Index Performance, 1957–1988. SOURCE: The Boston Company.

TABLE 13-3. Monthly Relative Returns on Stocks and Bonds vs. Prior Price Inflation Experience for 13 Countries, 1978–1987

	Regression Coefficients Between 12-Month Percentage Change in the Producer Price Index and Subsequent Asset Class Relative Performance		
Country	Stock/Bond	Stock/Cash	Bond/Cash
Australia	0.13	0.08	−0.06
Belgium	−0.43	−0.55[a]	−0.12[a]
Canada	2.34	1.43	−0.91
Denmark	0.60	0.13	−0.47
France	−0.14	−0.34	−0.20[b]
Germany	−0.98	−1.91[b]	−0.92[b]
Italy	−0.02	−0.75	−0.73[b]
Japan	0.46	0.45	−0.01
Netherlands	−0.62	−0.87[a]	−0.25
Sweden	−0.90	−1.36	−0.46
Switzerland	−1.45[b]	−1.81[b]	−0.35[b]
United Kingdom	0.17	−0.60	−0.78
United States	−0.18	−1.08[b]	−0.90[b]
Average	−0.08	−0.55[a]	−0.47[b]

SOURCE: First Quadrant Corp.
[a] Significant at 5% level.
[b] Significant at 1% level.

nored. Restricted credit hurts stock returns, while eased credit enhances them.

Inflation Rate Changes. Inflation has its own pervasive effect on the markets. As discussed in Chapter 5, Fama found that *unexpected* increases or decreases in the presumed inflation rate work their way through the pricing mechanism. However, surprises are indeed surprises, and it is doubtful that one can forecast them consistently. When inflation rises beyond expectations, bond investors face a cut in *real yield*. As nominal yields rise in turn to counteract this loss, bond prices fall. Unexpected changes in the inflation rate are highly significant to stock market returns as well.

Simple measures of inflation, such as the Consumer Price Index (CPI), are not dependable predictors of future stock and bond returns. The market seems to incorporate current inflation efficiently. Fortunately, rates of change in producer prices, which usually lead CPI inflation, provide better signals. Table 13-3 provides relationships of Producer Price Index (PPI) inflation with subsequent asset class relative performance for 13 countries from 1978 to 1987.

In every country tested, accelerating PPI inflation translated directly into eroding bond performance. In six of the thirteen countries, the bond/

cash relation was statistically significant, and in five of the six, it was significant at the one percent level. Such acceleration also weighs on the stock market, reducing stock market excess returns in nine of the thirteen markets. Five of the stock/cash relationships are statistically significant, and each of them is negative. In short, changes in PPI inflation provide useful signals.

Changing Return Prospects

Other things being equal (as they seldom are), price changes accompany changes in return prospects. With each down tick in a bond's price, its yield rises but its total return falls. For equities, as prices constantly change, so do return prospects. Enough change should lead to portfolio adjustments.

Bonds are simultaneously the most quantifiable and the least often quantified asset class. If relative yields of lower quality issues exceed historical norms, the prospect of higher returns by downgrading quality is enhanced. For example, if outstanding bonds issued by nuclear utilities with high start-up costs and heavy regulation are selling at a substantial discount to their nonnuclear counterparts, producing abnormally large yield spreads, they may have higher total returns in succeeding periods.

Even a measure as simple as the slope of the bond market yield curve is an indicator of bond performance relative to (short-term) cash equivalents. As Table 13-4 shows, if the yield curve is unusually steep (i.e., if bond yields are high relative to cash equivalent yields), the outlook is good for bonds. This relationship is statistically significant for over half of the countries tested. The table shows that if the yield curve is more positively sloped, measured relative to the average slope over the past 24 months, *subsequent* monthly bond returns tended to be higher.

This interpretation of steep yield curves is unconventional. The usual fear is that they foreshadow rising yields and falling bond prices. The empirical evidence tends to refute that apprehension. The relationship is imperfect, but suggestive enough to caution against joining the crowd thronging the exit.

THE TRANSACTION COST BARRIER

Inertia is no excuse for inaction, but transactions costs must give portfolio managers pause. Those costs can never be recovered and their cumulative erosion of value can be highly detrimental. The authors of Chapter 12 clearly are not proponents of excessive activity at the trading desk. In this, at least, they side with Buffett, who wonders at the inability of his fellow investors to sit quietly and focus only on value.

Portfolio revision is not a free good. In addition to the negative effect

TABLE 13-4. Monthly Relative Returns on Stocks and Bonds vs. Prior Bond/Cash Yield Spreads of 100 Basis Points or More for 15 Countries, 1978–1987

Country	Regression Coefficients Between 24-Month Bond/Cash Yield Spreads of 100 Basis Points or More and Subsequent Asset Class Relative Performance		
	Stock/Bond	Stock/Cash	Bond/Cash
Australia	−0.38	−0.34	0.05
Austria	−0.54	−0.14	0.40[b]
Belgium	0.01	0.10	0.08[b]
Canada	−0.05	0.19	0.24
Denmark	−0.02	0.24	0.26[a]
France	−0.04	0.28	0.32[b]
Germany	0.27	0.45[a]	0.19[a]
Italy	−0.12	−0.04	0.08
Japan	0.30	0.64	0.34
Netherlands	0.37	0.60[b]	0.23
Spain	−0.60	−0.50	0.10
Sweden	0.63	0.69	0.06
Switzerland	0.21	0.41	0.20[b]
United Kingdom	−0.10	−0.11	−0.01
United States	0.40[a]	0.60[b]	0.20[a]
Average	0.02	0.20	0.18[b]

SOURCE: First Quadrant Corp.
[a] Significant at 5% level.
[b] Significant at 1% level.

from fees brokers earn, trades themselves can impact security prices and thus subtract value at the outset. The astute portfolio manager seeks to understand trading costs and then to control or avoid them.

A variety of studies have addressed the issue, with startlingly diverse results: They conclude that equity transaction costs range from 10 to 500 or more basis points. The range of uncertainty is daunting.

There is no exact answer. Transaction costs consist of more than just commissions, as noted in Chapter 12. Market price changes before or after the trade or during the day are another inadequate measure. As Chapter 12 suggests, the real cost of transacting is the difference between realized price and the price that *would have prevailed in the absence of the order.* That cost is inherently unmeasurable. Furthermore, the trades one seeks but fails to execute impose yet another tariff, an opportunity cost. This cost may be more onerous than the others, and it is equally unknowable and unmeasurable.

Several research studies have attempted to pinpoint true transaction cost. They cannot realize their goal because traders, a resourceful lot, are skilled at devising ways to win whatever game portfolio managers decide to impose on them. Knowing the rules of the game, they may choose to transact or neglect to transact for reasons unrelated to investment. This gaming may threaten a less-skilled manager's performance and undermine the fiduciary aim of client service.

As noted in Chapter 12, trading costs take on the character of an iceberg. Commissions rise above the surface, visible to all. The submerged leviathan encompasses the market impact of trades and the imponderable cost of the trades that never happened.

The Measurement Puzzle: A Zero-Sum Game?

Buy-side trading is worse than a zero-sum game, even aside from commission costs. This depressing conclusion is even less hopeful than the common perception that each winner bests a loser. The latter view holds that if price rises in response to an order, the buyer incurs a *cost* while the seller reaps a *benefit*. Conversely, if the price falls, the buyer has taken the seller's measure. From this perspective, transaction costs look so trivial as to be unworthy of notice. That is a dangerous misapprehension, dependent on the false notion that price movements define market impact.

Those who promote this concept argue that some fortunate (prescient?) traders enjoy *negative* transaction costs at the expense of the unskilled or unlucky. But this is not the case. *Both* sides of the trade have to pay. In truth, if the first transaction were not there, one would have had to find someone else more reluctant to trade. *That* trade would probably have occurred at a less favorable price. Thus, the difference between *hypothetical* cost and *actual* cost is a part of the total tariff. It *cannot* be negative, nor can it be measured *accurately*.

Transaction Costs and Simulated Portfolios

Others, contemplating the considerable gaps in performance between simulated results of stock selection systems and the real-time records of managers employing such systems, come to a radically different conclusion. These researchers see true transaction costs as immense, as a direct reflection of the observed gaps. Certainly major differences between simulated and real portfolio performance exist, but transaction costs are only *one* of the reasons.

In one oft-cited simulation example, Value Line's Rank I stocks have dominated the Value Line mutual funds, which in turn have far outstripped the Value Line Index. Historians will remember, however, that a 1960s court order mandated delay between publication of Value Line rating changes and trading in their funds' portfolios. During this hiatus, subscribers skimmed some of whatever cream there might have been in the ratings. Hence, an important contributor to this particular performance shortfall was unrelated to transaction costs.

Those who concoct investment schemes from historical data often meet with disappointment when they extend them to the future. Ready access to computing power and historical prices provides an almost irresistible temptation to mine data to identify variables that *had* explanatory power. As Logue and Gultekin have noted in their writings, "if you torture the data long enough, it will confess to anything." The result is invariably impressive in retrospect, and there is ample commercial reason to disseminate it to the unwary. One never sees strategies (and rarely managers) that have underperformed up to now. The future reveals their weaknesses.

Buffett observed, "to a man with a hammer, everything looks like a nail." Seductively certain and available, price and volume data may suggest things that are not so. Simulations constructed with reported prices lack persuasive evidence that closing prices are tradable. Suppose the differences between them and reality amount to just a quarter point *each way*, *each trade*. These costs mount, particularly with the high turnover tactics that are the frequent result of this exercise.

Unexecutable trades exact their considerable toll, and considerations of prudence dilute the unalloyed message of the simulation. It may, for instance, deliver a lopsided portfolio replete with heavy exposure to one or a few industries or factors. Fiduciary concerns and even elemental self-interest may not permit slavish adherence to the dictates of any model, especially when the model points to trades that cannot be accomplished.

Portfolio performance rarely matches exuberant expectations because of real world considerations that are ignored in most simulation exercises.

Transaction Management

Affordable computing power, modern portfolio theory, and new investment vehicles provide an encouraging riposte to those arguing that trading costs are insurmountable. These innovations made the program trade a credible alternative to traditional execution. Suppose one trades on a blind basis, with the broker bidding *before* seeing the actual list of securities to be traded. Then, his bid is a slightly overstated measure of true cost. The broker expects, and probably receives, a profit for bearing position risk. The price for the program trade includes it.

Even on the most conservative basis (closing price guaranteed, with the list of securities divulged *after* the close), costs are affordable. Typical bids may range from $0.05 per share to $0.30 per share. Rarely, costs may be as high as 2 percent of the trade's value. Even at the extreme, this change is hardly prohibitive.

The portfolio's assumed bid-ask spread is another measure of cost. Figure 13-2 shows the spread as a percentage of the index itself for the issues comprising the S&P 500 over the 18-month period from early July 1987 to early January 1989. (The actual maximum one-day spread of 4.8 percent on October 21, 1987 is not reflected, because the data were plotted every other day.) Three observations are noteworthy:

1. Because the spread reflects two-way market impact, a reasonably accurate assessment of one-way cost is *half* of this spread.
2. The chart gives undue weight to relatively small issues. In the real world, dealing with block trades may cost more in bid-ask spread terms.
3. On the other hand, *package trades*, conveying lack of specific knowledge, are less threatening to brokers than single stock transactions. Therefore, quoted spreads reflect their reduced fear of being caught holding the bag.

Avoiding the Pitfalls

For those who persist in trying to measure the unmeasurable, here are some suggestions: First, eliminate unexecuted trades by forcing execution. This avenue is impractical for most investment strategies. Alternatively, an investor could eschew trading individual securities and depend solely on programs, forcing trades and determining a true cost: the program bid. All but asset allocators and passive managers (who transact in packages) are likely to disdain this option.

As a last, complicated, and inherently inaccurate resort, there are numerous schemes to evaluate traders that can at least provide clues to real costs, even though they may err in identifying skill. These schemes still incur the imponderable expense of encouraging gaming. The traders *will* win that game, but the portfolio manager's clients must not lose it.

To get low costs, the manager should trade portfolios. Failing that, he should trade individual securities *very* carefully. Under normal circumstances, the trading desk should feed orders into the market only when it is receptive. Alternatively, accommodating brokers usually consent to reduce exposure to specific risk by taking the other side of the trade. They offer this service warily, hoping that the investor knows nothing hidden from them. Their price must reflect the chance that the seller has valuable knowledge, costing clients real money.

Along with knowledge of clients and the markets, managers need another sort of wisdom: awareness of themselves. They must know where they fall in the trading classification system discussed in Chapter 12. Are they "value-based" or "information-based" traders? Managers should take care to avoid overestimating their information and strive to adopt the protective

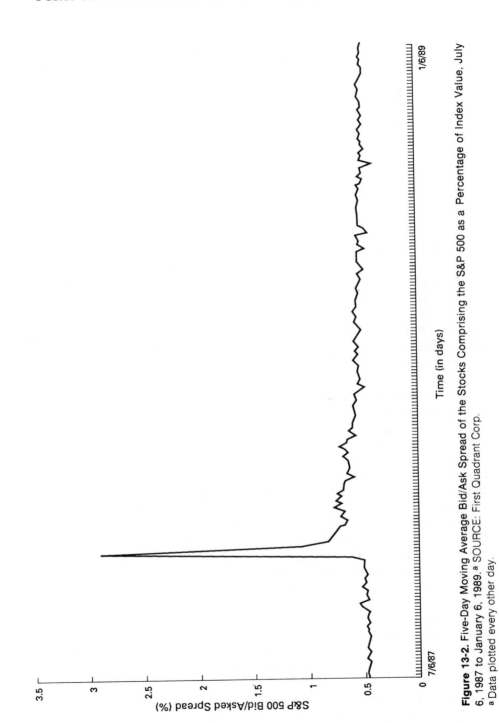

Figure 13-2. Five-Day Moving Average Bid/Ask Spread of the Stocks Comprising the S&P 500 as a Percentage of Index Value, July 6, 1987 to January 6, 1989. [a] SOURCE: First Quadrant Corp.

[a] Data plotted every other day.

coloration of the "informationless trader." In reality, that term likely approximates a manager's *true* armory when venturing into the trading jungle.

PRINCIPLES OF MONITORING AND REBALANCING

Investment monitoring and revision is a continuous and complicated process. The process requires the manager: (1) to be aware constantly of shifts in client circumstances and in the investment constraints he faces; and (2) to understand changes in the capital markets and the way they relate to the client's situation. Each portfolio revision leads inevitably to a new focus for the monitoring process.

Asset Mix Rebalancing Benefits

Drifting Mix. Clients and their investment managers work hard to have their normal asset policy mix reflect an educated judgment of their appetite for reward and their aversion to risk. That having been done, however, the mix often drifts with the tides of day-to-day change. Any slippage matters because ultimately it must be rectified.

There are only two sensible views of asset allocation. Either active shifts are assumed to add value, or else market efficiency is assumed to preclude profitable switching among asset classes. *All too many investors behave as though neither of these applies!* How many investors permit their asset mix to drift with the whims of the markets (assuring overweighting at market highs and underweighting at the lows)? How many investors were still liquidating their bond holdings in 1981 and their stocks in late 1974 in a futile effort to avoid a disappointment they had already suffered? Neither a drifting mix nor after-the-fact shifts in mix is intellectually consistent with either view of asset allocation. Simple rebalancing can provide the necessary measure of control over a drifting mix. It is worthwhile if properly managed.

Acknowledging their skepticism toward historical simulations, the authors now propose to construct one to test the benefits of systematic rebalancing. Like all such models, it leans heavily on the past as a predictor of the future. Similarly, it is rigidly mathematical.

Disciplined Rebalancing. Ambachtsheer argues persuasively in Chapter 4 that portfolios consisting of 60 percent stocks and 40 percent bonds are a satisfactory compromise for the typical pension fund. This mix is a reasonable base from which to quantify the likely benefit from disciplined rebalancing.

Assume an investor wishes to maintain the stated policy mix of 60 percent stocks and 40 percent bonds throughout the simulation, that is, rebal-

TABLE 13-5. Comparison of Results From Rebalancing to Maintain a 60/40 Mix vs. a Drifting Mix

12 Months Beginning in January of	Rebalancing Return	Drifting Return	Difference in Return
1973	− 12.69%	− 13.13%	0.44%
1974	− 15.32	− 14.21	− 1.11
1975	24.06	21.86	2.20
1976	20.57	20.26	0.31
1977	− 4.93	− 4.90	− 0.03
1978	3.29	3.03	0.25
1979	9.55	9.93	− 0.38
1980	15.69	17.80	− 2.10
1981	− 4.54	− 4.67	0.13
1982	30.60	29.08	1.52
1983	12.79	13.80	− 1.00
1984	9.75	9.13	0.62
1985	31.96	31.82	0.13
1986	20.61	20.12	0.50
1987	2.93	1.78	1.16
1988	12.73	12.93	− 0.20
Average	9.82	9.66	
Maximum	31.96	31.82	
Minimum	− 15.32	− 14.21	
Median	12.73	12.93	
Standard deviation	13.83	13.57	

SOURCE: First Quadrant Corp.

ance stock and bond positions to 60/40 equilibrium monthly. Transaction costs of 10 basis points each way are assumed to be attainable using futures. No other vehicle is so inexpensive. Indeed, it is probably impractical to rebalance extensively in the cash markets because of trading cost considerations.

Over the 16 years 1973–1988 covered in Table 13-5, simple rebalancing produced an average annual return of 9.82 percent, 16 basis points over the results for a drifting mix. Note that the rebalanced portfolio median return is slightly less than that of the drifting portfolio. Its standard deviation is also marginally higher (13.83 percent versus 13.57 percent). These results suggest reality. By rebalancing into more variable return assets when the markets decline, the portfolio stands to lose more than the drifting mix does. Fortunately, riskier assets usually provide superior long-term returns.

Coherent rebalancing enhances performance, more often than not, as it maintains control. "More often than not" means just that. It does not work in every year, or even in every market cycle, but it should work over time. Under these assumptions, the incremental return is earned with turnover of just 0.90 percent per month. Historically, the benefit justifies this minimal activity.

Maintenance of the asset mix at 60/40 is exquisitely boring. Disciplined rebalancing eliminates periodic departures from the policy mix. It can produce real world benefits over and above those depicted earlier. Rebalancing makes sense: It requires no belief in market timing and is easy to sell to clients. *More important, it provides an effective way to dissuade clients from abandoning policy at inauspicious moments.* Once they sign on to the concept, clients are more likely to stay the course.

Easy to accomplish, rebalancing adds modest value that compounds significantly over time. It is boring indeed, but it earns its keep by helping to avoid two expensive alternatives: drifting mixes or inopportune changes in mix.

Disciplined Rebalancing vs. Ad Hoc Changes. The introduction of ad hoc mix changes reflecting the pervasive tendency to shift after the fact in the direction of the most recent market move expands the annual advantage of the simple systematic rebalancing strategy to 39 basis points. In this example, the simulated rebalancing portfolio of Table 13-5 is compared with a simulation of ad hoc trend-following shifts in asset mix, such as those that have hurt the image and performance of the institutional investing world over the years. This example postulates responsive shift in asset mix in the same direction as the previous change in asset mix triggered by the market. If a stock market decline forces the portfolio from a 60/40 stock/bond mix to 55/45, assume a further trade that pushes the mix to 50/50. Thus, the temptation to move into the better performing asset class relates directly to the move generated by the market itself. In short, the model buys winners and sells losers.

Table 13-6 illustrates the benefits of systematic rebalancing. While a standard 60/40 portfolio rebalanced each month generated an annualized return of 9.82 percent, simulated ad hoc shifts in response to the drifting markets reduced this return by 39 basis points. Rebalancing recaptures performance on a periodic basis, with value added in two out of every three years.

Rebalancing does not help in every year. For example, in 1980, stock returns surpassed bonds rather persistently through the year. As a result, a rebalancing strategy had its adherents constantly moving money into bonds, which continued to underperform. This cost 372 basis points that year. The opposite happened in 1975, when stocks soared in the first half of the year and bonds won out later, such that the rebalancing strategy won by 487 basis points.

Once again, rebalancing incurs a cost in both median return and in variability. These results suggest that portfolio insurers and others who sell or buy after the fact reduce risk. Ironically, that is true, but when markets

TABLE 13-6. Comparison of Results From Rebalancing to Maintain a 60/40 Mix vs. Ad Hoc Trend-Following Changes in Asset Mix, 1973–1988

12 Months Beginning in January of	Rebalancing Return	Ad Hoc Changes Return	Difference in Return
1973	– 12.69%	– 13.63%	0.95%
1974	– 15.32	– 12.98	– 2.34
1975	24.06	19.20	4.87
1976	20.57	19.82	0.75
1977	– 4.93	– 4.79	– 0.14
1978	3.29	2.65	0.64
1979	9.55	10.00	– 0.44
1980	15.69	19.42	– 3.72
1981	– 4.54	– 4.78	0.24
1982	30.60	27.91	2.69
1983	12.79	14.49	– 1.69
1984	9.75	8.63	1.12
1985	31.96	31.67	0.29
1986	20.61	19.62	1.00
1987	2.93	0.82	2.11
1988	12.73	12.87	– 0.15
Average	9.82	9.43	
Maximum	31.96	31.67	
Minimum	– 15.32	– 13.63	
Median	12.73	12.87	
Standard deviation	13.83	13.32	

SOURCE: First Quadrant Corp.

fluctuate, insurance techniques are a certain way to get rich more slowly. Trading against portfolio insurers is profitable if it can be accomplished at low cost. By using the futures markets, that is possible.

The Burden of Excess Cash. Unintended cash reserves do not relate to the needs of long-term investors. What is worse, they sap portfolio returns over any extended period. *In this context, cash can be a high risk investment.* If interest rates decline sharply, investment income will decline and opportunities for attractive longer term investments most likely will have been missed.

Because cash looks safe in the short run, its return implications are straightforward. Over the period 1926–1988, cash equivalents underperformed stocks and bonds by about 600 and 100 basis points, compounded, respectively. Thus, assuming a 60/40 stock/bond mix for the typical diversified investor, cash equivalents cost that investor about 400 basis points annually on the amounts involved. For the proverbial long-term client, cash produces low returns at implausibly high "risk," contradicting one of our professional precepts.

TABLE 13-7. Comparison of Results From Rebalancing to Maintain a 60/40 Mix vs. Ad Hoc Trend-Following Changes Plus Maintenance of a 10 Percent Cash Position, 1973–1988

12 Months Beginning in January of	Rebalancing Return	Ad Hoc + 10% Cash Return	Difference in Return
1973	−12.69%	−11.52%	−1.17%
1974	−15.32	−10.02	−5.30
1975	24.06	16.93	7.14
1976	20.57	17.92	2.65
1977	−4.93	−3.75	−1.17
1978	3.29	3.08	0.20
1979	9.55	9.88	−0.32
1980	15.69	18.36	−2.66
1981	−4.54	−2.53	−2.01
1982	30.60	25.80	4.81
1983	12.79	13.80	−1.00
1984	9.75	8.75	1.00
1985	31.96	29.35	2.60
1986	20.61	18.61	2.00
1987	2.93	1.15	1.78
1988	12.73	12.25	0.47
Average	9.82	9.25	
Maximum	31.96	29.35	
Minimum	−15.32	−11.52	
Median	12.73	12.25	
Standard deviation	13.83	11.80	

SOURCE: First Quadrant Corp.

For the past decade, cash equivalents have accounted for some 11 to 15 percent of U.S. corporate pension assets. This fact is particularly significant because over this period the amount of these assets nearly quintupled. With a typical diversified portfolio outperforming cash by about 400 basis points a year, pension cash holders' returns were more than $100 billion less than if their funds had been fully invested in stocks and bonds.

Endowment funds, despite serving obligations that they hope will be perpetual, maintained even higher cash positions, to their considerable detriment. Investment managers working into the night would be unlikely to ever add enough value to offset these unnecessary performance leaks. Portfolio managers should always be alert to the opportunity to redeploy cash.

Table 13-7 again compares disciplined rebalancing versus ad hoc changes, but also assumes that the latter approach maintains 10 percent of the portfolio in cash reserves. Cash retained for benefits payments and cash reserves held by equity and bond managers can add up to a larger figure than this. In this example, the hypothetical pension sponsor, burdened with idle cash and with ad hoc shifts in the asset mix, experiences returns that average 57 basis points per year less than those provided by disciplined rebalancing. Historically, the typical sponsor actually has done somewhat worse than this.

In 1975, the combination of rebalancing and reinvesting all idle cash helped, increasing portfolio returns by 714 basis points. In 1974, however, this strategy produced a negative return differential of 530 basis points. Nonetheless, if it is assumed that a balanced portfolio typically outperforms cash by 400 basis points, then investing idle cash reserves, averaging perhaps 10 percent in the typical portfolio, should add about 40 basis points of return to a fully invested portfolio. Considering the benefit that should be derived from rebalancing versus ad hoc changes, the 57 basis point return advantage shown in Table 13-7 seems conservative.

Asset Mix Changes Based on Market Timing. Many aspire to time the markets, but the achievement of this goal is beyond the capabilities (and courage) of most. It demands the confidence to depart from a normal investment stance when the market offers an unusual opportunity. Those periodic opportunities arrive when one asset or class declines to an attractive price or when another rises beyond it. Strangely, at those times there tends to be no shortage of players eager to take the other side of the trade.

In the fall of 1987, portfolio insurers and other trend followers evidenced the conventional behavior contrarians aim to exploit. Contrarians tend to stabilize markets, by providing liquidity to those who have recently discovered a need for it and, conversely, delivering securities to those who perceive an overwhelming pressure to own them.

Can Ad Hoc Tactical Shifts Add Value? They certainly can. Are they likely to add value? Let's look at one piece of evidence in seeking that answer. Brinson, Hood, and Beebower [1986] examined the 10-year performance of 91 large U.S. pension plans. The results, in Table 13-8, show that market timing costs the average pension sponsor 66 basis points of annual average return over the course of a decade, supporting the conclusion of the simulation results in Table 13-6. The damage of market timing induced shifts in asset mix dwarfed the shortfall attributable to security selection over that span. The most fortunate sponsor added just 25 basis points from timing, while the most hapless sponsor forfeited 268 basis points annually over a decade.

The difference between the typical allocation result shown here and rebalancing that *adds* value is highly significant. After 10 years, a rebalanced $1 billion portfolio (earning 10.11 percent annually) might attain a net gain of $155 million over typical (i.e., timing included) institutional allocation (earning 9.44 percent). Much of this advantage comes from avoiding untimely shifts in asset mix. Although the process is discontinuous and no more predictable in the short run than any other aspect of investing, disciplined re-

TABLE 13-8. Annualized 10-Year Returns and Standard Deviations of 91 Large U.S. Pension Plans, 1974–1983

	Average Return	Minimum Return	Maximum Return	Standard Deviation
Portfolio Total Returns				
Policy mix	10.11%	9.47%	10.57%	0.22%
Policy mix and timing	9.44	7.25	10.34	0.52
Policy mix and selection	9.75	7.17	13.31	1.33
Actual portfolio	9.01	5.85	13.40	1.43
Differential Active Returns				
Timing only	(0.66)%	(2.68)%	0.25%	0.49%
Security selection	(0.36)	(2.90)	3.60	1.36
Other	(0.07)	(1.17)	2.57	0.45
Total active return	(1.10)	(4.17)[a]	3.69[a]	1.45[a]

SOURCE: Brinson, Hood, and Beebower [1986].
[a] Column not additive.

balancing evidences compelling merits. Clients who adopt it will win in the long run.

Investment committees share the common human characteristic of banding together to withstand an unfriendly (or merely unfamiliar) environment. Convincing them to sign on to the suggested simple, systematic rebalancing procedure discussed here means they will be adopting a portfolio management control feature that provides the opportunity for adhering to investment policy consistently and dynamically.

Tactical Asset Allocation: Theoretic Underpinnings

Active allocation among securities classes complicates the lives of managers, but as explained in Chapter 7, such tactics can add value. What is the market environment? What can be done about it? Instinct advises seeking solace in reduced anxiety. But no investor can win that way. Only by being different can he come out on top. The problem is to distinguish between being contrary to a misguided consensus and merely being stubborn.

Systematic asset allocation depends on three assumptions. First, the markets tell investors *explicitly* what returns are available. Second, relative expected returns reflect investors' current consensus. If expected equity returns are particularly high compared to bond expected returns, the market is clearly according a substantial risk premium to stocks. It does this when investors in general are uneasy with the outlook for stocks. Third, measurements of prospective returns provide useful clues to actual realized returns. These crucial assumptions merit scrutiny.

Markets Tell Explicitly What Returns Are Available. Cash yields reveal the immediate nominal return accorded short-term players. Assuming no change in interest rates, yield to maturity is the nominal reward on default-free bonds. Thus, at least for these asset classes, there is *objective knowledge* of prospective returns. Educated estimates of equity returns can be made in many ways, including earnings yield, dividend yield plus growth, or the dividend discount model's internal rate of return. Inevitably, reality will not quite match these expectations. Nevertheless history suggests that simple objective measures provide a useful, objective guide to future rewards.

Even disciplined return estimates for different asset classes arguably make the error of comparing apples and oranges. The return on cash, assured only over a short span, is fundamentally different from the uncertain (and decidedly long-term) outcome from stocks. However, when the market falls, pricing stocks to reflect a demand for higher returns, further declines merely enhance *rational* expectations for the future, even as they ruin investors' sleep. The pricing mechanism corrects itself eventually, as it always has.

Relative Expected Returns Reflect Consensus. The second assumption underlies widely held beliefs about securities markets. When investors see more risk out there, they demand payment for assuming it. In the 20 years following the deepest point of the Great Depression, equity yields were significantly higher than the yield on bonds. Apprehensive of a replay of the depression, stockholders demanded a compensatory premium. Ultimately, the markets rewarded those willing to bear equity risk. Conversely, as recently as 1981, demoralized bond investors priced those securities to reflect their unprecedented volatility amid fears of rebounding inflation. Here, too, willingness to embrace the out-of-favor asset class bore fruit. Each of these episodes had a particularly satisfying outcome, but they are hardly unprecedented. The investment world persists in unraveling excesses even if the exact timing eludes us.

Expected Returns Provide Clues to Actual Returns. Departures from equilibrium compress a proverbial spring that drives the system back towards balance. If 10 percent bonds produce zero return (by declining in price enough to offset the coupon), they then yield more to a prospective holder. Because this process is inherently finite, these bonds, short of default, will eventually produce their promised returns. Bond price changes, moving cyclically, exhibit negative serial correlation, a characteristic prized by contrarian asset allocators.

In the same way, differences between expected return on equities and realized return persist over time, but only if earnings growth estimates are inaccurate. They typically are, of course, but the law of large numbers provides more confidence in estimating returns of classes of investments than those of their individual components.

Bond yields provide an objective measure of prospective long-term bond

TABLE 13-9. Monthly Relative Returns on Stocks and Bonds vs. Stock Earnings Yields Net of Bond Yields for 15 Countries, 1978–1987

Country	Regression Coefficients Between 24-Month Stock Earnings Yields Minus Bond Yields Relative to their 24-Month Average and Subsequent Month's Asset Class Relative Return Performance		
	Stock/Bond	Stock/Cash	Bond/Cash
Australia	−0.48	−0.70	−0.22
Austria	0.11	0.24	0.13
Belgium	0.36	0.28	−0.09
Canada	0.44	0.75[a]	0.31[a]
Denmark	0.08	0.13	0.05
France	1.18[a]	1.57[b]	0.38[a]
Germany	0.66	0.92[a]	0.26
Italy	0.14	0.47	0.33[b]
Japan	4.16[a]	3.16	−0.99
Netherlands	1.32[b]	1.00[b]	−0.33
Spain	2.58[b]	2.42[a]	−0.16
Sweden	1.00	0.78	−0.23
Switzerland	0.96	1.39[a]	0.43[b]
United Kingdom	1.22[a]	0.82	−0.34
United States	0.49	0.84[b]	0.35
Average	0.95[b]	0.94[b]	−0.01

SOURCE: First Quadrant Corp.
[a] Significant at 5% level.
[b] Significant at 1% level.

rates of return. Similarly, earnings yields on stocks provide a crude but effective valuation measure of future stock returns. Table 13-9 shows that *expected* relative returns, represented by stock earnings yields minus bond yields, compared with the prior 24-month average of this difference, can predict *realized* relative performance over spans as short as *one month*. In 15 different countries, a one percentage point difference in relative expected return translated into a sometimes large number of basis points in relative stock market performance over the succeeding month. This magnification of prospective returns in realized returns is no surprise. Assuming markets in equilibrium with expected returns remaining constant over time, expected and actual performance are equal. Here, reality exceeds expectations because actual relative returns correct from transitory extreme disequilibria.

Portfolio managers concentrate on risk. They must respect their clients' tolerance for it or risk losing them. Years ago, Charley Ellis advocated testing prospective clients with a simulation device that generates the raw emotions of seeming to lose money one had thought one had. The Ellis device could provide useful insights into client risk tolerance, valuable because risk tolerance is often apparent only after it has been exceeded, which frequently leads the client to seek alternatives such as manager replacement. Regrettably, no device can simulate the feeling of losing real money.

Performance standards must be set that make sense for the client. The risks undertaken on his behalf should relate to that benchmark. In striving to surpass it, the investment manager must be as certain as possible not to be a loser. Furthermore, portfolios should be redeployed only at key turning points. Successful asset allocation comes to the fore in turbulent markets, while it may make only modest contributions in quiet times. This suggests that thoughtful managers should hoard precious transactional ammunition for a worthy target.

Tactical Allocation Simulation for Rebalancing

What is the theoretical potential for switches among asset classes? The obligatory caveat applies: The following simulation rests on history and may not represent the future. The model incorporates some of the relationships explored earlier, along with others that aim to take the pulse of market psychology. Relationships derived from the past, however diligently crafted, are merely interesting. They have their uses, and this is one of them.

The assumptions for the model simulating tactical asset allocation allow a plus or minus 15 percent change in asset mix from the norm, which is defined as 60 percent stocks/40 percent bonds. Therefore, the equity position can be as low as 45 percent or as high as 75 percent and the bond position may vary equivalently. With both stocks and bonds held at their bearish minimum (45/25), cash reserves would be as high as 30 percent. These are reasonable bounds for most individuals and institutions. Indeed, investors may well experience this kind of range under ordinary circumstances through asset mix drifts, *without* any disciplined approach for maintaining the appropriate balance.

This simulation uses a simple process to determine active portfolio management strategies. If the equity risk premium over bonds or cash, measured relative to historic averages, is at least one standard deviation above the historic norm, hold a maximum stock position. If the premium stands one standard deviation below normal, revert to minimum stock exposure. The same holds true for the bond maturity premium over cash yields for bond maximum or minimum exposure. Finally, if both the equity risk premium and bond maturity premium stand one standard deviation below normal, retreat to cash. Over half the time, either stocks or bonds are at their minimum or maximum exposure in the simulation. As such, this is an aggressive approach that seeks to identify and exploit above average (and below average) risk premiums.

A few additional premises underlie this simulation:

TABLE 13-10. Comparison of Results From Tactical Asset Allocation Portfolio Rebalancing vs. a Normal 60/40 Automatically Rebalanced Portfolio

12 Months Beginning in January of	Tactical Return	Normal Return	Difference in Return
1973	−7.47%	−12.67%	5.20%
1974	−6.15	−15.30	9.15
1975	31.44	24.10	7.34
1976	21.87	20.59	1.28
1977	−4.42	−4.92	0.50
1978	6.98	3.30	3.68
1979	12.89	9.57	3.32
1980	23.56	15.74	7.82
1981	3.27	−4.53	7.80
1982	33.03	30.63	2.40
1983	16.92	12.81	4.11
1984	13.40	9.77	3.63
1985	30.00	31.98	−1.97
1986	19.93	20.64	−0.71
1987	11.95	2.98	8.97
1988	12.97	12.74	0.23
Average	13.76	9.84	
Maximum	33.03	31.98	
Minimum	−7.47	−15.30	
Median	13.40	12.74	
Standard deviation	12.49	13.83	

SOURCE: First Quadrant Corp.

1. Futures contracts are an efficient and low cost way to allocate among asset classes.
2. Rebalancing adds value when done properly, and it should be done continuously.
3. Cash equivalents are inefficient and are assumed to have been removed from the normal asset mix as an investment alternative, although it may be used for tactical purposes.

The result is more than interesting, as shown in Table 13-10. Average return exceeds that of the normal or static 60/40 mix portfolio by 392 basis points annually. In a departure from the model explored earlier, both the median return and standard deviation dominate the disciplined rebalancing strategy (the static 60/40 mix, the returns on which differ slightly from the rebalancing returns in Tables 13-5, 13-6, and 13-7 because transaction costs are not subtracted). Somewhat lower returns in the two halcyon years of 1985 and 1986 seem a modest price to pay for what one might have earned. The required monthly turnover of 8.92 percent is considerable, but not far in excess of the institutional norm in the 1980s. The average deviation of the asset mix from the normal 60/40 portfolio is 11 percentage points—enough to attract the attention of the client, trustees, or appropriate committee but not large enough to engender alarm.

As shown in Figure 13-3, over a span of 16 years, the simulated performance edge of tactical over normal portfolio reallocation compounds impressively. Note that the y-axis plot is on a logarithmic scale. Although only an optimist could assume that these relatively modest allocation shifts will be as productive in the future, retention of even a fraction of the historic benefit would be valuable.

Finally, Figure 13-4 provides a graphic presentation of the extent of the exposure relative to the normal portfolio. The black sections, representing tactical reversions to cash, show departure from the assets of long-term choice.

Some of these incremental returns were probably achieved at the expense of managers who made ad hoc judgmental shifts in assex mix in a futile attempt to realize forgone *past* returns. The opportunity to enhance returns so spectacularly must surely diminish as more managers use disciplined approaches that avoid the errors of the past.

Rebalancing Without Futures

Some institutions cannot, or are just unwilling to, employ futures (or options) instruments in spite of their documentable attractions. For those institutions, there is only one, unattractive alternative: higher costs and less opportunistic trading.

The simulation presented in Table 13-11 differs from its predecessor (Table 13-10) in two respects. First, stock transaction costs amount to 200 basis points *each way* and costs for their bond counterparts amount to 100 basis points. Few investors would expect to pay more. Second, the simulation employs a more conservative implementation strategy than the previous example. Statistically, this means exploring the limits of the investment constraints only when a market such as the stock market is 2.5 standard deviations more attractive than its principal competition, such as the bond market. This policy contrasts with the previous simulation where maximum positions came in response to a one standard deviation opportunity.

Taken together, these changes cost money. Excess average return declines more than one third to 235 basis points, from 392 in the prior example, while variability increases slightly. As partial recompense, required turnover declines from 8.92 percent per month to 3.56 percent as the model rejects trades that it would have allowed under the earlier ground rules.

When considering adoption of an active allocation strategy, a manager needs to understand the client's willingness and ability to rebalance in an
(*text continues on page 13-32*)

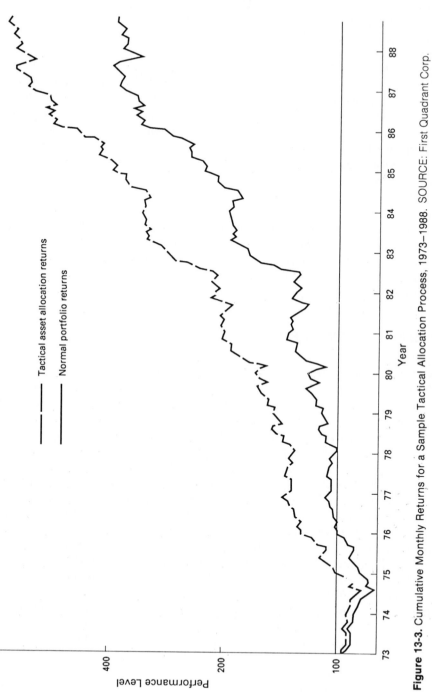

Figure 13-3. Cumulative Monthly Returns for a Sample Tactical Allocation Process, 1973–1988. SOURCE: First Quadrant Corp.

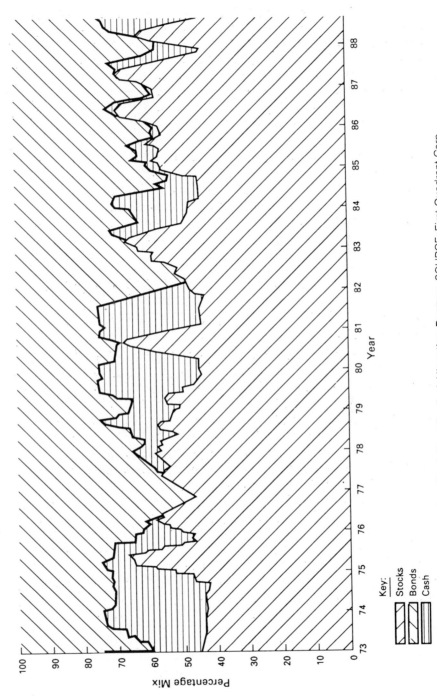

Figure 13-4. Asset Mix Over Time in a Disciplined Tactical Allocation Process. SOURCE: First Quadrant Corp.

TABLE 13-11. Comparison of Results From a Tactical Asset Allocation With High Transaction Costs Portfolio Rebalancing vs. a Normal 60/40 Automatically Rebalanced Portfolio

12 Months Beginning in January of	Tactical Return	Normal Return	Difference in Return
1973	−8.96%	−12.67%	3.70%
1974	−9.88	−15.30	5.42
1975	30.61	24.10	6.51
1976	20.43	20.59	−0.16
1977	−4.66	−4.92	0.25
1978	3.98	3.30	0.68
1979	11.56	9.57	1.98
1980	19.28	15.74	3.54
1981	1.81	−4.53	6.34
1982	33.15	30.63	2.52
1983	12.49	12.81	−0.32
1984	11.98	9.77	2.21
1985	31.75	31.98	−0.23
1986	21.15	20.64	0.51
1987	8.73	2.98	5.75
1988	11.58	12.74	−1.16
Average	12.19	9.84	
Maximum	33.15	31.98	
Minimum	−9.88	−15.30	
Median	11.98	12.74	
Standard deviation	13.15	13.83	

SOURCE: First Quadrant Corp.

active mode. The manager must exercise intelligent disciplines and make them part of the allocation framework. This is hard work, but it will pay off when emotion threatens to override intellect.

REBALANCING WITH STOCK SCREENS

A number of vendors offer stock screening models for use in managing portfolios, including rebalancing activities. Some of these models have added considerable value over time, but they also have some important shortcomings. Typically, transaction costs are omitted when these models are evaluated. While active managers deliver results *after* transactions costs, screening model vendors, who do not include such costs in the return equation, create an obvious favorable bias for screen results versus actual results. In addition, as long as the screen is equally likely to favor smaller stocks as larger ones, the model exhibits bias toward the smaller issues in its universe.

Why? Because there are far more small stocks than large, so more small stocks are selected than warranted by their share of aggregate equity market value. So, during the several years following mid-1983, the underperformance of smaller stocks relative to the market averages has revealed a weakness of such screening models. This experience is just the opposite of the experience over many years prior to mid-1983. In sum, because of the valuation, risk, and transaction cost characteristics of small versus large stocks, model results should not be compared with capitalization-weighted indexes such as the S&P 500. Thus, stock screen models must be evaluated carefully, objectively, and accurately to avoid misleading and inaccurate expectations.

Return Erosion

Although simple logic insists that transaction costs subtract from performance, every stock selection model suggests that more frequent rebalancing produces greater return before transaction costs. Jones [1988] has produced some interesting research that deals with the problem of elusive and often noncomparable data. His work provides valuable clues to the possible costs of translating theoretical models into actual performance.

The Jones model is a product of tests covering the 20 years ending in 1987. Incorporating 12 separate component models that have worked historically, this approach groups them into six categories and weights them equally to create a combination more powerful than the individual components. The Jones model deals with a universe of approximately 500 stocks, comparing results with equal-weighted returns for that universe. Thus, it avoids spurious comparisons with capitalization-weighted indexes. However, small stock bias and absence of transaction cost effects remain.

Jones calculates an *information coefficient* (IC) that reflects the correlation between the model's ranking and subsequent return over the indicated period. The *t*-statistic measures the significance of the IC. The higher numbers are best in each case, with an IC of 1.00 showing a perfect positive relationship between variables. A *t*-statistic greater than 2.0 implies statistical significance. Table 13-12 suggests that the model can deliver powerful results; it should, given its genesis in the data used in testing its results.

The results of Jones's research are confirmed by the comparisons in Table 13-13. With the exception of the price volatility model, the individual models *worked* during this period. That is, their top quintile demonstrated higher alphas (risk-adjusted performance) than their bottom quintile. The multifactor model dominated the individual models with a performance spread of 17 percentage points between the top and bottom quintiles. The best of the individual models, a classic dividend discount model, delivered a spread of about 15 percent, providing support to the dividend discount model approach.

TABLE 13-12. Average Information Coefficients (ICs) and t-Statistics for 12 Factor Models and One Multifactor Model for a Universe of 500 Stocks by Holding Period, 1968–1987

Factor Model	Holding Period							
	3 Months		6 Months		1 Year		2 Years	
	IC	t	IC	t	IC	t	IC	t
Value								
Dividend discount	0.07	5.6	0.08	6.3	0.10	8.2	0.12	10.6
K-ratio	0.05	2.9	0.05	3.2	0.07	4.5	0.11	7.8
Yield								
Cash flow	0.04	1.8	0.05	2.2	0.08	3.3	0.11	4.7
Earnings	0.04	2.3	0.05	2.6	0.07	3.7	0.10	5.8
Momentum								
Earnings	0.07	5.0	0.08	5.5	0.07	6.2	0.06	6.4
Price	0.06	3.3	0.09	5.1	0.12	7.1	0.09	6.2
Growth								
Historical	0.05	2.6	0.08	3.2	0.10	3.6	0.11	3.7
Sustainable	0.04	2.1	0.05	2.4	0.06	2.8	0.07	3.2
Risk								
Price volatility	0.05	2.0	0.07	3.0	0.10	4.1	0.14	6.3
EPS uncertainty[a]	0.03	1.4	0.03	1.8	0.05	2.4	0.05	2.1
Liquidity[a]								
Capitalization	0.08	3.3	0.11	5.1	0.17	7.4	0.25	11.5
Analysts' coverage	0.08	4.8	0.11	7.4	0.15	10.3	0.21	12.9
Multifactor model	0.11	6.7	0.14	8.6	0.18	11.5	0.22	15.3

SOURCE: Goldman, Sachs & Co.

[a] Ranked low to high.

PORTFOLIO MONITORING AND REBALANCING

TABLE 13-13. Top vs. Bottom Quintile Portfolio Results With Quarterly Rebalancing for 12 Factor Models and One Multifactor Model for a Universe of 500 Stocks, 1968–1987

| | Top Quintile | | | Bottom Quintile | |
Factor Model	Beta	Alpha	Turnover[a]	Beta	Alpha
Value					
Dividend discount	1.04	6.25%	73%	1.14	−8.55%
K-ratio	1.08	2.37	72	0.98	−4.43
Yield					
Cash flow	1.03	4.06	53	1.03	−3.23
Earnings	1.00	4.64	72	1.07	−3.18
Momentum					
Earnings	0.98	6.08	112	1.11	−6.31
Price	1.01	7.39	208	1.13	−5.51
Growth					
Historical	1.23	1.01	33	0.95	−2.22
Sustainable	1.17	2.86	53	0.89	0.24
Risk					
Price volatility	1.36	−0.63	28	0.73	0.49
EPS uncertainty[b]	0.92	2.34	78	1.12	−3.51
Liquidity[b]					
Capitalization	1.28	4.78	19	0.77	−2.05
Analysts' coverage	1.19	4.13	33	0.87	−3.89
Multifactor model	1.08	8.19	75	1.06	−8.85

SOURCE: Goldman, Sachs & Co.
[a] Average annual percentage turnover in portfolio.
[b] Ranked low to high.

Introducing Turnover

Table 13-13 appears here for another reason: It shows presumed turnover for each model with quarterly rebalancing to keep its ranking current. Practitioners can make their own use of this information, observing the differences in turnover indicated among the 13 models.

Jones's results show that for portfolio managers who favor momentum models, turnover will probably be relatively high (but not necessarily higher than the recent institutional norm). For those who favor illiquid issues, turnover should be low. That is good, of course, because trading is difficult and costly for them.

The multifactor model fulfilled its promise in the abstract. Those who choose to follow it or its competitors face the challenge of converting it to real performance, net of transactions costs, in the future.

The Jones model results in Table 13-14 show that alpha or risk-adjusted performance is higher with more frequent rebalancing when one-way transaction costs amount to less than 2 percent. Most practitioners should be

TABLE 13-14. Annualized Risk-Adjusted Returns for Top Quintile of Multifactor Stock Selection Model vs. Goldman Sachs Equal-Weighted Universe Based on Different Rebalancing Frequency and Transaction Cost Assumptions, 1968–1987

One-Way Transaction Costs Assumed	Annual Alpha	
	Quarterly Rebalancing	Annual Rebalancing
0%	8.19%	6.30%
1	6.43	5.45
2	4.43	4.52
3	2.45	3.59
4	0.55	2.65

SOURCE: Goldman, Sachs & Co.

able to surmount that hurdle. However, virtually all the benefit of quarterly rebalancing disappears if costs exceed 4 percent, despite the impressive historic power of this model. But annual rebalancing retains some value even at these high transaction cost levels.

ACTIVE MANAGEMENT/REBALANCING: WHY BOTHER?

Is active management dead? Today, after all, institutional managers essentially *are* the market. Managers who succeed in a given year have no better than an even chance of winning in the next. Only one of four exceed the median manager in two consecutive years and one of eight for three such years. Does it necessarily follow that trying to select managers is futile? It might seem so, but these figures obscure a subtle but significant nuance. More managers produce excellent or miserable results than chance alone would predict.

As demonstrated in this section, *there are managers who add value.* Because relative performance is a zero-sum game by definition, the fateful corollary must also hold true: Another universe of losers exists. What *no one* can determine satisfactorily is the attribution of performance among managers. The real source of a manager's success or lack thereof eludes existing statistical tools, unless results can be examined over a span of time that is too lengthy to be useful.

Table 13-15 presents year-by-year returns of equity portfolios from 1979 to 1988, using the SEI performance data base. If success were a random

TABLE 13-15. An Evaluation of Equity Portfolio Performance via Upper vs. Lower Quartile Results, 1979–1988

SEI One-Year Results	1988	1987	1986	1985	1984	1983	1982	1981	1980	1979
25th percentile	21.5%	6.3%	21.8%	36.6%	6.4%	25.5%	27.5%	0.2%	39.5%	26.6%
75th percentile	12.6	−0.8	14.2	29.4	−2.7	16.7	17.0	−9.8	26.6	16.5
Range[a]	8.9	7.1	7.6	7.2	9.1	8.8	10.5	10.0	12.9	10.1

Cumulative Results		2-Yr.	3-Yr.	4-Yr.	5-Yr.	6-Yr.	7-Yr.	8-Yr.	9-Yr.	10-Yr.
25th percentile		12.3%	14.6%	19.4%	16.8%	18.4%	19.3%	16.9%	18.5%	19.0%
75th percentile		7.4	11.1	16.0	12.9	13.9	15.1	12.6	14.8	15.4
Range[a]		4.9	3.5	3.4	3.9	4.5	4.2	4.3	3.7	3.6
Theoretic no-skill range[b]		5.6[d]	4.5[d]	3.8[d]	3.5	3.3	3.2	3.0	3.0	2.9
Theoretic skill range[c]		5.9	4.9	4.3	4.1[d]	3.8[d]	3.8[d]	3.7[d]	3.7[d]	3.6[d]

SOURCE: First Quadrant Corp. and SEI Corp.

[a] Spread between 25th and 75th percentile equity portfolios.

[b] Assumes that no "skill" exists: All managers have results that are median plus or minus some random "value added."

[c] Assumes that "skill" exists: Half of all managers are "winners," with results that are normally one percent above the median; half are "losers," with results that are normally one percent below the median; all managers exhibit some randomness in performance which, in any particular year, can swamp their "skill" results.

[d] Designates the range that best matches the observed range. Note that all long-term results better fit the view that skill exists, while short-term results appear more consistent with a random walk.

process, the margin between the winners and losers would converge over time (approximately with the square root of the time covered). If the gap between the 25th percentile portfolio and the 75th percentile portfolio is 8 percent in two successive years, and if results are random (in other words, if winners and losers each have equal likelihood of success or failure in the subsequent year), then the two-year annualized spread between the 25th and 75th percentile portfolios should be 5.6 percent (8 percent divided by the square root of 2). The second part of the table shows some convergence, but long-term convergence (over 5 to 10 years) is not as convincing as the random process theorists would suggest that it should be.

Assume a world in which half of all managers are winners and half are losers, and that the winners normally beat the median by a percentage point while the losers lag by a like amount. In any given year, the managers of the 25th percentile portfolio consist of some who got there through skill (winners) and some who got there by luck (losers who happened to strike it lucky that year). By the same token, managers at the 75th percentile consist of some who deserve to be there (losers) and some who got there through luck (winners who had an off year). With this assumption, the spread between the performance of the 25th percentile and 75th percentile portfolios narrows over time, but less so than with the theoretic "random walk" expected results. Intriguingly, the range that is observed in the real world essentially stops converging after four years. This is precisely the pattern that would be observed in a world in which long-term results are not random, a world of winners and losers. The long-term results are *not* consistent with a true random walk.

Table 13-16 displays SEI results during the years 1981 to 1985. If skill were nonexistent, approximately one of 32 managers should exceed the median for five consecutive years. Likewise, one unfortunate manager should underperform the median that often. Survivor bias culls the roster of losers, so definitive conclusions cannot be drawn on that side, but the winners show up roughly four times as often as they should if talent played no role. Once again, the data are more consistent with a Darwinian world divided into winners and losers. These results are more discriminating than most active managers or their clients would dare to expect.

Ironically, institutional clients with resources that might prove useful in picking managers are the most likely to embrace passive investing. Their size inhibits mobility and knowledge feeds their skepticism. Less sophisticated clients, lacking the resources to select profitably, are more hopeful. They provide the real opportunity for active managers.

If the average money manager cannot win, what hope does an institutional investor have of winning? As indicated earlier, institutional investors essentially *are* the market and the market cannot beat itself. Any success an institutional investor hopes to attain must come at the expense of the competition. There is compelling evidence that some *do* succeed.

TABLE 13-16. An Evaluation of Actual vs. Theoretical Manager Results to Assess Investment Management Skills Using the SEI Funds Evaluation Data, 1981–1985

Manager Description	Period Covered	Position in SEI Rankings	Percentage of Managers in This Category		
			Actual[a]	Theoretical[b]	Theoretical[c]
Balanced	5 years	Top quartile	1.3%	0.1%	0.8%
Balanced	5 years	Above median	8.5	3.1	7.4
Balanced	5 years	Below median	2.0	3.1	0.9
Equity	5 years	Top quartile	1.7	0.1	0.8
Equity	5 years	Above median	11.5	3.1	7.4
Equity	5 years	Below median	2.1	3.1	0.9

	Percentage of Managers Beating Median		
	0/5 or 5/5 Years	1/5 or 4/5 Years	2/5 or 3/5 Years
SEI Equity Funds[d]	13.6%	35.0%	51.4%
SEI Balanced Funds[d]	10.5	31.5	57.9
Theoretical:			
Random 50/50	6.2	31.3	62.5
3-year survivor bias[e]	4.2	25.0	70.8
Skill 65/35[f]	11.9	34.6	53.5

SOURCE: First Quadrant Corp. and SEI Corp.
[a] Actual distribution of 1981–1985 results per SEI Funds Evaluation.
[b] Assumes no skill. All managers exhibit random results.
[c] Assumes that all managers fall equally into two camps: those with skill (and a 65 percent likelihood of adding value in any year) and those without skill (and only a 35 percent likelihood of adding value in any year); further supposes that half of those with three consecutive below-average years disappear from the sample.
[d] Distribution of 1981–1985 results, per SEI Funds Evaluation.
[e] Any manager lagging the median three successive years is presumed to drop from the sample. This would exclude all 0/5 managers, most 1/5 managers, and some 2/5 managers.
[f] Managers presumed to fall into two equal camps: Half exhibit skill, with a 65 percent chance of beating the median in any year; half have negative skill, with only a 35 percent chance of beating the median in any year.

TRADING'S POSITIVE SIDE

This chapter implies a view of models and trading costs that may not be popular on Wall Street. There is another side to the story that deserves attention. Traders provide liquidity, one of the most precious attributes of our capital markets. At the same time, commissions indirectly fund investment research, which contributes to the efficiency that makes investment management a challenging and potentially rewarding occupation. Also, re-balancing is a necessary aspect of portfolio management; doing it on a cost effective basis is an important ingredient in determining the success of the portfolio manager's efforts to realize the client's investment objectives.

SUMMARY

Even efficient markets allow room for the most competent and disciplined portfolio managers to help to realize their clients' goals. Whatever market inefficiencies exist provide the nimble and the wise opportunities to profit from the errors of the crowd. The manager should start by understanding his or her clients. Nothing is more important than the client's inherent tolerance for risk. Each client is unique; so should be the manager's understanding of the client's needs. When those needs change sufficiently, transaction costs assume a secondary role.

The investment decision process must include disciplined analysis of market opportunities. When consensus perceptions of risk exceed objective risk prospects, the markets reward those with the courage to act. Nothing undermines investment success so perniciously as emotion—the markets never compensate comfort. When the economic, political, and regulatory environments change enough, the perceptive investment manager will act—except when the shift is already reflected in the market's valuation, as it often is.

Managers must accord markets the respect they deserve. Implementation of portfolio strategies and tactics must be as rigorous as the investment decision process. Legitimate chances to improve on diversified portfolios are rare. It pays to be wary of the multitude of vendors whose commercial interest argues otherwise. Excepting the market makers, there are no winners in the transactions game.

Normal policy, while hardly sacred, is the beacon; one should generally steer toward it. Even if the value of a disciplined framework for opportunistically shifting portfolios is discounted, there is still the need to rebalance portfolios periodically. After-the-fact moves between asset classes impose terrible costs, actually *destroying* value. Investors should resist, at whatever cost, the inevitable pressures to indulge in them.

FURTHER READING

Since publication of the first edition of this volume, the costs and potential benefits of portfolio rebalancing have received increasing attention. Nevertheless, its Chapter 13 on monitoring and rebalancing portfolios by John Maginn and Jim Vertin is worth re-reading. Textbooks by Jones, Tuttle, and Heaton [1977] and Sharpe [1985] provide useful background, as does the compilation edited by Arnott and Fabozzi [1988]. Kirby [1984] presents a valuable rejoinder to rebalancing's advocates.

BIBLIOGRAPHY

Arnott, Robert D. "Risk and Reward: An Intriguing Timing Tool." Salomon Brothers Inc., April 4, 1987.

Arnott, Robert D., and Frank J. Fabozzi. *Asset Allocation*. Chicago: Probus, 1988.

Arnott, Robert D., and Robert M. Lovell, Jr. "Resisting the Mounting Pressures for a Shift to Conservatism." *Financial Analysts Journal*, November/December 1988.

Arnott, Robert D., and James N. von Germeten. "Systematic Asset Allocation." *Financial Analysts Journal*, November/December 1983.

Bader, Lawrence N., and Robert D. Arnott. "Pension Funding Under the Omnibus Budget Reconciliation Act of 1987." Salomon Brothers Inc., January 18, 1988.

Bagehot, Walter (Jack L. Treynor). "Money Will Not Manage Itself." Reprinted in *The Journal of Portfolio Management*, Spring 1975.

Brinson, Gary P., L. Randolph Hood, and Gilbert L. Beebower. "Determinants of Portfolio Performance." *Financial Analysts Journal*, July/August 1986.

Buffett, Warren E. "The Superinvestors of Graham-and-Doddsville." *Hermes, Columbia Business Review*, 1984.

Crowell, Richard A. "You CanNOT Live With One Decision." *The Journal of Portfolio Management*, Fall 1977.

Dunn, Patricia C., and Rolf D. Theissen. "How Consistently Do Active Managers Win?" *The Journal of Portfolio Management*, Summer 1983.

Etzioni, Ethan S. "Rebalance Disciplines for Portfolio Insurance." *The Journal of Portfolio Management*, Fall 1986.

Hill, Joanne M. "Is Optimal Portfolio Management Worth the Candle?" *The Journal of Portfolio Management*, Summer 1981.

Hill, Joanne M., and Frank J. Jones. "Equity Trading, Portfolio Trading, Portfolio Insurance, Computer Trading and All That." *Financial Analysts Journal*, July/August 1988.

Ippolito, Richard A., and John A. Turner. "Turnover, Fees and Pension Plan Performance." *Financial Analysts Journal*, November/December 1987.

Jones, Charles P., Donald L. Tuttle, and Cherrill P. Heaton. *Essentials of Modern Investments*. New York: John Wiley & Sons, 1977.

Jones, Robert C. "Introduction to the Multifactor Model." Goldman, Sachs & Co., July 1988.

Kirby, Robert G. "The Coffee Can Portfolio." *The Journal of Portfolio Management*, Fall 1984.

Kritzman, Mark. "How to Detect Skill in Management Performance." *The Journal of Portfolio Management*, Winter 1986.

LeBaron, Dean. "A Psychological Profile of the Portfolio Manager." *The Journal of Portfolio Management*, Fall 1974.

LeBaron, Dean, and Evan Schulman. "Trading: the Fixable Leak." *The Journal of Portfolio Management*, Fall 1981.

Lovell, Robert M., Jr. "Alternative Investments." *Financial Analysts Journal*, May/June 1980.

McClay, Marvin. "The Penalties of Incurring Unsystematic Risk." *The Journal of Portfolio Management*, Spring 1978.

Merton, Robert C. "On Market Timing and Investment Performance. An Equilibrium Theory and Value for Market Forecasts." *Journal of Business*, July 1981.

Murphy, J. Michael. "Why You Can't Win." *The Journal of Portfolio Management*, Fall 1977.

Perold, André F. "The Implementation Shortfall: Paper vs. Reality." *The Journal of Portfolio Management*, Spring 1988.

Perold, André F., and William F. Sharpe. "Dynamic Strategies for Asset Allocation." *Financial Analysts Journal*, January/February 1988.

Rendleman, Richard J., Jr. and Richard W. McEnally. "Assessing the Costs of Portfolio Insurance." *Financial Analysts Journal*, May/June 1987.

Rubinstein, Mark. "Portfolio Insurance and the Market Crash." *Financial Analysts Journal*, January/February 1988.

Sharpe, William F. *Investments*, 3d ed. Englewood Cliffs, N.J.: Prentice-Hall, 1985.

Shiller, Robert J. "Do Stock Prices Move Too Much to be Justified by Subsequent Changes in Dividends?" *American Economic Review*, June 1981.

CHAPTER 14

Evaluating Portfolio Performance

Peter O. Dietz

Jeannette R. Kirschman*

MONITORING INVESTMENT STRATEGY AND MANAGER SKILLS

From the investor's point of view, the purposes of performance measurement are to identify skill at portfolio management, to provide evidence that favorable performance coincides with the investment skills that were claimed by a particular manager, and to monitor the investment strategy that has been developed based on investor objectives. From the investment manager's perspective, performance measurement should provide feedback concerning whether results coincide with expectations.

The portfolio strategy developed to meet defined investment objectives and constraints must take into account the investor's time horizon and tolerance for risk. Some of the possible objectives of investors include:

- High total rate of return
- A large real (inflation-adjusted) rate of return
- Maximization of current income or yield
- A high after-tax rate of return
- Income growth equal to or greater than the increase in inflation
- Preservation of capital
- Superior risk-adjusted return

All of these considerations must be included in performance measurement.

* The authors note their thanks to David Carino, David M. McMillan, and Nola Williams for their assistance in providing the sections on evaluating bond, equity, and real estate performance.

EVOLUTION OF PERFORMANCE MEASUREMENT

The evolution of performance measurement is summarized in the following calendar of developments in portfolio management and performance measurement:

Years	Action Taken by Portfolio Managers	Performance Measurement
1945–1955	Buy bonds	None
1955–1965	Buy stocks	None
1965–1975	Switch to last year's best investment vehicle	Risk-adjusted measurement
1975–1985	Diversify the investment portfolio	Adjustment for economic/statistical/theoretical limitations of measurement systems
1985–1988	Use of derivative securities	Application of normal portfolios and performance attribution

Prior to the mid-1960s, little performance measurement existed, even in the institutional market, and what did exist was primarily a measure of internal rates of return, generally computed for periods of one year or longer. An internal rate of return is the actual return earned on the initial portfolio and on any net contributions for the period covered. Internal, or dollar-weighted, rates of return are appropriate for such purposes as actuarial assurance of meeting pension obligations. However, because they are influenced to a large degree by cash flows (such as contributions to or distributions from a retirement fund), they are not appropriate for comparisons to other portfolios or to market indexes, and they may obscure measurement of the portfolio manager's skill. A far better measure of manager performance is a time-weighted rate of return.

Time-Weighted Returns

Since 1966, time-weighted rates of return have been the standard comparative measure in the industry. They are used to compute the return earned on the beginning portfolio for any given time period, with a number of methods used to eliminate the impact of cash flows. Thus, time-weighted rates are much more appropriate than internal rates for comparative purposes. Although time-weighted rates are currently accepted, the following historical discussion provides insight into the problems of performance measurement.

Time-weighted rates of return were first introduced by Dietz [1966a],[1]

---

[1] In his initial work, Dietz called the time-weighted return method the average return method.

followed by the first major study of performance measurement by the Bank Administration Institute (BAI) [1968]. At that time, the concept of time-weighted rates of return was a major breakthrough for pension fund sponsors as well as other institutional investors. The mutual fund method of unit value accounting, which puts everything on a dollars-per-unit-purchased basis and automatically provides data for calculating time-weighted returns, became universally accepted.

Since the late 1960s, the initial time-weighted return formulas have been expanded and improved as computer developments have allowed for more sophisticated, detailed, and accurate measurements. However, the basic theory has continued in force. Extensions of the original concept have included risk-adjustment procedures introduced by Treynor [1965], Sharpe [1966], and Jensen [1968], which arrive at risk-adjusted returns and capital market statistics such as alpha (α), beta (β), standard deviation (σ), and correlation coefficient (ρ), as discussed in Chapter 2.

Prior to 1965, returns were seldom related to a measure of riskiness. Dietz's work relating returns to their standard deviation was subsequently modified by tying return to risk as measured by return covariance with a market portfolio. This definition of risk is based on the capital asset pricing model (CAPM) developed by Lintner [1965], Mossin [1966], and Sharpe [1964], and is represented by relating return to beta, or equity systematic risk, as in Figure 14-1(a). Figure 14-1(a) shows a security market line (SML) drawn between the risk-free rate of return (R_f) and the expected return on an economy-wide market index security (R_m), such as the S&P 500, that is given a beta of 1.0 as developed in Chapter 2. Figure 14-1(b) shows a characteristic line that relates portfolio return to market return.

In the early 1980s, the robustness of CAPM in its traditional form was challenged by the arbitrage pricing theory (APT), whose chief proponents were Ross [1976] and Roll [1978].

A fuller discussion of the advantages and limitations of the various risk-adjusted measures requires an understanding of the basic principles of measuring rate of return on a non-risk-adjusted basis. The basic issues involved in performance measurement, including valuation methodology, accounting basis, length of time period, and the problems associated with multi-asset portfolios, are described in the next two sections.

PRINCIPLES OF PERFORMANCE MEASUREMENT

Portfolio management begins with a portfolio of securities and an investor; performance measurement begins with portfolio valuations and transactions. In other words, performance measurement starts with accounting data and translates that into rates of return. Although neither performance measure-

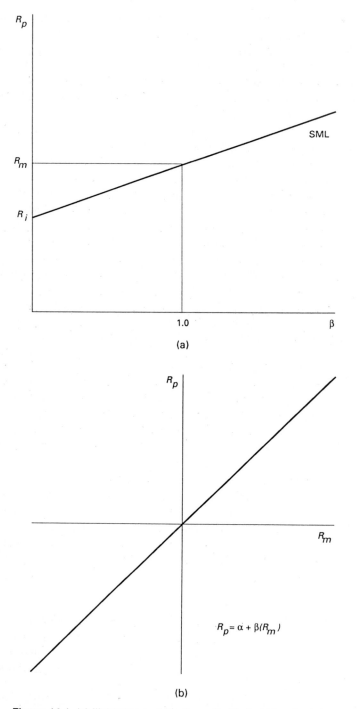

Figure 14-1. (a) Illustration of the Security Market Line Based on the
Capital Asset Pricing Model; (b) Illustration of a Characteristic Line
Relating Individual Security Return to Return on the Market.

ment nor accounting is an exact science, because performance measurement is based on accounting data, it is important that the accounting data be accurate and consistent.

Even an educated first-timer into the real world of performance measurement is generally surprised at the amount of judgment that can go into the computation of the finished accounting product that becomes the raw data for performance measurement. In addition to statistics such as alphas and betas, performance measurement deals with the raw accounting data fed into programs that relate to valuation methods, accrual basis versus cash basis, and trade-date accounting versus settlement-date accounting. This chapter highlights where differences in interpretation occur and the views of opposing sides in any controversy.

Recording the accounting data is not difficult. Basically only four types of transactions occur: purchases, sales, income, and contributions or distributions. On occasion, a conversion, merger, stock dividend, or stock split may occur. None of these transactions is difficult to account for. Beyond those bookkeeping entries lie more theoretical issues, which are discussed here.

Valuation Methods

Equities. In measuring performance, investment portfolios should be valued at their current market value; however, it is difficult to determine exactly what current market value is. In general, investments are valued at the "best available" price.

For common stocks, preferred stocks, and convertible preferred stocks that are listed on one or more exchanges, the best available price is generally the closing composite price. In the United States, the composite includes trades on the American, Midwest, New York, Pacific, Philadelphia, Boston, and Cincinnati stock exchanges and as reported by the National Association of Securities Dealers and Instinet. Most mutual funds continue to use New York Stock Exchange closing prices so that they can determine their net asset value and process that day's investments and liquidations prior to the close of their business day at 5:00 p.m. Eastern time.

For over-the-counter issues, the generally accepted source for prices in the United States is the National Association of Securities Dealers Automated Quotation System (NASDAQ). The NASDAQ prices printed in the *Wall Street Journal* and picked up by the pricing services are the 4:00 p.m. Eastern time intradealer bid and asked prices for actively traded issues and the best bid-asked ranges as of 4:00 p.m. Eastern time for less actively traded issues. Most mutual funds use the mean between the bid and asked prices, while most other investors use the more conservative bid price.

Bonds. Bonds continually provide a valuation problem for portfolio managers and recordkeepers, as most bonds are not traded on exchanges (even though many are listed) and dealers are reluctant to report trade prices to any central data gathering organization. Bond trades on exchanges generally involve small lots of less than $10,000 par value, and therefore prices are not necessarily representative of prices realized for lots at the $100,000 and $1,000,000 (and higher) par value trade level of institutional investors.

Obviously, the bond dealer community is the best source for prices. Some mutual funds arrange with bond market makers to receive price quotations daily on a routine basis. Most institutional investors rely on pricing services such as Telstat, Interactive Data Corporation, and Merrill Lynch. U.S. government and agency issues are usually priced at the prices listed in the *Wall Street Journal,* which are defined as "representative over-the-counter quotations based on transactions of $1 million or more as of 4:00 p.m. Eastern time."

Matrix Pricing Method. Some pricing services use a matrix pricing method to estimate bond prices. A matrix is a multidimensional representation that tracks a number of different variables, depending on the complexity of the pricing algorithm. Such variables might include coupon rate, maturity, duration, sinking fund characteristics, call feature, the issuer's industry or sector, quality rating, and liquidity. The matrix method groups bonds according to their values along the various matrix scales or bases for categorizing bonds. The pricing matrix uses actual trader quotes for pricing a key bellwether issue in each cell. These prices are then used as the basis for estimating the price of other cell-inhabiting bonds with similar features.

In 1982 Telstat developed a "bond valuation model" that uses actual trade prices reported by banks and bond dealers in a detailed matrix, taking into account other bonds of the same issuer, to arrive at bond values.

At various times in the past, Frank Russell Company has compared bond prices reported by pricing services and found that, although prices on individual issues may vary on an overall basis, for a total bond portfolio, the reported prices are quite close to actual prices. Occasionally they are not and this divergence has been the cause of some controversy. However, a partial analogy to the stock market can be used to temper this controversy. Suppose an investor holds a $200 million portfolio invested in 50 different issues. At least 100,000 shares of some issues would be held, a lot size so large that it is unlikely that it could be sold at the closing composite price. Hence, even with accurate, readily available pricing data, the aggregate value of large blocks of stocks is not subject to estimation with assured accuracy. With bonds, the problem is even worse because of the lack of a central source for pricing data for the valuation process.

Non-U.S. Securities. In general, non-U.S. equities are priced at their closing price on each country's local stock exchange; and, as in the United

States, the dealer community in each country is the best source for bond prices. Most institutional investors rely on pricing services such as Extel Computing Ltd.

To arrive at an overall fund or portfolio valuation when foreign assets are held, a base currency must be established and the value of each investment must be converted to that base currency. For example, a U.S. corporate pension plan would use a base currency of U.S. dollars because the United States is the country of residence for that investor.

Significance of Pricing Errors. It is apparent from the preceding discussion that the valuation process is not exact, even with actively traded issues. From a pragmatic view, in the long run the issue will be sold and the pricing error term previously included in the performance measurement process will wash out during the period the issue was held. For example, if a bond purchased at 90 is priced at 85.50 and 95, respectively, at the end of the two subsequent quarters, and is then sold at the end of the third subsequent quarter for 98, the returns, based on price change only, will be -5.0, 11.1, and 3.2 percent, respectively, which compound to 8.9 percent. The same result is achieved by measuring point-to-point from 90 to 98. In other words, in this example it does not matter—for rate of return purposes—whether the intervening quarter-end prices were accurate.

However, inaccurate interim pricing may artificially magnify or reduce volatility measures. When income and the effect on the remainder of the portfolio are taken into account, some amount of distortion occurs. By default, this is accepted from a performance measurement viewpoint, but obviously the pricing error term is a constant source of frustration for those charged with the responsibility of computing unit values for pooled funds and per share net asset values for mutual funds.

Real Estate and Other Assets. Still other methods are needed for the valuation of real estate, private placements and other infrequently traded securities, and venture capital investments.

Real estate held in institutional portfolios is usually valued annually by an outside appraiser. Because that appraiser generally has been educated and trained in the profession, his appraised values are generally accepted. However, to compute acceptable time-weighted rates of return, valuations are required at least quarterly. Most real estate management firms have developed internal methods of determining market values on an ongoing basis for properties held in their portfolios, taking into account the state of the economy, inflation, income characteristics of the property, and capitalization rates, among other items. While the only practical approach is to rely on the valuations determined by the professional real estate manager, the appraisal process does tend to smooth out price changes that might be reflected in actual transactions. As discussed in Chapter 10, this has the impact of reducing volatility in any measurement process.

Valuation of private placements of bonds whose issuers also have publicly traded bond issues is not as controversial. The prices of publicly traded issues can be readily converted to the coupon rate and maturity of the private placement. Generally, a discount is taken from such an inferred value for the illiquidity inherent in the private placement feature. The amount of the discount varies and depends on the individual circumstances.

Where the issuer has no publicly traded bonds, the valuation involves a review of prices for bonds of similarly rated companies with similar coupon, maturity, duration, sinking fund requirements, and other features. Again, an appropriate discount for the private placement feature is applied.

For infrequently traded bond or stock issues, the analyst must do what he or she can. For audit purposes at year end, it is probably necessary to request, in writing, a reliable value from a market maker. For non-year-end periods, one or more market makers should be called for current quotations.

In sum, portfolio valuation sounds easier than it is. In many cases, several methods may be used and each would be considered correct. Valuation is one of the most important factors in performance measurement and is often overlooked in theoretical discussions. It is entirely possible that two identical portfolios could have different computed returns solely because of the market valuation methods employed, as discussed in Dietz and Williams [1970]. However, consistency is extremely important; in the long run, valuation differences tend to wash out.

Futures and Options. Derivative securities, including futures and options, can be defined as those whose values and cash flows are determined by the behavior of other securities called underlying securities.

Much controversy exists about measuring the performance of derivative securities. However, on close examination, that controversy is found to center on the *valuation* of those securities and, therefore, on the evaluation of performance of portfolios holding them. The actual *measurement* of performance involves the same mathematical computation as any other measurement of performance.

As pointed out in Chapter 11, derivative securities can be used to achieve a variety of objectives. For example, in the area of options, selling calls on an underlying portfolio (covered call writing) can be employed to gain additional income or to enhance future stock sales. Buying calls can be used to leverage an investment or, in combination with a cash equivalents portfolio, to participate in the equity market while limiting or eliminating the possibility of loss. In the area of futures contracts, stock index futures can be purchased to effectively convert cash held in a portfolio into equities or can be either bought or sold to hedge a manager's risk while a large portfolio of stocks is being either bought or sold.

Each of the many possible strategies involving derivative securities can lead to a different valuation method and a different way of evaluating performance. For example, a stock manager has a target sale price of $50 on a particular stock. As the stock price approaches $50, he sells a call option with a strike price of $50 for a premium of $2. If the stock price continues to increase, the stock will be called away and the seller will have received $52 per share ($50 stock price plus the $2 option premium). Obviously, the valuation when the transaction is completed is the $52 cash received. But, what if at the end of the month the stock's price is $49.50 (and the stock has not been called away) and the option price is $4.00? Two different valuations could be applied, depending on how the open option contract is viewed. First, if the manager wants to have the stock called away (i.e., he does not intend to repurchase the option), and the stock has not reached the strike price, the valuation could be $51.50 ($49.50 for the stock plus the $2 premium received). Or, second, if the option is viewed as a liability, the valuation could be $47.50 (the $51.50 computed previously less the $4.00 it would cost to repurchase the option).

Another strategy that involves selling covered calls is an *overwriting strategy*. In this approach, the underlying stocks are held in a portfolio managed by an equity manager and an option overwriting manager is employed to write calls against the portfolio. Generally, the option manager is given the mandate that no stocks may be called away, so he must always either repurchase the option in a closing transaction or let the option expire. Suppose he sells an option with a strike price of $50 for a $2 premium when the stock is at $45. If the stock price stays at $45 to the option expiration date, then he will have collected $2. If the stock price increases to $51, the option premium may rise to $4 (or more) and the option manager will have to buy it back for a net loss of $2. Because the option manager is not allowed to have a stock called away, the valuation will always be the net of cash received from the sale of the call option less the current price of the option.

Both of these strategies involve selling covered calls, yet the evaluation of performance should be different. The option overwriting manager may be evaluated by comparing incremental returns with other overwriting managers. However, much of his success is dependent on the stocks in the underlying portfolio and the trading activities of the equity manager.

Evaluating the performance of the equity manager who sells calls with the anticipation that stocks will be called away is also difficult. Is it enough to say that however much he receives from the sale of the call options is pure incremental return and leave it at that? Perhaps. A complete discussion of the strategies employing derivative securities, the valuation of the derivative securities under each strategy, and the evaluation of the performance of each strategy is beyond the scope of this chapter.

The authors do caution that when an investor employs a manager who uses derivative securities or gives a manager authority to use derivative securities, the method of valuation of the derivative securities and the determination of how performance will be evaluated should be agreed upon in advance.

Accrual Basis vs. Cash Basis

Accrual basis refers to an accounting method that includes accrued income (income earned but not yet received) in the portfolio value and also records security transactions, with offsetting receivables and payables, on the trade date rather than on the settlement date. The *cash basis* accounting method recognizes income only when cash is received and also records security transactions on the settlement date when cash is received or paid.

It is extremely important to include accrued income in portfolio valuations and performance measurement, particularly in bond portfolios where income is a primary determinant of the portfolio return. The return may be distorted significantly by including income only when it is received in cash. Accrued income is not as material for common stock portfolios, where income usually is a smaller portion of total return and is generally received on a quarterly basis.

Table 14-1 compares the two treatments of income on a single bond portfolio. It shows that the return would have been distorted by 5 percent (i.e., 3.0 versus −2.0 percent) for the first quarter and by 3.2 percent (i.e., 2.9 versus 6.1 percent) for the second quarter using the cash basis accounting method. This difference will continue until the bond is sold and the accrued income is received.

Trade Date vs. Settlement Date. The question of when a trade should be reported—when it is executed or when money changes hands—is actually a part of the accrual basis versus cash basis controversy, as stated previously.

Experience has shown that which date is used makes little difference in the rate of return, because a major market price change seldom occurs during the five days between trade date and regular settlement. Occasionally, however, a material price change does occur. Because of this and because it is true that once a purchase has been executed, the buyer benefits from any price increase (or suffers any price decline) regardless of what was actually paid for the purchase (and vice versa for a sale), the use of trade date basis is strongly recommended for accounting and portfolio valuation purposes.

TABLE 14-1. Comparison of Bond Returns on Accrual Basis vs. Cash Basis

	Accrual Basis	Cash Basis
Portfolio at beginning of quarter 1:		
12% short-term issue	$1,000,000	$1,000,000
Transactions at end of quarter 1:		
Short-term issue matures: Principal	$1,000,000	$1,000,000
Interest	30,000	30,000
Buy: $1 million 12% 10-yr. Treasury bond		
Principal	(980,000)	(980,000)
+ 5 mos. accrued interest	(50,000)	(50,000)
Portfolio at end of quarter 1:		
$1 million 12% 10-yr. Treasury bond	$ 980,000	$ 980,000
Accrued interest	50,000	0
Total market value	$1,030,000	$ 980,000
Quarterly return (first period):	$\left(\dfrac{1{,}030{,}000}{1{,}000{,}000}-1\right) \times 100 = 3.0\%$	$\left(\dfrac{980{,}000}{1{,}000{,}000}-1\right) \times 100 = -2.0\%$
Transactions during quarter 2:		
Interest received	$ 60,000	$ 60,000
Portfolio at end of quarter 2:		
$1 million 12% 10-yr. Treasury bond	$ 980,000	$ 980,000
Cash	60,000	60,000
Accrued income	20,000	0
Total market value	$1,060,000	$1,040,000
Quarterly return (second period):	$\left(\dfrac{1{,}060{,}000}{1{,}030{,}000}-1\right) \times 100 = 2.9\%$	$\left(\dfrac{1{,}040{,}000}{980{,}000}-1\right) \times 100 = 6.1\%$
2 quarters' return:	$\left(\dfrac{1{,}060{,}000}{1{,}000{,}000}-1\right) \times 100 = 6.0\%$	$\left(\dfrac{1{,}040{,}000}{1{,}000{,}000}-1\right) \times 100 = 4.0\%$

TABLE 14-2. Hypothetical Portfolios A and B in Market Period X

	Portfolio A			Portfolio B	
Investment Subperiod	Contributions	Market Value	Return	Contributions	Market Value
Beginning		$1,000.00			$100.00
1	$100.00	1,415.00	+30%	$100.00	245.00
2	100.00	1,661.50	+10	100.00	375.50
3	100.00	1,419.20	−20	100.00	389.60
4	100.00	1,666.12	+10	100.00	533.56

METHODS OF PERFORMANCE MEASUREMENT

Calculation of Rate of Return

The basic purpose of all rate of return calculations is to account for changes in asset value plus dividend or interest income plus realized capital gains or losses. These changes are then expressed as a percentage of initial capital value, adjusted for net contributions or withdrawals. As noted earlier, time-weighted rates of return are used in performance measurement because they minimize the impact of external cash flows—over which the portfolio manager has no control—on the rate of return calculation.

Internal or Dollar-Weighted Rate of Return. An example of the impact of external cash flows is shown in Table 14-2. The only two factors affecting the output of the internal or dollar-weighted rate of return method are: (1) beginning and ending market values and (2) the timing of net contributions. In the example, it is assumed that both portfolios were invested in the same assets. An examination of hypothetical portfolios A and B in time period X shows the results of an internal rate of return calculation. During period X, portfolio A had a compounded internal rate of return of 5.16 percent while portfolio B's return was 2.72 percent. Because the two portfolios were invested in the same securities, the difference in the internal rates of return is accounted for by two facts: (1) portfolio A benefited to a greater extent than did portfolio B by the high 30 percent rate of return during the first subperiod, when A's asset value was roughly six times B's, and (2) portfolio A also benefited as compared with B in later periods when much lower returns were experienced by A at a time when A's asset value was only three or four times the size of B's.

The internal rate of return method, then, weights the final overall return figure by the investment in the portfolio in each subperiod. As a result, different dollar size and growth of the portfolios have a strong influence on the final return figure. The example in Table 14-2 indicates that even though portfolios *A* and *B* were invested in the same securities and in the same proportions, the internal rate of return method produces inappropriate numbers if the purpose is to compare the performance of two portfolio *managers*. The internal rate of return method does give the most accurate rate earned on funds invested, which is important when making comparisons to a minimum acceptable return—for example, to a pension fund's actuarial return rate.

Time-Weighted Rate of Return. The time-weighted approach computes a rate of return for each subperiod. (As shown in Table 14-2, the subperiod rates are the same for each of the two portfolios, because the securities held and their weightings are the same for each.) These individual subperiod rates of return are then compounded (or *chainlinked*) to get a return rate for each portfolio for the entire period *X*. Thus, during period *X* a dollar invested in either portfolio *A* or *B* at the beginning of the period grew to $1.26. A compound rate of return for the *n* subperiods in period *X* can be found by taking the *n*th root. In this case, the 4th root of the 4th period terminal value of 1.26 gives a compound rate of 5.9 percent.

All algorithms for time-weighted rates of return currently in use are based on the original Dietz and BAI formulas.[2] Both methods assume all contributions occur at the midpoint of the specified time period. The Dietz method does this by assuming that one half of the net contributions are made at the beginning of the time interval and one half at the end of the time interval; portfolio beginning and ending values are adjusted by adding and subtracting half the contribution, respectively. The BAI algorithm solves for the rate of return by the process of iteration and assumes midperiod compounding.

For example, assume the following information for a portfolio for a specific time interval:

---

[2] The Dietz algorithm is:

$$R_i = \left(\frac{P_i - .5C_i}{P_0 + .5C_i} - 1 \right) \times 100$$

where:

P_0 = portfolio value at beginning of time interval *i*
P_i = portfolio value at end of time interval *i*
C_i = net contribution(s) during time interval *i*
R_i = rate of return for time interval *i*

The BAI algorithm is $P_0(1 + r_i) + C_i(1 + r_i)^{1/2} - P_i = 0$. By iteration solve for r_i and then $R_i = r_i \times 100$.

Portfolio value at beginning of time interval i	$10,000,000
Portfolio value at end of time interval i	12,050,000
Net contributions during time interval i	1,000,000

The Dietz method arrives at a rate of return of 10 percent via this calculation:

$$R_i = \left[\frac{\$12,050,000 - .5(\$1,000,000)}{\$10,000,000 + .5(\$1,000,000)} - 1\right] \times 100 = 10.00 \text{ percent}$$

The BAI method arrives at a return of 10.01 percent via this calculation:

$$\$10,000,000 (1 + r_i) + \$1,000,000 (1 + r_i)^{1/2} - \$12,050,000 = 0$$

$$R_i = r_i \times 100 = 10.01 \text{ percent}$$

CPPS Study. In a 1987 report to the Financial Analysts Federation (FAF), the Committee for Performance Presentation Standards (CPPS), chaired by Claude N. Rosenberg, recommended standards for investment management performance presentation. Included in the report is the statement, "Time-weighted calculation is the natural method; perhaps the FAF should recommend one preferred formula." While the authors agree with the intent of that statement, the time intervals used in the computation (as discussed in the next section) generally affect the returns more than whether the Dietz method or the BAI method is used to make the computation.[3]

Time Intervals. It is generally agreed that more frequent measurement periods (shorter time intervals) result in more accurate computations of returns. Ideally, portfolio valuations should be calculated whenever a contribution or distribution takes place; this would eliminate the necessity of making assumptions as to the timing of cash flows and would simplify return computations. However, as a practical matter trustee/custodian banks and investment management firms usually do not have systems in place that allow for valuation more frequently than monthly, nor has there been a great demand for such services from institutional investors.

Because employee benefit funds, other institutional investors, and individuals do not generally make contributions to or receive distributions from portfolios on a daily basis, monthly computations are normally sufficient. Computations at monthly intervals, and never less frequently than quarterly, are strongly encouraged.

On the other hand, registered investment companies (mutual funds) generally value their portfolios on a daily basis to arrive at the net asset value

---

[3] For a detailed discussion see The Committee for Performance Presentation Standards [1987].

per share to be used for shares of the fund that were purchased or redeemed on that day. Therefore, assuming their data are more reflective of actual market values, rates of return computed for mutual funds are the most accurate; all other returns are simply estimates.

There need not be a direct relationship between the time interval for valuation and the time horizon of the portfolio. For example, the time horizon of the portfolio may be 3, 5, or perhaps 50 years. But the investor would not want to wait 50 years to find out whether or not objectives have been met. Therefore, the time-weighted returns for shorter time intervals are computed and compared to objectives and alternative portfolios.

Day-Weighting Method. Recognizing that cash flows do not all occur at the midpoint of a time interval, and attempting to minimize the distortion that might result from such an assumption, some performance measurement algorithms *day-weight* cash flows. For example, if a contribution is made on the tenth day of a month, rather than assuming it was made at the midpoint of the month, the return algorithm is adjusted to treat it as having been in the portfolio for two-thirds of the month.

Using the previous example and the Dietz algorithm, the revised calculation would be

$$R_i = \left[\frac{\$12,050,000 - \left(\frac{30 - 20}{30} \times \$1,000,000 \right)}{\$10,000,000 + \left(\frac{30 - 10}{30} \times \$1,000,000 \right)} - 1 \right] \times 100 = 9.84 \text{ percent}$$

No one method consistently arrives at the most accurate time-weighted return. In any event, the purpose is to determine how well the manager is doing his or her job; therefore, small error terms in the rate of return calculations are tolerable, especially in view of the valuation problems discussed previously and the risk-adjustment issues still to be discussed.

Annualized Returns. Once the returns for individual time intervals are calculated, the time-weighted rate of return for sequential time intervals can be computed by chainlinking the results of the individual time intervals. If the sequential time intervals involved in the computation in total cover more than a one-year period, then the appropriate root is found to determine the annualized (compound) rate of return. For example, if the total time period is three years, then the 3rd root is taken to arrive at the annualized rate of return. *Annual returns* are those computed for individual one-year periods, whereas the term *annualized return* is used to designate the compound average annual return for a period longer than one year.

To compute a quarterly time-weighted rate of return from the returns of the three individual months, the returns are changed into return relatives (decimal form plus 1) and multiplied together to arrive at the quarterly return. Assuming the following set of monthly returns,

Month 1	+3.06%
Month 2	−1.95
Month 3	+5.01

then,

$$R_i = (1.0306 \times 0.9805 \times 1.0501) - 1$$
$$= 1.0611 - 1$$
$$= 0.0611$$

for a quarterly time-weighted return of 6.11 percent.

An annual rate of return is computed by chainlinking the results of the 12 individual months, or the results of the four individual quarters. For example, for the following four quarterly returns,

Quarter 1	+6.11%
Quarter 2	+4.06
Quarter 3	−3.54
Quarter 4	+2.95

the annual return calculation is

$$R_i = (1.0611 \times 1.0406 \times 0.9646 \times 1.0295) - 1$$
$$= 1.0965 - 1$$
$$= 0.0965$$

or an annual return (compounded quarterly) of 9.65 percent.

Annualized returns are computed by chainlinking monthly, quarterly, or annual returns in the same fashion and taking the appropriate root of the result. The root should be the number of years in the total time period (e.g., for three years, the 3rd root; for $4\frac{1}{2}$ years, the 4.5 root). An eight-quarter example, involving the 2nd, or square, root, is shown below:

Quarter 1	+6.11%
Quarter 2	+4.06
Quarter 3	−3.54
Quarter 4	+2.95
Quarter 5	+8.34
Quarter 6	+5.20
Quarter 7	−1.95
Quarter 8	+4.86

$$R_i = (1.0611 \times 1.0406 \times 0.9646 \times 1.0295 \times 1.0834$$
$$\times\ 1.0520 \times 0.9805 \times 1.0486)^{1/2} - 1$$
$$= 0.1335$$

The result, 13.35 percent, is the annualized or compound annual rate of return for the two years measured. Because of extreme fluctuations in monthly or quarterly returns due to market movements, annualized quarterly returns should never be computed with fewer than four quarters of data. The following example shows the unrealistic results of annualizing quarterly returns where only one quarter's return is used: The annualized rate of return based on a 20 percent positive quarter would be $[(1.20)^4 - 1] \times 100 = 107.36$ percent, while the annualized return based on a one-quarter return of -20 percent would be $[(0.80)^4 - 1] \times 100 = -59.04$ percent.

Portfolio Segment Measurement

For the various methods of performance measurement for total portfolios addressed in the preceding section, errors are possible as long as valuations are not performed at the time of each new cash flow. In dealing with portfolio segments, such as stocks, bonds, and convertibles, these errors in estimates may be even greater because accurate performance measurement would require valuations each time a purchase, sale, or income transaction took place. In general, cost-benefit analyses have shown that the additional accuracy does not warrant these costly computations so long as monthly asset valuations take place.

Segment measurement helps explain the total portfolio return and how it was achieved. For example, suppose the return for an equity-oriented total portfolio was only 5 percent for a quarter in which the equity market return was 10 percent. If the return on the equity segment of the portfolio was 12 percent, then that would indicate the manager was probably right about the stocks bought for the portfolio (i.e., his stock selection was good). However, the fact that about 70 percent of the portfolio was in cash had a detrimental effect on the overall return (e.g., the manager made a poor timing decision). On the other hand, if the equity segment return was only 7 percent, then the manager would have been wrong on two counts, stock selection and timing. A detailed method to analyze or decompose a portfolio is described in the section on performance attribution.

When dealing with a segment of the total portfolio, such as the equity or the fixed-income part, it is difficult to determine how cash contributions were allocated between the specific portions of the portfolio. That is, there is no practical way to know what portion of contributions was invested in common stocks and what portion in bonds. However, because net security purchases must equal the sum of contributions and cash investment income to the fund, an equivalent can be developed. The algorithms for total portfolio performance are thus altered so that the contribution term is replaced by the term net security purchases (gross purchases less sales) minus income and the total portfolio values are replaced by the segment values. In this way, performance of individual portfolio segments can be evaluated.

The returns for portfolio segments can be chainlinked to arrive at quarterly, annual, and annualized longer period returns using the same algorithms as for total portfolio returns.

Adjusting for Risk

A well-accepted theorem is that rate of return and risk are positively correlated. Therefore, no performance measurement process is complete without some attempt to measure the riskiness of the portfolio. The major methods currently used to calculate risk-adjusted performance measurement include the Treynor measure, the Sharpe measure, and the Jensen measure, which are discussed below.

The most fundamental notion of both security risk and portfolio risk is variability, that is, variability of interperiod results compared to average results over time. Basically, the notion is simple: A security with a return stream of 0.05, 0.05, 0.05, and 0.05 is more predictable (less risky) than a security with a return stream of 0.03, 0.07, 0.01, and 0.09, even though both securities have a mean return of 0.05. Most approaches to measuring variability or risk use the standard deviation of return distributions discussed in Chapter 2.

The standard deviation of return for securities follows the general notions of riskiness. That is, securities with high degrees of fundamental riskiness—having characteristics such as poor market liquidity, cyclical industry, high financial leverage, small capitalization, or long duration—have tended to have higher standard deviations than securities with the opposite characteristics. Thus, time series of Treasury bill returns generally have had smaller standard deviations than returns on long-term bonds and much smaller standard deviations than returns on equities. Among stocks, there is a fairly wide range of risk; for example, utility stocks usually have return distributions with lower standard deviations than stocks in the airline industry.

Standard deviation measures total risk, or variability. As demonstrated in Chapter 2, an alternative and more theoretically elegant approach is to partition total risk into its component parts, systematic and unsystematic risk. Systematic risk (measured by beta) is the component of a security's or a portfolio's volatility related to the market in general, while the unsystematic risk (total risk net of beta risk) measures the residual variability of a security after market-related risk is removed.

Once the riskiness of a portfolio has been measured, risk can be related to return to determine whether the return earned was sufficient to reward the investor for the degree of risk incurred. This is most commonly done by the use of a single index model, such as those proposed by Treynor [1965], Sharpe [1966], or Jensen [1968]. These single index models are described briefly below; a more complete discussion can be found in investment texts such as Reilly [1989].

Treynor Measure. Treynor suggested that the appropriate risk measure for a portfolio is its systematic risk, or beta. The Treynor measure (T) relates the rate of return earned above the risk-free rate to the portfolio beta during the time period under consideration. Thus,

$$T = \frac{R_p - R_f}{\beta_p}$$

or, in words,

$$\text{Treynor's measure} = \frac{\text{Excess return on portfolio } p}{\text{Beta on portfolio } p}$$

$$= \frac{\begin{array}{c}\text{Average rate} \\ \text{of return for} \\ \text{portfolio } p\end{array} - \begin{array}{c}\text{Average rate of} \\ \text{return on a risk-free} \\ \text{investment}\end{array}}{\text{Beta on portfolio } p}$$

where portfolio p's beta is the slope of the portfolio's characteristic line, which measures the portfolio's volatility relative to the market—that is, its systematic risk. An example of a characteristic line is shown in Figure 14-1(b).

The numerator of the T ratio, ($R_p - R_f$), is the risk premium earned by the portfolio and the denominator, β, is the measure of risk. Therefore, the T ratio indicates the portfolio's return per unit of risk. Because the risk measured is systematic risk, this ratio assumes nothing about the portfolio's diversification. The Treynor measure, then, implicitly assumes that the portfolio being measured is fully diversified.

Using this measure, numerous portfolios can be ranked relative to one another and to the market portfolio. Because higher T values give higher returns per unit of risk, risk-averse investors would seek to maximize this value. Because the market beta equals 1.0 (by definition), the market risk premium ($R_m - R_f$) becomes the slope of the SML as shown in Figure 14-1(a). Portfolios plotting above the SML have superior risk-adjusted performance.

Sharpe Measure. The Sharpe measure (S) also is based on the capital asset pricing model and relates return to the capital market line. This measure is similar to the Treynor measure except that the denominator used is the standard deviation, which measures total risk. Thus,

$$S = \frac{R_p - R_f}{\sigma_p}$$

Excess return on portfolio p is measured per unit of σ_p, the standard deviation of the portfolio's rate of return during the measurement period.

Because the numerator is the risk premium earned in the portfolio, the Sharpe measure indicates the return per unit of total risk. Both the Treynor and Sharpe measures assume a linear relationship between return and risk. For perfectly diversified portfolios, the two measures will give identical rankings because the total variance of the portfolio would be the same as its systematic variance. If a portfolio is poorly diversified, it can have a Treynor ranking different from its Sharpe ranking relative to other portfolios included in the rankings.

Jensen Measure. The Jensen measure or Jensen's alpha, also based on the CAPM, assumes that the realized rate of return on a portfolio is a linear function of the risk-free rate, plus a risk premium that is a function of the portfolio's systematic risk during the period of review, plus a random error term. Thus, using a time series linear regression format for realized rates of return, the model is

$$R_{pt} - R_{ft} = \beta_p(R_{mt} - R_{ft}) + U_{pt}$$

In words,

$$\begin{pmatrix} \text{Realized} & \text{Risk-} \\ \text{return on} & - \text{free} \\ \text{portfolio } p & \text{return} \end{pmatrix} = \begin{matrix} \text{function} \\ \text{(beta)} \end{matrix} \begin{pmatrix} \text{Realized} & \text{Risk-} \\ \text{return on} & - \text{free} \\ \text{market index } m & \text{return} \end{pmatrix} + \begin{matrix} \text{Random} \\ \text{error} \\ \text{term} \end{matrix}$$

or

$$\begin{matrix} \text{Excess return} \\ \text{on portfolio } p \end{matrix} = \begin{matrix} \text{function} \\ \text{(beta)} \end{matrix} \begin{pmatrix} \text{Excess return on} \\ \text{market index } m \end{pmatrix} + \begin{matrix} \text{Random} \\ \text{error} \\ \text{term} \end{matrix}$$

In equilibrium, in an efficient market one would not expect an intercept for the regression. However, if some portfolio managers can consistently select superior portfolios, they will consistently plot above the average represented by the regression line; that is, their actual returns will consistently be above expected (equilibrium) returns. This return differential can be measured by the regression intercept (alpha) term of the regression equation as follows:

$$R_{pt} - R_{ft} = \alpha_p + \beta_p(R_{mt} - R_{ft}) + U_{pt}$$

or verbally,

$$
\begin{array}{c}
\text{Excess return} \\
\text{on portfolio } p
\end{array}
=
\begin{array}{c}
\text{Unique} \\
\text{return} \\
\text{(alpha)}
\end{array}
+
\begin{array}{c}
\text{function} \\
\text{(beta)}
\end{array}
\left(
\begin{array}{c}
\text{Excess return on} \\
\text{market index } m
\end{array}
\right)
+
\begin{array}{c}
\text{Random} \\
\text{error} \\
\text{term}
\end{array}
$$

That is, α_p represents the unique return experience of portfolio p over time relative to market index m. Given enough time periods, the significance of alpha can be measured.

The Jensen measure, like the Treynor measure, assumes fully diversified portfolios. An additional problem with the Jensen alpha is that it is unique to a particular portfolio beta level; in other words, Jensen alphas in different risk classes should not be compared with one another. As discussed later, it is preferable to segregate portfolios into different management styles, each of which tends to have different systematic risk parameters.

Problems in Use of CAPM. The Treynor, Sharpe, and Jensen measures all assume (at least in their simplest form) that the relationship between risk and return is linear and remains linear throughout its entire range. Much research has shown that the relationship is not as simple as capital market theory would suggest and sophisticated methods for improving risk-return measurement have been recommended. Although the detailed mathematics are not discussed here, important insights are gained from understanding the following empirical problems inherent in the simplistic use of the CAPM methodology for ex-post risk adjustment:

1. The intercept of the empirically derived SML often differs significantly from the risk-free rate as approximated by actual Treasury bill return experience.
2. There is no generally accepted and universally applicable economy wide market index.
3. Statistical error is so large, because of large fluctuations observed in a limited sample of data, that statistically significant alphas seldom occur.
4. Errors in estimating beta may (or may not) produce offsetting errors in alpha, the measure of excess portfolio return.
5. Residuals from the characteristic line calculation frequently are not statistically independent across securities.
6. Residual risk appears to be nonconstant over time.

7. Beta estimates for individual stocks appear to be nonstationary.
8. Capital market line analysis does not tell how a manager achieved his or her return.

Arbitrage Pricing Theory Approach. Perhaps the most interesting of the proposed suggestions for improving risk-return measurement is an approach based on the arbitrage pricing theory (APT), discussed in Chapter 2. The major critique of CAPM is that the relationship between risk and return is more complex than expressed in a single-index model. The APT model is a multi-index or multi-factor model.

In a multi-index model, returns are explained by a variety of factors that may include, but are not limited to, the behavior of the overall market. The Roll and Ross model [1984] asserts that the risk elements that influence security returns are unanticipated changes in four economic variables: (1) inflation, (2) industrial production, (3) risk premiums, and (4) the slope of the term structure of interest rates.

Decomposition of Returns. Fama [1972] suggested an approach to the decomposition of portfolio returns. As indicated in Figure 14-2, he proposed that overall return can be attributed to (1) returns from the investor's targeted systematic risk level above the risk-free portfolio, (2) returns from the actual systematic risk the manager chose to take, and (3) returns from selectivity. The latter return is attributed to two sources: (1) diversification, the additional return that would just compensate the investor for the diversifiable risk randomly assumed by the manager, and (2) net selectivity, the actual results of (nonrandom) security selection compared to a naive portfolio at the chosen level of diversification. For a more complete discussion of Fama's methodology, see Elton and Gruber [1987].

Use of a Two-Parameter Measure. The validity of the APT, the combination of ex-post return measurement errors and ex-post risk measurement errors, and the nonlinearity of the total true risk-reward function provide a strong recommendation for a two-parameter measure, such as the relations between the rate of return and standard deviation used in the remainder of this chapter. Although portfolio rankings derived from two parameter measures are less precise than those provided by single-index models, the probability of drawing erroneous conclusions is also lessened. The assumption that one prefers the highest return for any given level of risk still holds.

Although great strides have been made in ex-post return measurement and risk adjustment, use of the CAPM methodology is most successful when augmented by the methods discussed below, as well as by personal knowledge of the manager's organization and detailed analysis of how the portfolio was invested.

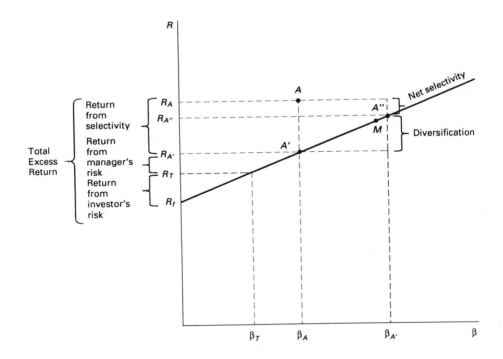

Key:

Part 1: Components of return from selectivity (all returns are excess returns)

$R_A - R_{A'}$ = Return from selectivity = Jensen differential return or Jensen measure of performance
= Return from incurring diversifiable as well as systematic risk
= Return from incurring the equivalent of $\beta_{A'}$ minus β_A of systematic risk

$R_{A''} - R_{A'}$ = Return from random non-diversification or from incomplete diversification but naive security selection
= Return from randomly bearing unsystematic risk

$R_A - R_{A''}$ = Return from net selectivity
= Return from incomplete diversification and deliberate security selection

Part 2: Components of return from (systematic) risk bearing

$R_{A'} - R_f$ = Return from bearing systematic risk level β_A
$R_T - R_f$ = Return from bearing systematic risk level β_T where β_T is investor's target risk level given to manager
$R_{A'} - R_T$ = Return from bearing systematic risk level $\beta_{A'}$ chosen by manager, rather than target level β_T

Figure 14-2. Decomposition of Portfolio Returns. SOURCE: Fama [1972].

EVALUATION OF INVESTMENT PERFORMANCE

Common approaches to performance evaluation that have been developed on a commercial basis are based on the theory discussed previously. They must be straightforward enough to be agreed upon and easily understood by both the owners of the capital to be invested and the professional managers of the portfolios.

As stated previously, any valid performance measurement method should begin by evaluating portfolios in risk-return space. Then, the job of analysis can proceed. The next section describes the process of performance attribution in general, and later sections focus more directly on analysis of fixed-income and equity performance. The major issues in each of the major portfolio segments involve the development of comparative measurement universes and appropriate benchmarks. Important investment issues are involved in the development of both; these are addressed in the sections on the evaluation of bond strategies and equity strategies later in this chapter.

Performance Attribution

The purpose of performance attribution is to trace the impact of all decisions made with respect to the management of the portfolio. These include the strategic policy decision, the asset allocation decision, and the security selection decisions. Picture this as a "top down" approach with policy decisions at the top and selection decisions at the bottom.

Strategic policy decisions involve setting a policy, or benchmark or normal portfolio, that defines the appropriate asset classes for long-run portfolio investment. This is the top-most level of a string of investment decisions that will impact the returns on the portfolio. It is the process described by strategic asset allocation in Chapter 7

The effect on performance of decisions made at this top level can be measured by comparing the returns of the policy portfolio to the returns of a naive portfolio. A naive portfolio is difficult to specify but can consist of any type of investment that the investor wants to compare against. Possible naive portfolios consist of portfolios allocated 100 percent to Treasury bill investments, 100 percent to equity investments, or to the average asset allocation weighting of all pension portfolios. The analysis in this section focuses on the impact of decisions made below the investment policy level.

Table 14-3 identifies three asset classes, weights, and benchmarks for the portfolio. For the measurement period, the actual portfolio is allocated to those three asset classes differently from the policy portfolio. For each asset class, the returns for the benchmark index and the returns for the actual portfolio are shown. Also shown are total returns for three portfolios: the policy portfolio, the allocated portfolio, and the actual portfolio. Finally, the table shows the allocation effect and the selection effect.

Allocation Effect. The allocation effect measures the impact of the decision to allocate assets differently than the policy portfolio. This decision is often referred to as either tactical asset allocation or market timing. Identifying the value added by the allocation effect is the same as identifying the value added by tactical asset allocation. To measure the performance of the

TABLE 14-3. Allocation/Selection Performance Attribution Analysis

Asset	Index Representing the Asset Class in the Policy and Allocated Portfolios	Weights Policy	Weights Actual	Asset Returns Index	Asset Returns Portfolio	Policy Portfolio	Allocated Portfolio	Actual Portfolio	Allocation Effect	Selection Effect
Stocks	Russell 3000 Stock Index	60.0%	50.0%	13.08%	11.75%	13.08% × 0.6	13.08% × 0.5	11.75% × 0.5	(0.28%)	(0.66%)
Bonds	Shearson Lehman Hutton Govt./Corp. Bond Index	30.0	30.0	6.56	8.44	6.56% × 0.3	6.56% × 0.3	8.44% × 0.3	0.00	0.56
Cash equivalents	U.S. Treasury Bills	10.0	20.0	4.77	5.53	4.77% × 0.1	4.77% × 0.2	5.53% × 0.2	(0.55)	0.15
Total return						10.29%	9.46%	9.51%	(0.83%)	0.05%
Total effect										

allocation decision, the returns of the appropriate benchmarks for each asset class are compared with the returns of the policy portfolio as a whole.

The allocation effect is calculated simply as the difference between the allocated portfolio return and the policy portfolio return. In this case, the allocation effect is -0.83 percent. The negative impact of the manager's decision to underweight equities and overweight cash equivalents has been identified and quantified without including the impact of individual security selection. That is, the allocation effect is the difference between the return the manager would have received had the indexes been bought in the actual weightings (the allocation portfolio return) and the return he would have received had the indexes been bought in the policy weights (the policy portfolio return).

Details of the calculation of the allocation effect are shown below.

$$
\left(
\begin{matrix}
\text{Actual} \\
\text{weight}
\end{matrix}
-
\begin{matrix}
\text{Policy} \\
\text{weight}
\end{matrix}
\right)
\times
\left(
\begin{matrix}
\text{Asset class} \\
\text{return} \\
\text{in policy} \\
\text{portfolio}
\end{matrix}
-
\begin{matrix}
\text{Total} \\
\text{return} \\
\text{on policy} \\
\text{portfolio}
\end{matrix}
\right)
=
\begin{matrix}
\text{Allocation} \\
\text{effect}
\end{matrix}
$$

$(0.50 - 0.60)$	$\times$	$(13.08$	$-$	$10.29)$	$= -0.28\%$	Equity allocation effect
$(0.30 - 0.30)$	$\times$	$(6.56$	$-$	$10.29)$	$= 0.00$	Fixed-income allocation effect
$(0.20 - 0.10)$	$\times$	$(4.77$	$-$	$10.29)$	$= -0.55$	Cash equivalent allocation effect
					-0.83%	Total allocation effect

A manager adds allocation value by deciding to take a larger position in an asset class that subsequently has superior performance relative to the total returns of the portfolio or taking a smaller position in an asset class that subsequently has poor performance relative to the total return of the policy portfolio.

A summary of the allocation effect is shown in the following table:

	Asset Class With	
Manager Allocation Decision	Superior Performance	Poor Performance
Overweight	+	−
Underweight	−	+

Selection Effect. The selection effect measures the impact of individual security selections on the total return of the portfolio. The question here is whether the manager made security selections better (or worse) than all of the securities in the benchmark index. The selection effect can be cal-

culated simply as the sum of the differences between the actual portfolio
return and the allocated portfolio return for each asset. It is the actual
(weighted) portfolio segment returns as compared to the returns the manager
would have had if he had bought the indexes themselves in the actual allocation weightings. The total selection effect for this example is calculated
as follows:

Stock selection effect		Bond selection effect		Cash selection effect		Total selection effect
	+		+		=	

$$\begin{bmatrix} (11.75 \times .5) \\ -(13.08 \times .5) \end{bmatrix} + \begin{bmatrix} (8.44 \times .3) \\ -(6.56 \times .3) \end{bmatrix} + \begin{bmatrix} (5.53 \times .2) \\ -(4.77 \times .2) \end{bmatrix} =$$

$$-0.66 + 0.56 + 0.15 = 0.05$$

The selection effect of 0.05 percent is the effect on the portfolio of the
manager's individual stock selection, bond selection, and cash equivalent
selection, without including the impact of the allocation effect.

Evaluation of Bond Strategies

As discussed in Chapter 8, bond portfolio managers use a number of quite
different strategies. An investor's choice of a particular manager may be
viewed as a choice at two levels: the choice of one strategy among alternative
strategies and the choice of a particular manager among alternative managers
pursuing the same or similar strategies. When evaluating portfolio performance, an investor or analyst should focus on which choice is being considered so as not to make inappropriate comparisons.

Two types of comparisons are useful: comparisons with similarly managed portfolios and comparisons with benchmarks. The most obvious way
to evaluate a portfolio manager's skill is to compare the manager with his
or her peers. Several firms gather performance information from managers
and publish summary statistics from the sample of portfolios. Some attempt
is usually made to classify the portfolios along broad strategy guidelines,
forming "style universes." For example, Frank Russell Company classifies
U.S. fixed-income portfolios into the styles listed in Table 14-4.

The styles are generally defined by traditional active management approaches: (1) those that anticipate changes in interest rates and modify portfolio structure accordingly, principally by shortening or lengthening duration; (2) those that anticipate interest rate changes to a lesser degree and
instead search for undervalued sectors or individual issues; (3) those that
specialize in a particular maturity range (i.e., short, intermediate, or long)
or in a particular sector (e.g., high-yield bonds, convertible bonds, or municipal bonds).

TABLE 14-4. Example of U.S. Fixed-Income Style Universes

Style	Comparison Indexes
Active duration accounts	Shearson Lehman Hutton (SLH) Aggregate
	SLH Government/Corporate
Active sector rotation accounts	SLH Aggregate
	SLH Government/Corporate
Intermediate bond accounts	SLH Intermediate Government/Corporate
Long-term bond accounts	SLH Long-Term Government/Corporate
Short-intermediate bond accounts	Merrill Lynch 1–2.99 Years Treasury Master
	Payden & Rygel 2-Year Treasury Notes
Short-term investment fund (STIF)	Salomon Bros. 6-Month Treasury Bills
and cash accounts	Commercial Paper
Convertible securities accounts	First Boston Convertible
	Goldman Sachs 100 Convertible
	Froley, Revy 30 Convertiible
High-yield bond accounts	SLH Government/Corporate
	Salomon Bros. High-Yield Corporate
Municipal bond accounts	SLH Municipal

SOURCE: Frank Russell Company.

A summary of universe performance typically is presented in a chart such as Figure 14-3, showing quartiles of the distribution of returns within the universe for various time periods plus comparisons with relevant bond index returns.

One problem with quartile chart comparisons is that they focus attention on return, drawing attention away from risk. An alternate way of summarizing universe information is to plot a measure of return against a measure of risk for all portfolios in a universe, creating a scatter diagram as in Figure 14-4. The measure of risk most commonly used in such diagrams is the standard deviation of return over a given length of time. There are, of course, other risk measures, such as duration and convexity, that are specific to bonds (see Bierwag [1987]). Nevertheless, similarly managed portfolios should be expected to produce similar risk and return, however measured. A large disparity for a given portfolio could be used as a basis for further investigation.

Universe Comparison Problems. Several problems should be acknowledged when making universe comparisons. The first problem is *identifying the appropriate universe*. If the purpose of the comparison is to evaluate skill among managers pursuing a given strategy, then the investor or analyst should consider whether the available universes conform well to the chosen strategy. Given the large number of techniques used by bond managers, those who create style universes face the fundamental dilemma of how narrowly to define the styles. Because no two managers are alike, one

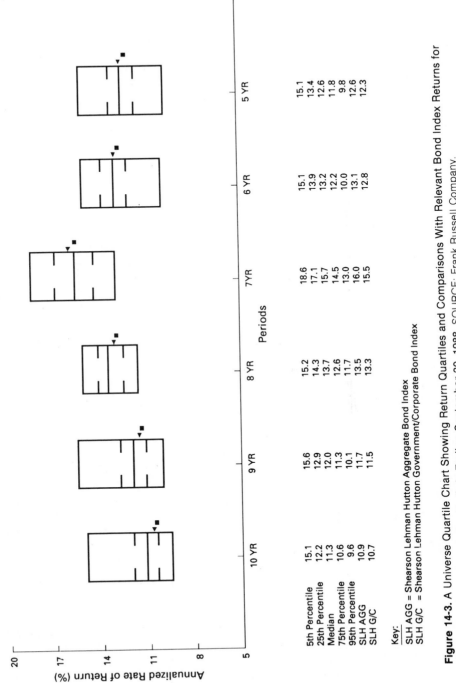

Figure 14-3. A Universe Quartile Chart Showing Return Quartiles and Comparisons With Relevant Bond Index Returns for Active Duration Accounts for Periods Ending September 30, 1988. SOURCE: Frank Russell Company.

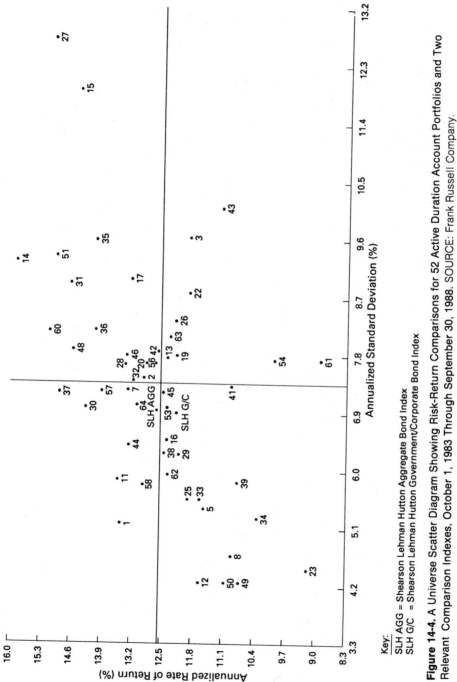

Figure 14-4. A Universe Scatter Diagram Showing Risk-Return Comparisons for 52 Active Duration Account Portfolios and Two Relevant Comparison Indexes, October 1, 1983 Through September 30, 1988. SOURCE: Frank Russell Company.

Key:
SLH AGG = Shearson Lehman Hutton Aggregate Bond Index
SLH G/C = Shearson Lehman Hutton Government/Corporate Bond Index

could, in principle, create a style for every manager, leaving no possible comparisons within styles. Therefore, styles are necessarily defined along broad strategy guidelines. Ultimately, a universe is appropriate for comparison with a given manager if the membership contains reasonable alternatives for the investor.

This consideration is particularly important when evaluating some of the newer strategies, such as dedication, immunization, or their many variations. By design, these strategies have return targets that are stated in absolute terms, and are tailored to a particular investor's specified liability stream (see Granito [1984] and Chapter 8). Unless the comparison portfolios are tailored for the same liability stream, for example, it would be invalid to compare performance of dedicated or immunized portfolios. For the same reason, it is inappropriate to include dedicated or immunized portfolios in universes of more traditional styles.

A second problem, closely related to the first, is *accurately classifying managers into styles,* even after settling on a classification scheme. The universe creator must ask the portfolio manager for detailed information about his or her investment process, objectives, constraints, and philosophy. Undoubtedly, the placement of a manager within a universe involves some subjective judgment.

A third problem involves the *length of time that performance is available* for a manager. All investments involve some risk, and superior or inferior performance for a given quarter may have been due to luck rather than skill. If so, it should not be expected to continue over many quarters. Unfortunately, actual performance over long periods may not be available. New accounts obviously will not have a long history of actual performance, and even accounts in existence for some time may undergo a change in personnel or a change in investment approach.

Despite these problems with direct comparisons against other managers, it is clearly natural for an investor to ask, "How did my manager's performance compare with others?" By observing consistently superior performance over a long time, an investor gains confidence that returns were earned more from skill than from luck. Observing inferior performance for a given period should not be interpreted as necessarily the result of bad decisions, unless further detailed investigations also support that conclusion.

Comparisons With Benchmarks. The other performance comparison that is commonly made is a comparison with a benchmark portfolio. In principle, a benchmark should be thought of as representing a feasible alternative to the managed portfolio under study. Often, an investor's wishes are communicated to the manager by assigning the manager a benchmark against which performance will be compared. When an asset allocation decision is made, or when the choice of a mix of strategies within the fixed-income asset class is made, it is usually made on the basis of the performance

of benchmarks that are believed to be representative of the alternative strategies. As with comparisons against universes, benchmarks that are appropriate for the given manager's strategies or styles should be used.

The most commonly used benchmarks are market indexes. Three major
indexes represent the broad U.S. fixed-income market: the Merrill Lynch
Domestic Master Index, the Salomon Brothers Broad Investment Grade
Bond Index, and the Shearson Lehman Hutton Aggregate Bond Index. Each
of these indexes is divided into many components representing segments of
the market.

In recent years it has become possible to obtain the performance of a
market index through the use of index funds. Market index funds are often
referred to as a passively managed alternative, but in fact, there is much
work involved in index fund management (see Mossavar-Rahmani [1987]),
and index fund managers do charge fees. Those fees, however, are usually
lower than those of active managers, justifying the notion of an indexed
alternative.

A comparison of a managed portfolio against an index can be used to
provide evidence of skill only if the index is appropriate for the manager's
style. As with universe comparisons, there is a fundamental dilemma in
defining styles. If the goal is to compare specific groups of managers, then
styles should be defined broadly and matched with an index that includes
the securities in which that style normally invests. The comparison indexes
used by Russell for the styles mentioned earlier are also listed in Table 14-
4.

Normal Portfolio Comparisons. Unlike universe comparisons, benchmark comparisons need not be restricted to broad style definitions. A benchmark or index can be tailored to a specific manager, creating what is known
as a manager's *normal portfolio* (see Robie and Lambert [1987]). The normal
portfolio represents the manager's neutral investment position, displaying
exposures to market characteristics that are the manager's averages over
time. The manager may deviate from the neutral position at any given time
and would be expected to do so when making active management decisions.
When comparing a manager's performance against such a customized index,
the question implicitly being asked is, "What value was added by those
active decisions?"

In practice, the problems facing normal portfolio creators are the same
as those facing universe creators in classifying managers. The analyst must
ask the manager detailed questions about process, techniques, and philosophy. The effort expended in the task may be useful not only for the purpose
of constructing the benchmark itself, but also for the simple purpose of
obtaining such qualitative knowledge.

In some situations, however, there may be an obvious benchmark for
comparison. In particular, dedication and immunization strategies have ex-

plicitly stated performance targets. For example, a zero coupon bond maturing at the stated horizon date may be an appropriate benchmark portfolio for an immunized portfolio.

As with universe performance comparisons, an investor should view benchmark comparisons as potential evidence supporting the conclusion that good management decisions were made, not as proof. A carefully selected benchmark lends more weight to the evidence.

Analysis of Sources of Return

A simple comparison of portfolio return against a benchmark can provide evidence of management skill, but such a comparison can only measure the net result of many separate decisions made by the manager. For example, a manager may make a duration adjustment in anticipation of a general interest rate movement while simultaneously selecting an apparently undervalued sector to overweight. The two decisions are conceptually distinct, but total return can only measure their combined effect.

To isolate the effects of such decisions, the interaction of duration and sector must be decomposed. Dietz, Fogler, and Hardy [1980] first proposed this idea, and Fong, Pearson, and Vasicek [1982] posed substantial methodological improvements. Several consultants and portfolio managers themselves use tools that are designed in the spirit of performance "attribution."

The intent of these tools is to determine how much of total portfolio return can be explained by pure interest rate movements and how much of the remainder can be explained by changes in relative valuation among market sectors. The residual is regarded as security specific return. By applying such an analysis of sources of returns to both a portfolio and to a benchmark, the differences can be interpreted as or attributed to the effects of management decisions. An analyst can then determine if the measured effects meet expectations.

This type of analysis requires information on the specific securities held in a portfolio as well as data from which to estimate parameters of the model. The data requirements are much greater than those of simple performance comparisons. In return for a greater investment in time, effort, and cost, such an analysis can provide great insight into an investment manager's decision process.

Example of Return Sources and Attribution. An example of the decomposition of and attribution for a manager's results is shown in Table 14-5. Here a manager's results are compared with a broad-based unmanaged index, with the decomposed returns of the managed portfolio being measured against the decomposed returns of a 2,100 bond universe. The results are

TABLE 14-5. Value Added by Active Fixed-Income Management

	Total Return	=	Yield to Maturity Effect	+	Interest Rate Effect	+	Sector Effect	+	Residual Effect
Short-term portfolio return	8.30%		4.06%		3.94%		−0.58%		0.88%
Less: Index return	10.44		3.92		8.20		(−1.68)		0.00
Management differential	−2.14%		0.14%		−4.26%		1.10%		0.88%
Long-term portfolio return	16.25%		3.63%		9.76%		−1.37%		4.23%
Less: Index return	10.44		3.92		8.20		(−1.68)		0.00
Management differential	5.81%		−0.29%		1.56%		0.31%		4.23%

shown for both a short-term and a long-term portfolio as compared with the 2,100 bond universe for one quarter in the early 1980s.

The returns are decomposed into the following effects:

1. *Yield to maturity effect,* an a priori known return assuming *no* change in interest rates, sector or quality differentials, or the like. It is the return from accruing income, the price change from amortization toward par, and the impact from riding the yield curve. It is a return that is totally external to management.
2. *Interest rate effect,* the return from the price change due to changes in the level and shape of the yield curve. This is an internal effect, or one that can be affected by the manager's actions.
3. *Sector effect,* return due to a yield spread shift because of a change in sector differentials. This is an internal effect.
4. *Residual effect,* return or external effect that is not measured by the model, usually because of random, unpredictable, and nonrecurring events.

The example shown in Table 14-5 covers a period during which interest rates declined. For the short maturity portfolio, there was a negative management differential, largely because of a poor interest rate forecast, even though that forecast was partially offset by good sector judgments and actions. In the long maturity portfolio, there was a large positive management differential but only about one-third of it was attributable to management's interest rate and sector or quality activity. About two-thirds was accounted for by external factors, especially residual factors. Thus, overall, the manager's quarterly results were poor in the short-term area and only moderately positive in the long-term area.

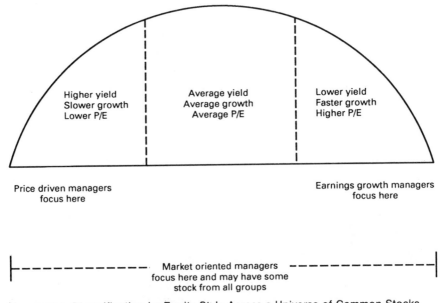

Price driven managers
focus here

Earnings growth managers
focus here

Market oriented managers
focus here and may have some
stock from all groups

Figure 14-5. Diversification by Equity Style Across a Universe of Common Stocks.
SOURCE: Frank Russell Company.

Evaluation of Equity Strategies

The universe of equity managers also contains a number of investment styles, with a multiplicity of logical divisions. Figure 14-5 shows one method of separating the equity market into sectors and the styles employed by managers in each sector. The two most distinctive styles can be termed *earnings growth* and *price driven*. The earnings growth manager tends to invest in companies with above average earnings growth, while the price driven manager tends to invest in stocks with below average price/earnings, price-to-book, or price-to-sales ratios or above average dividend yields, as explained in Chapter 9.

In addition to focusing on growth and price, many investors focus on small capitalization issues as a separate class. If this group is also taken into account, equity management styles can be viewed as shown in Figure 14-6. This schematic plots styles based on their emphasis on company size and earnings growth. An important aspect of the diagram is that it represents a spectrum of styles. While an understanding of manager style can be important to evaluating results, some managers defy clear-cut categorization and employ elements of various approaches.

Identification of Styles. Reiterating some of the material in Chapter 9, the following are descriptions of each style in Figure 14-6:

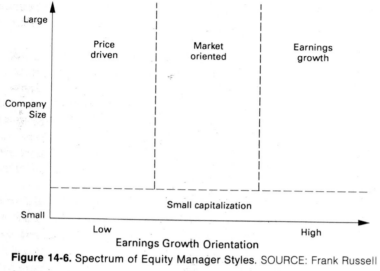

Figure 14-6. Spectrum of Equity Manager Styles. SOURCE: Frank Russell Company.

   1. **Price driven.** Managers in this group are frequently referred to as value-oriented investors. While there are differences in how these organizations define "value," an issue's current market price is generally the critical variable. For example, some organizations focus on companies with low absolute or relative price/earnings ratios (price is in the numerator), while others stress issues with above average dividend yields (price is in the denominator). Additional measures that may be used are price-to-book and price-to-sales ratios. A stock whose price has declined because of adverse investor sentiment may also attract certain of these managers. Historical growth and profitability characteristics of stocks held by price driven managers are frequently well below market averages, and overall characteristics are in sharp contrast to those of earnings growth managers.
   2. **Earnings growth.** Managers in this style devote their efforts to identifying companies with above average earnings growth prospects. In general, two basic categories of securities are owned: (1) companies with consistent above average historical and prospective profitability and growth and (2) companies expected to generate above average, near term earnings momentum based on company, industry, or economic factors. In the latter case, such securities may not have exhibited above average historical growth but are expected to do so over the near future. Managers in this style, frequently referred to as growth managers, are willing to pay above market multiples for the superior growth rate and profitability they anticipate. Other typical characteristics of this style are selection of higher quality companies; emphasis on consumer, service, health care, and technology stocks; and lighter weightings in cyclical and defensive stocks.

3. Market oriented. These managers do not evidence a strong preference for the types of companies emphasized in price driven or earnings growth portfolios. Instead, they generally select stocks from the broad equity market. A wide variety of managers fall into this category, including those with (1) growth and valuation characteristics similar to the market, (2) slight earnings growth or price driven biases not sufficient to place them in the price driven or earnings growth categories, or (3) a willingness to make significant bets in growth or value but no consistent preference for either.

4. Small capitalization. The major distinguishing characteristic of this style is a focus on small companies. In some cases, small companies are unseasoned and rapidly growing, but in other cases they are simply small businesses with long histories. Typical characteristics of small capitalization portfolios are below market dividend yields, above market betas, and high residual risk relative to broad market indexes. Just as in the large and medium capitalization segments of the marketplace, managers in the small capitalization area often focus on particular stock characteristics. Within the small capitalization sector, managers may have a price driven, earnings growth, or market oriented approach.

Price driven and earnings growth portfolios are normally at opposite ends of the systematic risk spectrum; therefore, differences in performance may be explained by a beta effect. However, because of measurement errors in equity market indexes, it is preferable to compare portfolios with those of similar objectives. In addition, a manager's focus on specific market sectors must be taken into account in comparing and evaluating performance.

Performance Comparisons for Mutual Fund Study. Figures 14-7, 14-8, and 14-9 demonstrate the effect equity management styles can have on performance. The results shown are for mutual fund groups for the five-year periods ending December 31 of 1975, 1980, and 1985, respectively. Note that in the first five years the capital market line is negative, whereas for the later periods it is steeply positive.

Figures 14-7 and 14-9 show that price driven portfolios had the best performance in the periods ending December 31, 1975 and December 31, 1985; conversely, small capitalization portfolios had the worst results in those periods. For the intervening period ending December 31, 1980, shown in Figure 14-8, the return patterns inverted; small capitalization portfolios experienced the best results, while price driven portfolios provided the worst.

In this example, riskiness was measured by use of the standard deviation of quarterly returns. Because beta (systematic or market risk) is only one portion of the risk measured by standard deviation, a pronounced beta effect is evident in only two of the periods. That is, higher standard deviation (higher beta) portfolios performed worse than both the market and lower risk portfolios in bearish market years (1971 to 1975) and better than the

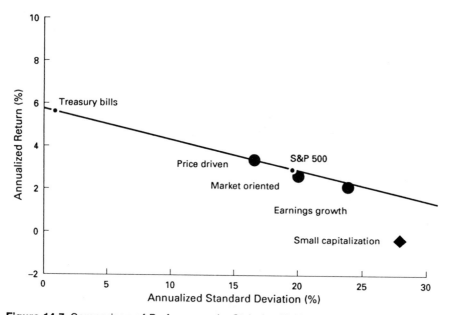

Figure 14-7. Comparison of Performance by Style for 92 Mutual Funds Consisting of 31 Earnings Growth, 25 Market Oriented, 20 Price Driven, and 16 Small Capitalization Funds for Five Years Ending December 31, 1975. SOURCE: Frank Russell Company.

market and lower risk portfolios in bullish years (1976 to 1980). The trend is not consistent, however; the five years ending December 31, 1985 includes mostly bull market years (1981 is the exception), yet over this period, the lower beta portfolios outperformed their higher risk counterparts.

In theory, optimally diversified portfolios would be expected to fall on the capital market line in an efficient market. The fact that they do not indicates either superior or inferior security selection, excess positive or negative returns from bearing nonmarket risk, or measurement error. It is likely that all three factors are present.

The mutual fund study shows that performance results are not necessarily a function of superior or inferior selection of issues within each market segment. A complete evaluation also takes into account the performance of a manager's market segment relative to the market as a whole. For example, in the five-year period ending December 31, 1975, small capitalization portfolios performed poorly in comparison with those of the other styles. The portfolios may have displayed superior selection of small capitalization issues, but because they had exposure to an underperforming market sector, selection relative to the broad market was poor.

Similarly, the term *measurement error* in performance evaluation does not refer to computational errors but, instead, implies that it may not be appropriate to measure small capitalization stocks against a capital market

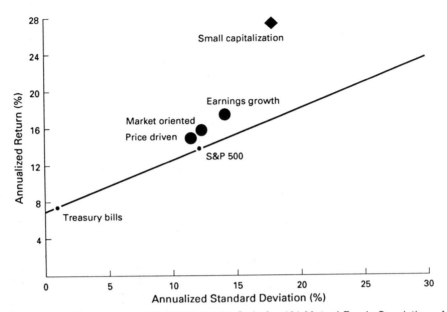

Figure 14-8. Comparison of Performance by Style for 101 Mutual Funds Consisting of 32 Earnings Growth, 25 Market Oriented, 23 Price Driven, and 21 Small Capitalization Funds for the Five Years Ending December 31, 1980. SOURCE: Frank Russell Company.

line estimated by the rate of return on Treasury bills and the return and risk on the S&P 500. A different, better tailored market index would be more appropriate in this instance, or perhaps the variation in results could be captured by use of an APT measurement model.

Benchmark Development. Because of the potential for measurement error, much effort has been devoted to developing benchmarks that are better than the initial indicators of manager skill. This problem was first raised by Roll [1978]. The results have included both (1) normal portfolios individually tailored to measure a single manager's approach and (2) a variety of new indexes, each of which is applied to groups of managers with similar styles.

Many market indexes are publicly available. For a number of years, the S&P 500 Composite Index was generally accepted as the comparative index for institutional portfolios. However, it suffers from three major technical problems that reduce its usefulness as a universal benchmark. These problems include large capitalization bias, double counting due to (corporate) cross ownership of equities in the index, and the fact that it only covers 65 to 70 percent of the value of all traded U.S. securities.

To overcome some of the measurement errors, Frank Russell Company developed a series of equity indexes as shown in Table 14-6. A variety of fundamental, size, and valuation factors were considered in the development

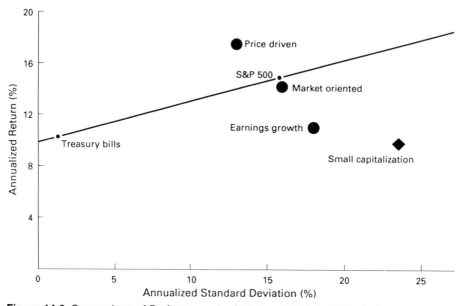

Figure 14-9. Comparison of Performance by Style for 103 Mutual Funds Consisting of 32 Earnings Growth, 25 Market Oriented, 23 Price Driven, and 23 Small Capitalization Funds for the Five Years Ending December 31, 1985. SOURCE: Frank Russell Company.

of the indexes, and the resulting stock universes were compared to actual managed portfolios to ensure that they were appropriate.

Figure 14-10 depicts the importance of the choice of a market index in performance measurement. For illustrative purposes, the capital market line has been drawn from the return on Treasury bills to the return on the Standard & Poor's 500, the Russell 3000 Index, and the Russell 2000 Small Stock Index. Each of these indexes is capitalization weighted. Portfolios plotted in the space between these lines would have a negative alpha (or unique return) using the S&P 500 as a market proxy and, simultaneously, a positive alpha compared to the Russell 3000 for the shaded areas and the Russell 2000 for the cross-hatched and shaded areas. For a small-capitalization portfolio, the Russell 2000, because of its small capitalization constituency, would clearly be the preferred benchmark.

To complicate matters further, the compounded 90-day Treasury bill rate may not be appropriate as a risk-free rate. In Figure 14-10, the Salomon Brothers three-month Treasury bill index provides the basis for the capital market lines. A 90-day holding period is assumed. In fact, the only risk-free investment available to the portfolio manager for the period December 31, 1984 to December 31, 1988 would have been a Treasury note or bond with a four-year maturity and a return of 10.5 percent; this was the only risk-free security with that particular maturity that could have been bought and held

TABLE 14-6. Examples of Style Indexes

Index	Manager Style for Which Index Is Designed	Description
Russell 1000 Index	Market oriented	Consists of the 1,000 largest capitalization U.S. stocks. Represents the broad universe of stocks in which most active money managers invest.
Russell Earnings Growth Index	Earnings growth	A subset of the Russell 1000. Characteristics include above average or accelerating growth, below average dividend yield, and above average return on equity, dividend growth, debt coverage, and return volatility.
Russell Price Driven Index	Price driven	A subset of the Russell 1000. Characteristics include below average price/book and price/earnings ratios, above average dividend yield, and below average volatility.
Russell 2000 Small Stock Index	Small capitalization	Consists of the smallest 2,000 stocks in the Russell 3000 Index[a] representing approximately 10 percent of the total U.S. market capitalization

[a] The Russell 3000 Index consists of the largest 3,000 U.S. stocks by market capitalization, representing approximately 97 percent of the U.S. equity market. Together, the Russell 1000 and the Russell 2000 make up the Russell 3000.

to maturity over the four-year time horizon with a relatively assured return. Because portfolio managers are always measured after the fact over a time period beyond their control, the risk-free rate more likely plots out as a narrow ellipse lying along the vertical axis of a risk/return diagram like Figure 14-10, rather than as a single point. The ellipse traces out the sharp fluctuations in return and the small but finite risk of the riskless asset. Thus, performance could be measured against a whole series of capital market lines.

Performance Comparisons Within Styles. The evidence provided in Figures 14-7, 14-8, and 14-9 suggests that a manager's performance should be compared not only with a specialized benchmark, but also with a universe of actual portfolios of the same investment style. These universes may be composed of mutual funds, pooled accounts (such as at commercial bank trust departments), or separately managed portfolios.

Figure 14-11 shows the quarterly four-year moving average returns of separately managed or separate account portfolio universes in the four equity styles described earlier. However, in this case the market effect has been removed and returns in excess of the Russell 3000 Index are shown. As can

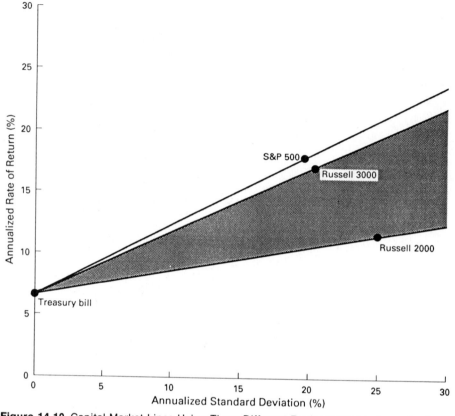

Figure 14-10. Capital Market Lines Using Three Different Equity Market Indexes for the Period December 31, 1984 to December 31, 1988. SOURCE: Frank Russell Company.

be seen, portfolios (stocks) tend to move in groups based on short-term market preferences. For example, earnings growth portfolios outperformed the market in the four-year periods ending December 1982 through June 1985. However, they seriously underperformed the market in essentially all of the four-year periods ending June 1986 through September 1988. This result could not be explained by the beta effect—rising or falling with the market for stocks—because the average annual return on the Russell 3000 during this period was 17.2 percent, giving the capital market line a positive slope.

Without style comparisons, traditional risk-adjusted measures such as the Sharpe or Treynor indexes or the Jensen alpha could be misleading even over periods as long as four years. For example, because of the nature of traditional risk-adjustment methods, earnings growth managers would have appeared to have earned superior results because of security selection for the four-year period ending September 1983 when, in fact, the results were

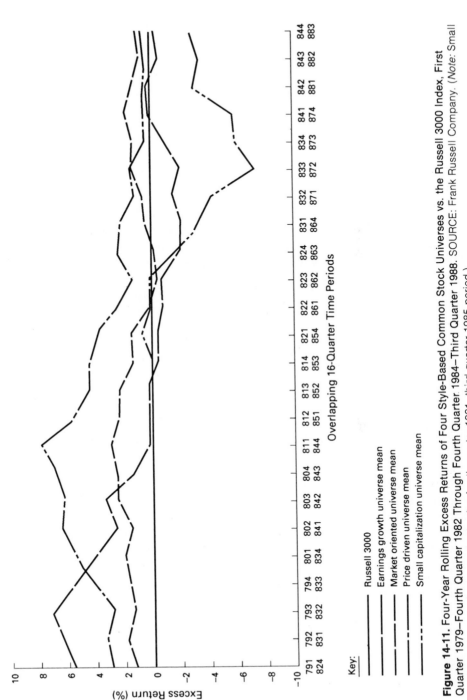

Figure 14-11. Four-Year Rolling Excess Returns of Four Style-Based Common Stock Universes vs. the Russell 3000 Index, First Quarter 1979–Fourth Quarter 1988. SOURCE: Frank Russell Company. (*Note:* Small capitalization universe plotted only after fourth quarter 1981–third quarter 1985 period.)

TABLE 14-7. Market Value Weightings of Two Hypothetical Equity Portfolios and the Market Index

	Portfolio Market Value Weightings		
Sector Profile	Portfolio A	Portfolio B	Market Index
Consumer	28%	40%	30%
Energy	24	30	26
Technology	8	20	10
Basic industry	25	5	22
Interest rate sensitive	15	5	12

primarily due to investor preferences as a whole. That is, because Figure 14-11 reports median performance for *all* earnings growth managers, it essentially says that earnings growth *stocks* performed well and the active managers of funds invested in them just went along with the stocks.

The formation of comparable manager peer groups has traditionally been more of an art than a science. A combination of quantitative and qualitative analysis should be used to group similar managers into appropriate universes. Factors reviewed include many measures of portfolio structure, performance correlations, and an analysis of the decision-making process based on lengthy in-person interviews. With technological advances over recent years, the use of quantitative techniques to determine manager style is increasing; factor analysis, in particular, is taking on greater importance.

Portfolio Analysis. Portfolio analysis helps both the investor and the investment manager to determine the reasons for overperformance or underperformance. One useful approach is a combination of equity profiles and an analysis of management effect.

As an example, suppose the industry profile of portfolios A and B and the market are as shown in Table 14-7. In the analysis of management effect shown in Table 14-8, the return for each economic sector is calculated and its impact (return × portfolio weight) on the total results for portfolio A, portfolio B, and the market is shown.

A quick glance at the total equity returns shows that portfolio B earned a superior return, while portfolio A's return was almost 10 percentage points lower than B's and almost 5 percentage points lower than the market. A cursory judgment might arrive at the conclusion that the manager of portfolio B was the superior manager; closer examination is needed.

An analysis of these two tables shows the following was true for portfolio A:

1. Diversification in terms of percentage distribution among sectors was very close to that of the market portfolio.

TABLE 14-8. Analysis of Active Management of Two Hypothetical Equity Portfolios Relative to a Market Index

	Analysis of Management Effect					
	Portfolio A		Portfolio B		Market Index	
Sector Profile	Absolute Return	Impact[a]	Absolute Return	Impact[a]	Absolute Return	Impact[a]
Consumer	21%	5.9%	19%	7.6%	20%	6.0%
Energy	30	7.2	70	21.0	50	13.0
Technology	10	0.8	8	1.6	20	2.0
Basic industry	28	7.0	22	1.1	25	5.5
Interest rate sensitive	15	2.2	30	1.5	10	1.2
Total equity return		23.1%		32.8%		27.7%

[a] Market value weighting from Table 14-7 multiplied by absolute return.

2. Three sectors of portfolio A (consumer, basic industry, and interest rate sensitive) performed better than the counterpart market sectors. These sectors comprised 68 percent of portfolio A versus 64 percent of the market portfolio.
3. Only two sectors of portfolio A (energy and technology) performed worse than the market sectors.

If it is assumed that the manager of portfolio A had said in advance that the stocks in the portfolio (1) would have market diversification and (2) would have high dividend yields, *and* during this time period the stellar performance of the energy sector was in low-dividend-paying issues, then the overall conclusion might be that portfolio A's manager did a pretty good job.
By comparison, the following was true for portfolio B:

1. In comparison to the market, the portfolio was overweighted in the combined consumer and technology sectors at 60 percent, versus 40 percent for the market portfolio.
2. Sector returns were all lower than the market except for the energy sector, where the manager had approximately a market weighting, and the interest-rate-sensitive sector, with a smaller-than-market weighting.
3. Essentially all of portfolio B's excess return came from the energy sector.

If it is assumed that the manager of portfolio B had said in advance that he would (1) invest the portfolio in growth stocks and (2) over- and underweight the portfolio in accordance with his anticipation of economic trends, then it is questionable whether the manager's performance was as good as the absolute return would indicate or simply a matter of lucky stock selection in the energy area.

From a manager's viewpoint, *A* would probably be pleased that the results coincided with his expectations. Manager *B* should review his economic analysis to determine why the consumer and technology sectors did not meet expectations as evidenced by their portfolio weightings.

Analysis of Extra-Market Risk Approach

Another approach to performance attribution is the system initially developed by Rosenberg [1978] and developed further by Rudd and Clasing [1982]. This type of system attempts to identify the economic factors that tend to drive market movements. The most widely used factor model is that developed by Rosenberg's firm, BARRA, which subdivides a portfolio's total return into market risk, industry risk, and 13 fundamental measures of *extra-market risk* or risk not associated with the market. The 13 extra-market factors are as follows:

1. Market (price) variability
2. Success
3. Size
4. Trading activity
5. Growth
6. Earnings growth
7. Book/price
8. Earnings variability
9. Financial leverage
10. Foreign income
11. Labor intensity
12. Yield
13. Low capitalization

The BARRA Model analyzes 60 descriptors, which are ratios or attributes of individual companies that are designed to capture all the important aspects of a company's operations. These descriptors are then combined into the 13 risk factors shown above, which are common across all stocks. To the extent that market prices are sensitive to these 13 factors, a portfolio's return can be analyzed in terms of its sensitivity to each of these factors.

Determining the precise number of factors to use and the nature of the individual factors is an imprecise science. For factors to prove useful to the analyst, they should be:

1. Interpretable or individually meaningful. Each factor should be

based on generally accepted and well-understood features of securities. Collectively the factors should express the key characteristics of a portfolio.

2. Incisive. A good factor divides the market into well-defined slices.
3. Interesting. A good factor consistently yields a significant positive alpha and accounts for significant variation in security returns.

Although much additional work remains to be done in the application of factor analysis to performance evaluation, progress thus far is encouraging.

EVALUATION OF REAL ESTATE STRATEGIES

As with the other asset classes, different equity real estate money managers have different levels of interest and skill in segments of the broad market. Some managers specialize in types of property; for example, a manager may be particularly skilled in assembling portfolios of retail properties—malls, strip centers, specialty centers—but less interested in or adept at buying central business district office buildings. Other managers may focus more specifically on the financial structure of the investments rather than on the type of real estate being underwritten. Still others may elect to buy property only in a relatively small regional market. This last strategy is consistent with the theory that primary real estate value accrues from location before anything else, and there is no substitute for thorough knowledge of a single area, however small.

Because of the relatively limited amount of information immediately available in real estate investing, performance comparisons are difficult and somewhat fraught with peril. Transactions are not always comparable to other potential transactions even in the same locale. Furthermore, virtually no real estate transactions are conducted in an open auction market as are those of stocks and bonds. Real estate purchases are most often private affairs worked out among acting principals.

Moreover, even if all data on all transactions were public, it is doubtful that a dependable price index could be constructed. Real estate is not liquid. Because it changes hands infrequently, there are few observations of trans-actions prices. Fewer still are the observations of transactions involving the same property. Hence the issue of performance comparisons in real estate remains somewhat troubling, particularly for those whose expectations about data availability stem from their work in the stock market.

Still, investors demand comparisons, both to ascertain the opportunity cost of investing in real estate over the other major asset classes and to establish the relative value of a particular project or portfolio manager. In this regard, the most used benchmark of real estate performance, the FRC

Property Index, described in Chapter 10, has characteristics that make it an important benchmark portfolio.

The dollar-based FRC Property Index is composed of over 1,000 non-leveraged, investment grade, income-producing properties. The returns are calculated based on individual property returns and the data are divided into four major categories of properties. Most importantly, the index is measured in the same way that most real estate portfolios are measured—by appraisal. Whatever lags or smoothing that may be endemic to the appraisal process exist in both index and portfolio nearly equally.

On the other hand, several features of this index may make its returns inappropriate for direct comparison with other assembled portfolio performance statistics. For example, because "membership" in the FRC Property Index is restricted to wholly owned properties, the potential effects of financing features cannot be included in the market values reported. By contrast, many assembled portfolios have nontrivial debt positions in the properties owned. Furthermore, because large retail projects are most often significantly leveraged, the FRC Property Index is underweighted in retail to the extent that retail deals have a greater than average propensity to be structured in this way.

In some cases, a more suitable portfolio benchmark might be a weighted average of portfolios composed of open-end and/or closed-end funds because these portfolios provide a more representative sample of financial structuring. Perhaps fund portfolios could be grouped by property characteristics to come up with a still more appropriate comparison. For example, in evaluating the managed performance of a portfolio of office properties, a comparison to other portfolios invested predominantly in apartments or warehouses would be unfair. A weighted average office property oriented fund would provide a more useful comparison.

Although these approaches provide measures that are better than nothing, they are still less accurate and applicable than an investor might desire. If the goal is to determine whether a manager has shown skill in selecting or managing properties, these benchmarks may prove incomplete and even incorrect. They must, therefore, be used with care. But as institutional investors increase their attention to this asset class, information will become more widely available. Continuing efforts are being made to construct larger and more complete data bases of property specific information so that more adequate benchmarks may be calculated.

One specific effort is the construction of a capitalization rate adjusted FRC Property Index, as explained in Chapter 10. By adjusting traditional, smoothed appraisal values for market capitalized cash flow valuations, this index has more realistic price and return volatility, making it a more realistic vehicle for risk/return comparisons.

PERFORMANCE FEES

Traditional investment management fees are based on assets under management. These types of fees reward managers to the extent that increasing returns increase the assets under management. Whether the performance comes from general market movements or from the manager's skill in security selection or timing is irrelevant.

Incentive fees attempt to tie managers' rewards more directly to their skill. A common structure for a performance fee calls for a base fee that is less than the manager's normal fee. The manager receives a bonus (incentive) as the portfolio return exceeds an agreed upon benchmark return or the return of an agreed upon customized normal portfolio. An appropriate benchmark or normal portfolio must be selected carefully, as discussed previously; benchmark misspecification can be a serious problem.

While incentive fees have intuitive appeal, great care must be taken in their specification. The client and manager must decide whether the fee will involve a penalty for underperformance, the length of the period over which the performance is to be measured, and the rate of take-down of the performance fee. Care must be taken that lucky performance is not rewarded and unlucky performance is not unduly penalized. Finally, the fee must be structured so that the manager has no incentive to arbitrarily change the risk structure of the portfolio. In the event a portfolio manager has below par initial performance, there should be no incentive for him to play "catch up" by increasing risk. Likewise, a manager who had outstanding initial performance should not be allowed to collapse his portfolio to the benchmark or normal portfolio merely to protect his incentive fees. Incentives should be rewards for superior active management undertaken at agreed upon risk levels.

PROBLEMS WITH PERFORMANCE MEASUREMENT

Client Pressures

One of the major problems with performance measurement is that some investors tend to measure results too frequently and to make judgments based on a time frame that is too short to be a true measure of significantly good or poor portfolio management. For accuracy of computations, performance should be computed as often as practical, but results should not be taken as significant by the investor or the investment manager until a reasonable period of time—such as a market cycle for equities or an interest rate cycle for fixed-income securities—has elapsed.

An investor often puts pressure on a portfolio manager because the portfolio's return is lower than other portfolios, especially in a comparative framework. At other times, the manager may perceive such pressure even if it does not exist. In either case, the manager may change management style or take more risk than he or she is comfortable with (or has agreed to take) in an attempt to "save the business." Although it cannot be proven statistically, one reason why some mutual funds outperform pension funds with similar goals and objectives is because the purchasers of mutual funds are less sophisticated and therefore have less influence over the activities of the portfolio manager.

Performance in Perspective

As one investor put it, "You can't eat relative performance." For many investors, such as pension funds, performance has direct cash flow implications. Shortfalls from the actuarial return rate may require alternate funding, such as increased contributions from the plan sponsor. In the case of an endowment fund, such shortfalls may require the invasion of principal to meet current budget requirements, or reductions in the budgeted disbursements themselves. Theoretical portfolio work has led many to define risk as variability of returns; however, many investors would agree that another relevant risk is the probability that the portfolio will not achieve a stated rate of return objective—a concept discussed in Chapter 7.

An investor's primary objective should be to obtain a real return—one that maintains or increases the purchasing power of the portfolio relative to its funding requirements. In other words, the portfolio objective stated in nominal terms must incorporate current cash flow needs, an adjustment for current and prospective inflation, and, where applicable, a margin of safety for forecast errors. While this objective should be incorporated in the asset allocation determination, not enough attention has been paid to setting portfolio objectives in real return terms or measuring performance in those same terms.

Liabilities are funded and cash is disbursed in absolute, not relative, terms. In essence, the most basic measure of portfolio performance is in absolute terms—the actual realized return for the time period involved, measured against the portfolio's return objective. As stated above, this measurement reflects primarily the appropriateness of the asset allocation decision or how well the investor's needs have been integrated with expectational factors. Relative return performance is primarily a measure of the appropriateness of individual asset selection and weighting—portfolio construction within asset categories—as compared with an appropriate market or asset index or bogey.

In Japan, the major emphasis in portfolio management is ordinary income and realized gains and losses. Under current measurement standards, unrealized gains are ignored. Unrealized losses, on the other hand, are recognized in a lower of cost or market valuation basis. This method puts an emphasis on cash returns and often leads to very conservative investment practices. While market valuation is recommended as the most appropriate measure of investment results, because it avoids the arbitrary separation of realized from unrealized gains, the Japanese emphasis on cash returns has considerable merit.

Finally, when evaluating investment performance, those involved often compare the results to the "median manager." There is not a *single* measurement of the median manager because of the differences in the data bases of the pension fund consultants. These differences include universe size, composition, and computation methods. In terms of composition, for example, some consultants' data bases are oriented toward bank trust investment operations, while others are oriented toward investment advisory firms. Smaller consulting firms tend to have more variation than the larger firms do.

As analysis is performed and subsets of the universe are examined, the differences become more significant because of the many variations in the data composition. For example, one large pension consultant has four or five equity investor style categories whereas another firm has almost twice as many. This difference is an important consideration in attempting to evaluate "value managers," for example, because there may be more than one type of value manager category. As a result, the median value manager in one universe may have 12 percent return performance whereas in another universe that manager may have 14 percent performance. Other differences may occur in how certain performance attributes are calculated, such as how performance is divided between industry selection and individual stock selection. These differences in reported performance are not a criticism of the consultants; they are simply the realities of investment performance measurement. Those involved in the measurement process need to be aware that such differences exist and that adjustments should be made in the interpretation of reported results.

SUMMARY

There are many pitfalls and unresolved issues in the process of performance measurement and portfolio analysis. Many decision makers place great emphasis on the niceties of quantitatively defined results. However, blind use of performance numbers can lead to erroneous conclusions and poor decisions. A whole industry has developed around ex-post measurement. Given how such measurement has sometimes been used by client-investors, there is a question whether it has really improved the return of the mutual fund investor or decreased the cost of providing pension benefits.

On the other hand, while a quantitatively based approach to performance evaluation has its shortcomings, the available alternatives are almost always worse. Performance measurement, judiciously analyzed in conjunction with other factors, can aid the careful investor, showing him or her how the decision-making process may be improved through time.

FURTHER READING

Time-weighted and dollar-weighted rate of return concepts are developed and explained in Dietz [1966a, 1966b] and Bank Administration Institute [1968].

There are many approaches to risk measurement and risk-adjusted performance. The historically significant works are: Jensen [1968, 1969], Fama [1968], Sharpe [1966], and Treynor [1965].

Performance attribution (the analysis of performance) is becoming more important to pension plan sponsors. Academic work in this area has been sparse, with most methods being developed commercially. Fama [1972] and Rosenberg [1978] deal with equity portfolios; Dietz, Fogler, and Hardy [1980] and Fong, Pearson, and Vasicek [1982] deal with fixed-income performance attribution.

Current methods of portfolio measurement and risk adjustment are widely used in the investment industry. However, there are both practical and theoretical limitations to these methods. These are highlighted in the following: Jeffrey [1977], Ferguson [1980], Roll [1980, 1981], and Stolte [1981].

COMPUTER APPLICATIONS

There are literally hundreds of performance measurement systems commercially available. The most popular, by type, are:

1. *Stand-alone (batch) performance measurement systems*—Typically provided to banks that lack an in-house performance module in their trust accounting system; National FSI and Catalytics.
2. *Time sharing portfolio management systems*—Shaw Data and Interactive Data Corp.
3. *Minibased, in-house portfolio accounting systems*—Nidsport-Data General and CDA-VAX.
4. *Microbased portfolio accounting systems*—Numerous packages available, some with performance measurement capability; one of the most successful to date is ADVENT.

BIBLIOGRAPHY

Arbel, Avner. "Generic Stocks: An Old Product in a New Package." *The Journal of Portfolio Management*, Summer 1985.

Arditti, Fred. "Another Look at Mutual Fund Performance." *Journal of Financial and Quantitative Analysis*, June 1967.

———. "Risk and the Required Rate of Return on Equity." *The Journal of Finance*, March 1967.

Bank Administration Institute. *Measuring the Investment Performance of Pension Funds*. Park Ridge, Ill.: Bank Administration Institute, 1968.

Barineau III, John. "Does 'Good Portfolio Management' Exist?" *Management Science*, February 1969.

Berkowitz, Stephen, Louis Finney, and Dennis Logue. *The Investment Performance of Corporate Pension Plans*. New York: Quorum Books, 1988.

Bierwag, Gerald O. *Duration Analysis: Managing Interest Rate Risk*. Cambridge, Mass.: Ballinger Publishing Company, 1987.

Bold, Bob L., and Hal Arbit. "Efficient Markets and the Professional Investor." *Financial Analysts Journal*, July/August 1984.

Bookstaber, Richard, and Roger Clarke. "Option Portfolio Strategies: Measurement and Evaluation." *Journal of Business*, October 1984.

———. "Problems in Evaluating the Performance of Portfolios With Options." *Financial Analysts Journal*, January/February 1985.

Bower, Richard S., and Ronald F. Wippern. "Risk/Return Measurement in Portfolio Selection and Performance Appraisal Models: Progress Report." *Journal of Financial and Quantitative Analysis*, December 1969.

Brinson, Gary P., Jeffrey J. Diermeier, and Gary G. Schlarbaum. "Composite Portfolio Benchmark for Pension Plans." *Financial Analysts Journal*, March/April 1986.

Brown, Keith C., and Gregory D. Brown. "Does the Composition of the Market Portfolio Really Matter?" *The Journal of Portfolio Management*, Winter 1987.

Buffett, Warren E. "The Superinvestors of Graham and Doddsville." *Hermes, Columbia Business School Magazine*, Fall 1984.

Camp, Robert C., and Arthur A. Eubank, Jr. "The Beta Quotient: A New Measure of Portfolio Risk." *The Journal of Portfolio Management*, Summer 1981.

Carlson, Robert S. "Aggregate Performance of Mutual Funds, 1948–1967." *Journal of Financial and Quantitative Analysis*, March 1970.

Chang, Eric C., and Wilbur G. Lewellen. "Market Timing and Mutual Fund Investment Performance." *Journal of Business*, 1984.

Cohen, Jerome, Edward Zinbarg, and Arthur Zeikel. *Investment Analysis and Portfolio Management*, 5th ed. Homewood, Ill.: Irwin, 1987.

Cohen, Kalman J., and Bruce P. Fitch. "The Average Investment Performance Index." *Management Science*, February 1966.

Cohen, Kalman J., and Jerry Pogue. "Some Comments Concerning Mutual Fund Versus Random Portfolio Performances." *Journal of Business*, April 1968.

The Committee for Performance Presentation Standards, The Financial Analysts Federation. "A Report on Setting Performance Presentation Standards." *Financial Analysts Journal*, September/October 1987.

Cranshaw, T. E. "The Evaluation of Investment Performance." *Journal of Business*, October 1977.

Davanzo, Lawrence E., and Stephen L. Nesbitt. "Performance Fees for Investment Management." *Financial Analysts Journal*, January/February 1987.

Dietz, Peter O. "Pension Fund Investment Performance—What Method to Use When." *Financial Analysts Journal*, January/February 1966a.

———. *Pension Funds: Measuring Investment Performance.* New York: The Free Press, 1966b.

———. "Components of a Measurement Model: Rate of Return, Risk and Timing." *The Journal of Finance*, May 1968.

Dietz, Peter O., H. Russell Fogler, and Donald J. Hardy. "The Challenge of Analyzing Bond Portfolio Returns." *The Journal of Portfolio Management*, Spring 1980.

Dietz, Peter O., H. Russell Fogler, and Madelyn Smith. "Factor Analysis of Manager Returns." Unpublished working paper, 1982.

Dietz, Peter O., and George P. Williams, Jr. "Influence of Pension Fund Asset Valuations on Rate of Return." *Financial Executive*, May 1970.

Dhrymes, Phoebus J. "The Empirical Relevance of Arbitrage Pricing Models." *The Journal of Portfolio Management*, Summer 1984.

Elton, Edwin J., and Martin J. Gruber. "Risk Reduction and Portfolio Size: An Analytical Solution." *Journal of Business*, October 1977.

———. *Modern Portfolio Theory and Investment Analysis*, 3d ed. New York: John Wiley & Sons, 1987.

Fama, Eugene. *Measuring the Performance of Pension Funds. A Supplement: Risk and the Evaluation of Pension Fund Performance.* Park Ridge, Ill.: Bank Administration Institute, 1968.

———. "Components of Investment Performance." *The Journal of Finance*, June 1972.

———. "A Note on the Market Model and the Two Parameter Model." *The Journal of Finance*, December 1973.

Ferguson, Robert. "Performance Measurement Doesn't Make Sense." *Financial Analysts Journal*, May/June 1980.

Fischer, Larry, and Roman Weil. "Coping With the Risk of Interest Rate Fluctuations: Returns to Bondholders From Naive and Optimal Strategies." *Journal of Business*, October 1971.

Fong, Gifford. "Bond Performance: Analyzing Sources of Return." *The Journal of Portfolio Management*, Spring 1983.

Fong, Gifford, Charles Pearson, and Oldrich Vasicek. "Bond Performance Analysis," presented to the Institute for Quantitative Research in Finance, May 1982.

Fox, Edward A. "Comparing Performance of Equity Pension Trusts." *Financial Analysts Journal*, September/October 1968.

Friend, Irwin, and Marshall Blume. "Measurement of Portfolio Performance Under Uncertainty." *American Economic Review*, September 1970.

———, and Jean Crockett. *Mutual Funds and Other Institutional Investors.* New York: McGraw-Hill Book Co., 1970.

Friend, Irwin, and Douglas Vicker. "Portfolio Selection and Investment Performance." *The Journal of Finance*, September 1965.

FRS Associates. *Pension Asset Management: The Corporate Decision.* New York: Financial Executives Research Foundation, 1980.

Fuller, Russell J. *Capital Asset Pricing Theories—Evolution and New Frontiers.* Charlottesville, Va.: Financial Analysts Research Foundation, 1981.

Gaumnitz, Jack E. "Appraising Performance of Investment Portfolios." *The Journal of Finance,* June 1970.

Gibb, William. "Critical Evaluation of Pension Funds." *The Journal of Finance,* May 1968.

Gordon, M., G. Paradis, and C. Rorke. "Experimental Evidence on Alternative Portfolio Decision Rules." *American Economic Review,* March 1972.

Granito, Michael R. *Bond Portfolio Immunization.* Lexington, Mass.: D.C. Heath and Co., 1984.

Grant, Dwight. "Portfolio Performance and the 'Cost' of Timing Decisions." *The Journal of Finance,* June 1977.

Grinold, Richard, and Andrew Rudd. "Incentive Fees: Who Wins? Who Loses?" *Financial Analysts Journal,* January/February 1987.

Gumpetz, Julian, and Evertee Page. "Misconceptions of Pension Fund Performance." *Financial Analysts Journal,* May/June 1970.

Guy, James. "The Performance of British Investment Trust Industry." *The Journal of Finance,* May 1978.

Henriksson, Roy D., and Robert C. Merton. "On Market Timing and Investment Performance. II Statistical Procedures for Evaluating Forecasting Skills." *Journal of Business,* 1981.

Horowitz, Ira. "The 'Reward to Variability' Ratio and Mutual Fund Performance." *Journal of Business,* October 1966.

Jeffrey, Robert H. "Internal Portfolio Growth: The Better Measure." *The Journal of Portfolio Management,* Summer 1977.

Jensen, C. Michael. "The Performance of Mutual Funds in the Period 1945–1964." *The Journal of Finance,* May 1968.

———. "Risk, the Pricing of Capital Assets, and the Evaluation of Investment Portfolios." *Journal of Business,* April 1969.

———. "Capital Markets: Theory and Evidence." *The Bell Journal of Economics and Management Science,* Autumn 1972.

Joy, Maurice, and Burr Porter. "Stochastic Dominance and Mutual Fund Performance." *Journal of Financial and Quantitative Analysis,* January 1974.

Klemkosky, Robert. "The Bias in Composite Performance Measures." *Journal of Financial and Quantitative Analysis,* June 1973.

———. "How Consistently Do Managers Manage." *The Journal of Portfolio Management,* Winter 1977.

Kon, Stanley J. "The Market-Timing Performance of Mutual Fund Managers." *Journal of Business,* 1983.

Kon, Stanley J., and Frank Jen. "Estimation of Time-Varying Systematic Risk and Performance for Mutual Fund Portfolios: An Application of Switching Regression." *The Journal of Finance,* May 1978.

Kritzman, Mark P. "Incentive Fees: Some Problems and Some Solutions." *Financial Analysts Journal,* January/February 1987.

Lee, Cheng, and Frank Jen. "Effects of Measurement Errors on Systematic Risk and Performance Measure of a Portfolio." *Journal of Financial and Quantitative Analysis,* June 1978.

Lehmann, Bruce N., and David M. Modest. "Mutual Fund Performance Evaluation:

A Comparison of Benchmarks and Benchmark Comparisons." *The Journal of Finance*, June 1987.

Levitz, Gerald. "Market Risk and the Management of Institutional Equity Portfolios." *Financial Analysts Journal*, January/February 1974.

Levy, Haim. "Portfolio Performance and Investment Horizon." *Management Science*, August 1972.

Lintner, John. "Security Prices, Risk, and Maximal Gains from Diversification." *The Journal of Finance*, December 1965.

Mains, Norman E. "Risk, the Pricing of Capital Assets, and the Evaluation of Investment Portfolios: Comment." *Journal of Business*, July 1977.

Malkiel, Burton. "The Valuation of Closed End Investment Company Shares." *The Journal of Finance*, June 1977.

Markowitz, Harry. "Portfolio Selection." *The Journal of Finance*, March 1952.

———. *Portfolio Selection: Efficient Diversification of Investments*. New York: John Wiley & Sons, 1959.

McDonald, John. "Objectives and Performance of Mutual Funds: 1960–1964." *Journal of Financial and Quantitative Analysis*, June 1974.

Mennis, Edmund A. "A New Method for Evaluating Pension Fund Portfolios." *The Journal of Portfolio Management*, Winter 1979.

Merton, Robert C. "On Market Timing and Investment Performance: An Equilibrium Theory of Value for Market Forecasts." *Journal of Business*, 1981.

Meyer, Jack. "Further Applications of Stochastic Dominance to Mutual Fund Performance." *Journal of Financial and Quantitative Analysis*, June 1977.

Mills, D. Harlan. "On the Measurement of Fund Performance." *The Journal of Finance*, December 1970.

Monroe, Robert, and James Trieschmann. "Portfolio Performance of Property-Liability Insurance Companies." *Journal of Financial and Quantitative Analysis*, March 1972.

Moses, Edward A., John M. Cheyney, and E. Theodore Veit. "A New and More Complete Performance Measure." *The Journal of Portfolio Management*, Summer 1987.

Mossavar-Rahmani, Sharmin. "Understanding and Evaluating Index Fund Management," in Frank J. Fabozzi and T. Dessa Garlicki, eds., *Advances in Bond Analysis and Portfolio Strategies*. Chicago: Probus, 1987.

Mossin, Jan. "Equilibrium in a Capital Asset Market." *Econometrica*, October 1966.

Pari, Robert, and Son-Nan Chen. "An Empirical Test of the Arbitrage Pricing Theory." *Journal of Financial Research*, Summer 1984.

Perold, André F., and Evan C. Schulman. "The Free Lunch in Currency Hedging: Implications for Investment Policy and Performance Standards." *Financial Analysts Journal*, May/June 1988.

Pohlman, R., J. Ang, and R. Hollinger. "Performance and Timing: A Test of Hedge Funds." *The Journal of Portfolio Management*, Spring 1978.

Record, Eugene E., Jr., and Mary Ann Tynan. "Incentive Fees: The Basic Issues." *Financial Analysts Journal*, January/February 1987.

Reilly, Frank K. *Investment Analysis and Portfolio Management*, 3d ed. Hinsdale, Ill.: Dryden Press, 1989.

Robie, Edgar A., Jr., and Peter C. Lambert. "Fixed Income Normal Portfolios and Their Application to Fund Management," in Frank J. Fabozzi and T. Dessa

Garlicki, eds., *Advances in Bond Analysis and Portfolio Strategies*. Chicago: Probus, 1987.

Robinson, Randall S. "Measuring the Risk Dimension of Investment Performance." *The Journal of Finance*, May 1970.

Rohrer, Julie. "Ferment in Academia." *Institutional Investor*, July 1985.

Roll, Richard. "Ambiguity When Performance Is Measured by the Security Market Line." *The Journal of Finance*, September 1978.

———. "Performance Evaluation and Benchmark Errors (I)." *The Journal of Portfolio Management*, Summer 1980.

———. "Performance Evaluation and Benchmark Errors (II)." *The Journal of Portfolio Management*, Winter 1981.

Roll, Richard, and Stephen Ross. "The Arbitrage Pricing Theory Approach to Strategic Portfolio Planning." *Financial Analysts Journal*, May/June 1984.

Rosenberg, Barr M. "Performance Measurement and Performance Attribution." Working Paper No. 75, Research Program in Finance, University of California at Berkeley, May 1978.

———. "Bond Performance Measurement," presented to the Institute for Quantitative Research in Finance, April 1980.

———. "Prediction of Common Stock Betas." *The Journal of Portfolio Management*, Winter 1985.

Ross, Stephen. "The Arbitrage Theory of Capital Asset Pricing." *Journal of Economic Theory*, December 1976.

———. "On the Empirical Relevance of APT: Reply." *The Journal of Portfolio Management*, Summer 1985.

Rothschild, Michael. "Asset Pricing Theories." Technical Working Paper No. 44, National Bureau of Economic Research, March 1985.

Rothstein, Marvin. "On Geometric and Arithmetic Portfolio Performance Indexes." *Journal of Financial and Quantitative Analysis*, September 1972.

Rudd, Andrew, and Henry K. Clasing, Jr. *Modern Portfolio Theory: The Principles of Investment Management*. Homewood, Ill.: Dow Jones-Irwin, 1982.

Sarnat, Marshall. "A Note on the Prediction of Portfolio Performance From Ex-Post Data." *The Journal of Finance*, June 1972.

Schlarbaum, Gary. "The Investment Performance of the Common Stock Portfolios of Property-Liability Insurance Companies." *Journal of Financial and Quantitative Analysis*, January 1974.

———. "Realized Return on Common Stock Investments: The Experience of Individual Investors." *Journal of Business*, April 1978.

———, **Wilbur Lewellen, and Ronald Lease.** "The Common-Stock Portfolio Performance Record of Individual Investors: 1964–1970." *The Journal of Finance*, May 1978.

Sharpe, William F. "Capital Asset Prices: A Theory of Market Equilibrium Under Conditions of Risk." *The Journal of Finance*, September 1964.

———. "Mutual Fund Performance." *Journal of Business*, January 1966.

Smidt, Seymour. "Investment Horizons and Performance Measurement." *The Journal of Portfolio Management*, Winter 1978.

Smith, Keith V., and Dennis A. Tito. "Risk Return Measures of Ex-Post Portfolio Performance." *Journal of Financial and Quantitative Analysis*, December 1969.

Stolte, Myron O. "Pension Plan Sponsors: Monitor Yourselves." *Harvard Business Review*, March/April 1981.

Treynor, Jack. "How to Rate Management of Investment Funds." *Harvard Business Review*, January/February 1965.

Treynor, Jack, and Kay K. Mazuy. "Can Mutual Funds Outguess the Market?" *Harvard Business Review*, July/August 1966.

West, Richard. "Mutual Fund Performance and the Theory of Capital Asset Pricing: Some Comments." *Journal of Business*, April 1968.

Williamson, Peter. "Measurement and Forecasting of Mutual Fund Performance: Choosing an Investment Strategy." *Financial Analysts Journal*, November/December 1972.

Index

[*Chapter numbers are boldface and are followed by a colon; lightface numbers after the colon refer to pages within the chapter.*]

A

ABO.   *See* Accrued benefit obligation

Accounting methods, **14**:10

Accrued benefit obligation (ABO), **4**:14–15, **7**:33, 34–35

Accumulated benefit obligation.   *See* Accrued benefit obligation

Accumulation phase, **3**:18

Ad hoc changes, portfolio rebalancing, **13**:20–21, 23–24

Adventurer personality, of client, **3**:8, 9

Advertised orders, **12**:44

Agency auction, **12**:38

Agency relationship, **12**:44

Aggregate capital market return formula, **5**:19

Aggregate economic output, **5**:17–18

Aggressiveness index, **3**:13

Alternative minimum tax (AMT), **3**:29, 32

American Institute of Real Estate Appraisers, **6**:53, 64

American option.   *See* Options

AMT.   *See* Alternative minimum tax

Annuities, **8**:16

Appraisal, real estate
cost approach, **6**:61
income approach, **6**:61–62
market data approach, **6**:62–63

Appreciation
office property, **10**:33–34
retail property, **10**:39–41

APT.   *See* Arbitrage pricing theory

Arbitrage, **5**:47
index, **9**:10–11
model, **6**:70, 71

Arbitrage pricing theory (APT), **2**:33–36, **5**:14–15, 23, 25, **6**:33, **14**:3, 22

Ask price, **12**:4

Asset allocation, **1**:7, **7**:1–69, **13**:18
accounts, **7**:68–69
active, **7**:44
analytic formulas, **7**:47–48
approaches, **4**:19–20
consultants, **7**:12–13
deviant beliefs about asset classes and markets, **7**:25, 44
dynamic, **7**:54
effect, **14**:24–26
futures in, **11**:25–30, 35
indexing effects, **7**:34–35
insured, **7**:25–27
integrated, **7**:21
international, **11**:28–30
options in, **11**:30–35
pure asset plays, **7**:68
reallocation, **7**:66–68
requirements, **5**:13
review, **7**:18–21
shadow mix, **7**:3–5
strategic, **7**:22–23, 54
tactical, **7**:24–25, 57–59, 63, **13**:24–29, **14**:24
three-way, **7**:3–5

Asset alphas, **7**:43–44

Asset class, **5**:13, 16–30, **6**:77–78, **7**:13, 16–18

Asset/liability management, **4**:41, 57, 60, 69, **8**:43, **11**:67–69

Asset management principles, **1**:6

Asset market, **2**:2–4
approach, **5**:46
forecast, **6**:18–19

Asset mix
decision, **7**:5–13
effective, **7**:63–66
policy, **4**:16–18

Asset pricing, **2**:25–36

Asset returns, **2**:4–9

[Chapter numbers are boldface and are followed by a colon; lightface numbers after the colon refer to pages within the chapter.]

[Chapter numbers are boldface and are followed by a colon; lightface numbers after the colon refer to pages within the chapter.]

*[Chapter numbers are boldface and are followed by a colon; lightface
numbers after the colon refer to pages within the chapter.]*

[*Chapter numbers are boldface and are followed by a colon; lightface numbers after the colon refer to pages within the chapter.*]

[Chapter numbers are boldface and are followed by a colon; lightface numbers after the colon refer to pages within the chapter.]

[Chapter numbers are boldface and are followed by a colon; lightface numbers after the colon refer to pages within the chapter.]

[Chapter numbers are boldface and are followed by a colon; lightface numbers after the colon refer to pages within the chapter.]

[Chapter numbers are boldface and are followed by a colon; lightface numbers after the colon refer to pages within the chapter.]

[Chapter numbers are boldface and are followed by a colon; lightface numbers after the colon refer to pages within the chapter.]

[Chapter numbers are boldface and are followed by a colon; lightface numbers after the colon refer to pages within the chapter.]

*[Chapter numbers are boldface and are followed by a colon; lightface
numbers after the colon refer to pages within the chapter.]*

*[Chapter numbers are boldface and are followed by a colon; lightface
numbers after the colon refer to pages within the chapter.]*